Josephus, Judea, *and* Christian Origins

Josephus, Judea, *and* Christian Origins

Methods and Categories

STEVE MASON

With the editorial assistance of
Michael W. Helfield

Josephus, Judea, and Christian Origins: Methods and Categories

P. O. Box 3473
Peabody, Massachusetts 01961-3473

ISBN 978-1-59856-254-5

The previously published chapters (notice of previous publication and permission to reproduce each are found on pp. ix–x) have been edited to provide consistency of spelling, abbreviations, and other stylistic matters for the reader. Chapter 3 has not been so edited according to the permission granted for its republication.

Printed in the United States of America

Second Printing—January 2010

Cover Art: Sarcophagus of the "Traditio Legis." Early Christian. Location: Museo Nazionale, Ravenna, Italy.
Photo Credit: Scala / Art Resource, N.Y. Used with permission.

Library of Congress Cataloging-in-Publication Data

Mason, Steve, 1957–
Josephus, Judea, and Christian origins : methods and categories / Steve Mason.
p. cm.
Includes bibliographical references and indexes.
ISBN 978-1-59856-254-5 (alk. paper)
1. Christianity—Origin—Historiography. 2. Jews—History—168 B.C.–135 A.D.—Historiography. 3. Judaism—History—Post-exilic period, 586 B.C.–210 A.D.—Historiography. 4. Josephus, Flavius. 5. Church history—Primitive and early church, ca. 30–600.—Historiography. I. Title.
BR129.M377 2009
270.1—dc22

2008031967

Dedication

For my colleague and friend, Dr. Stephen H. Ford, in gratitude for years of conversation about categories and methods

Table of Contents

Permissions

Chapter 2, "Of Audience and Meaning: Reading Josephus's *Bellum Iudaicum* in the Context of a Flavian Audience" was first published in *Josephus and Jewish History in Flavian Rome and Beyond.* Journal for the Study of Judaism Supplement 104. Edited by J. Sievers and G. Lembi. Leiden: Brill, 2005: 71–100. Used with permission.

Chapter 3, "Figured Speech and Irony in T. Flavius Josephus" was first published in *Flavius Josephus and Flavian Rome,* edited by Edmondson, Mason, and Rives © 2005: 244–88. By permission of Oxford University Press.

Chapter 4, "Contradiction or Counterpoint? Josephus and Historical Method" was first published in the *Review of Rabbinic Judaism* 6 (2003): 145–88. Used with permission.

Chapter 5, "Jews, Judeans, Judaizing, Judaism: Problems of Categorization in Ancient History" was first published in the *Journal for the Study of Judaism* 38.4 (2007):1–56. Used with permission.

Chapter 6, "Pharisees in the Narratives of Josephus" was first published as "Josephus' Pharisees: the Narratives," in *In Quest of the Historical Pharisees.* Edited by J. Neusner and B. Chilton. Waco: Baylor University Press, 2007: 3–38. Used with permission.

Chapter 7, "The Philosophy of Josephus's Pharisees" was first published as "Josephus' Pharisees: the Philosophy," in *In Quest of the Historical Pharisees.* Edited by J. Neusner and B. Chilton. Waco: Baylor University Press, 2007: 39–64. Used with permission.

Chapter 8, "The Essenes of Josephus's *Judaean War:* From Story to History" was first published in shorter form as "Essenes and Lurking Spartans in Josephus' *Judaean War:* from Story to History," in *Making History: Josephus and Historical Method.* Edited by Z. Rodgers. Leiden: Brill, 2006: 219–61. Used with permission.

Chapter 10, "'For I Am Not Ashamed of the Gospel' (Rom 1:16): The Gospel and the First Readers of Romans" was first published in *Gospel in Paul: Studies on Corinthians, Galatians and Romans for Richard N. Longenecker.* Edited by L. Ann Jervis and P. Richardson. Journal for the Study of the New Testament:

Supplement Series 108. Sheffield: Continuum (Sheffield Academic Press), 1994: 254–87. Reprinted by kind permission of Continuum International Publishing, Ltd.

Chapter 11, "Chief Priests, Sadducees, Pharisees, and Sanhedrin in Luke-Acts and Josephus" was first published in longer form as "Chief Priests, Sadducees, Pharisees and Sanhedrin in Acts," in *The Book of Acts in its Palestinian Setting.* Edited by R. Bauckham. Volume 4 of *The Book of Acts in Its First Century Setting.* 6 vols. Edited by B. Winter. Grand Rapids: Eerdmans, 1995: 115–77. Used with permission.

Preface

The task of collecting, arranging, and editing essays into the coherent sequence necessary for an effective book-long presentation brings with it many challenges. In this particular case the arrangement of Professor Mason's papers into three parts is his own and will be subsequently explained in the author's introduction. The decision, however, to include a cumulative bibliography along with ancient sources, ancient persons and places, and modern author indices at the end of the volume needs to be explained. I will elaborate upon these choices after first noting the origins of the two chapters that have not been previously published elsewhere (please reference the permissions [pp. ix–x] for the origin of most of the essays in this volume):

Chapter 1, "Josephus as Authority for First-Century Judea," was a presentation given by Professor Mason on October 17, 2006, before colleagues and graduate students gathered at the *Seminar on Ancient Judaisms and Christianities* (recently renamed *Culture and Religion in Antiquity*) at the University of Toronto.

Chapter 9, "Paul's Announcement (τὸ εὐαγγέλιον): 'Good News' And Its Detractors in Earliest Christianity," was a lecture delivered by Professor Mason on February 11, 2002 at the University of Minnesota in the Department of Classics and Near Eastern Studies.

With regard to the chapters previously published elsewhere, it should be noted that, with the exception of chapter 3, they have all been made to conform to the house style of Hendrickson Publishers. The third chapter, "Figured Speech and Irony in T. Flavius Josephus," retains the house style of Oxford University Press in accordance with the terms on which their permission was granted.

It is also apposite to mention that chapters 8 and 11 have been significantly modified since their initial publication. Chapter 8, "The Essenes of Josephus's *Judean War*: From Story to History," has been revised to take account of recent developments in the study of the Essenes. For chapter 11, "Chief Priests, Sadducees, Pharisees, and Sanhedrin in Luke-Acts and Josephus," the text has been considerably shortened to avoid duplication of material that now appears in earlier chapters.

With regard to the supplementary sections at the end of the book, the author and I have opted for a combined bibliography in order to avoid needless overlap from chapter to chapter. We believe, moreover, that the indices will be self-explanatory. We have chosen to omit a subject index because most content should be easy to locate via the chapter headings and subheadings or via the three indices.

On a final note, I would like to acknowledge Professor Mason's dedication as well as his collegiality, both of which, together, have made the experience of editing the essays in this volume a truly rewarding experience.

Michael W. Helfield, Toronto

Abbreviations

ANCIENT SOURCES

Abr.	Philo, *De Abrahamo* (*On the Life of Abraham*)
Abst.	Porphyry, *De abstinentia* (*On Abstinence*)
Adv. Iud.	Tertullian, *Adversus Judaeos* (*Against the Jews*)
Aen.	Virgil, *Aeneid*
Aesch.	Aeschylus
Ag.	Aeschylus, *Agamemnon*
Ag. Ap.	Josephus, *Contra Apionem* (*Against Apion*)
Ages.	Plutarch, *Agesilaus*
Ages.	Xenophon, *Agesilaus*
Agr.	Tacitus, *Agricola*
AJ (*A.J.*)	Josephus, *Antiquitates judaicae* (*Judean Antiquities*)
Anab.	Xenophon, *Anabasis*
Anach.	Lucian, *Anacharsis*
Anim. pecc. dign. cur.	Galen, *De animi cuiuslibet peccatorum dignotione et curatione* (*On the Diagnosis and Cure of the Errors of the Soul*)
Ann.	Tacitus, *Annales* (*Annals*)
Ant.	Josephus, *Antiquitates judaicae* (*Judean Antiquities*)
Ant. or.	Dionysius of Halicarnassus, *De antiquis oratoribus* (Περὶ τῶν ἀρχαίων ῥητόρων)
Ant. rom. or Ant. rom.	Dionysius of Halicarnassus, *Antiquitates romanae* (*Roman Antiquities*)
Anth.	Stobaeus, *Anthology*
Antid.	Isocrates, *Antidosis*
Ap.	Josephus, *Contra Apionem* (*Against Apion*)
Appian	Appian of Alexandria
Apol.	Justin, *Apologia* (*Apology*)
Apol.	Plato, *Apologia* (*Apology*)
Ar.	Aristophanes
Areop.	Isocrates, *Areopagiticus*
Arist.	Aristotle
Aristocr.	Demosthenes, *In Aristocratem* (*Against Aristocrates*)
ARN	*Avot de Rabbi Nathan*
Ath. pol.	Aristotle, *Athēnaiōn politeia* (*Constitution of Athens*)

b. Qidd.	Tractate *Qiddushin* of the Babylonian Talmud
Bell. Cat.	Sallust, *Bellum Catilinae* (*On the Catilinarian Conspiracy*)
Bell. civ.	Appian, *Bella civilia* (*Civil Wars*)
Bell. gall.	Gaius Julius Caesar, *Bellum gallicum* (*Gallic War*)
Bibl.	Photius, *Bibliotheca* (*Library*)
BJ (*B.J.*)	Josephus, *Bellum judaicum* (*Judean War*)
Bk(s).	Book(s)
Brut.	Cicero, *Brutus*
C. Cels.	Origen, *Contra Celsum* (*Against Celsus*)
Cal.	Suetonius, *Gaius Caligula*
Cat.	Cicero, *In Catilinam*
Cat.	Sallust, *Bellum Catilinae* (*On the Catilinarian Conspiracy*)
Cat. Mai.	Plutarch, *Cato Major* (*Cato the Elder*)
CD	*Damascus Document*
Celt.	Appian of Alexandria, *Gallic Wars*
Char.	Theophrastus, *Characteres* (*Characters*)
Charm.	Plato, *Charmides*
Cic.	Marcus Tullius Cicero
Cic.	Plutarch, *Cicero*
Civ.	Augustine, *De civitate Dei* (*The City of God*)
Claud.	Suetonius, *Divus Claudius* (*Divine Claudius*)
1 Clem.	*1 Clement*
Col	Colossians
Comm. Jo.	Origen, *Commentarii in evangelium Joannis* (*Commentary on the Gospel of John*)
Comm. Matt.	Origen, *Commentarium in evangelium Matthaei* (*Commentary on the Gospel of Matthew*)
Comp. Dem. Cic.	Plutarch, *Comparatio Demosthenis et Ciceronis* (*A Comparison of Demosthenes and Cicero*)
Conf.	Augustine, *Confessionum libri XIII* (*Confessions*)
Cons.	Boethius, *Consolatio*
1–2 Cor	1–2 Corinthians
Criti.	Plato, *Critias*
Ctes.	Aeschines, *In Ctesiphonem* (*Against Ctesiphon*)
De or.	Cicero, *De oratore*
Decal.	Philo, *De decalogo* (*On the Decalogue*)
Deipn.	Athenaeus, *Deipnosophistae*
Dem.	Demosthenes
Dem. ev.	Eusebius, *Demonstratio evangelica* (*Demonstration of the Gospel*)
Demetr.	Demetrius
Demon.	Lucian, *Demonax*
Descr.	Pausanias, *Graeciae descriptio* (*Description of Greece*)
Dial.	Justin, *Dialogus cum Tryphone* (*Dialogue with Trypho*)
Dial.	Tacitus, *Dialogus de oratoribus* (*Dialogue on Oratory*)
Dial. mort.	Lucian, *Dialogi mortuorum* (*Dialogues of the Dead*)

Diatr.	Arrian, *Diatribai* (*Dissertationes*) (*Dissertations*)
Dio Chrys.	Dio Chrysostom
Diog. Laert.	Diogenes Laertius
Dion. Hal.	Dionysius of Halicarnassus
Diss.	Gaius Musonius Rufus, *Dissertationum a Lucio digestarum reliquiae* (*Discourses to Lucius*). In C. E. Lutz, *Musonius Rufus: 'The Roman Socrates'*. New Haven: Yale University Press, 1947.
Dom.	Suetonius, *Divus Domitianus* (*Divine Domitian*)
DSS	Dead Sea Scrolls
Ebr.	Philo, *De ebrietate* (*On Drunkeness*)
Eloc.	Demetrius, *De elocutione* (*Style*)
Ep.	Julian, *Epistulae* (*Letters*)
Ep.	Phalaris, *Epistulae* (*Letters*)
Ep.	Pliny the Younger, *Epistulae* (*Letters*)
Ep.	Lucius Annaeus Seneca, *Epistulae morales* (*Moral Epistles*)
Ep. Afr.	Origen, *Epistula ad Africanum* (*Letter to Africanus*)
Eph	Ephesians
Epit.	Albinus, *Epitome doctrinae platonicae (Didaskalikos)* (*Handbook of Platonism*)
Eq.	Aristophanes, *Equites* (*Knights*)
Eusebius	Eusebius of Caesarea
Eth. eud.	Aristotle, *Ethica eudemia* (*Eudemian Ethics*)
Eth. nic. or *Eth. Nic.*	Aristotle, *Ethica nichomacheia* (*Nicomachean Ethics*)
Eup. simpl. med.	Pedanius Dioscorides, *Euporista,* or *De simplicibus medicinis* (*On Simple Medicines*)
Eus.	Eusebius
Exod	Exodus
Exord.	Demosthenes, *Exordia (Prooemia)*
Fab. Max.	Plutarch, *Fabius Maximus*
Fam.	Cicero, *Epistulae ad familiares* (*Letters to Friends*)
Fat.	Cicero, *De fato* (*On Fate*)
Fin.	Cicero, *De finibus* (*About the Ends*)
Flacc.	Philo, *In Flaccum* (*Against Flaccus*)
Fug.	Philo, *De fuga et inventione* (*On Flight and Finding*)
Gal	Galatians
Galb.	Suetonius, *Divus Galba* (*Divine Galba*)
Galen	Claudius Galenus
Geogr.	Strabo, *Geographica* (*Geography*)
Georg.	Virgil, *Georgica*
1 Glor.	Dio Chrysostom, *De gloria i (Or. 66)* (*Reputation*)
Glor. Ath.	Plutarch, *De gloria Atheniensium* (*On the Glory of the Athenians*)
Gos. Thom.	*Gospel of Thomas*
Grg.	Plato, *Gorgias*

Haer.	Irenaeus, *Adversus haereses* (*Against Heresies*)
Heb	Hebrews
Hell.	Xenophon, *Hellenica*
Heracl.	Euripides, *Heraclidae* (*Children of Hercules*)
Hermot.	Lucian, *Hermotimus (De sectis)*
Hist.	Tacitus, *Historiae* (*The Histories*)
Hist. conscr.	Lucian, *Quomodo historia conscribenda sit* (*How History Should Be Written*)
Hist. eccl.	Eusebius, *Historia ecclesiastica* (*Ecclesiastical History*)
Hist. plant.	Theophrastus, *Historia plantarum* (*History of Plants*)
Hymn. homer. cer.	anonymous, *Hymnus Homericus ad Cerem* (*Homeric Hymn to Ceres*)
Ign.	Ignatius
Il.	Homer, *Iliad*
Inst.	Quintilian, *Institutio oratoria* (*Training in Oratory*)
Isoc.	Isocrates
Isocr.	Dionysius of Halicarnassus, *De Isocrate*
Josephus	Titus Flavius Josephus
Juv.	Decimus Junius Juvenalis (Juvenal)
Lac.	Xenophon, *Respublica Lacedaemoniorum* (*The Constitution of the Lacedaemonians*)
Lapid.	Theophrastus, *De lapidibus (On Stones)*
Leg.	Cicero, *De legibus* (*On the Law*)
Leg.	Philo, *Legum allegoriae* (*Allegorical Interpretation*)
Leg.	Plato, *Leges* (*Laws*)
Life	Josephus, *Vita*
Luc.	Cicero, *Lucullus*
Luc.	Plutarch, *Lucullus*
Lucian	Lucian of Samosata
LXX	Septuagint
Lyc.	Plutarch, *Lycurgus*
m.	Mishnah
m. Qidd.	Tractate *Qiddushin* of the Mishnah
1–2 Macc	1–2 Maccabees
4 Macc.	*4 Maccabees*
Macr.	Lucian, *Macrobii*
Magn.	Ignatius, *To the Magnesians*
Mar.	Plutarch, *Marius*
Marc.	Tertullian, *Adversus Marcionem* (*Against Marcion*)
Mart.	Marcus Valerius Martialis
Mat. med.	Pedanius Dioscorides, *De materia medica libri quinque (Pharmacology in five volumes)*
Matt	Matthew
Med.	Marcus Aurelius, *Meditations*
Mem.	Xenophon, *Memorabilia* (*Remarkable Things*)

Men.	Lucian, *Menippus* (*Necromantia*)
Mil.	Plautus, *Miles gloriosus* (*The Braggart Soldier*)
Min. Fel.	Minucius Felix
Mor.	Plutarch, *Moralia*
Mos.	Philo, *De vita Mosis* I, II (*On the Life of Moses* 1, 2)
MS(s)	Manuscript(s)
Mut.	Philo, *De mutatione nominum* (*On the Change of Names*)
Nat.	Caius Plinius Secundus (Pliny the Elder), *Naturalis historia* (*Natural History*)
Nat. d.	Cicero, *De natura deorum* (*On the Nature of the Gods*)
Nav.	Lucian, *Navigium* (*The Ship*, or *The Wishes*)
Ner.	Suetonius, *Divus Nero* (*Divine Nero*)
Nigr.	Lucian, *Nigrinus*
Noct. att.	Aulus Gellius, *Noctes atticae* (*Attic Nights*)
Nub.	Aristophanes, *Nubes* (*Clouds*)
Num.	Plutarch, *Numa*
Oct.	Minucius Felix, *Octavius*
Od.	Homer, *Odyssey*
Op.	Hesiod, *Opera et dies* (*Works and Days*)
Opif.	Philo, *De opificio mundi* (*On the Creation of the World*)
Or.	Demosthenes, (*Orations*)
Ord. libr. eug.	Galen, *De ordine librorum suorum ad Eugenianum* (*On the Ordering of his own Books, to Eugenianus*)
OT	Sophocles, *Oedipus tyrannus* (*Oedipus the King*)
Pan.	Epiphanius, *Panarion (Adversus haereses)* (*Refutation of All Heresies*)
Pan.	Isocrates, *Panathenaicus*
Pan.	Pliny the Younger, *Panegyricus*
Paneg.	Isocrates, *Panegyricus*
Peregr.	Lucian, *De morte Peregrini* (*The Passing of Peregrinus*)
Perik.	Menander, *Perikeiromenē* (*Rape of the Locks*)
Phaed.	Plato, *Phaedo*
Phal.	Lucian, *Phalaris*
Phars.	Marcus Annaeus Lucanus (Lucan), *Pharsalia* (more properly *De bello civili* [*On the Civil War*])
Phil.	Cicero, *Orationes philippicae*
Phil	Philippians
Philo	Philo of Alexandria
Philostr.	Philostratus
Phld.	Ignatius, *To the Philadelphians*
Pis.	Cicero, *In Pisonem*
Pl.	Plato
Plac. Hipp. Plat.	Galen, *On the Opinions of Hippocrates and Plato*
Plaut.	Plautus
Plin.	Caius Plinius Caecilius Secundus (Pliny the Younger)

Plut.	Aristophanes, *Plutus* (*The Rich Man*)
Plut.	Mestrius Plutarchus (Plutarch)
Pol.	Aristotle, *Politica* (*Politics*)
Polyb.	Polybius
Pomp.	Plutarch, *Pompeius* (*Pompey*)
Prae. ger. reip.	Plutarch, *Praecepta gerendae rei publicae* (*Precepts of Statecraft*)
Praem.	Philo, *De praemiis et poenis* (*On Rewards and Punishments*)
Praep. ev.	Eusebius, *Praeparatio evangelica* (*Preparation for the Gospel*)
Praescr.	Tertullian, *De praescriptione haereticorum* (*Prescription against Heretics*)
Prob.	Philo, *Quod omnis probus liber sit* (*That Every Good Person Is Free*)
Prog.	Aelius Theon, *Progymnasmata*
Prog.	Hermogenes, *Progymnasmata*
1QS	*Community Rule*
Quaest. conv.	Plutarch, *Quaestionum convivialum libri IX* (*Convivial Questions*)
Quint.	Marcus Fabius Quintilian (Quintilian)
Red. sen.	Cicero, *Post reditum in senatu* (*After His Return to the Senate*)
1 Regn.	Dio Chrysostom, *De regno I (Or. 1)* (*Kingship 1*)
Rep.	Cicero, *De republica* (*On the Republic*)
Resp.	Plato, *Respublica* (*Republic*)
Rh.	Aristotle, *Rhetorica* (*Rhetoric*)
Rhes.	Euripides, *Rhesus*
Rhet.	Aristotle, *Rhetorica* (*Rhetoric*)
Saec.	Horace, *Carmen saeculare*
Sall.	Caius Sallustius Crispus (Sallust)
Sat.	Aulus Persius Flaccus (Persius), *Satirae* (*Satires*)
Sat.	Juvenal, *Satirae* (*Satires*)
Sat.	Petronius, *Satyrica*
Sat.	Quintus Horatius Flaccus (Horace), *Satirae* (*Satires*)
Silv.	Publius Papinius Statius (Statius), *Silvae*
Simpl. med. temp.	Galen, *De simplicibus medicinis (On Simple Medicines)*
Smyrn.	Ignatius, *To the Smyrnaeans*
Somn.	Philo, *De somniis* I, II (*On Dreams* 1, 2)
Soph.	Sophocles
Spec.	Philo, *De specialibus legibus* I–IV (*On the Special Laws* 1–4)
Strat.	Polyaenus, *Stratēgēmata* (*Stratagems*)
Strom.	Clement of Alexandria, *Stromata* (*Miscellanies*)
Suet.	Caius Suetonius Tranquillus
Superst.	Plutarch, *De superstitione* (*On Superstition*)
Symp.	Lucian, *Symposium*
Symp.	Plato, *Symposium*
Tac.	Publius (or Caius) Cornelius Tacitus (Tacitus)

Tert.	Quintus Septimius Florens Tertullianus (Tertullian)
1–2 Thess	1–2 Thessalonians
Tib.	Suetonius, *Divus Tiberius* (*Divine Tiberius*)
Tim.	Aeschines, *In Timarchum* (*Against Timarchus*)
Tim.	Plato, *Timaeus*
Tim.	Plutarch, *Timoleon*
Tit.	Suetonius, *Divus Titus* (*Divine Titus*)
Trall.	Ignatius, *To the Trallians*
V A	Philostratus, *Vita Apolloni* (*Life of Apollonius*)
Vect.	Xenophon, *De vectigalibus* (*On Taxes*)
Vesp.	Suetonius, *Divus Vespasianus* (*Divine Vespasian*)
Virgil	Publius Vergilius Maro
Virt.	Philo, *De virtutibus* (*On the Virtues*)
Vit.	Josephus, *Vita* (*Life*)
Vit. Const.	Eusebius, *Vita Constantini* (*Life of Constantine*)
War	Josephus, *Bellum judaicum* (*Judean War*)

GENERAL

ABD	*Anchor Bible Dictionary*. Edited by D. N. Freedman. 6 vols. New York, 1992
ALGHJ	Arbeiten zur Literatur und Geschichte des hellenistischen Judentums
ANRW	*Aufstieg und Niedergang der römischen Welt: Geschichte und Kultur Roms im Spiegel der neueren Forschung*. Edited by H. Temporini and W. Haase. Berlin, 1972–
B.C.E.	before the Common Era
C.E.	Common Era
CE	Common Era
CIJ	*Corpus inscriptionum judaicarum*
CIL	*Corpus inscriptionum latinarum*
CPJ	*Corpus papyrorum judaicarum*. Edited by V. Tcherikover and A. Fuks. 3 vols. Cambridge Mass.: Harvard University Press, 1957–1964
CRINT	Compendia Rerum Iudaicarum ad Novum Testamentum
d.	died
IG	*Inscriptiones graecae*. Editio minor. Berlin, 1924
JIWE	*Jewish Inscriptions of Western Europe*. Ed. D. Noy. 2 vols. Cambridge, 1995
JSJ	*Journal for the Study of Judaism in the Persian, Hellenistic, and Roman Periods*
LSJ	Liddell, H. G., R. Scott, H. S. Jones, *A Greek-English Lexicon*. 9th ed. with revised supplement. Oxford, 1996
op. cit.	in the work cited

PWRE	*Paulys Realenzyklopädie der classischen Altertumswissenschaft*
RB	*Revue biblique*
SEG	Supplementum epigraphicum graecum
TDNT	*Theological Dictionary of the New Testament.* Edited by G. Kittel and G. Friedrich. Translated by G. W. Bromiley. 10 vols. Grand Rapids, 1964–1976
viz.	namely
vs.	versus

Introduction

Several years ago an editor at Hendrickson graciously invited me to consider putting together a volume of my scattered essays. I felt honored. Like many academics, I had published papers in places not easily accessible—in now out-of-print *Festschriften* or other essay collections—and I was fairly sure that some of these had not been widely read. But then, as I began gathering the more obscure pieces and reading them through again, it struck me with certain clarity that many of them should remain precisely where they were, buried. This, therefore, is not that originally envisaged book of studies, united only by common authorship.

The only reason to produce a new academic book is to contribute something coherent for scholarly reflection. In the past year I began to think that a number of my published and unpublished papers, on Josephus, Judean society, and Christian origins, had such a unifying theme and so could usefully be brought together in one volume. Driving my research for a number of years has been a set of questions related to historical and literary-interpretative methods, and the relationship between these two. What is history? What does it mean to read Josephus (or any other ancient narrative)? What is the relationship between reading the narrative and reconstructing the past—whether the past behind the story or the past represented by the text's own existence as an artifact itself?

On the historical side of the ledger, one of my primary concerns has been with the appropriateness of our standard categories. Oxford philosopher Gilbert Ryle taught us to think in terms of "category-mistakes"—when we place phenomena in categories that do not fit,[1] and especially when we set out to compare two very different kinds of phenomena as if they belonged in comparable categories: apples and oranges, a platoon and an army, Judaism and Christianity. The more that I have worked on the Eastern Mediterranean under Roman rule, the more I have become convinced that some of our most basic analytical categories, such as "religion," "Judaism," and even "gospel," do not map onto ancient conceptions or language. And if they do not, what are the implications of that disparity for our analysis? What categories should we use instead?

And so, I seemed to have in hand the promise of a coherent contribution: "methods and categories" in the study of Josephus, Judea, and Christian origins. The remainder of this introduction will sketch the book's contents against the background of such a unifying framework.

[1] Ryle applied this above all to the notion of the "ghost in the machine": *The Concept of Mind* (London: Hutchinson's, 1949), 15–23.

The book comprises eleven chapters in three parts. Part 1 concerns the interpretation and historical use of Josephus. This is fundamental to everything else because, of course, Josephus is the chief narrative source for the history of Judea in the Herodian and early Roman periods. How can we use him, then, for that history?

Chapter 1, "Josephus as Authority," broaches the issue directly by exploring what Josephus's narratives are made of. Through an examination of illustrative episodes, I argue that using Josephus as a simple window into the past is, in effect, a category-mistake. He writes artistic narratives, not manuals of factual nuggets that may simply be appropriated as historical facts. That would be cheating. There is no way around the historian's arduous work of seeking to understand each kind of evidence contextually, constructing and testing hypotheses, and admitting when the evidence is insufficient to permit proper demonstration of these hypotheses. Crucially, where Josephus is our only source for specific events, personalities, intentions, and motives, which is often the case, we must face the fact that we have no way of testing hypotheses—and so we cannot claim to know. On the other hand, Josephus's narratives are themselves, as efforts at communication with real audiences, direct evidence for a new set of historical questions concerning the situation of a Judean living in Flavian Rome.

Chapters 2 through 4 develop this approach by examining the following issues more closely: the meaning of Josephus's narratives for specific audiences in Rome, how he published his works, what he assumed his audience already knew and did not know, and how this communicative context helped to shape his narratives (chapter 2); his pervasive use of irony in communicating with Roman audiences, the importance of that irony for understanding his narratives in their Flavian-Roman context, and the consequences for using Josephus as a historical source (chapter 3); and finally, the general problem of trying to extract historical facts from Josephus's narratives, with a critical survey of techniques that are often used, based on the method of "contradictory evidence" or reading against the grain (chapter 4).

If part 1 deals with Josephus's narratives, asking where we might go from there, part 2 asks about a number of first-century historical phenomena. The first chapter here (chapter 5) anchors the section by tackling the basic problem of historical categories for studying Judea and Judeans. There I ask about the language we so easily use in relation to "religion," and especially "Judaism." I try to show that, far from debating whether this last noun should be singular or plural, we need to face the fact that the word itself was not used, and that the exceedingly rare *Ioudaïsmos* appears to mean something else. Chapter 5 is thus a plea to align our categories—for the "emic" sorts of study we normally conduct—with those actually used by the ancients. Once we do that, and see that Judeans understood themselves as an *ethnos* comparable to other nations, it will have profound effects on our understanding of Judean life, Judean-Roman relations, what we call "conversion," and (though the topic is not developed here) the early Christian predicament in relation to Judean culture. Judean law, tradition, and custom (not "Judaism") was a very different cultural complex from belief in Jesus.

Chapters 6 through 8 are devoted to two features of the Judean cultural landscape that continue to fascinate scholars: Pharisees and Essenes. Chapters 6 and 7 deal with Josephus's portraits of the Pharisees (as narrative actors and as a philosophical school). On the one hand, I try to show something of how complex and fascinating those narratives are, and how small a supporting role the Pharisees play; then I move to the implications for trying to extract historical information from such a stylized presentation. In the case of the Essenes (chapter 8), I do something similar. But there I felt an obligation to discuss historical implications in conversation with the still-dominant hypothesis that the primary evidence for Josephus's (second-hand) report comes from the Dead Sea Scrolls found near Qumran. That hypothesis provides, I hope, a useful foil for my main task of reading Josephus's Essenes contextually. My argument is that when we read his Essenes in context, paying attention to his structures, language, and themes (something that has not often been attempted), it becomes increasingly difficult to imagine that the group he is describing were the people of the sectarian Dead Sea Scrolls.

Part 3 applies the same concerns for method and categories to Christian origins. Chapter 9 anchors that section with a survey, and attempt at "stratification," of a crucial term for early Christian communities: *euangelion*, usually translated as "gospel" and assumed to be shared by more or less all followers of Jesus. I argue, by contrast, that the evidence is better explained if this was understood to be a proprietary term of Paul's gentile mission (it was truly *his* Announcement). This accounts for Mark's embrace of the term, in sharp contrast to the hesitation of Matthew, Luke, and John. Only with the third generation did the term begin to be used in a proto-catholic sense—with the rougher Pauline edges smoothed off in the process. Chapter 10 applies this broad stratification to an interpretation of Paul's letter to the Romans (with whom he has not yet shared his *euangelion*) as an urgent and earnest letter sent to defend his much-maligned Announcement (Rom 1:16) before the most prominent Judean-Christian community in the world.

Finally, chapter 11 applies the same sorts of methodological concerns as chapters 6–8 to the two-volume master work in the New Testament, Luke-Acts. Again, the question concerns the presentation of the Pharisees and other leadership groups (especially, the Sanhedrin, chief priests, and Sadducees) in that work, and their functions in the narratives. The ultimate problem, again, is how to use this narrative for historical reconstruction.

All translations are my own unless otherwise indicated.

It remains to thank several parties to this experimental effort. First, I thank two of my doctoral students. Michael Helfield undertook many editorial tasks, including the preparation of a unified bibliography and two of the indexes. Michael's preface clarifies a few formatting issues. William den Hollander prepared the index for ancient persons and places. I am grateful to them both for their valuable help. Second, my long association with Hendrickson Publishers has always been a happy one. But it has never been more pleasant than now, in connection with this volume. Shirley Decker-Lucke, Allan Emery, and Sara Scott have been particularly encouraging, helpful, and professional. Third, as many of the essays indicate, I have been extremely fortunate to have a wide circle of outstanding scholars as friends, colleagues, and discussion partners. Even those who disagree with me most emphatically have been patient and generous in their criticism over the years. Although most of these essays are no more than five years old, re-reading them now brings home to me how far our exchanges over method have progressed. And they continue in an atmosphere of respectful engagement, as we challenge and learn from each other. I hope that these chapters may serve as useful reference points for those discussions and as stimuli for other students of this endlessly compelling and consequential period.

Part I

JOSEPHUS: INTERPRETATION AND HISTORY

Chapter 1

Josephus as Authority for First-Century Judea

The following study addresses what seems to me a fundamental problem in the use of Josephus's writings for studying Roman Judea, namely, his status as an *authority*. I begin from the observation that Josephus is, and has always been (though for changing reasons), regarded as the peerless authority for first-century Judea, and that this assumption runs even more deeply than we perhaps realize. My argument, simply, is that he should not be so regarded. This is not because he is unworthy or "unreliable" or only partially reliable—or because of anything to do with reliability. It is rather because the whole appeal to reliable authorities in the discipline of history is an error of categories. History has, or should have, a problem with authority.

After a consideration of the origins and bases of Josephus's authoritative status in antiquity and in modern times, I examine two case studies concerning matters for which he is generally assumed to be authoritative: the career of Pontius Pilate and the civil strife in Caesarea that, he claims, catalyzed the revolt. Finally, I offer some reflections on the nature of history and what it might mean to do history with Josephus's narratives.

Authority and Truth in Josephus: Origins and Character

Antiquity and the Middle Ages

It is widely observed that in the Greco-Roman world the competition for honor (φιλοτιμία) was a zero-sum game played by members of the elite classes; each prominent man tried to assert his *auctoritas* at the expense of his peers.[1] The writing of history was but one occupation of the same group that led all aspects of ancient society: as magistrates, councilors or senators, governors, priests, landowners, and military commanders (e.g., Thucydides, Xenophon, Polybius, Fabius Pictor, Cato the Elder, Cicero and Atticus potentially, Sallust, Caesar, Tacitus).[2]

[1] Cf. T. P. Wiseman, *Roman Political Life: 90 B.C.–A.D. 69* (Exeter: University of Exeter Press, 1985), 3–19.

[2] For the Roman elite and its values under the early Empire, see S. P. Mattern, *Rome and the Enemy: Imperial Strategy in the Principate* (Berkeley: University of California, 1999), 1–23, 162–211.

Works of history, increasingly supplemented by explicit autobiographical notes,[3] were an extension of political life. Like other forms of public benefaction and commemoration, but all the more because they sought to teach lessons to future statesmen, they reinforced their author's claim to recognition as social paragon and moral arbiter. As a branch of literature, history was produced and received according to the ubiquitous values of the rhetorical training in which the elite had been nurtured (Cicero, *De or.* 2.62–64).[4] Accordingly, the author's perceived character (ἦθος) was the crucial criterion for acceptance, as well as the basis for his appeals to reason (λόγος) and emotion (πάθος).[5] Character was considered a product of blood lines, familial and personal achievements (especially military), wealth, offices, powerful friends, and benefactions given and received.[6]

Such elite competition famously characterized the late Republic in Rome, where powerful men asserted their superior potency and status (*potestas, auctoritas, dignitas, virtus, gloria,* etc.), until Augustus found a way to achieve monarchical rule while preserving a veneer of republican values, drawing all glory to his own person. Tacitus remarks (*Ann.* 1.1; cf. *Agr.* 1.2–3) that the scope for personal assertions of authority has by his time shriveled to nothing, yielding instead to flattery of the supreme leader.[7] Prominent men largely stopped writing history or autobiography; even those who dabbled in biography risked danger if they seemed to praise models of dangerous behavior or implicitly criticize the regime.[8] These vicissitudes of history-writing reflect its extricable bond with the author's prestige. A historical account, if not merely for show or entertainment, was a major political-moral statement by an actor-author (*auctor*).

Greek cities did not cultivate the same opportunities for personal power as the Roman Republic did, but there too the writing of history had generally involved an eminent man's production of an authoritative narrative (e.g., Thucydides, Xenophon, Polybius). We see this in the "continuator" tradition, according to which each new historian sought to become the authority for his own age, taking up the past from the point at which an established writer had ended his narrative.[9] The process of continuation often combined a degree of deference with self-interested

---

[3]Cf. G. Misch, *A History of Autobiography in Antiquity* (trans. E. W. Dickes; 2 vols.; London: Routledge, 1950), 1:231–33. Two relevant cases are Nicolaus of Damascus and Josephus; the latter's substantial *Life* was written as an appendix to the *magnum opus,* to exhibit the author's character (*Ant.* 20.266–67; *Life* 430).

[4]On the passage, and Cicero's view of historiography in general, see A. J. Woodman, *Rhetoric in Classical Historiography: Four Studies* (London: Croom Helm, 1988), 70–216.

[5]For these three sources of proof see Aristotle, *Rhet.* bks. 1–2.

[6]On the crucial role of character in history–writing see J. Marincola, *Authority and Tradition in Ancient Historiography* (Cambridge: Cambridge University Press, 1997), 128–74.

[7]C. S. Kraus and A. J. Woodman, *Latin Historians* (Oxford: Oxford University Press, 1997), 88–97.

[8]Tacitus, *Ann.* 3.76; 4.43–5; 16.7, 22; Pliny, *Ep.* 1.17.3.

[9]Xenophon's *Hellenica* continues Thucydides' *History;* Polybius continues both Aratus and Timaeus, and is in turn continued by Posidonius and by Strabo's lost *History,* among others. On the continuator tradition, see Marincola, *Authority,* 237–57.

challenge. Even among the accounts we know about, we can identify rival efforts to become the continuator (e.g. Strabo and Posidonius after Polybius), and the extant writers often declare that they are challenging earlier authors who deal with the same periods (e.g., Polybius 1.3.7–10; 3.6.1–4, 9.1–5; 12.2; 16.4.1; Josephus, *War* 1.1–8; *Life* 336–367). Polybius's decision to begin where Timaeus had finished (1.5.2), implying a basic admission of authority, by no means prevents him from savagely attacking the same writer in the famous digression of book 12, further enhancing his own claim to trustworthiness.

When Josephus charges in his prologue to *Judean War* that his eloquent Greek contemporaries "write the history of the Assyrians and Medes, as though these events had been less finely reported by the ancient historical writers" (1.13), or "The industrious man is not the one who merely remodels another person's arrangement and order, but the one who, by speaking of recent things, thereby establishes the body of the history in a distinctive way" (1.16), he seems to expect applause for scoring a lethal point. Namely, whereas he is doing what Thucydides and Polybius did, establishing himself as the sole trustworthy authority for this contemporary subject, his critics (a different group from those already disparaged in 1.2–8 for having written up the war in second-rate sophistic terms) appear obsessed with merely rearranging the work of the established ancient authorities. By alternatively doing battle with current rivals and fending off criticism from others, he attempts to secure his place as the unrivalled authority for this crucial period of Judean and Roman history.

In *War*, consequently, Josephus justifies his beginning point on the Polybian ground that earlier periods have been tolerably well covered by others (1.17). He acknowledges that others have written about the recent war (1.1–8), but he seeks to replace their "sophistic" ephemera with an authoritative guide based on unique access to both sides of the conflict (1.1–3). In this respect, at least, he succeeded beyond his wildest dreams. He did indeed become the sole authority for the period—until today. That those rival accounts did not survive even to late antiquity, as far as we can tell, seems to reflect their massive prestige deficit: they lacked the authority that he enjoyed, chiefly by virtue of connections with the Flavian house (*Life* 361–367).

In the elite circles that produced ancient history we do not find authors inviting their audiences, in any systematic way, to consider a series of specific problems of fact, review the range of available evidence (catalogued and located), and reach logically probable conclusions. Greek and Latin lacked any term corresponding to our "evidence" in this sense, their "proofs" (e.g., τεκμηρία, ἀποδείξεις) being of a different, rhetorical kind,[10] and although Hellenistic and Roman-period historians liberally used the language of truthfulness, precision, and probability (e.g., ἀλήθεια, ἀκρίβεια, ἀσφάλεια), those terms had more to do with rhetorical than empirical concerns. Lucian even sounds like Ranke when he insists, "One task only is the historian's: to speak as it happened" (*Hist. conscr.* 39), until

[10] C. W. Hedrick, *Ancient History: Monuments and Documents* (Oxford: Blackwell, 2006), 18–19.

we recall that it is a teacher of rhetoric writing and we read the context, which lacks any directions for getting at the facts.

Here too Polybius provides illustrative material. He decries the widespread trust of Fabius Pictor, justified by admirers on the premise that the Roman historian was a senator and a contemporary of the events he described. Polybius insists that readers test "what is said" and not simply trust "the one saying it" (3.9.1–5). This reveals that critiques of authority could be asserted and heard, but also that deferring to accounts by prominent figures (such as a senator) was the normal reflex. He asks the reader to "test the facts" (or "circumstances") (ἐξ αὐτῶν τῶν πραγμάτων ποιεῖσθαι τὰς δοκιμασίας) and not to assume the senator's trustworthiness (3.9.5). Yet the example he provides as a critique of Fabius rests entirely on a matter of speculative judgment concerning Carthaginian motives (3.8.1–11)—nothing that can actually be tested. Or again, in his treatment of the Cleomenic War (229/8–222 B.C.E.), rather than interrogating the two main sources available to him as to their factual correctness, Polybius rejects Phylarchus's account out of hand, on the basis of that author's repugnant political sympathies, choosing rather "to follow Aratus"; Phylarchus's "falsehood" (τὸ ψεῦδος, 2.56.2) consists in his alleged bias toward the Spartans, excessive sympathy with the plight of their allies, and failure to mention the nobility of Megalopolis, Polybius's own city (2.56–63). Consequently, Aratus's account is simply "true," whereas Phylarchus's is just as surely "false" (2.56.2). Truthfulness in history-writing was for him inseparable from *moral trustworthiness.*

Thus, although Polybius is regarded as one of the more careful historians, when he comes to divulge his methods for ascertaining facts he is disarmingly quick to invoke character-based criteria and "probability" arguments based upon character.[11] He justifies his prefatory account of the first Punic War on the grounds that the two existing sources are biased toward either the Romans or the Carthaginians: his truthfulness will consist in his *avoidance of such bias,* praising even enemies and chastising even friends (1.14.1–8). We find the same understanding of truth or accuracy as avoidance of partisanship among his many Greek and Roman successors, famously in Tacitus's promise to write *sine ira et studio* (*Ann.* 1.1), and spelled out in Lucian of Samosata's well-known essay on *How History Should be Written:*[12] "This, then, is what the historian should be: fearless, incorruptible, free, a friend of frank speech and truth, who calls a fig a fig and a trough a trough, as the comic writer says" (*Hist. conscr.* 41). "Truth" here is tested by freedom from bias; the crucial question of *how one knows* is all but ignored.

It would be easy, but surely misguided, to trivialize this understanding of balance and frank speech toward friends and enemies as the essence of "truthfulness." To be sure, it was part and parcel of the larger moral-rhetorical context

---

[11] Who advised young King Philip to conduct his impious assault on Thermos? Even one who was not present, Polybius avers, *may discern from the character of his two advisors* that it must have been Demetrius (5.12.5–8).

[12] *Hist. conscr.* 8–13. See in general Woodman, *Rhetoric,* 70–116, esp. 73–75.

of ancient historiography that one appear to speak the truth fearlessly. But this preoccupation had real meaning in the social context in which histories were "published"—which is to say orally, before an immediate live audience.[13] Authors had to be reminded and cajoled to remember indeterminate future *readers* (Lucian, *Hist. conscr.* 13, 40) because inevitably one wrote for one's local peer audiences (*Hist. conscr.* 10). In such public contexts everyone understood that, although it was easy to speak ill of enemies not present, it really did take courage not to flatter the powerful, especially if they or their friends were present at a recital, and genuine moral fortitude to openly criticize them. Nevertheless, this is not what we normally mean in the first instance by truthfulness and accuracy, and the difference is vast.

So, when Josephus speaks about writing the truth (ἀλήθεια) with precision (ἀκρίβεια; *War* 1.6, 9, 17, 30; 7.454; *Ant.* 1.4; *Life* 360–361, 364–367; *Ag. Ap.* 1.6, 50), his meaning is clear from the context. Whereas other writers in Rome are predictably flattering those now in power, while denigrating the defeated Judeans (*War* 1.2, 6–8), he will set the record straight and tell the truth, *which is to say,* he will not overcompensate by praising his compatriots too much, but will give due praise and blame to both sides (1.9). The opposite of truth here is not simple factual error, but *bias.*[14] The post-Enlightenment notion of facts *in themselves,* which impose themselves on all neutral observers no matter what their social status, and which deserve to be studied precisely for their intrinsic merit, in order to "get it right," is a different concept altogether—and still a long way off.

Except in his opening claim to eyewitness status (*War* 1.2–3), which cannot account for much of the narrative content,[15] Josephus's *War* and *Life* divulge little about the sources of his knowledge.[16] *Judean Antiquities* is different: not a war monograph, it presents itself as the translation of another corpus, the sacred texts of the Judeans (*Ant.* 1.5–10), and along the way cites many other supporting documents and texts by name. But even there Josephus makes it clear that his priestly status and peerless character are the principal guarantees of his truthful interpretation, the authority behind the artful creation of this "useful" and "beautiful" work (*Ant.* 1.9).[17] No one else could have produced it, he declares, citing his combination of illustrious ancestry and unique achievement (20.266–267), and that is presumably why he was pressed into doing it (1.10).

---

[13] Lucian, *Hist. conscr.* 7, 29; cf. R. J. Starr, "The Circulation of Texts in the Ancient World," *Mnemosyne* 64 (1987): 213–23.

[14] Marincola, *Authority,* 158–74.

[15] That is, he cannot have known *by personal observation* anything until about 50 C.E., when he turned thirteen, or anything that occurred in the towns where he was not present (including, presumably, the crucial events in Caesarea from 59 to 66, at *War* 2.266ff.), or in besieged sites where he was not on the inside—notably Jerusalem.

[16] In *War* itself Josephus reveals little about his sources, though he leaves openings when he mentions deserters from besieged sites or the old woman and children who survived Masada (*War* 7.399). Only in *The Life* (358–367) and *Against Apion* (1.50–56) will he indicate more solid resources: an allegedly extensive correspondence with King Agrippa II and consultation of the Roman generals' *commentarii.*

[17] *Ant.* 1.6–9; 16.187; 20.266–267.

Throughout his entire corpus, Josephus obviously bends episodes to his narrator's will. To take a small but telling example: when the wealthy Maria addresses the infant she is about to eat (inside besieged Jerusalem, the story being known to Josephus and the Romans *by rumor; War* 6.214) she expounds upon the evils of "war, famine, and civil strife" (6.205). This little speech conveniently reprises a programmatic triad from the prologue (1.27), the three evils for which Josephus has since blamed the rebels (4.137; cf. 375–376), and what the Romans recognize as the Judean plight (6.13); most strikingly, it anticipates Titus's restatement of the same triad when he hears of the enormity a few sentences later (6.215–216). It is more or less impossible that these characters were all so obliging to the narrator, and that he happened to know and report it. He does not invite his audiences to investigate the basis of his knowledge. Like his contemporary historians, he is saying in effect: "Trust me: I know what happened and especially *what it means for us.*"

Historical works, then, along with treatises on ethnography and geography, cosmology, physics, biology, and astronomy/astrology, were part of the bulwark of accepted authority in antiquity. We can only be astonished at the degree to which Roman leaders and authors deferred to such recognized sources for their information about the cosmos, foreign peoples, and distant places. Although more accurate information was often available from merchants and travelers with first-hand experience, lacking the prestige of the established authorities those sources were generally ignored.[18] Notwithstanding occasional outbreaks of the empirical impulse, chiefly among sub-elite specialists, deference to authority would remain the dominant mode of learning throughout the Middle Ages; only a Copernican revolution could overthrow it.

Although none of the rivals Josephus mentions in *War*'s prologue has left traces for comparison with his own work, the legacies of Nicolaus of Damascus and Justus of Tiberias help to put this issue of authority in relief. Nicolaus was a highly educated and skillful writer, whose public career had given him unmatched access to the most powerful men alive, and so to the best information of his time.[19] Yet, although sections of his 144-volume *Universal History* have survived in relative plenty (via the 10th-century *Excerpta* of Constantine Porphyrogennitus), nothing remains of his detailed accounts of Judea or King Herod, though he wrote copiously of both; we know these parts only through what Josephus—the new authority on Judean matters—adapted from Nicolaus for his own purposes.[20]

---

[18]On the deference to authority in all spheres of knowledge see Mattern, *Rome,* 24–80; C. R. Whittaker, *Rome and Its Frontiers: The Dynamics of Empire* (London: Routledge, 2004), 63–87.

[19]The standard account remains B.-Z. Wacholder, *Nicolaus of Damascus* (Berkeley: University of California Press, 1962).

[20]A concise survey of Josephus's *Nachleben,* including the insightful contrast with Nicolaus and Justus, is in S. Bowman, "Josephus in Byzantium," in *Josephus, Judaism, and Christianity* (ed. L. H. Feldman and G. Hata; Detroit: Wayne State University Press, 1987), 362–85; for this point, 367.

Justus of Tiberias was evidently also a talented writer, as secretary and protégé of King Agrippa II (*Life* 40, 336). He too must have had access to precious information, and modern scholars would be delighted had his work survived. Yet Justus found little uptake among the Christian authors who preserved Josephus, and his works, though they seem to have treated Judean affairs almost exclusively, disappeared entirely.[21] We know about Justus only through Josephus's criticisms of him, and those criticisms would echo through the ages. Early on, Justus lost the competition for prestige: once Josephus was regarded as *the authority* for Judea, his rival had no chance. Eusebius's ready endorsement of Josephus's moral critique of Justus (*Hist. eccl.* 3.10.8) shows that the contest had long been settled by the fourth century. The ninth-century Patriarch Photius claims to have read Justus's work, and briefly indicates its contents (*Bibl.* 33), although he devotes nearly half of this entry to restating with enthusiasm Josephus's dismissal of Justus. By the time of the *Suda Lexicon* in the tenth century, the entry on Justus merely cites Josephus as a sufficient repudiation (I.450: "He took it upon himself to compile a Judean history and write certain commentaries; but Josephus exposes this fellow as a fraud, for he was writing history in the same period as Josephus").[22]

Plainly, the very different evaluations of Josephus and his near contemporaries by the Christian writers whose judgments determined what would be copied for survival had little to do with any critical investigation of their accounts. It had everything to do with a presumed *moral* compatibility that was buttressed by Josephus's overwhelming prestige. After the initial boost provided by his Flavian social connections, a curious thing happened to Josephus's legacy. The Judean community declined utterly to show an interest in their famous son. This is the flip-side of the authority question, for no matter how good his *information* might have been, he was—like Phylarchus to Polybius—perceived as morally reprehensible and *therefore* as an *untrustworthy guide* (see already Josephus's response to moral criticism in *War* 3.438–442; *Life* 416, 425). Christian authors took up Josephus's work with enthusiasm, however, precisely because they found him as congenial as his compatriots had found him objectionable. At least a dozen Christian authors of the second and third centuries, from Theophilus of Antioch to Tertullian and Origen, use Josephus as an authority,[23] but they do not explain *why* they credit his works.

Eusebius is important because he not only makes extensive use of Josephus;[24] he also explains why. He introduces him as "the most distinguished of historians

---

[21] Justus's history may, however, have provided the basis for Julius Africanus's historical schema, which furnished a foundation for many later chroniclers: see Bowman, "Byzantium," 366.

[22] This language (ἐπεχείρησε μὲν καὶ αὐτὸς Ἰουδαϊκὴν ἱστορίαν συντάξαι) closely matches Josephus's descriptions at *Life* 40, 338.

[23] Cf. M. E. Hardwick, *Josephus as an Historical Source in Patristic Literature through Eusebius* (Atlanta: Scholars Press, 1989), 10, 31, 34, 49, 60.

[24] See S. Inowlocki, "The Citations of Jewish Greek Authors in Eusebius of Caesarea's *Praeparatio Evangelica* and *Demonstratio Evangelica*," (M. Litt. thesis. Oxford University: Faculty of Oriental Studies, 2001). The tenth-century *Lexicon* (entry, "Jesus [Ἰησοῦς],

(ἐπισημότατος ἱστορικῶν) among the Hebrews"[25] (*Hist. eccl.* 1.5.3; cf. 1.6.9). After uncritically endorsing Josephus's claims to comprehensive knowledge (cf. *War* 1.3), he elaborates that the historian was

> the *most renowned* (ἐπιδοξότατος) man of the Judeans at that time, not only with his compatriots but *also among the Romans*, such that he indeed was *honored* by the erection of a statue in the city of the Romans, and the works composed by him were *considered worthy* of [deposit in] the library. (*Hist. eccl.* 3.9.1–2)

Eusebius reinforces Josephus's *credibility* (πιστεύεσθαι) by endorsing his claims against his rival Justus of Tiberias (*Hist. eccl.* 3.9.3), accepting Josephus's assurances that such powerful figures as King Agrippa and his family as well as the *imperator* Titus all vouched for the *War*'s accuracy (3.9.10–11; cf. *Life* 361–363). The *Suda Lexicon* will reiterate many of the same points: Josephus was a lover of the truth (φιλαλήθης), who spoke of both the Baptist and Jesus and James, and whose fame led to his being honored with a statue (I.503–504). Josephus's authority sprang ultimately from the esteem in which powerful Romans had first held him.[26] Here was a Jerusalemite of impeccable social standing before the war, who had nevertheless castigated the Judean rebels, also describing in lurid detail the fall of Jerusalem—thereby seeming to demonstrate the fulfillment of Jesus' predictions (e.g., Origen, *C. Cels.* 2.13.68–85).

Josephus, of course, had made no connection between the fall of Jerusalem and Christian claims, but it seemed possible to use him in this way: a Judean witness who wrote with unrestrained emotion about the alleged failings and crimes of his contemporaries. His pervasive celebration and defense of Judean law and culture could either be minimized, as it was by Origen, who famously credited him with being "not far from the truth" (*C. Cels.* 1.47; *Comm. Matt.* 10.17), and by Eusebius, or it could be squarely faced and exploited, as it was by the fourth-century writer we know as Pseudo-Hegesippus. This author wrote (*De excidio* 2.12): "However, it was no detriment to the truth that he [Josephus] was not a believer; but this adds more weight to his testimony: that while he *was an unbeliever*, and though *unwilling* that this [the *testimonium flavianum*] should be true, he has not denied it to be so." Hegesippus felt strongly enough about the authority of Josephus's *witness* ("an outstanding historian," 1.1), yet *also* about his being too Jewish, that he wrote a new history of Jerusalem's fall—now in "truthful" Christian terms.[27] Again, the authority of the new version would rest not in independent investigation of what had happened, but on the combination of moral congeniality and accreditation by worthy (fourth-century) contemporaries. It would take another 1,350 years

---

Christ and our God," item 229, line 164) identifies Josephus as the historian to whom Eusebius often referred.

[25] For the positive valuation of "Hebrew" in Eusebius, see Inowlocki, "Citations," 52–64, 112–21.

[26] Hardwick, *Patristic Literature*, 74.

[27] Passages cited here are from the opening paragraph of the work. A concise introduction to Pseudo-Hegesippus in relation to Josephus is A. Bell, "Josephus and Pseudo-Hegesippus," in *Josephus, Judaism, and Christianity* (ed. Feldman and Hata), 349–61.

for the Cambridge mathematician and heterodox theologian William Whiston to press the adoptionist line of Origen and Eusebius as far as actually making room for Josephus within the Christian fold—now as an Ebionite bishop.[28] Either way, Josephus's prestige remained unmatched, even by works such as that of Ps.-Hegesippus, through the Middle Ages and into modernity.

Josephus's Authority in Modern Scholarship

Writers of the modern *Umwelt* manuals in the nineteenth and twentieth centuries would continue to use Josephus as their generic *Companion to the* NT, but their rationale was fundamentally different from that of the church fathers. As the basis for their esteem, Josephus's personal prestige gave way to a conception of *raw facts* and *sources* presumed to be embedded in his accounts.

If it is possible to speak of the Enlightenment as a coherent movement, its defining trait was the repudiation of all so-called knowledge derived from authorities. Common reasoning applied to repeatable observation became the only acceptable way of knowing, in a world now grown up and free of tradition's tutelage.[29] Like other disciplines, history needed rescuing from accrued sacred tradition. Once the clear-sighted critic had burned away the thick patina of clerical orthodoxy, it was hoped, the plain facts of astronomy, biology, physics, geography, and history—for Deists, the very words of God—would impose themselves on honest and neutral thinkers, demanding a new view of the world.

Ancient history did not immediately take up the positive "scientific" logic of the Enlightenment. The *philosophes* of the eighteenth century, in a striking parallel to their ancient elite counterparts, viewed history as but one of their many encyclopedic pursuits, and they shunned specialization in the field as pedantic. Though sometimes diligent in examining sources, they tended to write sweeping interpretative histories accompanied by vigorous moral assessment based in universal principles. In their animus against Christianity they were hardly objective, though they believed their harsh assessments justifiable in the service of truth.[30]

The accommodation of history to the new scientific conception of independent facts came chiefly in the nineteenth century. Historians such as B. G. Niebuhr and Leopold von Ranke insisted, against the Enlightenment synthesizers, on studying the details of particular places, states, and individuals without assuming the normativeness of a universal "natural law," as the Enlightenment had done, and therefore also withholding moral judgment. Their prime directive was to get the facts correct and only afterwards, where possible and with great care, to move

[28]So "Dissertation 1" attached to W. Whiston's ubiquitous 1737 translation of Josephus.

[29]Immanuel Kant's *Was ist Aufklärung?* (1784) is a classic statement. The opening paragraph declares: "'Have the courage to use your own understanding' is therefore the motto of the Enlightenment."

[30]An excellent analysis, with vastly more nuance than I can attempt, is in P. Gay, *The Enlightenment: An Interpretation* (New York: Knopf, 1969), 368–96.

up to general statements drawn from these particulars. The momentum in history was moving decisively away from the grand narratives preserved from antiquity, driven by universal principles of nature and morality, toward the atoms thought to constitute the surviving evidence, whether these were found in material remains, in non-literary documents, or in sources distilled from the surviving literary texts (a specialty of Niebuhr).[31]

The scientific turn in history proved its value in the later nineteenth century as thousands of material remains from antiquity were found, cataloged, and interpreted: coins, papyrus documents, funerary and civic inscriptions, and remains of monuments. This gathering of new evidence generated dictionaries, encyclopedias, and other reference works of hitherto unimaginable quality, considerably refining our understanding of social, cultural, legal, and linguistic variation in antiquity. This fund continues to provide the basis for much of our analysis of antiquity.

A problem, however, was that the new enthusiasm for raw data and particular facts tended to create the expectation that *any and all such data,* once discovered, could be treated in the same way, no matter where they originated—for a fact was a fact. This mood conditioned also the interpretation of literary texts, including Josephus's works. The scholar's aim was now to get past the subjective, moralizing interpretation of the author to the facts beneath, or, if not the facts, to the earliest and least corrupted sources behind the extant writings.

Although the presence of two or more overlapping literary sources for an event, or confirmation of certain items by archaeology, made this task of extracting facts appear reasonable, the problem of what to do when only one narrative survived—this is most often the case with Josephus—would take much longer to be recognized as a general problem, with the "linguistic turn" in historical study since the 1960s. In the meantime, because of his intersections at some points with other texts and material remains, Josephus and his hypothetical sources tended to be accepted by default, unless there was a specific reason to reject them: if the passage in question did not seem obviously colored by his "biases." It was as though Josephus had *inscribed* or *mirrored* the realities of life in some kind of neutral, value-free language.

Such a distinctively modern adoption of Josephus as preserver of facts is embodied in Emil Schürer's *History of the Jewish People in the Age of Jesus Christ.* This manual justifiably remains a standard reference work, following extensive revision by the Oxford-based team from the 1970s, if only for its wealth of references. Its stated purpose is to assist the NT scholar in relating "Jesus and the Gospel" to "the *Jewish world* of his time"[32]—not to Josephus's narratives. Given Schürer's heavy reliance on Josephus, it is remarkable that his introduction fails even to mention the man by name, let alone the credentials or fame—or the

[31] See G. G. Iggers, *The German Conception of History: The National Tradition of Historical Thought from Herder to the Present* (Middleton: Wesleyan University Press, 1968), 3–123—with valuable correctives to Ranke's familiar image in North America.

[32] Schürer-Vermes, *Jewish People,* 1:1.

statue!—that had so impressed his ancient and medieval users. The modern historian implies rather that he is dealing with *facts in themselves,* and not with the messy problems of a human personality and bias. We are in a completely different world from that of Eusebius, though both authors depend crucially on Josephus's works.

Schürer's introduction, for example, already contains a number of statements that he presents as facts, though they merely reword Josephus. This continues throughout the work, as a few random instances will illustrate. "Antipater was now all-powerful at court and enjoyed his father's absolute confidence. But he was *not satisfied. He wanted total power and could hardly wait* for his father to die."[33] "But Sabinus, *whose conscience was uneasy* because of the Temple robberies and *other misdeeds,* made off as quickly as possible."[34] "His [Philip's] reign was *mild, just, and peaceful.*"[35] All this is Josephus, not fact. How can we in the twenty-first century know about such internal motives and moral qualities, which we would hesitate to ascribe even to living politicians about whom we have much more independent information? Schürer's positivist method made it seem acceptable to treat Josephus's gripping stories as though they provided data. He did not explain *how* he made this transition from story to history, or indeed whether he recognized that a transition was involved.

In Schürer, then, we see the quiet transmogrification of an artistic story into fact. Such handling of Josephus as an information portal drove the entire NT-backgrounds industry through the late nineteenth and twentieth centuries. For example, the many scholarly biographies of King Herod before Peter Richardson's 1996 study—Schalit is a partial exception—were to a large degree paraphrases of Josephus: thoughts and motives attributed to the king by Josephus, for the sake of a compelling first-century story crafted for a Roman audience, were assumed by scholars to reflect the monarch's actual mental world.

Two particularly striking examples are the popular 1964 book by the scholar who translated Josephus's *War* for Penguin, G. A. Williamson's *The World of Josephus,*[36] and Cleon Rogers's 1992 reference work *The Topical Josephus,* with the telling subtitle: *Historical Accounts That Shed Light on the Bible.*[37] In each

---

[33] Ibid., 1.324.

[34] Ibid., 1.332.

[35] Ibid., 1.339.

[36] Boston: Little, Brown, 1964. Williamson describes the Judean-Roman war in ostensibly factual terms: "On the other [Judean] side was a motley host, torn by dissension and bloody strife, and led by rival self-appointed chieftains lusting for power . . ." (p. 17). Yet this merely translates Josephus's distinctive, thematic lexicon of στάσις, λῃσταί, and τύραννοι. Or again, Gessius Florus was "heartless, dishonest, disgusting; he filled Judea with misery, accepting bribes from bandits" (p. 145). Williamson is not about to accept everything Josephus says, but his opening critical questions reflect the limits of his skepticism. Are Josephus's narratives, he asks, "as objectively true as we would wish them to be? . . . Is it within our power to separate the true from the false, to distinguish the sober statement from the gross exaggeration?" (p. 21).

[37] Grand Rapids: Zondervan, 1992. Rogers cites Josephus's assessment of Herod's military virtue (*War* 1.230) and proceeds to "demonstrate the validity" of this assessment—by

case the author takes over Josephus's language bodily, presenting it as though it were a factual record—along with the usual cautions about biases and the need for skepticism.

Although many scholars are more cautious, this is usually a quantitative rather than qualitative difference: they simply doubt *more*.[38] Few hesitate to reproduce as facts those passages they consider unproblematic, overlooking problems such as Josephus's structures and diction. The series Compendia rerum iudaicarum ad Novum Testamentum (CRINT) is a partial exception, for it includes expert essays by Attridge[39] and Feldman[40] that at least point toward important aspects of Josephus's artistry. But these essays have little discernible effect on the rest of the collection.

Problems with the Traditional Approach: Two Case Studies

Pontius Pilate in Judean War

In spite of its evident appeal and ubiquity, this approach to Josephus is fatally flawed by its failure to take account of what the atoms that constitute his narratives are: *his* diction, structures, themes, and literary devices. Rather than descending into the pit of abstract theory here, I invite consideration of two case studies, which plainly reveal at least some dimensions of the problem: Josephus's treatment of Pontius Pilate's prefecture and the role of Caesarea in the outbreak of war with Rome. For reasons of limited space, we focus on the accounts in his *Judean War*, with only glances at the later works. Here we are dealing with material that seems "historical," both in the sense that there is little in it of the wondrous or paranormal and in the sense that editorial "biases" do not seem to obtrude in significant ways. Accordingly, these episodes have been largely taken over verbatim into modern histories on the relevant topics.

Pilate is a figure of obvious importance for all students of first-century Judea and Christian origins. He governed Judea for at least ten years, for as many as eighteen or nineteen if Daniel Schwartz is correct.[41] Either way, it was an unusually long tenure, and Pilate's relationships with the local elite decisively shaped

---

citing examples of Herod's valor from Josephus (pp. 18–20). Yet this demonstrates only that Josephus's narrative holds together, not that it reflects reality. The paraphrase of Josephus continues: "When Nero heard the news of Roman losses in Judea, he was inwardly very much upset, even though he outwardly tried to conceal these concerns (*War* 3.1–3)" (p. 121).

[38] An example is the justly influential study by E. P. Sanders, *Judaism, Practice and Belief, 63 BCE–66 CE* (Philadelphia: Trinity Press International, 1992), which, in spite of its corrective virtues and abundant insights, regularly slides without warning between Josephus's story and the actual past: 92, 140–141, 380–385.

[39] CRINT 2.2 (Assen: van Gorcum, 1984): 185–232.

[40] CRINT 2.1 (Assen: van Gorcum, 1988): 455–518.

[41] D. R. Schwartz, *Studies in the Jewish Background to Christianity* (Tübingen: Mohr [Siebeck], 1992), 182–217.

Judean-Roman relations there in the period before Josephus's birth in 37. Yet in *War* Josephus relates only two episodes from Pilate's long career in Judea, both of which resulted in "huge disturbances." One concerns his introduction of military standards into Jerusalem, the other his appropriation of temple funds to build an aqueduct for the city (2.169–177). *War*'s material is of brief enough compass that I can quote it in full.

> [169] After being sent to Judea as procurator (ἐπίτροπος) by Tiberius, Pilatus introduces into Hierosolyma—by night, concealed (κεκαλυμμένας)—the images (εἰκόνας) of Caesar, which are called "standards." [170] After daybreak this stirred up a huge disturbance (μεγίστην ταραχὴν ἤγειρεν) among the Judeans. For those who were close to the spectacle (τὴν ὄψιν) were shocked at their laws' having been trampled (πεπατημένων)—for they think it proper to place no representation (δείκηλον) in the city. And [in addition] to the indignation (ἀγανάκτησιν) of those in the city, the people from the countryside streamed together in concert (ἄθρους). [171] They rushed to Pilatus in Caesarea and kept pleading for him to take the standards out of Hierosolyma and to preserve their ancestral [customs] (τηρεῖν αὐτοῖς τὰ πάτρια). But when Pilatus refused, they fell down around his residence, prone (πρηνεῖς καταπεσόντες), and held out (διεκαρτέρουν) motionless for five days and nights alike.
>
> [172] On the next [day], Pilatus sat on a tribunal-platform (ἐπὶ βήματος) in the great stadium and, after summoning the rabble (τὸ πλῆθος) as though truly intending to answer them, gives the soldiers a signal, according to a scheme (δίδωσιν τοῖς στρατιώταις σημεῖον ἐκ συντάγματος), to encircle (κυκλώσασθαι) the Judeans with weapons. [173] As the column was positioned around three-deep, the Judeans were speechless at the unexpectedness of the spectacle (πρὸς τὸ ἀδόκητον τῆς ὄψεως). After saying that he would cut them to pieces if they would not accept Caesar's images (εἰ μὴ προσδέξαιντο τὰς Καίσαρος εἰκόνας), Pilatus nodded to the soldiers to bare their swords (γυμνοῦν τὰ ξίφη). [174] The Judeans, just as if by an agreed signal (καθάπερ ἐκ συνθήματος), fell down in concert, (ἀθρόοι καταπεσόντες) bent their necks to the side (τοὺς αὐχένας παρακλίναντες), and cried out (ἐβόων) that they were ready to do away with themselves rather than transgress the law. Pilatus, who was overwhelmed by the purity of their superstition (δεισιδαιμονίας ἄκρατον), directs [his men] immediately to carry the standards out of Hierosolyma.
>
> [175] After these events he set in motion a different kind of disturbance (ταραχὴν ἑτέραν ἐκίνει) by exhausting the sacred treasury—it is called the *corbonas*—on a water conduit; it conducted [water] from 400 *stadia* away. At this there was indignation among the rabble (τοῦ πλήθους ἀγανάκτησις ἦν), and when Pilatus was present at Hierosolyma they stood around his tribunal-platform and kept yelling at [him] (περιστάντες τὸ βῆμα κατεβόων). [176] But because he had foreseen their disturbance (τὴν ταραχήν) he had mixed in amongst the rabble (τῷ πλήθει) armed soldiers (τοὺς στρατιώτας ἐνόπλους ἐσθῆσιν) concealed (κεκαλυμμένους) in civilian clothes. Having prohibited them from using the sword, but having enjoined them instead to strike with sticks those who had begun shouting, he gives the agreed signal (σύνθημα) from the tribunal-platform (ἀπὸ τοῦ βήματος). [177] Many Judeans were lost from being hit by the blows, but many others from having been

> trampled under (καταπατηθέντες) by their very own [people] in the escape. Given the calamity (τὴν συμφορὰν) of those who had been taken, the beaten down rabble (τὸ πλῆθος) became silent.

Although these episodes are widely cited for the facts of Pilate's career, consideration of their literary and historical dimensions should give the historian pause.

With regard to literary characteristics, we first notice that the passage is replete with—is indeed *made up of*—Josephus's characteristic language, themes, and habits of speech. Here we see one of many cases in which the Judeans suffer the calamities (συμφοραί) foreseen and established as a major theme in the prologue (1.9, 11, 22, 27; cf. *Ant.* 20.166). Phrases indicating the "baring" of swords,[42] the inclining of necks,[43] the "concerted" movement of the Judeans, their "holding out,"[44] and their determination not to transgress the laws,[45] are characteristically and even distinctively Josephan. In this case, the "disturbance" (forms of which appear 184 times in Josephus) is caused by an equestrian "procurator" who provides the first clear example of a type introduced at 2.117: the governors dispatched to Judea were low-level and unworthy equestrians, in contrast to the distinguished senatorial *legati* who governed Syria (e.g., Varus, Petronius, Quadratus, Cestius). The Judean leaders had unsuccessfully petitioned Augustus to be attached to the *legati* in Syria (2.25, 90–91), who appear in Josephus as trustworthy administrators.

More specifically, these episodes illustrate the Judean virtues outlined in the recent Essene passage—steadfastness and contempt for death (2.138, 151–153)—and also prepare for increasingly important events to follow. The first is the more portentous "images of Caesar" episode when Gaius Caligula orders his legate Petronius to install his statue in the Jerusalem temple. When the people opposing Pilate are threatened with death "if they will not accept" Caesar's image, this language anticipates the order at 2.185. The later passage similarly cites the biblical prohibition of "representations"—this rare word appears only in these two passages in Josephus—and again has the masses willing to die rather than transgress the law prohibiting images (2.195). In the later passage too, the Syrian legate will be won over by the purity of their devotion (2.197–198). Still, being a distinguished leader of senatorial rank, Petronius behaves with much greater wisdom than Pilate, initiating a dialogue with the elite on a separate track from his speeches to the mob (2.199).

The complex of incidents based in Caesarea that Josephus will present as a main cause of the revolt will also be filled with language recalling these episodes: a disturbance (ταραχή) caused by a governor (2.266, 296) and calamity (συμφορά). The same *dramatis personae* are constantly present: the impulsive

---

42 Also at *War* 2.213, 619; *Ant.* 14.463, though not attested before Josephus.

43 Also at 1.618; 6.224.

44 Josephus uses this verb a noteworthy fifteen times (exceeded by Diodorus, but more frequent than in other historians); καρτερία is a paramount Judean virtue for him.

45 Although such phrases are found elsewhere, Josephus's use of them in about sixty-five cases gives frequency much higher than in other writers (compare ten occurrences in Philo).

rabble, the spirited youths, and the notable, principal, or powerful men. Gessius Florus, the later procurator who allegedly ignited the war will, while staying in the Herodian palace in Jerusalem, have a "tribunal platform" brought in to hear the Judeans (2.301), from which he will dispense orders for a massacre by the same auxiliary cohorts (2.308).

As for historical considerations: this introduction of standards reportedly occurred during a single night in Jerusalem, and evoked a massive protest in Caesarea beginning the next day. In *War* Josephus relates very little of what the historian would need to know about the incident's context and causes, of Pilate's aims as governor, or the state of relations between governor and governed. *Who* introduced the standards into Jerusalem, and for what purpose? If a military unit escorted them, as one would assume, which one? Had they not carried standards bearing images—normally indispensable to military cohorts—before this? Were these particular standards different in form or unusually offensive (because of *Caesar's* image)? Did Pilate's concealment of them, by night, represent an effort to *avoid* giving offense in a necessary military operation or, on the contrary, a plan to humiliate the Jerusalemites by a *fait accompli*? Did his removal of the standards at the end of the story entail also a change of cohorts?[46] And how can human beings remain motionless, unless in comas, for five days and nights?

In *War,* Josephus implies that he should simply be trusted: this was a scandalous disturbance caused by Pilate, which evoked characteristic Judean courage in the face of death, and it happened as he tells it.

The parallel in *Antiquities* 18.55–59 says more, but the additions mainly create further difficulties: "having resolved upon the dissolution of the Judean legal system" (ἐπὶ καταλύσει τῶν νομίμων τῶν Ἰουδαϊκῶν ἐφρόνησε), we are now told, Pilate moved his auxiliary army to winter quarters in Jerusalem instead of their normal base in Caesarea. Previous governors had avoided the provocation of imperial standards in Jerusalem, but Pilate deliberately ignored this by wintering his army there. But if the auxiliary force normally in Caesarea (three, four, or five cohorts?) was moved to Jerusalem, why did Pilate himself remain in Caesarea, still with a sizeable force? His alleged program of abolishing the Judean laws was surely too grand for an equestrian *praefectus,* inconceivable in the context of Roman-provincial relations,[47] and described in language suspiciously reminiscent of the events that provoked the Hasmonean revolt (2 Macc 2:22; 4:11; 4 Macc 5:33). Such language is used elsewhere in Josephus only of Julius Caesar's resolve to abolish *Roman* democracy and law (*Ant.* 19.173) or Gaius Caligula's attack on Judean laws (19.301); Pilate was not in this league. If Pilate did have such ambitions, how is it that neither the hostile contemporary writer Philo nor the gospel writers mention such an assault, and Josephus himself passes over it in

46 Cf. C. H. Kraeling, "The Episode of the Roman Standards at Jerusalem," *HTR* 35 (1942): 263–89, esp. 265, 271–73; H. Bond, *Pontius Pilate in History and Interpretation* (Cambridge: Cambridge University Press, 1998), 79.

47 See C. Ando, *Imperial Ideology and Provincial Loyalty in the Roman Empire* (Berkeley: University of California Press, 2000).

War, where he presents the "procurators" in the darkest of colors? Further, having the cohorts winter in Jerusalem with their standards was a rather subtle and doubtful way of achieving such a purpose. Again, if the icon-bearing standards were the cause of such outrage, how does one account for Philo's contemporary story that Pilate aroused popular indignation by his introduction of *aniconic* shields into Jerusalem (*Legat.* 299–305), which Eusebius (*Dem. ev.* 8.122–123) and many scholars conflate with this episode? And if Pilate had such a plan to abolish Judean law, why does he end up calming the masses by removing the *images,* but not the wintering army (*Ant.* 18.59)? Josephus's narratives are opaque with respect to all such underlying realities.

However one resolves such problems, the disturbance caused by the aqueduct project must have been entirely different, in historical terms. Building such a conduit (*War* makes it fifty miles long; *Ant.* 18.60 quietly halves the length) would have required at least a year, more likely two or more, and imagining the historical realities involved is exceedingly difficult. A new aqueduct of any significant length was a mark of prestige and a major practical benefit for the fortunate city, but notoriously expensive to build. Financing typically required a combination of imperial grants, community funds, and private donations. In the provinces the Roman governor had the decisive role in arranging finances for such projects: gathering donations and community funds (possibly encouraged by a partial rebate of tribute), seeking the emperor's approval, commissioning engineers to design and lay out the aqueduct, and possibly requesting help from the imperial *fiscus* (cf. Pliny, *Ep.* 10.90).[48]

Such real-life considerations remind us how very little Josephus has disclosed in his highly stylized description of Pilate's aqueduct. Was it in fact Pilate's initiative to build this conduit, or was it that of the Jerusalem leadership, or of a prominent citizen, or some sort of joint effort? Given that these water systems required professional planning, because of the strict technical requirements concerning elevation and grade, *who designed and built the aqueduct*? Archaeology reveals that Jerusalem's aqueduct system was complex, dating from different periods.[49] Which part(s) did Pilate build? Was his contribution, indeed, a completely new structure, an extension of existing structures, or a repair project? Did Pilate or the local leaders also arrange for private donations, in the usual way, aside from the resort to the temple treasury that sparked the demonstrations? (Even if the temple treasury was exhausted, as Josephus claims, it may well not have covered the entire cost.) Who if anyone mediated Pilate's raiding of temple funds? Did he storm the temple with a cohort of soldiers? Josephus does not say he did, and we might have expected him to do so in such a hostile portrait of Pilate if he had known of such a thing. It seems more likely that some unnamed temple officials cooperated

---

[48] On the usual procedures see P. Leveau, "Aqueduct Building: Financing and Costs," in *Frontinus' Legacy: Essays on Frontinus'* de aquis urbis Romae (ed. D. R. Blackman and A. T. Hodge; Ann Arbor: University of Michigan Press, 2001), 85–101, esp. 91.

[49] See D. Amit, J. Patrich, and Y. Hirschfeld, eds., *The Aqueducts of Israel* (Portsmouth: Journal of Roman Archaeology, 2002), esp. A. Mazar, "A Survey of the Aqueducts to Jerusalem," 210–42.

with Pilate, perhaps also joining in the planning, though we cannot know. But if they did, and if we knew the answers to any of these other questions, the picture would look very different.

Possible scenarios abound, any of which could provide the back story to Josephus's impressionistic account. It could be that an intended benefactor died or became insolvent, and the inability to fulfill his commitment forced Pilate to turn to a greater use of community funds, putting pressure on the temple treasury. It is entirely possible that the Roman *fiscus* was involved in some way, even indirectly: by rebating tribute or by contributing technicians, surveyors, auxiliary soldiers, or materials—such as lead. Moreover, at what point in this long process did some groups become disaffected, and why at that point? Was the aqueduct completed, half-finished, or merely in a planning stage? If it was only in the planning or surveying stage, how could the treasury have been exhausted? If it was nearing completion after a couple of years, why did the riots occur only now, and reportedly in a single encounter? Josephus gives the occasion as Pilate's visit to Jerusalem (from his base in Caesarea), but he had to visit several times a year; and if the populace had been enraged, they could always have challenged him in Caesarea as they did in the standards episode. What triggered the protest, and who constituted the upset mob? Was this also an internal protest against the temple leadership for authorizing the project? Were personal squabbles and alliances involved?

On all these important questions, about which the historian would need to have information in order to develop any responsible reconstruction, Josephus is completely silent.

A final problem is the very different nature of these two Pilate episodes, if considered historically. For Josephus as author works hard to help his audience overlook such differences between them, and the historical problems that one might ponder, by assimilating one episode to the other. He wants to present two similar "disturbances" provoked by this unworthy Roman governor. Notice the deliberateness in his parallel structures: both episodes involve life-threatening protests by indignant masses before Pilate and his soldiers, secret plans and signals, encirclements and weapons, a hearing before the governor's tribunal-platform, and potentially fatal consequences.[50]

[50] K.-S. Krieger (TANZ 9; *Geschichtsschreibung als Apologetik: bei Flavius Josephus* [Tübingen: Francke, 1994], 32–42) is followed by H. Bond (*Pilate,* 49–62) in arguing that these two episodes in *War* support the narrative aims as follows. The first shows the Judeans peacefully resisting Pilate, with a good outcome; in the second, they respond militantly with fatal consequences. This difference highlights the moral: "either accept Roman rule peacefully and its governors will show consideration or resort to violence and risk certain annihilation at the hands of Roman troops" (Bond, *Pilate,* 56). Both scholars note the different number, configurations, and emphases of the Pilate episodes in *Antiquities* and argue that those stories likewise serve its different agenda. This explanation is perhaps too mechanical, however. Neither response by the Judeans is violent: the first creates a "huge disturbance," with outraged masses streaming into Jerusalem and then Caesarea to protest; the second explicitly has them yelling at Pilate, but there seems to be no reason in the narrative to exclude such abuse from the first story—not enough of a difference, at any rate, to treat the stories as models of two different kinds of behavior.

Josephus reinforces the assimilation by repeating key vocabulary from the first episode in the second ("disturbance," "indignation," "rabble," "prone," "tribunal-platform," "surrounding," "concealed," "sword," "agreed signal," "trampled"). In part, this repetition creates dramatic irony: the concealed standards anticipate the soldiers' concealed weapons; the trampling of the laws leads to the physical trampling of Judeans; and whereas the Roman forces train hard to remain in close order, the indignant Judean masses move in close order spontaneously. They also instinctively act *as if* by an agreed signal, whereas the auxiliary soldiers really need *their* secret signals to be carefully planned. Not only has Josephus hammered these two stories into a matching pair; he has also assimilated them to his narrative tendencies, everywhere exploiting his own meaning-charged lexicon.

Although such an investigation makes clear the extent to which Josephus controls and constructs his episodes from his language, while neglecting basic historical questions, none of this deterred Schürer or his many followers in the NT-*Umwelt* industry. Schürer has the historical Pilate *begin* his (10- or 18-year?) tenure in Judea with the standards episode simply because it is the first of the two stories in Josephus. He portrays as historical the masses besieging Pilate for *five days and nights* without moving, Pilate's clever plan and "agreed signal," the Judeans' defiance with "bared necks," the shrieking mob protesting the aqueduct, the concealed clubs, and the merciless beating of the people.[51]

I chose the Pilate episodes for illustrative purposes because they represent a best-case scenario for the historian, since here Josephus is not our only source of contemporary information. We have also Pilate's contemporary Philo, the trial narratives in the gospels and occasional notices elsewhere in the NT, some coinage from Pilate's term of office, and the famed *tiberieum* inscription from Caesarea.[52] From all this we can easily confirm a hypothesis that a Pontius Pilatus did govern Judea under Tiberius and that his title was "prefect" rather than Josephus's "procurator" (unless both titles were simultaneously operative). We also have enough independent and multiform evidence, it seems to me, to declare it more probable that he took up office in 18 than in the accepted year, 26 C.E.[53] But *what Pilate did* during his long stay in Judea, and *why he did it*—in other words, the nature of his tenure as governor, and the very thing that concerns historians most of all—seem impossible to recover, even where we have several lines of independent evidence. For the vast majority of cases, where Josephus provides the sole evidence, we simply have no means of recreating the past that he knew from his surviving works of art.

Reading Josephus's narratives is very much like watching a well-made film on ancient history: Ridley Scott's *Gladiator* or the BBC-HBO series *Rome*. We

---

Most importantly, Josephus appears to have tried hard to assimilate one story to the other (as argued here).

[51] Schürer-Vermes, *Jewish People,* 1:384–85.

[52] A. Frova, "L'Iscrizione di Pontio Pilato a Cesarea," *Rendiconti Istituto Lombardo* 95 (1961): 419–34.

[53] Cf. Schwartz, *Studies,* 182–217; K. Lönnqvist, "Pontius Pilate—An Aqueduct Builder?—Recent Findings and New Suggestions," *Klio* 82 (2000): 458–74.

know that the production was well researched and that it is *based on* much reliable information. But it is quite obviously an artistic construction, with every element calculated to contribute to the whole effect. Knowing that real ancient conditions lie behind the production does not help us to know whether or to what degree any particular episode or character has a basis in reality: it sometimes happens that the most compelling parts are pure invention, whereas the least appealing elements have historical roots. But we can know that only when we have access to independent evidence. For Josephus's works, he is in effect the producer, screenwriter, director, set-designer, and sometimes leading actor. Where his artistic production is our only surviving testimony to events, we have no way of turning that work of art by itself into real events.

Caesarea's Role in the Outbreak of Revolt

I have suggested that one function of the Pilate episodes in *War* is to prepare for the complex of incidents in Caesarea that, according to Josephus, played a major role in precipitating the revolt. But the Caesarea complex in *War* also illustrates a different kind of problem for the historian, in its fundamental differences from a parallel account in *Antiquities*.

That these basic differences have been largely overlooked is a symptom of the accepted scholarly approaches to Josephus, which have focused on historical realities behind the text and not on the narrative itself. But if we read the Caesarea stories in *War* and *Antiquities* as distinct narratives, we become aware of Josephus's remarkable freedom as a writer, which in turn ought to prompt sobering questions about the underlying historical realities. The differences are all the more troubling here because in both accounts Josephus claims that the Caesarea incidents were a significant cause or pretext of the war (*War* 2.285; *Ant.* 20.183–184). But what exactly happened, and how did this lead to war?

War's account is surprising in many respects, if we read it without assimilation to *Antiquities* (thus, as his first audiences heard it), and it reflects Josephus's disciplined posture as author. Throughout the developing narrative of *War* 2, he usually withholds explicit moral judgment—sometimes to an astonishing degree—as he describes the behavior and human foibles of his actors. The "spirited" or hot-headed elements among the youth are not blamed for behaving as they do, even if their actions produce disaster: they cannot be other than what they are. The same is largely true of the equestrian governors or Syrian legates, or of the mob in general. In the case of Caesarea, the dispassionate tone may cause us to miss what Josephus actually says, especially if we import other and later stories of Judean suffering at the hands of their Greek neighbors.

The Caesarea story opens with a clear statement that the Judeans of that harbor city fomented civil strife, or started a quarrel, or formed a faction (στασιάζω—a highly charged term in this work) against their Syrian neighbors. Why?

> [265] And whereas this war was being fanned every day, [266] a different kind of disturbance involving Caesarea compounded [matters], after the Judeans who

> were mixed in [with the population] formed a faction against the Syrians there. For whereas the former reckoned the city to be theirs, saying that its founder had been a Judean (this was Herod the king), the others, though they conceded that the *colonizer* was a Judean, nevertheless insisted that the city was in fact one of Greeks, for in dedicating it to Judeans he [Herod] would not have set up statues and shrines. [267] Because of these [matters] both sides kept contending: their rivalry progressed to weapons, and every day the more spirited ones from both sides were plunging ahead into battle. For the senior Judeans were not able to restrain their own agitators, and to the Greeks it seemed a disgrace to be in a weaker position than the Judeans. [268] These [the Judeans] had the advantage in wealth and strength of [their] bodies, the Greek [side] in protection by the soldiers—for the bulk of the military force there had been enlisted by the Romans from Syria and, just like relatives, they were ready for acts of assistance. (*War* 2.265–268)

Josephus has already authoritatively described Herod's foundation of Caesarea as a port open to the world, marked by colossal statues, temples, theatres, and quinquennial games (1.408–415). In that early description, he says that Herod dedicated the city to the province of Syria, the harbor to sailors along the coast, and the glory of the place to Caesar Augustus (1.414). H. K. Beebe has compellingly argued that Herod offered Caesarea to the Romans as a counterweight to Jerusalem,[54] a place where Greco-Roman culture and trade could flourish and the military could act freely. Such a status is amply confirmed by successive governors' use of the site for their headquarters, and by its "re-foundation" by Vespasian after 70 as *Colonia Prima Flavia Augusta Caesarensis.*[55]

Yet in the present story, Josephus describes a Judean community with many who, "mixed in" among a mainly non-Judean population, have grown so wealthy and strong enough that they boldly attempt to remake the city as "theirs" (οἱ μὲν γὰρ ἠξίουν σφετέραν εἶναι τὴν πόλιν).[56] They build their case on the remarkable premise that Herod, the founder, was after all a Judean (2.266). Josephus withholds judgment on this claim, as also on the Syrian counter-argument that even before Herod the city was Greek, and that in any case Herod himself would not have set up the shrines and statues if he was dedicating it to Judeans—a line of thought that matches Josephus's earlier description quite closely, down to the key verb ἀνατίθημι. The audience should simply know that this is an implausible stretch on the part of the Judeans.

For the Judeans to make the city "their own"—that is, Judean rather than Greco-Roman in character, like Jerusalem presumably—would be a tall order indeed: it would require the dismantling of the most prominent landmarks (the colossal statues on either side of the port entrance, the massive temple to Rome and

---

[54]"Caesarea Maritima: Its Strategic and Political Importance to Rome," *JNES* 42 (1983): 195–207.

[55]B. H. Isaac, *The Near East under Roman Rule: Selected Papers* (Leiden: Brill, 1998), 94–98.

[56]Correctly L. I. Levine, "The Jewish-Greek Conflict in First Century Caesarea," *JJS* 25 (1974), 387: "Thus we find a Jewish community daring to seek control of a Greco-Roman city, an attempt without parallel in antiquity."

Augustus that faced the harbor, all the prominent cultural and entertainment facilities, and countless other structures and established procedures, including the very calendrical basis of city life).

Josephus goes on to describe the hostilities that resulted from this bold attempt: in his narrative, the Judeans are the main instigators.

> [269] It certainly was a concern of the prefects to check the disturbance: constantly arresting the more belligerent [men], they would punish them with lashes and chains. But the sufferings of those who were arrested did not produce a turnaround or anxiety in those left behind; rather, they were provoked even more toward civil strife. [270] On one occasion, when the Judeans had been victorious, Felix went into the marketplace and directed them, with a threat, to withdraw. When they did not comply, he sent his soldiers against [them] and did away with*[57] a great number, whose property was then also plundered.

It is *their* leaders who cannot restrain their own factionalists or agitators (στασιασταί); the Greek side, embarrassed to be considered weaker than the Judeans, reacts to the provocation (2.267). Josephus claims, however, that the Judeans enjoyed both superior wealth and greater physical vigor (2.268).[58] This general statement is supported by the first example of fighting that he gives (2.270): the victorious Judeans can only be stopped by the governor's personal intervention with a military cohort. If we read the preceding sentence (2.269) contextually, it seems that the instigators at this point, whom the city's military prefects are mainly occupied with identifying and punishing, are Judeans.

---

[57] The asterisk here and in the following translations signifies a present-tense Greek verb translated in the past for best English usage.

[58] "Strength of body" (ἀλκὴ σώματος) is characteristic of *War*'s lexicon (2.376, 476, 580; 4.503; 6.55, 81, 331; 7.232; note also 2.60; *Ant.* 6.21; 17.278). At 2.580 Josephus will claim that strength of body (and exaltation of soul) have allowed the Romans to master most of the inhabited earth. This collocation is also attested, though not common, before Josephus: Euripides (*Rhes.* 382); Diodorus Siculus (2.39.2; 4.26.3; 17.100.5; 18.70.3), and Philo (*Ebr.* 174; *Mos.* 1.259; *Virt.* 46). The plural here (σωμάτων ἀλκή) could be construed either as a claim of greater physical vigor among the Judeans—"the strength of [their individual] bodies," as in the similar constructions at 2.376; 6.331; *Ant.* 6.21—or in the sense that the Judeans's strength consisted in their numerical superiority: they had the advantage of "the strength that comes from having many *bodies.*" The parallel account does not help because it mentions only their greater wealth (*Ant.* 20.175). Although Levine ("Conflict," 382–83; 1975a: 22) and Feldman (*Jew and Gentile in the Ancient World: Attitudes and Interactions from Alexander to Justinian* [Princeton: Princeton University Press, 1993], 120) understand the issue as numerical, my translation reflects Josephus's usage elsewhere. The Judeans of Caesarea thus compare favorably to the Germans, renowned for the strength and size of *their bodies* (2.376). Indeed, physical strength on the Judean side is assumed in the later story (2.286), where their youths undertake to prevent construction by a Greek resident near the synagogue—and can only be restrained by the governor's military forces. Further, having a numerical advantage would mean enjoying a majority, whereas Josephus's language ("mixed in" at 2.266) and the massacre at 2.475 suggest a Judean minority, no matter how successful and wealthy it was, as do general considerations related to the decidedly Greek character and constitution of the city.

However that may be, the upshot of the conflicts resulting from the Judean bid is that the governor Felix dispatches embassies from both sides to Nero (presumably in the late 50s), for an adjudication of the Judeans' appeal and the Syrians' rejection of it (2.270): "But since the civil strife was continuing, he selected the notables from both [groups] and sent them as emissaries to Nero so that they could negotiate concerning their rights." This in itself is a striking moment: the freedman governor has enough of a sense that the Judeans might be successful that he, after trying to stop the violence, supports a hearing in Rome. At this point in *War,* Josephus puts the issue in suspension while he continues a chronological narrative of the governors following Felix (Festus and Albinus).

The technique of suspending a story and then returning to announce its outcome is a familiar device in *War.* Although Josephus could have anticipated the outcome at this point (and he does that in some other cases), here he prefers to keep the audience waiting, until Gessius Florus is in office in about 66 C.E. The delay allows him to tie Nero's eventual decision directly to the outbreak of revolt in that year.

So we move forward to 2.284, where we learn that the Greeks of Caesarea were successful, after all, in making their case for their ongoing control of the city. Josephus takes this opportunity to date the onset of war and in the next sentence begins to explain the connection.

> (14.4) [284] Now at this point the Greeks of Caesarea, having won from Nero [the right] to control the city, brought back the documentation of the verdict, and the war took its beginning in the twelfth year of Nero's *imperium,* in the seventeenth of Agrippa's kingship, the month of Artemisius. [285] Given the magnitude of the calamities [that arose] from it, it [the war] did not have a worthy justification. Namely: the Judeans in Caesarea, having a meeting [place] beside a site whose owner was a certain Caesarean Greek, tried hard and often to acquire the spot, offering a price many times its worth; [286] but while disdaining their appeals, with added insult he himself built across the site, constructing workshops. He was thus leaving them a passageway that was both narrow and constrained in every direction. So at first, the more hot-headed of the youths were plunging ahead and trying to hinder construction. [287] But while Florus was restraining these [people] from violence, the powerful [men] of the Judeans, among whom was Ioannes the public contractor, being at a loss, persuaded* Florus with eight talents of silver to prevent the project. [288] Yet he, being [interested] only in the taking, after promising to cooperate in everything, took [the money], absconded* from Caesarea to Sebaste, and abandoned* the civil strife to its own devices, as though having sold the Judeans a license to fight.
>
> (14.5) [289] The next day being the seventh, when the Judeans had assembled in their meeting [place] a certain Caesarean agitator turned over a belly-style [container], placed it beside their entryway, and began sacrificing birds on it. This provoked the Judeans beyond remedy, on the ground that their laws had been outraged and their site polluted. [290] Whereas the stable and mild element considered it proper to retreat to the governors, the factious element, having become inflamed by virtue of youth, were burning for a fight. The agitators among the Caesareans also stood ready—for by a plan they had sent forward the man performing the sacrifices—and so an engagement soon came about. [291] Iucundus, the cavalry commander as-

signed to prevent [this], came forward and took away* the belly-style [container]; he kept trying to end the civil strife. But as he was proving unequal to the violence of the Caesareans, the Judeans seized their laws and withdrew to Narbata; a district of theirs is called thus, lying sixty stadia from Caesarea. [292] The twelve powerful [men] with Ioannes went to Florus at Sebaste, where they began lamenting bitterly about what had been done and begging him to help, discreetly reminding him of the eight talents. He, however, arrested and confined the men—charging them with removing the laws from Caesarea!

(14.6) [293] At this there was indignation among those in Hierosolyma, though they checked their tempers. But Florus, as if he had signed a contract to fan the flames of war, sent to the temple treasury and extracted* seventeen talents; he had pretended that [it was] for Caesar's needs. [294] Confusion immediately began to grip the populace: they ran together into the temple and with piercing shouts kept calling upon the name of Caesar, begging him also to free them from the tyranny of Florus. [295] Some of the agitators had screamed the most shameful insults and, carrying around a reed basket, were demanding bits of change for him as though he were destitute and needy. He was not put off from his love of money by these [insults], but was all the more driven by rage to pursue wealth.

[296] At the very least he should have gone to Caesarea and extinguished the fire of the war beginning from there and disposed of the causes of the disturbance—for which [task] he had indeed taken compensation. Instead, he charged against Hierosolyma with an army of both cavalry and infantry, so that he might do his deeds with Roman weaponry, and strip the city through [the use of] anxiety and threats.

This part of the story also deserves fuller consideration than we can give it here. But the gist is that, notwithstanding Nero's decision, the Judeans of Caesarea continue to try changing the facts on the ground to their advantage. Namely, they establish a meeting place adjacent to some land owned by a Greek, and then attempt to buy up that land from him at many times its face value. This confirms the impression established at the outset of superior Judean wealth. The Greek, however, is uncooperative—for the understandable reason, we soon learn, that he has purchased the property *in order to develop it.* Indeed, he soon builds workshops right across it, no doubt now (in the story) partly out of spite at the Judean attempt, and this leaves the Judeans a very narrow passageway to enter their meeting-place.

Although Josephus again withholds comment on either side's motives, this is an impressively even-handed description. It is not often observed that, if the Greek was being inconsiderate in building so close to the edge of his land, that problem can only have arisen in the first place if the Judeans had built *near to the edge of their* land, perhaps—as the narrative implies—with the firm expectation of buying up the adjacent parcel and having a larger combined space, in which their meeting place would be more central. Josephus describes the resulting animosity as the predictable result of normal squabbles: one side provokes the other; the other responds with spite.

Following the pattern already established, it is the younger Judean men who at first try to interfere with construction on the Greek's land, as young men are wont to do, while their elders prefer to gather a massive sum of money (eight talents of silver) for an attempt to bribe the governor to intervene on their side and simply stop the building by his authority (2.287)—not because this course of action is right (or wrong), but because it is the kind of thing that should work. The governor declines to do so, not because he is above bribery, but quite the opposite: he pockets the money but then conveniently leaves town. Josephus remarks that it is as though he had sold the Judeans a license to fight; they continue to be the main agitators to this point. Throughout, however, Josephus continues withholding the expected "bourgeois" moral judgments.

And so it goes. The conflict rapidly escalates, particularly after a young Greek agitator (this is the first time we meet one) is dared by his comrades to overturn one of the Greek storage jars near the Judeans' land (therefore near the narrow pass they must use to enter their building) and begin sacrificing a series of birds. The Greeks know that this will provoke a fight, and the youths on both sides have at it. An auxiliary cavalry prefect arrives and tries to stop the commotion—by snatching away the Greeks' makeshift altar—a practical and disinterested intervention aimed at ending the present provocation, without regard for the larger issues. Some of the Judean leaders are now worried enough to take their Torah scrolls and leave for nearby Narbatene, while a delegation heads to Florus in Sebaste to tactfully remind him of the bribe they have paid. He, in his insouciant greed, charges them with having removed their law scrolls from the city!

Only now, as all of the stock character types come to interact, do we begin to understand the connection between these seemingly minor and local Caesarean events and the outbreak of war. According to Josephus, it all boils down to the low character of the Roman governors (an ongoing theme of *War*), in this case Gessius Florus. There are no heroes in this narrative: everyone behaves badly—or at least, as people always do behave. It is the central task of a governor, however, to manage tensions, by careful cultivation of the local elites on all sides, and thus to keep a lid on things. Because Gessius was in Judea mainly to improve his material situation, however—a characterization that would come as no surprise to upper-class Romans—he ignored this most basic duty and, on the contrary, allegedly *undertook to fan the flames of war as a means of diverting imperial attention from his own crimes.* In Caesarea he found a local but potentially virulent conflict, which he could exacerbate through studied neglect, and in which he could be sure to involve the Jerusalemites. Although the citizens of the mother-city had otherwise determined to check their indignation over Caesarea (2.293), he egged them on by first plundering the temple for seventeen talents, and then pursuing a reckless course of diplomatic sucker-punches, provocation, and violent reprisal at every opportunity. Tensions in Caesarea will also lead to a massacre of the Judeans there, which in turn will spark violent Judean raids on all the Greek cities of the coast, the Decapolis, and southern Syria, which in turn will generate massacres of the Judean populations in those cities (2.457–498). That entire complex of hostilities will finally demand the intervention of Cestius Gallus (2.499–458), whose defeat by Judean rebels will create the unstoppable conditions for war. So Josephus claims, and it is a riveting story.

Even this brief sketch will suffice, I hope, to show how pointless it is to characterize Josephus's *War* by simple slogans: that he wrote as a Flavian lackey or mouthpiece, or to absolve himself and his class from war guilt, or to blame the revolt on a handful of "rebels." Such captions do not represent the complexity and multi-layered nature of the narrative. As he makes clear in the prologue, the basic ethos of the *Judean War* is that of a tragedy: the story abounds in suffering, sorrow, calamity, lament, and wailing caused by fortune's unpredictable turns and reversals, but in which context people usually act according to type, from familiar motives. It is a tragedy without heroes. Incidentally, the story brings out the subordinate themes of Judean strength and gubernatorial malfeasance, among others.

The parallel account in *Antiquities* must be treated even more briefly. It will suffice here to point out the very different character of the story. In this later work, the whole episode of the attempted land purchase, with its serious consequences and serviceability to Florus as a vehicle for provoking revolt, is absent. So Josephus must take an entirely different tack.

The *Antiquities* version also has two parts. The first, recalling the *War* counterpart, concerns the Judeans' bid for "primacy" (20.173: πρωτεύειν) over the Syrians of Caesarea, which again leads to violence.

> [20.173] And now civil strife arose among the Judeans inhabiting Caesarea, against the Syrians in the same place, concerning equality of citizenship rights. For, whereas the Judeans were asserting their primacy on the ground that the founder of Caesarea had been their king, Herod, a Judean by ancestry, the Syrians conceded the point about Herod but insisted that Caesarea had formerly been called Strato's Tower, and that at that time there had been not a single Judean inhabitant. [174] When the prefects in the area heard these things, they seized those responsible from both sides and tortured them with beatings, and thereby suppressed the disturbance for a while. [175] But the Judeans who were in the city, made confident [or daring] by their wealth and on that account holding the Syrians in contempt, kept slandering them, expecting to provoke them to anger. [176] These [the Syrians], while inferior in resources were feeling courageous because most of those doing military service there under the Romans were either Caesareans or Sebastenes, and so for a while were also using abusive language against the Judeans. And then they began throwing stones at each other, until many were injured—on both sides, but still the Judeans would win.
>
> [177] When Felix observed that this rivalry had become a sort of war, he sprang forward and appealed to the Judeans to stop; when they did not comply, he armed his soldiers and sent them out against them. He did away with many of them, though he took more alive, and sent [soldiers] to raid some of the houses belonging to those in the city, which were full of goods. [178] Now the more reasonable and preeminent of the Judeans became alarmed for themselves and appealed to Felix to recall his soldiers with a trumpet-call, and spare them for the sequel [or spare what they had left], and give them [a chance for] regret at what had been done. And Felix obliged them. . . . [A report follows on factional strife among the chief priests in Jerusalem.] Thus did the violence of the [chief priests'] troublemakers prevail over all justice. [182] When Porcius Festus had been sent by Nero as successor to Felix, those who

> were prominent among the Judeans living in Caesarea went up to Rome, bringing accusations against Felix; he certainly would have faced retribution for his crimes against the Judeans if Nero had not yielded to the persistent appeal of his [Felix's] brother Pallas, holding him in the highest regard at just that time.

In this *Antiquities* account Josephus heightens the Judeans' confidence and also its corollary, a powerful disdain for their Syrian-Greek neighbors: from their position of greater wealth, the Judeans hold the poorer Syrian population in contempt and keep slandering them in the hope of provoking a fight (τῷ πλούτῳ θαρροῦντες καὶ διὰ τοῦτο καταφρονοῦντες τῶν Σύρων ἐβλασφήμουν εἰς αὐτοὺς ἐρεθίσειν προσδοκῶντες, 20.175). When this behavior eventually succeeds in provoking violence, Felix intervenes with troops to stop the Judean instigators (20.177).

At this point the story departs markedly from *War*'s account. Here, the Judean leaders of Caesarea fully admit their error, begging for pardon and a second chance (20.178: καὶ φείσαθαι τὸ λοιπὸν αὐτῶν δοῦναί τε μετάνοιαν, 20.178), which the procurator graciously grants them. In *Antiquities,* as far as the literary audience knows this marks the end of the Judeans' quest for primacy in Caesarea. There is no need for an embassy to Nero, as in *War,* because the matter has been forcibly settled by the governor.

Just as *War*'s sequel, concerning the land dispute exploited by Felix, has no parallel in *Antiquities,* so the later work has a sequel that is not only absent from *War* 2, but completely changes the picture created there. Namely:

> [183] Furthermore, the prominent Syrians in Caesarea persuaded Beryllus—he was Nero's tutor, entrusted with the administration of Greek correspondence—by giving him a vast sum, to request a letter from Nero canceling the Judeans' equality of citizenship with them. [184] So Beryllus made his appeal to the *imperator* and succeeded in getting the letter written. This furnished the causes of the bad things that followed for our nation: for *when the Judeans of Caesarea learned* what had been written, they engaged all the more in civil strife against the Syrians *until indeed they ignited the war.*

Antiquities relates that, soon after the arrival of Felix's successor Festus (in ca. 60), the Syrian Caesareans, apparently continuing to resent their humiliation by their Judean neighbors, send their own delegation to Rome. This embassy prevails upon Nero's secretary[59] to secure from him an annulment or cancellation (ἀκυρόω) of the already existing Judean equality (*Ant.* 20.183–184: παρὰ τοῦ Νέρωνος αὐτοῖς ἐπιστολὴν ἀκυροῦσαν τὴν Ἰουδαίων πρὸς αὐτοὺς ἰσοπολιτείαν), and it is this decision by Nero, which comes already during Festus's term in the early 60s, that will be a major cause of the war. That is because it prompts the disappointed Judeans to greater aggression against their neighbors (20.184): "when the Judeans of Caesarea learned what had been written, they engaged all the more in civil strife against the Syrians until indeed they ignited the war" (πυθόμενοι γὰρ οἱ κατὰ

[59] For Beryllus, see M. Griffin, *Nero: the End of a Dynasty* (London: B. T. Batsford, 1984), 32, 46, 55.

τὴν Καισάρειαν Ἰουδαῖοι τὰ γραφέντα τῆς πρὸς τοὺς Σύρους στάσεως μᾶλλον εἴχοντο μέχρι δὴ τὸν πόλεμον ἐξῆψαν). We should apparently understand that, since the Judeans have recently aimed at primacy in Caesarea, with a corresponding loss of Syrian standing, this retaliatory revocation of their existing political standing naturally inflames them all the more (20.183–184).

The basic differences of content and chronology between the Josephus's stories ought to be the starting-point for historical analysis. Did Felix authorize a delegation to make the case for Judean primacy in Caesarea before Nero? Did Nero delay his decision by several years (perhaps until Poppaea's death in 65), finally rejecting the Judean case when Gessius Florus was governor? Did the Judeans nevertheless press on with trying to acquire larger community holdings in Caesarea, causing a fierce backlash that Florus would later exploit to conceal his crimes? So *War* claims. Or was an initial Judean bid for primacy immediately cut short by Felix because of the disorders it generated, and abandoned by the Judean leadership? And was this resulting ill will the basis for a successful secret maneuver by the Syrians of Caesarea, during Festus's term in Judea, to have Nero revoke Judean rights in the city? Was this revocation of Judean equality a major cause of the war? So *Antiquities.*

These differences have been more or less ignored by commentators, who tend to see only trivial variations of language in describing the same reality, and so pick and choose elements from each story for a composite "historical" picture.[60] So Lee Levine (emphasis added): "With but few exceptions Josephus's account is *limited to a narration of events* and the two sources *basically agree.*"[61] Or Aryeh Kasher: "Theoretically speaking, the dispute was founded on two interrelated questions, which could actually be considered as two sides of the same coin: Which of the two parties deserved the status of *primi inter pares,* in the framework of the legal and organizational-political equality (termed *isopoliteia* by Josephus) which had prevailed in the city since its foundation by Herod?"[62]

No doubt the confusion arises in part from Josephus's reference to ἰσοπολιτεία at the very beginning of the Caesarea cluster in *Antiquities* 20 (173), followed by explanatory γάρ and an account of the Judeans' bid for primacy, which in turn sounds like the first part of *War*'s story, to which it is assimilated by scholars. But ἰσοπολιτεία is not used in *War,* because the issue does not arise there—not, at least, as something *lost* by the Judeans of Caesarea.[63] Only in the second *Antiquities* episode does ἰσοπολιτεία arise explicitly.

---

[60] E.g., Schürer-Vermes, *Jewish People,* 1:465–66.

[61] Levine, "Conflict," 380.

[62] A. Kasher, *Jews and Hellenistic Cities in Eretz Israel: Relations of the Jews in Eretz-Israel with the Hellenistic Cities During the Second Temple Period (332–70 CE)* (Tübingen: Mohr [Siebeck], 1990), 254.

[63] Conflating the two accounts would require, among other things (some problems are noted in Schürer-Vermes, *Jewish People,* 1:467 n. 45), that Nero's agreement to *deprive* the Judeans of equality (*Ant.* 20.183–84) was somehow tantamount to turning down their request for control of the city (*War* 2.284). But the verb used of Nero's response to Beryllus's intercession in *Antiquities* (ἀκυρόω) normally, and always elsewhere in Josephus

Two readings of the ἰσοπολιτεία theme in *Antiquities* 20 appear most plausible. The more obvious one is that Josephus announces the general theme in the opening topic sentence (20.173), and then narrates a balanced account of two communities each trying to displace the other: the Judeans first attempt to remove Greco-Syrian equality in the city, but consequently, thwarted in this aim, suffer a corresponding loss of their own rights. Given that the abstract noun appears only in this story (20.173, 183) in all of Josephus's thirty volumes, we should hesitate before investing the term with any precise legal significance; he need only be offering a general category for the competition over rights. He does not mention it in the first *Antiquities* section because what the Greco-Syrians have is more than equality—*it is a Greek city*—just as he does not mention "primacy" in the latter half (because it was not something the Greeks needed to seek). In favor of this reading is the elaboration of Judean hostility toward the Greco-Syrians in the former half: by upping the ante in this way, and having the Judeans actively abuse their neighbors in their bid for supremacy, Josephus prepares for a compensatory move on the Greco-Syrian side.

The problem with this reading is that ἰσοπολιτεία is, after all, not mentioned in the former half but is attached explicitly only to the Judean side in the second part of the story. This circumstance suggests another reading, namely: in the topic sentence (20.173) Josephus is only letting the audience know *in advance* where the story will end up, with a Judean loss of equality in Caesarea. In the former half he supplies a background story to explain how that result came about:[64] in seeking *primacy* the Judeans overreached and ended up losing even what they had.

The technique of announcing an outcome and then filling in a longer or shorter back-story is characteristic of Josephus. But the difference between these

(*Ant.* 11.17; 14.216; 18.304), refers not to the denial of a request but to the *overturning or cancellation of an existing decree* or decision—a ψήφισμα, δόγμα, or ἐντολή. In the Caesarea story of *Ant.* 20, the verb cannot mean that Nero turns down a Judean petition for primacy because the Judeans themselves have voluntarily abandoned that bid already under Felix; Nero is responding to a contrary appeal from the Syrians. The Judean delegation after Festus's arrival (*Ant.* 20.182) sets out to accuse Felix of general maladministration; Nero does not hear an appeal for primacy from them.

[64]The technique of announcing a theme long before he develops it, like that of suspending a conclusion, is characteristic of Josephus. Most obviously, the prologue to *War* (1.10–11, 24) claims that the war was caused by internal civil strife, led by "tyrants." Yet *War* 1 does not deal with such matters, and even bk. 2 hardly mentions tyrants as it charts the many causes of the war. Civil war and tyranny only become important after the middle of the work (midway through bk. 4), with the death of the chief priests who had been directing affairs, and especially from bk. 5. They do not govern the entire narrative, even though they appear as guiding themes in the prologue. Also in some particular episodes Josephus provides a topic sentence that does not match the main story immediately following, but only its final outcome (e.g., Pilate's generation of a "disturbance" at 2.175 [where the immediate sequel is about his building of the aqueduct, which secondarily created a disturbance]; the claim of Pharisaic and popular opposition to John Hyrcanus, grounded in jealousy over his success, at *Ant.* 13.288 [though in the story that follows, he is the Pharisees' devoted disciple, and only as a result of Sadducean machinations does he eventually find himself in conflict with them and the masses, at 13.296–98]).

two readings is not great: it involves only the question whether Josephus intends his headword ἰσοπολιτεία to apply to both halves of the *Antiquities* account or only the latter. Irrespective of that decision, the story is clear enough: an aggressive but unsuccessful bid by the Judeans of Caesarea to make the city Judean is eventually countered by a successful Greco-Syrian scheme to remove their political standing in the city altogether. What lies behind this in concrete terms is a tantalizing problem, but unanswerable from Josephus's highly schematic narrative. Crucial for the purposes of this chapter, however, is the simple point that in *Antiquities* Josephus retells the story of Caesarea, and how it became a flashpoint in the build-up to war, in a completely different way from the story in *War*. Whatever else we want to say about this matter, we cannot deny that he exhibits breathtaking freedom as a narrator to redraw stories with new personnel, dates, locations, causal connections, and outcomes.

Failure to recognize this technique has led scholars both to homogenize the two different parts of the story in *Antiquities* 20, overlooking essential elements of the first part, *and* to conflate all of this with *War* 2. This peculiar hybrid has in turn produced considerable speculation about the historical meaning of ἰσοπολιτεία in Caesarea,[65] along with a strong tendency to see the whole complex as but another example of Judean suffering at the hands of hostile neighbors. Yet one of the few points of strong agreement between *War* and *Antiquities* is Josephus's insistence on the aggressive nature of the Judean bid for primacy, based on superior wealth and strength.

From the Caesarea complexes I would like to draw two points relevant to our theme. First, Josephus's narratives are much more interesting *as narratives* than is usually assumed—not least because he so effectively combines vivid characterization and emotional impact with restraint in moralizing. This is not ideological work, but a rich and multi-layered pragmatic-political history, portraying the aims, virtues, and failings of all those on all sides who contributed to the Judean war with Rome. Heroes and villains are few, as the bulk of the narrative charts

[65]In one study ("Conflict," 384; but cf. his *Caesarea under Roman Rule* [Leiden: Brill, 1975], 22–23, 29), for example, Levine insists that the Judeans cannot have had equal civil rights in the first place, as "annulment" of them presupposes, because "the Judeans were demanding some such recognition, and it was this quest [*sc.* for ἰσοπολιτεία] that brought on the hostilities in the first place." But this confuses the two parts of *Antiquities'* story: in the first part the Judeans were not initially seeking equality, but rather (as Levine also observes) *primacy and control;* when they later have their equality canceled, that is the result of a separate action on the part of the Syrians, long after they have given up their bid for primacy. Kasher ("The *Isopoliteia* Question in Caesarea Maritima," *JQR* 68 [1977]: 24; *Hellenistic Cities,* 202) challenges Levine by arguing that that the Judeans of Caesarea had already been granted separate but equal political status by Herod, not as part of the main *polis,* but as a πολίτευμα under their own laws. He cites the labels that Josephus uses for the notables, dignitaries, and leaders of the Judean community there as proof of the existing πολίτευμα ("*Isopoliteia,*" 18–19). But such terms are ubiquitous in Josephus and not sufficiently technical to inform us about the specific historical situation here. For further discussion see the essays in T. L. Donaldson, ed., *Religious Rivalries and the Struggle for Success in Caesarea Maritima* (Waterloo: Wilfrid Laurier Press, 2000).

ordinary human foibles and their unintended consequences. Josephus's latitude in rewriting the same events combines with his absolute freedom over the initial structure, content, and diction, as we saw in the Pilate episodes, to create a truly artistic production, for which he is producer, director, screen-writer, set designer, narrator, and occasional actor.

Second, this narrative richness only exacerbates the problem of getting behind Josephus's narratives to real historical persons and events. To this problem we now return, with the material considered above as grist for the mill of reflection on method.

Reflections on Historical Method

Standard Approaches

How *does* one, then, reach behind Josephus to historical reality *where he is our only "source"* for the phenomenon in question? We shall return briefly to the different problem of doing history where multiple sources overlap. But where Josephus provides our sole access to events, as is most often the case with first-century Judea, four standard scholarly approaches to the extraction of factual information have dominated the field: (1) efforts to winnow or distil a factual residue from Josephus's narratives; (2) extrapolation of general reliability from archaeologically verifiable items; (3) exploiting apparent contradictions, doublets, and "seams" to isolate or even reconstruct Josephus's own sources; and (4) applying the same principle of contradiction to identify items that seem inimical to Josephus's literary aims, which he must therefore have included not from literary bias but because they actually happened. I offer a comment on each method before summary judgment.

1. The vast majority of scholarship that uses and cites Josephus opts for a simple winnowing method. Underlying this procedure are two assumptions: (a) that material created or influenced by Josephus's dreaded biases must never be mistaken for fact. But (b), since his manner of writing was to collect facts, like self-contained nuggets or gems, and to surround them with his biased commentary, the commentary can be lifted or evaporated off to leave a factual residue. This project can only be justified, however, by an extremely weak and inadequate apparatus for identifying "bias": usually, one excludes only what is patently aggrandizing, with respect to Josephus or his patrons, along with the miraculous or bizarre. Otherwise, as we see with Schürer and his many imitators, the narrative is simply cut from the "literary" column and pasted into the "historical," and phrases such as "Josephus reports that . . ." (if present at all) become the functional equivalent of "It happened thus. . . ." The cases we have examined, however, demonstrate that Josephus's investment in the most seemingly pedestrian stretches of his narrative is much deeper than this conventional procedure allows.

2. Many archaeologists are bullish, so to speak, on Josephus's stock as an accurate reporter. Their expressed reasoning is that the correspondence between what they find in the ground—in the south-west corner of Herod's temple mount, at Caesarea, Masada, Herodion, reinforced and breached walls at Gamala and Iotapata—and Josephus's description of the same sites requires us to admit that he is a fairly accurate historian.[66] This verdict, however, reflects category confusion. If a modern historian inquires into the physical layout of coastal Caesarea and its harbor, say, then we have *independent evidence* available in Josephus and archaeology, but the archaeology is decisive. If our question is about events described in Josephus's narrative, however—whether the masses streamed from all over Judea to surround the governor's residence in Caesarea, remaining motionless for five days and nights, or whether Felix dispatched embassies to Nero to settle the Judeans' bid for primacy—archaeology has nothing directly to say about the matter. In principle, it is always possible that an artifact will be found that documents a particular person's actions. But this almost never happens for first-century Judea, where the recovered sites, epigraphy, coins, and papyri clarify only general conditions, and the personal names they produce are often hard to connect with those in literary texts. Thus, even if Josephus had written something akin to a historical novel, using real settings but *entirely invented characters, plots, and events,* archaeology would still be compelled to give much the same positive verdict on his "reliability."

3. As in most fields of classical and biblical studies, in the study of Josephus's works the half-century from about 1870 to the 1920s was a period in which scholars were fascinated with what must have seemed an exhilarating quest: to recover the sources Josephus used. The underlying logic of this enterprise was that most ancient authors, certainly Josephus, could better be described as compilers or anthologists than as creative authors. In Josephus's case, given prevailing views about the normativeness of rabbinic Judaism, it was assumed that an Aramaic-speaking Pharisee (as he was almost universally understood to be) was incapable of producing not only the fine Greek language that we see in much of his work, but especially the abundant allusions to classical models of historiography, tragedy, and rhetoric. The source critics reasoned that wherever one encounters anything other than a simple, smooth-flowing narrative (which itself, however, *might* have been borrowed from someone else if it is too smooth)—where we see repetition of vocabulary or doublets in content, a change of vocabulary for the same object, concentrations of *hapax legomena,* a shift of mental or geographical perspective, an abrupt digression or change of subject, an inserted schematic summary, or a reference to some work by the author that we do not possess—all such items likely arise from his (often incompetent) soldering together of sources.

Already in 1920, Richard Laqueur wrote what seemed then to be the obituary for this approach, when he demonstrated that exactly the same phenomena can be

[66] E.g., M. Broshi, "The Credibility of Josephus," *JJS* 33 (1982): 379–84; also the essays by D. Syon and M. Aviam in *The First Jewish Revolt: Archaeology, History, Ideology* (ed. A. Berlin and A. Overman; London: Routledge, 2002).

found throughout Josephus's conflicting and choppy accounts of *his own career;* in that case, they cannot result from an ignorant compilation of sources. Since Laqueur's time, many of source criticism's underlying assumptions about Josephus's education and worldliness have also been systematically dismantled. For some decades, scholars realized that, however we explain all the complications of his narrative, we must reckon with Josephus as a genuine author. Strangely, however, full-blooded source criticism enjoyed something of a mini-revival in the early 1990s.[67]

It stands to reason that Josephus, like most ancient and modern writers, was occasionally influenced in his lexical choices or even sentence structures by his sources. But how can we know *where* this happened? And can we hope to reconstruct the source bodily? Those are the questions that seem impossible to answer affirmatively. With the Pilate episodes, for instance, Josephus must have known also this material from oral or written sources, since it happened before he was born. Yet we have seen there that he has fully accommodated the two episodes to his language and themes in general, to the narrative development in *War,* and each story to the other. Sustained examination of the biblical paraphrase in *Antiquities* abundantly confirms that Josephus fashions and controls his material: even though we know in that case that he used the Bible, and although we still have many versions of "rewritten Bible" for comparison, critics cannot yet agree on the kind of biblical text(s) Josephus was using. This is because his reworking is so thorough.[68] The very atoms and molecules from which the story is constructed are Josephan, and if we remove Josephus from the text there is no coherent remainder.

Because he took the same approach throughout his narratives, we can (*a fortiori*) have little hope of recovering otherwise *unknown* sources. Since Josephus's literary art demonstrably involves changes of narrative voice, complexity of character development, calculated repetition of charged language, variation of diction, and diversionary excursus, it seems impossible to devise criteria based on such phenomena for extracting sources. Attempting such recovery would require a sort of literary Heimlich maneuver, performed on someone who has long since digested the item being sought. The result is likely to be neither appealing nor useful.

4. The most far-reaching proposal in recent decades for excavating historical gold from the (allegedly) baser metal of Josephus's narratives hinges on the principle of identifying contradictions or reading against the grain. The logic here is that Josephus wrote to convey certain strong ideas; for example, it is alleged that he wanted to absolve himself and members of his aristocratic peers from

---

[67] Schwartz, *Agrippa I: The Last King of Judea* (Tübingen: Mohr [Siebeck], 1990), 2–3; R. Bergmeier, *Die Essener-Berichte des Flavius Josephus: Quellenstudien zu den Essenertexten im Werk des jüdischen Historiographen* (Kampen: Kok Pharos, 1993).

[68] See the survey by L. H. Feldman, "Use, Authority, and Exegesis of Mikra in the Writings of Josephus," in *Mikra: Text, Translation, Reading and Interpretation of the Hebrew Bible in Ancient Judaism and Early Christianity* (ed. M. J. Mulder and H. Sysling; Minneapolis: Fortress, 1988), 455–66.

complicity in the war, insisting that it was driven by a mere handful of rogue actors. Since Josephus would not invent material at odds with his purposes, any material that contradicts his aims is likely to be there *because* it is historical, included because he could not in good conscience avoid mentioning it.[69] In relation to the war against Rome, some scholars believe that they can learn from Josephus things that he did not intend to say, through a kind of cross-examination of our long-dead writer. Using him against himself, they challenge his claims and thereby reconstruct a more adequate historical reality.[70]

For a detailed exploration of this method, please see chapter 4 in this volume, "Contradiction or Counterpoint?" The main problem with it is that it must reduce Josephus's complex narrative to a sort of slogan or thesis, against which "contrary" evidence may be especially valued; but if the narrative is filled with demonstrably deliberate and artful tensions, the rationale for such a procedure collapses. Reconstructing the real past is not as simple a matter as positing Josephus's thesis or "position" and then finding things that contradict it.

General Considerations

To speak more generally, all these efforts to wring facts from Josephus overlook two fundamental problems: the nature of language and the nature of history. As to the former: it seems obvious that, with the possible exceptions of mathematical and musical notation, there is no such thing as neutral language. We may come close with single-word questions (Height? Eye-color? Age?) and answers (180 cm, blue, 50). But as soon as we begin to use sentences, we must interpret; we cannot simply mirror phenomena as experienced by all participants from all perspectives. This is as true of the television Evening News (perhaps more insidious because less widely recognized) as it is of Josephus, though in Josephus's case the problem should be especially clear. There is therefore no prospect of converting any narrative into a simple reflection of real events. To do so would require a kind of alchemy: making make one sort of thing into something else entirely. Or, to return to the image of Josephus as producer, writer, director, set designer, and sometimes actor: trying to extract the real Pilate from Josephus's narratives would be much like trying to extract the real Commodus or Marcus Aurelius from Ridley Scott's film *Gladiator.* In both cases we know that the work of art we are watching has a basis in past reality, but unless we have independent evidence concerning the real figures and events, we cannot get beyond the art, to know whether the characters portrayed really existed or to what extent they matched

[69]The principle that "incidental" evidence, out of keeping with a source's general aims, is for that reason more valuable, is discussed in R. G. Collingwood, *The Idea of History* (London: Oxford University Press, 1976), 256–82; M. Bloch, *The Historian's Craft* (trans. P. Putnam; New York: Alfred A. Knopf, 1953), 61. But these historians observe that such incidental evidence is usually exposed by a second, independent line of evidence.

[70]M. Goodman, *The Ruling Class of Judea: The Origins of the Jewish Revolt against Rome AD 66–70* (Cambridge: Cambridge University Press, 1987), 20–21; J. J. Price, *Jerusalem under Siege: The Collapse of the Jewish State, 66–70 C.E.* (Leiden: Brill, 1992), 33, 186.

the reality. It is no less misguided to draw facts from Josephus than it would be to approach the screen at a showing of *Gladiator* and hope to reach out and touch a real character.

An even more basic problem is that the standard approaches mistake the character of history. We know about the human past in two principal ways: through what has been handed down to us as grateful but passive recipients, through *tradition,* and by the active and disciplined pursuit of our questions about the past, irrespective of whether any group saw fit to transmit information, which is to say through *history.* The nineteenth and twentieth centuries hosted much debate about the true nature of history: whether it is best pursued according to biographical, political, social, economic, social-scientific, or narrative (postmodern) programs. However one resolves those issues, what distinguishes all history since Herodotus applied the word for investigation or research (ἱστορίη) to the past is the authoritative position of the historian: the one who determines the questions, gathers evidence, develops and tests working hypotheses. Unlike tradition, which has a sociological function in preserving group memories and values, history begins with a historian's problem, the careful examination of relevant evidence in situ, and then the generation and testing of possible hypotheses. To the extent that we imagine ourselves called upon to declare one piece of evidence—Josephus or Tacitus or Augustus's *res gestae*—reliable or unreliable, we are shirking the work of history to engage in a more or less critical traditionalism. In its academic context, history is a form of *scientia* or *Wissenschaft,* the methodical pursuit of a problem. Declaring any ancient writer historically reliable or unreliable as such (or partly reliable, etc.) is in this context meaningless.

Thus, a fixed chasm exists between Josephus's artful portraits of Pontius Pilate or Caesarea, which belong to a much larger narrative, and the specific questions *we* might have about the length of Pilate's term in office, his involvement with Roman personalities and politics under Sejanus, or his aims and policies in Judea. We pursue our questions by articulating them as precisely as possible, gathering the evidence that bears on the problem, and producing hypotheses. The most probable hypothesis will be the one that best explains how the range of surviving evidence came into being. Where we enjoy independent lines of evidence, especially if one line involves material remains, we may entertain some hope of resolving modest questions.[71]

Where we have only one *narrative* source, however, and no other evidence can be brought directly to bear, we have an insurmountable problem. The best explanation of Josephus's narratives will normally be Josephus's interests as author and artist, beyond which we cannot reach. Speculation based on hunches about seeming incongruities has no place to gain traction, to move it beyond speculation. Only where we have a second or third independent narrative that overlaps in significant measure can it become a meaningful exercise to test a hypothesis concerning the lost reality that produced those different artifacts. Even in Pilate's case, where we do have at least three (depending on how one counts the gospels)

[71] See the discussion attached to n. 53 above, on Pilate's term in office.

independent literary portraits—in Philo, Josephus, and the gospels—each one may be so thoroughly accommodated to its narrative context that the problem of the historical Pilate remains intractable. If Pilate's term was as long as eighteen years, the snippets provided by the ancient authors appear paltry indeed; we need only compare the difficulty of figuring out the real President of the United States or Prime Minister of Britain, for whom we are overwhelmed with a daily flood of information.

It might be objected to the model of historical investigation outlined here that it seems to entail an assumption of objectivity or neutrality on the part of the *modern investigator*.[72] If we reject the notion of finding facts in ancient authors, why do we think that our own narratives will be any less freighted with our assumptions, values, and language games? For my part, however, I see no connection between understanding history as investigator-driven, evidence-based, and argumentative—what I have argued for here—and any such illusion of conceptual or linguistic neutrality. What distinguishes our historical work from ancient historical narratives is *not* its neutrality. It is rather that history for us takes the form of argumentation, not authoritative narrative. Our written work is in the nature of reporting on historical experimentation: outlining the problem, the evidence, the possible hypotheses, and the results, so that others may work through the reasoning process with us. When our historical work is done we may dare to produce narratives from it, ultimately, but these must still be supported at each point by the results of specific investigations. Because *our aim*—and here we differ fundamentally from a Thucydides, a Josephus, or even a Herodotus—is to invite others to retrace the analysis that has led to our conclusions, we must write in a publicly accessible way, avoiding highly charged idiosyncratic or emotional language that draws from our personal authority and cannot be shared among critical international audiences.

This is far from any claim to neutrality: the point is rather that, in our unavoidable (but unashamed) particularity of style and expression, we seek nonetheless to use a discourse that is as open as possible to the language worlds of others, that offers as many points of connection as possible with other intelligent critics as they reexamine our evidence. In publishing, we invite critical reviews, which are in any case sure to follow. In our conception of history, appeals to our own character or personal trustworthiness (*ethos*), or attempts to elicit specific audience emotions (*pathos*) as a means of persuasion, should have yielded more or less entirely to *logos*-appeals.

Conclusions

I have tried here to probe the unquestioned status of Josephus as unrivalled authority for the history of early Roman Judea. In general, I have argued that history ought to be no respecter of such authority; in particular, that coming to

[72] One recent example of the criticism is Hedrick, *Ancient History*, 17–22.

terms with the content of Josephus's narratives makes clear their limitations as mirrors of episodes in Judean history. We must not rely on Josephus, *not* because he is any more "unreliable" than any other ancient writer but because, like all of them, he crafts a work of art. His work may be relied upon to fulfill its own aims, but not as a window to real events. We cannot rely on Josephus (or Tacitus or others) because historical problems that we define for investigation can only be pursued and resolved, if they *can* be pursued and resolved, by evidence that we identify, gather, and control—in the sense of being able to check it. Where Josephus provides our only account(s) of episodes in Judean history, we still know nothing about them, but only *that* he said what he said. The default posture of the historian about the underlying events must be agnostic, in advance of a disciplined investigation.

So far my conclusions are antagonistic to long-prevailing methods used to study Josephus. To end on a more constructive note, I wish to suggest three more promising approaches. First, where Josephus's narratives overlap with material evidence or with other literary accounts (as in the case of Pilate's career), it becomes at least plausible to formulate certain kinds of historical problems for which independent lines of evidence exist to be explained and, therefore, which we may hope to solve with some greater measure of confidence.

Second, although the content of particular episodes lay entirely in Josephus's gift, the larger portrait he paints of Judean society must have been one that seemed realistic to someone of his status, background, and temperament. The institutions, groups, and general social conditions that he portrays must have been broadly amenable to his interpretations. This is so for two reasons. First, it defies belief that, given the countless changes and contradictions in specific points over his thirty-volume corpus, he could have sustained a purely imaginary background world. Second, Josephus would have opened himself to pointless criticism from his many contemporaries who also knew general conditions in Judea if he wholly manufactured the basic scenic elements. Still, this is only to say what we might say of Ridley Scott's *Gladiator:* that it authentically conveys many general conditions and certain values from the author's perspective. The problem arises if we wish to press any particular element of the general picture, in the absence of independent support.

Josephus's most direct usefulness to the historian, finally, may lie in territory that is not part of his traditional use at all, but in which we are beginning to make strides. A Roman citizen and resident of the capital throughout his literary career, this author of thirty volumes is not only the most prolific extant writer from Flavian Rome; he is also the only surviving historian from those fateful decades. From a wide variety of archaeological (numismatic, epigraphical, papyrological, and monumental), literary (poetic, rhetorical, biographical, and later historical), and prosopographical evidence, we enjoy a fairly nuanced picture of many aspects of Josephus's lived environment in Flavian Rome, though large gaps remain—not least concerning the expatriate Judean community at that time. Since both the broad Roman context and a large number of specific phenomena are available to us, and since Josephus wrote in the first instance for immediate audiences in

Rome, everything he writes is potentially valuable evidence for the life of a Judean aristocrat in Flavian Rome. Since every sentence is a calculated transaction between this author and his Roman audience, we can in principle, with a measure of plausibility provided by supporting evidence, hope to understand better the specific historical phenomena that his author-audience exchanges represent.

Josephus thus becomes, along with such figures as Plutarch and Dio Chrysostom, a rich source of insight into Roman-provincial relations under the principate, and the community of foreign elites in the capital. The value of his narratives may lie less in what he *writes about* than in what he actually *says:* his language, its implicit assumptions, and its likely effects. Without losing their enormous value as narratives about Judea (both for their general picture and for specifics that may be combined with other lines of evidence), when contextualized as products of Flavian Rome Josephus's works invite also many new kinds of historical questions and hypotheses. The following two chapters endeavor to develop this line of investigation.[73]

[73] See also S. Mason, "Flavius Josephus in Flavian Rome: Reading on and Between the Lines," in *Flavian Rome: Culture, Image, Texts* (ed. A. J. Boyle and W. J. Dominik; Leiden: Brill, 2003), 559–89. Not to be neglected is also the world of the Greek statesman under Roman rule, to which Josephus belongs in some measure. This is the theme of two essays I have forthcoming: "Of Despots, Diadems, and *Diadochoi:* Josephus and Flavian Politics," in *Writing Politics in Imperial Rome* (ed. W. J. Dominik and J. Garthwaite; Leiden: Brill, 2008), and "Josephus, the Greeks, and the Distant Past," in *Antiquity in Antiquity* (ed. K. Osterloh and G. Gardner; Tübingen: Mohr [Siebeck], 2008).

Chapter 2

Of Audience and Meaning: Reading Josephus's *Judean War* in the Context of a Flavian Audience

Victor Tcherikover's 1956 essay, "Jewish Apologetic Literature Reconsidered,"[1] showed that Alexandrian-Jewish literature, which had hitherto been considered apologetic, polemical, and missionary work aimed at an undifferentiated Gentile audience, must in fact have been directed—almost entirely—at the Jews of Alexandria. Having established this point, Tcherikover called for a reappraisal of this literature in its concrete historical environment, in light of Egyptian papyri, ostraca, and inscriptions. Understanding a text's audience, he realized, makes all the difference to interpretation: "If our opinion is right and every literary work reflects the ideas of a certain group of people [i.e., the author and first audience], then we have to know exactly where this group lived, when this work was written and under what historical conditions it was conceived."[2] Audience matters.

In the study of Josephus, questions of audience have not usually been considered crucial for interpretation. Then again, interpretation itself has not been a priority: we have until recently lacked even elementary attempts at sketching the structures, themes, and characteristic language of Josephus's major works.[3] The *meaning* of the text has most often been located rather in the interplay between our author and his sources: because he altered the Bible (or Nicolaus, etc.) in manner X, he must have meant or thought Y.[4] Although Josephus's use of sources is an indispensable avenue of inquiry, and may reveal to scholars something of his interests as an author, it leaves unsettled whether any particular audience would have been able to follow this use of sources: the question of what he wished to

---

[1] Victor Tcherikover, "Jewish Apologetic Literature Reconsidered." *Eos* 48 (1956): 169–93.

[2] Ibid., 186.

[3] Cf. P. Bilde, *Flavius Josephus between Jerusalem and Rome: His Life, His Works and Their Importance* (JSPSup 2; Sheffield: JSOT Press, 1988), 71, 92 [under "Literature"].

[4] See for example L. H. Feldman, *Studies in Josephus' Rewritten Bible* (Leiden: Brill, 1998); C. Begg, *Josephus' Account of the Early Divided Monarchy (AJ 8.212–420): Rewriting the Bible* (BETL 108; Leuven: Leuven University Press, 1993); C. Begg, *Josephus' Story of the Later Monarchy* (BETL 155; Leuven: Leuven University Press, 2000); F. M. Colautti, *Passover in the Works of Josephus* (Leiden: Brill, 2002), 13–83; D. R. Schwartz, "Josephus and Nicolaus on the Pharisees." *JSJ* 14 (1983): 157–71; Schwartz, *Agrippa I*, 1–38.

communicate. Josephus's audience may have been recognized by scholars as an introductory issue for the right sort of textbook, but since few if any studies of Josephus count as textbooks, audience questions have mostly been treated piecemeal and vaguely.

One surprisingly durable view holds that Josephus wrote *War* as Roman propaganda, whether on the basis of a comprehensive Roman source[5] or translating an Aramaic version intended for the Parthian empire (cf. *War* 1.3, 6). The *Antiquities* and later works were, according to this view, instruments of repentance or at least opportunistic rehabilitation, directed at "Roman authorities" to win support for a putative new rabbinic leadership at Yavneh, or perhaps at the Yavnean rabbis themselves.[6] Scholars who have found such a radical disjunction in Josephus's literary career unpersuasive have usually adopted the diplomatic solution that he wrote for everyone: Romans and Greeks and Jews.[7] But where and how he should have reached these vaguely conceived parties remains unclear. Finally, in keeping with Tcherikover's question about Alexandrian-Judean literature—"What interest, indeed, could a Greek reader have for the practical prescriptions of Judaism?"[8]—some scholars have insisted that only other Judeans could have been much interested in, or able to comprehend, the writings of this displaced compatriot, no matter what Josephus said about his expected audience.[9]

Underlying my argument in this essay is the proposition that Josephus's audience matters for interpretation. Thus I agree with Tcherikover, not only in his particular conclusions about Alexandrian-Judean literature, but more importantly in his (largely neglected) method and argument. Tcherikover regarded a couple of Philo's works (*Legatio ad Gaium* and *Against Flaccus*) as exceptions to his general position, for they seemed obviously targeted at Roman officials; he

---

[5] W. Weber, *Josephus und Vespasian: Untersuchungen zu dem jüdischen Krieg des Flavius Josephus* (Hildesheim: Georg Olms, 1921 [1973]); cf. H. Lindner, *Die Geschichtsauffassung des Flavius Josephus im Bellum Judaicum* (Leiden: Brill, 1972).

[6] With different emphases and nuances, R. Laqueur, *Der jüdische Historiker Flavius Josephus: Ein biographischer Versuch auf neuer quellenkritischer Grundlage.* (Darmstadt: Wissenschaftliche Buchgesellschaft, 1970), 126–27; H. Rasp, "Flavius Josephus und die jüdischen Religionsparteien." *ZNW* 23 (1924): 46; H. St. J. Thackeray, *Josephus: The Man and the Historian* (New York: Ktav, 1929), 27, 52, 56; M. Smith, "Palestinian Judaism in the First Century," in *Israel: Its Role in Civilization* (ed. M. Davis; New York: Harper & Brothers, 1956), 72; J. Neusner, *From Politics to Piety: The Emergence of Pharisaic Judaism* (Englewood Cliffs, N.J.: Prentice Hall, 1973); S. J. D. Cohen, *Josephus in Galilee and Rome: His Vita and Development as a Historian* (Leiden: Brill, 1979), 86, 145, 209; H. W. Attridge, "Josephus and His Works," in *Jewish Writings of the Second Temple Period: Apocrypha, Pseudepigrapha, Qumran Sectarian Writings, Philo, Josephus,* (ed. M. E. Stone; Philadelphia: Fortress, 1984), 200–203; S. Schwartz, *Josephus and Judaean Politics* (Leiden: Brill, 1990), 10, 199–201.

[7] G. E. Sterling, *Historiography and Self-definition: Josephus, Luke-Acts, and Apologetic Historiography* (NovTSup 44; Leiden: Brill, 1992), 297–308; Bilde, *Josephus*, 77–78.

[8] Tcherikover, "Apologetic," 178.

[9] E. Migliario, "Per l'interpretazione dell' Autobiografia di Flavio Giuseppe," *Athenaeum* 69.1–2 (1981): 92, 96, 136; T. Rajak *Josephus: The Historian and His Society* (London: Duckworth, 1983), 178 (the Jewish Diaspora was Josephus's primary audience).

also thought that Josephus's later works were written for Gentiles,[10] though he left *War* unmentioned. But if we apply the same sort of historical logic to Josephus's *War,* written in Rome, that Tcherikover used for Alexandrian-Judean literature, we should conclude that Josephus wrote in the first instance—without precluding secondary and tertiary readerships—for sympathetic or at least tractable audiences in his adopted home city of Rome, who shared with him an elite education and world of discourse. These groups included some fellow-Judeans (*Ioudaioi*) in Rome (*Ag. Ap.* 1.51), though he wrote with special concern for Greeks and Romans in the capital.

Although it would be ideal to spell out some consequences of this conclusion for understanding Josephus's *War,* lack of space precludes that kind of exploration here. The interested reader may wish to consult chapter 3 in the present volume and another essay of mine[11] on those questions. In the present study I attempt, with sharper focus than I have been able to indulge elsewhere, the nature of Josephus's expected audience; in the conclusion I shall merely suggest some of the consequences explored in the other essays, to which this study is logically preparatory.

Audience Matters for Interpreting Communicative Texts

Because interpretation of Josephus has usually ignored or abstracted the question of audience, it seems necessary to begin by establishing the otherwise trite premise that *audience does matter* for understanding a work's aims.[12] The point seems straightforwardly provable. *If* an ancient author writes to communicate, and not merely for personal satisfaction, then he writes to communicate *with someone.* It follows that in composing his work he must take into account the existing *knowledge base* of the intended recipients (e.g., linguistic, historical, geographical) as well as their *interests, values, and attitudes.* A text is not self-interpreting: it has no independent meaning. It is rather a medium or "middle term" between two parties, a set of codes left by an author for a skilled readership or—with other sensory cues added—an audience to decipher. For example,

[10] Tcherikover, "Apologetic," 183.

[11] S. Mason, "Flavian Rome," 559–89 (chiefly on *Antiquities,* though with some attention to *War*).

[12] The reticence about "aim-" or "intention-" language that one often meets in classical, biblical, and humanistic scholarship represents, as far as I can see, in part a misapplication of W. K. Wimsatt's "intentional fallacy" (of 1946 vintage), developed in relation to belletristic literature, especially poetry, and by no means uncontested even there (see T. Eagleton, *Literary Theory: An Introduction* [Minneapolis: University of Minnesota Press, 1996]), 38–46. Eagleton aptly observes (p. 44), "Most literary theories, in fact, unconsciously 'foreground' a particular literary genre, and derive their general pronouncements from this." Since the author of *Judean War* declares intentions (1.1–30) and writes a narrative that fulfills them, I see no problem in discussing the book's aims, or indeed Josephus's aims by implication, as long as we bear in mind that our accounts can never be exhaustive and that the man Josephus behind the work remains unknown in most respects.

a page of Aristophanes is completely unintelligible to those without knowledge of the script; someone else might be able to identify the characters as Greek without being able to read them; another person might have the ability to read them syntactically but without grasping the referential sense; yet another might make decent sense of them but, lacking appropriate historical knowledge, miss elements of wit or nuance that an interpreter with such contextual knowledge would notice. Any set of written codes requires such interpretation, and anyone who sets out to communicate verbally has no choice but to bear in mind the abilities of the expected decoders.

This does not imply that communication is ever perfect, or even that an author/speaker intends it to be so: we have all used phrases, images, or allusions because they are particularly satisfying to us, whether or not our audience ever detected the significance *for us*. (If they do, it is a bonus.) Still, as long as we aim chiefly to communicate, we can do so only with an assessment of our audience's knowledge and sympathies.

In this chapter, I mainly assume that Josephus wished to communicate. The question becomes, then: *With whom*?

Let us begin with basics. The fact that he wrote the extant *War* in Greek requires that he composed for people who could understand this language. More than that, however, he wrote a particular kind of Greek, different in pitch, tone, diction, and syntactic sophistication from the language of Jewish Greek compositions of the preceding centuries, from such contemporary texts as the New Testament's Mark, John, or Luke-Acts, or from Chariton's *Chaereas and Callirhoe*. Josephus's writing is much closer to that of contemporary and later statesmen-teachers: Plutarch, Dio Chrysostom, Aristides, and Lucian. Like them, he shows himself keenly sensitive to questions of style (*War* 1.13; 7.455; see further below). *War*'s opening sentence comprises 264 words (on Niese's punctuation), half a dozen *μέν* . . . δέ constructions along with other binary contrasts, and a number of rare words or formations.[13] The work as a whole scrupulously avoids the clashing of vowels ("hiatus"), à la mode, and particularly in the opening and closing sections favors old-fashioned Attic spelling.

These traits do not bespeak an easy capitulation to fashion, for they required sustained artistic effort, especially from someone for whom Greek was a second language. As critics have long observed, however, *War* is in fact a fine specimen of the developing Atticistic Greek so popular among the Greek revivalists of Josephus's time.[14] Surprisingly, it contains the first attestation of many words and phrases that would become popular in the authors named above, members of the "Second Sophistic."[15] Josephus also happens to share much of their outlook on

---

[13]Rare words: ἀτυχήματα, 1.12; ἐφρεάζω, 1.13; προϊστορέω 1.15, ἀρχαιολογέω, διεκοδικός, 1.18, comparative of προγενής at 1.18. Unusual formations (not used again in Josephus, for example: the neuter substantives τὸ *νεωτερίζον* in 1.4, τὸ κελτικόν in 1.5, τὰ στρατιωτικά, 1.5; τὸ ληστρικόν in 1.11.

[14]Thackeray, *The Man and the Historian*, 104.

[15]I refer the reader to my commentary on *War 2,* which is vol. 1b of *Flavius Josephus: Translation and Commentary* (Leiden: Brill, 2008).

issues of internal state (*polis*) government and external relations with Rome, and like them he seems to draw much of this from Polybius.[16] *War* contains arguably the richest surviving example of the Greek historical prologue (*War* 1.1–30),[17] and the narrative is conspicuously sensitive to the prescriptions of rhetorical training: variation in scene and diction, speeches and other major digressions, colorful battle accounts. It is replete with evocations of Greek epic and tragedy.[18]

Given that Josephus will not maintain *War*'s literary standards in his later compositions, falling into what seems his unaided natural voice by *Ant.* 20–*Life*,[19] one must ask why he went to all this trouble in his definitive work, during his first decade in the capital. It would be bizarre to imagine him doing so for mere self-gratification, or if he wrote for audiences who did not care about such things. It seems impossible to avoid the conclusion that he expected an audience who would appreciate or even require these touches.

In modern scholarship, classicists have shown a more determined interest in the concrete conditions of publication, in the situations of authors and audiences from Aristophanes to Virgil to Dionysius to Pliny the Younger,[20] than have their counterparts in biblical, postbiblical/intertestamental, and New Testament literatures—the other principal constituencies for the study of Josephus. This may be because, with the notable exception of the apostle Paul (the vast library of scholarship on his letters deals very much with contexts and audiences),[21] the authors and provenances of biblical, postbiblical, and early Christian texts are usually difficult or impossible to know. From that side of the scholarly world, therefore, one might object that the study of ancient texts obviously *does not* require knowledge of first audiences. But such a position would only make a virtue of necessity. The

[16]See A. M. Eckstein, "Josephus and Polybius: A Reconsideration," *Classical Antiquity* 9 (1990) for specific parallels; A. M. Eckstein, *Moral Vision in the Histories of Polybius* (Berkeley: University of California Press, 1995) for Polybius in general.

[17]For the standard tropes of ancient prologues, see H. Lieberich, *Studien zu den Proömien in der griechischen und byzantinischen Geschichtsschreibung. I: Die griechischen Geschichtsschreiber* (Munich, J.G. Weiss, 1899); D. C. Earl, "Prologue-Form in Ancient Historiography," *ANRW* (1972) 1.2:842–856; and, with (happily) significant attention to Josephus, J. Marincola, *Authority.*

[18]See H. Chapman, "Spectacle and Theater in Josephus's Bellum Judaicum" (PhD diss., Department of Classics, Stanford University, 1998), 208.

[19]Josephus's last work (*Against Apion*) returns to a highly polished rhetorical style.

[20]W. R. Connor, *Thucydides* (Princeton: Princeton University Press, 1984), 12: "The study of the audience of ancient literature is one of the most pressing items in the agenda of classical studies." For convenient demonstration, one might consider the treatment of each author in E. J. Kenney and W. V. Clausen, eds., *The Cambridge History of Classical Literature* (Cambridge: Cambridge University Press, 5 vols., 1982–1989); more generally, C. Salles, *Lire à Rome* (Paris: Les Belles Lettres, 1992); E. Fantham, *Roman Literary Culture: From Cicero to Apuleius* (Baltimore: Johns Hopkins University Press, 1996)—a detailed survey of literary contexts or audiences—and C. Pelling, *Literary Texts and the Greek Historian* (London: Routledge, 2000), 1–17.

[21]See e.g., W. A. Meeks, *The First Urban Christians: the Social World of the Apostle Paul* (New Haven: Yale University Press, 1983); C. J. Roetzel, *The Letters of Paul: Conversations in Context* (Louisville: Westminster John Knox Press, 1991).

fact that we lack much evidence for the authorship and context of most biblical and postbiblical literature is lamentable. This lack does not stop critics in those fields from endlessly formulating hypotheses about the audiences of the Deuteronomistic Historian, *Wisdom of Solomon, 4 Maccabees,* or even Q—proof of the question's importance. Scholars simply lack the supporting material to make compelling cases. In the case of Josephus, however, the situation is much more akin to that of most classical authors: we know his name, rough dates, career outline, and place of writing. We also have a decent picture from various sources of the general environment in Flavian Rome,[22] and Josephus's writings contain significant references to conditions and even a few persons in that environment. To neglect the fundamental question of his expected audience would therefore be irresponsible.

Before moving to the particular evidence for Josephus's audience, I pause to elucidate one further point. My working hypothesis is that Josephus wrote to communicate, but there are many levels and kinds of communication. For the sake of simplicity, I suggest that verbal communication (on one plane at least) ranges between the poles of the obvious or basic conveyance of meaning and subtle, figured, or partially hidden modes. On the plain-sense extreme, we simply try to get across an unambiguous message—as when visiting a foreign country, when our ability to use the codes and our knowledge of audience are severely limited—without causing either mirth or ambiguity. In such contexts there is little room for irony, humor, sarcasm, or other higher dimensions of communication. In these cases, one must spell out everything.

Yet in Greek and Roman rhetoric such obvious writing was often considered pedestrian, even demeaning to the audience, who should be left to complete the story for themselves so as to feel respected by the author/speaker. So Demetrius (*Eloc.* 222): "It is a slur on your hearer to tell him everything as though he were a simpleton."[23] One can only write artfully in this way, however—saying things without actually saying them, leaving things for the audience to discover—when one knows the audience. In the case of Josephus it is especially important to consider this higher level of communication because it was so widely embraced in Flavian Rome, where it could be dangerous to speak frankly.[24] Although we lack the space in this essay to explore Josephus's uses of figured language,[25] it is important to remember these possibilities because they further illustrate the importance of audience for interpretation: it is only when we posit a certain kind of audience knowledge that we can detect such plays.

---

[22]See e.g., A. J. Boyle and W. J. Dominik (as referenced in n. 11 above).

[23]Further on artful modes of discourse: *Eloc.* 287–98. Cf. Quintilian (*Inst.* 9.1.14, 2.65) on figured speech: "a hidden meaning, which is left to the hearer to discover."

[24]See F. Ahl, "The Art of Safe Criticism in Greece and Rome," *AJP* 105 (1984); V. Rudich, *Political Dissidence under Nero: The Price of Dissimulation* (London: Routledge, 1993) and V. Rudich, *Dissidence and Literature under Nero: The Price of Rhetorization* (London: Routledge 1997); S. Bartsch, *Actors in the Audience: Theatricality and Doublespeak from Nero to Hadrian* (Cambridge, Mass.: Harvard University Press, 1994).

[25]See ch. 3 and my essay in n. 11 above.

Josephus's Audience in Rome: The Evidence

At least five considerations place it beyond doubt that Josephus wrote his Greek *War* to communicate with an elite audience in the capital city.

1. In the ancient world, publication was normally a local and social project. The ground on which Tcherikover decisively refuted abstract assumptions about apologetic and missionary purposes in Alexandrian-Judean literature has generally been ignored. Against the then common assumption (he said) that ancient authors reached their audiences much as we reach ours, Tcherikover pointed out crucial differences between ancient and modern publication[26]—or at least the process of making a work public (see below). Since all dissemination of literature depended upon copying by hand, it was inevitably a local affair in the first instance.[27] Book production was dependent largely on the stature or *auctoritas* of the author and/or his patron: "the main condition for the distribution of a book within a society was, that the author should be rooted in that society."[28] The Jewish authors had audience/reader groups around them. This recognition by itself obviated implausible notions about the Mediterranean-wide ambitions and reach of Judean literature from Alexandria.

Quite right. But then, Josephus too must have had a local audience in Rome, and written *for* that audience. To apply Tcherikover's challenge to Josephus's works, one should not conclude that he too wrote for Judeans. One should rather examine all the available evidence concerning his method of writing and publication, considering the ways in which these clues reflect Josephus's context in Rome.

Since Tcherikover's time an array of studies has made the point repeatedly and for various kinds of literature[29] that bringing out a book was a social and local enterprise. It will be most efficient to sketch some salient results of these studies as a point of reference for better understanding Josephus's remarks in the following sections of this chapter. I refer the reader to the studies themselves for full documentation.

Publication as we understand it did not exist in antiquity. This may seem obvious, but it needs emphasis because most studies of Josephus appear to assume that seven-volume corpora on rolls, such as his *War,* could be distributed to any audience he desired. Starr appropriately suggests: "The term 'publish' should not be used because it unavoidably bears a burden of modern implications."[30]

---

[26] Tcherikover, "Apologetic," 171–74.

[27] See also Starr, "Circulation."

[28] Tcherikover, "Apologetic," 173.

[29] P. White, "The Friends of Martial, Statius, and Pliny, and the Dispersal of Patronage," *HSCP* 79 (1975): 299; T. P. Wiseman, *Roman Studies: Literary and Historical* (Liverpool: F. Cairns, 1987), 252–56; Starr, "Circulation"; W.V. Harris, *Ancient Literacy* (Cambridge, Mass.: Harvard University Press, 1989), 222–29; Salles, *Lire à Rome,* 94–110; Fantham, *Literary Culture,* 120–21, 183–221; D. S. Potter, *Literary Texts and the Roman Historian* (London: Routledge, 1999), 23–44.

[30] Starr, "Circulation," 215 n.18.

Technology available to us, from the printing press and its digital successors to convenient travel and electronic communication, has spawned the publishing industry. In this environment, we divide book production cleanly into two phases: the preparation of the work, which is our task as authors and is essentially *private* (the degree to which we involve others is discretionary), and the work's *publication,* when it goes out to the audience. Conditions created by mass production, editorial and marketing staffs, and modern delivery services dictate that while writing, we meet our audiences only *in our imaginations.* We may try to keep them constantly in view, so that the resulting text (or codes) will match their competencies, but it is the publisher's task to find that imagined audience in reality. We hand over a finished work and the publisher produces hundreds or thousands of copies, using advertising, placement in appropriate sales venues, and mass-mail resources to control the distribution of the work. In principle all such distribution depends on the publishing firm, which monitors usage for any infringement of their corporate ownership (copyright) of the work. Revision of a book, should we desire it, is a large and expensive undertaking—impossible without the publisher's agreement and further investment. For us, then, book-writing is essentially an impersonal or asocial exercise, which can be initiated anywhere in the world if we have the requisite technology.

In the ancient world, the complete absence of such technology meant that there was *no clear line* between writing and publication, which is why we probably should abandon the latter term as Starr suggests. Preparing a book was almost inevitably a *local* and *social* project. Evidence from a sufficient variety of sources throughout the late republic and early empire (e.g., Cicero, Horace, Martial, Statius, Pliny the Younger, Tacitus, Lucian) creates a consistent picture along the following lines. An author normally composed a work gradually and by constant revision, presenting it in stages to ever-widening concentric circles, moving from closest friends to more remote associates through a combination of oral recitation and distribution of partial drafts.[31] The cycle of oral presentations typically began in the intimate setting of a private residence, perhaps at a dinner party, and moved as the author gained confidence in the work to rented auditoriums. The oral dimensions of this entire process, even with written texts, should always be kept in mind. Apart from scribes and other bookish types, people did not often sit down to pore over thirty- or even seven-scroll corpora such as Josephus's, with uncial lines lacking word dividers or much in the way of punctuation. The simple act of reading would itself normally involve a slave reciting stretches of a text to his master.[32] (Letters, poems, and epigrams were another story.) The leisured classes commonly attended recitals to keep themselves abreast of current work.

This process of writing and testing one's work was chiefly *where the author met his intended audience:* in the give and take of presentation and circulation of

---

[31] See ibid., 213.

[32] C. Fornara, 31; Fantham, *Literary Culture,* 202–203, 214–16; Potter, *Literary Texts,* 106–10.

drafts among trusted acquaintances, receiving challenges from them, and ongoing correction. Salles observes: "The success of a literary work depended equally on the activity of the coteries, the public readings, and the representations of the author to his associates; but in all this, dissemination remained in a 'closed circuit.'"[33] Some authors apparently rested content with the narrowest circles of such oral/aural exposure. Horace contrasts his practice to that of the frivolous, who allegedly recite anywhere and to anyone (*Sat.* 1.4.73): "I reserve the reading of my work for my friends alone."[34] Pliny allows that he begins with his respected friends (whose criticism he still fears), but then recites (*recito, lego*) and sends (*trado*) to ever-larger audiences in the quest to perfect his work (*Ep.* 7.17). He concludes: "I am positive that any work must be revised more than once and read to a number of people if it is intended to give permanent and universal satisfaction" (*Ep.* 7.17.15; see also 5.12). Here we have to do with cycles of preparation in a social context, at any phase of which an author could simply choose to halt the project. If he did, we could not say that the work was "unpublished," since it had already reached some levels of the author's society. Nor, conversely, can we say that completion of the work would imply much wider circulation.

To be sure, there was a natural point of completion for a book long in preparation, at which point it might be appropriate to make gift copies to the dedicatee (if there was one) and a small circle of associates. Yet the need for manual reproduction meant that each copy was also in some way a new work; the necessity of correcting each copy was well known.[35] Because finality was not possible in the way it is with printed texts, however, deliberate revision was also relatively easy with each new copy, a condition that precludes our concept of a fixed text. Thus the "finished" copy was no different in principle from earlier drafts, except that the author was provisionally more satisfied with it and so may have distributed it with a stronger sense of completion. But further revision was common, and it was a significant concern to authors that an inferior version had larger circulation than the better one.[36] Any number of subsequent "editions" could be created with successive copies, as a result of further dialogue with the recipients of gift copies. Therefore, no clean division between preparation and publication of a book was possible.

For present purposes, the main consequence of this is that the entire process remained local. Even the further distribution of books after completion occurred mainly among close acquaintances: "The channels of circulation ran from one friend to another, never between strangers. . . . This probably restricted both the number of texts in circulation and the number of people to whom particular texts were accessible."[37]

---

[33] Salles, *Lire à Rome,* 156: La succès d'une œuvre littéraire dépend simultanément de l'activité des cénacles, des lectures publiques, des envois de l'écrivain à ses relations, mais, par ces procédés, la diffusion se fait en «circuit fermé».

[34] Ibid., 156.

[35] See Potter, *Literary Texts,* 33–37.

[36] Ibid., 29–33.

[37] Starr, "Circulation," 216–17.

An illustration of the inappropriateness of our assumptions about book production for understanding Josephus's world is furnished by the phenomenon that most closely approximates modern publication: the handing over of the book rolls to others—friends, a library, or even a bookseller. Thus was the work "made public." Paradoxically, however, whereas publication for us is the point at which we *begin to reach* the audience we envisaged while writing, via our publisher's controlled distribution, for the ancients this handing over (ἔκδοσις)[38] of the work to others was the beginning of the author's effective *loss of control* over audience. Anyone who wished could now have the rolls copied from exemplars, whether from friends' copies or through custom orders from booksellers. Occasionally, to be sure, copies of books made it to far-flung locales as gifts or via booksellers. Such booksellers as there were, however, lacked a distribution system: it seems that they did not transport (much less import) books in bulk but had copies produced on order from exemplars they either owned or could secure. In a world of widespread illiteracy and poverty, where books were passed avidly among friends in elite circles, the book trade seems to have been "merely an ancillary system of circulation beside the private channels. . . ."[39] In any case, the authors could have had no idea about this added use, and therefore could not have counted on it while writing. Rather, *they met their intended audiences while preparing their works.*

One aspect of bringing a work to the attention of one's friends and associates, of "publication," deserves closer attention, both because it is furthest from our experience in a text-conditioned world and because of the possible light it throws on Josephus's situation. The custom of hearing texts recited, namely, was confined neither to Rome nor to the more entertaining genres, such as poetry. Recitation was a widespread practice in the Mediterranean and it was used also for historical works. In Rome, the process of disseminating new histories was comparable with practices for other genres because there were no professional historians in the first century: the field was open to anyone who could make a claim to credibility. As Tacitus's *Dialogue on Oratory* (*Dial.* 3) and the so-called progymnasmata (pre-rhetorical handbooks) plainly show, all those with advanced education in rhetoric felt able to compose in any genre: "training in exercises is absolutely useful not only to those who are going to practice rhetoric but also if one wishes to undertake the function of *poets or historians or any other writers*" (Aelius Theon, *Prog.* 70; cf. 60). Pliny too assumes that histories were being recited alongside tragedy and poetry (*Ep.* 7.17.3). In the Roman period it was widely reported that Herodotus, the father of history a half-millennium earlier, had recited much of his work, which indeed bears many marks of oral performance.[40] (Even his younger contemporary Thucydides, the model of dense historical writing, may

---

[38]Cf. B. van Groningen, "EKDOSIS," *Mnemosyne* 16 (1963): 1–17; Potter, *Literary Texts*, 32.

[39]Starr, "Circulation," 221.

[40]R. Thomas, *Herodotus in Context: Ethnography, Science, and the Art of Persuasion* (Cambridge, Cambridge University Press, 2000), 249–69; L. Kurke, "Charting the Poles of History: Herodotos and Thoukydides," in *Literature in the Greek World* (ed. O. Taplin; Oxford: Oxford University Press, 2000), 118–22.

have recited some of his work.)[41] Although it might seem bizarre to moderns that audiences would sit through sessions long enough to cover much historical narrative,[42] we should remember that in many parts of the world even today it is common to listen to political speeches of several hours' duration.

In Josephus's time, Tacitus portrays Maternus (under Vespasian) feverishly rewriting his life of Cato because the previous day's *recitation* had generated concern about its potentially dangerous resonances (*Dial.* 3). It seems likely that figurative references (*figurae*) in a history by Hermogenes of Tarsus, which prompted Domitian to execute him (Suetonius, *Dom.* 10.1), were also detected through oral presentation, for this victim is mentioned among others who gave offense to the emperor *in their performances* (Suetonius, *Dom.* 10.3–4). Writing in the 160s, Lucian of Samosata frequently observes that he has come to know the histories being composed concerning the recent Parthian campaign by *hearing* authors in various Greek cities: "So then, I'll relate to you what I recall hearing certain historians earlier in Ionia—and, by God, in Achaea just recently—relate about this very war" (*Hist. conscr.* 14). He claims to have walked out early from one such reading, because he could predict the clichéd narrative to follow (*Hist. conscr.* 15). He sarcastically describes one recital in which the author's grandiloquent prologue failed to match up to the paltry narrative that followed: "Those who have been listening (οἱ ἀκούσαντες) immediately call out to them 'A mountain was in labour!'" (23). The situation that he describes assumes that the speaker presented a substantial amount: enough for the audience to complain about early expectations unfulfilled.

In sum: making books public in the Roman world was a matter of disseminating the work orally and in draft copies through ever widening circles of friends and associates: it was local and social. It is difficult to imagine how Josephus could have been free of the constraints and conditions of his time.

2. The specific evidence for the publication of *War* seems indeed to require that he followed the normal practices. This evidence falls into two parts: first, references in later works to his preparation and dissemination of *War* and second, clues within the prologue about his situation while writing.

First, then, two substantial passages from Josephus's later works deal with his writing and dissemination of *War*: the closing sentences of his digression against Justus of Tiberias in *Life* 361–366 and a piece of his digression on Judean (vis-à-vis Greek) historiography in *Against Apion* 1.46–56.

In the former place, Josephus asserts that Justus's patron and employer King Agrippa II had been in frequent contact with himself while he was writing *War*.

> [364] And the king, Agrippa, wrote sixty-two letters attesting to [my] transmission of the truth. Two of these I have actually appended, in case you insist on knowing from them what was written:

[41] S. Hornblower, *Thucydides* (London: Duckworth, 1984), 29; M. Munn, *The School of History: Athens in the Age of Socrates* (Berkeley: University of California Press,

[42] To recite Herodotus's narrative would require between one and two 24-hour days (Kurke, "Charting," 119).

> [365] King Agrippa, to dearest Josephus, Greetings! I went through the volume with greatest pleasure, and it really seems to me that with superior care you have precisely described what you have portrayed. [366] *Send me the rest also.* Be well.
>
> King Agrippa, to dearest Josephus, Greetings! From what you have written, you look as though you need no instruction—[we can read you] instead of our learning everything from the start. *Whenever you next meet me, I myself will inform you of many things that are not [widely] known.*

Two further points emerge here with some clarity—even if Josephus invented the letters or exaggerated the contact, since he is presumably evoking a plausible scenario. First, Josephus circulated pieces of *War* to others, including Agrippa, while he was writing ("Send me the rest also. . . ."; "I myself will inform you"), not merely on completion. Notice the single "volume" (ἡ βίβλος) in Agrippa's comment. Second, this exchange involved at least some personal contact ("Whenever you next meet me. . . ."). If these letters are indeed exemplary of the rest, they reveal their limited function. Josephus and Agrippa were close enough geographically that they could exchange such notes easily (presumably at least 124, counting both directions). But the notes themselves were brief and pointed; serious discussion was reserved for face-to-face encounters, which must therefore also have occurred easily enough. Although Agrippa wants to impart more information to Josephus, he is content to leave the matter until *whenever* (ὅταν) they should next meet. No travel plans need to be discussed.

In *Against Apion* 1.46–49, Josephus describes his process of carefully gathering information during and after the war, and then speaks of his period of composition in Rome (notice incidentally the complete lack of reference to an Aramaic precursor): "Then, taking advantage of leisure in Rome, with all the work [πραγματεία· argument? material?] now ready and at my disposal, and after I had consulted [or: arranged, furnished, engaged] certain collaborators for the Greek sound, thus I accomplished the transmission of the events" (*Ag. Ap.* 1.50). In Josephus's enlistment of co-workers (συνεργοί) or literary friends[43] in the capital for this massive project, we again witness a social affair and not the work of an isolated author. Another point raised by this notice concerns Josephus's ability in Greek, since the collaborators helped particularly with the Greek sound (or possibly "language": φωνή), a question to which we shall return presently.

Both passages present intriguing information about those who first received copies of *War* upon its completion. *Life* 361–362 has Josephus delivering (ἐπιδίδωμι) the written materials (τὰ βίβλια) to the imperators, Vespasian and Titus, when the events had scarcely passed, and likewise immediately (εὐθύς) delivering (same verb) the *historia* to "many others" (ἄλλοις δὲ πολλοῖς). Some of these latter had participated in the conflict, including Agrippa and certain of the king's relatives. *Against Apion* 1.51–2, however, notoriously describes these same transactions differently. Josephus *gives* the volumes (ἔκδωκα τὰ βίβλια) first to Vespasian and Titus as also "to many of the Romans who had fought along-

[43] There is no reason to imagine Thackeray's "literary assistants" or slaves (LCL, 1929: 105) here; see Rajak, *Historian,* 63.

side them," but then *sells* others to "many" of his own people (πολλοῖς δὲ τῶν ἡμετέρων ἐπίπρασκον). Among these purchasers is King Agrippa, the king's brother-in-law Julius Archelaus, and an elusive "most dignified Herod."[44] All are described as fully trained in Greek wisdom (1.52; cf. *Life* 359), a point that seems to be offered as a reason why, though Judeans, they would be interested in the Greek-language book. If so, that would suggest that other Judeans who lacked such Greek culture would not be interested.

It is in the nature of traditional Josephus scholarship that attention has focused largely on the dating problem created by Josephus's presentation of the work to Vespasian, who died in 79 (although book 7 in its current form has been thought to have been written after that date),[45] and on Josephus's apparent mendacity in claiming in one place that he gave copies to Agrippa and family, in the other that he had *sold* these copies. But for our purposes there are more important things to be learned. Namely, Josephus's audience—even in the sense of the first recipients of his finished, "final" copies—was local, in keeping with the normal practices considered above. His delivery of copies to individuals who were resident in Rome during much of the 70s (Agrippa and his sister arrived in 75)[46] confirms the picture developed above of a proximate network of interested associates.

Josephus qualifies the adjective "many" (of his fellow-Judean recipients) with only three examples, all of whom were of the highest rank. They were fairly distinguished Roman citizens, they spent much of their time in the capital, and they were fully conversant with Greek culture. We have no reason, then, to imagine massive sales of *Judean War* to Judeans around the Mediterranean—a technically implausible project in any case. The identity of the "many" Romans who had fought alongside Vespasian and Titus who received copies, is similarly puzzling. There too, "many" seems typically rhetorical (an exaggeration common also in modern scholarship). We should not imagine the distribution of Josephus's *War* to the legionary camps in Judea or elsewhere, in the vein of Thomas Paine's pamphleteering during the American revolution, but should probably look for a few prominent officials worthy to be mentioned alongside the *principes*. Obvious candidates are the surviving legionary legates from the war, such as: Sextus Vettulenus Cerialis (*legio V Macedonica*) and M. Titius Frugi (*legio XV Apollinaris*), the former of whom Josephus had once accompanied on a reconnaissance trip (*Life* 420; cf. *War* 6.236–237); the tribune Nicanor, who had reportedly been a friend of Josephus (*War* 3.344–346); and Masada's conqueror L. Flavius Silva Nonius Bassus.[47]

---

[44] As N. Kokkinos in *The Herodian Dynasty: Origins, Role in Society and Eclipse* (Sheffield: Sheffield Academic Press, 1998) observes, the name *Iulius* suggests that Archelaus's family had become Roman citizens already in the time of Herod. Herod "the most dignified" he identifies as Herod VII, the last man known to bear the famous name, son of Aristobulus III (son of Herod of Chalcis), a cousin of Agrippa II who like him grew up in Rome.

[45] Cohen, *Galilee and Rome*, 84–90; Schwartz, *Judaean Politics*.

[46] Dio 66.15.3–4; Kokkinos, *Herodian Dynasty*, 329.

[47] For fuller discussion see W. Eck and H. Cotton, "Josephus's Roman Audience: Josephus and the Roman Elites," in *Flavius Josephus and Flavian Rome* (ed. J. Edmondson, S. Mason, and J. Rives; Oxford: Oxford University Press, 2005).

Even if we think of "publication" as the dissemination of finished copies, then, Josephus's audience seems to have been limited, local, and Roman. There is no reason to imagine that he produced more than perhaps a dozen copies for such associates—about what we would have expected in light of general conditions. Absent from Josephus is any suggestion that his work was in demand through Roman booksellers—the venue for purchasing texts to which one had no access via friends—even though there is some evidence that they were becoming more commonly used in his period.[48] They still seem to have been rare in the western provinces at least: Pliny expresses (possibly feigned) surprise that there was *a* bookshop even in Lyon, center of the Three Gauls (*Ep.* 9.11.2). Josephus's audience in *War*'s first phases of reception appears to have been local.

This picture of dissemination through growing concentric circles of associates does not materially change even if we accept Josephus's word that Titus privileged Josephus's account, affixed his authorization to the volumes, and ordered their publication (τὰ βιβλία δημοσιῶσαι προσέταξεν, *Life* 363), which may have meant nothing more than deposit in one of the new imperial libraries.[49] Primary distribution would still have been among locals who wished to have copies made of the library master.

Second, with regard to clues within the prologue, we turn to the prologue of *War*, the impression of local engagement is confirmed also for the period during which Josephus was preparing the work. Evidence here indicates that he was making the work public in the familiar ways: meeting his intended audiences, circulating partial drafts, targeting those willing to hear him, receiving criticism along with praise; he was fully involved in the literary thrust-and-parry of Roman society.

Consider carefully the language of the opening sentence:

> [1] Whereas, with respect to the war of Judeans against Romans . . . those who did not happen to be at the events, but *are collecting* (συλλέγοντες) random and incoherent tales through hearsay, *are writing them up* (ἀναγράφουσιν) sophist-like, [2] while others who were there *are misrepresenting the events* (καταψεύδονται τῶν πραγμάτων), either through flattery toward the Romans or through hatred toward the Judeans—their compositions comprise denunciation in some cases and encomium in others, but nowhere the precision of history—; [3] I, Josephus . . . have set myself the task of providing a narrative in the Greek language.

Although commonly available translations (such as Whiston and Thackeray for Loeb) represent the italicized verbs by the English perfect, indicating *completed accounts* against which Josephus reacts after the fact, in modern-scholarly fashion, his Greek portrays a much livelier and more fluid situation. He knows what other writers are *currently* doing. But how could he know this, if they have not yet "published" by disseminating completed works? Josephus has evidently seen advance copies or extracts via friends or he has heard some of these people recite, or both.

---

[48] Starr, "Circulation," 222.

[49] Eusebius (*Hist. eccl.* 3.9.1–2), significantly calling Josephus the most renowned Judean of his time also among the Romans, who had a statue erected in his honor, claims that his works (λόγοι) were included in Rome's library—which one, we are not told.

It appears, similarly, that others have heard and responded to his *War*—before he composes this prologue. Quite unexpectedly, having outlined the main themes of his narrative (1.1–12), he turns to criticize certain eloquent Greeks (1.13–16). These men admittedly excel in speech-craft, he says, and yet they choose for their subjects the ancient conflicts between Greeks and Persians ("Assyrians and Medes"—for effect): a fairly direct attack on the tendencies of the Greek revival discussed above.[50] Of interest here is not only that Josephus again seems well aware of what his contemporaries are writing, but also that *they are fully apprised of his work:* they have "abused" him for it. What else are we to make of this lengthy and peculiar paragraph? These eloquent men "position themselves as judges" over great recent events (*sc.* the Judean war): "which expose the ancient wars as paltry by comparison, *while abusing those who rival them for honor*—in relation to whom, even if they prove superior in speech-craft, they are inferior in choice of subject." Oblique though this passage may be, for understandable reasons in a dignified prologue, it seems to show Josephus again in vigorous debate with other writers in the capital. He can even take advantage of traditional Roman stereotypes of the Greeks,[51] as money-grubbing windbags (1.16), to drive home his attack.

So Josephus has produced an account of the war, which eloquent Greeks have dismissed, while they occupy themselves with the past glories of Hellas. One of the main issues in their abuse is Josephus's Greek style and perhaps accent, which are ongoing issues of sensitivity for him (e.g., *Ant.* 20.263; *Life* 40; cf. *War* 1.16 with *Ag. Ap.* 23–24). If we wished to put all the pieces together, then, it would be easy to suppose that he secured the help of friends with better Greek than his (*Ag. Ap.* 1.50), "for the Greek sound," precisely because of such prepublication criticism. This atmosphere of sniping at another's diction and style was characteristic of the Greek revival[52] and it is clearly reflected in the work of the Syrian Lucian.[53] But all of this criticism happened before Josephus came to write the current prologue to *War.*[54] We can only make sense of such evidence if he and his contemporaries knew each other's work in progress, quite possibly through recitation, though we cannot prove that. Josephus's remark even in the version of the prologue that has come down to us—"I shall not conceal any of my own misfortunes, since I am *about to speak to those who know [them]*" (μέλλων γε πρὸς εἰδόντας ἐρεῖν; 1.22)—though susceptible of other meanings, tends to

---

[50]See E. L. Bowie, "The Greeks and Their Past in the Second Sophistic," *Past and Present* 46 (1974): 3–41; S. Swain, *Hellenism and Empire: Language, Classicism, and Power in the Greek World, AD 50–250* (Oxford: Oxford University Press, 1996).

[51]See J. P. V. D. Balsdon, *Romans and Aliens* (Chapel Hill: University of North Carolina Press, 1979), 30–54.

[52]See Bowie, "The Greeks," 1974.

[53]See Lucian's *Pro lapsu inter salutandum* and *Pseudologista;* also Swain, *Hellenism and Empire,* 43–64.

[54]For other readings of *War* 1.13–16, some of which indeed speculate about Josephus's conditions in Rome, see S. Mason, *Flavius Josephus on the Pharisees: A Composition-Critical Study* (Leiden: Brill, 1991), 71–75.

confirm the oral dimension of publication. At the very least, it reminds us that Josephus knew his audience, and they knew him.

Finally, the most obvious statements about intended audience in *War*'s prologue take nothing away from the foregoing discussion, though they are implausibly sweeping. In *War* 1.3 Josephus claims to write for those under Roman hegemony (τοῖς κατὰ τὴν Ῥωμαίων ἡγεμονίαν), as a counterpart to the equally vague "upper barbarians" graced with his prior accounts of the conflict in Aramaic.[55] A little further along (1.6), having enumerated (and wildly exaggerated) various groups among those Aramaic-speaking recipients—Parthians and Babylonians, etc.—he correspondingly elucidates the readership of his current work: "Greeks, and those of the Romans who did not take part in the fighting" (*War* 1.6). But we have already seen that he actually delivered completed copies of *War* to those who *had* participated: Vespasian and Titus, their generals, Agrippa and his relatives (*Life* 361–363; *Ag. Ap.* 1.51–52). Rhetorical motives are at work in both passages: there to stress that his knowledgeable recipients would have objected had he misrepresented the facts, here to emphasize his didactic purpose: therefore, he need not write for those who fought in the war. Then again, he has just claimed that even those who *were* present are writing their accounts from prejudice rather than fact (*War* 1.1–2). All of this highlights the rhetorical malleability of such programmatic statements, in contrast to the more concrete evidence concerning audience.

Still, we need not doubt the sincerity of such broad descriptions in general—cf. *Ant.* 1.5: *Antiquities* is for "the whole Greek world"—*as long as* we remember that this was not a practical goal. Every self-respecting author, from Thucydides (1.22.4; cf. Josephus in *Ag. Ap.* 1.53) to Pliny the Younger (*Ep.* 7.17.15: *quod placere et semper et omnibus cupias*), strove to write for posterity or for the world. But they all had more immediate audiences and aims in view. I leave it to an expert in Thucydides—the paradigm of the writer for posterity—to make the point: "Thucydides, like Herodotus, clearly intended his work to endure, like a monument in stone. But all monuments are established for an immediate purpose."[56] Josephus's hope for a hearing across space and time has been fulfilled beyond his wildest dreams, but that does not change the fact that he wrote *War* with a concrete audience and situation in view.

The remaining three lines of evidence that he wrote for (and received) a local Roman audience may be summarily presented.

3. The narrative assumes ignorance of basic Judean realia, but substantial knowledge of Roman history. The following examples are representative.

War's audience is apparently not expected to know anything significant about even the most famous figures of Judean history in the centuries preceding the revolt: the Hasmoneans, including Judah Maccabee (*War* 1.36–37), or Herod the

[55] The Aramaic precursor to the Greek *War* is best understood as some sort of concise communication(s) issued from Jerusalem or at least Judea, not as a *Vorlage* in any proper sense—or indeed as a composition from his Roman period.

[56] Munn, *School of History*, 316.

Great (1.181, 203–204). All these men receive full introductions at first mention. As for Judean culture, Josephus must explain that on the seventh day Judeans abstain from labor (1.146), that Sepphoris is a city of Galilee (1.170), that the high priestly office requires freedom from physical defect (1.270), that Judean law (not an obscure one, note, but the second commandment) forbids representation of living creatures (1.650), that a feast called "Unleavened," also known as *Pascha* (no Aramaic is assumed), is a feast involving pilgrimage and many sacrifices (2.10–11), that another known as "Fiftieth" (i.e., Pentecost) takes its name from the interval following Passover (2.42), that a certain (i.e., nazirite) vow requires shaving of the head (2.313), and that Judean law (viz. Deut 21:21) prescribes the immediate burial of corpses (4.317). Although the audience seems to have an idea about the coastal cities of Phoenicia—Berytus (a Roman colony) may be mentioned alongside Tyre, Sidon, Byblos, and Ptolemais without explanation (1.422)—they are assumed to know nothing at all about Judean or Galilean geography and topography. Even Jerusalem and its temple (5.136–229) must be described in detail, as also the two Galilees (1.22; 3.35–44).

All this is basic information. Of course, King Agrippa's relatives and presumably even Roman commanders from the conflict would know it, but Josephus apparently has in view a local Roman audience that needs such explanations. Their lack of knowledge about matters Judean is thrown into sharp relief by what Josephus apparently does expect them to know—*Roman* history and politics.

Although he can also introduce minor Roman figures, of a century or more past, in the way he introduces the major Judeans (e.g., *War* 1.205: Sextus Caesar, a relative of the great Caesar who was at that time governor of Syria), the audience receives no such help with important Roman personalities. Thus, Josephus first mentions Marc Antony, Augustus, and Marcus Agrippa without introduction (1.118) and describes Scaurus as the general who had been sent to Syria by *Pompeius Magnus* (notice the transliteration from Latin, rather than the Greek equivalent Μέγας)—assuming audience familiarity with Pompey if not Scaurus.[57] Even Pompey's father-in-law [Q. Caecilius Metellus Pius] Scipio, his associate in the eastern *imperium*, acquitted on a charge of *ambitus*, famous in Rome and discussed by Julius Caesar, Cicero, and Livy, can be mentioned (1.185) without introduction. Josephus likewise assumes that [P. Licinius] Crassus and his notorious Parthian campaign (53 B.C.E.) are well known to the audience (1.179). And in 1.183 we find the telling chronological pointers, "When Pompey fled with the Senate across the Ionian Sea, [Julius] Caesar now being master of Rome and the world," which expect rather a lot from the audience. (When did Pompey flee with the Senate, then?) At 1.242 he casually mentions the "death of Cassius at Philippi" (in 42 B.C.E.), again expecting audience knowledge of a period so famous among Romans.

Especially telling, it seems, are *War*'s first references to Queen Cleopatra, for example (1.243): Marc Antony was "now a slave to his desire for Cleopatra." The

[57]The Latin nick-name appears even more strikingly, without need of "Pompey," at 5.409.

dark portrait of the Egyptian monarch intensifies in 1.358–368, where Josephus speaks of Antony's gradual destruction through enslavement to his desire for Cleopatra and now also of her "thirsting for the blood of foreigners." This is obviously not a detached description, but highly tendentious rhetoric especially suited to the standard Roman image of the eastern seductress, who had provided the basis for much of Octavian's anti-Antony propaganda.[58] Indeed, memories of Cleopatra may well have contributed to Titus's need to dismiss the Judean Queen Berenice from his house and bed in 79 C.E., before acceding to the principate—not another Cleopatra![59] Josephus assumes here both the subject knowledge and the values of a Roman audience.

Further examples abound. In *War* 1.243 and 1.284 [M. Valerius] Messalla [Corvinus], the eminent Roman general and orator, literary patron of Ovid and Tibullus (64 B.C.E. to 8 C.E.), is mentioned quite incidentally as "Messala." Yet both contexts have to do with oratory: defending Herod and Phasael before Antony and speaking for Herod's kingship in the Senate (40 B.C.E.). The audience should presumably understand the significance of this particular character. At 1.364 Josephus casually mentions the outbreak of war at Actium (31 B.C.E.; cf. 1.398).

At 1.400 Josephus remarks that, "In Caesar's affections, Herod stood next after Agrippa, in Agrippa's next after Caesar." But this assumes audience knowledge of the very close relationship, nowhere explained, between Augustus and his son-in-law M. Vipsanius Agrippa. *War* 2.25 is even more telling. First, [P. Quinctilius] Varus, legate of Syria in 4 B.C.E., notorious in Josephus's Rome for his loss of three legions in the Teutoburg forest in 9 C.E.,[60] is introduced without elaboration (as in the prologue, 1.20; see below). Then Augustus convenes an advisory council, in which Josephus pointedly remarks that "for the first time he also seated Gaius, the son [he] adopted from Agrippa and Iulia his daughter." It is a pointed reference ("for the first time"), but what *is* the point—since neither Gaius nor Julia will appear again in *War*? This notice could only have meaning for an audience familiar with the sad history of Augustus's family: the marriage of the princeps' daughter to his loyal friend Agrippa, the birth of their son Gaius and Augustus's hopeful adoption of him as successor, and the later tragedy of the young man's death in 4 C.E., which so fatally shaped the subsequent imperial succession.

That such assumptions about the audience's Roman knowledge do not derive from Josephus's sources (such as Nicolaus) is clear because they continue throughout. In *War* 2.247 Josephus introduces the new governor of Judea, Felix, as the *brother of Pallas*. But this identification only works if Pallas himself was already known to his audience. Marcus Antonius Pallas was indeed notorious in élite Roman circles as the stereotypical too-powerful freedman in Claudius's court (Suetonius, *Claud.* 28; Tacitus, *Ann.* 12.53). Similarly, in 2.250–251 Jose-

[58] E.g., *Cambridge History of Classical Literature* 2.3: 39, 57, 93, 102.

[59] Cf. Suetonius, *Tit.* 7 and thereto B.W. Jones and R. Milns, *Suetonius: The Flavian Emperors, A Historical Commentary* (London: Bristol Classical Press, 2002), 107.

[60] E.g., Velleius 2.117–121; Tacitus, *Germ.* 37.5; *Ann.* 1.3, 43, 55, 57–62, 65, 71; 2.41, 45; Cassius Dio 56.18–22.

phus prescinds from exploring the horrors of Nero's reign because they are well known to his audience. Notice again both the *content* of the audience's assumed knowledge and Josephus's hostile *tone* concerning Nero, which matches elite Roman attitudes of the late first century.[61] According to Suetonius (*Ner.* 57) and Tacitus (*Hist.* 1.4), the masses rather liked Nero and mourned his death. Josephus, however, shares the scandalized outlook of the elite authors. Finally, in 4.496, he likewise avoids exploring the Roman civil war following Nero's death on the ground that these events are well known (δι' ὄχλου πᾶσίν ἐστιν) and they have been written up by many, "Greeks as well as Romans." Both of these appeals to audience knowledge, from experience and from current books, make the best sense in the context of his Roman environment.

Josephus's pointed reference to works by *both* Greek *and* Roman authors raises the important question whether his efforts at fashionable and high-level Greek somehow restrict his audiences to Greek- *rather than* Latin-speaking circles in Rome. Such an assumption would, however, misunderstand Roman literary culture, which was fully bilingual. The fact that Josephus wrote in Greek was simply a result of necessity: even with a functional literacy in Latin, he would not have hoped to compose at a level high enough for elite consumption, whereas he could (and did) manage this in Greek. But we have many solid clues that he could read Latin as needed.[62] An elite audience in Rome, even if Roman by birth, was able to function well in Greek.

In sum: Josephus's assumption that his audience is schooled in Roman conditions is thrown into sharp relief by his expectation that they know nothing (necessarily) about Judean culture.

4. The prospectus of the narrative that Josephus provides in *War*'s prologue (1.17–30) conspicuously reaches out to a Roman audience. This fact on its own—though not to my knowledge discussed before—seems decisive for the question of Josephus's expected audience. If one compares the Polybian-style table of contents that Josephus provides with the actual narrative to follow, one discovers that he has consistently shaped the prospectus to appeal to Roman interests, while downplaying or omitting altogether features of the narrative—no matter how large or important in the narrative context itself—that will require careful introduction.

This is immediately apparent from the personal names given. Of the Judeans, only Herod son of Antipater (who was in any case world-famous) receives mention

---

[61] Cf. *War* 2.184 on Gaius Caligula, who cut off the cream of nobility in his country and then extended his design to Judea.

[62] These include not only antecedent probability (after years spent with Roman officers and guards in captivity, then in the capital itself) but also more concrete indicators. Josephus apparently used the generals's *commentarii* (field notes) as sources (*Life* 358; *Ag. Ap.* 1.56); his *War* shows many parallels with Julius Caesar's highly esteemed *Gallic War* (not least *War* 2.119; cf. *Bell. gall.* 1.1) as well as Sallust's widely read *Catilinarian Conspiracy;* and by the time he writes *Ant.* 18–19 he almost certainly borrows heavily from Latin sources for the detailed description of Gaius's accession to the principate (T. P. Wiseman, *Death of an Emperor: Flavius Josephus* [Exeter: University of Exeter Press, 1991]).

(1.19–20). Even though the narrative to follow is about the Judean revolt and so deals at great length with such figures as John of Gischala, Simon bar Giora, and Eleazar son of Yair, Josephus leaves these men unnamed in the prologue, referring only in a general way the Judean "tyrants" and their differences (1.24). By contrast, a number of Romans receive anticipatory billing: not only Vespasian and Titus, who figure repeatedly (1.21, 23, 24, 25, 28, 29), but also rather less important figures in Josephus's narrative such as Pompey (1.19), [Gaius] Sossius (1.19), *Augustus* (1.20; in Latin transliteration rather than the Greek equivalent Σεβαστός), *Quintilius* Varus (1.20; simply Varus at 2.25), Cestius [Gallus] (1.20), and Nero (1.20, 21). Josephus includes names that will be immediately meaningful to his envisaged audiences and readers, but omits those that will sound alien or perhaps generate adverse responses without careful introduction.

Still more important are the prospectus's lack of proportion and disparity of theme vis-à-vis the narrative. For example, *War* 1.19–20 passes over most of the long and detailed book 1, concerning the Hasmonean dynasty and Herod's colorful career, focusing only on Roman involvement in the region. This Roman political and military emphasis continues throughout, with some astonishing results. Josephus omits from book 2 the entire Herodian succession story (2.1–117), the three philosophical schools (especially Essenes), the governors of Judea, and King Agrippa's strenuous efforts before the war; from book 3, almost everything that does not relate to the activities of Vespasian and Titus, including Josephus's own military career (the focus of that book); from books 4 to 6 almost everything—the capture of Gamala, Tabor, and Gischala, the growth of serious factionalism in Jerusalem, the arrival of the Idumeans and the pivotal murder of Ananus and Jesus (4.233–333), as well as other crimes against the sanctuary, though these are pivotal in the book's theme and structure. Most significantly, he leaves out of the prospectus the narrative's many examples of Judean courage, resourcefulness, and partial success (5.71–97, 109–135, 258–330), as also the Romans' long hard struggle to take Jerusalem, which was delayed by the temporary victories of the Judeans (6.12–92, 129–192). He omits reference to his own final speech (6.99–110) and his relay of Titus's speech (6.124–128), as well as the worst horror of the famine: Mary's cannibalism (6.193–219). In their place, he highlights only a few paragraphs toward the end of book 4 and the beginning of book 5 concerning Nero, the *Roman* civil war, and Vespasian, some exotic information about the temple and its priests, the unnamed Judean tyrants and bandits, the suffering they inflicted on the Judeans, and the Roman desire to spare his compatriots (1.21–28).

If we had only this latter half of the prologue, we might suppose that *War* was indeed an instrument of Roman propaganda on the old view, but it is crucial to remember that this outline does not in fact match the content of the book. It seems rather carefully crafted to hook the audience in—a Roman audience—while reserving detailed reinterpretation of *War* for the appropriate time. Josephus has already signaled that he will counter the prevailing jingoistic accounts with a balanced viewpoint (1.2–3, 6–10), but the force and consequence of his revisionist view must await careful articulation in the story itself.

5. Josephus uses the major theme of his *War*, civil war (στάσις οἰκεία), to connect the Judean situation with the Roman. He introduces the theme of στάσις in the prologue (1.10), makes it the first word of the narrative proper (1.31), and refers to the theme often throughout. *War* is in many respects the story of a Judean civil war: aristocrats such as Josephus had gone to great lengths to suppress it, but they failed, so that behind the scenes of an ostensible war with Rome lay a full-scale internal conflict.

Most scholars trace this Josephan theme to Thucydides' classic treatment of civil war at Corcyra (3.82–84),[63] and one even tries to interpret *War* as an ongoing intertextual play vis-à-vis Thucydides.[64] It takes nothing away from the helpfulness of these analyses—Thucydides *does* remain a fund for historians throughout this period—to observe that Josephus as author does not connect the Judean *stasis* with Thucydides or Greek problems half a millennium before his time. He rather connects the Judean *seditio*, and programmatically, with the many *Roman* civil wars, especially the one concluded just before his arrival with Titus in Rome, which was also fresh in the experience of his Roman audience.

Already in the prologue (*War* 1.4), Josephus describes the period of momentous change (κίνημα) in which the Judean war erupted as one in which internal Roman affairs were also becoming diseased (νοσέω)—a verb commonly applied in Greek and Latin literature to the blight of factionalism.[65] Twice again in the opening prospectus he makes the same link, by distinguishing the Romans from Pompey (1.19) and by mentioning the upheavals (μεταβολαί) in Rome at the time of the Judean war (1.23). Josephus appears to suggest that the civil war or sedition that afflicted the Judeans and led to fateful Roman intervention in their politics was a phenomenon entirely familiar to the Romans themselves, not—as Nicolaus of Damascus (*War* 2.92) and many others would claim—a distinctive ethnic trait of the Judeans.

In book 1, these connections are too frequent to itemize, as the Roman civil wars and their protagonists furnish the whole backdrop for the later Hasmonean period and for Herod's masterfully shifting allegiances. At 1.216–219, for example, Josephus pauses the narrative to describe the outbreak of civil war (πόλεμος ἐμφύλιος), internal factionalism (διαστασιάζω) and upheaval (κίνημα) *in Rome*, assuming the audience's prior knowledge of the figures and events mentioned.

After book 1 Josephus takes the narrative back to Rome with great frequency: 2.24–38, 90–110 (Augustus ponders Herod's will), 2.204–217 (Claudius's accession

---

[63] E.g. Rajak, *Historian*, 91–94; L. H. Feldman, *Josephus's Interpretation of the Bible* (Berkeley: University of California Press, 1998), 140–48; Gottfried Mader, *Josephus and the Politics of Historiography: Apologetic and Impression Management in the Bellum Judaicum* (Leiden: Brill, 2000), 55–103; cf. J. J. Price, *Thucydides and Internal War* (Cambridge: Cambridge University Press, 2001) on the Thucydidean background.

[64] Cf. Mader, *Politics* in the previous note.

[65] Thucydides 2.48–59; Plato, *Resp.* 5.470c, *Soph.* 228a; Sallust, *Bell. Cat.* 36.5; *Hist.* 2.77m; Tacitus, *Ann.* 1.43.4; *Hist.* 1.26.1; cf. E. Keitel, "Principate and Civil War in the *Annals* of Tacitus," *AJP* 105 (1984): 320 and n. 32.

and Agrippa I), 2.245–251 (Claudius decides the Judean quarrel with Samaritans; accession of Nero), 3.1–8 (Nero hears of the Judean revolt and sends Vespasian), 4.440 (revolt of Vindex), 4.491–502 (Roman civil war after Nero's death), 4.545–549 (Roman civil war again). The purpose of these references becomes clear from Josephus's language at 4.545. While describing the violent conflict between Simon bar Gioras and John of Gischala's Zealots, he observes: "Not only in Judea were there civil war and sedition, however, but also across Italy"—citing the struggles of Galba, Otho, and Vitellius (4.545–549). This ongoing comparison is strengthened when, a few paragraphs later, he turns to describe Vitellius's behavior as "a savage tyrant" (4.596) and the actions of that general's army in the city of Rome: reckless looting and slaughtering of the wealthy (4.586–587)—just like the Judean tyrants in Jerusalem. Several paragraphs near the end of book 4 are devoted to a graphic day-by-day portrait of the end to the civil war in Rome (4.630–655), but this occurs immediately before Titus is sent to end the civil war in Jerusalem (4.656–663). Titus is reportedly quite aware, as Vespasian had been, that the problem in Jerusalem is essentially a *civil war* among Judean factions (5.1–3), not a matter of the Judean people's opposing Rome *en bloc*.

The fitting end of the civil-war theme coincides with the close of the main story. It is the joint triumph of Vespasian and Titus in Rome, concerning which Josephus comments (7.157): "For on this day the city of the Romans celebrated *both* victory in the campaign against her enemies [sc. the Judeans] *and* the end of civil disasters [sc. among the Romans]—and thus the beginning of hopes for prosperity." The very next paragraph, collapsing about four years, covers the dedication of the Forum of Peace in Rome (7.158–162). Vespasian's triumph over internal chaos, with his sons as insurance against bloody succession contests in the near future, coincides with decisive victory over foreign enemies. From Josephus's perspective, similarly, the end of Judea's civil war has renewed the promise of peace.

Josephus continually reverts to affairs in Rome not only because that is the natural reference-point for his envisaged audience in the city, but also in order to make the Judean conflict more intelligible and less alien, by implicit comparison with the capital's own vividly remembered struggles. Every statesman knew that civil war (στάσις, *seditio*) was a perennial threat,[66] and the Judeans could hardly be singled out for odium because the disease had affected their society so dramatically.

Conclusion

To conclude: the general conditions of composing and disseminating literature in the first century, along with explicit indicators in Josephus's writings about *War*'s circumstances and assumptions he makes about his audience's knowledge and values all point in a single direction. He wrote his finest work with a sophisti-

[66] This is, e.g., the dominant theme of Plutarch's *Praecepta gerendae reipublicae*.

cated Roman audience in view, one that was fully at home in elite discourse about politics and constitutions, and one that had a taste for fine writing.

Here I can only hint at some important consequences that flow from identifying Josephus's audience. Only when such concrete conditions are ignored, it seems to me, can Josephus be interpreted as a mouthpiece of Roman propaganda, in the traditional way. Abstracted from such a context, for example, his flattery of Vespasian and Titus, along with his acknowledgment of Roman fortune, might easily be read as an effort to persuade fellow-Judeans around the Mediterranean to acquiesce under Roman rule.

Once he is placed in his Flavian Roman context, however, everything changes. We no longer expect him to spell everything out, since we can see that he relies upon prior audience knowledge and values. Once we take on board the nature of Flavian self-representation in post-70 Rome, as the conquerors of a rebellious people, as those who have defeated a weak race and its deity by means of their virtue, generalship, and support from Roman deities, everything in *War* takes on a completely different hue. Now we can begin to take seriously Josephus's claim that he is writing to balance the record with a fair treatment of his people (1.1–3, 6–9). Now his ongoing emphases on Judean valor, toughness, and contempt for death, along with their talent for outwitting the famous legions, become more meaningful as a challenge to the dominant portrait. Now we may see his flattery of Vespasian and Titus, by contrast, as no more than *de rigueur,* and we may become more attentive to cracks in this portrait. These cracks are to be found especially in the famous theme of Titus's clemency, which in fact makes the young emperor out to be somewhat gullible on the battlefield, a decent humanist faced with Judea's wily war-fighters—certainly, deserving no *credit* for Jerusalem's fall. And we become alive to the possibilities of irony. Whereas most scholars have treated the presentation of the eighteen-year-old Domitian in 7.85–88 as obsequious flattery, even redating book 7 to Domitian's reign in part to account for this apparent groveling (it "extols Domitian's prowess"),[67] against the background of a Roman audience's likely knowledge[68] it seems more plausible that Josephus was practicing "the art of safe criticism"[69] through an obvious and excessive flattery.

Audience matters: the stakes are enormous.

[67] Cohen, *Galilee and Rome,* 87.

[68] Suetonius, *Dom.* 2; Tacitus, *Hist.* 4.75–85.

[69] See Ahl, "Safe Criticism," n. 24.

Chapter 3

Figured Speech and Irony in T. Flavius Josephus*

In a programmatic article of 1984 Frederick Ahl called for a reappraisal of Graeco-Roman literature against the recognition that the ancients were partial to 'figured' speech. Many preferred Odysseus' way (deferring to 'crooked-counselled' Zeus) to that of Thersites, the plain-speaking fool whom the wily hero attacked (*Il.* 2.211–77; Ahl 1984: 174–79; cf. Lateiner 1995). Any Scythian could reveal his mind (Demetr. *Eloc.* 216, 297); only a man of refinement could craft his language so as to embed important discoveries for the audience to make (Ahl 1984: 196). This refracted manner of speech was called ἔμφασις in ancient rhetoric—in diametric opposition to our usage of the English descendant (Ahl 1984: 176–79) and also Greek usage in other contexts. In a world in which elusive language was valued, even the most egregious kind of flattery, so repugnant to modern readers of the Flavian poets for example, might turn out to be skillfully manipulative of its willing victim. Ahl cites the case of Juvenal's fisherman, who reeled in Domitian with the outrageous claim that an unusually large fish he offered the emperor had presented itself, eager to be served on the imperial table (Juv. 4.69–71; Ahl 1984: 197–98).

Several studies in the past decade have excavated the related phenomena of 'doublespeak', 'dissimulation', and 'dissonance' in the history and literature of the early principate (Rudich 1993: xvii-xxiv, 1997; Bartsch 1994: 63–97). Augustus and Tiberius encouraged language games among the elite by extending the capital charge of 'diminishing the majesty of the Roman people' (*maiestas*) to include slander, or perceived slander, of the *princeps* (Suet. *Aug.* 55; Tac. *Ann.* 1.72; Dio Cass. 57.22.5; cf. Bartsch 1994: 66). Throughout the first century senators increasingly accommodated themselves to the new pretences, though the resulting internal dissonance could become unbearable. Titius Rufus committed suicide in 39 CE while awaiting trial for 'having declared that the Senate thought one thing but propounded another view' (Dio Cass. 59.18.5; cf. Rudich 1993: xxiii).

*Thanks to members of the SBL Josephus Seminar and the Jewish Studies Seminar at Wolfson College, Oxford, also to Martin Goodman, Christina Kraus, Christopher Pelling, Joseph Sievers, and Jane Lightfoot for critique (much of which remains in play, alas). I prepared this study while enjoying a Killam Research Fellowship (administered by the Canada Council for the Arts), a research grant from the Social Sciences and Humanities Research Council of Canada, and a Visiting Fellowship at All Souls College, Oxford.

Says Rudich, 'It was an uncanny world of illusion and delusion, of ambivalences and ambiguities on all levels of social interaction' (1993: xix).

Whereas the satirical verse of a Juvenal positively invites ironic analysis (Romano 1979) and a recent study of the Domitianic *Argonautica* by Valerius Flaccus can devote a substantial final chapter to dissimulation as theme and meta-theme (Hershkowitz 1998; 224–47), with the notable exception of Tacitus (e.g., Leeman 1973: 169; Keitel 1984; Plass 1988; O'Gorman 2000) and Xenophon perhaps (Nadon 2001: 1–3; 160–66), historians have not often attracted such readings (but Węçowski 1996). Given both a general taste for elusive language in antiquity and the specific constraints of imperial Rome, however, we should at least ask about the ironic dimensions of any text we study from the period.

Among Flavian authors, nowhere is the dearth of scholarly attention to artful speech more patent than in the case of Titus Flavius Josephus, new citizen and prolific historian. Traditional scholarship on Josephus had scarcely credited him with the intelligence needed for sustained seriousness (Bilde 1988: 123–41), a precondition of irony. Now we have conquered that summit, from which we can glimpse many promising trails, we may be tempted to rest content with our new image of Josephus as earnest historian, ardent apologist, and creative author (Bilde 1988: 141–71). My goal here is to press further and ask how his works were read in Flavian Rome, and whether they shared in the language games then current. To what degree did he plant seeds of self-mockery, arising from his peculiar situation, in his compositions? Did he leave signals for his audience that there was more for them to discover than he had plainly said? Might even some of his much-discussed flattery of the Flavians be better understood as ironic fish stories?

Pursuing irony in Josephus draws our attention not only to the challenging political threads that he might have woven between the lines of a seemingly straightforward narrative, but also to his rhetorical aesthetics in general, and the interposition of a certain playful distance between himself and his language (Kierkegaard 1965 [1841]: 292; Muecke 1969: 159–215; Fowler 2000: 8–9). Inasmuch as it reveals the gap between one's inner disposition and what one says, an ironic outlook is the basis, and literary irony the quintessential manifestation, of rhetoric. The two come together, for example, in Robert Lamberton's keen observation about Plutarch (2001: p. xv): 'Plutarch all too often turns his eloquence to the task of demonstrating a point while leaving in us the suspicion that he would be equally capable of arguing the contrary position.' Rhetorical expertise, the goal of ancient education, enabled its practitioners to make any case whatsoever as the situation demanded (Cic. *Brut.* 93.322; cf. Marrou 1956: 285; Kennedy 1994: 102–27; Cribiore 2001: 220–44). If sincerity (*sine* + *ceres*) signifies 'the absence of wax', rhetoric was all about wax (cf. Demetr. *Eloc.* 296): wax tablets that could be inscribed, erased, and re-inscribed as desired. Looking for irony in Josephus takes us to that rhetorical pulse in his writing and illuminates his historiographical values.

After an attempt to clarify terms, I shall proceed through Josephus' narratives in order.

IRONY: DEFINITIONS, MEANS, AND ENDS

Irony and its Relatives: A Brief Family History

What I seek to open up in this exploratory essay is hard to reduce to a single category, for it has to do with Josephus' art as an author, his attitude toward his own writing and portraiture. In particular I wish to investigate the degree to which he, by the evidence of the text, remained detached from the compositions he created, exercising that 'Herrschaft über den Stoff' which allowed him the transcendental smile of Romantic irony. Ludwig Tieck (in Wheeler 1984: 19):

> In most definitions irony is taken too one-sidedly, too prosaically and too materially. Hegel misunderstood Solger on this point. He imagined, that Solger was thinking about common irony, that crude irony of Swift. But already in Plato, it is clear that there is another completely different higher irony. The irony of which I speak is not derision, mockery, persiflage or what in a similar vein is usually understood by the term. Rather irony is the most profound seriousness, yet bound up with play and genuine joviality.

We are already here perhaps en route to the position that all human language, because contingent and constructed, is ironic. But whatever philosophical merits that position may have (Rorty 1989), I do not intend to go so far here—and render pointless any investigation of irony in Josephus. If we stay with Romantic irony as point of reference, and include also standard forms of literary or dramatic irony, we shall at least retain some sort of criteria for making arguments. The question is whether Josephus was capable, like Plato, Shakespeare, and Goethe, of recognizing the contingency of his language and his situation, such that he could combine earnest thematic and character development with the playfulness of language that visits only when art is not wholly identified with the artist's ego. A. W. Schlegel (1846 [1808]: 369) wrote, contrasting Shakespeare with other poets:

> Most poets who portray human events in a narrative or dramatic form take themselves a part; and exact from their readers a blind approbation or condemnation of whatever side they choose to support or oppose. The more zealous this rhetoric is, the more certainly it fails of its effect. . . . When, however, by a dexterous manœuvre, the poet allows us an occasional glance at the less brilliant reverse of the medal, then he makes, as it were, a sort of secret understanding with the select circle of the more intelligent of his readers or spectators; he shows them that he had previously seen and admitted the validity of their tacit objections; that he himself is not tied down to the represented subject, but soars freely above it; and that, if he chose, he could unrelentingly annihilate the beautiful and irresistibly attractive scenes which his magic pen has produced.

I realize too well that pursuing such questions threatens a hopeless lack of precision in analytical categories, and futility in the means of proof. An immediate objection might concern the identification of the real Josephus with the implied author and possibly the narrator too; similar hesitation attends questions of 'audience'. By 'Josephus' I mean the implied author (not necessarily the narrative voice or the real Josephus); by 'audience', however, I mean both the implied audience and his first real audiences in Rome, since we can draw some general conclusions about real conditions among literate Romans in the early 80s from outside the text of Josephus. The best analytical categories I can produce are 'irony', with its many valences, and 'figured speech'. My first task is to survey the ancient terminology that most closely approximates these categories—itself used quite differently by different ancient critics, however—and to show some connections and disjunctions with our theme. Then I shall offer summary remarks on what we often call 'literary irony'—though a modern development, necessarily part of this investigation. But I am primarily searching for moments in Josephus' narratives where a certain detachment from his language, a willingness to 'play' with language even in very serious contexts, and so an ironic posture, come forward.

It would be useful in a study such as this to consider the Greek and Latin forebears of irony, εἰρωνεία and *ironia,* and how they were used in antiquity along with complementary vocabulary for figured speech. There is to my knowledge no existing study that considers all of these questions together. Given space constraints here, however, four summary points must suffice.

1. In much Greek literature, εἰρωνεία indicates nothing more than a distasteful evasiveness or lack of candour, and an εἴρων is a person exhibiting these traits (Thomson 1926: 3; Dem. *Exord.* 14.3; *Or.* 4.7.5, 37.5; Plut. *Fab. Max.* 11.1; *Tim.* 15.7; *Mar.* 24.4; 43.3; *Luc.* 27.4; *Pomp.* 30.6).

2. With Plato (*Resp.* 337a; cf. *Apol.* 37e; *Symp.* 216e; *Grg.* 489e), Aristotle, and many subsequent authors, εἰρωνεία gained prestige by its association with Socrates (Cic. *Brut.* 292–93; Quint. *Inst.* 9.2.46; Plut. *Quaest. conv.* 612d.12; Lucian *Demon.* 6.1; *Dial. mort.* 7.5.17; Diog. Laert. 2.19).[1] Wherever he was viewed as the embodiment of the εἴρων, the word group signified not simple dissimulation but a strategic, knowing self-deprecation or pretended innocence in combination with equally strategic praise of others. Although Aristotle can position εἰρωνεία (understating one's knowledge) and ἀλαζονεία (overstating it) as equally undesirable opposites, with honest assessment (ἀλήθεια, παρρησία) the preferred middle way (*Eth. Nic.* 1108a, 1127a), he is usually more lenient with the 'Socratic' fault of εἰρωνεία (*Eth. Nic.* 1127b.30–31; cf. *Rh.* 1419b.8).

3. Cicero and Quintilian fully incorporate irony into their discussions of rhetoric, further dignifying it in the process. Although they continue to associate it chiefly with Socrates (*Brut.* 292; *De or.* 2.269), they disagree about its precise meaning, and whether it can be adequately rendered by such Latin words as *dissimulatio* (so Cic. *De or.* 2.269; *Luc.* 15.18) or *illusio.* Quintilian makes the latter connection in places (*Inst.* 6.6.54–7; cf. 9.50), on the ground that irony involves intending the opposite (*contraria*) of what one says (*Inst.* 9.2.65), but elsewhere he insists upon using the Greek word because there is no precise Latin equivalent (*Inst.* 9.2.44–6).

[1]Note the subtitle of Kierkegaard's 1841 book on irony: *with constant reference to Socrates.*

4. When ancient writers wanted to highlight the shared but unstated understanding between author and audience, they tended to use terms other than εἰρωνεία and *ironia*. They spoke of figured (τὸ ἐσχηματισμένον, σχήματα, σχηματίζω), refracted, or encoded speech (ἔμφασις, ἐμφαίνω) (Demetr. *Eloc.* 287–98). Significantly, they often mention εἰρωνεία in the same context, as a *near* equivalent (Demetr. *Eloc.* 291; Quint. *Inst.* 9.2.65). In his discussion of figures of speech (*figurae*, σχήματα), Quintilian observes that common usage in his day, following the fourth-century BCE critic Zoilus, narrows the sense of *figura* (and σχῆμα) to the case in which 'the speaker pretends to say something other than that which he actually does say' (*Inst.* 9.1.14). He also describes an unnamed figure according to which:

> we excite some suspicion that our meaning is other than our words would seem to imply (*quod non dicimus accipi volumus*); but our meaning is not in this case contrary to that which we express, as is the case in εἰρωνεία, but rather a hidden meaning which is left to the hearer to discover' (*latens et auditori quasi inveniendum*). (*Inst.* 9.2.65)

Although he distinguishes this from εἰρωνεία , it sounds very close to what we often call irony. He gives the figure no name, however, because his contemporaries all but reserve the generic term *figura* for it. This *figura* or σχῆμα is also very close to ἔμφασις—so close, he muses, that the two may be identical (*Inst.* 9.2.65).

Since contemporary ironologists find definition of their subject impossible (Muecke 1969: 14; Knox 1972; Fowler 2000: 7–8), they often prefer to test for its presence by a matrix of conditions. For present purposes I borrow the product of someone else's labours. In his classic study D. C. Muecke finds three 'essential elements' in literary irony (Muecke 1969: 19–20):

> In the first place irony is a double-layered or two-storey phenomenon. At the lower level is the situation either as it appears to the victim of irony (where there is a victim) or as it is deceptively presented by the ironist (where there is an ironist). . . . At the upper level is the situation as it appears to the observer or the ironist. The upper level need not be *presented* by the ironist; it need only be evoked by him or be present in the mind of the observer. . . .
>
> In the second place there is always some kind of opposition between the two levels, an opposition that may take the form of contradiction, incongruity, or incompatibility. What is said may be contradicted by what is meant . . . ; what the victim thinks may be contradicted by what the observer knows. . . .
>
> In the third place there is in irony an element of 'innocence'; either a victim is confidently unaware of the very possibility of there being an upper level or point of view that invalidates his own, or an ironist pretends not to be aware of it. There is one exception to this; in sarcasm or in a very overt irony . . .

In brief: 'the art of irony is the art of saying something without really saying it. It is an art that gets its effects from below the surface' (Muecke 1969: 5). On the dramatic level, then, we shall be looking for evidence that Josephus expected his audience to understand more than he explicitly said, where this 'more' stands in some tension with the facile sense of the voices in his narrative. Beyond that, we seek evidence of his posture as author vis-à-vis his narratives.

Means: Two Kinds of Irony

The issue of the clued-in observer, crucial to figured speech, ἔμφασις, or irony in modern senses, suggests a classification of irony according to this criterion: What *are* the possible sources of audience knowledge? At bottom are only two possibilities: either the author (or speaker) furnishes the audience with the necessary information in some other place, outside the ironic episode itself, or he expects them already to possess the extra-textual resources that they need in order to close the circuit. Let us call these two cases text-dependent and audience-dependent irony, respectively. Josephus will use both, but in order to see how he works it is useful to keep the distinction in mind.

Text-dependent irony is the simpler and less risky of the two forms. An author wants to ensure that an audience, or an indefinite number of audiences, will detect his intended irony. So he frames the ironic story within an authoritative statement, for the audience alone, of facts unknown to characters in the story. This was the way of Greek New Comedy. Menander and his peers wrote plays that were largely self-contained, with the necessary information embedded in the work itself. That is perhaps why these Greek plays were so portable for adaptation in other contexts, for example with Plautus and Terence (the latter of whom dropped this element, however, leaving his work harder for us to grasp).[2] Authoritative prologues, often from a divine being, guaranteed the audience's readiness to follow the plot and thereby created 'New Comedy's major effect, dramatic irony' (Ireland 1995: 19; cf. Zagagi 1994: 142–43; cf. Balme 2001: xix). It is because of this reliable foreknowledge that the audience of Menander's *Aspis* (97ff.) knows that Smikrines will be frustrated in his attempt to seize his niece's fortune—for the heir still lives; understands what the misanthrope and the love-struck young man of the *Dyskolos* do not know about each other; and is immediately ready to find hilarity, as the *Miles gloriosus* begins, in the *alazon*'s confident ignorance of what is happening next door (Plaut. *Mil.* 79–145).

Comedy was by no means the only venue for such self-contained textual irony. The most famous example is probably the Gospel of John, which includes an authoritative divine prologue (John 1.1–18) concerning Jesus' heavenly origin (cf. John 3.11–21; 5.19–47; 6.35–58; 8.12–58; 10.1–38). The repeated claims of ignorant characters in the story to *certain knowledge* of Jesus' origins (John 1.45–6; 6.42; 7.41–3) are devastating because the audience—any audience at any time—knows otherwise.

Audience-dependent irony is what the ancient critics had in mind when they discussed 'figured speech' (above). It was also the way of Old Comedy, which was filled with topical references to conditions in Athens around the year 420: many

[2] I thank Dr. C. S. Kraus for this observation about Terence.

of the main characters are famous figures from the period (Ireland 1995: 1–2). Because of the tacit connections with current affairs, the genre is not easily portable: a modern reader of Aristophanes can only appreciate these references through diligent background study, and a basic aim of the commentary in modern editions is to put the reader in the picture. Greek tragedy and later pantomime also depended upon the audience's familiarity with traditional story lines from epic poetry and myth, presented again in new forms. It was prior audience knowledge of the plot that gave poignancy to Oedipus' vow to find and punish the one who was polluting Thebes (Soph. *OT* 135–45). The watchman of the *Agamemnon* can only 'speak to those who understand, and remain a mystery to those who do not' (Aesch. *Ag.* 39; cf. Ahl 1984: 180).

Audience-dependent irony can be subtler and more effective than text-driven irony, though it is riskier because it operates without the safety net of authoritative guides. The author must be sure not only that the audience will know certain crucial items but, in potentially dangerous contexts, that they will not read the wrong sort of irony into his presentation. In the case of Rome, Shadi Bartsch traces the development of topical allusions on the stage from the late Republic, when these were largely effected by authors and actors through stress and gesture, through the early principate, when the actors and playwrights backed away from such signals out of fear, and audience detection became the definitive side of the ironic dialectic (Bartsch 1994: 71–82). In the absence of obvious clues, it was always possible that an audience's determination to discover topical allusion would itself generate subversive interpretations that had never been intended (Bartsch 1994: 67–8).

Any proposal concerning audience-dependent irony in Josephus will in the nature of the case be more open to debate than observations on language-plays that receive explicit textual authorization. But that should not prevent us from asking the question and making proposals with good reason.

Ends: Elite Discourse and Managing the Masses

In the Flavian period, virtually everyone in elite circles appears to have been speaking and writing elusively (and allusively) at times, relying upon their audiences to make inferences. Under Domitian, Quintilian observes that the 'figured controversies' discussed above were much in vogue, used with great frequency (*qua nunc utimur plurimum . . . quod et frequentissimum est*) (*Inst.* 9.2.65). He recognizes three contexts for this language: when it is unsafe to speak frankly, or unseemly to do so, or merely for subtle effect. Under the first heading he insists that one may address tyrants without danger 'as long as the form of speech is susceptible of a different interpretation', for 'if [the risk is neutralized] by ambiguity of expression, everyone will approve of his cunning' (*Inst.* 9.2.67). Another rough contemporary of Josephus, Dio Chrysostom, states more bluntly that during Domitian's reign, in which he himself was exiled, 'it used to seem necessary to everyone to lie, on account of fear' (πᾶσιν ἀναγκαῖον ἐδόκει ψεύδεσθαι διὰ φόβον; *Or.* 3.13).

So candid confrontation was out and either lying or irony was in. This point was not lost on the *principes,* who accordingly became accomplished irony-detectors. They sought out figurative sedition in plays, recitals of poetry, gestures, and literary allusions in all genres, trying to censor what Rudich calls the 'uncontrollable subtext' (Rudich 1997: 11). Members of the senatorial class were vulnerable also if they unwisely referred to exempla from the republican era, especially Brutus and Cassius: the senator Cremutius Cordus, prosecuted in 25, is a famous example (Tac. *Ann.* 4.34–5). Under Nero, by contrast, Seneca prudently denied Stoic justification to Caesar's assassins (*Ben.* 2.20.2). Tacitus reports other examples of sensitivity to this issue (*Ann.* 3.76; 16.7, 22), as does Pliny (*Ep.* 1.17.3; cf. MacMullen 1966: 1–45; Salles 1992: 70–75). Suetonius mentions a number of persons convicted on the basis of their plays (*Cal.* 27.4; *Ner.* 39.3; *Dom.* 10.4; cf. Bartsch 1994: 78–9). It seems that Domitian, possibly inspired by competing senatorial factions (Syme 1983: 122–24), was closely attuned to such figural representation, especially from the autumn of 93 (Jones 1992: 122–25)—just when Josephus published his *magnum opus* (*AJ* 20.267). He executed Hermogenes of Tarsus for certain allusions (*figurae*) in his history (Suet. *Dom.* 10.1), the younger Helvidius Priscus for having allegedly criticized the emperor's divorce in a farce concerning the legendary Paris and Oenone (*Dom.* 10.4), Rusticus Arulenus and Herennius Senecio for praising long-dead critics of Nero and Vespasian (Suet. *Dom.* 10.3–4; Tac. *Agr.* 2.1; Plin. *Ep.* 7.19.5; Dio Cass. 67.13.2). If the need for irony was so obvious in Domitian's Rome, we must wonder whether and how Josephus accommodated himself.

Whereas Quintilian's three contexts for figured speech all apply to the internal discourse of the elite classes, there was a much older and more widely distributed currency of misdirection in relations between the ruling class and the masses they governed. We see this already in Aristotle, who insisted that the great-souled man speak the truth without fear in *almost* all circumstances:

> It is also necessary that he [*sc.* the great man, μεγαλόψυχος] be both candid in hatred and candid in affection, because concealment (τὸ λανθάνειν) implies fear . . . ; for in view of his disdain [for others' opinions] he is frank and truthful, *except of course whatever [he says] by way of irony, to the masses* (πλὴν ὅσα μὴ δι' εἰρωνείαν πρὸς τοὺς πολλούς). (Arist. *Eth. Nic.* 3.28; 1124b, line 1)

Even if we should render εἰρωνεία here as 'dissimulation' vis-à-vis the masses, when the deceit is shared among one's peers it becomes irony.

In Josephus' day, Plutarch confirms that Roman hegemony had rendered it an even more urgent necessity to dissemble to the always restive and impetuous masses. Plutarch advises the statesman first to listen and learn about his people's distinctive character, so that he might accommodate himself and win their confidence (*Prae. ger. reip.* 799b–800a). Compare Josephus' first actions in Galilee (*Vit.* 30–61). The statesman must also possess great rhetorical skill (*Prae. ger. reip.* 799b–800a, 801a–804c) for 'softening by persuasion and overcoming by charms the fierce and violent spirit of the people' (801e). Given the inevitability that the masses will dislike politicians, the latter must often resort to clever schemes.

They might, for example, arrange for some colleagues to speak against a measure in the assembly and then be won over by the others, so that they bring the audience along with them (813a-c). Plutarch emphasizes that the chief task and test of the statesman under Roman rule is to maintain peace, avoid internal conflict (στάσις), and keep Roman forces from needing to enter the scene (814f–816a). This all intersects more or less perfectly with Josephus' expressed motives and language in his autobiography (below). Such laudable realism was to be sharply distinguished, of course, from the sordid business of 'flattering the mob' (κολακεία or *adsentio* directed to the *plebs,* δῆμος, *vulgus;* cf. Roller 2001: 110), which is what one's demagogic rivals did (cf. Hands 1959 on Sallust).

IRONY IN JOSEPHUS' *JUDAEAN WAR* AND *JUDAEAN ANTIQUITIES*

These constraints of literary culture in Flavian Rome seem to require that we ask certain questions of Josephus' narratives.

The Judaean War

His earliest extant composition is a Greek account of the recent war in Judaea. He claims to have completed much of it while Vespasian lived (*Vit.* 359–61; *Ap.* 1.50–1), though there is good evidence that Titus was emperor when the bulk of it was released, and that volume 7 was finished only under Domitian or even later (Cohen 1979: 87–8; Schwartz 1986; Cf. Barnes, Ch. 6 above [in the original work]). In this work Josephus relies to a significant degree upon his audience's knowledge for ironic effects: in his overall portrait of the Judaean-Roman war and the Flavian rulers' role therein; in his flattery of the imperial family; and in his use of the 'civil war' motif. Where it is politically innocuous to do so, he also sets up a text-driven irony, unmistakably signing it as such for the audience's benefit.

The Fall of Jerusalem and the Flavians' Role

Nothing about the new regime could have been clearer to residents of Flavian Rome than its investment in the recent subjugation of Judaea (cf. Levick 1999: 53–4). Since the essays in Part II of this [the original] volume consider the evidence in detail, I shall not repeat it here. The main points come out in the inscription on the arch of Titus that formerly stood in the Circus Maximus: under his father's guidance Titus had 'subdued the people of the Judaeans and destroyed the city of Hierosolyma' (*gentem iudaeorum domuit et urbem hierusolymam . . . delevit; CIL* 6.944). Everyone knew what 'subdued' and 'destroyed' meant: a barbarian *urbs direpta,* demolished by the irresistible ferocity of Roman arms and then given to the soldiers for revenge (Ziolkowski 1993; cf. *BJ* 6.403–8). The joint triumph of 71 concealed nothing of the Roman severity but rather gloried in it, magnificently portraying for those who had not witnessed the events 'whole battalions of the enemy slaughtered . . . an area all deluged with blood . . . . fire engulfing sanctuaries and the collapse of houses upon their owners' (*BJ* 7.143). Titus was assumed to have a character eminently suited to making war: in the decade following the war, while he was assisting his father in the principate, he apparently had a reputation for such extreme brutality (*saevitia*) that people feared his accession—so, at least, Suetonius (*Tit.* 1, 6–7).

Tacitus' truncated presentation of the Judaean people (*Hist.* 5.1–13), in which he argues that their rites and customs are at sharp variance with those of the Romans (*Hist.* 5.4–5), is offered as background to the war itself (5.2). His portrait, combined with a variety of later statements (Origen *C. Cels.* 5.41; Min. Fel. *Oct.* 10, 33; Philostr. *V A* 5.33) and especially the coins and monuments of the 70s and 80s, presents a fairly coherent picture of perceptions in the capital. Namely, this was an external war (*bellum externum*) of the Roman people against a troublesome foreign nation (Mattern 1999: 151, 168, 193). Its conclusion, the irrefragable defeat of the Judaeans and their protective deity, was due to the virtue of the Roman generals (now *principes*), their military superiority, and the favour of Roman deities.

In case anyone had missed these points, a crop of new histories was appearing that stressed the same themes—in highly rhetorical fashion, according to Josephus (*BJ* 1.1–2):

> Whereas] those who did not happen to be at the events, but are collecting random and incoherent tales through hearsay, are writing them up sophist-like, while others who were there misrepresent the events, *either through flattery toward the Romans or through hatred toward the Judaeans—their compositions comprise denunciation in some cases and encomium in others,* but nowhere the precision of history. . . .

While residents of Flavian Rome could have had little doubt about the meaning of the war for the new rulers, nothing could be clearer in Josephus' history than his claim that Jerusalem fell *not* because of any foreign power but because a *civil war* provoked divine punishment: the Judaean God's purging of his own house to rid it of the pollution caused by 'tyrants' (*BJ* 1.9–10). In this, the Romans were but useful pawns (cf. *BJ* 6.410–13), accomplishing under divine manipulation what the nation's leadership itself had been unable to do. Quite irrespective of the Romans, Josephus invokes:

> a certain ancient saying (τις παλαιὸς λόγος) that the city would be captured and the holy sanctuary burned down by right of war (νόμῳ πολέμου) whenever factionalism (στάσις) should arrive and domestic hands (χεῖρες οἰκεῖαι) should take the lead in polluting the sacred precinct of God. (*BJ* 4.388)

The Romans had had no intention, in particular, of destroying the temple:

> That it was internal factionalism (στάσις οἰκεία) that brought it down, and that the Judaean tyrants drew both the *Romans' unwilling hands* and the fire upon the sanctuary, Titus Caesar—the very one who destroyed it—is witness. . . . And since *no foreigner was the cause* of these things, it was not possible to keep control over one's lamentations. (*BJ* 1.10–12)

The point is reiterated as necessary: see especially *BJ* 4.397; 5.19, 28, 442–45; 6.128–30, 228. Near the close of the work, the rebel-leader Eleazar at Masada is allowed to comfort his doomed comrades with language that, albeit from a different frame of reference, intersects with the author's on this point:

> Neither pin the blame on yourselves *nor credit the Romans*, that this war against them has ruined us all; for it is not by their strength that these things have happened, but a more powerful cause has come and furnished them with the appearance of victory (τὸ δοκεῖν ἐκείνοις νικᾶν παρέσχηκε). (*BJ* 7.360)

Two essays in this [original] volume (Barnes, Rives) deal with the problem that Josephus' effort to remove Titus from involvement in the temple's destruction fits ill both with the Flavians' celebration of this event and with an alternative account, apparently from Tacitus (preserved in Sulpicius Severus and Orosius), according to which Titus firmly decided that the temple *should* be destroyed. In other words, Josephus makes claims in his narrative that sharply diverge from what his audience understands. Whereas those contributions propose historical solutions to the problem, I would observe that on the narrative level this particular issue of Titus' decision about the temple serves a much larger ironic scheme.

Josephus' entire *War* undermines, albeit in the nicest way, the Flavian presentation of this conflict: 'Er kämpft um seinen persönlichen Beitrag zur Weltgeschichte and muß diesen Kampf selbst gegen das flavische Geschichtsbild durchführen' (Lindner 1972: 65). Even his famous prediction of Vespasian's rise and his ordering of the various legions' acclamations are uncomfortably at odds with the Flavian self-portrait (Lindner 1972: 61–8, 82–4). While he repeatedly adduces Titus' clemency (but see below), he precludes any notion that this was a *Judaean* revolt or war against Rome, that the Judaeans were inferior in courage or cleverness to the Roman legionaries, and that the Romans subdued a recalcitrant people by force of arms, the aid of Roman deities, or the virtue of their generals. Nor does Josephus permit the Romans to occupy the consummate place in world history (cf. *BJ* 5.367). This is *vom Haus aus* a Judaean story told by an aristocrat from Jerusalem (*BJ* 1.3), deferring to prophetic themes (from Jeremiah and Daniel) about the rise and fall of nations under divine supervision and about God's concern to punish those who violate his law and sanctuary (Lindner 1972: 25, 33, 43–4; Mason 1994).

Even without the other literary accounts in circulation, the basic ingredients of Josephus' theme, like the stories of Helen, Achilles, or Iphigeneia for audiences of tragedy, would have been known to his public in advance. All the major protagonists who had survived were familiar in Rome: the conquering generals Vespasian and Titus; Josephus himself, whose personal (mis)fortunes he claims are known to the audience (*BJ* 1.22); the faithful client king Agrippa II, who had received singular honours and now passed a good deal of his time in the capital (Dio Cass. 65.15.4); his sister Berenice, who had achieved another sort of fame as Titus' erstwhile lover (Tac. *Hist.* 2.2; Suet. *Tit.* 7.1); the brothers, sons, and nephews of the Judaean convert, King Izates of Adiabene, whom Titus had sent to Rome as hostages against the loyalty of their country because of their prominence in the revolt (*BJ* 6.356–57); and the factional chiefs, Simon bar Giora (since executed) and John of Gischala, who had both been exhibited in the triumph of 71 (*BJ* 6.433; 7.118, 154–55, 263–66), whom Tactius also mentions (*Hist.* 5.12).

Broadly speaking, then, the entire *War* is ironic in a way that not all histories are. The *Antiquities* (below) stands in marked contrast on this point. Although the very broad outlines of Polybius' or Livy's histories, or Tacitus' *Annals*, were known to their audiences, those audiences did not have the vivid presence of characters, material, and atmosphere complementing Josephus' monograph on the recent war. Because of this immediate knowledge, every ploy of the rebel leaders, their every mistaken motive and deceitful speech, has a tragic-ironic quality: the audience knows full well where their policies will lead. On tragic themes and tropes of the narrative other than those discussed here, the Stanford dissertation by Honora Chapman (1998) is generally persuasive and highly illuminating.

Flattery of the Flavians

We may take it for granted that the rival accounts of the war flattered Vespasian and Titus, both on *a priori* grounds and because of Josephus' characterization (*BJ* 1.2) and counter-ploy: he argues that too much vilification of the Judaeans actually diminishes the achievement of the Roman ruling family (1.8):

> I just do not see how those who have conquered insignificant people should seem to be great. And they [these writers] respect neither the length of the war, nor the mass of the army engaged on the Roman part, nor the greatness of the generals, who sweated so much in the vicinity of Jerusalem. I suppose that, by denigrating their [the generals'] achievement, they regard them too as unworthy!

Obviously Josephus' rivals do not intend, in their energetic praise of the Flavians' accomplishments, to disparage the imperial family. Josephus has caught them, however, in a rhetorical trap: 'Your denigration of the Judaeans implies that the emperors' victory was not very impressive!' The trap only works if everyone understands that flattery of the imperial family is non-negotiable, regardless of the facts. Josephus' rivals must now amend their accounts, he sarcastically implies, to make the Judaeans better enemies in order to aggrandize the Flavians. By driving home the rhetorical nature of imperial praise, this ploy raises the question whether Josephus' own apparent flattery of the Flavians was not often intended, and understood by his first audiences, ironically.

The issue is highlighted by Josephus' repeated resort to this ultimate weapon, what we might call the *argumentum ad dignitatem Caesaris*. In *BJ* 1.16 he will charge that the Greeks who are preoccupied with their own ancient histories are neglecting the glorious deeds of the leaders. In *BJ* 2.26–36, Josephus presents two speeches by accomplished orators on the subject of King Herod's royal succession. The first speaker, who opposes Herod's son Archelaus, goes through a brilliant series of arguments at great length, with choice diction and abundant witnesses for each point, challenging Herod's mental competence when he made the will that appointed Archelaus. The speaker who supports Archelaus, however, can be brief: in that contested will, Herod appointed Caesar the arbiter. Was Herod competent when he chose Caesar? Augustus tells Archelaus that he is a worthy successor to his father (*BJ* 2.37).

Point: flattery of the *princeps* is non-negotiable, and it is something of a game to see who can configure an argument most favourable to Caesar. In such passages as these, Josephus tips his hand with respect to his ensuing flattery of Vespasian and Titus, furnishing the reason for doubt mentioned by Quintilian (above).

A prime candidate is his claim, in a speech crafted for the character Josephus before the walls of Jerusalem, addressed to the recalcitrant rebels inside, that the springs feeding Jerusalem flow more copiously now, with Titus' presence (παρουσία) in the region (*BJ* 5.409–11; cf. Paul 1993: 64–6). The rebels should see this as proof that God has fled the sacred places of Jerusalem to stand with Titus—and capitulate. We may find here either a raw, obsequious flattery or an irony that his literary audience (excepting Titus) should immediately recognize. All indications favour the latter option. Whatever the historical facts about Jerusalem's springs were, no reader would expect the hardened inmates of the city to agree with Josephus' claim as to cause: even if the springs *had* recently opened up, this could as easily signify divine support for the rebels and their own newly arrived leaders. Josephus comments elsewhere that the rebels were quick to interpret signs in their favour (*BJ* 6.285–87, 291, 312–15; cf. Tac. *Hist.* 5.13). Further, he claims that the same thing happened with the springs hundreds of years earlier, when the king of Babylon besieged the city (*BJ* 5.411), though there is no hint of that miracle in the Bible. In connection with that Babylonian destruction of the city, Josephus' speech has already established his signal points: the Judaean God is in control of affairs, now as then; in both cases he has required the Jerusalemites to surrender their city to the enemy as punishment; Josephus is a Jeremiah-like figure (*BJ* 5.391–93). All of this undercuts any notion that he is attempting special flattery of Titus. At most, the gushing springs are a sign from God that it is time to give up. But the good possibility that no one else knew about these bountiful springs, either in the Babylonian period or now as Josephus stands before the city, raises the prospect that he is telling a story that his literary audience should recognize as akin to that of Juvenal's fisherman.

Yet more striking in this vein is Josephus' oily description of Domitian's abortive campaign in Gaul and Germany at the very beginning of Vespasian's reign (*BJ* 7.85–88). Hearing of a revolt (of Batavian auxiliaries and Treveri under Civilis and Classicus), Domitian did not hesitate, in spite of his youth (eighteen), to assume a Caesar's responsibility. 'Enjoying his father's manliness by natural inheritance and having perfected his training beyond that suited to his age, against the barbarians he immediately marched. They, crumbling at the report of his approach, gave themselves entirely over to him, finding subjection under the same yoke again (ὑπὸ τὸν αὐτὸν πάλιν ζυγὸν ὑπαχθῆναι), without suffering disaster, a great advantage over their fear' (*BJ* 7.87). When he had 'put all the affairs of Gaul in order' he returned to Rome to illustrious honour and universal admiration (*BJ* 7.88).

The question of ironic intention here can be settled easily enough. Is it more likely that Josephus' Roman audience was willing to be persuaded of these events, or that he and they both understood this as mocking flattery of Domitian—saying the opposite of what everyone knew to be the case? Two considerations tell in favour of the latter option. First, the language is patently hyperbolic and implausible: Domitian's single-handed determination to shoulder the burden of empire, the keenness of the fearsome barbarians to kneel again under his yoke if they can only be spared a confrontation with the eighteen-year-old. Like Juvenal's fish, they spontaneously present themselves for Domitian's pleasure.[3]

Second, it seems likely that Josephus' audience knew a very different version of events. Suetonius has the young Domitian arrogantly undertaking an *unnecessary* campaign, against the wishes of his absent father's advisers (*Dom.* 2), which reluctance would make sense in terms of their worry about the new dynasty's succession given that Titus was also on campaign in Judaea (Jones and Milns 2002: 124). Suetonius claims that Domitian was later rebuked by his father for these rash actions and forced to learn his place by living with him in Rome. Tacitus has the new emperor's son, whose youth is disdained by the rebel leaders (*Hist.* 4.75), entirely accountable to Vespasian's trusted general Mucianus (4.80, 86: *pars obsequii*). They both head to the theatre of the Gallo-German revolt, only to find before crossing the Alps that the uprising has already failed at the hands of Cerialis' seven legions; so their contribution is not needed (*Hist.* 4.85). Tacitus circulates reports that Mucianus refused the prince's request for his own command, thinking it wiser that the young man not interfere with the glory of others (*Hist.* 4.85), and even that Domitian sought (unsuccessfully) to take over Cerealis' forces in order to challenge either his father or his brother (*Hist.* 4.86). Realizing that his youth is treated contemptuously by all of these generals, Domitian withdraws in pique even from those minimal imperial duties he had heretofore involved himself with. Both the tone and the content of this account flatly contradict Josephus' extremely flattering revision.

If even the core of what is common to Suetonius and Tacitus was widely known, and this abortive campaign had been a humiliating episode in the adolescent Domitian's life—leaving aside their hostile assessments of Domitian's motives in detail (Jones 1992: 16–17)—, then Josephus' audience must have recognized his praise as mocking flattery. Josephus did not need to mention the embarrassing story at all, but that he chose instead to present a version diametrically opposed to the one commonly known (if it was) creates irony. This kind of flattery fulfills its ironic mission because the only person in a position to debunk such outrageous claims without incurring suspicion of *maiestas* is the object, Domitian, and he is not about to do so (cf. Ahl 1984: 198). The story hangs there for all to see, a source of quiet ridicule. While 'damning with faint praise' can be effective, the victim is likely to be at least as aware of the slight as observers; damning with hyperbolic praise is the more effective because it locks the victim in a cage of self-congratulation, intensifying the observers' delight.

[3]Jones and Milns (2002: 124) aptly cite Sil. *Pun.* 3.607–8 in comparison: 'even when you were a boy, the yellow-haired Batavians feared you'.

Titus' Clemency

It appears that much of the rest of Josephus' flattery of the Flavians would similarly have been understood ironically by his first audiences. All other things being equal, clemency is a good, Caesar-like quality in a general (Yavetz 1975: 424–25; Meier 1982: 15–25). In Josephus' praise of Titus' clemency, however, we find some small but telling cracks. On the one hand, he includes plenty of evidence for Titus' cruelty, or his allowance of it on the part of his soldiers (*BJ* 3.304, 329, 501; 5.289–450; 7.23, 37–9; Yavetz 1975: 415). On the other hand, Josephus indicates that he himself was considerably more astute than the Roman general, who in his determined trust and simplicity (πιστεύσας ἐξ ἁπλότητος), for example, failed to see the dangerous ruse that a Judaean soldier named Castor was trying to put over on him. Although Roman warfare was all about stratagems (στρατηγήματα; cf. Frontinus' book on the subject in the Flavian period), Titus' naiveté nearly caused Roman deaths in that encounter. Whereas Josephus understood the trick from the start, Titus had to learn the hard way that 'in hostilities mercy was mischievous' (*BJ* 5.329).

The episode is introduced by a remarkable editorial observation from Josephus. While the Judaean combatants, he says, were careless of their own suffering (ἀμελοῦντες τοῦ παθεῖν), considering their own deaths as trivial if they could but kill one of the enemy (*BJ* 5.316):

> Titus, on the other hand, was taking precautions for the security of his soldiers as much as for their victory. Saying that charging without circumspection amounted to desperation, whereas true valour came only with precaution and not creating suffering (μόνην δ' ἀρετὴν τὴν μετὰ προνοίας καὶ τοῦ μηδὲν τὸν δρῶντα παθεῖν), he directed that his troops make themselves men in ways that were risk-free (ἐν ἀκινδύνῳ τῷ κατὰ σφᾶς ἐκέλευσεν ἀνδρίζεσθαι).

Now, there is a striking parallel to this in Velleius Paterculus' portrait of his hero Tiberius (115.5). When the emperor was still a general fighting the Dalmatians:

> *numquam adeo ulla opportune visa est victoriae occasio, quam damno amissi pensaret militis semperque visum est gloriosissimum, quod esset tutissimum.*

> No opportunity for victory seemed to him timely for which he would have to pay with sacrifice of his soldiers; always, the course that was safest seemed to him also the most glorious.

Yet Anne Eriksen observes what a sharp departure this was from traditional Roman values with respect to military virtue (2002: 113–14), values that have been convincingly articulated for the early empire by Susan Mattern (1999: 162–222). Although precaution (πρόνοια) was of course a virtue for generals and others, like clemency, one could have too much of a good thing. It is hard to imagine that, in a narrative that often praises death-defying courage (sometimes encouraged by Titus himself) on both the Roman and the Judaean sides (3.149, 153–54; 5.305–6, 315–16; 6.33–67, 147–48), and in the context of post-war Rome, appearing as a risk-averse general could redound to Titus' glory.

Titus' preoccupation with clemency (to the point of gullibility) and security (to the point of timidity) comes through clearly in an earlier, paradigmatic episode concerning the only siege entrusted to the young general while his father Vespasian still had theatre-command of the legions: the taking of Gischala, the northern-Galilean base of the notorious rebel leader John (*BJ* 4.84–120). When Titus offers the Gischalan population terms of surrender, rather than devastation by his thousand-strong professional cavalry, John ('a trickster of extremely wily character', 4.85) replies at some length that Titus must (δεῖν) first allow them to observe the approaching sabbath, on which they were forbidden either to fight or to make peace. 'Even the Romans' surely know the requirements of the sabbath, and Titus would have nothing to lose by giving the extra day, for he could guard against flight by camping around the city's perimeter (ἐξὸν περιστρατοπο-δεύσαντα παραφυλάξαι, 4.101). Unbelievably, Titus is not only persuaded by this gambit (πεισθῆναι Τίτον τῇ σκήψει, 4.104)—Josephus further observes that John bluffed him (ἐσοφίζετο τὸν Τίτον, 4.103)—but he fails to take even the elementary safeguard *recommended by John* of camping around the town. Instead, he withdraws his force to the secure embrace of the Tyrian possession Kedasa (4.104). Josephus notes that this was 'rather far' from Gischala; in fact the site, Kedesh-Naphtali, lies about 10 kilometres to the North-East of Gischala. Titus' withdrawal to this stronghold predictably allows not only John himself but a vast train of combatants along with their families to make their escape during the night, unimpeded. Our author stresses the peculiarity: 'At nightfall John, since he observed not a single Roman guard around the town (οὐδεμίαν περὶ τῇ πόλει Ῥωμαίων ἑώρα φυλακήν), seized the opportunity' (4.106). Neither Josephus nor Vespasian nor any other imaginable general could have behaved in this way—even if Josephus graciously credits the failure to divine supervision ('preserving John to bring final ruin upon the city of the Jerusalemites', 4.104).[4]

In Josephus' narrative the innocent Titus does not learn from any of these encounters, but continues to show gentle patience and mercy while the Judaean fighters cause him and his soldiers extreme anxiety and loss of life by *their* clever stratagems and daring (*BJ* 6.12, 29–32, 78–9, 152–56, 190)—usually admirable traits in Josephus. While he watches one of his valiant soldiers being hacked to death by Judaeans, we are told, Titus really wants to help but cannot because of his location (τόπος), while those Romans who could help refrain because of fear (*BJ* 6.89). And his men frequently disobey his orders, or act without them. As a large number of them are perishing in flames, and Titus is rushing about in his

[4]Titus' biographer, B.W. Jones, notices the disparity between the more official portrait of Titus in Suetonius, *Div. Tit.* 4.3 (1989: 132–34) and Josephus, especially in light of this episode. His approach is to privilege Josephus' account historically: *even* he, 'in his authorised version of the wars' (1989: 128 n. 9), preserves evidence of for a picture of Titus that is different from his reputation (1989: 130, 132). I would rather insist that this different picture of Titus is fully thematized in Josephus, established from the *War*'s prologue and continuing throughout: it is part of Josephus' aim to undermine Flavian propaganda by withholding the *credit* for Jerusalem's fall from Titus. It does not necessarily take us any closer than Suetonius to the historical Titus.

remote viewing post urging those nearby to do something, the burning men are said to die cheerfully nonetheless, moved by their general's emotive shouts (*BJ* 6.183–84). How does all of this square with Titus' post-war image in Rome?

Even after Titus hears about the abomination of Mary's cannibalism in the city and determines (again) to move decisively against the rebels, his assaults are repelled by the Judaeans' clever tactics, resulting in great loss of Roman life (*BJ* 6.214–27). Yet again he must reconsider his 'clemency': 'Titus, as he observed that sparing these foreign sacred precincts had meant only injury and slaughter for his troops, ordered them to set the gates on fire' (*BJ* 6.228). Josephus continually stresses, however, Titus' helplessness in the face of divine control. The general convenes his famous war council and decides after all to extinguish the flames around the temple in order to preserve it (*BJ* 6.236–43), then makes firm plans to occupy the sacred fortress on the following day (6.249). But God thwarts his plans (*BJ* 6.250), having ordained that the polluted sanctuary must go at the appointed time. So, while his soldiers have continued their combat, Titus, who 'happened to be resting in his tent after the fighting', can only be informed about the temple's fate (*BJ* 6.254); he has no say in the matter. His utter helplessness is obvious: he shouts and waves to no avail; his own legionaries pretend not to hear him; he is unable to restrain the impetuosity of his frenzied soldiers.

Indeed, only after the temple has been set ablaze, and the long conflict is all but concluded, and after yet further exasperation with the remaining rebels, to which he gives vent in a speech, does Titus *finally* decide that 'everything from now on would go according to the law of war (πολέμου νόμῳ). To the soldiers he gave the signal to burn and plunder the city' (*BJ* 6.353). A truly decisive move!

On one level, all of this might have had a certain plausibility for a war-experienced audience, since it was an open secret that commanders could not manage their soldiers in such circumstances (Ziolkowski 1993: 79–87), though military leaders worked hard to maintain the image of control (Ziolkowski 1993: 89). But Josephus chooses what and how to narrate, and so we must ask how Titus' 'clemency' in his narrative came across to a Roman audience—especially if the audience already shared Suetonius' perception of Titus as a brute before his accession (*Tit.* 1, 6–7).

Against the background of the audience's prior experience in Rome, this whole presentation appears ironic. Josephus plays with the theme of Titus' clemency, using it to portray him as an innocent caught in the wily war-fighting of the Judaeans, in which Josephus himself was fully adept. At the same time, his notice that Titus finally decided to unleash the typical Roman hell on the enemy give him a narrative exit strategy for explaining the outcome that the audience well knew. I do not wish to deny the possibility of a historical kernel to Josephus' perception of Titus' clemency (*BJ* 3.408; 4.628; cf. Yavetz 1975: 431), but only to propose that Josephus held this motif at some distance from his earnest views—'at play seriously', in Cicero's phrase (*severe ludas; De or.* 2.269). While systematically undermining the Flavian representation of the war, he offered Titus the naïve clemency of a humanist (cf. *BJ* 6.356) as consolation prize. Contrast Josephus' own vaunted clemency in the *Life* (*Vit.* 99–103, 169, 307, 329, 375, 385, 388), which is made effective by a peerless grasp of military stratagem (*Vit.* 148, 163, 169, 265, 379).

Zvi Yavetz refined the customary explanation of Josephus' praise for Titus' clemency—as propaganda for the regime—by positing a specific historical context: in the late 70s Titus needed material to remake his violent image (1975: 426–30). Nevertheless, Yavetz does not think that history-writing is an effective means of propaganda, that Josephus' marginal position in Rome could have made his work very important for Titus (1975: 431–32), or that Jews who had such a vivid picture of the real Titus could have been persuaded by Josephus' presentation (1975: 424). In the end, he seems to decide that the *War* was mainly a personal effort of good will by a faithful, but largely irrelevant, client. My analysis asks whether *anyone* in Rome, with the exception of Titus himself,[5] could have been persuaded. If not, and Josephus portrays Titus' clemency so enthusiastically in contradiction of what his Roman audience knew to be the facts (both from their own experience and from his narrative), Josephus was creating irony. The many strings attached to Josephus' flattery diminish the likelihood that it was meant to persuade anyone but Titus. In view of the generally high quality of the work, its survival into the period of Christian hegemony (whence its transmission was assured), and the indications of its initial reception (*Vit.* 361; *Ap.* 1.50; Eus. *Hist. eccl.* 3.9), it is hard to believe that Josephus' *War* was quite as marginal as Yavetz feared. It seems more likely to me that Josephus, who otherwise shows himself skilled in figured speech, used his favoured position to engage in a 'safe criticism' that also strove to defend his people from post-war hatred.

Civil War in Judaea and in Rome

Let us return to the theme of internal dissension as the cause of Jerusalem's fall. Although prologues are not always helpful guides to a historian's actual narrative, Josephus does in fact carry this theme through his narrative, the very first word of which is σάσις (*BJ* 1.31; cf. 1.24, 25, 27; 4.371, 388; 5.2, 15, 20, 257). While sitting in Rome and addressing Roman audiences, surrounded by the evidence of Roman victory and in the face of all the resentment and reprisal that such victories inevitably bring, Josephus has the clarity of vision to write a subversive history that displaces the Romans as victors in any meaningful sense. He is attempting nothing less than a comprehensive vindication of Judaean tradition in apparent contradiction of the facts.

In adducing the theme of internal sedition (στάσις οἰκεία) Josephus touches upon a potent issue for a Roman audience of the Flavian era. Somewhat strangely, scholars usually discuss this important Josephan theme abstractly, with direct

[5]I confess to some puzzlement as to how Titus himself could have accepted such presentations of his actions. The best I can propose is that he did not endorse them, but the gain in this portrait of extreme clemency was acceptable to him as the lesser of evils, hardly worth challenging to prove his generalship, which was already obvious to all from the result. He could use Josephus' help with the clemency argument, however, even if it was overdone.

reference to Thucydides 3.82–4—half a millennium before Josephus' time (Rajak 1983: 91–4; Feldman 1998: 140–48; Mader 2000: 55–103; cf. now Price 2001 on Thucydides). Yet civil war (*bellum civile*) was arguably the most prominent theme in Roman literature from Cicero, Sallust, and Caesar through Lucan, Tacitus, Florus, and (if we may include him) Appian (cf. Keitel 1984; Henderson 1998). The Flavians' prestige rested symbolically upon their victory over a foreign people in Judaea, but practically upon their success in bringing internal stability to Rome after the bloody civil war of 68–69, following Nero's death. Early in his prologue Josephus himself makes this connection (*BJ* 1.4):

> For during this, the greatest period of change, as I stated, *while among the Romans domestic affairs were becoming diseased* (ἐνόσει), the revolutionary bloc of the Judaeans reached its peak in those turbulent times with respect to numbers and also in resources.

The reference to *stasis* in Rome as 'disease', a classic metaphor,[6] confirms that Josephus plays his narrative against the background of his audience's knowledge. Indeed, his account will repeatedly allude to recurring civil wars in Rome and dwell on some of the famous Roman protagonists (e.g., *BJ* 1.23, 183, 187, 216, 218–19, 359–60, 370, 386–92; 2.204–13, 250–51; 4.491–6). Yet since he does not explicate these parallels with Judaea, but only suggests them, the irony depends upon the audience to supply the back-story. His brief discussion of the civil war prior to Vespasian's accession (*BJ* 4.491–96, 501–2), at a crucial moment in the Judaean civil war (4.503), drives the point home: 'All these matters I may be excused from narrating in detail because they are common knowledge: they have been written up by many Greeks and also Romans' (4.496). He expects his audience to employ their extra-textual knowledge in interpreting his narrative, to realize that the Judaean civil war, though it attracted Roman legions, is no different from their own common experience. The war was in no way, therefore, a Judaean *national* revolt against Rome.

Text-Dependent Irony

Although Josephus must use 'emphasis', exploiting the audience's prior understanding, in his ironic representations of Titus and Domitian, when he comes to the Judaean rebels he may be as direct as he wishes: they have no powerful supporters. His textual irony is most obvious when he flags it with εἰρωνεία and σχῆμα language, sometimes together (e.g., *BJ* 2.29). The rebel leaders are not merely the confidently mistaken victims of his authorial irony, but they themselves also try to practise irony on their publics, which makes them appear doubly foolish.

About one third of the occurrences of the εἴρων-word group in Josephus fall in the fourth book of the *War,* where the rebels' activities are featured. First, they effect an inversion of Judaean tradition, mixing irony (παρεκίρνατο δὲ τοῖς

---

[6]Keitel 1984: 320 and n. 32, citing Pl. *Rep.* 470c, *Soph.* 228a; Hdt. 5.28; Soph. *Ant.* 1015; Sall. *Cat.* 36.5; *Hist.* 2.77M; Tac. *Ann.* 1.43.4; *Hist.* 1.26.1.

δεινοῖς εἰρωνεία) with their other horrors by electing through lots their own, non-hereditary high priest; they do this under the pretext (πρόσχημα) that it was the more ancient custom (*BJ* 4.152–54).

Later, when Josephus' former Galilean rival John of Gischala enters Jerusalem, he conceals the fact that he has been driven there by the Roman advance, and emptily boasts that the Romans will never take Jerusalem:

> He also spoke ironically about the ignorance of the inept [Romans] (καὶ κατειρωνευόμενος τῆς τῶν ἀπείρων ἀγνοίας), that even if they should take wings (ἂν πτερὰ λαβόντες), the Romans would never surmount the wall of Jerusalem—those who already suffered so terribly [sc. the Romans] throughout the villages of Galilee also breaking their machines against the walls there (*BJ* 4.127).

Yet the literary audience knows in hindsight the truth about this man, now a perpetual prisoner in Rome, and indeed that the Romans *will* bring 'wings' (i.e., the *alae* of cavalry)[7] and engines; they will not only surmount but bring down Jerusalem's walls. John is thus a pathetic would-be hero, imagining that he can outwit fate.

Later in this volume comes a passage in which εἴρων-words appear three times along with two occurrences of σχῆμα. The scene is constructed ironically. An eminent citizen named Zacharias has become a target of the Zealots and Idumeans in Jerusalem, allegedly because of his wealth and virtue. Rather than killing him outright, because they are tired of indiscriminate slaughter (*BJ* 4.326–34), the rebels cleverly plan a show trial, empanelling seventy citizens as judges for the purpose. The judges should know, however, what they are expected to decide in view of a massacre just completed. They are charged to assume the *role* (or figure) of judges, as in a play (περιθέντες δ' αὔτοις ὥσπερ ἐπὶ σκηνῆς σχῆμα δικαστῶν; *BJ* 4.336). In the event, contrary to plan, the prosecutors are unable to offer convincing evidence for their charge that Zacharias has held treasonable communications with Vespasian. So, with unimaginable innocence, the citizen judges vote to acquit him. The result:

> A cry went up at this acquittal (πρὸς τὴν ἀπόλυσιν) from the Zealots, and they were all aggravated at the judges for not perceiving the ironic nature of the authority they had been given (ὡς μὴ συνιεῖσι τὴν εἰρωνείαν τῆς δοθείσης αὐτοῖς ἐξουσίας; *BJ* 4.342)

To make their point, the Zealots move forward and dispatch their intended victim on the spot, punning that this was *their* verdict, and now the man has received a more perfect acquittal (ἀπόλυσις—i.e., 'release' from life). The language of irony also appears in the introduction to the story, where Josephus speaks of ironic trials and courts (*BJ* 4.334), and again in the middle, where the Zealots must restrain themselves from expressing rage at Zacharias for his defence, to maintain the 'façade [or figure] and ironic nature' (τὸ σχῆμα καὶ τὴν εἰρωνείαν) of

---

[7]The word-play works even though Josephus elsewhere uses Greek ἴλη for Latin *ala:* the word πτερά occurs only here in his corpus.

the trial (4.340). Notice that even Josephus' explanation of the name 'Zealot' has them using language ironically (κατειρωνευόμενοι; *BJ* 2.270).

These few examples from Josephus' most famous and controversial work, which is the foundation of the paradigm according to which he was a Flavian propagandist (Laqueur 1920: 126–27; Weber 1921: *passim;* Thackeray 1929: 27–8), will show I hope that asking new questions of the narrative may produce a very different reading. Once the question about irony has been asked, shafts of light flood in from all directions and give a possibly more satisfying account of this expert narrative than the rather sorry counsel about Flavian propaganda.

Careful investigation of the ironic dimensions of the *War*'s major speeches and prologue (*BJ* 1.1–30), both strategically important for the narrative, will no doubt repay the effort. In the prologue, for example, there is irony in Josephus' casting his people as barbarian (*BJ* 1.3, 6) while writing in high Atticizing style, yet appealing to Roman sympathies and attacking 'real Greeks' (*BJ* 1.13–16). The speeches are mines of ironic manipulation. Josephus' *tour de force* on the traditional pacifism of the Judaeans (*BJ* 5.390) would have impressed anyone who knew either the Bible or Roman commonplaces about a bellicose Judaean history. King Agrippa's masterful deliberation on war contains a number of assertions the audience knows to be invalid: the Gauls and Germans have willingly submitted to Roman rule (*BJ* 2.371–73, 377; but 1.5; 4.440–41; cf. Suet. *Ner.* 40–46; *Galb.* 9.2; 11; 16.2; Tac. *Hist.* 1.6, 8; 5.12–37, 54–79) and the Adiabenians would never join such a serious fight (*BJ* 2.389; but 2.520; 5.474; 6.356). Eleazar ben Ya`ir's deliberative speech on suicide at Masada is the ironic pinnacle: he openly reflects on the crimes committed by his band (*BJ* 7.332, 359) and resorts to a desperate rhetorical justification of suicide as the natural course (*BJ* 7.341–57), in contrast to Josephus' earlier and equally rhetorical speech against suicide (*BJ* 3.361–82; cf. Ladouceur 1987). But space does not permit a more thorough examination of irony in the *Judaean War.*

The Judaean Antiquities

Because I have devoted a parallel essay to exploring what Josephus' *magnum opus,* the *Judaean Antiquities,* might have meant for a Roman audience, the briefest sketch must suffice here.

The *Antiquities,* to which *Life* is an appendix, was published in 93 or 94 (*AJ* 20.267), a sensitive time in Domitian's Rome, for members of the elite at any rate (Syme 1983: 122–26). The core of the narrative (vols. 1–13), on Judaean 'antiquity', does not seem to depend upon prior audience knowledge. Josephus insists rather that his account is something new and unique, bringing to a Greek-speaking audience (*AJ* 1.10, 12) fundamental information about Judaean origins: their constitution, history, and culture (1.5, 10; 20.229, 251, 261; cf. *Ap.* 2.287). He must introduce each biblical figure (e.g., *AJ* 1.34 [Adam], 36 [Eve], 1.52, 154–60 [Abraham]), and he pauses frequently to explain even the most elementary Judaean customs and terms (e.g., *AJ* 1.128–29; 3.317; 14.1–3, 186–87; 16.175; 17.254; *Vit.* 1,

12). There is every reason to think that the audience was much the same as *War*'s, for he does assume their knowledge of, or at least their access to, the earlier work (e.g., *AJ* 1.1–4, 6, 203; 13.72, 173, 298; 18.11; 20.258–59; *Vit.* 27, 412; cf. *BJ* 7.454 and *AJ* 1.12).

Notwithstanding the very different character of this book, which is free of *War*'s pervasive tragic ethos, Josephus has abundant opportunities for ironic composition at the thematic level. He seems, for example, to exploit his audience's knowledge of Roman political and historiographical traditions. His account of the Judaean constitution is that of a decidedly anti-monarchical, senatorial aristocracy (*AJ* 4.223; 6.36; 11.111; 14.91), and this even leads him to introduce a senate into his paraphrase of the Bible (*AJ* 5.15, 43, 55, 135). Although the people demand a king (*AJ* 6.36; cf. Cic. *Rep.* 2.12.23; Livy 1.17.3), the subsequent rule of Tarquin-like kings in Judaea is disastrous (*AJ* 10.143–44; 13.300–301; 14.41; cf. Cicero, *Rep.* 1.40.62; cf. 2.30.52). Josephus writes his history as a kind of serial biography, focusing upon individual character, which he develops by means of moralizing obituaries (cf. Cicero, *Rep.* 2.31.55). The role of moral exempla in Roman historiography, by way of comparison, is the subject of C. Kraus's essay in this volume.

More specifically, one finds numerous points of intersection between Josephus' narrative of Judaean origins and traditional accounts of Rome's beginnings. Both constitutions were the embodiment of natural law (Cic. *Leg.* 2.5.13; cf. 1.6.20–12.34; Joseph *AJ* 1.18–30) and both featured the role of priests and piety (*AJ* 3.159–87; 3.214; 4.184, 304; cf. Cic. *Rep.* 2.13–14; *Dom.* 1.1; Dion. Hal. *Ant. Rom.* 2.58–66; Plut. *Num.*). Both constitutions are free of the unseemly myths that plague the Greeks (*AJ* 1.22–3; Dion. Hal. *Ant. Rom.* 2.18.3). The archetypal demagogue in Josephus' narrative, a jealous aristocrat who amassed a following and generated a civil war (*stasis*) of unprecedented scale (*AJ* 4.12–20), has many parallels to Catiline (cf. Cic. *Cat.* I-IV; Sall. *Cat).* Josephus' epitomes of the constitution emphasize the characteristically Roman virtues of austerity, discipline, justice, and humanity (Polyb. 6.7.5–8, 48.3, 56.1–5; Sall. *Cat.* 11–13; Livy 1.pref.9–12, 18.4; Cic. *Rep.* 1.27–28; Plut. *Cat. Mai.* 1.3–4; 2.1, 3). Moses and Romulus begin and end their lives in strikingly similar circumstances: exposed in rivers at birth as objects of a king's wrath (*AJ* 2.218–23; Livy 1.4.1–6; Dion. Hal. *Ant. Rom.* 1.79.4–7), enveloped in clouds at the end, generating speculation about apotheosis (*AJ* 4.326; Cic. *Rep.* 2.10.17 Livy 1.16.1; Dion. Hal. *Ant. Rom.* 2.56.2). Since Josephus does not explicitly connect his portrait with the Roman parallels, however, we are dealing here with audience-dependent irony.

The most effective irony in the *Antiquities* comes in the ample stretches of narrative that Josephus devotes to affairs in Rome between Tiberius' last days and Claudius' accession (*AJ* 18.205–304; 19.1–226). It was in these closing books that a Roman audience encountered thoroughly familiar names: here, I submit, we can have little doubt that he expected them to read between the lines. We know Demetrius' advice (*Eloc.* 292–93) about criticizing a reigning tyrant obliquely, by targeting *someone else* with similar traits. Ahl plausibly suggests that Quintilian, while advising his students how to critique 'those tyrants' (*illos tyrannos*), was really teaching them about dealing with the current regime. He further argues that Tacitus and Suetonius were writing with one eye on their own times when they exposed the crimes of earlier monarchs (Ahl 1984: 190, 206). If we bear these considerations in mind, Josephus' Roman narrative, which labels *all* the emperors 'tyrants' (*AJ* 19.187, 230), appears to brim with ironic possibilities for an audience in Domitian's Rome. For example, it becomes ironic for such an audience that the stereotypical succession woes of the tyrannical King Herod should have been brought for arbitration to Augustus (*AJ* 17.304–20), whose own problems in finding a successor were legendary (Syme 1939: 418–39).

Though any criticism of a previous emperor could be a sensitive matter, Josephus' narrative subject, Tiberius, and his current patron Domitian had some striking parallels. Both were absent from the capital for long periods, giving the impression of aloofness and arrogance (Jones 1992: 26–8) and requiring a secretarial post *ab actis senatus,* so that they could remain informed of senatorial discussions; this appointment fell into disuse between their reigns (Tac. *Ann.* 5.4; Southern 1997: 50). Both were bald (Syme 1983: 135), childless, and devoted to astrology (Suet. *Tib.* 14; *Dom.* 15–16). Indeed they were born, made Caesar, and designated *princeps* under the same three astrological signs (Scorpio, Cancer, Virgo; cf. Sauron 1991: 39) and, if one accepts Sauron's reconstruction of Tiberius' magnificent cave at Sperlonga (1991: 19–39), Domitian's Alban villa was a deliberate imitation of Tiberius' retreat (cf. Jones and Milns 2002: 165). Suetonius famously alleges that Domitian's reading was confined to Tiberius' acts and memoirs (*commentarios et acta, Dom.* 20.3). After the fire of 80 CE, Domitian was concerned to rebuild (among other things) the *domus Tiberiana* on the Palatine, which had become the imperial residence, and which he connected with his own new palace (Jones 1992: 89). Though we should not conclude from these parallels that Domitian was universally seen as a 'new Tiberius', they would presumably have encouraged an audience listening to specific criticisms of Tiberius *on these issues* to make connections with Domitian.

Against this background it becomes ironic that Josephus should dwell on Tiberius' problems with the succession, in a highly sarcastic story. The emperor finds himself absurdly trapped in appointing an heir (*AJ* 18.205–27)—such a victim of horoscope-addiction, Josephus moralizes, that he unwillingly and bitterly saddles himself with Gaius as heir (*AJ* 18.211–23; *contra* Tac. *Ann.* 6.46). Tiberius begs Gaius to keep his grandson Gemellus alive on the ironic grounds that it will be dangerous for Gaius if he isolates himself as ruler and that the Gods will punish monarchs who behave contrary to the law (*AJ* 18.222–23). It is ironic that Josephus' leading exempla of monarchical rulers in Rome, Tiberius and Gaius (*AJ* 18.226; 19.2), should both behave so high-handedly towards the traditional nobility, in story time, as Domitian was doing in real time (Suet. *Dom.* 12.1–2; Dio Cass. 68.1.1–2). And it is ironic that in Josephus' narrative the senator Gnaeus Sentius Saturninus should be given a forum to extol aristocracy, to denounce Julius Caesar and his successors as tyrants (*AJ* 19.173–74), and to praise Gaius' assassins as worthy of even greater honour than Brutus and Cassius (*AJ* 19.182–84)—those names so dangerous to utter.

Thus, having straightforwardly made his case for the aristocratic Judaean constitution in the first part of the *Antiquities,* when he comes to discuss the Roman constitution under the emperors Josephus resorts to irony or 'figured speech', allowing (and intending) his audience to make the connections.

IRONY IN THE *VITA*

Although Josephus' one-volume autobiography has been studied more intensively than his larger compositions, scholarly attention has focused almost exclusively on the historical issues behind the text and not on the narrative as such. Lacking the space here to tackle the introductory issues, I simply declare my understanding of the book's purpose (cf. Mason 2001: xxvii-l).

Josephus frames the *Life* as an exposition of his character (*Vit.* 430) on the evidence of his ancestry and *curriculum vitae* (*AJ* 20.266). This frame matches the content well enough: after sketching his glorious ancestry and precocious youth, he turns to his public life (*Vit.* 12), presenting in some detail the five months that, as far as we know, constituted his only real claim to political achievement. In keeping with this restricted focus, Josephus offers the work as his *commentarii* (cf. ὑπομνήσω; *AJ* 20.267). Like *commentarii,* it gives the impression of having been hastily written, and its episodes often recall the exploits of Julius Caesar in his famous *commentarii* (the *Gallic War*). Josephus' many hapless opponents are brought forward in series and dispatched with glee. Their vices and abject failure serve mainly to highlight his virtues (cf. *Vit.* 34–42, 46–61, 63, 70–76, 85–103, 336–72). I no longer find compelling the customary view that a book by one of those rivals, Justus of Tiberias, was the principal reason for Josephus' writing the *Life.*[8]

Text-Dependent Irony

Within this highly rhetorical construction of Josephus' career, irony plays a crucial role. Because the audience is unfamiliar with many of the actors and the story, text-created irony dominates. That is, early in the book Josephus explicitly sets up an ironic situation, which he then pursues consistently to the end. Whereas we earnest scholars have tended to use this text to blame him for his double dealing and lies, it should be obvious from the way he relishes his deceptions that he expects a different response, namely: praise for the statesmanlike way in which he handled the ineluctably ironic situation of the revolt.

[8]Pace, e.g., Schürer 1901–11: I. 59, 97; Niese 1896: 228–29; Luther 1910: 8, 65–81; Laqueur 1920 [1970]: 44–55, 75–83; Drexler 1925: 293–312; Thackeray 1929 [1967]: 5–12; Schalit 1933: 67–95; Gelzer 1952: 89; Shutt 1961: 6; Barish 1978: 64; Mason 1991: 316–24. Some crucial criticisms of the standard view were made by Cohen 1979: 121–37 and Rajak 1983: 154. Cf. Mason 2001: xxvii–l.

Let us join the narrative at *Vit.* 17. After an embassy to Nero's Rome (further below), which proves the young aristocrat's abilities (*Vit.* 13–16; cf. Plut. *Prae. ger. reip.* 10.804D-12.806F), he is back in Jerusalem assuming a position of leadership, but facing a popular demand for secession from Rome (*Vit.* 17). Here he begins to establish the ironic situation. He first makes a dutiful attempt at the candid speech (παρρησία) recommended by Aristotle for most cases (*Vit.* 17–19):

> I tried to restrain the insurgents and charged them to think again. They should first place before their eyes those against whom they would make war—for not only with respect to war-related expertise but also with respect to good fortune were they disadvantaged in relation to the Romans—and they should not, rashly and quite foolishly, bring upon their native places, their families, and indeed themselves the risk of ultimate ruin. I said these things and was persistently engaged in dissuasive pleading, predicting that the outcome of the war would be utterly disastrous for us. I was not convincing, to be sure, because the frenzy of the desperadoes prevailed.

When he fails with frankness, however, he resorts without hesitation to the doublespeak that Aristotle identifies as appropriate in dealing with the mob (*Vit.* 20–23).

> I became anxious now that by saying these things constantly I might incur hatred and suspicion, as though conspiring with the enemy, and I would risk being taken and done away with by them. . . . . [I] held discussions with the chief priests and principal men of the Pharisees. Extreme fear took hold of us as we saw the populace with weapons: we were unsure what we should do ourselves and were unable to halt the revolutionaries. Given the clear and present danger to ourselves, we began saying [or kept saying] (ἐλέγομεν) that we concurred with their opinions. But we counseled them to stand fast, even if the enemy soldiers had advanced, so that they should be given credit for justly taking up weapons in defence. We did these things hoping that before long Cestius [Gallus, governor of Syria] would come up with a large force and halt the revolution.

Here Josephus parades before the literary audience his calculated effort to deceive the common folk, confiding what he could not have said in story time: his internal hope that legions from Antioch would solve his problem. The ironic game, then, has begun.

But it has only *just* begun. In *Vit.* 30–61, Josephus anticipates Plutarch's advice by gathering intelligence about the state of play in each Galilean centre under his charge. In the course of this he learns about Agrippa's viceroy Varus, a past master of demagoguery. Varus used to invent slanders against his rivals and his patron, attribute the slanders to some other group that was troubling him, then execute those people in pretended indignation that they should have said such things (*Vit.* 50, 55)! So in one stroke he got rid of them and put into circulation rumours harmful to his more powerful enemies. The atmosphere is thick with disinformation.

By the time he has gathered this intelligence, Josephus himself is fully committed to the deception game. His first action in Galilee is to summon the council of Tiberias (*Vit.* 64), before whom he *claims* (ἔλεγον) that the Jerusalem council has instructed him to demolish the house of Herod Antipas on the ground that it contains animal images (*Vit.* 65). Some of the more refined councilors, led by one Capella, strongly disagree with the plan, though they eventually are persuaded by Josephus (*Vit.* 66).

If this story is taken straightforwardly, to the effect that the Jerusalem leaders in fact ordered the destruction of Antipas' house, which is how scholars usually take it (Luther 1910: 17–8; Drexler 1925: 297–98; Goodman 1987: 218; Price 1992: 32), it creates a number of problems. First, even though he has just described his most recent instructions from Jerusalem (*Vit.* 62–3), Josephus has mentioned nothing at all about attacks on royal property, which appear quite out of character with the leaders' reported sentiments. Second, he uses the same ironic code (λέγω) as in *Vit.* 22, where we know that it indicates duplicity. He *said* that the Jerusalem leaders had sent him to demolish the house, but had they really? Third, in spite of his declaration and the alleged urgency of the matter (*Vit.* 65: τάξος), Josephus presently departs for Upper Galilee (*Vit.* 67). Fourth, when a Tiberian faction led by one Jesus attacks the palace in Josephus' absence, he becomes furious *because* they have acted contrary to his intention (*Vit.* 68). Finally, he recovers as much as possible of the pilfered furnishings and hands them over to none other than Capella's group—the refined men who had objected to the operation in the first place. Josephus tells the literary audience plainly that he had wanted to return the goods to King Agrippa (*Vit.* 68). This account, then, makes sense only if it is read ironically: Josephus had no intention of actually raiding royal property, but boldly declared his intention to do so in order to consolidate his support base among the militant Tiberians, in keeping with the policy announced at *Vit.* 22. On this reading, the passage provides no support for the common historical argument that either Josephus or the Jerusalem council was aggressively prosecuting the revolt at this time (*contra* the scholars mentioned above). He is illustrating his ability to control the masses with deception.

The Josephus character in the *Vita* is not the only one playing a double game. One of the three factional leaders in Tiberias, Justus, 'although he kept pretending to be in doubt about the war, was actually longing for revolutionary activities' (*Vit.* 37). Hoping to build his own power base, Josephus asserts, Justus made preposterous claims about the injured status of his city to the Tiberian mob (*Vit.* 38). With his usual resignation about mob fickleness (cf. *AJ* 3.24–7, 68–9, 295–315; *Vit.* 77, 103, 113, 140, 149, 271, 315, 388), our narrator continues (*Vit.* 40):

> By saying these things, he won over the mob (προετρέψατο τὸ πλῆθος). For he was rather good at manipulating the populace and at overcoming the better arguments of disputants by craftiness and a kind of guile through words. In fact, he was well trained in the Greek sort of education (καὶ γὰρ οὐδ' ἄπειρος ἦν παιδείας τῆς παρ' Ἕλλησιν) . . . .

Here Josephus confronts Justus' demagogic dissimulation with the old charge against the sophists: the Tiberian makes the worse argument appear the better one (Ar. *Nub.* 94–8, 112–18; Isoc. *Antid.* 15; Pl. *Apol.* 19b; Arist. *Rh.* 2.24.11.1402a). Josephus' characterization of this skill as *Greek* appears to presuppose a Roman audience, for Roman authors had a long (rhetorical) tradition of expressing contempt for deceptive Greek ways, over against their own putative simplicity and faithfulness.[9] Whereas the character Justus attempts dissimulation in the story, vis-à-vis the mob, the author Josephus neutralizes it with an irony that he expects his audience to appreciate.

We next meet another skilled pretender, John of Gischala, who *claims* (ἔφασκεν) that he wants to raid some imperial grain storehouses in order to rebuild the walls of his native town from the proceeds, though his real motives are quite different (*Vit.* 71). Later, John will request Josephus' permission to take physical therapy at the baths near Tiberias, his real goal being to inspire defection from Josephus in the region (*Vit.* 85–7). And after a failed attempt at revolt he will insist with oaths and vows that he has played no role in these unfortunate events (*Vit.* 101).

Josephus, for his part, continues undaunted in his own campaign of deception, which becomes ironic when it is shared with the audience. Only because he wants to keep an eye on the Galilean leadership, 'on a pretext of friendship' (ἐν προφάσει φιλίας), as he says, he designates seventy of them his 'friends' (φίλιοι) and travel companions; they will accompany him in the trial of cases—but really as hostages for the loyalty of the people. Josephus is disarmingly candid about this pretence (*Vit.* 79).

Josephus' cheerful willingness to deceive the masses confronts the *Life*'s audience in the incident with the Dabarittan young men (*Vit.* 126 ff.). These youths rob the wife of the king's administrator, Ptolemy, and bring the plunder to their ostensible rebel leader Josephus. With the literary audience, now, he can be straightforward about his alleged intention, thirty years earlier, to return the goods to their rightful owner (*Vit.* 128): 'Wanting to preserve these things for Ptolemy, I asserted (ἔφην) to those who had brought them that it was necessary to keep them *so that the walls of Jerusalem might be repaired* from their sale.' Josephus assumes the audience's understanding that one simply does not declare one's true intentions before a mob. While reassuring the masses in this way, he secretly hands the gear over to friends of the king for safe conduct back to Ptolemy (*Vit.* 131).

When this secret action is leaked, however, the frenzied mob makes a charge on Josephus' residence. Courageously walking out to meet them, he digs even deeper into pretence, winking ironically at the audience as he narrates. First, he begs for mercy, conceding that he may indeed have seemed to commit an injustice (*Vit.* 139). Observing that his incipient contrition favourably affects the mob, he fabricates the entirely new proposition that he had actually wanted to keep the captured goods as a surprise—for *rebuilding the walls of noble Tarichaea* (*Vit.* 142)! On a roll now, our reporter decides to gild the lily (*Vit.* 142):

> For because I understood well that this city, so hospitable toward foreigners, was eagerly accommodating such men as these, who have left behind their native

[9] Polyb. 6.56; 31.25.4; Plaut. *Asin.* 199; Cic. *Brut.* 247; *Flac.* 9, 24, 31, 57; *Tusc.* 4.33.70; 5.20.58; Sall. *Iug.* 85.32–3; Luc. 3.302; Tac. *Ann.* 14.20; *Dial.* 28.4–29.2; cf. Balsdon 1979: 30–54; Segal 1987: 37–8; Gruen 1992: 52–83, 223–71.

> places and made common cause with our fortune (ἡμετέρας τύχης), I wanted to construct walls....

Although in *Vit.* 143 and 162 Josephus will refer to some resident aliens in Tarichaea, he has already (*Vit.* 112–13) made an issue of the Tarichaeans' scandalous lack of hospitality towards the dignitaries who had fled from Agrippa's territory to live among them (cf. *Vit.* 149–54). It is also ironic that he should speak of 'sharing our fortune', since he has consistently placed fortune (τύχη) on the Roman side (*Vit.* 17; cf. *BJ* 2. 360, 373, 387, 390; 3.368; 5.367; 6.409–13). When the fickle Tarichaeans predictably respond to this new building proposal with huzzahs, but the visitors in Tarichaea become envious, he spontaneously adds that of course he planned to fortify those other locations as well (*Vit.* 144).

The decisive incident for establishing Josephus' ironic posture in the first half of the *Vita* comes when he interviews the Tiberian leaders Justus and Pistus, his prisoners, after giving them a generous dinner. Hear his own description (*Vit.* 175–78):

> After the banquet I said: 'I myself know very well that the power of the Romans is utterly overwhelming; but *I* have kept quiet about it because of the bandits.' I counseled them to do the same, to wait patiently for the necessary amount of time and not become upset with me as general, for they would not easily have the chance to encounter someone else who was similarly mild. I also reminded Justus that before I came along from Jerusalem, the Galileans had cut off his brother's hands, adducing wrongdoing prior to the war in the form of forged letters by him....

This encounter recalls quite plainly the opening scenes of the revolt in *Vit.* 17–22: the wiser leaders decide upon a policy of duplicity because they realize that straightforward opposition to the sentiments of the masses is pointless and perilous. The audience can feel only contempt for such parochial naïfs as Justus and Pistus.

Josephus and the Delegation from Jerusalem

With the arrival of a delegation from Jerusalem, led by Jonathan but initiated by John of Gischala in connivance with his high-ranking friends, the narrative becomes an ironic duel, from which only one party can emerge successful.

Jonathan and his three companions are allowed the first shot. Once again, Josephus makes explicit the ironic framework: he offers an ostensibly trustworthy narration of the delegation's mandate: to bring him back dead or alive (*Vit.* 202). It is not only the literary audience that is in on the secret, however, for Josephus explains that his character in the story also received this crucial intelligence through a friendly informer (*Vit.* 204). When the audience shares knowledge with the author and character Josephus, of which the delegation members are confidently unaware, we have an impressive ironic situation akin to that of New Comedy. This is the background against which all of the delegation's subsequent dissembling must be read.

Anticipating their arrival in Galilee, Josephus hastily assembles an army of 8,000 men and heads to the western extremity, as he explains, of Galilee. He hurries there, he says, on the pretext (σκηπτόμενος) of preparing for battle with the Roman (tribune) Placidus (*Vit.* 212–15). But why should he head so quickly for the western extremity, only to make believe that he is preparing for battle? As soon as he has set up camp, Jonathan's delegation arrives in southern Galilee and writes requesting an interview. Observe the ironic nature of their letter (*Vit.* 217–18):

> Jonathan and those with him,
> who have been sent by the Jerusalemites,
> To Josephus
> Greetings!
>
> We were sent by the principal men in Jerusalem, when they heard that John of Gischala had often plotted against you, to reprimand him and to exhort him to submit to you for the duration. Because we want to deliberate together with you about what still needs to be done, we invite you to come to us quickly—but not with many others, for the village would not be able to accommodate a mass of soldiers.

If anyone doubts that *Life* has a playful undercurrent, here we can have no more doubt. The literary audience knows with certainty that this letter turns the facts on their head: the delegation does not intend to discipline John, the man responsible for their mission (*Vit.* 189), and their reason for wanting Josephus to come with only a few soldiers has nothing to do with a lack of accommodations. There are shades here of the fawning letter with which Nero reportedly invited Domitius Corbulo to Cenchreae, calling him 'father' and 'benefactor', only to have him killed upon arrival (Dio Cass. 63.17.5–6; Rudich 1993: 98–9).

It is a futile attempt, however, because Josephus has not only anticipated their request but also placed their true motives beyond doubt by interrogating their courier (*Vit.* 220–25). And *now* we learn the reason for his sudden excursion west (*Vit.* 226–27):

> Josephus,
> To Jonathan and those with him,
> Greetings!
>
> I am pleased to discover that you have arrived in Galilee in good health, especially because I shall now be able to pass over to you the care of local affairs as I return to my native city [Jerusalem]. I have been wanting to do this for a long time! I would have come to you not only at Xaloth, but further, and without being directed to so; but I beg your understanding that I am not able to do this because I am closely guarding Placidus in Chabolos. He has a plan to go up into Galilee. So, *you* come to *me* when you have read the letter.
>
> Be well!

Every single statement here is obviously false. Josephus has no intention of coming to meet them in Xaloth, the southern-most point in Galilee, from which they might spirit him away to Jerusalem with minimal bother. He has planted himself deep in Galilee so that if they wish to take him they will need to get through his (allegedly) vast army of Galilean supporters. Josephus expects a literary audience that is ready to admire him and even to laugh with him at his brilliant subversion of the delegation's attempted game.

Unlike the overly confident delegates, he is a master of the art of deception and so arranges tight security for the conveyance of his letter (*Vit.* 228). That Josephus has wounded them in this first round is abundantly clear from their curt response (*Vit.* 230):

> We charge you to come three days from now, without armed soldiers, to the village of Gabaroth, so that we can hear fully the complaints that you have made against John.

Though now seemingly willing to enter the Galilean heartland, they do not buy Josephus' claim that he is busy guarding Placidus, because they require him to travel to Gabara. This town has already been introduced (*Vit.* 123–25; cf. 233–34, 313), however, as the only centre in lower Galilee completely loyal to John. The battle of wits continues.

Josephus now reiterates the ironic framework: he has fully understood from the beginning the delegation's intention to fight him, and so relates that he advanced not to Gabara, as demanded, but only as far as his own secure fortress of Iotapata (*Vit.* 188; cf. 332, 412)—with 3,000 armed troops. From there he writes to indicate that he has known their game all along (*Vit.* 235):

> If you want *me* to come to *you* at all costs, there are 204 cities and villages throughout the Galilee. I will come to any of these you desire, except Gabara and Gischala: the one is John's native place, and the other his ally and friend.

Realizing that Josephus has seen through his charade, Jonathan abruptly stops writing (*Vit.* 236). Confrontation is now inevitable.

Their final scene of conflict is Tiberias, where again the parties compete in duplicity. The delegates' opening effort is characteristically lame. After stirring up disaffection there, they hear of Josephus' arrival. He narrates (*Vit.* 273–75):

> They came to me and, after greeting [me], kept saying [or began to say] (ἔλεγον) that they considered it fortunate that I was thus involved in the Galilee, that indeed they rejoiced together [with me] at the honour in which I was held. For, they claimed (ἔφασαν), my reputation made them look good, since they had been my teachers and were currently my fellow-citizens; in fact, they kept saying (ἔλεγον) that my friendship was more appropriate to them than John's was. Though eager to depart for home, they would wait patiently there until they should place John at my mercy. While saying these things (ταῦτα λέγοντες) they swore in confirmation the most dreadful oaths that we have, on account of which I considered it improper to mistrust them. Indeed, on account of the next day's being a sabbath, they appealed to me to make my lodging elsewhere: they asserted (ἔφασκον) that the city of the Tiberians ought not to be burdened [with troops].

This paragraph gives the flavour of the mutual deceptions, often hilariously reported, that colour Josephus' final relations with the delegation (*Vit.* 280–83, 288–89), though we lack the space to follow them through. After further attempts to outsmart Josephus and mislead the masses, the individual delegates fall victim to assorted traps laid by him. In the end, they all return to Jerusalem defeated and cowed, whereas Josephus wins resounding support for his leadership from the capital (*Vit.* 331–35).

Of the *Life*'s many other examples of ironic narrative, note in particular the digression against Justus (*Vit.* 336–67). There, having flaunted his ability to persuade others of things that were untrue, and after citing the testimony of King Agrippa II as proof of his veracity in the *War* (*Vit.* 361–66), Josephus suddenly shows an awareness that he too might be seen as a victim of irony. What if Agrippa's praise was only an example of the same diplomatic dissembling? Apparently, Justus had not raised this possibility, for Josephus indignantly anticipates it with these words (*Vit.* 367): 'He [Agrippa II] was not flattering my finished history with "truth", for that would not have occurred to him; nor was he being ironic (οὐδὲ εἰρωνευόμενος), *as you will claim,* for he was beyond such bad character.' No other line in Josephus' entire corpus is so revealing of his self-consciousness in creating ironic worlds: he has no ultimate defence against the charge that his own supporters have misled him, just as he has misled others. It is not, after all, the practice of deception that matters, but the character of the deceivers.

Audience-Dependent Irony

Alongside the pervasive narrative irony of the *Life,* one must ask whether Josephus' brief Roman episodes at the beginning and end of the narrative appeal to a Roman audience's extra-textual knowledge—in much the same way as the Roman material of *AJ* 18–19. At least one episode appears to do so. In the story of his mission to Rome as a young man, to secure the release of some noble colleagues being held by Nero, our author seems to rely upon audience knowledge and also sentiments (*Vit.* 16):

> After we had come safely to Dicaearcheia, which the Italians call Puteoli, through a friendship I met Aliturus: this man was a mime-actor (μιμόλογος), for Nero an obsession (μάλιστα τῷ Νέρωνι καταθύμιος) and a Judaean by ancestry. Through him I became known to Poppaea, the wife of Caesar, and then very quickly arranged things, appealing to her to free the priests. Having succeeded, with enormous gifts from Poppaea in addition to this benefit, I returned home.

Josephus courageously travels to Rome to secure the release of noble friends unjustly held by Nero. But how was a young Judaean to make his way in the world capital, to reach even the emperor? According to him he did not actually need to see the emperor: he had only to persuade a showman whom Nero fancied, who helped him reach the emperor's wife, and the deed was done. In other words, at this point (63 or 64 CE) Nero's court was effectively run by actors and Poppaea.

I submit that a Roman elite audience would find particular enjoyment in this little story. In the late Republic and early Empire, show people had an ambiguous social position: loved by the masses, influential through their performances, hence a potential threat to autocratic rulers (Yavetz 1969:9–37); therefore occasionally exiled, but often seconded to the staffs of such monarchs (like astrologers); generally despised by aristocrats, however, as commoners of too great influence (Purcell 1999:181–93; Leppin 1992:135–55, 160–63; cf. Dio Chrys. 32.4). The 'bad' emperors were generally characterized by senatorial writers as dominated by their freedmen and women. If we throw uppity stage people into this mix, none was more vilified than Nero. Apparently fascinated by actors and acting, he sang and played the lyre, and insisted on joining (rigged) Greek competitions (Suet. *Ner.* 20–24; Dio Cass. 62.9). He bestowed large gifts on actors and athletes (Suet. *Galb.* 15) and was famously fond of a pantomime named Paris, who allegedly acquired considerable influence as a result (Tac. *Ann.* 13.20–22), but whom he later executed, reportedly from jealousy (Dio Cass. 62.18.1). Josephus appears to signal Nero's weakness for actors ironically when he describes Aliturus as μάλιστα τῷ Νέρωνι καταθύμιος (heart-throb or special obsession of Nero).

Given that Josephus has narrated events from the reigns of Tiberius, Claudius, and Gaius in ways that suggest critique of the current regime, we should ponder the illocutionary significance also of this Roman adventure. This is especially so because it appears that Nero was widely understood as an ironic cipher for Domitian, called by some the 'bald Nero' (Juv. 4.38; cf. Mart. 11.33; Syme 1983: 134; Bartsch 1994: 90–3). Domitian promoted several of Nero's advisers, including some who had been ignored by his father (Jones 1992: 51–4), though admittedly he also supported some associates of Nero's opposition, even marrying Corbulo's daughter (Jones 1992: 168–69). Juvenal claims that under Domitian, criticism of Nero's praetorian prefect Tigellinus was sure to bring an author's death (Juv. 1.155–71). In 86 CE Domitian established the quadrennial Capitoline Games, in Greek style, clearly modeled upon the now defunct Neronia (Jones 1992: 103). Further, the honour of the ordinary consulship for 96 was given to Manlius Valens, an aged 'relic' of Nero's reign (Syme 1983: 134; Dio 67.14.5). Most significant for our purposes, both Nero and Domitian had favourite actors named Paris (Suet. *Ner.* 54; *Dom.* 3; Dio Cass. 63.18.1). Both Parises were executed by their masters (in 67 and 87 CE, respectively), allegedly on charges related to jealousy (Dio Cass. 67.3.1; cf. Suet. *Dom.* 10).

When Domitian's 'terror' of late 93 began, among its first casualties were the relatives and friends of Nero's victim Thrasea Paetus (Syme 1983: 134). Domitian also executed Nero's secretary (*a libellis*) Epaphroditus for his role in that emperor's death, allegedly as a cautionary example to his own staff (Suet. *Dom.* 14.4). The younger Pliny seems to have this execution in mind when he contrasts Domitian's punishment of those who criticized Nero with Trajan's toleration of censure for past emperors; he cites Domitian's treatment of those who ended Nero's life (*Pan.* 53.4). In making his point he sarcastically denies that, having avenged Nero's death, Domitian would take criticisms of Nero, one so like himself (*de simillimo*), as personal opposition. Even if Pliny exaggerates Domitian's sensitivity to the Nero parallel in order to flatter Trajan, the execution of Epaphroditus might by itself constitute further evidence of the connection, especially if Suetonius' ambiguous language means that Domitian had also made Epaphroditus *his* secretary.

Bartsch convincingly argues (1994: 92–3, 245 n. 66, 277 n. 23) that Domitian's evident failure to punish all authors of hostile references to Nero (e.g., Mart. 4.63; 7.21, 34; Stat. *Silv.* 2.7.100, 118–19) need not indicate his lack of concern about the matter, for other emperors deliberately ignored provocative allusions in order to avoid giving them credence (1994: 82–90).

The question of possible parallels between Josephus' Aliturus and the two Parises is all the more intriguing because Aliturus has turned out to be such an elusive fellow. Not only did this putative favourite of Nero somehow escape the notice of every other extant commentator on Nero's reign, in contrast to Paris (e.g., Tac. *Ann.* 13.19–27; Suet. *Ner.* 54; Dio Cass. 62.18.1), but it has proven impossible to find even one other man, among the extensive material and literary remains of the Graeco-Roman world and Greek-language Judaism,[10] with the name Aliturus (or Ἁλίτυρος). Construed as a Greek word, the name would mean something like 'salt cheese', and it is difficult to imagine the circumstances under which one would acquire it. It is tempting to imagine that Josephus invented his *mimologos* in order to create a safe substitute for Nero's Paris, given the danger of Nero-Domitian parallels. If Josephus had met Paris, he would no doubt have wished to avoid using the name in Domitian's time—especially if he wanted to describe the man as Nero's heart-throb.

Nor is it difficult to speculate as to how he came up with Aliturus as an ironic alternative. It could simply be a made-up masculine name that sounded like *aliter* ('otherwise'), or it could have its full weight as future active participle of *alo* ('feed, nourish, support, sustain, maintain'), which is virtually identical with one of the three roots of *paris,* construed as a Latin verb in the second person singular (perfect subjunctive): *pasco.* The other possible roots are *paveo* (to be afraid, terrified, tremble with fear [perfect subjunctive]) and *pario* (give birth, spawn, produce [present indicative]). The Roman elite, who seem to have enjoyed puns on personal names (Corbeill 1996: 57–98), might have appreciated the effort of a foreign nobleman to find such a label for Nero's actor-friend. Of course, I have no way to render historically probable this solution to the problems connected with Aliturus. Even if Josephus did not invent Aliturus but really met a man with this name, it appears that he intends a degree of ironic humour in his telling of the episode, which does not seem necessary to the account.

In any case, the text-driven irony alone will suffice to show that in *Life* Josephus conjures up a Tacitean world of appearances detached from reality: everyone attempts to mislead everyone else for his own advancement. Josephus happily

[10] Examining Solin 1982, 1996; Fraser and Matthews 1987; Traill 1994; Osborne and Byrne 1996; Lozano Velilla 1998; Horbury and Noy 1992; Noy 1993, 1995.

participates in the game. The differences in his case are (a) that his dissembling was within the sphere of responsible statesmanship, unlike the attempts of his demagogic rivals, and (b) because he succeeded over his rivals, by virtue of sterling character and divine assistance, he was later able to transform his dissimulation into an ironically humorous narrative for an appreciative audience.

CONCLUSION

Ahl's programmatic essay includes this observation (1984: 182):

> The result of this difference of perspectives [between ancient readers attuned to figured speech and modern readers] has been, and continues to be, a radical misunderstanding of ancient authors who use figured speech extensively. Chief among the victims are authors of Quintilian's own day when the need for *schema*—in the sense that he, Zoilus, and Demetrius use the term—was high.

The foregoing essay will have succeeded if it has brought the most prolific (extant) Roman author of Quintilian's day, Titus Flavius Josephus, into view as a heavy user of figured speech and irony. It is in the *Life* that Josephus most vividly portrays himself as a master of oblique discourse, misdirection, and irony. But there is more than enough in the *War* and *Antiquities* to show that he was comfortable in the métier of ironic portraiture, playfully developing his very serious themes, all the way along. I hope to have shown that the stakes are high for understanding Josephus' narratives. There are implications too for the use of Josephus in historical reconstruction—a subject for another occasion (cf. Mason 2003 [chapter 4 in this volume]).

Chapter 4

Contradiction or Counterpoint? Josephus and Historical Method

Per Bilde's comprchensive 1988 study of Josephus included some startling observations. Nearly 1,900 years after the death of the famous Judean priest, who is unrivalled among ancient historians for the size of his citation index, Bilde could find little by way of an outline for Josephus's *magnum opus,* and nothing at all on its purpose: "In general, it is almost impossible to refer to any literature concerning Josephus's aim in *Ant.*"[1] Even in the case of the more famous *Judean War:* "To the best of my knowledge, no contribution to a discussion of the arrangement and plan of *Bell.* is to be found."[2] One deduces the same condition from Louis H. Feldman's detailed bibliographies published in the 1980s, whose hundreds of rubrics include no separate categories for the structures, aims, or audiences of Josephus's major compositions.[3] Reluctance to read Josephus with attention to such "introductory" questions has no doubt resulted from the preoccupations of his users, who have tended to seek out one-for-one correspondences between discrete passages in his works and external phenomena—theological, archaeological, historical.[4]

Much has changed in Josephan studies, or perhaps "Josephan studies" has only existed, since the 1980s. The narrative-centered approaches that Bilde perceived as new[5] have in the meantime assumed primacy. This rise in narrative interest is no random fluctuation: the Rengstorf/Schalit *Concordance* (1968–1983),[6]

---

[1] P. Bilde, *Josephus,* 102; cf. 92 on the outline question.

[2] Bilde, *Josephus,* 71. See also 118 on *Against Apion.*

[3] L. H. Feldman, *Josephus and Modern Scholarship (1937–1980)* (New York: de Gruyter, 1984); L. H. Feldman and H. Schreckenberg, *Josephus: A Supplementary Bibliography* (New York: Garland, 1986); L. H. Feldman and G. Hata, *Josephus, the Bible, and History* (Detroit: Wayne State University Press, 1989), 330–448. This is of course no criticism of Feldman, who was merely using appropriate categories for the published scholarship.

[4] See Bilde, *Josephus,* 126–41, on "the classical conception of Josephus."

[5] Programmatic studies, though not yet systematic efforts at composition criticism, were Helgo Lindner, *Die Geschichtsauffassung des Flavius Josephus im Bellum Judaicum* (Leiden: Brill, 1972); Harold W. Attridge, *The Interpretation of Biblical History in the Antiquitates Judaicae of Flavius Josephus* (Missoula: Scholars Press, 1976); and Feldman's many essays on biblical interpretation, largely reprised in his *Studies in Josephus' Rewritten Bible,* Supplements to JSJ 58. Leiden: Brill, 1998. An important precursor was André Pelletier, *Flavius Josèphe, Adapteur de la Lettre d'Aristée* (Paris: Klincksieck, 1962).

[6] K. H. Rengstorf, *A Complete Concordance to Flavius Josephus,* 4 vols. (Leiden: Brill, 1973–1983); A. Schalit, ed., *Namenwörterbuch zu Flavius Josephus* (Leiden: Brill, 1968).

Heinz Schreckenberg's text-critical and bibliographical studies,[7] Feldman's annotated bibliographies,[8] and a growing bank of digital tools[9] have finally provided the resources for systematic study of these complex multi-volume accounts. Since the early 1990s, in turn, international scholarly conferences, graduate seminars, dissertations, and collections of essays on Josephus have begun to proliferate. This comes after almost a century of near dormancy, when his literary biases were considered obvious and his narratives unworthy or insusceptible of detailed examination. Still, work within the new paradigm has been partial and tentative: we lack the larger synthetic interpretations missed by Bilde, and we have hardly begun to explore the rhetorical dimensions of Josephus's narratives, let alone more exotic literary possibilities. Yet the movement toward reading *Josephus through,* and not merely reading *through Josephus* to external realities, now provides the dominant agenda.

This growth in the Josephus industry has of course not pre-empted the ongoing use of his narratives for the reconstruction of ancient Judean realia. Whether or not historians of pre-70 Judea would describe themselves as "Josephus scholars," they necessarily rely to a large extent upon his accounts. It often appears, however, that interpreters of the narrative and historians preserve two solitudes. In this chapter I propose to bring the two interests into direct engagement. I do so with some trepidation, because in order to demonstrate the stakes I must consider cases, and since these cases have already attracted historical analysis I must take issue with others. I hope that the refutational side of this rhetoric will be read in the context of the constructive argument. My purpose is to show for Josephus what has often been demonstrated for other classical authors:[10] that literary concerns have direct consequences for the historical use of the text. It is at bottom a fundamental issue of method.

In general terms: we shall see that historical users of Josephus have often found in *narrative contradiction* the key to a less-varnished truth, or perhaps more reliable sources, behind his tendentious accounts. Yet identifying contradictions presupposes an adequate assessment of the narrative's shape, themes, and rhetorical dimensions. Historical work, alas, too often depends upon reductive appraisals of Josephus's literary tendencies, and thus, of what counts as contradiction. When this happens, our rigorously rebuilt reality may turn out to be little more than our imaginative riffs on his grace notes. To what extent are the alternative melodies that we think we have composed actually harmonies or contrapuntal themes borrowed from the master score?

---

[7] H. Schreckenberg, "Die Flavius-Josephus-Tradition in Antike und Mittelalter," ALGHJ 5 (Leiden: Brill, 1972); Schreckenberg, "Rezeptionsgeschichtliche und Textkritische Untersuchungen zu Flavius Josephus," ALGHJ 10 (Leiden: Brill, 1977).

[8] See n. 3.

[9] Notably the *Perseus Project* (http://www.perseus.tufts.edu/) and the *Thesaurus Linguae Graecae* (TLG) from the University of California at Irvine.

[10] See conveniently David S. Potter, *Literary Texts,* 20–78; Christopher Pelling, *Greek Historian,* 1–81.

Methodological Collisions—and Stand-Offs

I described the literary and historical analysis of Josephus as two solitudes, but the passing ships have occasionally collided. The figure who most regularly turned up at the scene of the collision was the late Horst Moehring of Brown University. In his essay for *ANRW*,[11] in his critique of Shaye Cohen's book, *Josephus in Galilee and Rome*,[12] and in Daniel Schwartz's reflections on "composition criticism" vis-à-vis Moehring,[13] we have, to switch metaphors, the makings of a methodological stare-down. The nature of this deadlock and some reasons for Moehring's role as *provocateur* are worth pondering by way of orientation to the problem.

Composition Criticism and Historical Reconstruction

Moehring's 1957 dissertation on "novelistic elements" in Josephus[14] took its departure from Martin Braun's 1934 study of novelistic writing in Greco-Oriental context.[15] Integrating Josephus's biblical paraphrase into this comparative field, Braun had determined that our author expertly refashioned his source material so as, in part, to produce novelistic-erotic effects. An example is the steamy episode of Joseph and Potiphar's wife, which Josephus entirely rewrites vis-à-vis Genesis with erotic overtones echoing the classical story of Phaedra and Hippolytus.[16] Josephus must be responsible for the novelistic reshaping, Braun had shown, because the language and themes that color this story show up throughout his writings. As Braun had seen presciently, Josephus's biblical paraphrase requires attention to his narrative art. Because his sources are more or less known there, we can observe him rewriting his material to make serious apologetic points but also to entertain.

Since Braun's time, incidentally, this basic conception of Josephus as true author has been illustrated a thousand-fold for the biblical paraphrase in *Antiquities*. Louis Feldman, Christopher Begg, Étienne Nodet, and others have shown Josephus regularly ironing out conflicts, dropping doublets and other inconvenient items, rearranging sequences, and weaving his thematic threads through the whole tapestry, even at the finest level of detail.[17] As soon as we abandon the

---

[11] Horst R. Moehring. "Joseph Ben Matthia and Flavius Josephus," *ANRW* 2.21.2:864–917 (New York: de Gruyter, 1984).

[12] Horst R. Moehring, "Review of Shaye D. J. Cohen, *Josephus in Galilee and Rome: His Vita and Development as a Historian* (Leiden: Brill, 1979)," *JJS* 32 (1980): 240–42.

[13] Schwartz, *Agrippa I.*

[14] Horst R. Moehring, "Novelistic Elements in the Writings of Flavius Josephus." PhD diss., University of Chicago, 1957.

[15] Martin Braun, *Griechischer Roman und Hellenistische Geschichtsschreibung* (Frankfurt: Klostermann, 1934). ET: *History and Romance in Graeco-Oriental Literature* (Oxford: Blackwell, 1938).

[16] Braun, *Romance* (see n. 15), 92–105.

[17] Already Braun's contemporary, B. Heller, "Grundzüge der Aggada des Flavius Josephus," *MGWJ* 80 (1936): 237–46; more recently T. W. Franxman, *Genesis and the Jewish*

hoary Destinon-Hölscher notion of large intermediate sources, whose authors had already done the heavy lifting for a Josephus imagined as inept *Redaktor*,[18] we must reckon with his traits as an author. Abundant and irrefragable evidence in the biblical paraphrase shows him to have been a careful and creative writer—there at least.

Although he did not know this wealth of confirmatory scholarship, of course, in his dissertation Moehring set out to determine whether such features as Braun had uncovered in the biblical paraphrase extended also to Josephus's Herodian and early first-century material in *War* 1–2 and *Antiquities* 14–18. He concluded that they did. For example, the emotional triangle of excessive love, jealousy, and suspicion characterizes a number of Josephus's entertaining stories, no matter what their source, where they fall in his narratives, or what assistants he may have employed while writing. The stories of jealous King Herod, libidinous Marc Antony, and Paulina the victim of seduction (*War* 1.438–440; *Ant.* 15.23–28; 18. 66–84) share similar motifs with episodes in the biblical paraphrase. The words and phrases of these passages are amply paralleled elsewhere in Josephus.[19] So they must all be his contribution. With this extra-biblical material in evidence, Moehring confidently concluded, "Josephus can justly be called the author, in the true sense of this term, of the works ascribed to him: even when he borrows and even when he uses assistants, he impresses his own personality upon his work."[20]

Because composition criticism cut its teeth on the biblical paraphrase, to a large extent it obviated historical questioning: few scholars would dream of pressing that narrative for its veracity. In extending his researches to the postbiblical period, however, Moehring had to face the controversial implications of his literary analysis for historical work. Recognizing the wholly crafted nature of the material he examined, he tended to view it as more or less free literary creation with no necessary connection to what really happened.[21]

About two decades after Moehring defended his dissertation at Chicago, Shaye Cohen submitted his to Columbia. Cohen tried to reconstruct Josephus's Galilean career by first examining the way in which *War* and *Antiquities–Life* are related to their sources, then surveying the relevant parts of *War* and *Life* to identify the literary tendencies of each, and finally using that knowledge to determine which text was closer to the facts in each case. One of his basic methodological criteria was bias: where an apologetic interest can be identified (for example, in his [alleged] claim of allegiance to the Pharisees), the datum in question is doubt-

---

Antiquities of Flavius Josephus (BibOr 35; Rome: Biblical Institute Press, 1979); Feldman, *Studies; Josephus's Interpretation of the Bible* (Berkeley: University of California Press, 1998), 3–220; Begg, *Account; Story;* É. Nodet, *La Bible de Josèphe* (Paris: Cerf, 1996).

[18] J. von Destinon, *Die Quellen des Flavius Josephus in der Jüd. Arch. Buch XII–XVII—Jüd. Kreig. Buch I* (Kiel: Lipsius, 1882), 19–39; Gustav Hölscher, "Josephus," *PWRE* 18 cols. 1966, 1981–83, 1992–93.

[19] E.g., Moehring, "Elements," 84–92, 142–43.

[20] Ibid., 145.

[21] Ibid., 64, 87, 144.

ful or spurious.[22] Space does not permit a survey of Cohen's many and nuanced historical conclusions here. In a review of the book that resulted from the dissertation, however, Moehring chastised him for having even tried to reconstruct Josephus's career from such narratives as *War* and *Life*. Rejecting what he described as a common but "naïve view that historians of the Greco-Roman age can be made to yield information that would allow us to reconstruct the 'historical facts' of Hellenistic Judaism . . . ," Moehring passed this verdict:

> Cohen seems to believe that it is actually possible to separate "fact" from "fiction." He fails to realize that every single sentence of Josephus is determined and colored by his aims and tendencies. . . . To assume that what Josephus added to the facts is fiction merely indicates a complete misunderstanding of Hellenistic historiography, including that of Josephus.[23]

In Moehring's own *ANRW* essay surveying Josephus on Jewish-Roman relations, which carried his composition-critical program yet further into what most consider the "historical" period, true to his word he pointedly eschewed "the actual historical development of this relationship," insisting again, "It is entirely useless to make any attempts to separate in Josephus any supposedly 'objective' passages from any supposedly 'subjective' interpretations."[24]

In his 1982 article on Masada, an apparently chastened, though possibly ironical Cohen concluded his survey of the literary sources with mere historical "conjectures." To this word he attached this revealing footnote: "Those who believe that ancient historians may study historiography but must not attempt to reconstruct historical events (like the reviewer [i.e., Moehring] in *JJS* 31 [1980], pp. 240–242), will prefer to admit ignorance."[25] So: a stand-off.

Recovering Sources through Narrative Contradiction

Daniel Schwartz offered a different kind of response to Moehring's position. He felt the need to justify a source-critical approach to the life of Agrippa I in a time (1990) when *kompositionskritische* study, most fully articulated by Moehring, had set the program. In pointed contrast to that method, Schwartz argued that in the latter volumes of *Antiquities* Josephus juxtaposes his sources with so little editorial intervention that "proper methods will allow him [the modern historian] to dissect the narrative, recreate Josephus's tabletop [i.e., his sources], and then ignore Josephus and do the job of historical reconstruction himself."[26]

---

22 Cohen, *Galilee and Rome,* 107, 144, 197.

23 Moehring, "Review of Cohen," 241.

24 Moehring, "Joseph ben Matthia," 868.

25 S. J. D. Cohen, "Masada: Literary Tradition, Archaeological Remains, and the Credibility of Josephus," *JJS* 33 (1982): 385–405.

26 Schwartz, *Agrippa I,* 2. Although he immediately retreats from the forcefulness of this image, on the ground that Josephus's interventions are not *utterly* insignificant, he maintains that this picture is basically sound.

The "proper methods" advocated here are, as Schwartz observes,[27] those of the older source criticism. Namely, the critic must be alert to perceived inconsistencies in the form of outright contradictions, editorial seams, doublets, parallel versions, and differential vocabulary, all of which betray sources not fully digested. This approach to Josephus had enjoyed nearly universal assent between 1870 and 1920, and continued to set the tone for decades afterward. For example, Heinrich Bloch (1879) had argued that, since Josephus in *Antiquities* has the tendency to disparage King Herod, passages in which he recognizes the king's virtue or piety must be vestiges of a pro-Herodian source (likely Nicolaus of Damascus).[28] Justus von Destinon (1882) insisted that Josephus could not reasonably be credited with the lists of high-priests that appear in the course of his narrative and (with some differences) in a final summary, so this interest must come from his sources.[29] Gustav Hölscher (1916) had likewise made inconsistency and contradiction the chief criteria for his thoroughgoing reassignment of Josephus's works to intermediate and ultimate sources:[30] Josephus could not have written anti-Pharisaic passages, for example, because he was a Pharisee.[31] Schwartz continues to support these criteria for identifying Josephus's sources.[32] Significant differences between his method and that of the older *Quellenforschung* are his emphatic denial that recognizing such an anthologizing technique should diminish Josephus's talents in our esteem[33] and his admission that he cannot identify sources with "mathematical precision." But then, since no historian can claim certainty, he allows, this is not a problem after all.[34]

Significantly for us, Schwartz positions his work in contrast to that of Moehring and Bilde by correlating their composition criticism with historical solip-

---

[27] Schwartz, *Agrippa I,* 3.

[28] H. Bloch, *Die Quellen des Flavius Josephus in seiner Archäologie* (Leipzig: Wiesbaden: M. Sändig, 1968), 112. But it is Josephus's practice throughout *Antiquities–Life* to present such balanced character portraits: *Ant.* 5.317; 8.211 (Solomon); 6.166, 344–350, 378 (Saul); 13.318–319 (Aristobulus); 13.380–383 (Aexander Jannaeus); 13.430–432 (Alexandra Salome); 19.208–209 (Gaius Caligula); *Life* 189–192 (Simon son of Gamaliel). Cf. Livy's balanced and sympathetic assessments of his characters (*Livy* [Foster, LCL 1: xxv]), Tacitus's explorations of his subjects's psychological make-ups and motives (R. Syme, *Tacitus* [Oxford: Clarendon, 1958] 1:138–165; Ronald Mellor, *Tacitus* [London: Routledge, 1993], 68–86), and the famously even-handed moral assessments of Plutarch's *Lives.* See also Feldman, *Interpretation,* 197–204, on Josephus's "psychologizing" tendency.

[29] Destinon, *Quellen,* 29–31. But Josephus has an abiding personal concern with the high-priestly succession: *Ant.* 16.187; *Life* 1–6; *Ag. Ap.* 1.30–36. Cf. Clemens Thoma, "The High Priesthood in the Judgment of Josephus," in *Josephus, the Bible, and History* (ed. Feldman and Hata), 196–215.

[30] Hölscher, "Josephus," cols. 1970–71.

[31] Hölscher, "Josephus," col. 1936. But it is not evident that he either was or wanted to be seen as a Pharisee; cf. Steve Mason "Was Josephus a Pharisee? A Re-Examination of Life 10–12," *JJS* 40 (1989), 31–45; more generally, *Flavius Josephus on the Pharisees: A Composition-Critical Study* (SPB 39; Leiden: Brill, 1991).

[32] See also Schwartz, "Josephus and Nicolaus on the Pharisees," *JSJ* 14 (1983), 157–71.

[33] Bloch, however, already insisted that Josephus combined his sources artfully, never as a mere "Compilator" (Bloch, *Quellen,* 7).

[34] Schwartz, *Agrippa I,* xiv.

sism and agnosticism: it is a "point of view which assumes that Josephus was an author, and that his work's prehistory is probably unrecoverable and in any event uninteresting."[35] He divides critics into a group that *cares* about history and one that does not: "The alternative [*sc.* to pursuing history through the recovery of sources] is not to do history at all, and, indeed, some Josephus scholars call for just that, claiming that Josephus should be used only as evidence for himself."[36] He describes these two methodological alternatives as matters of fashion and style: source-critical questions "went out of style, for various reasons," but "there are some indications that the pendulum of fashion might be swinging back."[37]

Although Schwartz properly challenges Moehring's implication that narrative criticism somehow precludes historical reconstruction, it is not clear that his study fully comes to terms with the more central claims of composition criticism. Adopting the standard source-critical criteria (above) for disambiguating sources, it begins by citing four contradictions between the story of Agrippa I in the *War* and the *Antiquities* parallel.[38] Without further ado Schwartz reasons, "These four contradictions, within the space of *BJ*'s brief narrative, *imply* that Josephus had two sources regarding this period."[39] The remainder of the book fleshes out these newly discovered sources, along with one other—a lost composition by Philo. Schwartz allows that he first became aware of the different sources for Agrippa when he observed the sudden switch from the Greek city name Dicaearcheia to the Latin Puteoli at *Antiquities* 18.160–161, where the switch accompanies a difference of perspective—from Cypros's to Agrippa's.[40] This difference of nomenclature for the Italian port comes up repeatedly in his argument.[41]

Particularly noteworthy is Schwartz's characterization of one source discovered by his analysis: a novelistic *Life of Agrippa*. He postulates that this imagined work had two distinctive motifs: the changing fortunes of the hero and the diminution of the divine role.[42] Thus, in passages credited to this source, Agrippa is not punished for transgression as characters typically are in *Antiquities* and as Agrippa is in the other sources for this period (e.g., Philo); rather, he appears as a victim of changing fortune. Schwartz draws parallels with the biblical portraits of Joseph, for sudden turns of fortune, and Esther, for the divine retreat from the story. The hypothetical *Life of Agrippa* was therefore a novelistic work based on the model of biblical figures who had succeeded in foreign courts.[43]

This analysis is curious, however, because it overlooks important features of Josephus's narrative. For example, the prologue to *Antiquities* highlights the trope "change of fortune(s) [or luck]" (τύχη, *Ant.* 1.6, 8, 13), a prominent theme

35 Ibid., xiii.
36 Ibid., xiv–xv.
37 Ibid., xiii–xiv.
38 Ibid., 3.
39 Ibid., 4; emphasis added.
40 Ibid., xv.
41 Ibid., 6–7, 50, 178.
42 Ibid., 33–35.
43 Ibid., 35.

of both this work (cf. *Ant.* 2.39; 11.56; 14.9, 97; 15.179) and the earlier *War* (e.g., 1.353, 374; 2.140, 357–387 [360]; 3.9, 354, 396; 5.367; 6.110, 127). No other source is needed to explain this. Further, it is a much-discussed feature of Josephus's biblical paraphrase that he diminishes the role of God.[44] The inexorable consequences of the Judean constitution, which punishes vice and rewards virtue (*Ant.* 1.14, 20), typically function without recourse to explicit divine intervention. Josephus emphasizes human motivations and expresses caution about miracles.[45] It seems that attention to the larger literary themes of Josephus's works has direct implications for the postulation of sources. Likewise, the theme of prospering in the courts of foreign rulers, which the young Agrippa embodies in his Roman sojourn and Schwartz attributes to the hypothetical biographical source, is quintessentially Josephan. The biblical Joseph and Daniel, who famously prospered on foreign soil, are—with Jeremiah—Josephus's best-loved models, crucial to his literary self-representation.[46] Schwartz, then, has not characterized the hallmarks of a source as much as the hand of Josephus himself. It is difficult to see how the resort to sources can be justified on such grounds.

Is the literary/historical impasse that Schwartz observes really a matter of taste, or is it question of method after all? The latter, surely. The older source criticism ground to a halt not merely because of changing fashion but because in 1920 Richard Laqueur demonstrated how arbitrary it was.[47] He did so by analyzing the different portraits of Josephus's career in *War* and *Life*. Since these portrayals diverge in many respects, and yet Josephus himself provided the fund for both, the contradictions cannot easily be attributed to different sources.[48] Laqueur applied this lesson to the Herodian sections of *War* and *Antiquities*, showing that here too the author's "coloring" (*Färbung*) of the narrative,[49] notwithstanding the possibility of new sources, accounted for the most important changes.[50]

In similar fashion, the contradictions that Schwartz finds between *War* and *Antiquities-Life* on Agrippa do not "imply" different sources because it is char-

---

[44] Feldman, *Studies*, 196; cf. G. E. Sterling, "The Invisible Presence: Josephus's Retelling of Ruth," in *Understanding Josephus: Seven Perspectives* (ed. Steve Mason; Sheffield: Sheffield Academic Press, 1998), 130.

[45] See Feldman, *Interpretation*, 205–14 ("Detheologizing").

[46] D. Daube, "Typology in Josephus," *JJS* 31 (1980): 26–36; Steve Mason, "Josephus, Daniel, and the Flavian House" in *Josephus and the History of the Greco-Roman Period: Essays in Memory of Morton Smith* (ed. F. Parente and J. Sievers; Leiden: Brill, 1994), 161–91; Feldman, *Interpretation*, 335, 629–31.

[47] Richard Laqueur, *Der jüdische Historiker Flavius Josephus: Ein biographischer Versuch auf neuer quellenkritischer Grundlage* (Darmstadt: Wissenschaftliche Buchgesellschaft, 1970). Laqueur saw the problem as discipline-wide, and his study as a corrective applicable to other ancient texts (p. 129). For the revolution in Livy studies, see T. J. Luce, *Livy: The Composition of His History* (Princeton: Princeton University Press, 1977), xv–xvii. A recent, witty statement on the general shift in studying classical texts is in J. Henderson, *Fighting for Rome: Poets and Caesars, History and Civil War* (Cambridge: Cambridge University Press, 1998), 21.

[48] Laqueur, *Historiker*, 6–128.

[49] Ibid., 168.

[50] Ibid., 128–230.

acteristic of Josephus, in keeping with ancient rhetorical practice,[51] to tell the same story differently on each new occasion. A pivotal episode in his Galilean career, for example, was the campaign of a delegation from Jerusalem to oust him from leadership. It is stunning how differently this story, which occupies about a third of the autobiography (*Life* 189–335), is reported there over against the *War* parallel. He names the four delegates differently and gives them different (mutually exclusive) familial and party relationships.[52] Indeed, the basic chronologies of the two narratives are incompatible.[53] Further, in the *Life* Josephus creates doublets before our eyes—of the very kind that source-critical method would attribute to distinct sources if Josephus were not obviously the author. *War*'s single Tiberian revolt (*War* 2.614–625) becomes two distinct episodes (*Life* 85–103, 271–308), apparently for literary reasons.[54] In other passages Josephus repeats himself almost verbatim (*Life* 373, 394).[55] Such awkward features of his own style are quite as dissonant as the contradictions that Schwartz adduces as evidence of source vestiges.

As for the distinction between Dicaearcheia and Puteoli at *Antiquities* 18.160–161, in his autobiography (*Life* 16) Josephus himself juxtaposes the two names. Since he writes from personal experience, it is not plausible to posit two sources there.[56] Elsewhere too, and commonly in *Antiquities* 18–19, he alternates the names of peoples and places, evidently for the sake of variety.[57] Why, then, should

---

[51] For example R. Cribiore, *Gymnastics of the Mind: Greek Education in Hellenistic and Roman Egypt* (Princeton: Princeton University Press, 2001), 238. Pelling (*Greek Historian,* 49–52 and works cited there) shows that Plutarch, Josephus's rough contemporary, made similar sorts of changes in stories told more than once.

[52] *War* 2.628: Joesdrus son of Nomicus, Ananias son of Sadok, Simon and Judas the sons of Jonathan, not himself a delegate, and therefore brothers. But *Life* 196–98. Jonathan leads the delegation, which contains no brothers and no Judas, but an Ananias, Jozar, and Simon of different family and party backgrounds (though Ananias and Jonathan are both Pharisees and laymen).

[53] *War:* (1) the Dabarittans' robbery through the Tarichaean revolt (*War* 2.595–613), (2) a single Tiberian revolt (2.614–625), (3) the delegation episode (2.626–629), and (4) the Tiberians' appeal to Agrippa II, prompting Josephus's illusory marine invasion (2.632–645). *Life:* a *first* Tiberian revolt (*Life* 85–103) precedes the Dabarittans' robbery and the Tarichaean revolt (*Life* 126–48), and the Tiberians' appeal to Agrippa prompting Josephus's fake naval assault (*Life* 155–174) occurs before the delegation episode (*Life* 189–335).

[54] Cohen, *Galilee and Rome,* 81–82, notices the doublet but remarks only that it prevents one from recovering the draft (ὑπόμνημα) that he thinks underlay *The Life.* For an argument about its role in the structure of *The Life,* see Steve Mason, *Life of Josephus: Translation and Commentary* (vol. 9 of *Flavius Josephus: Translation and Commentary;* ed. Steve Mason; Leiden: Brill, 2001), xxv–xxvi.

[55] Also noticed by Cohen, *Galilee and Rome,* 81.

[56] Schwartz, *Agrippa I,* 7 n. 8, acknowledges Josephus's own usage here, but does not appear to see the consequence that Josephus could juxtapose both terms, for at 178 he calls Dicaearcheia "Josephus's usual name for the city."

[57] Cf. Πάρθος (e.g., *Ant.*13.385, 18.96, 317, 325, 340, 355) and Παρθαῖος (e.g., 13.384; 18.98, 313, 318, 334, 339, 348) for Parthian; Περαῖος (*War* 2.59; *Ant.*17.276) and Περαΐτης (*War* 2.520, 566; 3.11) for Perean; Γαλααδίτης (*War* 1.89; *Ant.*7.230, 232, 272,

the shift at *Antiquities* 18.160–161 imply different sources? Finally, Schwartz does not explain why the very section of *Antiquities* he would like to assign to incompatible sources, books 17 to 19, exhibits an impressive, if bizarre (mock-Thucydidean), stylistic conformity.[58] This homogeneity renders it all the more difficult to conclude that Josephus preserved his sources on Agrippa I with such light editing that they are still excisable.

Schwartz is undoubtedly correct, in my view, that Josephus may have preserved a word or phrase here and there from his various sources.[59] My challenge concerns his use of perceived contradiction to attempt a more precise delineation, then characterization, of otherwise lost sources—reconstituting the eggs from which the cake was baked. It is an uncomfortable fact for the more ambitious varieties of source criticism[60] that Josephus has the authorial habit of repeating and contradicting himself, and of varying his terminology. These oddities call for analysis, but they may result from a variety of causes (e.g., sloppiness, rhetorical artifice, multiple editions, copyist's interventions, and yes, sources); they do not *ohne weiteres* imply incompatible sources.

The diverse perspectives of Moehring, Cohen, and Schwartz begin to create a map of the field in the 1980s and 90s. On one side is the position that the text is more or less opaque, blocking appreciable light on underlying realities. On the other side is the effort to wring historical facts or at least recoverable sources from Josephus on the basis of perceived inconsistencies. In spite of Moehring's apparent moratorium on history, historically minded scholars have continued undaunted in their quest to distill something reliable, which is to say non-Josephan, from his literary bequest.

We lack the space to review all of the strategies proposed for achieving this goal. In non-specialist literature (including NT studies and Roman history) one still often encounters the positivistic equation of "Josephus tells us that . . ." with "It happened thus." Even otherwise unimpeachably critical scholars have assumed

---

387) and Γαλαδηνός (*Ant.* 4.173; 5.254; 6.71, 72, 73) for Gileadite; Ἐσσαῖος (*War* 1.78, 213, 567; 3.11; *Ant.*13.311; 15.371; 17.346) and Ἐσσηνοί (*War* 2.119; 5.145; *Ant.*13.171–72; 13.298; 15.372; 18.18–22; *Life* 10–12) for Essene(s). In the case of "Parthian," at least, in the volumes under discussion by Schwartz, Josephus almost systematically alternates between the two forms. On the names for the Essenes in Josephus, see my "What Josephus Says About the Essenes in His *Judean War,*" part 1 [cited 6 October 2008]. Online: http://orion.mscc.huji.ac.il/orion/programs/Mason001.shtml.

[58] On the peculiar style of *Ant.* 17–19 see Thackeray, *The Man and the Historian,* 108–20; R. J. H. Shutt, *Studies in Josephus* (London: SPCK, 1961), 68–75; Rajak, *Historian,* 235. Schwartz ultimately concedes that he has not found a significant difference of style in his alleged sources (*Agrippa I,* 176). There, accordingly, he insists only that occasional vocabulary and much of the perspective of the source are preserved intact. This appears to me likely, but a problematic modification of his original project (above), for if Josephus rewrote his material in this Thucydidean style, then surely it is not possible to reach past Josephus to his sources.

[59] Ibid., 176.

[60] An extreme case is R. Bergmeier, *Die Essener-Berichte des Flavius Josephus: Quellenstudien zu den Essenertexten im Werk des jüdischen Historiographen* (Kampen: Kok Pharos, 1993).

the negative side of this logic: his silence about X means that "there is no evidence of X," and so X did not exist or happen.[61] Of course, many items in Josephus's narratives are partly paralleled in other texts, which provide some leverage;[62] others can be checked against archaeological finds.[63] Even where Josephus is our sole reporter, scholars have employed sociological models[64] and/or paradigms of Roman administrative practice as tests of his portraits.[65] The problem here is that he was under the inescapable rhetorical obligation of writing what his first audiences, who knew these political and social conditions far better than we, would consider plausible;[66] any challenge from us on this basis is therefore courageous. For the range of historical events to which Josephus offers our only access, scholarship tends to fall back upon perceived internal contradictions.

Narrative Contradiction and Historical Reality

Just as Schwartz expresses gratitude for such tensions in the belief that the sources they reveal will take us closer (than Josephus) to "what really happened,"[67] others have argued that Josephus's perceived contradictions preserve valuable

[61] E. P. Sanders and Lester L. Grabbe both argue from the alleged lack of "evidence" for Pharisees' activity between 6 and 66 C.E. that in that period the Pharisees were a small group lacking much influence. See Sanders, *Judaism, Practice and Belief, 63 BCE–66 CE* (Philadelphia: Trinity Press International, 1992), 386; Grabbe, *Judaism from Cyrus to Hadrian* (Minneapolis: Fortress, 1992), 2:470. But Josephus has very little to say about Judean affairs in this period.

[62] Even with two or more independent texts, we are not necessarily out of the woods—if the texts in question share similar biases and draw from the same rumour pool: cf. Tacitus, Pliny, and Suetonius on the first-century emperors and their women.

[63] M. Broshi ("The Credibility of Josephus," 379–84) proposes (p. 384): "Josephus' data are in many instances accurate, and that they stem from reliable sources." But his argument incidentally shows that the only textual data susceptible of such confirmation are more or less trivial scenic elements, and their accuracy says little about the truth of the *narratives*. A good historical novel could have its credibility proved in much the same way.

[64] See Rajak, *Historian*, 7–10, 104–43; R. A. Horsley and J. S. Hanson, *Bandits, Prophets, and Messiahs: Popular Movements at the Time of Jesus* (New York: Harper & Row, 1988), xviii–xxvi.

[65] Martin Goodman, *The Ruling Class of Judea: The Origins of the Jewish Revolt against Rome AD 66–70* (Cambridge: Cambridge University Press, 1987), relies heavily upon the standard Roman use of local elites as trusted collaborators to explain events in Judea. But his use of this model seems contradictory. Early in the book he argues that by about the year 50 C.E. the Romans had already lost confidence in the ability of the post-Herodian Judean aristocracy to win the trust of the populace, and were withdrawing their own trust (46–49). "Sixteen years or so before the revolt the Roman authorities already lost confidence in the ability of the Judean ruling class to fulfil its function" (49). If so, one might have expected the revolt to be the last straw, leading to the postwar dissolution of the Judean ruling class in Roman eyes. Goodman later insists, however, that *only* the heavy involvement of the ruling class itself in the revolt could explain the Romans's failure to reinstate the Jewish leaders after the war—in contrast to their general policy of supporting local elites (235–39).

[66] See Pelling, *Greek Historian*, 42.

[67] Schwartz, *Agrippa I*, xiv.

historical data. Indeed, alleged contradictions have become the basis for entire alternative histories of the causes and course of the Judean-Roman war of 66–73 C.E. Let us consider first the merits of the principle of contradiction, then some examples of its application to *War.*

Contradiction as Method

It is a broadly accepted principle in historical research that the investigator needs to tease out from sources what Marc Bloch famously called "unintentional evidence," which is "the evidence of witnesses in spite of themselves."[68] The underlying theory is that history is not a scissors-and-paste operation, rearranging the transmitted statements of sources, but an exercise of the critical imagination. The historian poses particular questions of the past, marshals relevant evidence and seeks to understand it *in situ,* tries to explain that evidence against a developing hypothesis, and ultimately seeks to persuade others who know the evidence. Given a literary source's inescapable shaping of the past according to both the author's conscious program and unconscious biases and language, the "ready-made statements" of sources can never be directly usable to the historian; they are not subject to immediate acceptance or rejection as simply true or false.[69] Rather, the statement has no historical value until the investigator can integrate it into her hypothesis, the theory of the case, in some way.

In R. G. Collingwood's example, even if someone should come forward and tell an investigator, "I killed John Doe," the investigator is not entitled to assume that statement as a fact, but must rather initiate her own critical assessment: "This person is telling me that he killed John Doe. *Why* is he telling me that?"[70] Until an investigation can show probable results based upon independent lines of evidence, the statement hangs there as an unsubstantiated claim. The historian's investigation may end up supporting much or part of a source's statement, but only *a posteriori.* Either to accept the source as valid until proven wrong or to reject it as untrue until proven correct would be equally misguided. We simply *do not know* until a convincing case is made with respect to particular questions.

Items in the source's statement that seem to contradict the author's deliberate point, however, or incidentally throw light on issues different from those being addressed, hold special promise for the investigator: they may not be as crafted as the author's considered statements about the issue at hand. This is just the sort of artless evidence that detectives look for, which then becomes grist for the cross-examination mill in trial. Accordingly, cross-examination, with its aim of exposing facts inconvenient to the witnesses, lies at the heart of the historical enterprise.[71] It is important to note, however, that such tensions

---

[68] M. Bloch, *Craft,* 61.

[69] Collingwood, *Idea,* 256–57.

[70] Ibid., 275.

[71] So already Thucydides 1.20–21; Polybius 1.15.6–11; 4.2.3. Cf. Bloch, *Craft,* 64; Collingwood, *Idea,* 25, 256–82.

within a source's statement normally come to light through questions prompted by a *second, independent line of evidence.*[72] It is the links between two or more independent sources, especially where incidental remarks in one enhance features of another, that lend force to a hypothesis.[73] If investigators have only one informant and no other testimony or material evidence, no matter what hunches they may entertain they will be unable to make their theory of the case probable before a critical jury. And this is the central problem for reconstructing much first-century Judean history: we are often dependent upon Josephus alone. The evidence of his narratives for any particular individual, group, or event is so refracted, slight, and isolated that it will permit a number of alternative explanations.

In the case of the Judean-Roman war, Martin Goodman and Jonathan Price are influential detective-historians. Their precise aims and arguments differ, but their methods and results overlap significantly. Both set out to write a new history of the war, Goodman focusing on the problem of origins, Price on the task of writing an "internal history of the war."[74] Both must depend exclusively upon Josephus for much of the reconstruction. Yet both agree against Josephus that the ruling class of Judea played a much larger role in the conflict than he allows. Most important for us, both arrive at this conclusion by giving the criterion of contradiction a fundamental role. Goodman will

> discover facts which I believe that he [Josephus] knew well but at which he preferred only to hint. . . . I shall rely heavily on Josephus's detailed narrative, attaching special significance to every snippet of information which appears to contradict the main thrust of his apologetic. There are *many such items,* and *their survival in such numbers confirms their reliability.*[75]

Similarly Price:

> A piece of information that contradicts any tendentious statement or motif can generally be trusted, for Josephus would have no reason to make up uncooperative details (assuming he did not intend to undermine his serious purposes).[76]

---

[72]For example, most scholars agree that Jesus' baptism by John is one of the few secure points in the life of the historical Jesus (see E. P. Sanders, *Jesus and Judaism* [Philadelphia: Fortress, 1985], 11, 191–92). They often emphasize that the story contradicts the gospel writers' effort to subordinate John. True, but the several lines of independent evidence for Jesus' baptism and for John's independent following seal the issue.

[73]For example, the accepted view that the Hasmonean revolt was precipitated by internal rivalries in high-priestly circles, not simply by an evil regime's forcing itself without cause upon the Judeans, as tradition has it. Those internal conflicts are an integral part of 2 Maccabees' theological explanation, but they are also revealed in 1 Maccabees (e.g., 1:11), which otherwise draws sharp lines between the "Israel" and the wicked Gentiles. Cf. D. J. Harrington, *The Maccabean Revolt: Anatomy of a Biblical Revolution* (Wilmington: Michael Glazier, 1988).

[74]J. J. Price, *Jerusalem under Siege: The Collapse of the Jewish State, 66–70 C.E.* (Leiden: Brill, 1992), xi.

[75]Goodman, *Ruling Class,* 20–21.

[76]Price, *Siege,* 186.

Price observes, "Thus we arrive at the conclusion [about aristocratic involvement in the war] contrary to Josephus's but best explaining his own evidence . . . ."[77] The underlying principles are familiar in the field: Heinrich Luther (1910) was followed by many in arguing that Josephus's actions—the facts (*die Tatsachen*)—refuted his *claims* about his own reluctant participation in the war.[78]

Goodman's assertion that unintentional evidence abounds in Josephus, and Price's implication that there is a sufficient amount of non-tendentious material for a subversive history, might create some initial unease. As with any other prized commodity, the value of unintentional evidence is directly proportional to its rarity. The logic of its usefulness requires that the author worked hard at making a coherent statement. If he did not care for consistency, or altogether failed to control his material, then he might have recklessly included all sorts of incoherent stuff, in which case "contradictory evidence" would have little meaning and less value. If we seem to be knee-deep in contradictions of the "main thrust of his apologetic," then perhaps we ought to consider whether we have adequately described that main thrust, also whether minor or contrapuntal thrusts properly count as contradictions, revealing vestigial evidence of the historically desirable kind.

The Basic Contradiction: Claims vs. "Recorded Actions"

Goodman and Price consider the essential contradiction in Josephus's *War* to be between his claims and the actions he reports. He frequently asserts, namely, that the Judean elite—priests, chief priests, principal men, notables, the powerful—opposed the war with Rome (e.g., *War* 2.316, 320, 410–411, 417, 422, 428). He declares that, following the governor Florus's reported massacre of some 3,600 Jerusalemites, "every priest and every minister of God (πᾶς ὑπερέτης τοῦ θεοῦ)" implored the people not to respond violently to this outrage, but to salute the governor's troops as he had demanded, in order to deprive him of any further provocation and so spare the temple (*War* 2.321). At the same time, Josephus mentions a number of nobles who were initially disinclined to oblige the priests (*War* 2.322). After further outrages committed by Florus, an alleged reckless youth named Eleazar, son of the High Priest Ananias and captain of the temple, persuades the officiating priests (τοὺς κατὰ τὴν λατρείαν λειτουργοῦντας)—presumably the very "ministers" who had earlier appealed for acquiescence—now to stop offering the sacrifice for foreigners, thus laying the foundation for revolt (*War* 2.408–410).

From there, things get messy. After a series of massacres of Judean communities in neighbouring cities and the Jerusalem rebels' remarkable defeat of the Syrian governor Cestius Gallus's Twelfth Legion, Josephus claims that many distinguished Judeans fled the city, while those who had defeated Cestius convinced

---

[77]Ibid., 33.

[78]Heinrich Luther, *Josephus und Justus von Tiberias: Ein Beitrag zur Geschichte des jüdischen Aufstandes* (Halle: Wischan & Burkhardt, 1910), 15.

the remaining Romanizers (ῥωμαϊζόντων), "either by force or by persuasion," to join the war effort (*War* 2.562). This radical militarization of a populace that finds itself under constant threat and humiliation, along with the silencing of voices that favor accommodation, is to be expected under such circumstances and has many parallels even in modern democracies. It is difficult or impossible, however, to identify the heart-felt beliefs of the players in such a crisis: Josephus himself, appointed general of the Galilee (*War* 2.568), was one; another was the chief priest Ananus II, joint supreme commander. Josephus has Ananus working with those who rejected accommodation with Rome (*War* 2.647–650), but strategically, like himself according to *Life* (17–22, 175–176)—still hoping to bring the populace around to a saner view (*War* 2.651; cf. 4.319–321).

In attempting to expose Josephus's contradictions, Price first proposes that his assertion that "the entire Jewish aristocracy" opposed the war is contradicted by information Josephus himself provides about aristocratic leaders (e.g., Eleazar son of Ananias, Ananus II, Jesus son of Gamalas) who helped lead the revolt. In the next paragraph, however, he concedes that Josephus has explained the aristocrats participation in the revolt: "This all makes a neat picture."[79] If we should be indulgent with Price's language about it "all" making a neat picture—as we should, in view of his earlier verdict that "this answer is partial and unsatisfactory"[80]—then perhaps we should be equally forgiving with respect to Josephus's exaggeration that "every" priest came out to appease Florus (*War* 2.321), and not charge him with a "patent untruth."[81]

Josephus does not exactly say that "the entire aristocracy" opposed the revolt; it is after all he who spells out the exceptions and qualifications (above). If he characterizes the priests, chief priests, nobles, or principal men as holding a common view, in opposition to the war, while also pointing out exceptions, this is only standard practice. Sallust writes an entire book about Catiline's aberrant behavior and opposition to "the Senate," while also allowing that he and many of his followers were senators (*Bell. Cat.* 16.4–17.6; 31.4–9; cf. 29.1–2). Similarly, in maintaining that the Judean elite, of which he was a part, opposed the war, Josephus does not contradict himself if he allows that some youthful aristocrats favored revolt, or if he claims that under those extenuating circumstances he and his peers also joined the war effort. It is only a question of how plausible the explanation is.

Against the fairly consistent explanation of the aristocrats' behavior that Price grants Josephus, he contends, "But as far as their recorded actions speak, they were devoted and energetic leaders who prepared the Jewish defense quite competently: they fortified Jerusalem . . . ."[82] So also Goodman: "the historian's apologetic must be rejected in its entirety, for the revolutionary *actions* taken by many members of the ruling class are too well documented to deny."[83] (The

[79] Price, *Siege*, 187.
[80] Ibid., 32.
[81] Ibid., 33.
[82] Ibid., 32.
[83] Goodman, *Ruling Class*, 167.

documentation, note, is *in Josephus*.) For both scholars, Josephus's notices that many aristocrats remained in Jerusalem until near the end of the revolt most impressively "showed that these men were committed to fight on behalf of the independent Jewish state."[84] Goodman and Price thus apply the insight of personal ethics that "actions speak louder than words." Yet there are problems with such a historical-political application of this personal-moral maxim.[85]

First, the proposition that political leaders' public actions reveal their true viewpoints is dubious at best. Who would have imagined, on the basis of Marcus Aurelius's ongoing and brutal military campaigns, if these had been the only things known of him, that he could have penned the private *Meditations* or the affectionate and sensitive letters to his teacher Fronto? Are his actions a more reliable guide than his writings to his real thoughts? Under the Principate it appears that Roman senators routinely calculated both words and actions as necessary: only their private thoughts remained impenetrable—or so they hoped.[86]

Modern politicians regularly demonstrate the need to speak *and* behave in the way that their constituents demand, against understood penalties ranging from ouster to assassination.[87] In a recent interview with American media, Saudi Prince Bandar bin Sultan reflected:

> My family has been in a leadership position (*sic*) since 1747. Now, you can call us many things, but politically stupid we are not. And we make our decisions based on one simple fact. Does it sound good [in] downtown Riyadh or not? . . . We are constantly keeping our thumb on the pulse of our people.[88]

The actions and speech of those in government are normally calculated to avoid domestic conflict in the first instance, not to reveal their deepest convictions. In times of war, military officers often privately oppose their missions while performing their duties with energy and ostensible commitment.[89]

We have valuable insight as to how members of ancient aristocracies saw their roles under Roman hegemony in the *Advice to Public Figures* by Josephus's contemporary Plutarch. Plutarch's essay shows that the prime directive of the

[84] Goodman, *Ruling Class*, 168; cf. Price, *Siege*, 32.

[85] In essential agreement with what follows, but with some different assumptions: Rajak, *Historian*, 78–173, esp. 128–36.

[86] See Rudich, *Political Dissidence*; idem., *Dissidence and Literature*; Bartsch, *Actors*.

[87] Consider the assassinations of Egyptian President Anwar Sadat and Israeli Prime Minister Yitzhak Rabin, and the reflection of Yasser Arafat (CNN World Report interview, November 12, 2000) that if he had accepted Prime Minister Barak's offer at Camp David 2000, he would be "drinking coffee with Rabin."

[88] "Interview, Bandar bin Sultan," *PBS Frontline* (September 2001): http://www.pbs.org/wgbh/pages/frontline/shows/terrorism/interviews/bandar.html. For other examples, see E. L. Rogan, "Jordan and 1948: The Persistence of an Official History," in *The War for Palestine: Rewriting the History of 1948* (ed. E. L. Rogan and A. Shlaim; Cambridge: Cambridge University Press, 2001), 104–24.

[89] Examples abound in Vietnam and the Balkan conflicts; the best documented example may be Admiral Wilhelm Canaris, head of German military intelligence during most of World War II.

local elites, to keep the masses quiescent, was widely understood. The statesman, Plutarch says, must not impose his views on the mob, but rather take time to study the people and learn their desires, so that he can win their trust while *gradually* steering them to a better course (*Prae. ger. reip.* [*Mor.*] 799b–801c). Further, given that the masses will inevitably dislike politicians and ignorantly oppose policies that work for their welfare, leaders must often resort to clever schemes and duplicity (*Prae. ger. reip.* [*Mor.*] 813a–c): "there are many unprofitable measures which the statesman cannot avert by direct means, but he must use some sort of roundabout and circuitous methods" (δεῖ τινὸς ἁμωσγέπως καμπῆς καὶ περιαγωγῆς; *Prae. ger. reip.* [*Mor.*] 818f). In this model, the worthy goal of ruling nobly, according to virtues grasped only by the elite, justifies almost any manipulation of popular sentiment. Another of Josephus's contemporaries recommends the philosopher's life because he assumes that anyone seeking office *must* pander to the masses (Dio Chrysostom, *1 Glor.* 66). A certain amount of "contradiction" will therefore be apparent to critical observers of almost any politician's career, other than that of a tyrant.

These assumptions are the very ones with which Josephus claims to have operated, and which he expected his audience to appreciate. In *Life* he presents his Galilean career as if it were a systematic application of Plutarch's prescriptions. Since he deliberately portrays the ultimately unsuccessful efforts of his class to maintain the popular trust (e.g., *War* 2.417–429; *Life* 17–22), and since he provides a narrative in support—he and his peers aggressively fortified sites, trained armies, and gave battle to the Romans as required—such "recorded actions" of the aristocrats do not furnish *contradictory* evidence, running counter to his agenda. They are an integral part of his agenda, of what Josephus wants to say. He boasts of his ability—I am neither accepting nor rejecting his account here—to deceive the masses in order to govern wisely and (for a time) save the pitiable mob from their dangerous wishes.[90] Since he eagerly retails his more belligerent actions in support of this programmatic duplicity, they seem to have no probative value *qua* contradictory historical data. Price contends that the Judean elite's activities "far exceeded what was required for mere pretense."[91] I am not sure where the threshold for "mere" pretense lies, but propose that it is the pretenders who have the motive to maintain their façade most energetically; within Josephus's narrative world, the vigor of the pretense is determined by the stakes (cf. *Life* 22, 175).

Thus, even if we had *recorded* actions of the Judean leaders, it would be impossible to determine from them the personal views of the leaders, who are by definition in a position of compromise and public performance. We should not apply the earnest ideals of liberal democracies, and assume that public figures would not have involved themselves in causes to which they were opposed. And we do not after all have recorded actions, but only Josephus's narratives: multidimensional and many-layered, describing the complex human realities faced by

[90] So *Life* 22, 79, 128–132, 144–148, 175–178, 226–227.

[91] Price, *Siege,* 32.

the governing élite, which he expects his contemporaries to understand—whether or not the story happened as he describes it. To get behind these narratives by identifying supposed thematic contradictions is no simple matter.

Independent Evidence in the Life?

Before we turn to more specific examples of proposed narrative contradiction, we need to determine whether Josephus's two or three narratives (*War* and *Antiquities-Life*) should be considered a single account for historical purposes or independent lines of evidence. It is a crucial question because, if Josephus has preserved independent sources for the same episodes, then we shall be on much safer ground in building historical hypotheses. Marc Bloch again: "At the bottom of nearly all criticism there is a problem of comparison."[92] We have seen that Josephus rarely agrees with himself when he retells the stories of *War* in *Antiquities-Life*. This prompts us to ask whether the contradictions between these compositions entitle us to treat them as independent, to use one as evidence against the other. This would be the case if, as many scholars think, *Life* was written under the duress of another author's challenge and incorporated elements of that lost work.

The theory, worked out most fully by Luther in 1910[93] and since then the common opinion, shared by Goodman and Price,[94] is that Josephus wrote his autobiography mainly because of Justus of Tiberias. In the 90s Justus published a work that challenged Josephus's *War* on numerous points while also disparaging our author's character. He alleged Josephus to have been a rebel warlord who incited Justus's home city of Tiberias and perhaps all Galilee to revolt, who championed the Judean war in general and worked in alliance with the Galilean bandits, living in luxury as a tyrant. He pursued anti-Roman and anti-royal activities, took bribes, and raped women.[95] Since Josephus's "life" confines itself disproportionately to the period of his Galilean command, and includes an explicit response to Justus's attack (*Life* 336–367), scholars have supposed that this book was written chiefly as a defense against Justus. If so, then Justus's account may be partially reconstructed by a mirror-reading of *Life*—by asking, "What must he have said to elicit this response from Josephus?" To the extent that the content of the *Life* is determined by Justus's hidden hand, it might become quasi-independent testimony to the crucial early stages of the war.

Seductive though this response-theory is—I speak as one formerly charmed—it cannot bear scrutiny. The following considerations, some raised by others, are

---

[92] Bloch, *Craft*, 110.

[93] Luther, *Justus*.

[94] Goodman, *Ruling Class*, 156; Price, *Siege*, 65.

[95] So Luther, *Justus*, 65–82; H. Drexler, "Untersuchungen zu Josephus und zur Geschichte des jüdischen Aufstandes," *Klio* 19 (1925): 277–312, esp. 293–99; Abraham Schalit, "Josephus und Justus," *Klio* 26 (1933), 67–95; Tessa Rajak, "Justus of Tiberias," *CQ* 23 (1973): 345–68, esp. 354–58; Cohen, *Galilee and Rome*, 126–28; M. Vogel, "Vita 64–69, das Bilderverbot und die Galiläapolitik des Josephus," *JSJ* 30 (1999): 65, 72.

cumulatively fatal.[96] The *Life* does not defend Josephus's *War;* it contradicts *War* in almost every place where their stories overlap, and most of these contradictions cannot plausibly be traced to Justus's influence.[97] The structure of the little book gives no prominence to Justus, one of the less visible of Josephus's many adversaries. When Josephus does finally respond, near the end, his vague and sarcastic remarks presuppose an uncritical audience—not one that needed winning back from Justus's camp. In any case, since Josephus's reputation in Rome rested upon his former life as a Judean general, who had energetically fought against Rome (*War* 1.3; cf. Suetonius, *Vesp.* 5.6; Dio 65.1.4), he would have had nothing obvious to fear from a rival who exposed his anti-Roman activities a quarter-century earlier. Efforts to meet these objections with the argument that the kernel of the *Life* had been written much earlier, for different purposes, and that Josephus dusted it off and spliced in new material to meet Justus's challenge,[98] do not explain the stylistic and structural unity of the book.[99]

The *Life* presents itself not as a defense but mainly as a celebration of Josephus's character (*Ant.* 20.266–267; *Life* 430), illustrated by his pedigree as well as his military-political career, the latter of which seems to have occurred only in the period represented by the book. It is a cheerful and proud appendix to *Antiquities:* "about the author," so to speak. Much of what appear to modern scholars as shameful confessions forced by a rival account are presented rather as part of a deliberately ironic program, for which he expects the audience's admiration.[100]

Here is one example of the way in which the assumption that Justus's challenge lies behind the *Life* might lead us to misread the text's plain indicators. If Justus had criticized Josephus for being zealously anti-Roman in the war, and if the charge had stung Josephus, we might have expected him to downplay or disguise his military activities. This is indeed what Goodman finds there: "Josephus in the *Vita* tries to minimize his own operations against Roman forces in Galilee."[101]

But Cohen has aptly observed that the *Life* shows Josephus eager to claim credit as a general who fought the Romans.[102] The entire story takes place before Vespasian's arrival in Galilee, so that Josephus's military actions were at best skirmishes, and with royal (i.e., Agrippan) auxiliaries rather than Roman legions. Yet Josephus proudly dons the mantle of "general": even though his triumviral mission (*Life* 29) did not inevitably suggest this language, it is pervasive

[96] On the restricted scope of Justus's influence, see also Cohen, *Galilee and Rome,* 144–70, and Rajak, *Historian,* 154. On Josephus's primary concern with his own character, see Bilde, *Josephus,* 108–9; J. H. Neyrey, "Josephus's *Vita* and the Encomium: A Native Model of Personality," *JSJ* 25 (1994), 177–206.

[97] See ch. 3 in the present volume.

[98] E.g., Laqueur, *Historiker,* 121–22; Matthias Gelzer, "Die Vita des Josephos," *Hermes* 80 (1952): 88; Cohen, *Galilee and Rome,* 77.

[99] See Thackeray, *The Man and the Historian,* 18–9; Schalit, "Justus," 67–95; Mason, *Life of Josephus,* xxi–xxvii.

[100] See Mason, *Life of Josephus,* xxxiv–l.

[101] Goodman, *Ruling Class,* 168; cf. Drexler, "Untersuchungen," 302.

[102] Cohen, *Galilee and Rome,* 151–52.

in the *Life*.[103] He seems to exaggerate his military achievements, most noticeably in *Life* 187–188, where he lists his numerous fortifications, which are not wholly supported by the narrative, and in *Life* 82, where he mentions a list of alleged conquests in which he did not exercise his conqueror's right to retribution—though again, the number of those conquests appears inflated against his own narrative.[104]

Even particular military engagements appear inflated. Although he says that the decurion Aebutius refused to confront him out of fear (*Life* 119–120), nothing in the narrative indicates that Aebutius even registered Josephus's presence in the area, let alone that he was gripped by fear. Likewise our general vaunts his success in checking Neapolitanus the prefect, without troubling to explain what this "prevention" consisted in (*Life* 121). He asserts, without providing evidence and against antecedent plausibility, that the Roman tribune Placidus was intimidated by his mere presence in a town 7.5 miles away (*Life* 213–214). And the account of his defeat of Agrippa's commander Sulla (*Life* 399–406) is almost comical for its avoidance of actual physical confrontation—he injured his wrist while falling from his horse—and its assertions about his opponent's fear. It seems difficult to maintain, then, that in the *Life* Josephus has the literary goal of *downplaying* his military encounters with Roman and royal forces, as one might expect if he were responding to Justus.

If my interpretation of *Life* as a free composition (i.e., not written under duress) is correct, this work does not offer any simpler or purer material for getting behind Josephus's presentation to the truth, but obfuscates matters yet further by overlaying newly invented claims upon his older literary creations in *War*. He carefully chooses what to include that will promote his virtues, without much regard for what he has already said in *War*.

Applying the Principle of Contradiction

Especially since research on half of his corpus—the biblical and early post-biblical paraphrase (*Ant.* 1–13)—has shown Josephus carefully managing his words and phrases, the proposition that in portraying the first century he began to leave in contradictory items because of his conscientiousness as a historian[105] carries a heavy burden of proof. A few examples will show that this burden is not easily borne.

High-Priestly Infighting (στάσις)

Goodman grounds his argument concerning the causes of the Judean revolt in putative incidental clues in Josephus that the rebellion was actually driven by

---

[103]He uses στρατηγός sixteen times, usually of himself; στρατήγημα, στρατηγία, and στρατηγέω five times each.

[104]See Mason, *Life of Josephus*, 67–68 nn. 441–46; 95–96 nn. 814–34.

[105]So Goodman, *Ruling Class*, 21.

elite, high-priestly factions who sought to establish their power in an independent Judean state. It is crucial for his thesis that this evidence be incidental, for if it were part of Josephus's crafted portrayal of the revolt then it would not provide the lever he seeks, to uncover what was *concealed* by Josephus. So he selects four "neglected" passages near the close of *Antiquities* (20.180–181, 197–203, 208–210, 213–214) that describe high-priestly misconduct. Each concerns an episode from the late 50s and early 60s concerning, respectively, the misbehavior of the new high priest Ishmael's men (*Ant.* 20.179–181); Ananus II's illegal execution of James and others (20.197–203); Ananias's capitulation to the *sicarii,* which resulted in the release of violent men from custody (20.208–210); and the fighting that broke out when King Agrippa II replaced Jesus son of Damnaeus with Jesus son of Gamaliel (Gamalas?) as high priest (20.213–214). None of these passages actually says anything about high-priestly factions in the context of the revolt against Rome; that link is supplied by Goodman (followed here by Price).[106] Proposing that these episodes of conflict in fact reveal deeper political alliances in chief-priestly circles, which Josephus conceals in *War* because he wishes "to exculpate his own class from blame for the revolt,"[107] Goodman tries to pry open a window on the various factions quests for power that allegedly ushered in the revolt.

For Goodman, this internal strife (στάσις) among the chief priests acquires historical importance not only because it contradicts Josephus's main purpose but also because it is mentioned "in passing": it does not reflect Josephus's own ideology or literary interpretation *because* it is not a biblical-Jewish category:

> The significance of this emphasis by Josephus on the dangers of social division lies precisely in the fact that unity is not one of the Old Testament virtues. . . . . Josephus's adoption of it [the unity/conflict antithesis] in explaining his own society probably reflects, then, *not ideology but the actual state of affairs.*[108]

Goodman supports this remarkable conclusion with the observation that Tacitus (*Hist.* 5.12) was independently "astonished" to see internal strife among the Judeans just at the point when they were under dire threat. He uses this supposedly non-ideological evidence in Josephus in support of his thesis: though Josephus suppressed it in *War,* he knew that chief-priestly factions were behind the revolt.

In trying to argue the incidental character of the στάσις motif and the high-priestly power struggles, Goodman begins on a shaky foundation. As others have shown, the στάσις theme constitutes the principal thesis of *War,* announced in the prologue (*War* 1.9–10; cf. 1.25, 27, 31, 67, 88, 142; 2.418, 419, 434, etc): Jerusalem owed its destruction to domestic strife (στάσις οἰκεία) led by those seeking power for themselves (τύραννοι). The theme assumes a prominent place also in *Antiquities–Life* (e.g., *Ant.* 1.117, 164; 4.12–13, 140; 13.291, 299; 18.8; *Life* 17, 134).[109]

---

[106] Price, *Siege,* 29.

[107] Goodman, *Ruling Class,* 20.

[108] Goodman, *Ruling Class,* 19–20, emphasis added.

[109] Rajak, *Historian* 91–4; Feldman, *Interpretation,* 140–48; Gottfried Mader, *Politics,* 55–103.

That Josephus goes to such great lengths to describe the "unprecedented" sedition (στάσις) perpetrated by Korah and his followers (*Ant.* 4.12–59), and that he employs the theme so programmatically in his autobiography (e.g., *Life* 17, 87, 264, 424), suffice to show that this language was an essential component of the world of discourse he expected to share with his audience, not simply a factual characterization of observed phenomena in Judea.

Before Josephus, Greek and Latin authors had often explored the phenomenon and language of civil war.[110] From Cicero (*Cat.* I–IV), Sallust, and Caesar to Lucan, Tacitus (*Hist.* 1–5), and Appian, the horror of civil war (*bellum civile*) was arguably the most familiar topic in the Roman repertoire (cf. Virgil, *Aen.* 1.124–156). This painful legacy had hardly been ended by Augustus's peace, alas, but overtook the city yet again in the dreadful year of the four emperors (69 C.E.), which happened to coincide with the recent Judean civil war that is Josephus's theme.[111] Given the recent history of Rome, the prominence of the unity/disunity theme in Roman authors,[112] and Josephus's concern to link the Judean civil war with the recent Roman one (e.g., *War* 1.4; 4.496), it is unlikely that either Tacitus, principal historian of 69 C.E. (cf. *Hist.* 1.2),[113] or Josephus merely reported what he saw, "astonished," without trafficking in the semantics of civil war. We cannot grant this language special status as if it were incidental to (much less contradictory of) Josephus's literary aims.

As for the *high-priestly* infighting, this too is a set piece of the *Antiquities* narrative. The high priesthood is a core concern in Josephus's *magnum opus*[114] as the guarantor of the aristocratic constitution established by Moses (*Ant.* 1.5, 10, 13, 15; 4.45, 184, etc.; 20.229, 251, 261; cf. *Ag. Ap.* 2.287—reflecting on *Antiquities*). Ac-

[110]The *locus classicus* is Thucydides 3.82–84, but see also Herodotus (*Hist.* 1.59.3, 60.2, 150.1; 3.82.3; 5.28.1; 6.109.5); Isocrates, *Paneg.* 4.79, 114, 174; Plato, *Leg.* 1.628C, 629C–D; *Resp.* 4.470B; Aristotle, *Ath. Pol.* 5.2–3; 13.1; *Pol.* 1265B; Diodorus Siculus 9.11.1; 11.72.2, 76.6, 86.3, 87.5; Plutarch, *Mor.* 813a, 823f–825b; Dio Chrysostom, *1 Regn.* 1.82; Pausanias, *Descr.* 3.2.7; 4.18.3. See H.-J. Gehrke, *Stasis: Untersuchungen zu den inneren Kriegen in den griechischen Staaten des 5. und 4. Jahrhunderts v. Chr* (Munich: C. H. Beck, 1985); A. W. Lintott, *Violence, Civil Strife and Revolution in the Classical City, 750–330 BC* (London: Croom Helm, 1982); "Civil Strife and Human Nature in Thucydides" in *Literary Responses to Civil Discord* (ed. J. H. Molyneux; Nottingham: University of Nottingham, 1993), 25–32; J. J. Price, *Thucydides and Internal War.*

[111]Josephus himself draws the parallels between Rome and Judea: *War* 1.4–5, 23–24; 4.486–503. From the vast literature concerning the impact of the "civil war period" on Rome, I cite only R. Syme, *The Roman Revolution* (Oxford: Oxford University Press, 1939), 440–524; P. Zanker, *The Power of Images in the Age of Augustus* (Ann Arbor: University of Michigan, 1988); E. S. Gruen, *The Last Generation of the Roman Republic* (Berkeley: University of California Press, 1995), 405–97; K. Galinsky, *Augustan Culture: An Interpretive Introduction* (Princeton: Princeton University Press, 1996); J. Henderson, *Fighting for Rome;* M. B. Roller, *Constructing Autocracy: Aristocrats and Emperors in Julio-Claudian Rome* (Princeton: Princeton University Press, 2001), 17–63.

[112]Some Romans reflected, for example, that their own internal dissension had been responsible for famous defeats (Livy 4.31.2–5; 5.6.11–27).

[113]See Keitel, "Principate," 306–25.

[114]See Thoma, "High Priesthood."

cording to Josephus, however, power struggles within the upper priesthood began as soon as the institution of high priest was created—with Korah, who challenged Aaron (*Ant.* 4.12–59). The struggles continued with the meddling Abiathar, who was removed in favor of Zadok (*Ant.* 8.9–10), with the notorious trio Onias, Jason, and Menelaus (*Ant.* 12.154–236), then with Hyrcanus II and Aristobulus II (14.4–32), whence they have persevered into Josephus's own time. Moreover, he frequently (as he points out) retells the story of the historic high-priestly schism that resulted in the construction of a rival temple in Egypt (*Ant.* 20.236–237; cf. *War* 1.33; 7.422–432; *Ant.* 12.387–388; 13.62–73, 285). So although one might imagine that it was contrary to the "main thrust" of an ideal, harmonious, temple-based portrait to keep discussing high-priestly rivalries, Josephus develops the motif with some consistency. We have no option but to conclude that high-priestly infighting provides a counterpoint to his more prominent theme of the constitution's faithful preservation by the priesthood. This is not contradictory evidence. Although Josephus does not include specific divine punishment of these offenses, the book ends on the eve of Jerusalem's destruction (*Ant.* 20.223), and he points forward to the catastrophe, which *War* has already recounted in detail: "From that period especially, it fell to our city to become ill, with everything degenerating to the worst" (*Ant.* 20.214; cf. 166, 218). This was for him the consummate punishment.

It seems arbitrary, then, to excise only these latest high-priestly offenses, in *Antiquities* 20, to assert that their presence contradicts Josephus's narrative aims, and then to leap from such specific incidents to incipient high-priestly factions eager to lead the fight against Rome. Rather, the high-priestly στάσις of *Antiquities* 20 fully supports larger narrative concerns about the efficacy and vicissitudes of the constitution, including the alternating theme of power struggles. This is not a buried historical treasure concerning the origins of the revolt, for the chief priests could have been the most cantankerous men imaginable without having had any desire to revolt from Rome.

Eleazar: Young Aristocratic Rebel

If there is for scholarship on the war an apparently solid historical wedge, seeming to run counter to the author's aims, it is Josephus's story of Eleazar, son of the former high-priest Ananias. In *War* 2.408–410, Josephus describes as "a foundation of the war" (πολέμου καταβολή) the action of this reckless young man (νεανίας θρασύτατος), who was temple supervisor (στρατηγός), and his priestly followers: they refused to accept any gift from a foreigner, and therefore—Josephus makes this connection—ended the customary daily sacrifice on behalf of Rome and the emperor.[115] Although they were admonished by "the chief priests and the notables," they stubbornly resisted. Josephus allows that many priests and others participated in this action, but attributes its success

[115] According to *Ag. Ap.* 2.77, it was the Judeans who supplied the sacrifices, and this seems implied also by *War* 2.197. Philo, *Leg.* 157, 317 claims that the emperor paid. The practice may have changed over time.

chiefly to the rebels' regard for Eleazar's position of leadership (ἀφορῶντες εἰς τὸν Ἐλεάζαρον στρατηγοῦντα). So the main ingredients of the story are that a prominent young member of the Judean nobility turns bad, by virtue of his prestige providing leadership for a larger body of priestly and non-priestly rebels (οἱ νεωτερίζοντες).

Goodman, Price, and others[116] argue that Josephus's identification of the chief priest Eleazar as a rebel contradicts his narrative aims. Supposing that his purpose is to absolve "the ruling class" or "the aristocracy" of blame for the revolt, they infer that the involvement of a high priest's son is something Josephus would have preferred not to divulge. He had enough of a conscience as a historian, however, that he had to let the unpleasant truth stand. Even still, his desire to limit the culpability of the ruling class is clear from his isolation of Eleazar as the solitary bad apple. This unwillingly-conceded story therefore becomes a precious window into historical reality: one can extrapolate from it an "Eleazar faction" suppressed by Josephus, and from there argue for the dedication of significant groups among the ruling class to the revolt, in spite of Josephus.[117]

A contextual reading, however, suggests that this historical construction, whatever other arguments may be adduced, lacks evidence that runs contrary to Josephus's narrative interests. In fact, the Eleazar story embodies many of his most characteristic devices. Thucydides and Polybius, two of his well-known models, already had much to say about "hot-headed youth" and the perennial conflict between generations.[118] This theme was also famously developed by Aristotle (*Rhet.* 2.12.3–16.1389a–b), for whom the chief characteristics of the young were raging desire (many variants of ἐπιθυμία), hot temper (θερμότης), impulsiveness, lack of self-control, gullibility, and susceptibility to false hope; "they are hot-blooded (διαθέρμοι) by nature." The image of the rash young man (*iuvenis ardens*)[119] was common in Roman literature, and that of the young aristocrat who tried to lead the populace in challenging the elite establishment was well-trodden turf.[120]

It is a narrative theme that Josephus appears to find compelling, for he resorts to it often as an explanation of almost any sort of rebellious or imprudent activity.[121] The motif is so archetypal that he presents it as a great virtue that he,

---

[116] Goodman, *Ruling Class,* 154–60; Price, *Siege,* 31–2, 186; Cohen, *Galilee and Rome,* 184–86; Drexler, "Untersuchungen," 278–81; Krieger, *Apologetik,* 222–26; J. S. McLaren, *Turbulent Times? Josephus and Scholarship on Judea in the First Century* (Sheffield: Sheffield Academic Press, 1998), 268–77, esp. 273.

[117] So Goodman, *Ruling Class,* 158–59.

[118] See Rajak, *Historian,* 93; Mader, *Politics,* 69–72, who note e.g. Thucydides 1.42.1, 72.1, 80.1; 2.8.1, 11.1, 20.2, 21.2; 6.18.6. For Polybius, see Eckstein, "Josephus and Polybius," 175–208 (esp. 192–4).

[119] Catullus, *Carmina* 62.21; Livy 1.46.2; Virgil, *Aen.* 6.5.

[120] Some obvious cases are Sulla, Marius, and Catiline; also the youthful Pompey and Octavian. See the thorough discussion in E. Eyben, *Restless Youth in Ancient Rome* (London: Routledge, 1993), 1–66.

[121] *War* 1.109, 117; 2.225, 286, 303, 595; 4.128, 133; *Ant.* 8.209; *Life* 12, 36, 80, 126–129. See Feldman, *Interpretation,* 111–12; Krieger, *Apologetik,* 207 ("ein Topos seiner Darstellung"), 222–26.

at age thirty, was able to overcome the normal rashness of his age (*Life* 80). But his self-control was rare. *Judean War* has Queen Alexandra keeping her younger son Aristobulus away from public life because of his hot-headedness (*War* 1.109), and the later rebels gaining many of their followers from the impulsive young (*War* 2.225, 286; 4.128; *Life* 126–129). It was youthful passion that led the young Israelites to cohabit with the Midianite women, forcing an early crisis in Judean identity (*Ant.* 4.131–144). Along with this assumption of youthful impulsiveness in Josephus goes the image of the bad seed: the youth who squanders the glory inherited from his fathers. The pattern appears as early as Adam's son Cain (Καις, *Ant.* 1.53), the fratricide, and recurs in the genealogies of kings and high priests.[122] In his account of the sedition (στάσις) led by the demagogic aristocrat Korah and his 250 *unnamed upper-class accomplices* (*Ant.* 4.14–59), in spite of his biblical source Josephus furnishes the culprit, like our Eleazar, with a distinguished ancestry (*Ant.* 4.14, 19, 26). This allows him both to introduce aristocratic competition into the mix and to evoke the bad-seed motif, which he later declares a general principle. At a pivotal moment in his narrative, he observes that the prophet Samuel's sons became clear exemplars of the rule that good and moderate parents often produce evil children, and vice versa (*Ant.* 6.33–34). Eleazar serves Josephus's rhetorical interests, and those of ancient audiences, admirably.

Finally, the pattern of singling out one individual such as Korah or Eleazar for moralistic appraisal is basic to both Roman historiography and Josephus's narrative art. Rhetoric traded in the praise and blame of individuals, and a rhetorically driven historiography was no different. Josephus's histories and those of his contemporaries often read as serial biographies, turning from one individual to the next as exempla of virtue or vice.[123] That Josephus named Eleazar in order to shield others from complicity in the revolt seems an unnecessarily specific explanation, given his general tendencies.

These considerations, along with the fact that the passage is dramatically told and freighted with Josephus's charged language,[124] render it unlikely that Eleazar's action was something he was forced by his historian's conscience to admit, against his preference as composer. Once again we have counterpoint, adding human depth and contrast to the main theme of aristocratic opposition to the war.

It would be ironic if Drexler and Krieger were correct in surmising that the historical Eleazar was not even that young—on the basis of *Antiquities* 20.208, which has him in the presumably senior position of temple captain (στρατηγός) already while Albinus was governor (62–64 C.E.).[125] Josephus's claims about Eleazar's youth may be as tendentious as anything else in the narrative.[126] Even if

[122] *Ant.* 5.339; 7.162; 9.185/205; 10.37; 13.300–301.

[123] Kraus and Woodman, *Latin Historians,* 88–97; Feldman, *Interpretation,* 74–5.

[124] For example, reckless youth (νεανίας θρασύτατος), cf. *War* 7.196; *Ant.* 16.67; *Life* 171, 220; a foundation of war (πολέμου καταβολή), cf. *War* 2.417; the pairing "chief priests and notables" (τῶν ἀρχιερέων καὶ τῶν γνωρίμων), *War* 2.240, 243, 301; revolutionaries (νεωτερίζοντες), some 30 times.

[125] Observed already by Drexler, "Untersuchungen," 278, and Krieger, *Apologetik,* 223.

[126] Goodman, *Ruling Class,* 171.

Eleazar was indeed still a "youth," given Josephus's interest in the themes of the bad seed and the rash youth he may well have inflated the man's historical role. What if (historically) it was only the later murder of his distinguished father Ananias by the rebel scion Menahem (*War* 2.433) that brought Eleazar into the conflict (2.433, 441), and his supporters' execution of Menahem and destruction of the Roman garrison that vaulted him to leadership of a rebel faction (2.443–560), but Josephus played up or created the earlier action in the temple out of hindsight, so as to include another moralizing rash-youth story?[127] It is entirely proper for historians to recognize the tendentiousness of Josephus's narratives, but what if there are no non-tendentious bits to save the day for us?

Let us take the case of Eleazar further. Having asserted the existence of an Eleazar faction that Josephus would have preferred to conceal, Goodman analyzes an earlier passage, before the introduction of Eleazar (*War* 2.301–304). There the "chief priests, nobles, and most eminent citizens" refuse to oblige Gessius Florus when he demands to know the identity of those who have mocked him by taking up a collection, after he seized seventeen talents from the temple treasury (*War* 2.293–295). In reply to the governor's demand, the leaders in the story insist upon the peaceful intentions of the people, imploring Florus to pardon the few offenders for the good of the many. They justify their plea by noting that any such large mob would include some who were reckless and foolish (θρασυτέρους . . . ἄφρονας) on account of their youth—again, the rash youth *topos* (*War* 2.303). Further, it was now practically impossible to find the culprits because everyone would deny involvement.

Observing that the leaders' claim to be unable to identify the culprits is disingenuous, an obvious failure to fulfill the obligation of the ruling class toward the Roman authorities (*viz.*, to maintain law and order), Goodman argues that the real cause of their reluctance must have been their desire to protect someone. Given the putative youth of the offenders, the ones protected must have been younger members of the ruling class, in particular those gathered around Eleazar son of Ananias. Eleazar's father and his father's friends would naturally have been concerned to shield them. Thus, it is not so much the elders in the story, but much more Josephus the author who works to conceal the involvement of aristocrats in revolutionary actions.

Yet this analysis faces insurmountable methodological objections. First, it is arbitrary to reject one part of Josephus's story—his own explanation of the context—while preserving another—Florus's search for his mockers—as if *that* were simply a fact requiring historical explanation, and then reasoning as to why the characters (in Josephus's story) really acted the way they did. This is like asking why, setting aside the context provided by Shakespeare, Romeo *really* killed him-

[127] This would resolve the "contradiction" between Eleazar's opposition to his father in the sacrifice story and utter devotion to him in avenging his death; it would also provide a psychologically compelling reason for him to have joined the revolt, and would explain his strong personal following. I am not advocating this hypothesis, but wish to stress how little we can know.

self. The whole account is crafted by Josephus, and it serves his narrative. The story humiliates Florus before the reader by displaying the cruel governor's personal weakness, vanity, and ineffectiveness, while contrasting the wisdom of the Judean chief priests and their associates. Rather than capitulating to the governor's impulsive demand for satisfaction, these distinguished Judean leaders appeal (unsuccessfully) to his better nature, affording him every opportunity to scale down the rising tensions that he has provoked. Cleverly invoking the commonplace of hot-headed youth, these literary characters wisely pretend ignorance of the perpetrators' identities.

Further, just as Josephus shows no hesitation in naming the bad seed Eleazar in the matter of rejecting foreign sacrifices, he will continue to chart this man's tragic course of rebellion, which will result in the murder of his own father and uncle by that lower-class interloper Menahem (*War* 4.225–245). Since Josephus appears determined to use Eleazar as an example of youthful folly and its consequences, it is hard to see why he would have tried to cover up his earlier involvement in the foolish humiliation of Florus if he had known of it.

Was Josephus a Wartime Partisan of Eleazar Son of Ananias?

A number of scholars have observed a contradiction between *War* and *Life* that they think proves Josephus himself to have been a partisan of Eleazar at one point. According to *Life* 17–21, soon after his return from Rome Josephus persistently engaged the would-be rebels of Jerusalem in dissuasive pleading, denouncing the folly of the incipient revolt. Seeing that his remonstrations put him in imminent danger, he withdrew into the inner temple as a secure place, since the fortress Antonia was already in rebel hands (*Life* 20). He did not come out again until it was relatively safe, when the rebel Menahem had been murdered (*Life* 21). The wrinkle, scholars observe, is that the *War* parallel (*War* 2.408–448, esp. 422–424) places the temple precincts to which Josephus retreated in the hands of Eleazar's partisans at this point, whereas Menahem's group held the Antonia and those aristocrats who opposed the war were confined to the upper city.

So, conflating the two stories, what was Josephus doing in the inner temple while it was under Eleazar's control? A common answer is that he accidentally reveals his own connection with Eleazar here.[128]

Yet this reasoning creates an absurdity: an author who vividly portrays his anti-rebel position in the *Life* describes himself as turning to the sacred temple's massive walls for protection from the rebels, but accidentally thereby reveals true and damaging evidence about his rebel past. If he knew that he had been a partisan of Eleazar and remembered the details, but was concerned to hide this allegiance, he should have chosen another site for his story of refuge from the rebels, or simply omitted the incident. He was under no obligation to say anything. If, on the other hand, he could not remember the facts or freely invented material

[128]Cohen, *Galilee and Rome*, 187, 194; Goodman, *Ruling Class*, 159; Price, *Siege*, 42–43 n. 130; Krieger, *Apologetik*, 227–29; Vogel, "Bilderverbot," 69–70.

without concern about contradiction, then the incident has no historical value. Josephus does not hint at any defensiveness about his past in this story and again, it is unclear why he should have been concerned about events twenty-five years earlier, given his present situation as a (well-ensconced) captured enemy general.

There are preferable explanations of the contradiction. To see their force we need to remember that *Life* almost always contradicts *War*, also that *Life*'s narrative operates according to its own rhetorical logic irrespective of *War* parallels. To read deep apologetic significance into this one detail, one would need to do the same with all the others, and that is not plausible. Better explanations are: (a) that Josephus forgot the detailed sequence thirty years after the fact, perhaps remembering—if *War* is correct—only that he had gone into the inner temple to confer with chief priests and other notables (so *War* 2.411–421) just *before* it was seized by the rebels (2.422), but incorrectly extending this stay until Menahem's death; or (b) although he more or less remembered the facts in proper sequence, they became cumbersome in the new context of the *Life*, where he was attempting a crisp one-sentence description of the plight shared by him and his upper-class colleagues. Since his Roman audience could not be expected to remember *War*'s minutiae or the topography of the temple precincts, he chooses the inner part of the world-famous fortress-sanctuary as a plausible safe retreat—untroubled, as always, that he is telescoping incidents. I do not know how to render either of these options probable, except that they have the support of Josephus's demonstrable freedom with his material.

Was Josephus a Wartime Partisan of Jesus Son of Gamaliel?

Although Goodman is among those who use *Life* 17–21 in this way, he finds Josephus's primary allegiance during the early revolt in the faction of the ex-high priest Jesus son of Gamaliel (Gamalas?), a principal partner in the war-time coalition led by Ananus II. Goodman argues that Jesus was one of the chief priests who sought power for himself in the imminent Jewish state, and so was a zealous rebel,[129] and then establishes Josephus's connection with Jesus from three textual data.

First, when John of Gischala's mission to the Jerusalem leaders is successful, according to *Life* 189–203, and the leaders empanel a delegation to remove Josephus dead or alive, Josephus learns of the move from his father via Jesus, "my friend and associate" (*Life* 204). In the *Life* narrative, this phrase has considerable significance. As in *War* Josephus has presented the Jerusalem leadership as fundamentally opposed to the revolt, and so as careful to place their own trusted men in positions of leadership, to manage it. Ananus, the leader of these men, first indignantly rejected the appeal of John's Pharisee friend Simon to move against Josephus, but eventually succumbed to Simon's bribes (*Life* 193–196). Though Jesus' role in the alleged bribery is not explained, he now makes an effort to let Josephus know what is coming.

[129] Goodman, *Ruling Class*, 139.

As for the phrase, "friend and associate" (φίλος καὶ συνήθης, matching the Latin pair *amicus* and *familiaris*), it is part of the stylized discourse of *Life*. Much of the movement in this story is propelled by such friendship bonds. The beneficial actions of the white knight Modius Aequus are explained on the basis that he was Philip son of Iacimus's "friend and associate" (*Life* 180). The Pharisee Simon son of Gamaliel caused serious trouble for Josephus in Jerusalem because he was John of Gischala's "friend and associate" (*Life* 192). Now, however, Josephus trumps John by having as "friend and associate" the even more eminent high priest Jesus, who alerts him to coming trouble. A signal proof of Josephus's character in *Life* is the way in which he treats his friends, or "friends and associates," those dependent upon his patronage. When Titus grants him anything he wishes from the rubble of Jerusalem, his main concern is for the freedom of his fifty "friends" and 190 "friends and associates" (*Life* 419; cf. 420). Given this context, it seems hazardous to follow Goodman's proposal that the phrase "friend and associate" at *Life* 204 *really*—inadvertently—exposes Josephus's membership in the rebel faction of Jesus. It seems arbitrary to excise this phrase, which appears deliberately chosen to stress that Josephus counted a high priest among his intimates, as historical code for a political alliance that Josephus would not wish to own.

As his second and third pieces of textual evidence for Josephus's membership in Jesus' rebel faction, Goodman adduces the eulogy at Jesus' death in *War* 4.322 and his failure to criticize Jesus for use of gang warfare, though he castigates the other chief priests, including Ananus, for their failings (*Ant.* 20.199–214).[130] This all seems confusing, however. The "eulogy" on Jesus at *War* 4.322 comprises fifteen Greek words—in the middle of the sublime praise of *Ananus*, killed at the same time. About Jesus Josephus says only, "though not comparable with Ananus, he stood far above the rest." This hardly betrays any special secret relationship. According to the narrative, Ananus and Jesus shared a noble vision of avoiding war if possible, managing it virtuously if not (*War* 2.647–651; 4.239–269, 319–325). Jesus was even accused of trying to betray the city to the Romans (*War* 4.245, 252). Nothing here inadvertently signals Josephus's affection for a former rebel-faction leader.

Goodman's reference to a "lack of specific criticism" of Jesus for his use of gang warfare is equally puzzling. Josephus relates how Jesus son of Damnaeus was removed from the high priesthood by Agrippa II and replaced by Jesus son of Gamaliel, a move that predictably (by this point in the narrative) sparked a conflict (στάσις) between the two. Their bands of followers hurled insults and stones at each other (*Ant.* 20.213). After noting that the royal descendants Costobar and Saul also used gangs to effect their will, Josephus concludes the paragraph (logically demarcated in the Loeb): "From that period especially, it fell to our city to become ill, with everything degenerating to the worst" (*Ant.* 20.214). Since this judgement evidently applies to all of the infighting just described, there seems no basis for exempting Jesus son of Gamaliel's followers, any more than one should exempt Jesus son of Damnaeus.

---

[130] Ibid., 165.

The Jerusalem Leaders and the Destruction of Images

A final piece of evidence often used to argue Josephus's rebel past is also revealing of the problems faced by anyone wishing to make historical deductions from his narrative alone. According to *Life* 65–69, at the outset of his Galilean administration Josephus summoned the principal men of Tiberias, including Justus of Tiberias:

> I started saying that I had been sent to them along with these men [his two colleagues] by the general assembly of the Jerusalemites, to persuade them that the house of Herod the tetrarch, which had been constructed containing animal forms (the laws forbid such construction), should be demolished. (*Life* 65)

Scholars have tended to take Josephus's statement at face value: this mission inadvertently reveals that both the Jerusalem council led by Ananus and Josephus himself, as the council's Galilean envoy, were anti-Roman and anti-royal zealots, committed to extirpating all symbols of foreign domination.[131] Josephus thus clumsily provided clear evidence in contradiction of his assertion that he and his peers opposed the revolt.

That apparently straightforward reading is, however, unlikely. The first clue is the opening phrase, "I started saying," which picks up the double game introduced at *Life* 22: "Given the clear and present danger to ourselves, we *said* that we concurred with their opinions." All the way through the text, Josephus and others *say* things that the reader knows well they do not believe.[132] In general, and in keeping with Plutarch's prescriptions for the statesman, Josephus tries to pacify the masses with his speech, telling them what he thinks they want to hear. In this particular case, the intended deceit is confirmed by the context: there is nothing in the preceding narrative to indicate that the Jerusalem leaders, who reportedly desire peace with Rome and King Agrippa (*Life* 21–23, 28–29), intended any such destruction of royal property.

Moreover, although he announces a directive to destroy the palace quickly, Josephus immediately departs for Upper Galilee (*Life* 67) without executing the supposed order. And when another man's followers proceed to burn and plunder the royal residence in his absence, Josephus becomes "furious" and quickly returns to rescue the plundered goods *for the king* (*Life* 68). Later in the story, similarly, Josephus will seize the goods plundered by the Dabarittan young men for surreptitious return to the king, while he fabricates a deliberate lie to cover this up (*Life* 130–131, 140–142).

Finally, whereas Josephus allows that he initially had trouble persuading the elite group around Julius Capella to agree to this action (*Life* 66), once the goods

---

[131] Luther, *Justus,* 17–8; Drexler, "Untersuchungen." 297–98; Goodman, *Ruling Class,* 218; Vogel, "Bilderverbot," 72–9; Price, *Siege,* 32, cites the episode as important evidence of the Jerusalem council's warlike agenda. Although he elsewhere allows (p. 67) that "this action is difficult to interpret," he treats it as a real action ordered by Jerusalem authorities.

[132] See *Life* 22, 39, 71, 128–130, 141, 263, 273–274, 282, 287–288, 291.

had been stolen he returned them precisely to *that group* for safe keeping (*Life* 69; cf. 295–296).

The basic point of this story, then, seems clear: it is the first of many demonstrations of Josephus's resourcefulness as general and statesman. He will use all manner of stratagems to lead the people effectively, and this appeal to the rebellious Tiberians' nationalistic-religious instincts is the only first example. Since that programmatic and consistent duplicity explains the episode, it is not plausibly read as contradicting his portrait, much less accidentally revealing his and the council's rebel intent in the Galilean campaign.

Getting Past Josephus?

Readers will recognize a family resemblance between my analysis here and that of James McLaren in his recent book on Josephus and historical method.[133] His basic principle is the pervasiveness of Josephus's bias, the inseparability of narrative and interpretation, and the consequent futility of protesting one's conceptual independence from Josephus while borrowing his material.[134] McLaren charts the ways in which even the most aggressively independent scholarly essays are, after all, dependent upon Josephus's conceptual framework,[135] and therefore insists on trying to understand Josephus's narratives *in situ* first, as an entirely distinct exercise from historical investigation, which the historian must control.[136] With all of this one should be in complete accord.[137]

Problems arise, however, in McLaren's execution of his proposals for historical reconstruction, the prospects for which remain fairly promising to him. To begin with, although he insists upon understanding Josephus contextually as a first step, his sketch of Josephus on first-century Judea conflates *War* and *Antiquities* as if they were of one piece. He justifies this by claiming that "to provide separate summaries would result in unnecessary repetition."[138] The difficulty is that Josephus *did* find some value in repeating the same stories in different ways, in keeping with the different structural and rhetorical contexts of each work. There seems no way around the interpreter's obligation to read each one in context.

According to McLaren, the way forward is for historians to take up individual case studies, relinquishing Josephus's causative-interpretative framework altogether and examining particular *incidents* according to their internal

---

[133] McLaren, *Times?*

[134] Ibid., 18, 67, 76–7, 200–1.

[135] Ibid., 179–218.

[136] Ibid., 21, 290.

[137] In quite the same spirit is Mason, *Pharisees,* 1–53. Although I charted a program of "composition-criticism," focused on Josephus's narratives only, as prolegomenon to future historical work, McLaren (p. 233 n. 4) presents me as doing this in order "to explain the significance of the various references [to the Pharisees] in relation to the historical situation." I did not attempt a historical investigation there.

[138] McLaren, *Times?* 21–22.

characteristics. By way of example, at the end of his book he identifies twenty-three such incidents (admittedly, in a "subjective and arbitrary" way)[139] from Josephus's narrative of 66 C.E. Then he chooses three of these for analysis, with the historian now ostensibly in control, ignoring Josephus's connections and alert to connections that Josephus does not make.[140] But what does it mean to analyze an "incident" without reference to Josephus's framework? What exactly is one analyzing? Evidently, one is still dealing with Josephus's narrative: "The narrative of Josephus can be used to explore the actual situation independent of the framework established by Josephus."[141] This seems to undercut McLaren's larger (and proper) position that framework and narrative are inseparable.

When McLaren comes to recover the concealed back-story of these case studies, now truly without any guidance from Josephus, he is understandably in the realm of speculation, left trying to convert a string of mere possibilities into a probability.[142] Given that we have a single narrative source for the events in question, there appears to be no way to render any such speculations historically probable. At the end of the day, and in spite of highlighting many crucial issues, McLaren has no alternative but to seek a way of transforming a single narrative into historical description.

Conclusion

My aim here has been to bring the burgeoning literary study of Josephus into direct engagement with the ongoing historical use of his writings. Although these two modes of scholarship usually operate in isolation, they are connected in a dialectical relationship, of which this essay has emphasized one side: from text to reconstruction. I have also narrowed the field (mainly) to problems concerning which Josephus is our sole source of information. This is not the place for a full discussion of historical method in ideal circumstances, where the investigator has independent lines of literary and material evidence (e.g., aspects of Herod's, Gaius's, or Tiberius's reigns, or Parthian royal succession) and constructs a hypothesis to explain the entire array. Where we have only Josephus's narrative, as we do for the key events and players of the Judean-Roman war, how may we reconstruct the events that lay behind it?

My conclusions are negative and positive. Negatively: where we have only one relevant narrative and no other evidence, we cannot hope to produce probable solutions to our historical questions, for at least three reasons. First, our questions are not those of Josephus. We do not ask (as historians) whether the fall of Jerusalem's temple meant the defeat of its patron deity, or whether the Judeans as a nation were faithful imperial citizens or hostile to humanity. We might ask

[139] Ibid., 261.
[140] Ibid., 264–88.
[141] Ibid., 286.
[142] Ibid., 281–82.

about the social and economic relations between Galilee and Jersualem or between villages and cities in Galilee, or about the outlook of Ananus II or Eleazar son of Ananias. In the service of his own questions, to be sure, Josephus occasionally comments upon such issues, but he does not ask *our* questions, and therefore does not marshal the evidence known to him (no doubt considerable) and argue methodically from it. It is as though he has chiseled out a sculpture of the image before him and we, lacking either the model he saw or the material he discarded, would try to represent the model better, sculpting a new figure from his; it cannot be done. Since he was the one who knew the evidence, but he chose not to ask or answer our questions, we have no recourse. His account will always be the best explanation of his evidence, until we have independent access to that lost material. This does not mean that he is right, but only that we cannot hope do better while his evidence remains lost to us.

Second, the consequence of this for historical argumentation is that, where Josephus's narrative is the only evidence to be explained, we have no way of making a hypothesis probable. Was Eleazar an important young aristocrat who headed a principled rebel faction, which embarrassed Josephus as he struggled to conceal it? Or was he a more esteemed fellow in his late thirties who entered the conflict when his distinguished father was murdered, and whose partisans led him to fill the power vacuum created by Menahem's death, but whose role Josephus magnified and back-dated in order to help with his literary tropes? Or was he something else entirely? With one complex narrative to test our hypotheses against, we can propose almost anything and find ways to explain the evidence; so large and diverse was Josephus's rhetorical storehouse. Our situation is not much different from that of the criminal investigator offered a piece of hearsay evidence[143] about a matter he was not pursuing, and for which there is neither physical evidence nor a second witness: nothing needs explaining but the statement itself. Our situation is worse, because we cannot interrogate Josephus.

Third, Josephus's shaping of his material is not limited to programmatic sections, such as prologue, speeches, asides, and epilogues, but affects his very words, phrases, and syntax. His language is largely about virtues and vices; piety toward the deity and justice toward humanity; chance, fate, and human will; "seeming" in contrast to "being"; pollution, punishment, and lament; traditional customs and laws over against innovations; notables, principal men, and chief priests facing revolutionaries, bandits, impostors, and zealots; civil war and its manifold evils. This world of discourse, his medium of communication with like-minded audiences of the late first century, has no independent existence. We have no way to transmogrify selected pieces of it into something more neutral, to decode it, disinfect it, or distill from it a residue of factual statements. That

[143] We should always remember that Josephus was not an eyewitness to most of what he reports: virtually any event in *Antiquities* (he did know customs that were observed in his day) and most of *War* (the first book and a half along with most of bk. 7 were beyond his time and place; for the events of bks. 4–6 he was a Roman prisoner with no direct access to events in Jerusalem).

would require magic or alchemy, not history. Though they are histories by ancient standards of genre, his narratives contain much of the dramatic, tragic, and poetic. It is not possible to detach even one item or case from "Josephus's framework," for that framework is pervasive and fully wrought, animating all of its constituent atoms.

Specifically, I have weighed the proposal that Josephus's internal contradictions are the key to uncovering the truth, or more reliable sources, behind his narratives. Examination suggests, however, that these too are part of the story's textured fabric. Josephus did not write simple stories laden with clumsy contradictions. His prologue to *War* claims that others were doing that, whereas he promises a balanced account that considers all sides of the picture (*War* 1.2, 7–9). Whether or not he has fairly characterized his rivals, he has in large measure achieved the balance he promised. He gives variety and depth to his compositions through management of plot and sub-plot, dominant and subordinate theme, exempla of vice as well as virtue, earnest pleading offset by rhetorical or novelistic tropes, recurring thesis and antithesis (cf. μέν . . . δέ), and scenes set in Judea, Galilee, Babylonia, and Rome. Josephus uses melody, harmony, and also counterpoint to craft compelling stories of human behavior. In the cases we have considered, proposed contradictions are part of the story, varying the theme while also strengthening it.

The upshot: we have no place to stand that affords traction for getting behind Josephus. We might prefer one hypothesis or another on the basis of taste. We might have strong impulses about particular passages: "Why would Josephus lie about this?" or "It seems like Josephus is not being straightforward here." But comparison of the overlapping material in *War* and *Life* should warn us against relying upon hunches, "inherent plausibility," or the appearance of duplicity as guides. Any effort to extract some strands from Josephus's tapestry while leaving others will seem more or less arbitrary to those with different tastes.[144]

Let me end on a more constructive note. Even where Josephus's narrative provides the only information we have, it may still be possible to do history if we can take a more expansive view of the project. First, on the principle that "the journey is the destination," we may construct hypotheses for heuristic purposes only, abandoning any claim to probability. The very process of constructing models that match parallel circumstances in other parts of the Roman empire or in later periods of civil war or in "failed states" can have some value in keeping

[144]For example, Price (*Siege,* 2) contends that "Jeremiah [Josephus's literary model for dealing with foreign domination] was remembered only after the disaster [of 70]." On 2–11, by contrast, he more or less accepts as historical Josephus's entire story of the build-up to war from 63 B.C.E.: Josephus's characterizations of Herod and the false prophet Theudas, the thorough corruption of Cumanus, and even the "seeds" (Josephus's language) of the later revolt. Yet the tables could as easily be turned. Reconstructing the causes of a catastrophe, in this case the build-up to the war, is a normal exercise after the fact. There seems no good reason, however, to assign Josephus's fairly sophisticated, structurally crucial use of Jeremianic and Danielic themes in *War* (cf. Lindner, *Geschichtsauffassung,* 33, 43, 53) to a notion "remembered" only after the war.

us aware of the range of *possibilities* underlying Josephus's artful stories. There is indeed "no harm in asking."

Second, we may shift our sights from the events *behind* Josephus's accounts to the compositions themselves as historical phenomena, produced in particular circumstances.[145] This refocus opens a fully historical, not merely literary, set of questions: How did Josephus publish his works? Who constituted his first audiences? Who were his patrons and friends? How were such narratives read in Flavian Rome? Even if many of these questions, too, do not admit of probable solutions, the last one at least offers the prospect of solid results. It is feasible to read the rich and copious narrative while bearing in mind questions about Josephus's audience: What does he assume about their knowledge and attitudes—toward him and Judean culture? What are the closest parallels in Greek and Roman literature, and how might his audience's knowledge of these parallels influence their understanding? Does Josephus employ irony, depending upon his audience's prior knowledge? What does he assume that they consider plausible? This kind of study is promising because we have a wide range of independent evidence concerning Flavian Rome, and some clues about publication and audiences. Most important, the abundant evidence of Josephus's narratives invites us to test them against various historical backgrounds. This too is valuable historical work, recovering in depth a real person in a concrete context.

[145] For a general formulation of these issues see Pelling, *Greek Historian*, 37–43.

Part II

JOSEPHUS AND JUDEA

Chapter 5

Jews, Judeans, Judaizing, Judaism: Problems of Categorization in Ancient History

An early review of *Flavius Josephus: Translation and Commentary* (Leiden, Brill, 2000–) took issue with my editorial decision to use "Judean" rather than "Jewish" for Ἰουδαϊκός in the titles of *War* and *Antiquities,* and with Louis Feldman's use of "Judeans" for Ἰουδαῖοι in the particular volume in question.[1] The reviewer fairly objected that this non-standard lexical choice, for an important issue, was insufficiently justified in the commentary.[2] She was right. Although I had supplied a footnote at the first use of "Judean" in the introductory essay,[3] the in-text citation format required notes to be few and brief. The following chapter is my effort to explore the problem more adequately. This is not for the sake of the commentary alone. I offer it also as a contribution to a fundamental question in historical research: the problem of appropriate categories. On each point, documentation could be multiplied; in view of this chapter's length I have tried to restrict annotation to what was necessary for the argument.

Given the theological context of some "Jew-Judean" debates, especially in relation to the Gospel of John,[4] let me stress at the beginning that my interests are historical and philological: to engage the mindset, values, and category formations of the ancients. How did *they* understand the phenomena their world presented to them, and what do *their* terms reveal about their values and assumptions?

---

[1] I wish to thank and indemnify John Barclay, Lincoln Blumell, Carl Ehrlich, Louis Feldman, Michael Helfield, Tommaso Leoni, Martin Lockshin, Hindy Najman, Stuart Parker, Sarah Pearce, James Rives, and Zuleika Rodgers, who have generously offered critical engagement with drafts of this long paper; Balbinder Singh, for a helpful discussion of Orientalism; the Social Sciences and Humanities Research Council of Canada, which continues to fund my research. I dedicate the essay to Professor E. S. Gruen on his retirement, a small token of gratitude for his magnificent scholarship on large questions and for his personal encouragement in countless ways.

[2] S. Pearce, "Review of *Flavius Josephus: Translation and Commentary* vol. 3" *JJS* 55 (2004): 169–70.

[3] L. H. Feldman, *Judean Antiquities 1–4* (vol. 3 of *Flavius Josephus: Translation and Commentary;* ed. S. Mason; Leiden: Brill, 2000), xiii.

[4] E.g., M. F. Lowe, "Who Were the ΙΟΥΔΑΙΟΙ?" *NovT* 18 (1976): 103–30; J. Ashton, "The Identity and Function of the Ἰ'ΟΥΔΑΙΟΙ in the Fourth Gospel," *NovT* 27 (1985), 40–75; R. A. Culpepper, "The Gospel of John and the Jews," *RevExp* 84 (1987): 273–88.

This is not to say that categories extrinsic to a culture under study are *eo ipso* inappropriate. If we wish to understand the assumptions and values of the ancients, we must take very seriously Herodotus's observation (2.184) that the difference in the thickness of Persian and Egyptian skulls was attributable to their different customs concerning head-covering; we would compare his remarks with similar analyses elsewhere. But if our interest is anthropological, in the facts of human skull sizes, we may not simply believe Herodotus as to the fact or its explanation. We would then need a method that was independent of ancient views, one that found its warrants in data available to us for analysis today. Such "etic" analysis[5] is valuable and necessary in social-scientific study: demographics, anthropology, economics, comparative ritual, diet, and linguistic traits—though people of the time knew nothing of the analyst's terms of reference. Just as a modern physician may inspect my colon, on the basis of scientific study of colonic behavior in general, caring only about what I might divulge concerning testable symptoms but otherwise caring nothing about my values, so a social-scientific historical inquiry may apply external questions and categories to ancient society. But in such externally driven analysis, valid criteria must be repeatable by all researchers ("objective" in that sense), logical, precise, verifiable, and falsifiable. The "emic" side of the historical project, by contrast—the quest after Dilthey's *Erlebnis* or Collingwood's "inside of events," the ancients' thought patterns, categories, and language[6]—requires our empathic entry into their own worlds of discourse. Although some may wish to argue that "Judaism" is a stable and verifiable category extrinsic to the ancients' language, that does not seem to be the assumption of most scholarship on this period. In any case, this chapter pertains to the emic exploration of categories used in studying ancient *Iudaea* and *Iudaei* / Ἰουδαῖοι.

My argument is that the crucial categories in this field, though usually invoked to explain what the ancients actually thought and felt, are neither emic (because they were not known then) nor yet etic (because they are not precise, observer-independent, publicly arguable, or falsifiable), and are therefore beyond the historian's reach. Using categories that were actually current in antiquity forces us to reorient our thinking about their world-views.

The past several decades have witnessed a profusion of synthetic studies of ancient Judaism: Palestinian, Galilean, Hellenistic, rabbinic, "intertestamental," early, middle (formerly "late"!), normative, common, diasporic Judaism—and for some, indeed, "Judaisms." The appropriate adjective, the number of the noun, the scope of diversity, problems of leadership and authority, the impact of 70/135 C.E. on Judaism, boundary issues ("Who was a Jew?"), and overlaps with a Christianity increasingly seen as diverse—including the problem of "the parting (or not) of the ways" between these two "religions"—have been promi-

[5]K. L. Pike, *Language in Relation to a Unified Theory of the Structure of Human Behavior.* Glendale: Summer Institute of Linguistics, 1954); M. Harris, "History and Significance of the Emic/Etic Distinction," *Annual Review of Anthropology* 5 (1976): 329–50.

[6]Collingwood, *Idea,* 213.

nent areas of debate.[7] Even a study as thoroughly revisionist in other respects as Seth Schwartz's recent *Imperialism and Judaism* is concerned with the nature of Judaism, indeed with "the core ideology of Judaism"—as if that were an emic category.[8]

It takes nothing away from the importance of these contributions in other respects to observe that no term equivalent to "Judaism" (much less "Judaisms") appears in the first two centuries B.C.E. and C.E. How could the ancients have expressed the same concept? Or did they recognize it at all? Is the distance between their terminology and ours so great that we should hesitate to use the term in describing Roman-era realities? Let us explore "Judaism," then, as an entrée to the closely related categories of "religion" and "Jews."

Searching for Ancient Judaism

We begin with some observable facts. First, no ancient Hebrew or Aramaic words map closely to our "Judaism." The *Yehudim* were known from the time of the Babylonian Exile (ca. 586–537 B.C.E.) as the people of *Yehudah,* or the region was known as their place, but there was no corresponding system of *Yahadut: Yehuda-ness* or *Yehuda-ism,* or Shaye Cohen's "Jewishness."[9] Second, the Greek and Latin words that appear to correspond, namely Ἰουδαϊσμός and *Iudaismus,* have a different and peculiar history. The Greek is used four times by one Jewish author in the unique situation of the 160s B.C.E., or by his epitomator some years later (in 2 Maccabees), and once by an author inspired by this work (in 4 Maccabees). It turns up again in *Ioudaios*-authored compositions only in two third-century C.E. inscriptions. The term does not appear at all in the large Greek-language corpora by Philo and Josephus, who both wrote extensively about *Ioudaioi* and their ways, *or in literature by any of their compatriots.* Greek and Latin authors mention the *Ioudaioi* and their laws or customs dozens of times, but it did not occur to them to invoke Ἰουδαϊσμός / *Iudaismus.* Why not? Third, though the apostle Paul and Ignatius had initiated Christian usage in narrowly restricted contexts, Christian writers from 200 to 500 C.E. *did* employ these terms liberally.

---

[7]Jacob Neusner's prodigious output specifying the contexts of rabbinic compositions and working out the historical implications of such analysis has set much of the current agenda. An accessible summary of some key points is in *Studying Classical Judaism: A Primer* (Louisville: Westminster John Knox, 1991). Among the most useful collections illustrating the range of perspectives are R. A. Kraft and G. W. E. Nickelsburg, eds., *Early Judaism and its Modern Interpreters* (Philadelphia: Fortress, 1986); Neusner's "Approaches to Ancient Judaism" series (Atlanta: Scholars Press, for "University of South Florida Studies in Religion," 1991–99); and his (with A. J. Avery–Peck) *Judaism in Late Antiquity,* Part 3: *Where We Stand: Issues and Debates* (4 vols.; Leiden: Brill, 1999–2000).

[8]S. Schwartz, *Imperialism and Jewish Society, 200 B.C.E. to 640 C.E.* (Princeton: Princeton University Press, 2001), 9, 103.

[9]S. J. D. Cohen, *Beginnings of Jewishness: Boundaries, Varieties, Uncertainties* (Berkeley: University of California Press, 1999). יהדות seems first attested in the fifth-century C.E. (?) *Esther Rabbah* 7.11, appearing there only once.

Our first task is to understand why a term that bears such enormous weight in scholarly discourse has such an elusive history in ancient texts.

Translators have not been as reticent as the ancients, but occasionally supply "Judaism" or "the Jewish religion" where the terms above are absent from the texts. They do this, for example, where conversion is the issue (*m. Qidd.* 3.5, Neusner trans.; *Acts* 14:43 NRSV) or for such phrases in Josephus as "the ancestral [traditions] of the *Ioudaioi*" ([ζηλοῦν] τὰ πάτρια τῶν Ἰουδαίων; *Ant.* 20.41) or "the customs of the *Ioudaioi*" (τὰ Ἰουδαίων ἔθη; *Ant.* 20.17, 38, 75, 139, Feldman trans. for Loeb). Yet Josephus's terminology comes from a different conceptual framework, as we shall see.

The virtual absence of Ἰουδαϊσμός from non-Christian Greek and Latin authors—all Gentiles and all *Ioudaioi* with the exception of two small texts and two late inscriptions—already indicates that the term's meaning or connotations restricted opportunities for its use. It could not, therefore, have meant the "Judaism" that we so readily employ.

Modern European languages distinguish perhaps five senses of *-ism* words, namely: (1) an action or its result (criticism, plagiarism, embolism, exorcism, synergism); (2) a system, principle, or ideological movement (Anglicanism, Marxism, Liberalism, Communism, Hinduism, McCarthyism; more generically, imperialism, feminism, theism); (3) a peculiar idiom in language (an Americanism, Britishism, Latinism; archaism, barbarism, solecism); (4) a pathological condition or disease (alcoholism, rheumatism); and (5) a criterion of prejudicial discrimination (racism, sexism, ageism). Of these five, only (1) and (3) have parallels in ancient Greek. The modern category (2), in which "Judaism" is generally understood to fall, as a term denoting a system of thought and practice, has no counterpart in Greek or Latin before the third century C.E. The rare form Ἰουδαϊσμός is therefore a "false friend" to the English -isms of system.

The Greek -ισμός noun represents in nominal form the ongoing action of the cognate verb in -ιζω. Common verbs such as ὀστρακίζω, φροντίζω, ὑβρίζω, νεωτερίζω, βαπτίζω, λογίζομαι, and σοφίζω produce -ισμός counterparts, denoting the action involved: ὀστρακισμός, φροντισμός, ὑβρισμός, νεωτερισμός, etc.[10] Such verbs often generate also a *nomen agentis* in -ιστής, indicating the practitioner or representative of the action: an ὀστρακιστής, φροντιστής, ὑβριστής, and so forth. This Greek pattern matches that of the English group (1) above.

Of greatest relevance here is the subset of these word groups derived from ethnic roots. Several such words had currency already in classical Athens, especially: μηδίζω / Μηδισμός; περσίζω / Περσισμός; λακωνίζω / Λακωνισμός; and ἀττικίζω / Ἀττικισμός. It is worth pausing for a moment over these forms, not only because of their formal similarity to ἰουδαΐζω / Ἰουδαϊσμός but also because of their programmatic status in Greek literature and thought.

[10]H. Dörrie, "Was ist 'spätantiker Platonismus'? Überlegungen zur Grenzziehung zwischen Platonismus und Christentum," *Theologische Rundschau* 36 (1971): 285–86; L. R. Palmer, *The Greek Language* (London: Faber, 1980), 252.

In these early examples the -ίζω verb indicates the "going over to, adopting of, or aligning with" a people or culture other than one's own.[11] Inasmuch as fidelity to one's *ethnos* and ancestral customs was considered an axiomatic duty (further below), such a change to other allegiances was normally to be deplored. The paradigmatic example of Medizing / Medism established this negative tinge: it was applied to those Greek cities (e.g., Thebans, Thessalians) and individuals (e.g., Pausanias) who had collaborated with, sought terms with, or outright defected to, the Persians during their invasions of mainland Greece in the early fifth century B.C.E.[12] The charge of Μηδισμός against the Spartan nobleman Pausanias is tellingly elaborated as "contempt of the laws [of his native Sparta] and imitation (ζήλωσις) of the barbarians . . . ; all the occasions on which he had in any way departed from the prevailing customs (τῶν καθεστώτων νομίμων) . . . " (Thucydides 1.132.1–2).

Since "Medism" was not a culture or belief system, but something that one *did*, Μηδισμός forms are best rendered either by the gerund, "(the) Medizing," or with the hybrid suffix *-ization* ("*Medization*"). Either captures the noun's -ίζω base in a way that the English *-ism* of systems does not. English has not preserved a parallel form to the ethnic -ισμός words. Our English *-isms* in category (2) above seem to take more from the Greek *nomen agentis* -ιστής, possibly also from a late-antique Latin development that we shall observe below.

The severely restricted use of Ἰουδαϊσμός appears to be explained, further, by the circumstance that ethnic -ίζω / -ισμός normally occur *in explicit or implicit contrast with some other potential affiliation, movement, or inclination.* Indeed, the prospect of one new allegiance in -ισμός encouraged new coinages: "Engage not in *X-ismos,* but (to coin a word) in *Y-ismos*!" Thucydides' Thebans, standing accused by the Plataeans of Medizing (Μηδισμός), at a hearing before the Spartans, counter-charge their accusers of an equally reprehensible "going over to Athenians" (προσχωρέω πρὸς Ἀθηναίους): the Plataeans are accused of "forsaking *their* ancestral traditions" (παραβαίνοντες τὰ πάτρια; Thucydides 3.61.2). The Thebans' conclusion is lapidary: "So, as concerns our *involuntary* Μηδισμός, and your [Plataean] *voluntary* Ἀττικισμός, this is how we explain things" (3.64.5). Evoking Ἀττικισμός is a brilliant ploy before this audience to deflect serious charges.

Amid the conflicts of classical Peloponnesian politics, indeed, the main options were Atticizing and Spartanizing (Λακωνισμός). Xenophon has the

---

[11] Dörrie, "'Platonismus'," 252: "Fast immer bewahrt der, der ein solches Verbum gebraucht, kritischen Abstand: es schwingt ironischer Tadel mit, daß einer sein eigentliches Wesen verleugnet, um ein ihm fremdes Modell nachzuvollziehen. . . ."

[12] E.g., Herodotus 4.144, 165; 7.138–139, 205, 233; 8.30–34, etc.; Thucydides 1.95.5; 3.62.1, 63.1, etc.; Isocrates, *Pan.* 157; Demosthenes, *Aristocr.* 205. J. L. Myers ('Μηδίζειν: Μηδισμός,' *Greek Poetry and Life: Essays Presented to Gilbert Murray on His Seventieth Birthday,* ed. C. Bailey et al. [Oxford: Clarendon, 1936], 97–105) points out that *Medismos* became so entrenched a concept in the seventh to sixth centuries B.C.E., while Media was still a regional power and rival to Lydia, that it persevered as a label for those who aligned themselves with *the Persians,* the conquerors of the Medes, rather than the more accurate περσίζω / Περσισμός.

enlightened Athenian Callistratus recognize, before a Spartan audience: "Of each populace and city, some favor you, and some us; and within each city, some Laconize while others Atticize" (*Hell.* 6.3.14). More pointedly, Isocrates (*De pace* 108): "Did not the meddling of the Atticizers make the cities Lakonize? And did not the insolence of the Lakonizers force the same ones to Atticize?' Λακωνισμός enjoyed also another life in political and philosophical discussion, describing imitation of the admired Spartan regimen (e.g., Isocrates, *Pan.* 110). And Ἀττικισμός would later come to mean the affectation of a classical writing style against the evolving κοινή. Even with these more positive connotations, however, both forms retained the basic image of *aligning* oneself with something exotic or alien.

That brings us to ἑλληνίζω / Ἑλληνισμός and ἰουδαΐζω / Ἰουδαϊσμός, with which one might also compare ῥωμαΐζω (the -ισμός form there seems unattested) and βαρβαρίζω / βαρβαρισμός. The verb ἑλληνίζω is widely attested from classical Athens onward. Meaning essentially "to express oneself in Greek," it occurs chiefly in contexts where there are doubts about the speaker's ability because he is a foreigner or uneducated (e.g., Plato, *Charm.* 159a; *Meno* 82b; Xenophon, *Anab.* 7.3.25; Aeschines, *Ctes.* 172) or where there is an issue of linguistic purity over against contaminated forms (Aristotle, *Rhet.* 3.1407b, 1413b). Ἑλληνισμός may have been used in the same period to indicate the *resulting* pure Greek (cf. *latinitas*), in contrast to "barbarism" (βαρβαρισμός), and matching the English category (3) above, but we rely on later presentations of lost texts for such usage (e.g., Diogenes Laertius 7.59). The earliest surviving author who uses Ἑλληνισμός in this linguistic sense, in his own voice, is Strabo (4.2.28).

Famously, but with added significance given the foregoing analysis, the first attestation of Ἑλληνισμός is in the same second-century B.C.E. text, 2 Maccabees, that hosts the first occurrences of Ἰουδαϊσμός. Following the patterns we have already observed, Ἰουδαϊσμός appears to have been coined in reaction to cultural Ἑλληνισμός, which the author may also have been the first to use in the sense of "Hellenizing."

The verb ἰουδαΐζω is older than the cognate noun. LXX Esther 8:17 relates that, upon the success of the *Ioudaioi* in thwarting Haman, many of the Persians "were circumcised; they Judaized on account of their fear of the *Ioudaioi.*" Here the verb plainly denotes alignment with foreign law and custom, in keeping with the pattern.[13] All other attestations of the verb have a similar sense (e.g., Alexander Polyhistor *ap.* Eusebius, *Praep. ev.* 9.22.5; Plutarch, *Cic.* 7.6). Paul denounces Peter because, though Peter allegedly lives as a foreigner and not as a Judean (ἐθνικῶς καὶ οὐχὶ Ἰουδαϊκῶς), "you compel the foreigners to Judaize" (τὰ ἔθνη ἀναγκάζεις ἰουδαΐζειν; Gal 2:14)—a cultural movement that Paul connects tightly with circumcision and observance of Judean law (2:12, 21). The only two occurrences of the verb in Josephus, which come in close proximity, mean much the same thing. At *War* 2.454 he describes the slaughter of the Roman

[13] Carl Ehrlich points out to me that the uniqueness of this verb in the Greek Bible must be related to the fact that the underlying Hebrew verb form, מתיהדים, is hapax.

garrison in Jerusalem, which only Metilius survives—on his promise "that he will Judaize all the way to circumcision" (μέχρι περιτομῆς ἰουδαΐσειν). A few sentences later (2.463), when hostilities erupt between Judeans and Syrians, Josephus reports that the latter killed most of the *Ioudaioi* in their midst, while remaining suspicious of the many Judaizers in each city (ἕκαστοι τοὺς ἰουδαΐζοντας εἶχον ἐν ὑποψίᾳ).

Returning to 2 Maccabees, then, we need to ask how Ἰουδαϊσμός functions and whether it nominalizes the -ίζω verb in keeping with the same pattern. This is particularly important because of enormous weight placed upon these passages in scholarship, in spite of their scarcity. For example, Martin Hengel has famously defined Ἰουδαϊσμός, by way of introducing his *oeuvre* on "Judaism and Hellenism," in expansive terms: "the word means both political and genetic association with the Jewish nation and exclusive belief in the one God of Israel, together with observance of the Torah given by him."[14] So: the whole system of Jewish practice and belief. Yehoshua Amir even claims, with a similar perspective, that Ἰουδαϊσμός was a remarkable exception to standard Greek usage:[15]

> In the entire Hellenistic-Roman cultural realm, to the extent of our present knowledge, not a single nation, ethnic, or other group saw the need of creating a general term for all the practical and ideological consequences entailed by belonging to that group, with the exception of the Jewish people [*scil.* in Ἰουδαϊσμός].

And Daniel R. Schwartz claims that the latter half of the Second Temple period was increasingly characterized by Jewish self-understanding "as adherents of an *ism*": "'Judaism,' as opposed to Jewish territory or Jewish blood, became the only way of defining 'Jews' which was well founded in the logic and facts of Jewish existence."[16]

This seems a lot to claim for a word that is absent from all Hellenistic-Judean texts but 2 and 4 Maccabees, completely passed over by Greco-Roman observers of the *Ioudaioi*, and unparalleled even in contemporaneous Hebrew or Aramaic. A better explanation of this rarity, in light of the usage of parallel forms (above), seems to be that the particular circumstances calling for the usage of this word, which always risked negative connotations, rarely occurred.

In the abridger's introduction to Jason of Cyrene's work (2 Macc. 2.21), he sets out to tell the story of those who were assisted by heavenly interventions while they bravely vied for honor, which they did for the sake of *Ioudaismos* (ὑπὲρ τοῦ Ἰουδαϊσμοῦ), which activity consisted in "driving out the barbarian masses" (τὰ βάρβαρα πλήθη διώκειν).[17] Already here we have reason to think that Ἰουδαϊσμός is not a general term for "Judaism," but rather a certain kind

---

[14] Judaism and Hellenism (Philadelphia: Fortress, 1974), 1.2.

[15] "The Term *Ioudaismos* (ΙΟΥΔΑΙΣΜΟΣ), A Study in Jewish-Hellenistic Self-Identification," *Immanuel* 14 (1982): 38.

[16] Studies in the Jewish Background of Early Christianity (Tübingen: Mohr [Siebeck], 1992), 15.

[17] See J. A. Goldstein, *II Maccabees* (Anchor Bible 41a; New York: Doubleday, 1983), 192. Note the ironic use of "barbarian" for non-Judeans.

of *activity* over against a pull in another, foreign direction. The contest becomes clearer when the author invokes Ἑλληνισμός, which is also not a static system or culture, but an energetic movement away from one's own traditions to embrace foreign ones: a "Hellen*izing*." Jason and his group, the writer narrates, introduced foreign ways—Greek cultural institutions, education, sports, and dress (4.10–12)—into Jerusalem, with the result that

> there was such a pinnacle of *hellenizing* and an inroad of *foreignizing* (ἀκμή τις Ἑλληνισμοῦ καὶ πρόσβασις ἀλλοφυλισμοῦ), on account of the towering profanity of that impious high priest—not!—Jason, that the priests were no longer eager for the service of the sacrificial altar. Rather, disdaining the sanctuary and caring nothing for the sacrifices, they hurried at the summons of the gong to share in the illicit activity of the wrestling hall! Reckoning their ancestral honors as nothing, they regarded Greek distinctions as the finest.

Here, Ἑλληνισμός (like ἀλλοφυλισμός) cannot indicate a culture or system; it labels a *defection* that threatens the heart and soul of Judean tradition.[18] The situation becomes incalculably more serious after Antiochus IV's Egyptian defeat and reaction to news of Judea's revolt. At that time he introduces the cult of Zeus Xenios into the temple, proscribes all Judean customs, compels Judeans to eat pork and violate the Sabbath, and orders the execution of "those not preferring to go over to the Hellenic ways" (2 Macc. 6.1–9)—that is those who will not join in Ἑλληνισμός. The king's policy amounted to the dissolution of the ancestral Judean constitution (τὴν τῆς προγονικῆς πολιτείας κατάλυσιν; 8.17). The situation was dire, and Judas Maccabeus could find only about 6,000 men to stand with him in trying to prevent the catastrophe (8.1).

Judas's antidote to this *Hellenizing* (Ἑλληνισμός) was a counter-movement, a bringing back of those who had gone over to foreign ways: a "Judaizing" or Judaization, which the author of 2 Maccabees programmatically labels Ἰουδαϊσμός. The noun appears only in such contexts as these, evidently, because of its inherent sense of *(re)alignment.* This program of Judas Maccabeus and his Asidaeans in 2 Maccabees (cf. 14.6) is not then "Judaism" as a system of life, but a newly coined countermeasure against Ἑλληνισμός.

It is admittedly tempting to read the construction at 2 Macc 8.1 such that Judas called for the support of his relatives and "those who had remained *in Judaism*" (τοὺς μεμενηκότας ἐν τῷ Ἰουδαϊσμῷ), which might indeed work for this sentence in isolation. But if the author posits Ἰουδαϊσμός as a slogan for the Maccabean countermovement, as it seems, then it is preferable also here to see

[18]It is to J. C. Droysen's *Geschichte des Hellenismus* (Hamburg: F. Perthes, 1836) that we owe the use of Hellenism to mean the *civilization* of the Greek-speaking world after Alexander. A. Momigliano comments, "The originality of Droysen was to take Hellenism to mean, not specifically the way of thinking of Jews under the influence of Greek language and thought, but generally the language and way of thinking of all the populations which had been conquered by Alexander and subjected to Greek influence" ("J. G. Droysen Between Greeks and Jews," in *A. D. Momigliano: Studies in Modern Scholarship* [ed. G. W. Bowersock and T. J. Cornell; Berkeley: University of California Press, 1994], 147–161), 150.

Judas finding men who, like him, "had persisted in *the Judaizing* [program]"—that is, not simply clinging to their faith and *remaining Ioudaioi,* but striving to *bring back* other Judeans and reinstate the ancestral law. Such a reading best explains how the group in question immediately behaves as an effective guerrilla organization (σύστημα)—burning towns, capturing strategic sites, and becoming invincible to foreigners (8.5). All along they have remained active in "Judaizing" activities, and that is why they are ready for active service with Judas.

The final two occurrences of Ἰουδαϊσμός in 2 Maccabees come in the description of Razis, a champion of Jerusalem known as "father of the Judeans." The author relates (14.38) that "in the former times of hostility [or stand-off, or separation, ἀμειξία], he was brought to trial on the charge of Ἰουδαϊσμός—and indeed he had spent every ounce of energy, body and soul, for the sake of Ἰουδαϊσμός." As Goldstein observes,[19] Razis is a narrative counterweight to Alcimus earlier in the same chapter, the high priest "who had voluntarily *defiled himself* in the times of *ameixia*" (14.3).[20] Whereas Alcimus not only shared in but positively catalyzed the Hellenizing movement—understood as a "mixing in" or confusion (ἐπιμειξία) of alien traditions—Razis refused, and willingly paid for this resolve with his life. In this context, the charge of Ἰουδαϊσμός, along with the gloss concerning Razis' extreme exertions in its behalf, cannot simply mean that he *remained a Jew* or "within Judaism"; the high priest Alcimus was also a prominent *Ioudaios,* and even our hostile author concedes that he presented himself as acting in the interests of his people (14.6–10). Razis' Ἰουδαϊσμός appears rather to be the Maccabean (or the author's) program of *Judaizing:* of striving to restore Judean law and custom against a powerful countercurrent.

In the only other occurrence of Ἰουδαϊσμός in non-Christian Jewish-Judean literature, 4 Macc 4.25, the context is borrowed from 2 Maccabees. The chapter is about Jason's radical attempt, violently advanced by Antiochus IV, to dissolve (again καταλῦσαι) Judean law and the temple service. When the king's abolition of ancestral law met only active defiance, even from mothers with newborns (4.23–25), "through torture he tried to compel every member of the *ethnos* to eat polluted food and to swear off Ἰουδαϊσμός" (4.26). Once again, although a tolerable sense might be yielded by the traditional rendering "[abandon] *Judaism,*" it seems that Antiochus is most disturbed by the widespread opposition, Judaizing one might say, that has just been described.

That the five occurrences of Ἰουδαϊσμός in Jewish-Judean writings owe so much to one creative author, either Jason of Cyrene or his epitomizer, who seems to coin the word as an ironic countermeasure to Ἑλληνισμός, should caution

[19] Goldstein, *II Maccabees,* 484.

[20] Space does not permit extended engagement with Goldstein's argument (*II Maccabees,* 483–84) for the alternative MS reading ἐπιμειξία in the case of Alcimus, or his translation of this term as "peace" and the ἀμειξία of Razis' time as "war." Although such readings are possible, it seems that locating both Razis' Judaizing and Alcimus's self-defilement during the time of [the contest or struggle for] distinction or separation— i.e., when these qualities were called for—makes a better contrast, with the support of most MSS and a meaning of ἀμειξία that suits the context well.

us against adopting the word as if it were generally understood to mean the entire culture, legal system, and "religion" of the Judeans. Outside the Hellenizing emergency and later Christian circles (below), ancient authors found no occasion for its use—partly, it seems, because of the pejorative resonance of the *Medismos* family, which might obtain also if Ἰουδαϊσμός were used outside of the contrast with a clearly repugnant Ἑλληνισμός.

By far the preponderance of known occurrences of Ἰουδαϊσμός / *Iudaismus* is in Christian writings. This remarkable state of affairs deserves fuller examination than we can give it here. Among the earliest Christian authors, even still, Ἰουδαϊσμός was useful only in rhetorical contexts connected with the movement away from X and toward Y. There we meet a new contrasting coinage: as Ἰουδαϊσμός comes to assume the harmful role of Ἑλληνισμός in Maccabean literature, the antidote becomes either "The [Christian] Announcement" (τὸ εὐαγγέλιον) or "Christianizing" (Χριστιανισμός)—that is, a return to Christ against the dangerous pull of Judaizing (Ἰουδαϊσμός). Later Christian writers would find a substantially new use for the term, which we shall consider below.

Thus Paul's only employment of Ἰουδαϊσμός, in two contiguous sentences, comes in a letter devoted to the *problem* of Judaizing. A group of Gentile believers in Galatia, products of his mission there, have after his departure begun to prefer other Christian teachers who advocate the law of Moses; some of those persuaded even contemplate or undergo circumcision (Gal 1:6–9; 3:1–5; 4:21; 5:1–12). In writing to address this crisis, Paul first stresses his own *former* activity[21] in Ἰουδαϊσμός (τὴν ἐμὴν ἀναστροφὴν ποτε ἐν τῷ Ἰουδαϊσμῷ; Gal 1:13–14). It is not as though the Judaizers are doing something he has neglected, for the same mindset was part of his background; but he has deliberately abandoned Judaizing for the sake of The Announcement (or "gospel," τὸ εὐαγγέλιον). We do not know whether Paul ever "compelled Gentiles to Judaize" in his pre-Christian life, as he now charges Peter with doing (2:14). From the little that he says about it, his former Judaizing seems more in the spirit of Judas Maccabeus and Razis: a violent harassment of Jesus' followers (Gal 1:13) out of zeal, as he puts it, for the ancestral traditions (1:14). The Book of Acts (9:1–3; 22:3–5) indeed claims that Paul sought letters from the high priest, to arrest and return to Jerusalem those who had defected to this new "way." That would certainly fit with the sort of Judaizing activity we found in 2 Maccabees. However one assesses the accuracy of Acts on this score, in Galatians we see Paul clearly trying to block a Judaizing turn by citing his own abandonment of his earlier activity in Ἰουδαϊσμός to follow Christ—implying that his Galatian converts should follow suit. This restricted sense of Ἰουδαϊσμός seems confirmed by the fact that Paul uses it so rarely, and only in a context of extreme Judaizing. Although he often speaks in his other letters of the *Ioudaioi,* Moses, the Law, circumcision, and Sabbath (e.g., 1 Thess 2:14–16; Phil

[21] The accompanying noun ἀναστροφή is stronger than "[my former] life," as often translated (e.g., NRSV, ASV). It should indicate some sort of "bent, inclination" or "turning toward" something, "a going back" to it, or a "preoccupation" with it (cf. LSJ *s.v.*). The *zeal* mentioned in 1:14 confirms this sense.

3; 2 Cor 10–13; all of Romans), it never occurs to him in those places to invoke Ἰουδαϊσμός for those purposes.[22]

In the early second century, the Syrian Christian Ignatius of Antioch faced a similar Judaizing issue, and his language is revealing. People have been telling him, he complains (*Phld.* 8), that if they cannot find something in the ancient texts (i.e., in the Bible: ἐν τοῖς ἀρχείοις), they will not believe it in the Announcement (τὸ εὐαγγέλιον). Ignatius responds, "Now if someone propounds Judaizing to you (ἐὰν δὲ τις Ἰουδαϊσμὸν ἑρμηνεύῃ ὑμῖν), do not listen to him! For it is better to hear Christianizing (Χριστιανισμός) from a man who is circumcised than [to hear] Judaizing (Ἰουδαϊσμός) from a foreskinned man" (*Phld.* 6). That Ignatius considers movement in the one direction appropriate—*Ioudaioi* may and should join the ostensibly universalizing Christ-people, or *Christianize*—but the reverse (Judaizing) movement retrograde, is clear also from another letter (*Magn.* 10):

> It is bizarre to talk Jesus Christ and to Judaize (ἄτοπόν εστιν, Ἰησοῦν Χριστὸν λαλεῖν καὶ ἰουδαΐζειν). For Christianizing did not put its trust in Judaizing, but rather Judaizing in Christianizing (ὁ γὰρ Χριστιανισμός οὐκ εἰς Ἰουδαϊσμὸν ἐπίστευσεν, ἀλλ' ὁ Ἰουδαϊσμὸς εἰς Χριστιανισμόν)—in which [Christianization] every language, having trusted God, has been gathered (συνήχθη [perhaps a pun on *synagogue*, συναγωγή]).

The sense of Ἰουδαϊσμός is confirmed here by the proximity of the -ίζω cognate immediately before (followed by γάρ) and by the issue at stake, which plainly concerns movement from one group to another. Whereas the author of 2 Maccabees had championed Ἰουδαϊσμός as response to the threat of Ἑλληνισμός, Ignatius coins Χριστιανισμός as remedy for a threatening Ἰουδαϊσμός.

That Ἰουδαϊσμός did not yet mean "Judaism" as a comprehensive system and way of life (an English *-ism*) seems clear because throughout the first two centuries no other Christian text used the term: not the gospels of Matthew, Mark, Luke, or John, the *letter to the Hebrews,* Justin (even in the *Dialogue with Trypho, a Ioudaios*), Melito (even in the *Paschal Homily*), Irenaeus, the apologists, or Clement of Alexandria—though the issue was often precisely what we incline to call "Judaism." Late-antique Christian and modern-critical scholarly commentaries to these texts are *filled* with references to "Judaism," but there is no corresponding term in the Greek texts themselves.

---

[22]Remarkably, even scholars who recognize the link between Ἰουδαϊσμός and the verb in -ίζω, as well as the proximity of the two in this work, can insist on the standard of the noun. Representative is F. F. Bruce, *The Epistle to the Galatians: A Commentary on the Greek Text* (Grand Rapids: Eerdmans, 1981), 90: "The verb ἰουδαΐζω, of which it is a derivative, is found in 2:14, but there it is used of Gentiles 'judaizing', living like Jews, as in Esth. 8:17 LXX; Josephus, *War* 2.454, 463. Here Ἰουδαϊσμός means simply 'Judaism', Jewish faith and life (as in 2 Macc. 2:21, 8:1, 14:38; 4 Macc. 4:26)." In some recent scholarship, good questions have been raised about the standard translations (e.g., C. Stanley, "Neither Jew nor Greek," *JSNT* 64 (1996), 101–24; P. F. Esler, *Galatians* [London: Routledge, 1999], 3–4), though without the consequences of a thorough reappraisal (e.g., Esler, *op. cit.*, 66).

From the early third century, things begin to change dramatically among Christian writers. To the church fathers Tertullian (24 occurrences), Origen (30), Eusebius (19), Epiphanius (36 occurrences in the *Panarion* alone), John Chrysostom (36), Victorinus (about 40), Ambrosiaster (21), and Augustine (27) we owe a new use of Ἰουδαϊσμός and *Iudaismus,* now indeed to indicate the whole belief system and regimen of the *Ioudaioi:* a true "*-ism,*" abstracted from concrete conditions in a living state and portrayed with hostility. Among these authors, Ἰουδαϊσμός retroactively covers the whole history of the *Ioudaioi* under Asyrians, Babylonians, and Persians (*C. Cels.* 3.3); it is now host to various sects, including Pharisees and Sadducees (*C. Cels.* 3.12). But it has become a kind of intellectual diminutive, the *vestige* of a once-grand culture that, after paving the way for "Christianism," has lost all nobility.

Tertullian, writing in the early third century C.E.,[23] seems to be the pivotal figure, and there are good reasons why this should be so. Although we know little about his life, Tertullian's writings were crucial to Christian self-definition and in creating a Latin theological vocabulary.[24] Lacking verbs in *-izo,* Latin did not natively form *-ismus* nouns (rough equivalents came in other forms, for example in *-atio*), and those that we find in classical texts are borrowed from Greek. Almost completely absent from the Latin canon are the ethnically rooted *-ismus* words: even the rare λακωνισμός is written in Greek script by Cicero (*Fam.* 11.25.2). Given this general avoidance of *-ismus* forms, it is all the more striking that Tertullian should for the first time use both *Christianismus* (four times) and *Iudaismus* (about twenty-four times). Further, every occurrence of *Christianismus* is paired with *Iudaismus.* But the juxtapostion no longer highlights two possible directions of movement, as in Ignatius, the Greek -ίζω base having fallen away; now it contrasts a living system with a defunct precursor. Thus, Tertullian interprets Marcion's distinction between Law and Gospel as one between *Iudaismus* and *Christianismus* (*Marc.* 4.6); he declares that John the Baptist marked the end of *Iudaismus* and beginning of *Christianismus* (4.33); he paraphrases Paul to the effect that *Christianismus* had a noble lineage in Abraham, whereas the slave woman Hagar produced the legal bondage of *Iudaismus* (*Iudaismi servitutem legalem;* 5.4); and he asserts that Isa 3:3 predicted Paul's departure from Judea, "that is from *Iudaismus,* for the construction of *Christianismus*" (5.6).

From these passages it emerges that Tertullian requires formally parallel terms to contrast with belief in Jesus, and he resorts to the *-ismus* form to enhance the contrast. When he is not making such contrasts, he has a rich vocabulary for *Christiani* and their faith, and so does not need *Christianismus;* for the Judeans, however, choices are limited and so he employs *Iudaismus* often. This usage

---

[23]The chronology is finally established on rigorously historical grounds in T. D. Barnes, *Tertullian: A Historical and Literary Study* (Oxford: Oxford University Press, 1971), 30–56.

[24]See especially E. Osborn, *Tertullian, First Theologian of the West* (Cambridge: Cambridge University Press, 1997), e.g., xiii–xvii, 139–43; also B. B. Warfield, "Tertullian and the Beginnings of the Doctrine of the Trinity" in idem, *Studies in Tertullian and Augustine* (Oxford: Oxford University Press, 1930), 3–109.

strips away all that was different in Judean culture—its position among ancient peoples, ancestral traditions, laws and customs, constitution, aristocracy, priesthood, philosophical schools—abstracting only an impoverished *belief system.*

Whereas many of his predecessors, bothered by the charge of Christian novelty, had tried to find proto-Christians in either age-old Judean tradition or Greek philosophy, Tertullian famously rejected such strategies: "What indeed has Athens to do with Jerusalem?" "What agreement is there between the Academy and the Church?" (*Praescr.* 7).[25] Rather, Tertullian happily conceded the *novelty* of the Christian *disciplina* or *nomen* or *secta* (he rejects *factio* as a slur), which "is quite young, from the time of Tiberius (*quam aliquanto novellam, ut tiberiani temporis*), *as everyone knows and we fully grant*. . . ." (*Apol.* 21; cf. 5, 7, 40; *Nat.* 1.7; *Marc.* 1.16).[26] Marcion had also sought to separate following Jesus from Judean law or history, attributing the latter to a lesser God, but that solution was unacceptable to Tertullian because it left to the *Ioudaioi* an ongoing vitality—continuing with their laws as they awaited their Messiah (*Marc.* 3.23; 4.6). Marcion recognized the ongoing culture of the Judeans, and tried only to divorce his faith from it. For Tertullian, *Iudaismus* ended in principle with the coming of Jesus and it survives only vestigially.

His handling of Judean tradition is no more ambiguous than his attacks on Greek and Roman culture. In *Adversus Iudaeos* he insists that each element of the Mosaic Law was envisaged from the start as provisional (e.g. 4, on Sabbath: *ad tempus et praesentis causae necessitatem . . . non ad perpetui temporis observationem*). The abolition of the Law was fully predicted by the prophets (*Marc.* 5.4), as was the putative wretched condition of the Judeans after their rejection of Christ (*Marc.* 3.23). Because of their failure to accept Christ in the interval between Tiberius (i.e., Jesus' death) and Vespasian (Jerusalem's destruction), the Judeans' territory has been made desolate, their cities have been burned, and foreigners now devour their patrimony (*Adv. Iud.* 13). They *formerly* had a covenant with God, but it is over: they have been cast away because of their sin, and the Christians have taken their place (*Praescr.* 8).

Crucial here is Tertullian's decoupling of the Judean people from its land and legitimacy, therefore from what had made it *different in kind* from Christian belief. Chapter 21 of the *Apology* is a succinct statement. At first, he says, the Judeans enjoyed God's favor and greatly flourished as a people, with a large kingdom and great happiness (*felicitas*). But how deeply they have sinned in rejecting Christ "their own present ruin proves" (*probaret exitus hodiernus ipsorum*):

> Scattered, wanderers, exiles from their own sun and sky, they roam the earth *without a king, either human or divine;* to them is granted not even the foreigner's right to set foot once in their ancestral land. (*Dispersi, palabundi, et soli et caeli sui extorres vagantur per orbem sine homine, sine deo rege, quibus nec advenarum iure terram patriam saltim vestigio salutare conceditur.*)

---

[25] See, e.g., H. B. Timothy, *The Early Christian Apologists and Greek Philosophy: Exemplified by Irenaeus, Tertullian and Clement of Alexandria* (Assen: van Gorcum, 1973).

[26] It is telling that Tertullian, who so forcefully rejected existing categories for Christianity, would himself later join the apocalyptic New Prophecy of Montanus. Only an apocalyptic worldview (cf. also Paul) could care not at all about existing norms.

It is of this formerly great and blessed *ethnos* (*gens, genus*), now landless, abandoned, and eclipsed by *Christianismus,* that Tertullian uses the term *Iudaismus.* And this will be the new function of the word that had formerly found such patchy employment. For Christian authors, *Iudaismus* is Judean culture deprived of all that had made it compelling to Judaizers, an ossified system flash-frozen with the arrival of Jesus, which will now suffer—construed as a system of postulates—by comparison with *Christianismus.* As T. D. Barnes has observed, "For Tertullian (as for many later Christians) Judaism was an unchanging, fossilized faith, not to be taken seriously or deserving proper attention."[27]

Similarly, the fourth-century Victorinus will define *Iudaismus* with all sterility as "works of the law and keeping the Sabbath and circumcision" (*id est Iudaismus, opera legis et sabbati observatio at circumcisio; Comm. Gal.* 1.1.20). This way of defining the Other anticipates critiques of modern Orientalism, "in which one part, the Oriental, remains trapped, separate, unheard, though described to enable the freedom of the describing and defining party."[28]

Tertullian's verbal swordsmanship[29] could not be confused with a historical assessment of the Judeans' contemporary position. The "scattering" he adduces as though it were devastating had in fact begun many centuries before Jerusalem fell to Titus; even after 135 C.E., Judeans remained amply present in Judea/Palaestina—though outside of Jerusalem. Tertullian was writing at about the time that Judah the Patriarch was publishing the Mishnah, the first great compendium of *halakhah,* which along with the Tosefta reveals intense activity among a sizeable sector of the Judean elite.[30] A number of diaspora communities flourished from the second to the fourth centuries (e.g., Rome, Ostia, Stobi, Sardis, Aphrodisias, Dura), as both site remains and funerary inscriptions attest,[31] and other evidence confirms that Judaizing continued vigorously.[32] Tellingly, although non-Christian observers of the second to fourth centuries interpreted the catastrophes of 70 and 135 as great humiliations for the Judeans, this did not prevent them from regarding the Judeans as a viable *ethnos* among the others, with an established place in the world, a constitution, and an an-

---

[27] Barnes, *Tertullian,* 92.

[28] Z. Sardar, *Orientalism* (Buckingham: Open University Press, 1999), 116; cf. E. W. Said, *Orientalism* (New York: Random House, 1978), 236–240.

[29] See R. D. Sider, *Ancient Rhetoric and the Art of Tertullian* (Oxford: Oxford University Press, 1971), 127–128; cf. Barnes, *Tertullian,* 211–32. The opening characterization of Marcion and Pontus in *Marc.* 1.1 gives an idea of the orator's ability.

[30] A convenient collection of essays by experts on Judean leadership from 70 to 500 or so is in H. Shanks, ed., *Christianity and Rabbinic Judaism: A Parallel History of Their Origins and Early Development* (Washington, D.C.: Biblical Archaeological Society, 1996).

[31] E.g., P. Trebilco, *Jewish Communities in Asia Minor* (Cambridge: Cambridge University Press, 1991); L. H. Feldman, *Jew and Gentile in the Ancient World* (Princeton: Princeton University Press, 1993); L. I. Levine, *The Ancient Synagogue: The First Thousand Years* (New Haven: Yale University Press, 2000), 160–290.

[32] See L. H. Feldman, "Proselytism by Jews in the Third, Fourth, and Fifth Centuries," *JSJ* 24 (1993), 1–58; idem, *Jew and Gentile,* 288–415. One need not accept all of Feldman's arguments (e.g., in relation to population numbers) to affirm the general picture.

cestral homeland; they rather saw the Christians as the oddity for lacking such traditions (see further Part 3 below).

Writing a few decades after Tertullian, Origen is interesting because although nine of his thirty uses of Ἰουδαϊσμός appear in his eight-volume response to the philosopher Celsus, where the question of Christians and *Ioudaioi* comes often to the fore, all nine are Origen's own formulations, often in a pair with Χριστιανισμός (*C. Cels.* 1.2.2; 3.12.21, 13.11, 14.19). It was not the philosopher but the theologian who used these comparative categories.

By the time of Eusebius in the fourth century, Ἰουδαϊσμός is evidently a system of thought removed from real life in Judea, an abstraction to be treated theologically. For example, in his *Demonstration of the Gospel* he repeatedly defines Χριστιανισμός as "neither *Ioudaismos* nor *Hellenismos,*" but a *new and true* divine philosophy (*Praep. ev.* 1.5.12; *Dem. ev.* 1.2.1). Again: "For if Ἰουδαϊσμός was [note the tense: ἦν] nothing other than the constitution according to Moses, and Moses appeared long after the times of those mentioned [the patriarchs], then clearly those who lived before him, whose piety is attested, were not *Ioudaioi*" (*Dem. ev. 1.2.5*). Eusebius may signal his awareness of the relative novelty of this language when he writes with optative verbs: "One might suitably call (εὐλόγως ἂν τις ὀνομάσειε) the constitution ordered according to the law of Moses, connected with the one God above all, Ἰουδαϊσμός; and Ἑλληνισμός, in a word, the *superstitious belief* in many Gods, according to the ancestral customs of all the *ethne*" (*Dem. ev.* 1.2.2). Both categories are defined for the convenience of Christian apologetic, with all of the depth, diversity, and richness of the concrete cultures removed. In spite of evidence for the ongoing adoption of Judean law by others even in the fourth century (see Part 3 below), Eusebius posits the inapplicability of Moses's law to anyone except the *Ioudaioi* of Jesus' time in *Ioudaia,* as proof of the need for another, universal way—one that has now supplanted *Ioudaismos* (*Dem. ev.* 1.2.16–17).

A little later, Epiphanius (d. 403) ranges Ἰουδαϊσμός alongside Βαρβαρισμός, Ἑλληνισμός, Σκυθισμός, and Σαμαρειτισμός as an arch-faction (or heresy, αἵρεσις), the font of seven others (Pharisees, Sadducees, etc.). And the fourth-century Filastrius of Brescia focuses all of this with a creative interpretation of Psalm 1:1: "Happy is the man who does not abide in the counsel of the wicked—that is, of the pagans (*id est paganorum*)—and does not stand in the path of sinners—of the *Iudaei,* of course (*quippe iudaeorum*)—and does not sit in the seat of disease—especially, of the heretics (*utique hereticorum*)." He goes on to describe these three wicked tribes with substantives, as "of course (*quippe*) *paganitas, Iudaismus,* and all the heresies" (*et omni heresi; Diversarum haereseon liber* 29.15–20).

Why this development of *Iudaismus* as a static category occurred among Christians is not difficult to see. By about 200 C.E. the church was making headway as a popular movement, or a constellation of loosely related movements. In that atmosphere, in which internal and external self-definition remained a paramount concern, Tertullian and others felt strong enough to jettison earlier attempts at accommodating their faith to existing categories, especially efforts to portray themselves as Judeans,[33] and to see commitment to Christ as *sui generis.* Rather than admitting the definitive status of the established forms and responding defensively, they began to project the hybrid form of *Christianismus* on other groups to facilitate polemical contrast (σύγκρισις).[34] The most important group for Christian self-definition had always been the *Ioudaioi,* and so they were the group most conspicuously reduced to such treatment, which generated a static and systemic abstraction called Ἰουδαϊσμός / *Iudaismus.*

With this background in view, we may now turn to the two Greek inscriptions that mention Ἰουδαϊσμός. As usual, the chief obstacle to interpreting them is our complete ignorance about the lives of those represented. The first (*CIJ* 1.537; Noy, *JIWE* 2.584) is an epitaph from Rome or Porto, apparently from the third or fourth century, for one Cattia Ammias, daughter of the "father of the synagogue" Menophilus: "having lived well in Ἰουδαϊσμός, having lived thirty-four years with her spouse" (καλῶς βιώσασα ἐν τῷ Ἰουδαϊσμῷ, ἔτη ζήσασα τριάκοντα καὶ τέσσαρα μετὰ τοῦ συμβίου). That the author uses two synonymous verbs for living—one "in *Ioudaismos*" and the other with her life-partner for thirty-four years—seems to preclude Amir's translation: "lived with her spouse for thirty-four years a gracious life inside Judaism."[35] Although it could be that Cattia lived her whole life nobly (honorably, virtuously, finely) "in Judaism" as a system, in which case the epitaph's writers would have adopted the Christian usage of the period, the extreme rarity of the noun among the many hundreds of known Jewish inscriptions as in Jewish literature (above) should make us hesitate.

There is no reason why such language might not indicate a situation in which both father and daughter adopted a Judean way of life, or Judaized, and the epitaph writers honored her decision in the notice that "in Judaizing" she flourished. We know of at least fourteen explicit "proselyte" inscriptions,[36] and some of the many others that identify the deceased as a Ἰουδαῖος / Ἰουδαῖα or Ἰουδαϊκός might indicate either a convert[37] or a sympathizer-Judaizer.[38] So too the strik-

---

[33] Osborn, *Tertullian,* 118–19: "Tertullian shows a remarkable change in Christian attitude [*sic*] to Jews. . . . Tertullian is not afraid of Jews. The triumphant spread of Christian faith proves that a new covenant and a new law have been given."

[34] Germane observations are in J. Rives, "Christian Expansion and Christian Ideology" in *The Spread of Christianity in the First Four Centuries: Essays in Explanation* (ed. W. V. Harris; Leiden: Brill, 2005), 15–41, esp. 22–23.

[35] Amir, "*Ioudaismos,*" 36.

[36] Seven of these are in Rome (*CIJ* 1.21, 68, 202, 222, 256, 462, 523; Noy, *JIWE* 2.62, 218, 224, 392, 489, 491, 577); one (on the most probable reading) is from Venosa: *CIJ* 1.576 [Noy, *JIWE* 1.52]. For the rest see P. W. van der Horst, *Ancient Jewish Epitaphs* (Kampen: Kok Pharos, 1991), 70.

[37] Cresces Sinicerius from the Nomentana catacomb is designated *Iudeus proselitus* (*CIJ* 1.68; Noy *JIWE* 2.491). Especially in cases where the deceased lies in a burial complex with other *Ioudaioi,* the ethnicon alone *might* indicate a convert.

[38] R. S. Kraemer, "On the Meaning of the Term 'Jew' in Greco-Roman Inscriptions," *HTR* 82 (1989): 35–53. Cf. Cassius Dio 37.17.1 for the claim that *Ioudaios* was used also of those who lived according to Judean laws, though not actually (ancestrally?) *Ioudaioi* (further below) and van der Horst, *Epitaphs,* 68–70.

ing epithet "lover of [this] people" (φιλόλαος), which appears only in *Ioudaios*-related inscriptions as a real adjective, used of men also characterized "lovers of the commandment" (φιλόλαος φιλέντολος; *CIJ* 1.203, 509; *JIWE* 2.240), might indicate converts or sympathizers; in other Greek inscriptions it is a personal name (e.g., *IG* 2[2].175; 7.1888e; 7.2810; 9[2].470, 474a, 517, 553, 590, 1362). The second man, Pancharius, is said to have "lived well" (καλῶς βιώσας) in this condition, as a lover of the people—a striking parallel to Cattia's "having lived well in *Ioudaismos*." He was also a "father of the synagogue," like Cattia's father and Polycharmus below.

The more famous inscription (*CIJ* 1.694) occupies thirty-three lines of a monumental column reused for a church in Stobi, Roman Macedonia, and dates from the late third century C.E.:[39]

> Claudius Tiberius Polycharmus, who is also [called] Achyrius, the father of the synagogue in Stobi (ὁ πατὴρ τῆς ἐν Στόβοις συναγωγῆς), having enacted every policy in accord with Ἰουδαϊσμός (πολιτευσάμενος πᾶσαν πολιτείαν κατὰ τὸν Ἰουδαϊσμόν), has, in keeping with a vow, [given] the buildings [or house complex (τοὺς μὲν οἴκους)] and the *triclinium* along with the *tetrastoon* for the sacred space, from private funds, without touching in any way the sacred [fund]. But authority and control over all and every part of the upper areas shall be retained by me, Claudius Tiberius Polycharmus, and by my heirs for life. Whoever might wish to renovate any of what has been donated by me shall donate to the Patriarch 250,000 *denarii*. So I have resolved—and as for providing for the maintenance of the brick for the upper areas, [that falls to] me and my heirs.

Notice first that, if Polycharmus's Patriarch is the *Nasi* in Judea (Galilee), as appears likely, the inscription joins an array of evidence confirming the ongoing vitality of Judean life in the homeland through the third century.[40]

The inscription is curious in a number of ways, not least because of the tension between Polycharmus's exultation over his large gift and his defensiveness about what was *not* given but remains in his control. It is not about the man's inner life, but concerns his benefactions to the synagogue and the fate of the connected buildings. The clause of greatest relevance to us, usually rendered along the lines of "having lived my whole life *according to Judaism*,"[41] seems rather to have the standard political sense reflected in my translation above, given that the cognate πολιτεία is the object of the verb.[42] The context also has to do with public benefactions: on Hengel's convincing analysis, the donation of the principal rooms of a large private house for use as a synagogue. Thus, the patron grounds his appeal for respectful consideration of his rights in the claim that all his public activity has been in keeping with Ἰουδαϊσμός.

---

[39] Cf. M. Hengel, "Die Synagogeninschrift von Stobi," *ZNW* 57 (1966), 145–83; Levine, *Synagogue*, 254.

[40] See Hengel, "Stobi," 152–59 and notes, for a convincing argument about the Patriarch's identity.

[41] E.g., Levine, *Synagogue*, 252.

[42] For πολιτεύομαι in general see S. Mason, "Was Josephus a Pharisee?" 31–45.

Aside from Ἰουδαϊσμός, the meaning of which remains to be seen, there is nothing to identify Polycharmus's ethnicity. The title "father of the synagogue" might seem to suggest that he was a born *Ioudaios,* except that "father" and "mother" were honorific titles paralleled across the Mediterranean.[43] A well-known sarcophagal inscription from Rome (*CIJ* 1.523; Noy, *JIWE* 2.577) honors as "mother" of *two* synagogues Veturia Paulla, who was herself a convert (*proselyta*) at age 70. Indeed, Gentile patrons are elsewhere found donating buildings for synagogue use "out of their private funds," as here: Iulia Severa, high priestess of the imperial cult at Phrygian Acmonia, who constructed and donated a property in the first century C.E.;[44] Luke's friendly centurion (Luke 7:2–5), whose historicity is irrelevant for this purpose; and Tation the daughter of Straton from Phocaea in Ionia, who constructed both a house and an open courtyard out of her own resources as a gift for the *Ioudaioi* (ἐχαρίσατο τοῖς Ἰουδαίοις)—and they gratefully reciprocated with a golden crown and a place of honor (προεδρία).[45] One thinks also of the θεοσεβεῖς-donors of Aphrodisias, from the same period as the Stobi inscription and later,[46] or of the patronal *archisynagogoi*—not necessarily *Ioudaioi*—uncovered by Rajak and Noy.[47] A scenario in which Polycharmus was either a wealthy Gentile sympathizer or a convert,[48] who donated his private property for the sacred use of the *Ioudaioi,* seems at least as good an explanation of his civic policies "according to Ἰουδαϊσμός" (i.e., aligning himself with this foreign *ethnos*) as the assumption that he was a *Ioudaios* born and raised.

Whether such Judaizing explains the *Ioudaismos* that enabled Cattia to flourish and guided Polycharmus's public life, or whether their inscriptions were already influenced by the Christian tendency of the period to cite "Judaism" as a system, we cannot know. In any case, one could hardly argue on the basis of these two inscriptions, in the absence of literary support, that Ἰουδαϊσμός was an established usage across antiquity approximating our "Judaism" (as system).

---

[43] Levine, *Synagogue,* 404–5. He comments (405), "what is recorded could well fit the activities of any wealthy patron," though he detects a deeper involvement in synagogue activity on the part of Polycharmus.

[44] Trebilco, *Communities,* 58–60.

[45] Ibid., 110–11. A natural reading of the inscription—she bestowed this on the *Ioudaioi,* and the synagogue of the *Ioudaioi* honored her for it—suggests that Tation was not a *Ioudaia.* Trebilco seems certain that she was "a Jewish woman," but his justification (230 n. 34), that the inscription would read differently on the building itself, I find puzzling. For other privately donated synagogues, see Hengel, "Stobi," 162–64; Trebilco, *Communities,* 230 n. 34.

[46] From the vast literature: J. Reynolds and R. Tannenbaum, *Jews and Godfearers at Aphrodisias* (Cambridge: Cambridge Philological Society, 1987); L. H. Feldman, "Proselytes and 'Sympathizers' in the Light of the New Inscription from Aphrodisias," *REJ* 148 (1989), 265–305; van der Horst, *Epitaphs,* 71–72, 135–37; Trebilco, *Communities,* 145–66; M. P. Bonz, "The Jewish Donor Inscriptions from Aphrodisias: Are They Both Third-century, and Who Are the *Theosebeis*?' *HSCP* 96 (1994), 281–99.

[47] T. Rajak and D. Noy, "*Archisynagogoi:* Office, Title and Social Status in the Greco-Jewish Synagogue," *JRS* 83 (1993): 75–93.

[48] This was the view of H. Lietzmann in a brief note (inaccessible to me) mentioned by Hengel, "Stobi," 178.

Searching for Ancient Religion

Given that *Ioudaioi* of the half-millennium spanning the turn of the era did not describe what they did and thought as "Judaism," what language did they use? An obvious clue is provided by those places mentioned above where "Judaism" has been supplied by translators of our texts: "the ancestral [traditions] of the *Ioudaioi*" (τὰ πάτρια τῶν Ἰουδαίων; *Ant.* 20.41) or "the customs of the *Ioudaioi*" (τὰ Ἰουδαίων ἔθη; *Ant.* 20. 17, 38, 75, 139). What we find in these passages from Josephus is actually standard terminology—in other literature and in his narratives—for the laws and customs of ethnic groups: their νόμοι, νόμιμα, πάτρια, ἔθη, and combinations of these.

Notice, for example, how Josephus frames his rebuttal of Apion, a writer often described as "anti-Jewish," though Josephus casts him as anti-*Judean.* The issue is the treatment of one's *ethnos* by members of another, or *foreigners,* not the treatment of one "religion" by another. Josephus claims (*Ag. Ap.* 2.237) that it is traditional among the Judeans to preserve their own legal precepts or conventions (νόμιμα) and to refrain from criticizing those of foreign peoples (τῶν ἀλλοτρίων). Of Apion he remarks (2.144):

> Healthy-minded people need steadfastly to maintain their domestic laws concerning piety with precision (τοῖς μὲν οἰκείοις νόμοις περὶ τὴν εὐσέβειαν ἀκριβῶς ἐμμένειν) and not abuse those of others. But he [Apion] shirked his own, and spoke falsely about ours!

Josephus cannot talk about Apion as member of another *religion* because the category did not yet exist.

The concept of *religion,* which is fundamental to our outlook and our historical research, lacked a taxonomical counterpart in antiquity. Whereas we often study Josephus and Judea within departments devoted to the study of religion, if we try to produce the ancient terms that express this category we come up empty. Jonathan Z. Smith writes, "The term 'religion' has had a long history, much of it, prior to the sixteenth century, irrelevant to contemporary usage."[49] And Wilfred Cantwell Smith reports, in the context of eastern traditions, "I have not found any formulation of a named religion earlier than the nineteenth century."[50]

This problem is well known in non-western traditions, where scholars often observe that the West has imposed the category of religion upon them, creating a convenient menu of *-isms*—Confucianism, Taoism, Hinduism, Buddhism, Shintoism—for the western observer. Fung Yu-Lan pointedly called his work a *History of Chinese Philosophy* (even then clarifying "philosophy"), though he well realized that westerners normally viewed his material as "religion."[51] "Hinduism"

---

[49] "Religion, Religions, Religious," in *Critical Terms for Religious Studies* (ed. Mark C. Taylor. Chicago: University of Chicago Press, 1998), 269.

[50] *The Meaning and End of Religion: A New Approach to the Religious Traditions of Mankind* (New York: Macmillan, 1963), 61.

[51] *A Short History of Chinese Philosophy* (ed. D. Bodde; New York: Macmillan, 1948), 1–6.

furnishes an egregious example of the West's transforming or abstracting a whole culture into a belief system in order to simplify comparison with western faiths, though "the people involved could have had no use for a term or concept 'Hindu' or 'Hinduism.'"[52] I have already mentioned the familiar specter of Orientalism: the systematization, reification, and indeed creation of a concept called the "Orient," to be explored by outsiders as an object and to give contrastive relief to the "Occident" of the explorers.[53] Whereas these problems are much discussed in connection with the West's conceptualization of the Near and Far East, I am proposing that we misunderstand also the ancient homeland of Judaism and Christianity when we impose the modern category of religion upon it.

I do not mean to say that our western forebears were not *religious*. Rather, I mean this: Modern westerners recognize a category of life called "religion." We know (because we constructed these categories) that Judaism, Islam, and Buddhism are religions, whose representatives may take turns appearing on the religious features of BBC Radio or Canada's Vision TV; they are religions that may be studied in courses on religion, within departments for the study of religion. Since at least the American and French revolutions, this category has been isolable from the rest of our lives: religious systems may be adopted or abandoned. Whereas questions such as "Are you religious?" "What is your religion?" or "What do you think of religion?" are easily intelligible to us, there was no way to frame such questions in the ancient world, which knew no separate category of "religion," the various elements that constitute our religion being inextricably bound up with other aspects of their lives. Walter Burkert could write a magisterial treatise on *Greek Religion*, to be sure, but he had to concede in the introduction, "[Sacrifice-centered] ritual and myth are the two forms in which Greek religion presents itself to the historian of religion."[54] That is, two categories that *are ancient* lend themselves to critical study, but we cannot study an ancient category called religion.

When surveys of the Roman world come to speak of "religion," they often observe that no Greek or Latin (or Hebrew or Egyptian; cf. Indian and Chinese, etc.) word corresponds to our category—not even Latin *religio*.[55] After discussing government, the military, architecture, social and family life, such surveys ex-

---

[52] Smith, *Meaning*, 63–64.

[53] Said, *Orientalism*, 3–9; Sardar, *Orientalism;* A. L. Macfie, *Orientalism* (London: Pearson, 2002); I. Davidson and D. J. Penslar, eds., *Orientalism and the Jews* (Hanover: Brandeis University Press, 2005).

[54] Greek Religion (Cambridge, Mass.: Harvard University Press, 1985). On animal sacrifice as the essence of ancient ritual, see p. 55.

[55] E.g., A. D. Nock, *Conversion: The Old and the New in Religion from Alexander the Great to Augustine of Hippo* (Baltimore: Johns Hopkins University Press, 1998), 10–11; J.-A. Shelton, *As the Romans Did* (Oxford: Oxford University Press, 1988), 360–61; J. E. Stambaugh, *The Roman City* (Baltimore: Johns Hopkins University Press, 1988), 213–14; M. Beard, J. North, and S. Price, *Religions of Rome* (Cambridge: Cambridge University Press, 1998), 1.42–54; D. Feeney, *Literature and Religion at Rome: Cultures, Contexts, and Beliefs* (Cambridge: Cambridge University Press, 1998), 1–21; J. Ferguson, "Classical Religions," pp. 749–65 in *The Roman World* (ed. J. Wacher; London: Routledge, 2002), 2.749;

plain that what we seek to understand as religion permeated all of these parts and more of ancient existence, without yet being identifiable with any one of them. James Rives observes, "There instead existed in the Greco-Roman tradition a variety of modes in which people could think about and interact with the divine world. . . . These overlapped and interacted in various ways, but neither formed an integrated system nor sprang from a unified understanding of the divine."[56] Trying to isolate something approximating religion requires us to juggle mentally at least six different balls, including all the prominent spheres of ancient thinking about human life.

1. Centuries before the Hasmonaean revolt, Greek curiosity about the world's inhabitants had already generated a rich ethnographical enterprise, according to which the fundamental groups of the inhabited earth (οἰκουμένη) were the various peoples or nations (ἔθνη, *nationes*—nineteenth-century notions of "nationalism" being of course irrelevant), a terminology that stood in varying relationship to "tribes" (φυλαί, *tribus*). Far from being a term of scientific precision—we should not confuse the etic, social-scientific category of ethnicity, in all its complexity, with ancient usage[57]—ἔθνος could indicate groups of quite different constituency, history, and size, from Athenians to Medians, Libyans and Indians to Spartans.[58] Largely as a result of Herodotus's enormous influence,[59] later writers of diverse ethnic origins (including Strabo and Josephus) employed *ethnos* and its usual companions as an exceptionally robust taxonomy for classifying the social phenomena they saw around them.[60]

M. T. Boatwright, D. J. Gargola, and R. J. A. Talbert, *The Romans: From Village to Empire* (Oxford: Oxford University Press, 2004), 71–75.

[56]"Flavian Religious Policy and the Jerusalem Temple," in *Flavius Josephus* (ed. Edmondson, Mason, and Rives), 157. I was privileged to read the typescript of Rives's *Religion in the Roman Empire* (Oxford: Blackwell, 2006), which develops this principle with abundant examples and trenchant insight. Rives's categories do not precisely match mine, but they confirm the general picture below.

[57]Here I favor the position of D. Konstan, "Defining Ancient Greek Ethnicity," *Diaspora* 6 (1997) 97–110, in critique of J. M. Hall, *Ethnic Identity in Greek Antiquity* (Cambridge: Cambridge University Press, 1997): whereas Hall defines ethnicity in terms of common descent, Konstan emphasizes that the ancient term *ethnos* in all its elasticity was a phenomenon of discourse and not of fact. More recently, Hall's *Hellenicity: Between Ethnicity and Culture* (Chicago: University of Chicago Press, 2002), 1–29, draws a sharp distinction between ethnicity and culture on similarly etic grounds: genealogically based ethnicity is for him only one variety of "cultural" identity (p. 18). Although in his treatment of "Hellene, Hella" Hall is very sensitive to the emic/etic distinction, and criticizes J. L. Myers for transgressing it (p. 46), in the case of *ethnos* he seems to straddle both sides of the chasm.

[58]Cf. C. P. Jones, "*Ethnos* and *Genos* in Herodotus," *CQ* 46 (1996): 315–20.

[59]For Herodotus's ethnographical conceptions in historical context, see R. Thomas, *Herodotus in Context*, esp. 102–31; R. V. Munson, *Telling Wonders: Ethnographic and Political Discourse in the Work of Herodotus* (Ann Arbor: University of Michigan Press, 2001).

[60]For Josephus's debts to Strabo—and Polybius and Herodotus—see Y. Shahar, *Josephus Geographicus: The Classical Context of Geography in Josephus* (Tübingen: Mohr [Siebeck],

Each *ethnos* had its distinctive nature or character (φύσις, ἦθος), expressed in unique ancestral traditions (τὰ πάτρια), which typically reflected a shared (if fictive) ancestry (συγγενεία); each had its charter stories (μῦθοι), customs, norms, conventions, mores, laws (νόμοι, ἔθη, νόμιμα), and political arrangements or constitution (πολιτεία).[61] The diversity among ethnic characters was connected with, sometimes directly attributed to (e.g., in the Hippocratic *Airs, Waters, Places*), peculiar environmental conditions; later Platonists would link this diversity with the different characters of the regional deities assigned as guardians to the various ἔθνη (further below). Although political constitutions were understood to be different—and fascination with such difference drove ethnographic inquiry—every *ethnos,* whether governed by a monarch, an aristocracy, or some form of democracy, was assumed to have its leading men (οἱ πρῶτοι, ἄριστοι, ἐπίσημοι, etc.). This cultivated (πεπαιδευμένοι) class, including magistrates and priests, understood the traditions and, under the Roman empire, were responsible to their overlords for internal order. According to both insiders and outsiders, the Ἰουδαῖοι (just like Egyptians, Syrians, Romans, etc.) were an *ethnos* with all of the usual accoutrements; see Part 3 below. This fundamental category of ἔθνη with their laws and customs includes important elements of our "religion," in what we separate out as "religious law," customs, and charter myths. In the case of the Judeans, such laws and customs are often taken by scholars as equivalent to "the Jewish religion." But the political-ethnographic category of ἔθνος cannot simply be identified with "religion."

2. An ancient *ethnos* normally had a national cult (τὰ θεῖα, τὰ ἱερά, θρησκεία, θεῶν θεραπεία, *cura / cultus deorum, ritus, religio*), involving priests, temples, and animal sacrifice. This cannot be isolated from the *ethnos* itself, since temples, priesthood, and cultic practices were part and parcel of a people's founding stories, traditions, and civic structures. There was usually a close connection between the aristocracy and the priesthood, whether the priesthood was itself hereditary and the main base of the elite (as in Egypt, Judea, and the East) or the elite were expected to assume priestly functions once they acquired sufficient rank, on a rotating basis or for life (as in Greece and Rome). This was a world in which the Roman *princeps,* endowed with a sacred aura by the Senate, with the solemn title of *augustus,* was also high priest in the college of *pontifices;* the Judean high priest was the leading political figure of that state (whether independent or under

2004), 49–84, 130–73, 190–270. Although there is still a marked tendency (e.g., in Josephus studies) to assume that Hellenization and the Greek language were somehow alien to Judean thought, such that Josephus dressed his thoughts in Greek or "Hellenized" them as a deliberate prcess, that assumption seems to me misplaced. Just as modern colonial elites often found the English and French languages full of possibilities for reconceiving their peoples' place in the world, so too a member of the Jerusalem elite such as Josephus appears to have considered the standard Greek categories valuable for his actual thoughts as well as his language. Could he have thought the same thoughts in Aramaic, without Greek?

[61] Cf. S. Saïd, "The Discourse of Identity in Greek Rhetoric from Isocrates to Aristides," in *Ancient Perceptions of Greek Ethnicity* (ed. I. Malkin; Cambridge, Mass.: Harvard University Press, 2001), 75.

foreign rule); and Roman senators and military leaders offered sacrifice as part of their duties. The Roman Senate could only meet in a consecrated building.

Yet cult and *ethnos* may be distinguished for our purposes, partly because there was no one-for-one match between a people and a single cultic system. The major centers of the world (e.g., Rome, Lugdunum, Carthage, Antioch, Athens, Alexandria, Ephesus, Jerusalem) typically housed their civic cults in prominent sacred precincts (τέμενος, τὸ ἱερόν, *templum*), with a shrine or house (ναός, *aedes*) for the deity in question. But most cities were happy to host a number of cults, the relative importance of which could change over time, and cities also exported their ancestral cults to foreign centers along with their émigrés. Further, alongside the civic cults were quasi-private "mystery" cults,[62] for initiates only (e.g., the followers of Mithras, Cybele, and Isis, or the Eleusinian *mystai*), whether they had stable cultic centers (e.g., Eleusis) or depended upon itinerant charismatic adepts (e.g., Dionysus, Cybele).

The dispersed Judean communities did not for the most part[63] take their cultic apparatus with them, restricting its use to the mother-city Jerusalem. Although Judeans abroad regularly contributed to the maintenance of the Jerusalem cult and were expected to visit the metropolis for festivals whenever possible, travel conditions normally precluded this. As a result, the main communities of the Judean *ethnos* in Asia Minor, Hellas, and Italy had no visible cultic expression. Nevertheless, representatives of these communities (e.g., Philo and Josephus) wrote a good deal about the Jerusalem-based cult, even decades after the temple's removal, continually reinforcing the bond between their *ethnos* and the ancestral land.

Paradoxically, whereas the sacrificial cult was the ancient category that most conspicuously involved "religious" language, with respect to consecration, purity, and attendance upon the Gods, it is probably the one most alien to modern conceptions of religion.

3. The other side of the same paradox is that a category least likely to be connected with religion in our world, philosophy, was in its ancient form rather close to our religion. At least, many basic elements of western religion—a voluntary system of belief concerning ultimate things, especially the divine, matched by a regimen of practice ordering the life of the disciple, based in the study of authoritative written texts, and promoting clear ethical norms—and even more obviously on Samuel Johnson's definition of religion ("Virtue, as founded upon reverence of God, and expectations of future rewards and punishments"),[64] were to be found in ancient *philosophia*. Philosophers were the ones most likely to

---

[62] E.g., W. Burkert, *Ancient Mystery Cults* (Cambridge, Mass.: Harvard University Press, 1987).

[63] In addition to the famous Judean temple in Leontopolis, there is some slight evidence that other diaspora communities may have offered at least the Passover sacrifice (Philo, *Spec.* 2.145–146; *Ant.* 14.244–246, 257–258, 260), on which see Colautti, *Passover,* 232; E. S. Gruen, *Diaspora: Jews amidst Greeks and Romans* (Cambridge: Cambridge University Press, 2002), 117. Colautti argues (153–241) that Josephus was among those after 70 who tried to continue the Passover sacrifice in Rome (cf. *Ant.* 2.313).

[64] Dictionary of the English Language, 1755, s. v.

issue a call to virtue and uprightness (or "righteousness"), denouncing the destructive power of worldly attractions (cf. Lucian, *Nigr.*).[65] It was philosophy that hosted discussions about the nature of the divine and human responsibility or ethics. Philosophy encouraged one to ponder life's meaning, the existence of the soul, and the afterlife, and to behave in accord with this reflection, facing suffering and death with equanimity.[66] That is why Philo (*Prob.* 75–91, esp. 88; *ap.* Eusebius, *Praep. ev.* 8.11; *Vit. Const.* 2, 16) and Josephus (*War* 2.119, 166; *Ant.* 13.171–173; 18.12) describe groups that *we* incline to consider religious—Essenes, Therapeutae, Pharisees, and Sadducees—as *philosophers.* This was no deceit: they were using the most appropriate category. "Religion" was not in the lexicon.

4. Other salient aspects of what religion provides for us—rites of passage at birth, marriage, and death, primary education in the laws and the founding stories of the (sub)culture, consecration of food, formal commemoration of the departed—in antiquity came from familial traditions. Among the Romans, domestic worship encompassed veneration of both ancestors and the family's protective deities. In Judea and possibly elsewhere, Passover sacrifices were consumed by families.

5. Still other elements of what we find in church, synagogue, or mosque were to be found in ancient "voluntary associations" (*collegia,* θίασοι). These too have been widely discussed in recent scholarship, and not least because of their potential to illuminate aspects of our "religion."[67] Some associations were cultic, comprising devotees of a particular deity; others were for members of trade guilds; others were social and drinking clubs. Whatever their specific purposes, *collegia* tended to have regular celebratory meals involving sacrifice to the patron deity, and to mark at least some rites of passage for members, notably funerals. Although they included important elements our religion, again *collegia* did not come close to matching the whole conception in our world.

6. Two other ancient categories that included elements of our religion were astrology and magic,[68] both of which were associated with the expertise of Chaldaeans and Magi from Babylonia and Persia. Astrology flourishes today, of course, and retains connections with religion even now—largely displacing "organized religion" in some bookshops—whereas magic has become for us the domain of deception and sleight-of-hand, rather than the application of spells believed to be efficacious, as it was in antiquity. Both categories dealt with some of the same

---

[65] Still basic is Nock, *Conversion,* 14, 164–86.

[66] On the political consequences of philosophy, which invite comparison with the predicaments of some Christians, see R. Macmullen, *Enemies of the Roman Order: Treason, Unrest, and Alienation in the Empire* (London: Routledge, 1966), 1–94.

[67] E.g., P. A. Harland, *Associations, Synagogues, and Congregations: Claiming a Place in Ancient Mediterranean Society* (Minneapolis: Fortress, 2003) and the essays in J. S. Kloppenborg and S. G. Wilson, eds., *Voluntary Associations in the Graeco-Roman World* (London: Routledge, 1996).

[68] E.g., Macmullen, *Enemies,* 95–162; on religious aspects of magic, F. Graf, *Magic in the Ancient World* (trans. F. Philip; Cambridge, Mass.: Harvard University Press, 1997), 215–22.

questions concerning ultimate reality and fate, therefore with the problem of causation and the meaning of human life, which were taken up in philosophy from a different perspective. Magic involved prayer, and its formulas often included the names of deities (frequently garbled); prominent among these was Yahweh (or Adonai). Origen was well aware of this phenomenon. In supporting the antiquity of Judean tradition against the philosopher Celsus, he asserted that *many* nations recognized the ancient figures Abraham, Isaac, and Jacob as Israel's founders:

> Their names are so powerful when linked with the name of God that the formula "the God of Abraham, the God of Isaac, and the God of Jacob" is used not only by members of the Judean *ethnos* in their prayers to God and when they exorcise demons, but also by *almost all those who deal in magic and spells.* For in magical treatises it is often to be found that God is invoked by this formula (*C. Cels.* 4.33).

Since they trafficked in ultimate powers, astrology and magic must be included among the religious aspects of antiquity, though again they were not comprehensive enough to provide an equivalent to modern religion.

These are only the larger rooms in which we might look for religion in Greco-Roman antiquity. A more exhaustive survey would take us through political and military cultures, educational and athletic institutions, and large-scale public entertainments, including tragic performances based on ancient myths, all of which included sacrifice and attention to the deity. What we would recognize as "religious" activities were everywhere, but there was no phenomenon understood as "religion."

In the previous section we observed that by the fourth century Christians had established *Iudaismus* and *Christianismus* as formally contrastable systems. Were these putative belief systems, then, not getting close to "religions" as we understand them? They were getting close.[69] But with the triumph of Christianity in the West, the proscription of paganism, and the church's increasing involvement in state organs, Christian elements rapidly began to fill the spaces formerly occupied by Roman cults, civic leadership bodies, and philosophical schools. This led to a new integration of civic life, belief, and worship, for a millennium or so—with the much-maligned Jews left decidedly on the fringes, ultimately forced to convert or to leave many Christian states. Of the term *religio* in this context, W. C. Smith observes:

> Early Western civilization was on the verge, at the time of Lactantius [d. ca. 325 C.E.], of taking a decisive step in the formulation of an elaborate, comprehensive, philosophic concept of *religio.* However, it did not take it. The matter was virtually dropped, to lie dormant for a thousand years.[70]

It is only western modernity that knows this category of religion.

---

[69] For Christianity as in essence a new form of "religion," see Rives, "Christian Expansion," 32–33, 36–38, 41.

[70] Smith, *Meaning,* 28. See further P. Harrison, *"Religion" and Religions in the English Enlightenment* (Cambridge: Cambridge University Press, 1990), 1—arguing that the Enlightenment created the concept.

Searching for Ancient Jews

In the absence of either "religion" or "Judaism," I have argued, the *Ioudaioi*/*Iudaei* of Greco-Roman antiquity understood themselves, and were understood by outsiders, as an ἔθνος, a people comparable to and contrastable with other ἔθνη. It remains to elaborate this point and to draw consequences from it for historical work.

In form, Ἰουδαῖος is cognate to Ἰουδαία and indicates a "person of Judea," a Judean. It bears precisely the same relationship to the name of the homeland that Ἄραψ, Βαβυλώνιος, Αἰγύπτιος, Σύρος, Παρθυαῖος, and Ἀθηναῖος have to the names of their respective homelands. If one asked where a Babylonian or Egyptian or Syrian or Parthian was from, in what laws and customs they had been educated, the answer was apparent in their ethnic label. That was also the case with Ἰουδαῖος (= of Ἰουδαία), which should therefore be translated "Judean" by analogy. A hypothetically equivalent question today, "Where are Jews from?" would not admit of a straightforward answer because, although the name originates with יהודים, Ἰουδαῖοι, and *Iudaei,* the changes that produced our English word have removed any immediate association with a place (as have *die Juden, les juifs,* or modern Hebrew יהודים).[71] Even in Israel many Jews consider themselves to be "from" Poland, Russia, Yemen, or Iraq, and some preserve Ashkenazi or Sephardi traditions in dress, diet, outlook, and speech. Since 1948 it has been possible for Jews also to be "from Israel," but the ethnicon that corresponds to this homeland is "Israeli," not "Jew." Since the modern English "Jew" does not mean "of Judea" as *Ioudaios* did, the ancient term is more faithfully rendered "Judean."

Decisive for this question is not form, but actual usage: the universal tendency of ancient non-Christian authors to discuss the Ἰουδαῖοι alongside other ἔθνη. *Ioudaioi* were not often compared—as the Christians *were* compared (Celsus in *C. Cels.* 1.9, 68)—with members of cults (e.g., of Mithras, Cybele, Isis) or voluntary associations.

Strabo, for example (16.2.2), writes, "Some divide Syria as a whole into Coele-Syrians and Syrians and Phoenicians, and say that four other nations (ἔθνη) are mixed up with these: Judeans, Idumeans, Gazaeans, and Azotians. . . ." Although he distinguishes the philosopher-astrologers known as Chaldaeans from the tribe of the same name living in Chaldaea (16.1.6), Strabo sees no need for such a distinction in the case of Judeans: they constitute an ἔθνος parallel to other ἔθνη. So also 16.2.34–36: Judea as a whole (including Galilee and Samaria) is home to peoples of mixed stock (οἰκούμενα μικτῶν ἔκ τε Αἰγυπτίων ἐθνῶν καὶ Ἀραβίων καὶ Φοινίκων); the ancestors of those called Judeans are believed to be Egyptians. Moses, though an Egyptian priest, rejected *Egyptian, Libyan,* and *Greek* modes of representing the deity, and so took a number of reflective men with him to establish a different kind of rule (ἀρχή) and piety in Judea.

---

[71] Cohen, *Beginnings,* 69.

Though governed by tyrants, he says, the Judeans revered their acropolis (*scil.* the temple mount in Jerusalem) as a holy place.

Note especially Strabo's next paragraphs. This reverence for the seat and origin of government, he says

> is common among both Greeks and barbarians. For, being *polis*-connected (πολιτικοί), they live under a common constitutional order (πρόσταγμα); otherwise, it would be impossible for vast numbers to act together harmoniously with one another, which is just what it means to πολιτεύεσθαι. (16.2.38)

Strabo mentions two other ἔθνη that have likewise preserved the divine origins of their constitutions: Cretans and Spartans (16.2.38). For him and his audiences, to be a Judean was comparable to belonging to any other *ethnos.* Just as being an Egyptian or a Libyan or a Greek was *not simply a matter of geography* or of education or of "religion," so being a Judean could not be limited in any such way. It meant representing an entire local culture (no matter where one currently lived).

Posidonius, used as a source by Strabo, must have employed similar language. In a fragment preserved via Diodorus of Tarsus and then Photius (*Bibl.* 244), he speaks of the Judeans as the only *ethnos* of all (μόνους ἁπάντων ἐθνῶν) who were unwilling to join in Antiochus IV's commonality initiative (ἀκοινωνήτους εἶναι), which involved mixing *with every other ethnos* (τῆς πρὸς ἄλλο ἔθνος ἐπιμιξίας); they rather assumed a hostile stance toward all (πολεμίους ὑπολαμβάνειν πάντας). Such characterizations pervade ancient Greek and Latin literature, as a perusal of Stern's *Greek and Latin Authors on Jews and Judaism* would show.

Philo offers abundant material in this vein:[72] the Judeans are an *ethnos* (*Mos.* 1.7, 34; *Decal.* 97; *Spec.* 2.163, 166; 4.179, 224; *Virt.* 212, 226; *Prob.* 75), whose *lawgiver* Moses (*Mos.* 1.1; *Prob.* 43, 57, 68) gave them a *constitution* (*Virt.* 108). "The Judeans were foreigners (ξένοι), as I said before, the founders of the *ethnos*—on account of famine, through lack of food—having migrated to Egypt from Babylon and the upper satrapies" (*Mos.* 1.34). The translation of the Greek Bible is presented by Philo as an inter-state matter—the rendering of foreign laws into Greek through diplomatic missions (*Mos.* 2.31–33). Precisely as an *ethnos,* the *Ioudaioi* are in constant tension with Alexandrians and Egyptians (*not* with followers of Isis, or Stoics) over the issue of civic and political status (*Flacc.* 1, 21, 43, 191; *Leg.* 117, 170, 178, 194, 210). The *Essaioi,* a small subset of the populous Judean *ethnos,* may be compared with the Magi among the Persians or the gymnosophists among the Indians (*Prob.* 74–75).

Particularly telling is Philo's language in connection with what *we* normally describe as "religious conversion":[73]

---

[72] Cf. E. Birnbaum, *The Place of Judaism in Philo's Thought: Israel, Jews, and Proselytes* (Atlanta: Scholars, 1996), 50–58. Birnbaum also explores "Israel" as an internal designation, a term that merits further exploration across the board.

[73] So Cohen (*Beginnings,* 130) on this passage: "Philo clearly describes conversion *in theological terms*" (emphasis added).

> Having legislated for fellow-members of the *ethnos* (περὶ τῶν ὁμοεθνῶν), he [Moses] holds that newcomers must be deemed worthy of every privilege, because *they have left behind blood-relatives, ancestral home, customs, sacred rites* (γενεὰν μὲν τὴν ἀφ' αἵματος καὶ πατρίδα καὶ ἔθη καὶ ἱερά . . . ἀπολελοιπότας), *images of the Gods, the gifts and honors too.* . . . He directs those of the *ethnos* to love the newcomers, not only as friends and relatives, but as though themselves in body and soul. (*Virt.* 102–103)

Philo's language includes the whole range of ethnic associations, from land, kin, and custom to the cult and its associated phenomena. Shocking though it may seem, we consistently find both *Ioudaioi* and outsiders understanding "conversion" as in fact a movement from one *ethnos* to another, a kind of change in citizenship (further below). There was no "religion" to which one might convert, even if one had wished to do so. Taking on the Judeans' laws and customs was different from, and more than, being initiated in the cult of Cybele or joining a philosophical school, notwithstanding parallels to both. It was a change of ethnic-ancestral culture, the joining of another people, as it had been already of the biblical paradigm, Ruth: "your people shall be my people" (1:16).

Josephus is important because he consciously undertakes to explain Judean history, laws, and customs to apparently receptive audiences in Rome. His *Judean War* presents the *Ioudaioi* as an *ethnos,* caught up in the sort of crisis long familiar to Romans and Greeks; hence the strong influences in this work from Thucydides, Xenophon, the Athenian orators, Polybius, and Strabo. The Judean civil war that caused the conflict (*War* 1.9–10), he explains, nourished itself on an age-old struggle to define freedom and autonomy in the context of foreign domination.[74] Though these questions were delicately managed in Judea most of the time by the hereditary aristocracy (as in the rest of the Greek East), even under the severe stresses of Roman administrative incompetence, things fell apart with the murder by unworthy demagogues and their gangs of the most distinguished leaders (4.314–333; 7.267).

If *War* presupposes a Roman audience with significant interest in postwar Judea, the much longer *Judean Antiquities* claims to be written in response to demands for a readable translation of the Judean constitution (πολιτεία): its legal provisions, traditions, and the national history (*Ant.* 1.5, 10; 3.322; 4.45, 184, 191–198, 302, 310–312; 20.229, 251, 261; *Ag. Ap.* 2.287). Near the end (*Ant.* 18–20) Josephus both undertakes a vigorous critique of the current Roman system of government, which he pegs to an elaborate account of Caligula's death and Claudius's accession, and shows the great appeal of the Judean code to foreign rulers. All of this remains at the level of political discussion and comparison of *ethne,* as we have come to expect. These were Josephus's categories, strongly tinged with philosophy and cult; one cannot extract "religion" from this without tearing up his narrative fabric.

---

[74]E.g., *War* 2.22, 54, 80, 260, 264, 295, 300, 346, 348–349, 355–361; 4.320, 335, 358, 408; 5.28, 389, 396, 406; 6.215; 7.255, 325–329, 344, 351, 370, 372, 386, 410.

Josephus's most concentrated discussion of the character of the *Ioudaioi* comes in the work known as *Against Apion*. There he regularly juxtaposes Judeans with Babylonians, Egyptians, Chaldaeans, Athenians, and Spartans. Each of these peoples has a homeland, a lawgiver and laws, ancestral customs, sacred texts, priests and aristocrats, and a citizenship; so they may readily be contrasted and compared. He opens with a dismissal of Greek claims to superiority in history (*Ag. Ap.* 1.6), asserting that the Egyptians, Chaldaeans, and Phoenicians—he declines for the moment, he says, to include Judeans—have the most reliable records of the past (1.8–9). This kind of ethnic comparison continues throughout. Notice, for example, Apion's reported wonder that Ἰουδαῖοι could be called Alexandrians (Ἀλεξανδρεῖς); this makes sense only on Apion's assumption that these are parallel, and mutually exclusive, terms. Josephus's response confirms that the assumption is shared. Rather than suggesting that Apion has confused categories, that being a *Ioudaios* is actually a "religious" matter or the like, he accepts the ethnic character of these labels but accuses Apion of not looking hard enough for parallel cases of "dual nationality" (so to speak): the Antiochenes, Ephesians, and Romans are among those who extend their citizenship also to those from foreign ἔθνη (2.38–41). So it is in Alexandria, he claims, where Ἰουδαῖοι have equal rights. There are parallels here with modern discussions of identity in relation to immigrant groups: "Indo-Canadian" or "Chinese-Canadian." Yet admitting the complexities of such terms does not cause us to fall back upon "religion" or some other category for the non-Canadian half of the expression. Similar complications should also be manageable in our study of the ancient "Judeans."

The final quarter of the *Against Apion*, an extended panegyric on the Judean constitution, is thick with parallels between Ἰουδαῖοι and other nations, their laws and legislators (*Ag. Ap.* 2.160–163, 168–170, 172, 223–235, 239–270, 276–278, 281–286). Josephus and his audiences, as also his literary interlocutors, assumed that the Judeans were an *ethnos*—and this more than two decades after the fall of Jerusalem to Titus.

Some scholars, while conceding at least parts of this kind of analysis, have suggested nevertheless that at some point the conditions constituting the Judeans as an *ethnos* changed—their corporate identity was severed from considerations of land or state—and that after that point Ἰουδαῖος should, or sometimes should, be translated "Jew," given the word's new "religious" meaning.

Daniel R. Schwartz argues in one study that the development of the Ἰουδαῖοι from *ethnos* to religion began already with the Babylonian exile and was reinforced at several subsequent watersheds—Hellenization, the rise of sectarianism, Roman annexation of Judea, and the destruction of the temple—each of which widened the gap between what had once been joined together: worship of the Judean God and governance of the homeland.[75] The problem with this proposal is that every ancient *ethnos* experienced its own vicissitudes through the centuries from Alexander the Great to the Severans, say, without thereby altering its

[75]Studies, 5–15.

character as an *ethnos*. Cities in Hellas and Asia were destroyed or passed from native rulers to the Romans, but if the people survived they retained their ethnic identity. Every city or region under Roman rule faced the problem of maintaining its ancestral constitution under the domination of this foreign overlord, as the Judeans did, though they did not cease to be ἔθνη for that reason, and we do not translate their names differently because of this struggle.[76] Even in the capital, Roman rule and citizenship became gradually disconnected from residence in the city, offered to ever wider groups, without *Romanitas* thereby becoming a "religion." The meaning of "Roman," "Greek," and "Egyptian," to name a few, certainly becomes increasingly complicated over the centuries, but we do not abandon their traditional names for that reason. Why change "Judean," when the conceptual framework that gave the word meaning remained fully functioning, and there was no other ancient word to replace it?

Shaye Cohen has located the crucial conditions of change from *ethnos* to religion in the Hasmonean period, in the mass conversions of the neighbouring ἔθνη (Idumeans and Ituraeans) to Judean citizenship (πολιτεία). In his view, such conversion meant the end in principle of the exclusively *ethnic-geographical* meaning of Ἰουδαῖοι that had obtained until then.[77] He insightfully proposes that the Hasmoneans were modelling themselves on the Achaean League, a largely voluntary but partly compelled association of neighbouring peoples living under one set of laws, way of life, piety, and so on.[78] A secondary effect of this political change (i.e., of "Judaism" now as a matter of *citizenship* rather than of *ethnos*) was a religious one: in the same period we begin to find stories of individual Gentiles believing in the God of the Jews and so undergoing "religious" conversion.[79] In the process, Cohen proposes, just as the meaning of "Hellene" changed to become a *cultural* term—it "was completely sundered from any connection with the land or people of Greece"[80]—so also Ἰουδαῖοι became largely cultural (= *religious*): "Conversion to Judaism thus emerges as an analogue to conversion to Hellenism."

But "Hellenism" (Ἑλληνισμός) represented neither a culture nor a religion at this time (see part 1), and in the ostensibly parallel case of Ἰουδαῖος Cohen does not justify the slide from "cultural" (by putative analogy with "Hellene") to "religious" (a category he does not apply to "Hellene"):[81] "the Hasmonean period attests for the first time the idea of religious conversion: by believing in the God of the Jews and following his laws, a Gentile can become a Jew."[82] Cohen does not

[76] Many of the debates preserved by Polybius concerned this issue (cf. Eckstein, *Moral Vision*, 194–236), which is still a central theme in Plutarch's works, especially *Precepts of Statecraft* (*Praecepta gerendae reipublicae*, *Mor.* 798a–825f).

[77] Cohen, *Beginnings*, 70, 81, 90.

[78] Ibid., 125–29.

[79] Ibid., 137.

[80] Ibid., 134.

[81] E.g., Cohen, *Beginnings*, 136: "But by investing Judean identity with political or cultural (religious) content, the Hasmoneans were able to give outsiders an opportunity to attain membership in Judean society"; cf. 70, 79, 81.

[82] Ibid., 137.

show what ancient category this religious conversion fits into; two of his chief supports are the Christians Paul and Origen, though as we have seen they have a separate discourse.[83] Although he wishes to argue that Ἰουδαῖος from this period onward should often be rendered "Jew," he does not say why this should be so if (a), as he concedes, the newer senses do not supplant (but only supplement) the enduring ethnic meaning, and (b) the analogue *Hellene* does not undergo a change of translation, but still means "Greek" with all of its complicated meanings in play (indeed, the ethnic-geographic sense of *Hellene* remains crucial throughout the "Second Sophistic" at least);[84] the analogy breaks down if "Hellene" does not become a *religious* term[85] as Ἰουδαῖος is said to do. Why change the translation of *Ioudaios* alone?

In a recent study Daniel Schwartz argues that outside observers changed their understanding of what *Ioudaios* meant after 70 C.E., as they began to call *Iudaea* by other names, and that Josephus's works mirror this development—*War* using *Ioudaios* with standard ethnic connotations, *Antiquities* linking it with "religious" terms and concepts (such as νόμιμα).[86] Yet Schwartz's evidence for outsiders' descriptions of Judea depends heavily upon the literary licence of the Flavian poets: when they called the region "Idumea" they were not reflecting a change in their perception. Well before 70, other poets such as Virgil (*Georg.* 3.12) and Lucan (*Phars.* 3.216) could substitute Idumea for Judea,[87] and even Philo could call the region "Palestinian Syria" (*Prob.* 75); Louis Feldman has shown that the name *Iudaea* persevered for centuries after Hadrian's attempt to separate the *ethnos* from its ancestral city.[88] As for Josephus, Schwartz perhaps misreads the change of theme from *War* to *Antiquities,* so that νόμιμα (legal matters / precepts) and

---

[83] Ibid., 134. Paul should not be taken as representative of Judean views. Outside of Romans, from which the passage in question comes (Rom 2:28), he shows no interest in being seen as a *Ioudaios,* and his appeal here that being a *Ioudaios* is internal or spiritual only serves his rhetorical needs in this letter (cf. ch. 10 in the present volume). And Origen, as it happens, still often speaks of the Judeans as an *ethnos* (*C. Cels.* 1.14, 55; 2.8).

[84] Cf. Dio's speech to the Rhodians. From a large and growing literature: E. L. Bowie, "The Greeks," 3–41; S. Swain, *Hellenism and Empire* (Oxford: Oxford University Press, 1996). Josephus's comment about the "native" or "genuine" (γνήσιοι) Greeks at *War* 1.16 is part of this discourse. Julian's fourth-century letter to the Senate and people of Athens still depends heavily on their ethnic continuity.

[85] G. W. Bowersock, *Hellenism in Late Antiquity* (Ann Arbor: University of Michigan Press, 1990), 9–12, indeed charts a change in the meaning of Hellene/Hellenism, but this is part of the same process we have described in part 1, in connection with an ascendant *Christianismos.* Hall, *Hellenicity,* argues that Hellenic identity first emerged in the sixth century on an ethnic basis (with fictive kingship, 125–71), but that it was redefined in the fifth and fourth centuries as a cultural matter (172–228). But the historical conditions of these changes (a Thessalian motive to unite and dominate, then Athenian supremacy in a more broadly disseminated culture) have no analogy in Judea; and the date of this shift seems too early to support Cohen's analogy.

[86] "Herodians and *Ioudaioi* in Flavian Rome," in *Flavius Josephus* (ed. Edmondson, Mason, and Rives), 63–78, esp. 68–78.

[87] Cf. M. Stern, *Greek and Latin Authors on Jews and Judaism* (Jerusalem: Israel Academy of Sciences, 1976), 1:316 and n. 1.

[88] "Some Observations on the Name of Palestine," *HUCA* 61 (1996): 1–23.

ἔθη (customs) become for him *religious* terms. This is all standard political and ethnic language, however, as we have seen and as Josephus's very last composition (*Against Apion*), left out of account by Schwartz, makes clear through its ongoing comparison of constitutions, lawgivers, laws, and customs.

The variety of these—mutually exclusive—arguments for a change (or incremental changes) from ethnic-geographic to religious meanings of *Ioudaios,* over several centuries, inspire doubt that there *was* such a change in antiquity, of sufficient distinction that it calls for a new translation of *Ioudaios*—even for "political" and "religious" translations of the same word within a single passage of text.[89] The same Greek and Latin ethnica (*Ioudaios, Iudaeus*) remained in use: when much later Greek truly needed a different word for "Jews" it turned to Εβραίοι;[90] there was no need for a new name in antiquity.

A further consideration, neglected in these discussions as far as I can see, is the fundamental and repeated criticism of the Christians by Celsus (*C. Cels.* 2.1, 3) and Julian (*C. Gal.* 43a), long after any of the dates proposed for "the change." These philosophers charge that precisely because the Christians have broken with the established ethnic-ancestral tradition of the *Ioudaioi,* they have become an anomalous group: "Since the Christians have forsaken their traditional laws *and are not an individual ethnos like the Judeans,"* Origen complains in response, "they are to be criticized for agreeing to the teachings of Jesus" (*C. Cels.* 5.35). The claim would make little sense if Celsus and Julian considered the *Ioudaioi* no longer an *ethnos* at their times of writing. Indeed, all the non-Christian observers of the *Ioudaioi* we know about continue to understand them as a living *ethnos.*

Basic to the philosopher Celsus's image of the world was the notion that each nation follows its peculiar laws and customs. This was not only because different groups have different values and customs, as in traditional ethnography, but also because various "overseers" are set over the nations from the beginning. Each nation's practices are right when they are done in the way that pleases the overseer, but "it is impious to abandon the customs that have existed in each locality from the beginning" (*C. Cels.* 5.25).

So, he writes in the latter half of the second century C.E.:

> The *Ioudaioi,* having become an individual *ethnos* [after leaving Egypt], enacted laws in keeping with their local conditions, and *carefully maintain them until even now.* In *preserving their worship*—which, whatever its actual form, *is ancestral*—they act just *like other people:* each takes great care with its own ancestral traditions, no matter what they are, if they happen to be established (Ἰουδαῖοι μὲν οὖν ἔθνος ἴδιον γενόμενοι καὶ κατὰ τὸ ἐπιχώριον νόμους θέμενοι καὶ τούτους ἐν σφίσιν ἔτι νῦν περιστέλλοντες καὶ θρησκείαν ὁποίαν δή, πάτριον δ' οὖν, φυλάσσοντες ὅμοια τοῖς ἄλλοις ἀνθρώποις δρῶσιν, ὅτι ἕκαστοι τὰ πάτρια, ὁποῖά ποτ' ἂν τύχῃ καθεστηκότα, περιέπουσι). (*C. Cels.* 5.25)

[89] E.g., Cohen, *Beginnings,* 90.

[90] I am indebted to a Thomas W. Gallant of York University, in private communication, for confirmation of modern Greek usage.

Although he often disparaged the *Ioudaioi* as derivative from Egypt and among the least accomplished of ἔθνη, Celsus did not hesitate to include them as an *ethnos*. Indeed, he made his criticisms by contrasting *Ioudaioi* with other ἔθνη· just as Athenians, Egyptians, Arcadians, Phrygians, and the others put forward stories of their glorious beginnings, so too did the *Ioudaioi*—though in a naïvely inferior way (*C. Cels.* 4.36; cf. esp. 1.14). There is no hint here of any change in the perception of *Ioudaioi* as *ethnos* a century after the fall of Jerusalem.

Writing from the same Platonic tradition in the third century, Porphyry fully acknowledges the horrors that have befallen the *Ioudaioi,* from their insufferable treatment under Antiochus to the fall of Jerusalem and their exclusion from it under the Romans (*Abst.* 4.11), and yet none of this prevents him from considering them a living ἔθνος even now (ἔτι καὶ νῦν). It is impressive that, although Porphyry will devote his comments on the practices of the Judeans almost entirely to the Essenes, he enfolds this group in the cover of the Judeans. Why? This part of his work is about ἔθνη—cf. *Abst.* 4.5: "now turning to the other ἔθνη"—and the *Ioudaioi* are the appropriate sequel to Spartans and Egyptians (*Abst.* 4.1–10) in a survey of peoples who lead disciplined lives. The *Ioudaioi* are, in his mind and for his audiences, obviously a functioning *ethnos,* notwithstanding the idealizing character of this work.

In the mid-fourth century, even Julian remains clear on this point. His whole critique of the Christians ("Galilaeans") rests on the view, well established by now, that every *ethnos* has its own character (φύσις, ἦθος· Celts and *Germani* are fierce, Egyptians intelligent, Syrians unwarlike and delicate), partly determined by its physical environment (*C. Gal.* 143d–e), which character is also reflected in its ancestral laws, constitution, and customs (νόμοι, νόμιμα, τὰ πολιτικά ; *C. Gal.* 116a–b, 131b–c). The ethnic character is suited to, and granted by, the national God (*C. Gal.* 143a): "the ἔθνη, being administered by them, follow each domestic God according to its essential character" (*C. Gal.* 115d–e). In Julian's analysis the Christians are blameworthy, first, because they preferred the isolationist Judean *ethnos* to those of the Greek mainstream, from which most Christians originated and, second, because they *did not even remain* with Judean laws and customs, but went their own way (ἰδίαν ὁδὸν ἐτράποντο), rendering themselves neither fish nor fowl: they do not belong to any national tradition (*C. Gal.* 42e–43b). What Tertullian had tried to render a virtue—the unique form of Christian corporate identity—made them incomprehensible in Julian's traditional categories. The plan of his argument is first to show the inferiority of the Judean tradition and then to demonstrate that, nevertheless, it is a far better option than the Christians' abandonment of all ethnic traditions—those of their homelands and those of Judea. And his main criticism of the Hebrews-Judeans is that they have confused their local or national God with the Supreme Being (*C. Gal.* 141c–d). The resulting view that their God is jealous of other deities (*C. Gal.* 155c–161a) has prevented them from recognizing the Gods of other nations, making them "atheists." This (τὴν ἀθεότητα; *C. Gal.* 43b) is the only quality that the Christians have taken from them, not the Judean virtues related to discipline (*C. Gal.* 238c).

Throughout this discussion Julian resorts often to other ἔθνη, their laws and lawgivers, for comparanda. So he urges his audience to contrast the mildness and openness of Lycurgus, Solon, or the Romans (*C. Gal.* 168b–c, 171d). Or again, how can the Judeans claim to be so favored by their God, when the Egyptians, Chaldaeans, Assyrians, and Greeks can boast of so much more success (*C. Gal.* 176a–c)? In particular, he contrasts the grandeur and success of Rome, which has nonetheless never claimed exclusive truth for itself, with the enslavement and poverty of Judea (*C. Gal.* 193c–194d, 209–210). Julian's essay often reads like a negative print of Josephus's *Against Apion:* the categories—of ethnic comparison—are the same, reflecting abiding agreement on these assumptions over several centuries. Only the value judgments differ. But this confirms that, outside of the Christian circles to which Julian was so relentlessly hostile, the Judeans were still seen as one ἔθνος among many (*C. Gal.* 306b):

> The Judeans agree with the [other] ἔθνη, except in supposing that there is only one God. That is their peculiar thing, alien to us, because all other matters are in common with us: sanctuaries, sacred spaces, sacrificial altars, purifications, and certain observances, concerning which we [and the Judeans] differ from one another either not at all or only trivially.

Julian's encouragement of the Judean "patriarchs and chiefs" to restore the cult, "sacrificing according to the ancient manner" (τὸν παλαίον τρόπον θύοντας) in a rebuilt Jerusalem and temple (so Sozomen 5.22; Theodoret 3.15), was evidently tied up with his larger effort to restore temples and sacrifice in the face of Christian encroachment, according to the old ways. Again, he criticizes the Christians for having abandoned any ethnic roots and so for rejecting these traditional behaviors (cf. *C. Gal.* 343c–d, 346e–3477c; *Ep.* 20.453; 41.436c–d).

We would like to know more about how Judeans in the long period from 100 to 400 C.E.—the same interval that separates us from the early eighteenth century—viewed all of this, but a problem with the evidence must be squarely faced. Christian authorities of the mediaeval period decided which ancient works would be copied in their *scriptoria* for posterity, and most of them believed that Judean culture had lost its vitality with the coming of Jesus and the condign punishment of Jerusalem's fall. Accordingly, our evidence for the first half-millennium of the Christian era has a peculiar cast. For relations among Christians, Judeans, and "pagans" we have bookshelves full of church fathers and precious little else. Greek-language Judean texts, which engaged the outside world and interpreted Judean life in that context, were preserved until the fall of Jerusalem—the one who described this event becoming quasi-canonical—but fell off completely with Josephus's death. If such authors continued to appear thereafter, as seems antecedently likely, they suffered the same fate as Paul's opponents, Judaizers, "gnostics," Marcionites, Montanists, and all others considered beyond the Christian pale. The Christians borrowed from the Romans a historiography based on authority—rather than disinterested investigation of what happened—and so, once they had recognized an authoritative text for an issue or period, its competitors usually fell away: the case of Josephus's rival Justus of Tiberias (Josephus, *Life* 336–367) is instructive.[91] Every Greco-Roman intellectual who wrote about the Christians is known exclusively from the authoritative rebuttals of the Fathers: their own work was not copied by Christian scribes. Among Judeans, only intramural writings in Hebrew and Aramaic endured within the community (though still edited by medieval censors).

We have every reason, however, to suppose that Greco-Judean writers continued to appear after Josephus's death and continued to see themselves in the same ethnic terms as Josephus employs. This evidence ranges from the general—the ongoing appeal of Judean law and custom to outsiders, the Greco-Roman authors' criticism of Christians for not embracing Judean ethnic traditions (so, this remained an option), and their assumption that these traditions live still—to the specific.

For example, both Justin and Celsus, in the second century, exploit authentic-seeming Judean voices[92] (at least, not merely extrapolated from Judean-Christian debates reflected in the gospels), which they must know from their contemporary experience. Even in Justin's pale figure of Trypho, that voice is learned, engaged with the outside world, and confident about the continuing role of Judean ancestral traditions. To be sure, Origen polemically challenges the authenticity of Celsus's Judean, but he does so on the basis of personal knowledge from his own days in Caesarea (*C. Cels.* 1.28, 45, 49, 55). Such experience underlies his claim that the Judeans use the argument from spell formulas (above) to prove their antiquity to doubters (*C. Cels.* 4.33) and that the Judean "ethnarch," as a function of the world-wide *didrachma* tax now payable to Rome, enjoys considerable power—both formal and informal, including administering the death penalty, and indulged by his Roman masters (συγχωροῦντος Καίσαρος; *Ep. Afr.* 14). Far away in Macedonia, we have seen, a third-century benefactor demands a huge payment to the Patriarch for any alterations to the synagogue structure he has donated. A few decades

[91] Although even Josephus credits him with literary talent (*Life* 40–41, 340), Justus found no real uptake among Christian authors because he had lost the competition for status. Eusebius's adoption of Josephus's critique of Justus without quibble (*Hist. eccl.* 3.10.8) shows that the contest had since been settled. The ninth-century Byzantine Patriarch Photius claims to have read Justus, but he repeats with enthusiasm Josephus's dismissal of the contender: "And *they say* that the history which that man [Justus] wrote happens to be mostly fabricated, especially in what concerned the Roman war against the Jews and the capture of Jerusalem" (*Bibl.* 33; emphasis added). "They" are Josephus, and this verdict from Photius may have sealed Justus's posthumous fate. By the time of the *Suda Lexicon* in the following century, the entry on Justus depends entirely on Josephus: "[Justus] took it upon himself to compile [this is Josephus's language: *Life* 40, 338] a Judean history and write up certain commentaries, but Josephus exposes this fellow as a fraud—he was writing history in the same period as Josephus." In winning the fathers's confidence, Josephus displaced all other evidence. *A fortiori,* the dominance of the church fathers' analysis must have dramatically reduced the survival possibilities of any Greco-Judean efforts at self-definition in this period.

[92] On the authenticity of Trypho's voice, see S. G. Wilson, *Related Strangers: Jews and Christians, 70–170 C.E.* (Minneapolis: Fortress, 1995), 260–61; on Celsus's Judean, see now L. Blumell, "A Jew in Celsus' True Doctrine? An Examination of Jewish Anti-Christian Polemic in the Second Century" *SR* 36 (2007): 297–316.

later, in about 353 C.E., the Judeans of Diocaesarea (Sepphoris) revolted against Roman control, reportedly overrunning much of Palestine; the eastern Caesar, Gallus, put down their rebellion and razed Sepphoris (Socrates 2.33; Sozomen 4.7.5). Julian must have been aware of this powerful national-ethnic sentiment when a few years afterward he offered to relieve the Judeans' burdens and restore Jerusalem with its cult (*Ep.* 51).[93] Although the evidence for Judean perspectives on the world (outside rabbinic literature) is scarce, such indicators as these combine with the perceptions of outside observers to create the impression of a continuing sense of corporate ethnic identity, without radical redefinition after 70 or 135 (e.g., as "religion"), notwithstanding the temple's loss and the Judeans' exclusion from Jerusalem.

Space does not permit worthy engagement with Seth Schwartz's recent argument, tangentially relevant to my case, that from about 70 to 350 "Jewish" identity, or "the core ideology of Judaism" from before 70, nearly dissolved in Judea and elsewhere (emphasis added): "We *perhaps* need to assume that *some Jews retained a sense of being Jewish* if only to understand how northern Palestine could have become Jewish in a strong sense after 350."[94] His analysis combines and takes much further the scholarly recognition over several decades that (a) rabbinic literature reflects the concerns of a tiny elite and (b) material evidence indicates the limits of rabbinic influence on post-war Judea. Schwartz's exploration of coinage and iconography—suffused with pagan themes—in Galilean centers is learned and subtle, alongside which he adduces the alleged Roman practice of destroying autonomy and native forms of leadership (other than city councils) when they annexed territory. He proposes a massive "disaffection with and attrition from Judaism," "probably everywhere," after the failed revolts of 66–70 and 132–135.[95]

Interpretation of coins and symbols in the absence of written comment from the ancients is difficult, however, partly because of what Denis Feeney describes as "the capacity of educated Greeks and Romans . . . to entertain different kinds of assent and criteria of judgement in different contexts, in ways that strike the modern observer as mutually contradictory."[96] We cannot deduce conceptions from symbols. Evidence for mass defection from Judean laws following 70 or 135 seems unavailable, and vastly outweighed by evidence for Judaizing. Josephus must be ranked among those who most deeply mourned the loss of the temple (the subject of his *War,* e.g. 1.9–12), but he is also the most enthusiastic advocate of Judean law and custom, even decades after the destruction. If we should suppose that the defection occurred after 135, why not already after 70? But if after 70, how was the revolt of 132–135 possible? And if not after 70, why suppose it after 135? As for a radically new Roman administrative style after 135: when Judea was annexed in 6 C.E. no such consequences followed. The general character of pro-

---

[93] A recent discussion of the relevant texts and the letter's authenticity is in R. J. Hoffmann, *Julian's Against the Galileans* (Amherst: Prometheus, 2004), 177–83.

[94] Imperialism, 103–76, here 105.

[95] Ibid., 108.

[96] D. Feeney, *Literature and Religion at Rome: Cultures, Contexts, and Beliefs* (Cambridge: Cambridge University Press, 1998), 14.

vincial administration outside Egypt does not suggest a Roman bureaucracy in Judea (Palaestina) of such scope that it could or would manage local affairs.[97]

The greatest difficulty arises from Schwartz's conceptual-linguistic framework, illustrated in the following (emphasis added):

> We can only speculate about the character of *its Jewishness* before that date [350 C.E.]; for now it may prove instructive to imagine *Judaism*, or rather the disintegrated shards of *Judaism*, surviving as a *nonexclusive religious option* in a *religious system that was basically pagan*.[98]

The categories "Judaism" and "Jewishness" are neither present in the texts ("emic"), in which case we might evaluate what the ancients thought about them, nor etic, in which case we could gather data and measure them by agreed standards. What do these categories mean, then, and where are the criteria for evaluating them? If *cultus* is the issue, it was simply absent after the year 70; there could be no question of "fleeing" from it. If *ethnos*, law, and custom: it appears (above) that these remained intact after 135, even if they were reinterpreted then as they had also been at various points before 70.[99]

Scholars have raised two main objections to the translation of *Ioudaios* as "Judean." One is a common assertion that the word is a *geographical* term only, and is therefore only one aspect of identity and not the most important, not at all appropriate for the diaspora. One frequently meets the observation that in some passage (e.g., in Josephus) *Ioudaios* may mean "Judean" (i.e., in or belonging to the territory of greater or proper Judea), but in other passages the word has *no such geographical constraints and therefore* should be rendered "Jew."[100] The foregoing analysis, however, has tried to show that "Judean" does not have a geographical restriction, any more than other ethnic descriptors do. Such a restriction *in our minds* arises from the absence of a political entity called Judea today, so that when we hear the word we think first of an ancient place but not of the people. But just as "Roman," "Egyptian," and "Greek" (etc.), had a wide range of associations beyond the geographical, and they do not require us to substitute

---

[97] Cf. P. A. Brunt, *Roman Imperial Themes* (Oxford: Oxford University Press, 1990), 264–66, 267–81, 302–5; A. W. Lintott, *Imperium Romanum: Politics and Administration* (London: Routledge, 1993), 54–69, 132–53; generally, C. Ando, *Imperial Ideology;* E. Meyer-Zwiffelhoffer, πολιτικῶς ἄρχειν: *Zum Regierungsstil der senatorischen Statthalter in den kaiserzeitlichen griechischen Provinzen* (Stuttgart: F. Steiner, 2002).

[98] Imperialism, 105.

[99] Once we shift the framework from "Judaism" to Judean identity (the viability of the ethnos), it becomes impossible to know on historical grounds what would have happened to this identity if, e.g., Jason, Menelaus, and Alcimus had succeeded. Their intent does not appear to have been the dissolution of the *ethnos:* cf. 1 Macc 1:11 and E. J. Bickerman, *The God of the Maccabees: Studies on the Meaning and Origin of the Maccabean revolt* (Leiden: Brill, 1979), 24–31; K. Bringmann, *Hellenistische Reform und Religionsverfolgung in Judäa* (Göttingen: Vandenhoeck & Ruprecht, 1983), 99–111.

[100] E.g., Lowe, "'ΙΟΥΔΑΙΟΙ," 103–6; S. J. D. Cohen, 'ΙΟΥΔΑΙΟΣ ΤΟ ΓΕΝΟΣ,' in *Josephus and the History of the Greco-Roman Period* (ed. F. Parente and J. Sievers; Leiden: Brill, 1994), 26–27.

other terms when we refer to "Roman citizens" or call Lucian a "Greek," so too "Judean" should be allowed to shoulder its burden as an ethnic term full of complex possibilities. If modern Israel had been called "Yehudah," there would be Judeans today and the nomenclature of "Judean customs/traditions" (as in "the Judean community of Toronto") would not sound strange. In the Hellenistic-Roman period there *was* a Judea, which everyone knew about, and there were Judeans as surely as there were Egyptians and Babylonians. Translating "Judeans" requires us to locate ourselves in that other time, but that seems to be no bad thing for historians. Using two different translations for the same word, in this case uniquely, destroys the unified conception that insiders and outsiders evidently had of the *Ioudaioi.*

Again, the main impetus for redefining the *Ioudaioi* not as members of the living culture of Judea, but as a homeless and humiliated people in a perpetual state of aporia who could only cling to a few strange-seeming practices, came from Christian authors. The evidence for "anti-Judaism" among Christians (actually: *anti-Judean* sentiment, which resulted in the *construction* of "Judaism" as system; see part 1 above) need not be rehearsed here. From the beginning some Christian teachers found it important to their self-understanding to depict the *Ioudaioi* as bereft, cut loose, cast down, destroyed, even dead.[101] Origen is clear and typical:

> . . . and so God's watchful care (ἐπισκοπή) over the Judeans was transferred (μεταβιβάζουσαν) to those from the *ethne* [or Gentiles] who trusted in him. And one may see after Jesus's coming the Judeans entirely left behind (καταλελειμμένους) and possessing none of those things they considered awe-inspiring from antiquity; but there is not the merest hint of divinity among them. . . . For which *ethnos* except the Judeans alone has been banished from its mother-city and its own place along with the ancestral cult? (Ποῖον γὰρ ἔθνος πεφυγάδευται ἀπὸ τῆς ἰδίας μητροπόλεως καὶ τοῦ οἰκείου τόπου τῇ πατρίῳ θρησκείᾳ ἢ μόνοι Ἰουδαῖοι;) (*C. Cels.* 2.8)

Whereas scholars propose that the *Ioudaioi* had come to constitute a "religion" by Origen's time, having shed or diminished their geographical-ethnic character, his own view is nearly the precise opposite. His most plausible option for displacing them lies in observing that they now constitute *an ethnos only,* because they lack the cult (and so divine favor) that normally goes along with status as an *ethnos.* Whereas Tertullian has limited knowledge of contemporary realia in the Judean homeland, Origen lived in Caesarea and knows the reality well. He moves rhetorically from *Jerusalem's* current woes to the peculiarity of the Judeans' status among the *ethne,* but he cannot deny that they *are* an ancient and abiding *ethnos.* Describing them as having a *cultus without an ethnos,* or some such thing, would have been absurd; "religion" was not an option for him.

[101] Already Paul in 1 Thess 2:14–16 and Gal 3–4; Matt 8:11–12; 22:1–15. From a vast literature, P. Richardson, D. Granskou, and S. G. Wilson, eds., *Anti-Judaism in Early Christianity* (2 vols.; Waterloo: Wilfrid Laurier University Press, 1986), and J. Lieu, *Image and Reality: The Jews in the World of the Christians in the Second Century* (Edinburgh: T&T Clark, 1996) offer breadth and judicious analysis.

"Some Christian teachers," it must be said, because we should not forget the evidence in the margins for the ongoing appeal of Judean law and culture among other Christians, which must owe something to the Judeans' prestige as an *ethnos* of great antiquity with recognized laws. It is no romanticization to observe that Judea and its diaspora continued to offer Judaizers a civilization, a grounded culture with a full suite of law and custom, *not* merely a system of belief, as Christianity seemed to be—a form that still proved difficult to explain in existing categories.

The second objection to "Judean" has to do with what we normally label "conversion to Judaism," which has predisposed scholars to employ the language of religion. Cohen identifies the conversion of foreign peoples under the Hasmonaeans as the decisive moment in the development of a religious sense for *Ioudaios*. He had titled a famous article on the subject "Respect for Judaism by Gentiles According to Josephus"—though Josephus does not speak of "Judaism." Cohen's analysis there is at once puzzling and revealing of the category problem (emphasis added):

> For Josephus, then, "adherence" and "conversion" are *ill-defined concepts* that never receive extended discussion. (*Since they are not Josephan terms,* they appear in quotation marks throughout this essay.)

But what is one quoting, if not Josephus? Why not analyze Josephus's own language? How may one say that a certain concept remains "ill-defined" in Josephus when it simply did not exist there?

With respect to the lengthy narrative in Josephus (*Ant.* 20.17–96) on the conversion of Adiabene's royal family, Cohen makes the following argument (emphasis added):[102]

> Separate from, or in addition to, this ethnic-geographic meaning, Ἰουδαῖος can also have a *religious meaning.* A Ἰουδαῖος is someone who believes (or is supposed to believe) certain distinctive *tenets,* and/or follows (or is supposed to follow) certain distinctive practices, and/or is a member (or is supposed to be a member) of certain distinctive *religious organizations*—in other words, a Ἰουδαῖος is a *Jew, someone who follows Judaism,* the way of life of the Jews. The clearest Josephan examples of this usage occur in the *Antiquities'* account of the conversion of the royal house of Adiabene. . . . In these passages, *which speak about conversion to Judaism,* the ethnic-geographic meaning of Ἰουδαῖος is *entirely absent,* and *only a religious meaning* is intended. A Gentile can become a Ἰουδαῖος, a Jew.

The tacit complement to the final sentence appears to be, "A Gentile could not become a Judean."

Given that the categories "Judaism" and "religion" (or "religious organization") do not appear in Josephus and did not exist in his world, Cohen's analysis presents problems. In fact, the passage in question *brims* with the standard language of *ethnos,* law, and custom, as do Josephus's narratives generally. *He*

[102] Cohen, "*Ioudaios,*" 27.

does not speak of a "religious conversion," but rather of adopting or going over to *foreign laws, customs, and ways,* and that language is precisely what lends the story its force.

In the first part of this chapter, we observed the ancient prejudice against forsaking one's ancestral traditions in favor of *foreign* ones: even Medizing or Atticizing out of political necessity could bring retribution. Hellenizing, an issue also for Rome in her encounters with Greece,[103] became a life-or-death issue in Judea under Antiochus IV. Herodotus (4.76) illustrates the normal fear of foreign ways with his story of the sage Anacharsis, a Scythian who sought out Greek wisdom and, on returning home, was killed for celebrating foreign rites. Although Greeks and Romans were generally happy to tolerate foreign visitors or the addition of foreign customs to the native tradition, the Judeans posed a unique threat among the because adoption of their exclusive laws required abandonment of one's native traditions. We have seen this above in Philo's description of those choose to live under Judean law, and this is the world we enter in the story of Adiabene.

This is a *political* story, in keeping with the constitutional themes of *Antiquities.* The controlling theme is announced in the topic sentence (*Ant.* 20.17): Queen Helena and her son Izates "exchanged their way of life for the customs of the Judeans" (εἰς τὰ Ἰουδαίων ἔθη τὸν βίον μετέβαλον). In the elaboration at *Ant.* 20.34–36 we learn that a visiting Judean merchant had first taught Izates' wives "to worship God in the way that was *traditional* among the Judeans" (ὡς Ἰουδαίοις πάτριον ἦν), after which the king learned that his mother also "had been brought over (μετακεκομίσθαι) to their laws." Things come to a head at 20.38–39. Note the language here:

> When Izates discovered that his mother was very pleased with the *customs of the Judeans* (τοῖς Ἰουδαίων ἔθεσιν χαίρειν), he moved quickly to go over to them himself. Supposing that he could not be a real Judean unless he were circumcised (νομίζων τε μὴ ἂν εἶναι βεβαίως Ἰουδαῖος,[104] εἰ μὴ περιτέμοιτο), he was ready to do it.

Helena objects that this will be dangerous. Observe her reasoning:

> For he was a king, and it would generate massive ill will if his subjects should learn that he was devoted to *customs that were foreign and alien* to them (ὅτι ξένων ἐπιθυμήσειεν καὶ ἀλλοτρίων αὐτοῖς ἐθῶν): *they would not tolerate a Judean being their king.*

Although the Judean merchant assured Izates that he could worship the deity without circumcision "if indeed he had resolved to *emulate the ancestral traditions* of the Judeans" (20.41), another teacher, "reputed to be precise in the ancestral traditions," admonished him to go ahead with the crucial ritual (20.43). So he did, secretly. When his mother and the merchant found out, they became

---

[103] E. S. Gruen, *Culture and National Identity in Republican Rome* (Ithaca: Cornell University Press, 1992).

[104] Note the word-play in the rhyme of these two words.

apoplectic: "*because* his subjects would not tolerate a man ruling them who was a *devotee of foreign customs*" (20.47). Similarly, when Izates' older brother wished later to adopt Judean customs, the Adiabenian elite resolved to punish him "because he had come *to despise their own customs*" (μισήσοντα τὰ παρ' αὑτοῖς ἔθη; 20.77).

The civic, political, and social character of the Adiabenian royals' initiative is emphasized by Josephus. Helena soon visits Jerusalem, he narrates, where she will spend most of her remaining years; she brings in food supplies to alleviate famine and builds a palace along with other monumental structures, one of which will serve as her tomb (*Ant.* 20.49–53, 95–96; *War* 4.567; 5.147, 252–253)—the sarcophagus now housed in the Louvre. Likewise, Izates sends famine relief (20.53) and even dispatches his five young sons "to learn precisely our ancestral language and culture" (τὴν . . . γλῶτταν τὴν παρ' ἡμῖν πάτριον καὶ παιδείαν ἀκριβῶς μαθησομένους; 20.71). A couple of decades later, two relatives of Monobazus, king of Adiabene in the 60s, are credited with a crucial role in the Judeans' initial, successful attack on Cestius Gallus's Twelfth Legion (*War* 2.520). And "the brothers and sons of King Izates"—presumably, the very sons who had grown up in Jerusalem—were reportedly among the last hold-outs in September of 70, who sued for terms with an infuriated Titus; he took them to Rome as hostages for Adiabene's future quiescence (*War* 6.356–357). Mother, son, and grandchildren, therefore, were indeed "real Judeans," just as Izates had first desired. It is not possible to abstract from this dramatic political realignment an affair of "religion."

Josephus's brief account of another foreign king, Polemo of Cilicia, who had himself circumcised and took on the Judeans' customs in order to marry Berenice, gives the same impression. When she deserted him, Josephus says, Polemo was "at once *liberated from* the marriage *and from* persevering in the Judeans' customs" (τοῦ τοῖς ἔθεσι τῶν Ἰουδαίων ἐμμένειν ἀπήλλακτο; *Ant.* 20.146). Lacking the Adiabienians' enthusiasm for these foreign laws, evidently, the Cilician king's adoption of them had (in the story) proven a significant burden.

That adopting Judean laws involved a decisive shift from one *ethnos* to another is clear across the range of evidence. Even in the ahistorical and rarefied romance *Joseph and Aseneth,* Pentephres' daughter at first rejects her father's proposal out of hand *because she worships the Gods of the Egyptians* (2.4–5) and will not marry a man of *another race,* a former prisoner at that, and a Canaanite (4.12–13). When she finally decides to marry Joseph, accordingly, this entails the rejection of "the gods of the Egyptians'" (12.5), which in turn distances her from her parents (2.11).

Similar issues of ethnic and familial connections receive considerable play in Tacitus's famous description of the *Iudaei* (*Hist.* 5.1–13):

> For the worst element [from other nations], their ancestral devotions left scorned, kept sending tribute and levies to *that place* [Jerusalem], thus growing the wealth of the Judeans. (*Nam pessimus quisque spretis religionibus patriis tributa et stipes illuc congerebant, unde auctae Iudaeorum.*) (5.5)

This is all ethnic and political language: defaulting in basic respect for one's ancestral tradition, pursuing *foreign customs,* and even making an *alien city* wealthy. Judeans practice circumcision, Tacitus continues, in order to be recognized by this difference:

> And those who go have gone over *to their custom* practice the same thing. There is nothing they absorb more quickly than to disdain the Gods, to *abandon their ancestral land, to hold in contempt parents, children, brothers.* (*Transgressi in morem eorum idem usurpant, nec quicquam prius imbuuntur quam contemnere deos, exuere patriam, parentes liberos fratres vilia habere.*)

This is almost precisely what Philo says, except that he welcomes the transformation.

Most interesting is the language of the Roman senator Cassius Dio. He first explains (37.16.5) that "The region has been named Judea, and the people themselves Judeans" (ἥ τε γὰρ χώρα Ἰουδαία καὶ αὐτοὶ Ἰουδαῖοι ὠνομάδαται), confirming the translation advocated here. He goes on to describe their temple in Jerusalem, their beliefs, and practices, without any apology for speaking of the *Ioudaioi* as a functioning *ethnos* even at his time of writing in the third century. In translating this passage it seems impossible to justify any word other than "Judeans" for the *Ioudaioi,* given Dio's connection of the people's name with that of the place, under the same verb, though still the Loeb edition renders "Jews." Matters get very interesting with what comes next. Dio observes (37.17.1) that "this appellation [*Ioudaioi*] applies also to all the other people who emulate their legal code, even if they are of foreign ethnicity" (ἡ δὲ ἐπίκλησις . . . φέρει δὲ καὶ ἐπὶ τοὺς ἄλλους ἀνθρώπους, ὅσοι τὰ νόμιμα αὐτῶν, καίπερ ἀλλοεθνεῖς ὄντες, ζηλοῦσι). Plainly, as for Tacitus, it is remarkable to Dio that members of one *ethnos* should be able to identify with another one in this way. The language is explicitly ethnic, not "religious" (whatever that could mean). We must speak here of "Judeans," given the first part of the passage, and we have no basis for abruptly switching to "Jews" for the sequel about emulation of foreigners' laws. This perception of national betrayal was presumably the reason why, according to the epitome of Dio's later account, the prospect of "drifting off into the ways of the Judeans" (ἐς τὰ τῶν Ἰουδαίων ἤθη ἐξοκέλοντες) caused such upheaval among members of the Roman elite at the end of the first century (67.14.2; 68.1.2).

When we describe "conversion to Judaism" in the Roman world as if it were a religious phenomenon akin to something in modern experience, we fail to capture the main problem expressed by ancient observers, from the Adiabenian nobility to the Roman: they could not accept it *because* it involved a betrayal of the native *ethnos* and its ancestral traditions. The issue could not be for them, and it was not, framed as one of "religious" choice.

We close the circle by returning to Josephus's more systematic comments on adoption of Judean laws. We noted above his response to Apion's complaint that Judeans could not be Alexandrians. Later in the same volume he crafts a prospectus of the Judean constitution designed to obviate, among other things, the accusation of misanthropy, by demonstrating the Judeans' posture of humanity toward the world (φιλανθρωπία). An essential part of this posture is the welcome given to those from other ἔθνη (πρὸς ἀλλοφύλους) who wish to come and live under the highly philosophical Judean laws (*Ag. Ap.* 2.210). Here again, what we call "conversion" is actually a matter of adopting a *new citizenship.* Only so can we understand why Josephus contrasts the *Spartan* concern to protect their laws (paralleled also among the Athenians), which resulted *for them* in xenophobia and the expulsion of foreigners, with the Judeans' equal concern to protect their laws, accompanied however by a welcome extended to all those wishing to live under their laws (2.59–61).

Again, the available categories are ethnic and political, with a strong philosophical tinge. That *we* insist on the religious nature of conversion is our problem, a function of our time and place. Josephus and his Judean contemporaries did not see it that way. Since they knew no "religion" of "Judaism," there could be no "religious conversion" in modern senses.

Conclusions and Corollaries

It is quite proper that modern histories of the Jews or Judaism should track the vicissitudes of this people across millennia, in the same way that one may write histories of the English, Greeks, Italians, Germans, and Christians over twenty or more centuries. But in all such cases we recognize that ancient conditions, terminology, and categories were different from our own. Hellas was of course not modern "Greece"; the *Germani* of Tacitus or the later Angles were not without further ado "Germans" and "English." That the modern words "emperor," "prince," and "Kaiser / Czar" have developed from *imperator, princeps,* and *Caesar* does not justify substituting the modern terms for the ancient, because those words meant something different. In the same way, although "Jew" and "Judaism" have developed from Ἰουδαῖος / Ἰουδαϊσμός and cognates, the Greek and Latin terms carried a different charge in their ancient contexts. In many of these cases, there is no great harm in using the familiar terms for popular studies, which can gently explain the historical situation. For academic purposes, the simplest solution is often to use the ancient terms themselves in transliteration, as we often do for *princeps* and *imperator.* But this is of dubious merit in translation projects, and cumbersome in other efforts to make the fruits of scholarship more broadly accessible. In the case of *Ioudaios/Iudaeus,* the most adequate English option is "Judean," by analogy with the other ethnica alongside which ancient writers consistently place it.

The *Ioudaioi* of the Greco-Roman world remained an ἔθνος, a people associated with a place and its customs—no matter how far, or how long, they had been away from Judea. The many upheavals in Judean politics between 200 B.C.E. and 200 C.E. had no discernible effect on this category, any more than the destructions of Carthage and rebellious Corinth in 146 B.C.E., the many reversals in Macedonian or Spartan or Pergamene fortunes during the two centuries B.C.E., or the abrupt change in Egypt's status in 30 B.C.E., required a change of name for the people concerned. Carthaginians, Corinthians, Egyptians, and other peoples were still known by their traditional names, as living—if humbled—ἔθνη. So also, to themselves and outside observers, the *Ioudaioi* remained what they always had been: Judeans. There was no ready alternative, since the Greco-Roman world knew no category of religion, no *-isms* denoting religious allegiance, and no "Judaism."

The rare *Ioudaismos* ("Judaization") was usable only in the special context of movement toward or away from Judean law and life, in contrast to some other cultural pull. That is why the term is hardly ever used. *Ioudaismos* as a belief system and way of life—as a *concept* abstracted from the realities of Judea, Jerusalem, temple and priesthood, sacrificial cult, aristocratic governance, political constituton, ancestral laws and traditions—was the construction of an ascendant *Christianismos* from the third to fifth centuries C.E. *Christianismos* was itself a new and hybrid kind of group, which drew elements from *ethne,* cults, philosophies, *collegia,* and magical systems; it was also based initially in households.[105] After long struggles to define its place in the world by existing categories, some of its teachers began to turn the tables: they made a true *-ism* of what had been initially (in Paul and Ignatius) a conversionist calque on *Ioudaismos* and asserted its revealed normativeness, constructing both a static *Hellenismos* / *Paganismos* and a *Ioudaismos* as foils, to facilitate polemical contrast. It was not until the Enlightenment's encounter with world cultures that full-fledged "religion" appeared as an isolable category. Critical historical scholarship's use of these late-antique and modern constructions as if they were live possibilities in antiquity creates conceptual mismatches at every step.

If the foregoing argument is valid, important consequences follow, not least for the comparison of "Judaism" and "Christianity." It becomes increasingly clear being a "Judean" and being a follower of Jesus were incommensurable categories, rather like being a Russian or a Rotarian, a Brazilian or a Bridge player. Scholars know this well, but our continued use of "religion," as if this were the *genus* of which "Judaism" and "Christianity" were two *species,* tends to de-historicize and obfuscate the matter. Whereas the *Ioudaioi* were understood not as a "licensed religion" (*religio licita*) but as an *ethnos,* the followers of Jesus faced formidable problems explaining exactly what they were, and increasingly so as they distanced themselves from, and were disavowed by, the well-known *ethnos.* The single most pressing question for followers of Jesus, "Are we part of the Judean *ethnos* or not?" was finessed in countless ways. It seems to have been Tertullian's rejection of all such efforts that catalysed the newly confident program of Christian normativeness, with the reformulation of other options as pale imitations of its own *-ism.* Although that approach would soon dominate Christian discourse, it did not persuade everyone. The Judaizing that we observe among Gentile Christians from the first to the fourth centuries must have been due in some measure to a sense of Christianity's continuing vulnerability, still assailed by Julian in the mid-fourth century.

---

[105]Nock, *Conversion,* 187–211, esp. 205, 210–11; now Rives, "Christian Expansion," 32–38, 41.

Chapter 6

Pharisees in the Narratives of Josephus

What do we really know about the Pharisees? A hallmark of Jacob Neusner's scholarship is the maxim "what we cannot show, we do not know." More than three decades ago, he demonstrated that impatience in resolving historical questions about the Pharisees had led scholars to approach the evidence—i.e., the literary sources—in a jejune manner.[1] The result was a bewildering array of mutually exclusive hypotheses, each requiring assent to certain prior assumptions, and none susceptible of proof in a meaningful sense.[2] Neusner insisted rather that we first attend to the portrait of the Pharisees in each text as a construction suited to the work's interests, date, and audience—a principle he has applied systematically to rabbinic literature, with profound consequences for interpreters and historians alike. Only when the evidence is thus understood *in situ* can we reasonably formulate historical hypotheses to explain it.

In the spirit of Neusner's distinction between interpreting texts and historical reconstruction, my work has focused on understanding Josephus's narratives—most recently in the context of post-70 Flavian Rome, where Josephus's first audiences were to be found. This is itself a historical kind of interpretation, and a necessary propadeutic to efforts at reconstructing the history behind the texts. Yet it tends to sharpen the distinction between interpretation—focused upon the text as medium of communication—and reconstruction of realities behind the text.

This approach commends itself not because one should not *care* about the underlying history or the external referents, but rather because reconstruction of them, which remains an aspiration for most readers of Josephus, must be conducted with a rigor sufficient to explain all relevant evidence, whether literary or material.[3] In Josephus's case, the very richness and subtlety of the evidence render efforts to get behind it—to events as we might have seen them—fraught with peril. Archaeology or parallel literary accounts may provide independent confirmation of certain scenic elements (sites, buildings, distances, provincial administration, military practices, names of key figures) mentioned by Josephus; very rarely do

[1] From Politics to Piety: The Emergence of Pharisaic Judaism (Englewood Cliffs: Prentice Hall, 1973), 13.

[2] Examples in Mason, *Josephus on the Pharisees,* 1–10 and related notes.

[3] On the problem of historical method and the use of Josephus, see S. Mason, *Josephus and the New Testament* (2d rev. ed.; Peabody, Mass.: Hendrickson, 2003).

we have such other material for reaching behind Josephus's accounts of who did what, when, and why.

This and the next chapter are therefore about *Josephus's Pharisees,* not about *the Pharisees* as they understood themselves, or as we might have encountered them via time travel. This first chapter examines the role of the Pharisees in Josephus's narratives. Those passages in which he halts the action to present the Pharisees as a philosophical school, alongside Essenes and Sadducees, we shall reserve for the next chapter.

Any interpretation of Josephus's Pharisees must reckon with a basic fact, all too often overlooked. Namely, the group figures only incidentally in his thirty volumes: one could write a fairly detailed account of Josephus and each of his four compositions without mentioning the Pharisees. They are not even as prominent as other minor supporting players—Herod's executed sons, Parthian rulers (even Adiabenians), Arabians, Pompey the Great, the Egyptian Queen Cleopatra—let alone the major figures of Josephus's stories: biblical, Herodian, Hasmonean, or revolutionary.

In *Judean War,* the Pharisees are named in seven sentences in books 1 and 2. Although they shape the narrative in perhaps fifteen sentences all told, they do not appear in the main story (*viz.,* books 3–7). In the leisurely twenty-volume narrative of *Antiquities* they get more space, though again not in the trunk of the work anticipated in the prologue (*Ant.* 1.5–26), namely: books 1 through 11 or 12. As in *War,* Pharisees appear mainly in connection with the Hasmonean and Herodian sections of *Antiquities.* They account for some twenty of the 432 sections in book 13 (thus, one part in forty-two in that volume), and receive glancing mention in book 15, a paragraph at 17.41–45, plus a couple of sentences in book 18 (outside the schools passage there). In the 430 sections of Josephus's one-volume *Life,* an appendix to *Antiquities,* Pharisees appear at two crucial points (*Life* 12, 191–198; incidentally at 21). *Against Apion,* which explains and defends the Judean constitution and laws, omits them along with the other two schools.[4]

The four philosophical-school passages, subject of chapter 2 in this book, do not alter this impression of the Pharisees' narrative marginality. In *War* 2.119–166, Pharisees and Sadducees are both dwarfed by the Essenes. In *Antiquities* 13.171–173, each school receives one sentence. In *Antiquities* 18.12–15, the Pharisees again receive less attention (and praise) than the Essenes (18.18–20). And in *Life* 10–11, all three schools yield immediately to Josephus's beloved teacher Bannus.

We should realize from the start, then, that Josephus could have had no serious axes to grind concerning the Pharisees, or none that he expected to communicate to audiences who lacked our technologies for locating and assembling "Pharisee passages." A Roman audience could have been forgiven if, after hearing or reading Josephus, they did not remember much about this group. This does not mean that Josephus had no view of the Pharisees, which we might still discern in what he wrote—*because* we are interested in the question and it is easy for

---

[4]Essene positions, however, are now ascribed to the whole nation, as Porphyry seems to have realized (*Abst.* 4.11.1–2).

us to gather the material. But given the textual data, we should be wary of theories that make the Pharisee passages drive interpretations of Josephus's works or even his thought in general.

It may be tempting to elevate the historical worth of the few Pharisee passages in Josephus on the principle that, precisely because the group is not significant in his narratives, he had little stake in massaging their image; thus, his incidental remarks likely reflect the historical situation. Yet Josephus is an artful writer, entirely capable of exploiting for momentary purposes even the smallest bit-player—youthful hot-head, courageous fighter, would-be tyrant.[5] We cannot so easily escape the web of his narrative world, even in the case of minor players.

Here, then, is a survey of the Pharisees in Josephus's narratives.

In *Judean War*

Since the Pharisees appear almost exclusively in the Hasmonean and Herodian stretches of *War,* my sketch of the relevant context will focus on those sections in books 1 and 2, which are preparatory to the book's main story.

Josephus wrote *Judean War* in the difficult environment of Rome in the 70s. The recent victory of Vespasian and his son Titus was being exuberantly celebrated (in the triumph, the new monumental buildings, coins, arches, and literature) as a primary legitimation of Flavian authority.[6] Predictably, the conflict was being reported in fawning pro-Flavian "histories," to the severe detriment of the Judeans. Josephus responds to this situation with a work that will, he claims, attempt to restore some balance (1.1–2, 6–8). The first sentence identifies him as a proud aristocrat and priest from Jerusalem, who fought against the Romans at the beginning and was then compelled to watch from their side (1.3). This rare *curriculum vitae* allowed him enviable claim to the balance of perspectives that had been prized as the key to impartiality since Herodotus invented "history"—objectivity in the modern sense being not yet on the horizon—as well as the eyewitness access required by Thucydides and Polybius.

In a complex and often brilliant narrative, Josephus will develop some of the following thematic lines: the essential virtue of the Judeans and the dignity of their leaders; their long suffering under incompetent and corrupt Roman equestrian governors; the Judeans' manly virtue and contempt for pain and death (often contrasted with the behavior of hapless legionaries); the *gravitas* of

---

[5]Josephus's intricate handling of the biblical narrative is the best documented analysis of his narrative methods (Moehring, "Novelistic Elements"; Feldman, *Rewritten Bible;* idem., *Interpretation;* idem., *Judean Antiquities 1–4;* C. Begg, *Judean Antiquities 5–7* (vol. 4 of *Flavius Josephus: Translation and Commentary;* ed. Steve Mason; Leiden: Brill, 2004). For the historical implications, see Moehring "Joseph ben Matthia"; Steve Mason, "Contradiction or Counterpoint? Josephus and Historical Method." *Review of Rabbinic Judaism* 6 (2003): 145–88.

[6]See F. Millar, "Last Year in Jerusalem: Monuments of the Jewish War in Rome," in *Flavius Josephus* (ed. Edmondson, Mason, and Rives), 101–28.

their aristocratic leaders, who would either have fought a more successful war or reached respectable terms with the Romans, had they lived; the civil war that threatened and finally erupted when a few tyrants managed to overturn aristocratic control and so precipitate the final disaster.

The unifying theme of all this is the question of the Judean ethnic character. In antiquity it was widely assumed that behavior issued from one's innate character: both individuals and groups behaved the way they did *because* of their character. In the case of individuals, this principle may be seen in the rhetorical structure of legal defenses—the frequently used argument from "probability" appealed to the ancestry, familial glory, education, and virtue of the accused, with surprisingly little attention directed to the facts of the case: "The accused *could not* plausibly have done what he is charged with because of his character (including ancestry and glorious deeds)!"[7] Similarly, ethnographers, geographers, and historians tended to see correlations among the characters or natures of whole peoples, their environmental conditions, their political constitutions, and their national behavior.[8] Thus, when Tacitus sets out to describe the fall of Jerusalem in 70 C.E., he thinks it important to supply an explanation of the Judeans' origins, culture, and character (*Hist.* 5.1–6, esp. 2). Because the revolt against Rome was taken to be the expression of a rebellious and misanthropic nature, Josephus understood his task in similar terms but from the other side: to furnish a more accurate picture of that national character, along with a better explanation of the war's origins and outcome.

It is curious that Josephus should begin his account of the war in 66–73 C.E. with the Hasmonean revolt 250 years earlier, following that with a detailed portrait of King Herod (40–4 B.C.E.) and Archelaus (1.31–2.116). This is all the stranger because he then glides over the three decades from 4 B.C.E. to the mid-20s C.E. with almost no material. Among the many reasons one might adduce for this interest in Hasmoneans and Herods (beyond the formal justification in *War* 1.17–18) we should include the following. The Hasmonean story, remembered annually at Hanukkah, had provided inspiration for those dreaming of independence from Rome in the recent war.[9] Himself cherishing roots in the

[7]E.g., Aristotle, *Rhet.* 1.2.1–15.1356a; 2.1.2–3.1377b; Cicero, *De or.* 2.182; Quintilian, *Inst.* 5.12.10; Aulus Gellius, *Noct. att.* 4.18.3–5; J. M. May, *Trials of Character: The Eloquence of Ciceronian Ethos* (Chapel Hill: University of North Carolina, 1988), 6–8; G. A. Kennedy, *A New History of Classical Rhetoric* (Princeton: Princeton University Press, 1994), 102–27.

[8]Along with known works by Herodotus, Hecataeus, and Strabo (among many), note Plutarch (*Mor.* 799b–800a) on the distinctive character of each *polis,* and Quintus Curtius (8.9.20) on the environment and character of India and its inhabitants. For the classical grounding of this conception see Plato, *Resp.* 544d–591; W. Jaeger *Paideia: The Ideals of Greek Culture* (3 vols. Oxford: Oxford University Press, 1973), 2:320–47; B. H. Isaac, *The Invention of Racism in Classical Antiquity* (Princeton: Princeton University Press, 2004), 56–74.

[9]W. R. Farmer, *Maccabees, Zealots, and Josephus; An Inquiry into Jewish Nationalism in the Greco-Roman Period* (Westport: Greenwood, 1956); Martin Hengel, *The Zealots: Investigations into the Jewish Freedom Movement in the Period from Herod I until*

Hasmonean-priestly dynasty (*War* 5.419; *Ant.* 16.187; *Life* 1–6), Josephus retells the story so as to argue that the Hasmoneans actually created a Judean state only in alliance with the superpower Rome (*War* 1.38). Therefore, their storied and paradigmatic "freedom" was astute, but never absolute. In Josephus's narrative the Hasmoneans and King Herod (also Herod's father Antipater) demonstrate rather the *diplomatic skills* that the author attributes to members of the elite such as himself: a remarkable adaptability in making alliances as needed with almost anyone (e.g., various Seleucid pretenders or the successive strongmen of the Roman civil wars), *for the welfare of the Judean state.* Given that world powers come and go under inscrutable divine providence, as Jeremiah and Daniel had understood long before, this was the only feasible way of life for peoples such as the Judeans.[10] As it happens, Josephus's approach intersected well with contemporary political reflection among other elites in the eastern Mediterranean.[11]

Further, because the government of the Hasmoneans and then Herod saw the concentration of political power in one person, their cases brought to light the very problem that plagued all monarchies and Rome herself since the rise of dictators in the first century B.C.E., and especially since Augustus had carefully developed a *de facto* monarchy: if one person is entrusted with supreme power, how to secure a peaceful succession? What do we do for an encore? John Hyrcanus, though a successful and beneficent administrator, foresaw that his less pious and less fortunate sons would quickly trigger the downfall of the dynasty (*War* 1.68–9). In a similar vein, although Herod's reign was consumed by the making and canceling of wills, when he died in 4 B.C.E. the succession saga dragged on at great length in the hands of Augustus—whose own problems in finding and keeping an heir were notorious[12] (2.1–116). The problem of monarchy and its Achilles-heel, succession, will become a still more prominent issue in *Antiquities.*[13] In *War,* this issue is tied up closely with the work's central questions of political "freedom" and governance.[14] The whole project of the so-called tyrants, who will seize the revolt from the nation's aristocracy, is allegedly based on the monarchical principle: each one seeks to be supreme ruler for the basest of reasons, with no genuine concern for the welfare of the nation, no training in or understanding of governance, and no provision for the sequel.[15]

---

70 A.D. (Edinburgh: T&T Clark, 1989), 149–55, 171–73 (a history of scholarship on the question), 377.

[10] D. Daube, "Typology in Josephus," *JJS* 31 (1980): 18–36; S. J. D. Cohen, "Masada, Literary Traditions, Archaeological Remains, and the Credibility of Josephus." *JJS* 33 (1982): 385–405; Mason, "Daniel."

[11] G. W. Bowersock, *Greek Sophists in the Roman Empire* (Oxford: Clarendon, 1969); E. L. Bowie, "The Greeks"; Eckstein, "Josephus and Polybius"; idem., *Moral Vision;* Swain, *Hellenism;* S. Goldhill, *Being Greek under Rome: Cultural Identity, the Second Sophistic, and the Development of Empire* (Cambridge: Cambridge University Press, 2001).

[12] Syme, *Revolution,* 415, 419–39; W. Eck, *The Age of Augustus* (Oxford: Blackwell, 2003), 113–25.

[13] S. Mason, "Reading on and between the Lines."

[14] See ch. 3 in the present volume.

[15] E.g., *War* 2.443, 264; 4.177–178, 273–279, 397; 5.18–19, 363; 6.102.

We first meet the Pharisees of *War* when the Hasmonean dynasty is already well into its downward spiral, following the death of Hyrcanus I. This degeneration began with Aristobulus I, who assumed the diadem and thus transformed the state into a monarchy (*War* 1.70; 104–103 B.C.E.). In keeping with this tyrannical turn, he lost no time in murdering family members (1.71–84). His brother Alexander Janneus had a much longer and in some respects successful reign (103–76 B.C.E.), but it too was marred by tyranny (1.97). Josephus remarks that although Alexander seemed (δοκεῖν) to be moderate (1.85), he faced a mass rebellion of the people, which he put down brutally by killing some 50,000 of them (1.91).

When Alexander died, his wife Alexandra assumed the throne as queen. She was a ray of hope for the dynasty because she utterly lacked her husband's brutality (the narrator authoritatively reports): she not only had a *reputation* for piety (δόξαν εὐσεβείας); she really *was* a precise observer of the laws (1.108). This piety, however, was also her downfall, for it caused her to give far too much power to the Pharisees, whom Josephus now introduces as a group with a reputation for, or image of (δοκεῖν), precision in the laws (1.110). Josephus describes their relation to the queen with a striking verb, normally used of plants growing from the same root: the Pharisees grow alongside (παραφύονται) Alexandra and encroach on her authority parasitically.

Indeed, the Pharisees become the *de facto* government in many respects, exploiting the queen's naïveté to settle their own scores: they arrange for their enemies to be bound and banished, their friends to be recalled and liberated. Josephus remarks that whereas Alexandra bore all the costs of rule, the Pharisees enjoyed the real authority behind her protective screen (1.112). Although they were not mentioned in the Alexander narrative, they are evidently on the side of those who opposed Alexander, for they take revenge on the late king's advisors and friends; therefore, the eminent and distinguished classes (would Josephus locate his kind of people here?) have the most to fear from their revenge (1.113–114). Whereas Alexandra succeeded in controlling neighboring nations through shrewd military planning, Josephus opines, the Pharisees controlled her (1.112).

This account of Alexandra and the Pharisees moves the narrative along by offering an explanation for the continuing decline of the Hasmonean house. After the deep wounds inflicted on the body politic by Alexander, yet before the dynasty reaches its nadir in the rivalry between Alexandra's sons Hyrcanus II and Aristobulus II (which ushers in Roman rule), the potential of this just and pious queen to turn things around is undercut by her alliance with vindictive and aggressive Pharisees.

More specifically, the passage carries forward a number of key Josephan themes. Chief among these is the contrast between seeming and being, reputation and truth, illusion and reality, names or titles and actual authority. This sort of dialectic is Josephus's métier.[16] Just as the historical man lived and wrote in a

[16]Cf. Plato's programmatic distinction between the world of appearances, sense-perception, and opinion, on the one hand, and knowledge and the real on the other (*Resp.* 514a–517c). In Josephus's *War,* Hyrcanus II's mischievous courtiers complain that he has

world of "doublespeak," dissonance, irony, and indirection in imperial Rome, so Josephus the writer often has his characters (including himself) say things that the audience knows to be either completely or substantially false. It is a world of unsettling and constant double games, where nothing is what it appears to be. In Josephus, as in Tacitus, we see vividly the "rhetoricized mentality" fostered by Greco-Roman education for elite males.[17] In the story of Queen Alexandra, the image-reality dialectic is everywhere at work. Her husband had given the *impression* of moderation, but this turned out not to be the reality. She really *was* moderate and pious, but this led her to mistakenly yield power to the *seemingly* moderate Pharisees. Their invitation to power allowed the Pharisees, in turn, to assume the *real* authority of the state, leaving her the outward shell and *title*.

Other characteristic language of Josephus has to do with "precision" (ἀκρίβεια), or apparent precision, in interpreting the laws. He will return to the Pharisees' reputation for legal precision in several places, even in his autobiography when describing Simon son of Gamaliel.[18] Although it was long conventional for scholars to relieve Josephus of responsibility for hostile attitudes toward the Pharisees by attributing them to his (undigested) sources,[19] these connections of language and perspective preclude such maneuvers. Indeed, we already see here one likely reason for Josephus's hostility toward the group: himself a member of the priestly elite, which has been charged with preserving and interpreting the Judean laws ever since the time of Moses (see notes 30 and 51 below), the sudden rise to power of a popular and populist group, whose members lack the aristocratic culture that creates elite statesmen and who undertake to rid the state of their aristocratic enemies, could not but attract his ire.

This debut of the Pharisees in Josephus's narratives, which is also their fullest scene in *War*, is at best inauspicious. Their two fleeting appearances in the later story confirm their ongoing influence with the people, but our author is not interested in exploring this phenomenon for his audience.

In *War*, King Herod is mainly a virtuous figure: a tough, proud, generous, and wily Judean who constantly shows other nations what his people can do in military and diplomatic spheres alike. He is plagued by succession worries, however, and his downfall is attributed by Josephus to the women in his life (1.431, 568). It is in the latter half of the Herod story, which explores his domestic woes, that the Pharisees turn up as *agents provocateurs*. Josephus as narrator plainly disapproves of Herod's sister-in-law, the unnamed wife of Pheroras, who behaves

---

only the title (ὄνομα) and not the authority (ἐξουσία) of king (1.209). Later (1.561), Antipater pleads with his father not to leave him the mere title of king while others hold the real power. At 2.208, *princeps*-designate Claudius promises through Agrippa I that he will rest content with honor of the title or address (προσηγορία) while governing in fact through senatorial consultation. More generally on reputations or seeming in contrast to being: *War* 1.648; *Ant.* 17.41; 19; 332; *Ag. Ap.* 1.18, 67; Cassius Dio 36.11.

[17] Rudich, *Political Dissidence;* idem., *Dissidence and Literature;* Bartsch, *Actors.*

[18] *War* 2.162; *Ant.* 17.41; *Life* 191; cf. Mason, *Josephus on the Pharisees,* 89–113.

[19] Hölscher, "Josephus"; Schwartz, "Josephus and Nicolaus"; Sanders, *Practice and Belief,* 390.

insolently in public and conspires to turn the king's son Antipater against him (1.568–570). At a hearing of Herod's *consilium,* one of the charges brought against the woman is that she has "furnished rewards to the Pharisees for opposing him" (1.571). We should like to know much more, and *Antiquities* (below) develops the story, but here in *War* Josephus is not interested in explaining further; he merely cites this among several examples of the woman's alleged impudence. As for the Pharisees, who played such a large role in Alexandra's reign, it is clear only that they remain a significant presence and a source of trouble for Herod. Although we might expect Josephus to admire those who oppose kings, given his stated preference for aristocratic rule, his narrative is much more textured than such simple dichotomies would require. The Pharisees can oppose eminent citizens as well as kings, and in this case are allied with a troublesome woman; they do not seem to be Josephus's kind of people.

In *War* 2 Josephus mentions the Pharisees twice: first in the philosophical-schools passage that features the Essenes (*War* 2.119–166), which we shall consider contextually in the following chapter; second, in a brief notice about the constituency of the leading citizens at the outbreak of the revolt. Seventy years have passed in real time since the death of King Herod in 4 B.C.E.—Josephus does not, however, write in chronological proportion—and a lot has happened. Under the deteriorating maladministration of the later equestrian governors sent by Nero, predictable tensions threaten to explode in violence and civil war, while members of the elite struggle to keep a lid on things in order to avoid Roman intervention. A series of riots induces Queen Berenice and her brother King Agrippa II to try oratory, the ancient statesman's best friend, in order to calm the masses; but this ultimately fails (*War* 2.342–407). Some younger aristocrats, led by the temple commander, insist on suspending all sacrifices by foreigners and the daily sacrifice for Rome and its *princeps* (2.409–410). This defiant action advances the movement to war.

At this point Josephus remarks (*War* 2.411) that "'the elite' [or 'the principal men/the powerful': οἱ δυνατοί] came together in the same place (εἰς ταὐτό) with the chief priests (τοῖς ἀρχιερεῦσιν) and those who were eminent among the Pharisees (καὶ τοῖς τῶν Φαρισαίων γνωρίμοις)," to discuss the brewing crisis. Brief though it is, the itemization is suggestive: the principal men or aristocrats, based in the priesthood and so naturally accompanied by the super-elite chief priests, are now also joined by the most prominent men of the Pharisees. Elsewhere, Josephus almost formulaically pairs the elite (οἱ δυνατοί or similar) with the chief priests as Jerusalem's leaders (2.243, 301, 316, 336, 422, 428, 648), *without* mentioning the Pharisees. In one other place he adds to this formula (οἵ τε ἀρχιερεῖς καὶ δυνατοί) a vague third term, "and the most eminent [stratum] of the city" (τό τε γνωριμώτατον τῆς πόλεως) (2.301). If leading Pharisees were in his mind as he wrote that, however, he chose not to burden his audience with this information. So the notice at 2.411, that the standard pair of priestly elite groups met with the leading Pharisees at that crucial point, seeming to stress that they also convened in the *same place,* hints that such a coalition was unusual in more normal times—necessitated here, we infer, by the emergency.

Although we later learn that it was quite possible to belong to the priestly caste and be a Pharisee (*Life* 197–198), membership in the Pharisees being a voluntary affiliation, members of the hereditary priestly aristocracy needed no school affiliation to give them status, and many apparently had none. It was by definition the elite class, comparable to other aristocracies in the Greek cities of the eastern empire, to which the Roman governors turned (or were supposed to turn) for collaboration in administering the province.[20] Inclusion of the Pharisees' leading representatives in this emergency council thus appears to be a diplomatic necessity, part of the elite's effort to calm the masses. Such a conclusion anticipates what will be spelled out in *Antiquities* (13.297–298; 18.15, 17) that the Pharisees had avenues of access to the masses that the priestly aristocracy as a body lacked.

Josephus's first known work does not, then, give the Pharisees much play. And yet the author's disdain seems clear. He gives the impression of mentioning them only when he must in order to tell his story, while leaving many obvious questions unanswered. What exactly was their social status and composition? Who were their leaders? How did they acquire such powerful enemies, whom they purged under Alexandra? Why were they so popular among the masses, and such a threat to Herod? How did they acquire their reputation for piety and careful observance if they were so politically cunning (as Josephus claims)?

Recounting Herod's final days, Josephus describes a popular uprising led by two influential "sophists," who also had a *reputation* for precision in the ancestral traditions (δοκοῦντες ἀκριβοῦντα τὰ πάτρια) and consequently enjoyed a reputation of the highest esteem among the whole nation; they were personally courageous in defending the laws against Herod's clear violation—placing a golden eagle atop the sanctuary (1.648–650; 2.5–6). Although Josephus's characterization leads those of us with concordances to suspect that *he* understood the popular teachers to have been Pharisees,[21] he again fails to convey any such connection to his Roman audience (who therefore could not have known it). He will not include moral courage among the traits of his Pharisees.

A similar case concerns two leaders of the people whom Josephus admires for their indignation against the Zealots' atrocities, and their opposition to the Zealots' appointment of an illegitimate high priest (4.159–160):

> For those among them [*sc.* ὁ δῆμος] with a reputation for excelling (οἱ προύχειν αὐτῶν δοκοῦντες),[22] Gorion son of Joseph and Symeon son of Gamaliel, kept exhorting both the gathered assemblies and each individual in private consultation that it was time to exact vengeance from the wreckers of freedom and to purge those who were polluting the sanctuary; the most eminent of the chief priests, Jesus son of Gamalas and Ananus son of Ananus, while castigating the populace for lethargy, in the meetings, roused them against the Zealots.

[20] D. C. Braund, "Cohors: The Governor and His Entourage in the Self-Image of the Roman Republic" in *Cultural Identity in the Roman Empire* (ed. R. Laurence and J. Berry; London: Routledge, 1998), 10–24; Meyer-Zwiffelhoffer, πολιτικῶς ἄρχειν.

[21] So, e.g., Sanders, *Practice and Belief*, 385.

[22] This is favorite, formulaic language in Josephus.

This cooperative venture is presented in an intriguing manner: some very popular teachers, with rhetorical skill and special access to individuals as well as groups, join the chief priests in trying to calm the masses. One of the two men named is none other than Simon son of Gamaliel, whom Josephus will describe in a later work as a leading Pharisee (*Life* 190–191), and his illustrious family is well known from other sources (*Acts* 5:34; 22:3; *m. Sotah* 9.15 *et passim*). Josephus must have known that Simon was a Pharisee, but again he chose not to reveal this to his audience—just where he is praising the man's behavior without demurral. When he later decides to label Simon a Pharisee, in the *Life*, the context will be very different and harshly critical (see below).

Thus, Pharisees hardly appear in Josephus's *War*, though for the historian they have a tantalizing presence behind the scenes. A dispassionate observer might have related much more than Josephus does: he seems to forego every opportunity to say more than is required for a coherent story, in which the Pharisees feature mainly for their negative (anti-royal, anti-aristocratic) traits. Although *War* is filled with digressions of various kinds (note especially the lengthy celebration of the Essenes in 2.119–161, as also the topographical and geographical excursuses), the Pharisees are not a group on which he cares to lavish attention. What he chooses to disclose about them to his audience is rather one-sided and derogatory: they latch on to the powerful in order to cause trouble for the nation, though their influence *must* be reckoned with.

In *Judean Antiquities*

Whereas *War*, written in the darkest days of post-war Rome, tried to portray the admirable Judean character in and through an account of the war's origin and course, Josephus's *magnum opus*, published about fifteen years later (93/94 C.E.; cf. *Ant.* 20.267), takes advantage of the additional time and space to explore Judean culture on a larger canvas, in particular the constitution (πολιτεία) of the Judean people (1.5, 10).[23] A nation's mode of governance was generally considered an expression of its character: people get the constitution they deserve.[24] This axiom stood in some tension with the recognition that constitutions change over time, from monarchy to aristocracy or oligarchy to some form of "democracy" and back again, as also with discussions of the optimal constitution,[25] which presupposed that peoples had an element of choice in their mode of governance. Rome itself had famously emerged from ancient kingship through the "mixed constitution" of the Republic to the current principate—a *de facto* monarchy,

---

[23]Note the prominence of constitution language in strategic places: *Ant.* 3.84, 213; 4.45, 184, 191, 193–195, 196–198, 302, 310, 312; 5.98, 179; 15.254, 281; 18.9; 20.229, 251, 261; *Ag. Ap.* 2.188, 222, 226, 272–273. At *Ag. Ap.* 2.287 Josephus recalls that he wrote *Antiquities* in order to give "an exact account of our laws and constitution."

[24]Plato, *Resp.* 544d–91; Jaeger, *Paideia*, 2:320–47.

[25]Famously, the sixth book of Polybius's *History*.

though crucially not yet called kingship in Rome itself. Although Roman authors seem to have largely given up the sort of abstract constitutional discussions that Herodotus, Plato, Aristotle, and Polybius had indulged (but note Cicero's *Republic* and *Laws*), Josephus's younger contemporary Tacitus reveals the ongoing concern in elite circles with relations between a *princeps* (or emperor) and an aristocratic Senate.[26] All tied up in that discussion was the question of true *Roman* character. Contemporary Greek writers also devoted considerable attention to the problem of local constitutions and aristocracies in the context of a Roman super-power.[27]

In his *Antiquities* as in his *War,* Josephus shows himself fully aware of such questions (e.g., what sort of "freedom" should nations desire—untrammeled or conditioned by political necessity?), which had become pressing among Roman and Greek elites, especially in the waning years of Domitian's reign, when Josephus was writing. His detailed portrait of the Judean constitution and the vicissitudes through which it had passed reveals abundant parallels with the Roman experience, which have been examined in detail elsewhere.[28] Crucially, both nations decisively reject kingship, as the inevitable precursor of tyranny, and Josephus is vocal in his insistence that the Judean constitution is aristocratic-senatorial.[29] The nation is properly run, its ancient laws preserved and rightly administered, by people like his good self: the hereditary priests, who have always constituted—already in the time of Moses and Joshua!—the governing council or Senate (βουλή, γερουσία).[30] The essay known as *Against Apion* (2.145–196) will develop in moving, idealized terms this image of a hereditary priestly college under the orchestration of the high priest, as the most sublime form of constitution imaginable.

In *Antiquities,* which assumes the obligations of history-writing, the picture is messier than in the *Against Apion.* After the principle of aristocratic governance has been enunciated by Moses and his successors, the masses nonetheless clamor for a king (*Ant.* 6.33–4). It was widely acknowledged in Josephus's day that the masses of all nations preferred powerful monarchs—even if these vaulted to power through bloody coups—to the vagaries, corruptions, and inefficiencies of aristocratic bodies.[31] Kings tended to be more solicitous of their popular base: it was much easier to keep the tiny aristocracy in check than to deal with overwhelming popular animosity. So, although Josephus's Samuel forcefully advocates aristocracy (*Ant.* 6.36), he must yield to popular demands, and the era of

---

[26] R. Syme, *Tacitus* (2 vols; Oxford: Clarendon, 1958), 408–34; B. Otis "The Uniqueness of Latin Literature." *Arion* 6 (1967): 199; R. Mellor *Tacitus* (London: Routledge, 1993), 87–112.

[27] See note 11 above.

[28] E.g., Feldman, *Judean Antiquities 1–4* (both his detailed commentary and my introductory essay in that volume).

[29] *Ant.* 4.223; 5.135; cf. Mason, "Reading on and between the Lines."

[30] *Ant.* 4.186, 218, 220, 255, 256, 325; 5.15, 43, 55. For the priestly core of this senatorial aristocracy, see *Ant.* 3.188; 4.304; *Life* 1; *Ag. Ap.* 1.29–37; 2.184–86.

[31] E.g., Cicero, *Rep.* 2.12.23; Livy 1.17.3.

kings, with its inevitable decline into tyranny, begins (6.262–268). The destruction of the first temple and with it the monarchy of Judah clears the way for a new aristocracy (11.111), but this is undone by the later Hasmoneans (13.300), who once again assume the diadem and quickly lead the nation to disaster. Roman intervention restores the aristocracy yet again (14.91), though this gives way to the Herodian monarchy—as a function of the Roman civil wars, which featured their own (Roman) contenders for supreme power. In the symmetrical structure of *Antiquities,* the two great king-tyrants of Judean history, Saul (book 6) and Herod (15–17), occupy corresponding positions.

Josephus devotes a surprising amount of *Antiquities'* final quarter to parallel constitutional crises: the Judean problem of finding a successor to King Herod and the Roman succession woes following Tiberius and Gaius Caligula.[32] For the Judeans, after the debacle of Herod's son Archelaus, matters are resolved for some decades when a native aristocracy (including our author) is allowed to govern Jerusalem under the remote supervision of a respectable, senior-senatorial Roman legate based in Syria, to which province Judea is joined (17.227, 355; 18.1–3; contrast *War* 2.117). This arrangement preserves Judea's native traditions and collective local leadership while at the same time securing the people's freedom—i.e., *freedom from native tyrants.* When *Antiquities* closes, however, this arrangement is beginning to unravel with the first rumblings of civil strife (e.g., 20.205–214), which *War* has described in detail. The Roman constitutional crisis, for its part, is *never* resolved, leaving open the possibility that *Antiquities* functions in part as a critique of Rome's increasingly monarchical governance at Josephus's time.[33]

Because some of the Pharisee passages of *Antiquities* develop items mentioned briefly in *War,* we need to bear in mind that Josephus frequently recounts in *Antiquities* 13–20 and *Life* stories already told in *War* 1–2. In virtually every case of overlap, however, the retelling is markedly different. He is a zealous practitioner of what ancient rhetoricians called *paraphrasis* or *metaphrasis* (παράφρασις, μετάφρασις)—changing the form of expression while retaining the thoughts (Theon, *Prog.* 62–4, 107–110; Quintilian, *Inst.* 1.9.2; 10.5.4–11)—and he certainly pushes the limits of "retaining the same thoughts." Changes run from the trivial to the comprehensive: dates, relative chronology, locations, *dramatis personae* and their motives, details of scene, and numbers.[34] Given Josephus's demonstrable freedom in retelling stories, and in view of parallel phenomena in other contemporary literature from the Gospels to Plutarch,[35] efforts to explain such changes programmatically—with reference to putative shifts of historiographical outlook, religious affiliation, moral convictions, personal allegiances, or political necessity[36]—seem a waste of scholarly energy. If Josephus changes

---

[32] Wiseman, *Death of an Emperor,* 1991.

[33] Mason, "Reading on and between the Lines"; see also ch. 3 in the present volume.

[34] These parallels are explored in great detail by Laqueur (*Historiker*) and Cohen (*Galilee and Rome*). For a comparative table illustrating the degree of difference between *War* and *The Life,* see Appendix C in Mason, *Life of Josephus.*

[35] E.g., Pelling, *Greek Historian.*

[36] Programmatically, Laqueur, *Historiker;* Rasp, "Flavius Josephus."

more or less every story that he retells, we have more to do with the rhetoricized mentality mentioned above than with a new ideological program.[37] He seems to abhor the prospect of boring his audience, at least by retelling stories verbatim, and so he experiments with new literary and rhetorical configurations, careless of the historical casualties.

Typical of such changes is our first encounter with the Pharisees in *Antiquities,* in a brief statement about the three schools' views on fate (13.171–173). Even this concise presentation is irreconcilable with the sketch of the schools' positions on fate in *War* 2.162–166, though he refers the audience to the earlier work for details (see the following chapter).

In assessing the role of Pharisees in *Antiquities,* we must again maintain some narrative perspective. They do not figure in the main part of the work (books 1–12), which outlines the origins of the aristocratic constitution, its contents, and early changes. This absence cannot be merely a function of chronology—i.e., because there were no Pharisees in the time of Moses or Saul—for Josephus does not hesitate to mention other current issues or figures in the course of his biblical paraphrase (e.g., 1.94, 108, 151; 4.146, 161; 7.101; 8.46). If he had any interest in doing so, he might well have extolled the Pharisees' legal tradition, or at least mentioned it, while elaborating upon Moses's laws and constitution, which he elaborates precisely because they form the *living code* by which Judeans of his day govern their lives. His failure to mention Pharisees or the other schools in the core of *Antiquities* is noteworthy.

After the brief philosophical aside of *Antiquities* 13.171–173 just mentioned, the Pharisees next appear in connection with the greatest crisis in the Hasmonean dynasty: the transition from the illustrious period of "senatorial" self-rule, led by the virtuous hero and high priest John Hyrcanus, to the destructive monarchy-cum-tyranny initiated by his short-lived and tragically self-absorbed son, Aristobulus I (13.301). Like *War, Antiquities* presents Hyrcanus I as the Hasmonean ruler most favored by God, the apogee of the glorious family (13.300). Following a detailed account of his exploits (e.g., successful manipulation of Seleucid rivals, Judaization of Idumea, renewed treaty with Rome, destruction of Samaria), Josephus tells a story with no parallel in *War,* but which helps to explain the mysterious "growth" of the Pharisees alongside Queen Alexandra in *War,* as well as the Pharisees' behavior toward Alexander's friends as recounted in the earlier work. Yet the new episode has a ripple effect on the whole Hasmonean story, changing its contours in significant ways.

The scene is a banquet, to which Hyrcanus invites "the Pharisees" (all of them?) because, our author notes, the virtuous high priest was one of their students (13.289). Because they "practiced philosophy" (see chapter 2), and because he wished to live a just life, which training in philosophy should produce, he invited them to offer criticism of anything untoward in his behavior (13.290). They all praised his conduct, but a certain Eleazar, also present at the dinner, boldly demanded that he relinquish the high priesthood on the ground—a false rumor,

[37] Further Mason, *Life of Josephus,* xxxvii–xli.

Josephus claims—that his mother had been a captive, and so presumably raped (13.290–292). At this, *all* the Pharisees become indignant (13.292). Josephus does not say that Eleazar was a Pharisee, and we soon learn that non-Pharisees were also present. For certain Sadducees in attendance cleverly exploit this opportunity by asking the Pharisees what punishment they deem suitable for the offending man. When the Pharisees call for (merely) severe corporal punishment—lashes and chains, rather than death (Josephus notes editorially that the Pharisees by nature take a moderate position in relation to punishments [φύσει πρὸς τὰς κολάσεις ἐπιεικῶς ἔχουσιν, 13.294])—the Sadducees are able to convince Hyrcanus that their rivals *approved* of the man's outburst, in spite of what our narrator plainly says. The Sadducees' device for proving this, asking the Pharisees how they would punish Eleazar's outburst, after their unanimous condemnation of his words, appears to confirm that Eleazar was not one of their school.

In any case, the Sadducees' gambit is successful and leads the prince to abandon his affiliation with the Pharisees. His new embrace of the Sadducees is dramatic: it results in his "dissolving the legal precepts established by [the Pharisees] among the populace" (τὰ τε ὑπ' αὐτὸν κατασταθέντα νόμιμα τῶν δῆμων καταλῦσαι) *and punishing those who continued to observe them* (13.296). This radical turn sets off a public uproar.

A Roman audience might reasonably wonder what practical difference the change would make, and so Josephus hastens to explain that the Pharisees follow a special set of legal prescriptions (νόμιμα) "from a succession of fathers" (ἐκ πατέρων διαδοχῆς) *in addition to the laws of Moses*—the latter being famously followed by all Judeans; the preceding narrative of *Antiquities* 1–12 has explored this common constitution. This supplementary legal tradition is rejected by the Sadducees, who recognize only the "inscribed" laws (of Moses).

Although this passage has been adduced as evidence for the rabbinic doctrine of תורה שבעל פה or "Oral Law,"[38] Josephus does not mention such a thing. He first characterizes the Pharisees' special ordinances as "not written *in the laws of Moses*" (ἅπερ οὐκ ἀναγέγραπται ἐν τοῖς Μωυσέος νόμοις), attributing them rather to a succession of fathers. Although the following phrase, describing the Sadducees' view (*viz.*, "it is necessary to respect only those ordinances that are inscribed," ἐκεῖνα νόμιμα δεῖν ἡγεῖσθαι τὰ γεγραμμένα), might appear to suggest an oral law, if it were wrenched from its context, in context it plainly assumes the qualification in the preceding part of the sentence: the laws of Moses are contrasted not with *oral laws*, but with laws "from a tradition of the fathers."[39] The Sadducees reject the Pharisees' tradition not because no one thought to write it down somewhere, but because it is not part of Moses's constitution, which has been elaborated at great length. Josephus has never mentioned such a special tradition before, and he will not do so again outside of *Antiquities* 18.12 (recalling

[38] J. M. Baumgarten "The unwritten Law in the Pre-Rabbinic Period," *JSJ* 3 (1972), 12–14; E. Rivkin, *A Hidden Revolution* (Nashville: Abingdon, 1978), 41–42.

[39] So Neusner, *The Rabbinic Traditions About the Pharisees Before 70* (3 vols.; Leiden: Brill, 1971), 2:163; Mason, *Josephus on the Pharisees*, 240–43.

this passage in a later description of the Pharisees). When he speaks elsewhere of "the ancestral customs or laws" (οἱ νόμοι, τὰ νόμιμα, τὰ πάτρια ἔθη/νόμιμα), as he frequently does, he plainly means the laws followed by all Judeans, given by the lawgiver Moses, which he compares and contrasts to the laws of other nations.[40]

In this explanatory gloss on the Pharisees' tradition from "a succession of fathers," Josephus also makes explicit what the audience might already have inferred from his brief notices on Pharisees in *War:* whereas the Sadducean base is tiny and found only among the elite, the Pharisees have the support of the masses (13.298). This point will turn up repeatedly in the few lines devoted to Pharisees in the sequel. If Josephus wishes to leave any image of the Pharisees with his audience, it is that they have massive popular access, support, and influence.

Hyrcanus's break with the Pharisees and Josephus's explanation about their influence receive space at this juncture, apparently, because they are programmatic for the balance of the Hasmonean story. This rift was not merely a personal one: it had ramifications for the constitution of the state because it meant the dissolution of the Pharisaic jurisprudence that had been in place throughout Hyrcanus's reign. Although Josephus does not pause to explain *why* Pharisees were so popular, or the nature of their legal precepts, he does drop an important hint in the banquet story: their penal code was milder. He will confirm this point in a later note to the effect that Ananus II, the high priest who executed Jesus' brother James, was a Sadducee and *therefore* "savage" in punishment (*Ant.* 20.199).

A brief historical reflection may illuminate Josephus's biases. At face value, biblical law seems raw, unsystematic, and potentially severe. The various apodictic and casuistic declarations throughout the Pentateuch offer little by way of a real jurisprudence: rights of the accused, a system of courts, principles of advocacy, or procedures for hearing and sentencing.[41] Any self-consciously interpretative tradition, therefore, simply as a function of articulating general legal principles and procedures of prosecution and defense—e.g., that a certain number of judges must hear cases, with advocates for the accused—would tend to mitigate the Law's potential severity. Perusal of the Mishnah tractate *Sanhedrin,* which reflects one kind of elaboration, suggests that few accused persons could face capital punishment under its provisions. The school of Hillel, represented in the first century by Rabban Gamaliel and his son Simon, is particularly associated with leniency.[42] Without assuming any identification between Pharisees and tannaitic rabbis, we may still observe that Josephus's remarks on the leniency of Pharisaic jurisprudence

[40] Ibid., 96–106.

[41] The Bible requires execution by an "avenger of blood" not only for murder, idolatry, and blasphemy, but also for cursing parents (Exod 21:17; Lev 20:9), owning an animal that gores a person to death (if the animal has also harmed others, Exod 21:29), being a medium or wizard (Lev 20:27), violating the Sabbath (Exod 31:14–15; 35:2), kidnapping (Exod 21:16), and adultery (Lev 20:10). On corporal punishment (for unspecified offenses), see Deut 25:2–3.

[42] E.g., *m. Rosh HaShanah* 2.5; *m. Yevamot* 16.7.

seem antecedently plausible.[43] Anyone who wished to live by the Law had necessarily to interpret it, to resolve its various prescriptions in some way.[44] If the Sadducees took a deliberately minimalist approach, rejecting any explicit body of authoritative legal principle or case law, claiming to observe *only* what the Law specified, it stands to reason that their interpretations would be more severe. If so, it is telling that our aristocratic reporter has no interest in explaining the popular Pharisees' legal principles, much less in embracing or celebrating them.

But why would the Sadducees prescind so pointedly from the Pharisees' tradition, or apparently any other body of ordinances not in the laws? And how might Josephus's audiences have understood this difference? In pre-modern societies—recall even Dickens's *A Tale of Two Cities*—it was inevitably the poor who faced the full force of severe laws. Aristocrats might worry with cause about committing political offenses, but they were largely immune from the legal cares of the masses because of their social position, connections, and presumed noble character. *They* were not likely to be accused of theft or assault. In Rome, the position of city prefect (*praefectus urbis*) was created under Augustus mainly to deal with the petty crimes of slaves and freedmen, not the nobles.[45] The elite author Josephus himself claims to *favor* severity in law, even celebrating this as a virtue of the Judean constitution in contrast to the ever-softening codes of other peoples: whereas others wiggle out of their laws' ancient demands, Judean law *still* exacts the death penalty for adultery and rebellious children (*Ant.* 1.22; 4.244–253; 4.260–264; *Ag. Ap.* 2.276). It is understandable that in such contexts the masses would favor the party with the more lenient penal code, but the aristocrat Josephus takes a typically piteous view of the masses: the rabble or the mob, who are fickle and vulnerable to persuasion by almost anyone.[46] He explains only, and rather dryly, that Hyrcanus's break with the Pharisees and his dissolution of their jurisprudence resulted in popular opposition to the Hasmonean dynasty.

His disdain for the Pharisees, no matter how popular they may be (or *because* of a popularity he considers unfortunate), becomes obvious in the way he frames the story of their rupture with Hyrcanus. The episode itself, which is borrowed from oral or written tradition,[47] seems neutral or sympathetic toward the

---

[43] For a thorough examination of the humane character of Pharisaic jurisprudence, argued on the basis of rabbinic *halakhah,* see famously L. Finkelstein, *The Pharisees: The Sociological Background of Their* Faith (2 vols.; Philadelphia: Jewish Publication Society, 1938).

[44] On the need for *everyone* who wished to live by the Bible to fill its "gaps," and for a fascinating exposition of Pharisaic and other tradition in the context of rapidly growing literacy from the Hasmonean period, see A. I. Baumgarten, *The Flourishing of Jewish Sects in the Maccabean Era: An Interpretation* (Leiden: Brill, 1997), 114–36.

[45] Eck, *Age of Augustus,* 79. From the early third century C.E. Roman law would formalize the long-evident legal distinction between the mass of free citizens (*humiliores*) and the privileged (*honestiores*).

[46] E.g., *War* 2.234, 259–260, 321–332, 399, 406, 411–417, 427, 523–526; 5.527–528; *Ant.* 1.115; 3.24–27, 68–69, 295–315; 4.37; 19.202; cf. Polybius 6.9.8–9; 44.9; Cicero, *Rep.* 1.42.65; Tacitus, *Hist.* 1.4, 32.

[47] Mason, *Josephus on the Pharisees,* 219; cf. the similar story told of Janneus in *b. Qidd.* 66a.

Pharisees. It leaves the affiliation of the troublemaker Eleazar uncertain, while emphasizing that the Pharisees as a group praise John's conduct, and *all* of them (πάντες) condemn Eleazar for his impertinence (13.292). It is the *Sadducees* who mischievously implicate all Pharisees in Eleazar's views (13.293). On the basis of the account itself, therefore, it makes little sense for Josephus to blame the Pharisees. Yet he chooses to introduce the episode with a remarkable indictment: popular envy of the Hasmoneans's success was expressed *through the Pharisees in particular;* they were *especially hostile* to him, and "they have such influence with the rabble [note present tense] that even if they say something against a king and a high priest, they are immediately trusted" (τοσαύτην δὲ ἔχουσι τὴν ἰσχὺν παρὰ τῷ πλήθει ὡς καὶ κατὰ βασιλέως τι λέγοντες καὶ κατ' ἀρχιερέως εὐθὺς πιστεύεσθαι; 13.288). The animus of our aristocratic author apparently leads him to stretch his material out of shape. Since he will use very similar language when characterizing the Pharisees in later episodes, he seems to have an *idée fixe* concerning the group—no matter what the evidence he can adduce.

Although Pharisees do not appear by name in Josephus's account of Alexander Janneus's actions (as also in *War*), the king's deathbed scene in *Antiquities* clarifies for the first time that much popular resentment toward him has been generated by this popular group: Alexander realized that "he had collided with the nation because of these men" (13.402). If we read the Hasmonean narrative as a unity, this makes sense. The Pharisees and their legal system have been repudiated by Hyrcanus I, so that under Aristobulus I and Janneus the milder and more popular legal regimen has remained outlawed. This has been a factor in the masses' hatred for Janneus, to which the king has responded with extreme brutality. Only by such a coherent reading can we explain why Janneus now advises his wife, who is terrified at the volume of popular hatred she is about to inherit, to grant power once again to the Pharisees—in an ostentatious manner. Invite them even to abuse my corpse, the wily politician declares, for all they really desire is power, and if you give them this they will immediately turn sycophant and allow me a grand funeral (13.403)!

This hard-headed appraisal of "those *reputed to be* the most pious and most scrupulous about the laws" is patently disparaging, and yet Josephus as narrator does nothing to ameliorate it. On the contrary, Janneus's cynical prediction is borne out by the story: invited to share power with the widow Queen, the Pharisees give her husband a magnificent send-off, proclaiming what a just or righteous (δίκαιος) king they have lost, and exploiting their demagogic talents to move the masses to mourning (13.405–6).

The fuller narrative here vis-à-vis *War* thus creates a significantly different atmosphere. Whereas the Pharisees' growth appeared sudden in *War*, minimally explained as if the pious Alexandra had simply been duped by an unscrupulous band, in *Antiquities* the Pharisees' popular influence has been a central concern to the Hasmoneans all along. The Queen becomes a fellow-schemer in the calculus advanced by her dying husband in order to help quiet the people.

Josephus makes the connection with the earlier rupture explicit: Queen Alexandra "directed the rabble (τὸ πλῆθος) to submit to the Pharisees, and *she re-established whatever legal measures* (νόμιμα) the Pharisees had introduced in keeping with the 'fatherly tradition,' *which her father-in-law Hyrcanus had dissolved* (ὁ πενθερὸς αὐτῆς κατέλυσεν)" (13.408). This note signals the complete reformation of the legal code to the *status quo ante.* Josephus further strengthens the link with Hyrcanus's break from the Pharisees by reprising his editorial observation of *Antiquities* 13.288, now placing it on the lips of dying Janneus (13.401–2):

> For he declared that these men had vast influence (δύνασθαι δὲ πολὺ) among the Judeans, both to harm those they hated and to benefit those in the position of friends (βλάψαι τε μισοῦντας καὶ φιλίως διακειμένους ὠφελῆσαι). "For they are especially believed among the rabble concerning those about whom they say something harsh, even if they do so from envy (κἂν φθονοῦντες)." Indeed, he said that he had collided with the nation because of these men, who had been outrageously treated by him.

Though Janneus confesses his crimes here, strangely none of it helps the Pharisees' image. Josephus is too artful a writer to work with simple oppositions, such that where he is critical of a certain ruler, opponents of that ruler must therefore receive his favor. There are many shades of virtue in his narrative: a Janneus or a Herod can have serious flaws but still receive due credit for certain virtues, or sympathy for his plight. Yet the Pharisees consistently come out on the side of unprincipled demagoguery.

With more space available in the generous proportions of *Antiquities,* Josephus can elaborate on the Pharisees' disruptive activities under Alexandra, crisply asserted in *War.* Now we are told that they personally cut the throats of numerous powerful men who had advised King Janneus in his actions against opponents, systematically hunting down one after the other (13.410). This purge by Pharisees causes a counter-reaction amongst the elite (οἱ δυνατοί), who evidently include the military leaders: these rally around the Queen's younger son Aristobulus II, whose intercession wins them at least the privilege to live securely in royal fortresses, safe from the Pharisees (13.415). Significantly, Aristobulus himself makes a bid for supreme power *because* he foresees that if his ineffectual older brother, Hyrcanus II, should assume the throne, the family would be powerless to stop continued control by the Pharisees (13.423; cf. 408). But Hyrcanus II, who is already high priest, will *indeed* become king (14.4), leaving the audience to infer that Alexandra's reinstatement of Pharisaic jurisprudence remains in force (further below).

Given all of the nuanced exchanges that Josephus crafts in describing Aristobulus II—he with the friends of his father, Alexandra with her Pharisaic cohort—one might wonder whether the narrator really intends us to sympathize with the influential men now hiding from the Pharisees, for had they not overseen the brutal regime under Janneus? Josephus removes any doubt about this, however, in his obituary on the Queen in *Antiquities* 13.430–432. With the omniscient narrator's voice, he adopts the sentiments expressed by Aristobulus II (13.416–417): Alexandra should not have insisted on ruling, out of a personal power-lust (ἐπιθυμία) inappropriate to a woman, while she had grown sons more suited to the task (13.431). Without mincing words, Josephus declares that Alexandra's rule caused *all* of the disasters and catastrophes that would subsequently fall upon the Hasmonean house and lead to its loss of authority (13.432). This happened because she preferred present power to what was noble or right (οὔτε καλοῦ οὔτε δικαίου) and because she invited into government *those who held her house in contempt* (*sc.* the Pharisees), leaving the leadership bereft of anyone who was concerned for its well-being (τὴν ἀρχὴν ἔρημον τῶν προκηδομένων ποιησαμένη, 13.431). Again, Alexandra's rapprochement with the Pharisees allegedly had lasting ill effects.

Among the seven remaining volumes of *Antiquities,* the Pharisees appear as narrative actors in only three further episodes. These occur during the administration of Herod's father Antipater, the Roman-appointed governor while Hyrcanus II is high priest and quasi-royal *ethnarch;* under King Herod himself; and then at the annexation of Judea to Roman Syria.

The first episode shows Hyrcanus II in the unenviable position of trying to assert the national laws, in his responsibility as ostensible ruler, yet thoroughly intimidated by an already tyrannical young Herod (14.165). At first persuaded by the Judean elders and the mothers of Herod's victims that Herod has been practicing extra-judicial killing, Hyrcanus summons him to trial (14.164–169). But on his arrival, the council serving as his court is intimidated into silence. Only one Samaias (not further identified here) rises fearlessly to declare that if the council does not punish Herod, the young man will come back to punish them. Josephus adds that this indeed happened later, and paradoxically only Samaias would be spared—for he, realizing that they could not avoid divine retribution, would advise the people of Jerusalem to admit Herod as king (14.172–176).

When we next hear of Samaias, however, the story has changed. At 15.3 we learn that he is *the student* of a Pharisee named Pollio,[48] and that it was *the Pharisee* who had made the original prediction about Herod! Herod's gentleness toward the Pharisees, even when they resist his directives, is spelled out again at 15.370. Leaving aside the manuscript problems at 15.3, we may observe two important points here. First, in Josephus's narrative, Pharisees remain an influential part of the vestigial-Hasmonean (effectively Roman-Herodian) government under Hyrcanus II—just as Aristobulus II had feared while his mother Alexandra lived. Even Herod, once he is in ostensibly absolute control of Jerusalem, thinks it necessary to persuade (συμπείθω) Pollio and Samaias to take the oath of allegiance to him along with their fellow-Pharisees (15.370).

Second, however, Josephus continues to avoid clarifying the situation for his audience. While he is describing Samaias's personal virtues as a fearless speaker,

---

48 Although some MSS have Samaias here as the Pharisee, with a student also named (a form of) Samaias, this would only postpone the problem until 15.370, where the text clearly gives the relationship above. It seems clear that some copyists adjusted the names at 15.3 to remove the contradiction with 14.172–176; they either did not notice 15.370 or could not bring themselves to "correct" the text a second time.

he declines to identify him as a Pharisee; this identification he reserves for a later setting that highlights *Pollio's* advice to admit Herod to Jerusalem. There, however, the bold and accurate prediction (now by Pollio) of future punishment is recalled as a mere afterthought (15.4). Our aristocratic author shows no interest in explaining the continuing presence and popularity of the Pharisees. He certainly does not advertise them, though *we who are interested* can discover from such incidental clues that they remain in the background of his narrative.

Josephus's failure to identify Samaias as a Pharisee while he is admiring his actions may be comparable to the cases of the teachers in *War* 1 and the popular orators of *War* 4 (above), as well as another instance in *Antiquities* 20. That is the story of the high priest Ananus II's execution of James, brother of Jesus, which I have already mentioned. Josephus attributes the action by Ananus (whom *War* 4.319–325 lauds for his behavior during the early phase of the revolt) to the high priest's alleged youthful rashness and daring, as well as to his membership in the school of the Sadducees, "who are savage in contrast to all other Judeans when it comes to trials, *as we have already explained*"—an apparent reference to the banquet with Hyrcanus I, at *Antiquities* 13. 296. Josephus goes on to state that "those in the city who were *reputed to be most fair-minded and most precise in relation to the laws* (ὅσοι ἐδόκουν ἐπιεικέστατοι τῶν κατὰ τὴν πόλιν εἶναι καὶ περὶ τοὺς νόμους ἀκριβεῖς)," a remark recalling his earlier descriptions of the Pharisees, were deeply offended by the Sadducean high priest's action.

Whereas scholars often suggest that Josephus *means to indicate* Pharisees here, I think that we must respect his compositional choices. He could not plausibly expect his audience—any audience other than scholars with concordances—to read "Pharisees" here in *Antiquities* 20, without his spelling it out. Although his narrative might lead *us* to expect that he was *thinking* of Pharisees when he described these popular non-Sadducean exegetes, yet again he opts not to apply the label "Pharisee" just where he is praising the behavior of the group in question.

The next *Antiquities* episode in which the Pharisees appear is openly hostile. After Herod has killed his sons Alexander and Aristobulus (ca. 8 B.C.E.), another son, Antipater, rises to prominence while the beleaguered king, exhausted by intrigues, begins to fail (*Ant.* 17.18, 32). Antipater reportedly gains control over Herod's brother Pheroras, partly by influencing that man's wife and her relatives (17.34). Immune to Antipater's designs, however, was the king's sister Salome. She dutifully reported the conspiracy to her brother, though he was reluctant to believe her exaggerated accounts (17.38–40). So: a stalemate for the moment.

At this sensitive juncture, the Pharisees appear as the decisive factor in prompting the king to action against all these conspirators. In the crabbed Greek that Josephus adopts throughout *Antiquities* 17–19:

> There was also a certain faction of the Judean people priding itself on great precision in the ancestral heritage (ἐπ' ἐξακριβώσει . . . τοῦ πατρίου) and, of the laws, pretending (προσποιουμένων) [regard] for those things in which the Deity rejoices. To them the female bloc was submissive. Called Pharisees, they were quite capable of issuing predictions for the king's benefit, and yet they were plainly bent on combating and also harming him (εἰς τὸ πολεμεῖν τε καὶ βλάπτειν). (*Ant.* 17.41)

This editorial perspective, with its reference to harming those in power, recalls *Antiquities* 13.288, 401, and continues the well-established theme of the Pharisees' contentious disposition.

Josephus's attempt to justify such strong language in this case borders on the bizarre. First, when some 6,000 Pharisees reportedly refuse to take an oath of loyalty to Herod—whether this is the same event as in 15.370 is debatable—the troublesome wife of Pheroras pays their fine (*Ant.* 17.42). In gratitude, they manufacture predictions not for the king's benefit, but for *her* pleasure. They emptily promise that Herod and his descendants will forfeit the rule, which will fall to Pheroras and to her (17.43). Josephus claims that Herod heard about this *quid pro quo* through his sister Salome, and now was enraged enough to execute those Pharisees who were to blame, as well as a eunuch named Bagoas and one Karos, the former object of the king's desire (17.44). Most interestingly, the king also executed "the entire element of his domestic staff that had supported *what the Pharisee was saying*" (πᾶν ὅ τι τοῦ οἰκείου συνειστήκει οἷς ὁ Φαρισαῖος ἔλεγεν). The rhetorical personification in "what the Pharisee was saying" is especially striking because at *Antiquities* 18.17 (below) Josephus will use the same unusual turn of phrase.

He explains that Bagoas was executed because the eunuch foolishly embraced the Pharisees' prediction that *he* would be enabled to marry and father children, and that *he* would be called father of a future king-messiah figure (17.45). The prediction to Bagoas makes clear the vacuous and promiscuous nature of Pharisaic prediction in Josephus's hands: they happily stir up those who should be most loyal to the King with promises of incredible, mutually exclusive, outcomes. The effect upon the audience of Josephus's portrait here would presumably have been much like that created by his younger contemporary Juvenal when he spoke about Jewish fortune-tellers in Rome: "a Judean will tell you dreams of any kind you please for the minutest of coins" (*Sat.* 6.546). Tacitus comments more generally, in the context of imperial court astrologers, about the deceptions of those who bring the science into disrepute by describing what they do not know (*Ann.* 6.22).

For all its interest and oddness, this remarkable story of Pharisaic prediction is dropped quickly and Josephus returns to the main narrative. The Pharisee incident seems to be mentioned mainly because it provides the trigger for Herod to act more forcefully against Pheroras's wife, who is the main character in this part of the story (*Ant.* 17.46–51). This episode in turn opens the way for Pheroras's retirement from Jerusalem, and death, as well as Antipater's momentary rise and protracted, desperate fall (17.52–145, 184–187).

To give a sense of proportion, again: many individual speeches in that ensuing narrative are longer than this paragraph mentioning the Pharisees. It is in the psychological analysis of motives, virtues, and vices, to which speeches lend themselves, that Josephus's main interest as a historian lies. His description of the Pharisees is by contrast vague and impersonal: individual Pharisees are not named; they act as a sort of nefarious Greek chorus, *en bloc* and without benefiting from rounded portraiture.

Here again, Josephus passes up the opportunity to answer inevitable audience questions about the Pharisees: Where does their ability to predict come from? Why is Josephus so cynical about this ability? In what sense could they have manufactured predictions "for the king"? It is clear only, because he emphasizes the point, that the Pharisees' popularity keeps them near the center of power and able to cause serious problems for those who govern, no matter how ostensibly powerful the rulers may be. In Herod's case, the Pharisees are entirely on the wrong side, with the impious son Antipater, the disloyal brother Pheroras, his scheming wife, and their conspiratorial bloc.

Although the final discussion of the Pharisees in *Antiquities* (18.12–15, 17) has mainly to do with their philosophical tenets in relation to those of the other schools, and so will be considered in the next chapter, three statements in and around that passage complete *Antiquities*' treatment of the group.

First, as at *War* 2.118–119, Josephus's introduction of the three schools is prompted by his mention of Judas the Galilean (here Gaulanite), who initiated a popular rebellion when Judea came under direct Roman rule: in *War* as a province in its own right, here as a territory annexed to the province of Syria (17.355; 18.1–2). With extra space at his disposal, Josephus dilates on the novelty, strangeness, and inescapably dangerous outcome of Judas's absolute conception of "freedom" (ἐλευθερία): this notion sowed the seed of every kind of misery, starting a movement that would spin out of control, sparking civil war and the murder of fellow citizens, especially those of high standing, and resulting in the destruction of the temple (18.4–9). Curiously, however, Josephus now explains the popular appeal of Judas's message by explaining that the rebel leader won the support of a certain Saddok, *a Pharisee* (18.4): together they appealed to the nation (τὸ ἔθνος), and the people (οἱ ἄνθρωποι) heard what they said with pleasure (18.4, 6). Josephus reinforces this link among rebels, the masses, and Pharisees at the end of the schools passage, where he asserts that the ironically described "Fourth Philosophy"—this is not a *real* group, who called themselves by such a name (see the next chapter)—agrees with the Pharisees in everything *except* the rebels' more absolute devotion to freedom (ἐλευθερία, 18.23).

Against the old scholarly view that this connection with the Pharisees contradicts *War*'s isolation of Judas' rebel philosophy and newly dignifies the rebels,[49] Josephus's language implies the opposite relationship: it is rather the Pharisees who are *tainted* by their new association with rebels. Josephus's rejection of rebellion and *stasis* does not abate in his later writings. He writes as the aristocrat who, like Plutarch, is ever alert to prevent civil strife and unrest (cf. *Life* 17–22 *et passim*). *Antiquities* 18.3–11 is even more adamant than *War* 2.118 in repudiating Judas and his heirs. Therefore, Josephus's new identification of a prominent Pharisee at the source of Judas's rebel program can work only to associate the Pharisee with

[49] Rasp, "Flavius Josephus," 39, 44, 47; M. Black, "Judas of Galilee and Josephus's Fourth Philosophy," in *Josephus-Studien: Untersuchungen zu Josephus, der antiken Judentum und dem Neuen Testament, Otto Michel zum 70. Gerburtstag gemidwet.* (ed. O. Betz, K. Haacker, and M. Hengel; Göttingen: Vandenhoeck & Ruprecht, 1974), 50; G. Alon, *Jews, Judaism, and the Classical World* (Jerusalem: Magnes, 1977), 44–47.

despicable behavior. Saddok exploits the Pharisees' popularity with the masses, which is by now familiar to the attentive reader, to stir up the always pliable rabble for unworthy goals. Significantly, it is a chief priest, Joazar son of Boethus, who must work to pacify the people against such rebel leaders (18.3)—*here* is the representative of Josephus's values in the narrative—though Joazar's statesmen-like work is largely undone by Judas and the Pharisee.

Second, at *Antiquities* 18.15 Josephus remarks that "because of these [their philosophical views], they happen to be extremely persuasive among the citizens (τοῖς τε δήμοις πιθανώτατοι τυγχάνουσιν), and divine matters—prayers and sacred rites—happen to be performed according to the manner of interpretation of those men (ὁπόσα θεῖα . . . ποιήσεως ἐξηγήσει τῇ ἐκείνων τυγχάνουσιν πρασσόμενα)." This is followed by a difficult clause about the citizens' following "the way that prevails in/over all things, in both their regimen of life and their speech."[50] Note the double "happen to be," which applies more than the usual amount of distance between author and object of discussion: Josephus conspicuously withholds any personal investment in the group's popularity.

Third, any doubt about Josephus's evaluation of the Pharisees' popularity is removed by his further notice concerning the Sadducees. Recalling his earlier observation about the small elite base of the Sadducean school (13.297–298), he now remarks that

> this [Sadducean] doctrine has reached only a few, albeit those who are highest in standing (τοὺς μέντοι πρώτους τοῖς ἀξιώμασι), and almost nothing is accomplished by them. For whenever they enter into governing positions (ὁπότε γὰρ ἐπ' ἀρχὰς παρέλθοιεν), though unwillingly and under compulsion, they therefore [i.e., as a condition of public office] side with *what the Pharisee says* (προσχωροῦσι δ' οὖν οἷς ὁ Φαρισαῖος λέγει), because otherwise they would not be tolerable[51] to the masses. (18.15–16)

Although one or more of Josephus's references to the Pharisees, especially the more overtly hostile ones, have traditionally been ascribed wholesale to his undigested sources,[52] it is clear now that he is responsible for all of them. The striking similarity of language between this relatively neutral school passage and the preceding episode (in speaking of "what the Pharisee says/said"), along with the conspicuous share of both passages in the peculiar language experiments of *Antiquities* 17–19, and then the links between these passages and *Antiquities* 13 (e.g., the Pharisees' determination to "harm" rulers and their influence with the

---

[50] Greek, ἐπιτηδεύσει τοῦ ἐπὶ πᾶσι κρείσσονος ἔν τε τῇ διαίτῃ τοῦ βίου καὶ λόγοις. Although Feldman (in the Loeb edition) renders "by practicing the highest ideals," presumably in view of the preceding ἀρετή (often "virtue") αὐτοῖς [Feldman, "the excellence of the Pharisees"] in *Ant.* 17–19 ἀρετή need not mean moral virtue or excellence, but often retains its older sense of morally neutral strength or force (e.g., 17.44, 49, 171, 238, 277, 279).

[51] Greek ἀνεκτός· 7 of its 11 occurrences in Josephus are in *Ant.* 18, one of many features embedding this passage in the surrounding narrative.

[52] See n. 19 above.

masses), show that we are dealing with a consistent authorial hand—no matter how varied Josephus's underlying sources may (admittedly) have been.

To summarize thus far: Josephus features the Pharisees only briefly in *Antiquities,* and only after the main story (*Ant.* 1–12) is finished, in his narrative of the Hasmonean dynasty's decline. There he sets up a situation that will apparently endure until his own time. Namely, although John Hyrcanus threw over the Pharisees' legal prescriptions (νόμιμα) in a fit of pique engineered by the Sadducees, the popular animosity that this generated, which reached its height under Alexander Janneus, could not be sustained. Alexander's widow restored Pharisaic jurisprudence, and the group's hold on popular opinion has remained formidable ever since. Even King Herod could only execute a few of their leaders when they created serious difficulties for him; he had still to deal with the group, and by the time his son Archelaus was removed in 6 C.E. at least one of their leaders was ready to exploit their influence again for rebellious ends. Tellingly, Josephus's summary comments on the Pharisees' popularity are in the present tense, including his description of the Judean philosophies at 18.12–22. He gives no narrative reason to think that the Pharisees' influence waned appreciably through the period of his history.

What must impress the reader interested in the Pharisees is Josephus's lack of interest in the group: *we* must go looking for Pharisees in Josephus. He does not highlight their presence or answer obvious questions about their leaders, activities, legal principles, group structure, social composition, relationship to the ancient priestly Senate (as Josephus presents it), entry requirements, claims to special powers, or popular appeal (contrast the Essenes of *War* 2.119–161). That they are able to manipulate the masses for whatever end they wish, and often use this influence to harm the eminent—this is enough of an indictment for our aristocratic author. Apparently, he fails to answer obvious questions because he disdains the group and regrets their popularity, like that of the countless other demagogues in his stories (e.g., *Ant.* 4.14–20, 37; 7.194–196; 18.3–6; 20.160, 167, 172; cf. Sallust, *Cat.* 37.3).

In *Life*

Josephus's autobiography adds a fascinating personal dimension to the picture of the Pharisees developed in his two historical accounts. This one-volume work is an appendix to the *magnum opus,* a celebration of the author's self-acclaimed virtue (*Life* 430) elaborated against the standard ancient rhetorical criteria of noble ancestry (1–6), youthful exploits (7–19), military and political achievements (20–413), and benefactions given and received (414–430).

This self-introduction first mentions the Pharisees quite neutrally in conjunction with the other two schools (*Life* 10), only to say that in his youthful quest for philosophical training, self-improvement, and toughening (ἐμπειρία, σκληραγωγέω, πονέω), Josephus did not find any of these groups satisfactory; he refers the audience to his "frequent" (πολλάκις) earlier discussions for details. Fleeting though it is, this constitutes the final "school passage" (see the next chapter). For present purposes, however, we must deal with Josephus's claim that his lack of satisfaction with the schools led to his retreat to the desert, to live with the extreme ascetic Bannus for three years. It was this experience that finally answered his philosophical yearning (ἐπιθυμία, *Life* 11).

What comes next (*Life* 12) requires careful attention, for English-speaking scholars have almost always taken it to mean that Josephus either joined or wished to claim that he joined the Pharisees. Yet such a claim at this point would make no sense of the immediate context, where he has found the Pharisees and the other schools insufficient; only Bannus (whose ardent student, ζηλωτής, he became) has shown him the way. A sudden lurch toward the Pharisees would, moreover, come as a shock after Josephus's few and disdainful references to the group throughout *War* and *Antiquities.* And most important, such a reading cannot be sustained by the sentence in question (*Life* 12).[53]

At the age of 18 to 19, when his Roman contemporaries would have completed their higher studies in philosophy and/or rhetoric and begun to take up responsibilities in public life, this is precisely what Josephus claims to have done. He returned to the *polis* of Jerusalem (εἰς τὴν πόλιν ὑπέστρεφον) and, "being now in my nineteenth year, I began to involve myself in public life" (ἠρξάμην πολιτεύεσθαι). Although in Jewish and Christian literature the middle verb πολιτεύομαι can have the meaning "govern *oneself*" or simply "behave," it is clear from the immediate context here (preceded by *polis* and followed by his diplomatic trip to Rome, *Life* 13), from Josephus's usage of this verb elsewhere,[54] and from the closest parallels in contemporary Greek authors of Josephus's class (Plutarch, *Mor.* 798d–e, 800d, f, 813a, 804f), that he is describing his embarkation upon *adult political life,* something expected of all members of his class. Thus, "[after three years with Bannus], I returned to the city. Being now in my nineteenth year, I began to involve myself in *polis*-affairs [or 'become politically involved']."

But that is not the end of the sentence. Dependent clauses add, "following after [or 'following the authority of'] the school of the Pharisees (τῇ Φαρισαίων αἱρέσει κατακολουθῶν), which is rather like the one called Stoic among the Greeks." Clues about the intended sense of the first and crucial sub-clause include the following. First, the kata-prefix on the main participle suggests "following *after* someone's lead or following an authority"—rather than joining or becoming zealously involved with a group. (Contrast Josephus's experience as Bannus's *devotee,* ζηλωτής) Second, since this clause is dependent, Josephus's entry into *polis* life provides the basis or reason for his following the lead of the Pharisaic school. Third, we have seen that it is a minor theme of the later *Antiquities,* however grudgingly divulged, that the Pharisees and their program hold complete sway over the masses and therefore over political life. At *Antiquities* 18.15, 17 Josephus has said pointedly that whenever anyone comes into public

[53] For a full examination of the passage, see Mason, "Was Josephus a Pharisee?"

[54] *Ant.* 4.13; 13.432; 14.91; 15.263; 18.44; 20.251; *Life* 258, 262.

office, he must—*even if unwillingly* and by necessity—side with "what the Pharisee says." Just as his mention of the three groups at *Life* 10 refers the audience to earlier discussions, so also this notice about following the lead of the Pharisees in public life reminds the audience of what he has said just three volumes earlier. If even Sadducees coming into office must support the Pharisees' agenda, Josephus's observation that his own entry into public life required following the Pharisees' prescriptions does not imply any closer affiliation with the group than the Sadducees had.

Like *War* 2.411 (above), *Life* 21 makes only passing mention of the "principal men of the Pharisees" (τοῖς πρώτοις τῶν Φαρισαίων) alongside the chief priests, in the coalition trying to manage the clamor for war. Even more pointedly than *War, Antiquities* has insisted that the hereditary priesthood and its leaders constitute the proper ruling elite of Judea.[55] Since the time of Queen Alexandra, although Josephus has preferred to speak of hereditary aristocratic-priestly leadership, he has grudgingly acknowledged that the immensely popular lay movement of the Pharisees must always be reckoned with by those in power. Since Alexandra, at least, leading Pharisees have been able to exert considerable influence on those in power; we glimpse their presence in the highest councils under Hyrcanus II and Herod. As the war against Rome takes shape, *War* 2.411 and *Life* 21 furnish hints of what seems a closer, more deliberate and diplomatic alliance: leading Pharisees are specifically identified in the ruling coalition. This makes sense in Josephus's narrative world: in the national emergency created by popular and demagogic demands for rebellion, the chief priests need the influence of prominent Pharisees to help calm the masses.[56]

The next cluster of references to the Pharisees, which is the last among Josephus's known writings, may illustrate the sort of relationship between chief priests and leading Pharisees that he has suggested until now. Observe even here, during the early revolt, the divide that remains between even the most eminent Pharisees and the chief priests. This narrative section confirms that Josephus does not number himself among the Pharisees. Some of his most determined *adversaries*, however, are Pharisees or close friends of Pharisaic leaders. Josephus's career as Galilean governor-commander has placed him in roughly the same position—i.e., a successful leader undermined by jealous Pharisees—that he has repeatedly described as the typical situation for other rulers.

---

[55] E.g., *Ant.* 3.188; 4.186, 218, 222, 224, 304, 325; 5.15, 23, 55, 57, 103, 353; 10.12, 62; 11.8, 11, 17, 62, 139–140; 12.142; 13.166; 14.211; 20.6, 180–181.

[56] Although I am trying to interpret the narrative, one can imagine that such dynamics might have been in play historically. Whereas scholars like to pass judgment on whether certain chief priests, Josephus himself, or leading Pharisees were "pro- or anti-Roman," as if this were a fixed trait, Josephus's narrative resonates with our common experience of places caught up in unrest. Native leaders are often faced with conflicting allegiances: sharing popular resentment of intrusive great powers and wanting to express that outrage, yet trying to manage dissent in safe ways, while preserving their own lives (e.g., not being tarred as collaborators) and social stability; seeing the futility of reckless or implacable revolt and yet possibly agreeing at certain moments to guerrilla strikes for the sake of honor.

By *Life* 189–191, Josephus's Galilean command is facing increasingly energetic opposition from John son of Levi, from Gischala in Upper Galilee, who will eventually become one of the two chief "tyrants" of Jerusalem in the war against Rome. The strong man of his hometown, John at first tried to restrain his fellow-Gischalans from revolt against Rome (*Life* 43), much as Josephus tried to restrain the Jerusalemites (17), but John became outraged when nearby Greek cities launched attacks. These led him to fortify the walls of Gischala against future incursions (44–5). This taste of militancy, Josephus implies, paved the way for John's later emergence as rebel leader—solely, we are told, for the sake of personal power (*Life* 70). This change brings John into direct confrontation with Josephus, who has been sent by the Jerusalem council to govern all Galilee (*Life* 29, 62). The main expression of this conflict before the passage that interests us has been John's effort to inspire the major city of Tiberias to defect from Josephus (*Life* 84–104, 123); John had considerable success there, as also at Gabara (123–124).

The next we hear of John (*Life* 189–190), he is pulling out all the stops to contrive Josephus's removal from Galilee. He sends his brother Simon to Jerusalem, to ask the renowned Pharisee Simon son of Gamaliel to persuade the council to demand Josephus's recall. Josephus introduces this famous Pharisee in grand style: Simon son of Gamaliel was from Jerusalem (the greatest stage for any Judean aristocrat: cf. *Life* 7), of illustrious ancestry, and from the school of the Pharisees, "who have the reputation of excelling others in their precision with respect to the ancestral ordinances" (οἳ περὶ τὰ πάτρια νόμιμα δοκοῦσιν τῶν ἄλλων ἀκριβείᾳ διαφέρειν)—Josephus's standard description of the group (cf. *War* 1.110; 2.162; *Ant.* 17.41). But we have seen that such an introduction does not indicate his favor, for in the other cases the ensuing narrative undermines the Pharisees' reputation. So it is here. Although he acknowledges that Simon was a most capable politician (191), Josephus continues, "Being a long-time friend and associate of John [son of Levi], however, he was then at odds with me." The following account describes the eminent Pharisee's efforts to have Josephus removed, in terms that amount to a serious indictment of Simon's character.

Simon first tries a direct approach: attempting to persuade the chief priests Ananus and Jesus, who evidently retain executive authority even in the wartime coalition, to replace Josephus with John. But these priest-aristocrats, whose wisdom and probity Josephus had celebrated at length in *War* (4.314–325), dismiss the leading Pharisee's ploy as both unjust ("the action of sordid men"), since Josephus was an able and well-regarded leader, and impracticable—for the same reason (*Life* 194). When Simon fails with this forthright approach, he confidently promises John's men that he will nonetheless achieve his aim: not to worry! His new, secret plan is for John's brother Simon to bribe Ananus and his group with gifts (*Life* 195–196). This tactic succeeds, alas, so that even the chief priests now become complicit in seeking Josephus's removal from Galilee.

Needless to say, we might easily entertain doubts that the story represents historical reality: it plainly serves Josephus's interests to protest the chief priests' unwillingness to countenance the dishonorable process pushed by Simon. Yet we are trying to *interpret the narrative*, and Josephus's portrait is clear enough:

this famous Pharisee cannot direct policy himself, but must *try* to use his influence (deriving from the Pharisees' popular prestige) to convince the chief priests, the most powerful leaders, of his views. Remarkably, Simon is the only named Pharisee in Josephus besides Pollion (Samaias may be judged a Pharisee by association), and he benefits from a touch of Josephus's typical effort at rounded characterization of individuals. In spite of Simon's otherwise admirable qualities, his close friendship with Josephus's adversary John drives the prominent Pharisee to move against Josephus, even though the undertaking is patently unjust. Simon even corrupts the chief priests.

As a result of the head Pharisee's machinations, three other prominent Pharisees are recruited to act unjustly against Josephus. It is not clear whether the chief priests themselves comply with the whole appeal and agree to replace Josephus with John (*Life* 190), because they send a four-man delegation with armed escort to bring Josephus back dead or alive, and apparently to provide a substitute collective government (202). This delegation is on John's side (203), to be sure, but the council has sent four men in order to persuade the Galileans that somewhere among them will be found whatever qualities they admire in Josephus(!). In Josephus's sardonic enunciation of the comparison, we learn that all four are Jerusalemites like him; all are highly trained in the laws, as he is; and two of the men are priests, one of chief-priestly ancestry, thus more than compensating for the one priest Josephus (198). They ostensibly have the better of Josephus on all fronts.

Yet before he spells out this comparison, Josephus has also informed us that *three* of the four men—two of the laymen and the ordinary priest—were Pharisees (197). Significantly, Josephus does *not* adduce membership in the Pharisees as a point on which this group can be favorably compared with him. He does not say "they were three Pharisees in contrast to me, only one," though he does compare himself with them in ancestry, origin, and legal training. Why, then, does he identify the three as Pharisees? Obvious reasons are: (a) to explain how they all had a claim to education in the laws, given that two of them were not priests as he was (note the reminder that Pharisees enjoy a reputation for legal precision); and (b) to connect them with the leading Pharisee Simon, as opponents of the legitimate leadership of Josephus. His own position, by contrast, is connected with the nation's revered chief-priestly leadership under Ananus and Jesus (cf. *War* 2.563–568).

Once they arrive in Galilee to execute their mission, the behavior of this mostly Pharisaic delegation confirms—and helps to explain—Josephus's consistent portrait of the popular school as hostile toward the nation's priestly/royal elite. Josephus portrays the actions of their leader Jonathan, one of the three Pharisees (*Life* 197), as particularly reprehensible. He and his group lie and deceive, slander, engage in violence (202, 216–218, 237–238, 274–275, 282–282, 290–292), and even abuse the sacred Law (290–291) in their single-minded pursuit of Josephus—in spite of our author's self-reported uprightness and popular affection. Another Pharisee, Ananias, Josephus describes as "a vile and wretched man" (πονηρός ἀνὴρ καὶ κακοῦργος, 290). In the end, Josephus's divine protection and resourcefulness, complemented by the grateful devotion of the Galilean masses whom he has managed to win over by every possible stratagem, enable him to defeat the Pharisaic delegation and send them back cowering to Jerusalem (332). The council eventually dismisses the attempt of Simon the Pharisee to remove him (311–312).

Conclusions and Corollaries

Although my work since the published revision of my 1986 dissertation on Josephus's Pharisees (1991) has taken many new directions in exploring his rich and vast corpus—e.g., his rhetoric, the structure of his works, his audiences in Flavian Rome—these new perspectives mainly confirm my original sense of the way the Pharisees function in these narratives. Now more than ever I would stress how marginal the Pharisees were to Josephus's principal concerns: they do not appear in the main stretches of *War* (3–7) or *Antiquities* (1–12), or in the summation of the Judean constitution we know as *Against Apion*. Throughout his writings run many coherent lines of interest, concerning the character and constitution of the nation, and his own character as the Judeans' shining representative. To these interests, the Pharisees are more or less irrelevant.

Josephus assumes the position of a proud aristocrat, the spokesman for his nation after the disastrous war against Rome. He writes with sophistication, showing deep familiarity with the repertoire of elite political themes that was cultivated from Polybius through Diodorus and Dionysius to Josephus's contemporaries Plutarch and Dio Chrysostom, and on to Cassius Dio.[57] This is a world of discourse in which men of breeding and culture (παιδεία) are the only ones capable of leading their people with wisdom and restraint, resisting the reckless, emotional impulses that drive lesser characters: the mobs, youthful hot-heads, barbarians, and women. The job of the statesman (ὁ πολιτικός) is to protect the body politic from disturbance (στάσις), and Josephus's accounts are filled with the measures taken by his people's rightful leaders, from Moses and Aaron to himself and his aristocratic peers, to ensure the peaceful life of their citizens under the world's finest constitution.

In this narrative world, Pharisees appear as an occasional aggravation to the elite. They are a non-aristocratic group with enormous popular support and a perverse willingness to use that support demagogically, even on a whim, to stir up the masses against duly constituted authority—Hasmonean, Herodian, or Josephan. In *War,* the moment of Pharisaic ascendancy is the reign of Queen Alexandra, though Josephus says as little as possible about the group after that. In *Antiquities,* Alexandra's reign is again a watershed, but now Josephus offers a back-story, the preceding interval from Hyrcanus I to Alexandra, *as* a failed experiment in governance *without* the popular Pharisaic jurisprudence. Ever since Alexandra's reign, therefore—under Herod's government and through the first century until Josephus's time—the Pharisaic program has again been in place:

[57] E.g., Eckstein, *Moral Vision;* Swain, *Hellenism and Empire.*

one who accepts office must listen "to what the Pharisee says." We do not know, because Josephus does not explain, how his audience should have understood the mechanisms of Pharisaic influence, let alone the content of the Pharisees' jurisprudence or how it was implemented. He seems uninterested in moving from complaint to clarification. During the earliest phase of the war, at least, leading Pharisees are more deliberately welcomed by the priestly elite, as the latter use the popular party's influence to try to stem the tide of rebellion. Still, the priests retain control through the early phases, before the "tyrants" seize power following the murder of Ananus and Jesus (*War* 4.314–344). (note: I continue to speak of the story, not of the real past.)

Conspicuously, to us who are able to scrutinize the narratives (a pleasure not shared by many ancients), Josephus passes up many opportunities to mention Pharisees, especially in contexts that might have elicited his praise (e.g., the anti-Herodian teachers, Simon son of Gamaliel in *War,* Samaias, or those who opposed James's execution by a young Ananus II). Nor does he elucidate their group structure or explain their popularity. We must join some dots if we wish to understand. When he does mention them as players in the narrative it is usually to express annoyance at their influence and tactics. He retains the last word over his own mischievous Pharisee opponents in Galilee, however, in the self-aggrandizing *Life.*

Although my aim has been to construct an adequate synthesis of the Pharisees *in Josephus's narratives,* if this interpretation is successful it obviously undermines hypotheses about the historical Pharisees that are based upon significantly different interpretations of Josephus. For example, an influential theory has held that the Pharisees attained some power under Alexandra, then faded from political life under Herod (or earlier), to resurface only on the eve of revolt in 66. This theory depends upon the impression that Josephus's narratives (viewed rather positivistically, as if proportional records of events) highlight the Pharisees only at these points.[58] But we have seen that Josephus portrays the re-establishment of Pharisaic jurisprudence under Alexandra as a necessary condition of governance, which has persevered until his own time.[59] The theory of decline and reawakening is usually tied up with a surprisingly durable claim about Josephus's biases: that in *Antiquities* and *Life* he aligns himself with the Pharisees and advocates their (post-70, Yavnean) program—and so the fuller attention to Pharisees in *Antiquities* amounts to his endorsement of them as a new post-70 elite.[60] If the foregoing analysis is even roughly correct, however, such an assessment of Jose-

[58]Among relatively recent works, Grabbe, *Judaism,* 2:470–76; Sanders, *Practice and Belief,* 386.

[59]Whereas in historical reconstruction each reconstructed phenomenon must be argued separately, when interpreting a narrative we are entitled to accept conditions of Judean life painstakingly established by the author at one place (*Ant.* 13) and assumed again later (*Ant.* 18) as holding in the intervening narrative as well. He need not pause every few pages, especially when speaking of Roman or Babylonian affairs, to remind us that Pharisees are still influential with the Judean masses.

[60]Grabbe, *Judaism,* 2:474.

phus's aims is impossible. He limits discussion of the Pharisees and has a general interest in ignoring them (even in *Antiquities*), only occasionally exposing them as examples of the demagogic type that he and his audiences deplore.

It is worth stressing that Josephus was a uniquely positioned reporter who may have had special reasons for disliking such a group as the Pharisees. His aristocratic biases should therefore be checked, if possible, by sources closer to the popular levels where the Pharisees found their supporters. Even Luke-Acts, the two-volume work that is among the best (in literary terms) produced by the first generations of Jesus' followers, is more favorably disposed toward the Pharisees than is our elite priest (cf. Mason 1995).

It may be objected to my analysis that excision of the school passages for separate treatment (see the next chapter) skews the picture. There, if anywhere, Josephus achieves near neutrality in portraying the Pharisees; his comments about *their beliefs* are not hostile. And surely the school passages are also part of the narratives. This is all true. My proleptic response is that, while it has seemed efficient to accept the editor's proposal of reserving the school passages for a separate chapter, I have also commented here on the *narrative function* of those passages. They do not significantly alter the general portrait I have described. As we shall see in the next chapter, brief comparative sketches of two or three philosophical schools, especially on the central question of fate and free will, were literary conventions and can be found also in other elite writers. They are too schematic to be of much use, and of doubtful accuracy or consistency anyway: they seem to function mainly as display pieces for the author's erudition, providing a narrative diversion. They also place him above the fray of inter-school squabbles, showing that he is not bound by a particular doctrine. It was a natural option for someone of Josephus's presumed stature to describe in brief compass the range of Judean philosophical schools. Yet just as Cicero can be harshly critical of Epicureans in other contexts (*Pis.* 68–72), and yet still grant them a neutral place in his philosophical spectrum, so too the fact that Josephus can epitomize the Judean schools in such set pieces without overt judgment says nothing about his view of the group. That view is more likely to emerge in his narrative descriptions and moral evaluations of this group alone, which we have examined here.

Chapter 7

The Philosophy of Josephus's Pharisees

In the previous chapter, treating the roles of the Pharisees in Josephus's narratives, we noticed a telling remark. In his story about the banquet at which John Hyrcanus repudiated the Pharisees and their legal code, Josephus observes that the Hasmonean prince, then a student of the Pharisees, was intent on living a just (δίκαιος) life and on pleasing both God and his beloved teachers (*Ant.* 13.289). Josephus offers the editorial explanation, "for the Pharisees philosophize" or "practice philosophy" (οἱ γὰρ Φαρισαῖοι φιλοσοφοῦσιν).

Two points impress one immediately. First, the off-hand way in which he makes this remark suggests that Josephus's understanding of Pharisees as philosophers is ingrained, and not an artificial construction for the "school passages" (below). It is hardly plausible, in spite of longstanding scholarly assumptions,[1] that Josephus's sources are responsible for portraying as philosophical schools what were really "religious" groups, and that Josephus took over these sources in spite of his own knowledge and perspective. Those passages fit too well with his general and even incidental tendencies as an author.[2] Second, the explanation itself—Hyrcanus asks Pharisees for help in his pursuit of just or righteous living and in pleasing God *because they are philosophers*—drives home signal differences between modern philosophy and ancient φιλοσοφία or *philosophia*. (Can we imagine inviting the local philosophy department to dinner, to solicit their help in our quest to live a decent, God-fearing life?) Yet "justice" in all its valences—political, criminal, moral, religious—was indeed a central preoccupation of ancient philosophy.[3]

---

[1]E.g., Hölscher, "Josephus," 1949 n.*; G. F. Moore, *Judaism: In the First Centuries of the Christian Era* (New York: Schocken Books, 1958); M. Black, "The Account of the Essenes in Hippolytus and Josephus," in *The Background of the New Testament and Its Eschatology* (ed. W. D. Davies and D. Daube; Cambridge: Cambridge University Press, 1956), 172–82; M. Smith, "The Description of the Essenes in Josephus and the Philosophoumena." *HUCA* 35 (1958): 273–93; Schwartz, "Josephus and Nicolaus"; Bergmeier, *Die Essener-Berichte.*

[2]For criticism of source theories, see C. Burchard, "Die Essener bei Hippolyt: Hippolyt, REF. IX 18, 2–28, 2 und Josephus, Bell. 2, 119–61," *JSJ* 8.1 (1977): 1–41; A. I. Baumgarten, "Josephus and Hippolytus on the Pharisees," *HUCA* 55 (1984): 1–25; Mason, *Josephus on the Pharisees,* 176–77, 306–8, 384–98; D. S. Williams, "Josephus and the Authorship of *War* 2.119–161 (on the Essenes)," *JSJ* 25.2 (1994): 207–221.

[3]Plato's *Republic,* a dialogue on the meaning of justice, is only the most famous example. See Jaeger, *Paideia,* 2:198–208.

These observations already generate three tasks for this chapter, which attempts an adequate contextual reading of Josephus's Pharisees *as philosophical school,* namely, to survey the landscape of "philosophy" in Josephus's time; to investigate the larger uses of philosophy in Josephus's works; and then to examine the school passages in those works.

By "school passages," I mean those in which Josephus compares the Pharisees, Sadducees, and Essenes as philosophical schools, with generic terms such as αἱρέσεις (schools) or φιλοσοφίαι (philosophies). There are four such units in Josephus—*War* 2.119–166; *Antiquities* 13.171–173; 18.12–22; *Life* 10–11. Although the last of these adds little, referring the audience to "frequent" earlier discussions (see chapter 1), we shall consider it briefly by way of introduction to the theme. Another pericope, the "footnote" to Hyrcanus's banquet story (*Ant.* 13.297–298), nearly qualifies as a school passage, since it explains important differences between Pharisees and Sadducees; but we have examined that clarification as a narrative product in the previous chapter. Here, then, we shall focus on the three school passages of *War* and *Antiquities,* after initial sketches of philosophy in the Roman world and in Josephus. Although our focus will remain on the Pharisees, we cannot avoid considering this school in relation to the other two, because Josephus does so.

Philosophy in Roman Antiquity: Some Salient Features

I have noted that Josephus's brief reference to the three schools in his autobiography adds little *content* to our picture of their respective systems. Yet the passage does highlight an essential difference between ancient and modern categories, for it describes his youthful experimentation with the Judean schools in terms of *discipline, training,* and even *toughening:*

> When I was about sixteen years old, I chose to gain expertise (or experience, ἐμπειρία) in the philosophical schools[4] among us. There are three of these: the first, Pharisees; the second, Sadducees; and the third, Essenes, as we have often said. . . . *So I toughened myself* and, *after considerable effort* (σκληραγωγήσας οὖν ἐμαυτὸν καὶ πολλὰ πονηθείς), passed through the three of them. (*Life* 10–11)

[4]Greek, αἱρέσεις. In earlier Greek, the noun αἵρεσις indicated one's "choosing" or "taking"—in any field (Plato, *Phaedr.* 99b; *Soph.* 245b; *Phaedr.* 249b; Aristotle, *Ath. pol.* 3.6; *Eth. eud.* 1249b; Lucian, *Phal.* 1.9). Perhaps because the term came to be employed so frequently in philosophical-ethical discussion, concerning one's choice *of a way to live* (Lucian, *Hermot.* 21, 28), it had by Josephus's time become also a technical term for a philosophical school or sect (cf. Galen, *Ord. libr.* eug. 19.50; Lucian, *Demon.* 13; *Hermot.* 48; Diogenes Laertius 1.18–21; cf. 2.47). Diogenes notes that several others before him had written books "On the Schools" (περὶ αἱρέσεων; 1.19; 2.65, 87). Although Josephus can use αἵρεσις in its broader senses—the "taking" or "capture" of a town (*Ant.* 7.160; 10.79, 133, 247; 12.363, etc.); another sort of "choice" or "option" (*War* 1.99; 6.352; *Ant.* 1.69; 6.71, etc.)—in thirteen of its thirty-one occurrences it means for him "philosophical school" (*War* 2.118, 122, 137, 142, 162; *Ant.* 13.171–173; *Life* 191, 197). He freely interchanges φιλοσοφία and cognates (*War* 2.119, 166; *Ant.* 18.11, 23, 25). Thus he presents Judean culture as wholly comparable to Greek: it even has its own philosophies.

Hellenistic *philosophia*, "devotion to wisdom," was oriented toward discovering happiness or well-being (εὐδαιμονία, *felicitas*). But if one's well-being were to be secure, everyone realized, it needed to be grounded in reality.[5] Philosophy's great advantage was that it claimed to offer a safe, solid, reliable way to live one's life, neither reacting impulsively to circumstances, animal-like, nor resorting to unreasonable, superstitious coping mechanisms (Plutarch, *Mor.* 171e; Epictetus, *Diatr.* 3.23.34; Lucian, *Men.* 4; Justin, *Dial.* 8.1). As Aristotle's vast legacy illustrates, the ancient precursors of most modern disciplines, from physics, biology, mathematics, agriculture, and astronomy to political science, anthropology, psychology, language, and theology, not to mention metaphysics, logic, and ethics, fell within the purview of the ancient philosopher. At least by the Hellenistic and Roman periods, however, the more abstract aspects of philosophy had become harnessed to the quest for the virtuous and therefore happy life. In spite of the many differences among Greek philosophical schools concerning the workings of the cosmos, they largely agreed on the moral disposition that should result from philosophical study.

The label "philosopher" came, therefore, to describe a type of person: a man (usually) committed to simplicity of lifestyle, rational mastery of the desires and fears that drove other mortals, and direct, frank speech. Already for Cicero in the first century B.C.E., the categories "philosophy" and "philosopher" were more important than the doctrines of any particular school: he speaks of worthily undertaking the heavy obligations of "philosophy" (e.g., *Pis.* 58, 71–72; *Phil.* 8.10; *Red. sen.* 13). This recognition of philosophy as a pursuit requiring one's whole commitment appears frequently in authors of the first and second centuries C.E.[6] Probably the closest ancient parallel to modern evangelical conversion was the sharp turn to embrace the philosophical life, with its rejection of worldly values.[7] The existence of identifiable persons who had taken up such a life explains how Vespasian and Domitian could expel "philosophers" from Rome—when the latter had begun to express with annoying candor their views on the developing monarchy (Dio 66.13.1; Suetonius, *Dom.* 10). And it was not Stoicism or Epicureanism but *philosophy* that would later console Marcus Aurelius (*Med.* 1.6, 14, 16–17, etc.) and Boethius (*Cons.* 1.3.2, 5; 4.1.1).

---

[5]On happiness as goal, see Plato, *Resp.* 421b and especially Aristotle, *Eth. eud.* 1214a, 1217a, 1219a–b; *Eth. nic.* 1095–1097, 1099a, 1102a, 1153b, 1177a–b, etc.; Seneca, *Ep.* 15.1; Plutarch, *Lyc.* 13.1; 29.2–4; 31.1; *Comp. Dem. Cic.* 1.1; *Mor.* 5c, 24b–25a, 97d. The second- and third-century commentaries on Aristotle by Aspasias and Alexander feature εὐδαιμονία conspicuously.

[6]Dionysius of Halicarnassus, *Ant. rom.* 2.21.1, 68.2; 5.12.3; 11.1.4; *Ant. or.* 1.13; 4.13; *Isocr.* 1.9, 43; 4.21; 7.28; Dio Chrysostom, *1 Glor.* 1.9; 2.24, 26; 7.128; 12.9; 18.7; 20.11; 27.7, etc.; Epictetus, *Diatr.* 1.8.13, 15.t, 2, 4, 25.33; 2.11.1, 13, 14, 17.30, 24.15; 3.13.23, 31.22, etc.; Justin, *Apol.* 3.2.5; 4.8.2; 7.3.3; 12.5.4; 26.6.4; *Dial.* 1.3.7, 11; 6.3; 2.1.2, 4–5.

[7]Epictetus, *Diatr.* 3.21.20, 23.37; Lucian, *Nigr.* 1, 33–38; Diogenes Laertius, *Lives* 4.16; 5.22.12; Augustine, *Conf.* 3.4.7; cf. Nock, *Conversion*, e.g., 185; H. I. Marrou, *A History of Education in Antiquity* (trans. G. Lamb; Madison: University of Wisconsin Press, 1956), 206–7. It is no coincidence that second-century Christians, such as Justin Martyr, the author of the *Epistle to Diognetus*, Clement of Alexandria, and Augustine understood philosophy as the category best suited to explain their way of life—and conversion to that life.

One index to the comprehensive claims of ancient philosophy is what we might call the "Spartanization" of philosophy's image, by which I mean a resort to the highly disciplined community of classical Sparta as a paradigm of moral and political philosophy. We see a glimpse of this already in Xenophon's (fourth century B.C.E.) portrait of the Spartan leader Agesilaus, alongside whom he had fought. Observe his points of emphasis:

> No doubt it is thought to be noble to build walls impregnable to the enemy. But I at least judge it nobler to prepare for the *impregnability of one's own soul:* in the face of material gain and pleasures and fear [as did Agesilaus]. . . . It brought him great cheer also that he knew he was able to *adjust ungrudgingly* to the way the gods had arranged things, whereas he saw the *other man fleeing the heat and fleeing the cold alike,* through weakness of soul, emulating a life not of good men but of the weakest animals. . . . The man who is foremost in *endurance* (καρτερία) when the time comes for labor, in *valor* when it is a contest of courage, in *wisdom* when it is a matter of counsel: this, it seems to me at least, may rightly be considered *an excellent man* overall. . . . The virtue of Agesilaus appears to me to be a model for those wishing to cultivate manly excellence (καλὸν ἄν μοι δοκεῖ εἶναι ἡ Ἀγησιλάου ἀρετὴ παράδειγμα γενέσθαι τοῖς ἀνδραγαθίαν ἀσκεῖν βουλομένοις). (*Ages.* 8.8; 9.5; 10.1–2)

Tellingly, Xenophon's description of the philosopher Socrates' virtues hardly differs from this: philosophy enabled him to be a master of endurance in all seasons and situations (*Mem.* 1.2.1; cf. 2.1.20; 3.1.6), always able to control his passions, following a tough regimen (*Mem.* 1.3.5), relentlessly training his body and rejecting all forms of luxury and softness (*Mem.* 1.2.1–4). He lived in extreme simplicity, eating and drinking only the minimum necessary, and fleeing sexual temptation along with other harmful pleasures (*Mem.* 1.3.5–15). Well trained soldiers thus often possessed the virtues that philosophy aspired to inculcate by other means.

Later Cynics, Stoics, and others found the characteristics of classical Sparta's adult males—rigorous training, simplicity of diet and lifestyle, disregard for marriage and family, communal male solidarity, rugged adaptability to all hardships, disdain for conventional goods, keen sense of personal honor at all costs, and unflinching courage in the face of pain and death—stripped, as necessary of objectionably bellicose traits (Plato, *Leg.* 626c–d; Aristotle, *Pol.* 1333b)—the living enactment of their philosophical aspirations (cf. Plutarch, *Lyc.* 31.1–2).[8] Roman moralists, too, found the Spartiate model singularly appealing, and so exempted Spartans from their typical characterization of Greeks as effeminate, preening windbags. Old Sparta, notwithstanding its subsequent decline, seemed a model of Cato the Elder's Roman virtues enacted through the male elite of a whole society.[9] Polybius discussed Spartan-Roman parallels; Poseidonius speculated about genetic links between Spartans and Romans; and the Hasmoneans played up a genetic connection with Sparta.

---

[8] E. N. Tigerstedt, *The Legend of Sparta in Classical Antiquity* (2 vols.; Stockholm: Almquist & Wiksell, 1974), 1:228–2:30–48.

[9] A. Wardman, *Rome's Debt to Greece* (Bristol: Bristol Classical Press, 1976), 90–93.

Sparta was so attractive because it was a basic goal of ancient philosophical training to make the *practitioner impervious* to physical hardship, weakness, and desire, to the emotions and human suffering (two senses of τὰ πάθη). Many philosophers, including Seneca's teacher Attalus, prescribed harsh physical regimens with respect to food, drink, and sex; he even required his students to sit on hard seats (Seneca, *Ep.* 108.14).[10] Though possibly exaggerating, Lucian's *Nigrinus* observes that students of philosophy are commonly subjected by their teachers to whips, knives, and cold baths, in order to produce toughness and insusceptibility to pain (στέρρον καὶ ἀπαθές); students often expire, he claims, from the physical exertions required by other philosophers (*Nigr.* 28). At *Nigrinus* 27 he seems to quote a slogan about philosophical training, "with many compulsions and efforts" (πολλαὶς ἀνάγκαις καὶ πόνοις), which as it happens closely matches Josephus's language above. The final test of all this training, and so of one's worth as a philosopher, was the ability to face death itself with equanimity (e.g., Epictetus, *Diatr.* 3.26.11–14, 21–39).

Significantly, the only other occurrence in Josephus of the verb σκληραγωγέω, which he uses to describe his "toughening" through philosophy (above), concerns his Pythagorean-like Daniel and friends, who observe a vegetarian diet in Babylon (*Ant.* 10.190). Josephus claims that these young men thereby avoided making their bodies soft (μαλακώτερα). He has said nothing so explicit about such tough training elsewhere in his descriptions of the Judean schools, though his Pharisees (*Ant.* 18.12) and especially Essenes (*War* 2.122–123; *Ant.* 18.20) reportedly practice the simple life, avoiding luxury and softness.

The tendency that we have observed in the Roman period toward eclecticism among philosophers[11] was mirrored and facilitated by standard assumptions about the education of aristocrats. These men were cultivated to be all-around leaders, ready to meet any public need that might arise, as orators, lawyers and magistrates, governors, generals, landowners, priests, historians, poets, and philosophers. In the mix of training needed to produce members of the elite, Plutarch comments on the importance of philosophical education (*Mor.* 10.8a–b):

> One must try, then, as well as one can, both to take part in public life (τὰ κοινὰ πράττειν), and to lay hold of philosophy [note the generic category] so far as the opportunity is granted. Such was the life of Pericles as a public man (ἐπολιτεύσατο—same verb as in Josephus in *Life* 12; cf. chapter 1).

Cicero's intensive youthful training among several philosophical schools (*Fam.* 13.1.2; *Fin.* 1.16; *Brut.* 89.306–91.316), an exercise thought to instill the Roman-elite virtue of *humanitas*,[12] had become a model of liberal education. Going the

---

[10] M. L. Clarke, *Higher Education in the Ancient World* (London: Routledge, 1971), 93.

[11] Cf. Arnaldo Momigliano, *Quarto Contributo alla Storia degli Studi Classici e del Mondo Antico* (Rome: Edizioni di Storia e Letteratura, 1969), 240; A. Meredith, "Later Philosophy," in *The Roman World* (ed. J. Boardman, J. Green and O. Murray; Oxford: Oxford University Press, 1988), 288–307, esp. 290.

[12] G. B. Conte, *Latin Literature: A History* (Baltimore: Johns Hopkins University Press, 19940, 177.

round of the philosophies to gain breadth and perspective may not have been possible or desirable for everyone, but it was a typical course for certain determined young men of means (Lucian, *Men.* 4–5; Justin, *Dial.* 2; Galen, *De anim. pecc. dign. cur.* 5.102). Such worldly cultivation in *all* the schools precluded any gauche or possibly dangerous devotion to a single ideology; as Ramsay MacMullen observes,[13] "specialization in one school . . . belonged to pedants, not to gentlemen." Both the quest itself and the folly of embracing any single school's doctrines were satirized, two generations after Josephus, by Lucian in his *Philosophies for Sale.*[14] Thus, Josephus's determination to equip himself by training in the several Judean schools, in preparation for a public career, was a familiar experience in the Roman world.

Inevitably, to put it another way, philosophical perspectives became another element of the juggernaut of *rhetoric.* Whereas the principles of rhetoric had once fallen under the polymath-philosopher's scrutiny,[15] by Josephus's time philosophical themes had long since been fully incorporated under the mandate of rhetoric. Expertise in rhetoric was the ultimate goal and highest good of elite education in the Hellenistic-Roman world,[16] and the first-century rhetor Aelius Theon complains that too many students approach it without even a modicum of training in philosophy (59.1–7):

> The ancient rhetoricians, and especially the most renowned, did not think that one should reach for any form of rhetoric before *touching on philosophy in some way* (πρὶν ἀμωσγέπως ἅψασθαι φιλοσοφίας), thereby being expanded with a breadth of intellect. Nowadays, by contrast, most people are so lacking in paying attention to such teachings that they rush into speaking without taking on board even much of what are called general studies.

So those who had some claim to philosophical training might understandably flaunt their credentials, as Josephus does (*Life* 10–12). Philosophical issues such as those described above had become for them, just like the historiographical principles originally designed by Thucydides and Polybius to *distinguish* history from rhetoric,[17] rhetorical commonplaces or *topoi* (*loci*): stock items in a speaker's or writer's repertoire, around which accrued standard techniques of elaboration, illustration, and evaluation.

Because elite students were trained by rhetoric to write and speak in all genres (cf. Theon, *Prog.* 60, 70), and because philosophy was part of the elite repertoire, a cultivated man should be able to speak of it knowledgeably but without unseemly devotion. An important part of rhetorical training was mastering different kinds of what were called *ekphraseis* (ἐκφράσεις): focused, vivid digressions on key persons, environmental conditions (geographical or climactic), battle prepa-

[13] MacMullen, *Enemies,* 47.

[14] Cf., on Josephus, Rajak, *Historian,* 34–38.

[15] E.g., in Aristotle's famous three-volume, *Rhetoric.*

[16] See Marrou, *Education,* and now Cribiore, *Gymnastics,* for a vivid introduction to the world of elite education.

[17] Marincola (*Authority*) illustrates the point thoroughly.

rations and scenes of conflict, or objects such as building structures (Theon, *Prog.* 118–120; Hermogenes, *Prog.* 10). Though not as common as these other forms of digression, the comparison of philosophical schools shares the essential requirements of *ekphrasis:* diversion from the main narrative to make vivid some particular issue, in language suited to the subject. Philosophical comparison is a kind of *ekphrasis* that includes within it a theoretical *thesis* (Theon, *Prog.* 120–123). It is a matter of abstract controversy not involving specific persons or circumstances. Thus, a smattering of philosophical understanding and especially a repertoire of philosophical anecdote were useful items in the speaker's or writer's arsenal.

Like other members of his class, Josephus employs philosophical language not as a specialist or devotee, but as a man of the world who took the harder path and immersed himself in philosophy—Judean and Greco-Roman—as part of his education.

One upshot of this eclectic training was that authors who had enjoyed an aristocratic education felt comfortable tossing off the sort of philosophical discourse that Josephus writes for himself at Jotapata (*War* 3.361) or providing urbane asides for their audiences.

In particular, schematic comparisons of the various philosophical schools could be useful subjects for digression. Cicero, after his strenuous efforts to acquaint himself with Greek philosophy, describes the main Greek schools for his Roman audiences: Epicurean (*Fin.* 1–2), Stoic (*Fin.* 3–4), and Platonist (*Fin.* 5). He could also range the schools along a spectrum according to their views on Fate:

> It seems to me that, there being two opinions among the older philosophers, the one held by those who believed that everything occurred by Fate in such a way that Fate itself produced the force of necessity (this was the view of Democritus, Heraclitus, Empedocles and Aristotle), the other by those to whom it seemed that there were voluntary motions of the mind without Fate, Chrysippus wanted to strike a middle path, as an informal arbitrator. (*Fat.* 39; cf. *Nat. d.* 1.1–2)

Among historians, Tacitus, while commenting on Tiberius's devotion to astrology, pauses to remark on the various philosophical approaches to the same questions:

> Indeed, among the wisest of the ancients and among their schools you will find conflicting theories, many holding the conviction that the gods have no concern with the beginning or the end of our life, or, in short, with mankind at all; and that therefore sorrows are continually the lot of the good, happiness among the lesser sort. Others, by contrast, believe that, though there is a harmony between Fate and events, yet it is not dependent on wandering stars, but on primary elements and on a combination of natural causes. Still, they leave to us the choice of a way of life, maintaining that wherever the choice has been made there is a fixed order of consequences. (*Ann.* 6.22)

Like Cicero, he identifies the Fate/free will problem as fundamental: some deny that Fate determines human life at all; others find a certain (vaguely explained) symbiosis between Fate and events, while allowing freedom of human choice;

most think that a person's future is astrologically fixed at birth (*Ann.* 6.22). Later, Galen the polymath physician will routinely compare three or four schools on a given issue (*Anim. pecc. dign. cur.* 5.92, 102; *Plac. Hipp. Plat.* 7.7.22; *Ord. libr. eug.* 19.50.14), and Diogenes Laertius will plot the Greek schools along two lines of "succession" from ancient masters (1.13), or between the two poles of affirmative or dogmatic and negative or skeptical beliefs about the workings of the cosmos (1.16).[18] We have a parallel to this kind of comparison even from Greek India: when in the early second century B.C.E. King Menander goes in search of a wise man to help resolve his doubts, his Greek entourage inform him that there are six philosophical schools in India, each with its own master (*Milindapanha* 1.11).[19]

This is all (perhaps disappointingly) similar to Josephus's comparisons of the Pharisees, Sadducees, and Essenes, which also hinge on their views of Fate (below). In all of these texts, such summaries have the effect of elevating the author as a man of broad philosophical awareness far above the parochial views of any particular school. But we should not expect much illumination from Josephus's learned digressions, any more than we do from Tacitus's brief reflections on the various approaches to Fate. Josephus's three-school schematics are formulaic and, in relation to his larger narratives, of negligible size or significance.

In sum, the broad values of philosophy had by Josephus's time become fully assimilated to aristocratic Roman social values: personal honor, courage, simplicity of life, incorruptibility, frankness, liberality, mastery of the emotions by reason, imperviousness to the allure of pleasure, and contempt for suffering and death. Only men of such virtues (i.e., the elite) were thought capable of steering the ship of state and preserving it from the impulses of the masses or from rogue demagogues. An author of Josephus's standing should know and be able to explain the particular philosophical schools of his culture, yet with the requisite detachment from any particular one. He might be excused if during his idealistic youth he had indulged himself in philosophical devotion (as he did).[20] Yet civic-*polis* life required him to lay aside such indulgence. (See the analysis of *Life* 11–12 in the previous chapter.)

General Philosophical Currents in Josephus

To provide some perspective for Josephus's three school passages, we should first consider the broader philosophical themes that permeate his writings. Judean culture had for a long time appeared to some outside observers as distinctively philosophical, because of its acceptance of a single invisible God, its lack

[18] Hellenistic philosophers such as Chrysippus and Poseidonius often compare Stoics and Epicureans (according to extant fragments) while working out their own views, but they are in a different category from the aristocratic amateurs I am discussing here.

[19] I owe this reference to Richard Wenghofer, doctoral student at York University researching Greco-Roman ethnography.

[20] Similar youthful enthusiasm, appropriately abandoned for serious public life, is reported by Seneca, of himself (*Ep.* 108.22), and by Tacitus, of his father-in-law Agricola (*Agr.* 4.3).

of regional temples and sacrifice, its devotion to the study and interpretation of ancient texts, and the conspicuous daily regimen—in diet, calendar-based observance, and social restraint—of its representatives (Theophrastus *ap.* Porphyry, *Abst.* 2.26; Megasthenes *ap.* Clement of Alexandria, *Strom.* 1.15.72; Diodorus Siculus, 40.3.4; Strabo *Geogr.* 16.2.35; *Ag. Ap.* 1.179).[21] Tacitus, though no admirer of the Judeans in general, concedes the philosophical character of their piety in contrast with that of the Egyptians:

> Egyptians worship many animals and made-up images, but Judeans *conceive of* one deity, and *with the mind* only (*Iudaei mente sola unumque numen intellegunt*). Those who fashion representations of a god from perishable materials in human form [they consider] impious, for that which is supreme and eternal is neither susceptible of imitation nor subject to decay. Therefore they do not allow any images to stand in their cities, much less in their temples: not for kings this flattery, nor for Caesars this honor. (*Hist.* 5.5)

Judean insight into the ineffable nature of the divine plainly commands Tacitus's respect. Corresponding to such admiration among foreign observers—even if this was occasionally grudging—was a tendency among Greek-language Jewish-Judean writers from at least the second century B.C.E. to interpret their own tradition in philosophical terms (Aristobulus *apud* Eusebius, *Praep. ev.* 13.12.1, 4, 8; *The Letter of Aristeas;* 4 Macc 1:1; 5:4, 8, 23; Philo *passim*). In considering this issue, we must bear in mind that ancient writers did not have the option—open to us—of speaking about either *religion* or *Judaism*. Greek (as Latin and Hebrew) lacked either a word or a concept matching our post-Enlightenment category "religion," and therefore there could be no "Judaism" as such—and indeed there is no corresponding term in the extensive writings of either Philo or Josephus.[22] What we consider religion was woven into many different categories of life (e.g., cult, politics, family life, sports, games, and theater). Prominent among these categories, and one that included crucial aspects of modern religion (*viz.* moral exhortation, exposition of texts concerning ultimate questions, and an ethical system based thereon, freely chosen adoption of ["conversion to"] that system), was *philosophia*. Josephus is among those writers who vigorously promote the philosophical interpretation of Judean culture.

Though present from the beginning of *War,* this is clearest in his later works. Josephus claims that, because the constitution of Moses reflects natural law, anyone wishing to inquire more closely into the basis of Judean law will find the exercise "highly philosophical" (*Ant.* 1.25). He laces *Antiquities* with detours on geography, ethnography, astronomy, mathematics, plant and animal life, historiography, language, and other such tools of the savant's trade. He criticizes the Epicureans, a favorite target of Roman authors too,[23] for believing that the divine does not interfere in human affairs (*Ant.* 10.277; 19.28), and he occasionally

---

[21] Nock, *Conversion,* 62.

[22] As I shall show more fully in a forthcoming *JSJ* article, Greek *-ismos* nouns are a false friend to English *-isms* that indicate a system of belief and practice.

[23] Cf. Cicero, *Fam.* 3.9; 9.25; 13.1, 38; *Red. sen.* 6.14; Epictetus, *Diatr.* 3.24.

shares his own editorial observations on Fate and free will, the soul, and the afterlife (1.85; 6.3; 8.146; 12.282, 304; 19.325). He separately compares Essenes with Pythagoreans (*Ant.* 15.371) and Pharisees with Stoics (*Life* 12). In keeping with his claim to be thoroughly trained in the "philosophy" of the Judeans' ancient books (*Ag. Ap.* 1.54), he even asserts that the Judean law itself "philosophizes" on the vexed problem of Fate and free will (*Ant.* 16.398).

Particularly noteworthy is Josephus's emphasis on "happiness, well-being, prosperity" (εὐδαιμονία), a term whose importance to moral philosophy we have seen above. From the prologue onward, *Antiquities* insists that only the legal constitution bequeathed by Moses brings happiness (*Ant.* 1.14, 20). Josephus introduces this word some forty-seven times into his biblical paraphrase (*Ant.* 1–11), though it had not appeared at all in the other major effort to render the Bible in Greek, the Septuagint. What Moses received from God at Sinai promised, according to Josephus, "a happy life and an orderly constitution" (βίον . . . εὐδαίμονα καὶ πολιτείας κόσμον; 3.84). The Judean nation is singularly happy (εὐδαίμων), Josephus's Balaam says, happier than all other nations (πάντων εὐδαιμονέστεροι τῶν ὑπὸ τὸν ἥλιον), because it alone has been granted God's watchful care (πρόνοια) as an eternal guide (4.114).[24] This related theme of God's watchful care, or providence, was a preoccupation of contemporary Stoicism (e.g., Epictetus, *Diatr.* 1.6, 16; 3.17). In a number of places Josephus more or less equates God with Providence, Fate (εἱμαρμένη), and even Fortune (τύχη).[25]

Accordingly, Josephus portrays key figures in early Judean history as philosophers. Following Seth's descendants, who discovered the orderly array of the heavenly bodies (*Ant.* 1.69), Abraham inferred from the irregularity of these bodies that there was one ultimate God (1.155–156). With the mind of a true philosopher, he visited Egypt intending that "if he found it [what their priests said about the gods] superior, he would subscribe to it, or, if what he himself thought was found preferable, he would reorder their lives according to the more excellent way" (1.161). Anticipating Socrates, he employed a dialectical method to listen carefully to them, and then expose the vacuity of their arguments (1.166). So it happened that it was he who taught the elements of mathematics and science to the renowned Egyptians (*Ant.* 1.167–168).

Moses, the peerless lawgiver, himself studied nature in order to achieve the proper foundation for his laws (*Ant.* 1.18–19, 34). Like Plato (*Rep.* 3.386–417), the Judean lawgiver rejected out of hand the unseemly "myths" about the gods (*Ant.* 1.22–24). His greatness of intellect and understanding were apparent even in childhood (2.229–230). He "surpassed in understanding all who ever lived, and used his insights in the best possible ways" (4.328).

King Solomon, for his part, "surpassed all the ancients, and suffered in no way by comparison even with the Egyptians, who are said to excel everyone in understanding; in fact, their intelligence was proven to be quite inferior to the

---

[24] On *pronoia* in *Antiquities,* see Attridge, *Interpretation,* 67–70.

[25] At least, these are executive aspects of the divine (*Ant.* 10.277–280; 16.395–404; cf. *Ag. Ap.* 2.180–181).

king's" (*Ant.* 8.42). His knowledge covered not only the whole range of natural science—encompassing every creature in existence—but extended even to occult science: the techniques for expelling demons and effecting cures (8.44–49). These powers remain the unique legacy of the Judeans in Josephus's day (8.46). Josephus's Daniel is yet another kind of philosopher: he and his companions adopt a Pythagorean-like vegetarian diet, by which they keep their minds "pure and fresh for learning" (*Ant.* 10.193).[26]

It was apparently the philosophical character of the Judean laws, for Josephus, that facilitated the movement by other nationals to come and live under them—what we frame as "conversion." Josephus contrasts the Judeans' openness to receiving those who wish to come and live under their laws with Athenian and Spartan jealousy of their own respective citizenships (*Ag. Ap.* 2.255–263). In his glowing account of the Adiabenian royal house's "having been brought over" (μετακεκομίσθαι) to the Judean laws and customs, he acknowledges that these laws were foreign, and this created great risk for the royals. Standard English translations, such as the Loeb's "Jewish religion" for τὰ Ἰουδαίων ἔθη (lit. "the customs of the Judeans," *Ant.* 20.38) or "Judaism" for τὰ πάτρια τῶν Ἰουδαίων (lit. "the ancestral [laws, heritage] of the Judeans," *Ant.* 20.41), disguise this ethnic-national context, replacing it with comfortably modern categories such as "religion" and "conversion." Yet Josephus stresses the "foreign and alien" character of Judean laws in relation to the Adiabenians (*Ant.* 20.39: ξένων καὶ ἀλλοτρίων ἐθῶν; cf. 20.47), and it was precisely this issue of foreignness that bothered his Roman contemporaries: Tacitus and Juvenal considered it impious for Romans to adopt foreign laws, because it meant abandoning their own ancestral traditions in the process (*Hist.* 5.4–5; *Sat.* 14). This anomie involved in adopting the laws of another *ethnos* is partly resolved in Josephus by resort to the Judean constitution's uniquely *philosophical* character, for one cannot be faulted for converting to the philosophical life. Josephus's Abraham provides the model of the missionary philosopher (above), and the whole discussion of comparative constitutions that Josephus hosts in *Ag. Ap.* 2.146–196 is philosophical in nature.

In *Judean War*, Josephus's first work, he exploits philosophical themes in a subtler way. Without much using the explicit language of philosophy, he nevertheless crafts two erudite speeches, for himself and Eleazar son of Yair, on life, death, morality, and suicide—with demonstrable debts to Plato (*War* 3.362–382; 7.341–388).[27] Throughout the entire *War* he drives home the Judean-philosophical virtues of courage, toughness, endurance, and contempt for suffering and death. But the most compellingly philosophical section of the work, and a primary contextual reference-point for the Pharisees and Sadducees of *War*, is Josephus's lengthy description of the Essenes in *War* 2.119–161.

---

[26] D. Satran, "Daniel: Seer, Prophet, Holy Man." *Ideal Figures in Ancient Judaism: Profiles and Paradigms* (ed. J. J. Collins and G. W. E. Nickelsburg. Chico Calif.: Scholars Press, 1980), 33–48.

[27] Cf. M. Luz "Eleazar's Second Speech on Masada and its Literary Precedents," *Rheinisches Museum* 126 (1983): 25–43; D. J. Ladouceur, "Josephus and Masada." in *Josephus, Judaism, and Christianity* (ed. Feldman and Hata), 95–133.

Although there is much to say about *War*'s Essene passage, I wish to make only two points here. First, Josephus's Essenes exhibit the comprehensive life-regimen of a philosophical school that we have now come to expect. In describing so many aspects of this school—initiation requirements and oaths, disciplinary and expulsion procedures, daily regimen, leadership structure, treatment of private property, sexual relations and attitude toward children, dress, dining and toilet habits, purity measures, objects of study, manner of worship, view of the soul and afterlife—Josephus gives us the clearest picture anywhere in his writings of a Judean "school." And it emerges that they live out the highest aspirations of philosophy in the Roman world. We considered above the Spartanization of Greco-Roman philosophy. Very much like the Spartiates, Essenes live their whole lives under the strictest discipline, avoiding even the use of oil in personal grooming (*War* 2.123; cf. Plutarch, *Mor.* 237a; *Lyc.* 16.6; *Ages.* 30.3), which is otherwise ubiquitous in the Greco-Roman world. They too remove women from their company, hold all possessions in common, and share a common meal. They disdain equally the pleasures (2.122) and the terrors (2.152) that motivate most others.

Second, the Essene passage is a condensed version of Josephus's claims about *all Judeans.* We see this partly in *War* 2.152–153, where the Essenes display the same virtues of courage and toughness in the face of torture that characterize Judeans throughout the work (2.60; 3.357, 475; 5.88, 458; 6.42; 7.406), but most clearly in a comparison with *Against Apion.* There, what Josephus has said about the Essenes in *War* 2 is applied to all Judeans: *the whole nation* observes the laws with the strictest discipline and solemnity, lives in utmost simplicity, values virtue above all else, holds death in contempt (same phrases used as for Essenes), and keeps women in their place. Sex, among Essenes (*War* 2.161–162) as for all Judeans, is thus for procreative purposes only, and not for pleasure.[28] It is conspicuous, in light of the discussion above, that *Against Apion* compares the Judeans favorably with the Spartans, driving home the point that the glory days of that universally admired state are only a distant memory, whereas Judeans have continued to practice these virtues for many centuries until the present, as the recent war has demonstrated (*Ag. Ap.* 2.130, 172, 225–231, 259, 272–273). Josephus has entered the Judeans in the competition for most philosophical nation.

The third-century Platonist philosopher, Porphyry, seems to have seen these connections clearly. In the fourth book of his work *On Abstinence* (from animal food), soon after discussing the Spartans (4.3–5) he treats the Judeans (*Abst.* 4.11–14) as further models of a disciplined regimen. For evidence about the Judeans he devotes most of his account to *War*'s Essene passage (4.11.3–13.10, almost verbatim), although he claims to get his information from both *War* 2 and *Against Apion.* Since *Against Apion* does not mention the Essenes, it appears that Porphyry saw the striking similarities and so confused the Essene passage in *War* 2 with

[28] Ag. Ap. 2.145–146, 293–294, pieces of panegyric on the Judean laws, can be matched phrase for phrase with earlier descriptions of the Essenes. See also *Ag. Ap.* 1.225; 2.193–196, 199–202, 205, 223.

what Josephus ascribes to all Judeans in *Against Apion*, perhaps on the assumption that a whole nation could not sustain such a disciplined regimen.

The school passages, to which we now turn, are therefore only one example—a minor and perfunctory one—of the philosophical interests that run throughout Josephus's works. As an author he is much more interested in those larger issues of moral character, in relation to the Judeans as a people, than he is in the petty doctrinal differences of the schools. When he fleetingly compares the schools' positions on Fate and the soul, he is only doing what a man of his education should be able to do: explain to foreign audiences that his people too have schools, with such and such views. But the result smacks of conventionalism and suitable vagueness. Josephus does not have Cicero's taste or patience for detailed philosophical analysis.

Pharisees among the Three Judean Schools

Let us, then, consider in turn the three school passages identified above. Such an examination is more useful for understanding Josephus than for investigating the Pharisees. We shall find what seem to be quite deliberate inconsistencies. At the very least, however, a responsible assessment of the Pharisees among the school passages should provide some criteria for using these passages in historical reconstruction.

War 2.119–166 is paradoxical. On the one hand, Josephus appears to regard it as his definitive statement, for he will refer the audience to it in both of the later school passages, *Ant.* 13.173 and 18.11, as also at 13.298. On the other hand, the form of the passage is not standard. Since the Essene component of the description (*War* 2.119–161) consumes more than twenty times the space given to either Pharisees (2.162–163, 166a) or Sadducees (2.164–165, 166b), the Essenes cannot properly be considered part of a three-way comparison.

Because Josephus has chosen to feature the Essenes so elaborately, as towering examples of Judean virtue, instead of using a Ciceronian three-point spectrum he opts here for the sort of binary contrast between affirmative and skeptical positions that Diogenes Laertius (above) will employ: Pharisees affirm what Sadducees deny.

> [162] Now, of the former two [schools], Pharisees, who are reputed to interpret the legal matters with precision, and who constitute the first school, attribute everything to Fate and indeed to God: [163] although doing and not [doing] what is right rests mainly with the human beings, Fate also assists in each case. Although every soul is imperishable, only that of the good passes over to a different body, whereas those of the vile are punished by eternal retribution.

Affirmed by the Pharisees—after the reminder that they are reputed to be the most precise interpreters of the laws (2.162–163)—are: the connection of "all things with Fate and indeed with God" (εἱμαρμένῃ τε καὶ θεῷ προσάπτουσι πάντα); the immortality of the soul (ψυχήν τε πᾶσαν μὲν ἄφθαρτον); the passing of the good soul into another body (μεταβαίνειν δὲ εἰς ἕτερον σῶμα τὴν τῶν ἀγαθῶν μόνην); and the eternal retribution facing the vile (τὰς δὲ τῶν φαύλων αἰδίῳ τιμωρίᾳ κολάζεσθαι). The Sadducees (2.164–165) deny Fate, remove God from the scene (Epicurean-like), and reject survival of the soul with post-mortem judgment.

We lack the space here for a proper exegesis of these statements, but a few points are noteworthy. First, when it comes to the most important arena of Fate's intervention, namely in human behavior, Josephus qualifies the Pharisees' alleged pan-fatalism in a significant way (2.163): "Although doing and not [doing] what is right rests mainly with the human beings, Fate also assists in each case" (τὸ μὲν πράττειν τὰ δίκαια καὶ μὴ κατὰ τὸ πλεῖστον ἐπί τοῖς ἀνθρώποις κεῖσθαι, βοηθεῖν δὲ εἰς ἕκαστον καὶ τὴν εἱμαρμένην), whereas the Sadducees recognize human choice alone. This formulation preserves the ubiquity of Fate's activity for the Pharisees, allowing them to occupy the affirmative pole, but also reveals a degree of sophistication.

According to Cicero, the Stoic Chrysippus distinguished two kinds of causes: principal or antecedent (*causae perfectae et principales*) and "helping" or proximate (*causae adiuvantes et proximae; Fat.* 42).[29] When one pushes a drum down a hill, for example, the antecedent cause of its rolling is its particular nature (its rollability, so to speak). The push that starts the roll is an immediate, "helping" cause—and in every case of action such an initiating cause will be found. So for Josephus's Pharisees, humans have a certain nature, but Fate "helps" *in each action* by applying a sort of prod to that nature.

Of course, the relationship between determinism and free will has, in various guises (nature vs. nurture, heredity vs. environment), remained a central problem of philosophy. Plato deals in several contexts with the problem of causation in human affairs (e.g., *Phaed.* 80d–81d; *Resp.* 614b–621d; *Tim.* 41d, 42d, 91d–e). Aristotle credits nature, necessity, and chance with much influence, but he holds that the choice of virtue or vice lays "in ourselves" (*Eth. nic.* 3.3.3–5.2). From rabbinic literature, a parallel to Josephus's statement is often drawn from a saying attributed to R. Akiva in *m. Avot* 3.15: "*All is foreseen,* yet freedom of choice is given" (Danby translation). But the key phrase (הכל צפוי) may mean only that all is *observed* (by God), and so one ought to be careful how one exercises free choice.[30]

These observations about Fate and human virtue in Josephus's Pharisees prompt a second point: that his language is wholly conventional in relation to Greek philosophy. Diction and phrasing alike—"doing the right thing" (Aristotle, *Eth. nic.* 1105b; Lucian, *Anach.* 22), "rests with human beings" (*Eth. nic.* 3.1.6, 5.2), "every soul is imperishable" (Plato, *Meno* 81b), "passes over into a different body" (Plato, *Meno* 81b; *Phaed.* 70c, 71e–72a), "eternal retribution" (Philo, *Spec.* 3.84;

[29]For this and other verbal parallels with Cicero's Chrysippus, see George Foot Moore, "Fate and Free Will in the Jewish Philosophies According to Josephus," *HTR* 22 (1929): 384.

[30]S. Schechter, *Aspects of Rabbinic Theology: Major Concepts of the Talmud* (New York: Schocken Books, 1961), 285.

cf. the classical Greek examples offered by Josephus himself at 2.156)—are well attested in other writers on similar subjects.

Josephus's language is not only classic-philosophical, however. It also turns up often in other parts of his narratives: describing Essenes, for whom he uses nearly indistinguishable language concerning the soul and punishments (2.154–155, 157; *Ant.* 18.18); describing Sadducees, for whom he uses the same language concerning human volition (2.165; *Ant.* 13.173); describing Pharisees in other passages (especially *Ant.* 18.12–15); and describing a number of other figures, including his own views as character and as narrator.[31]

Finally, although Josephus uses conventional philosophical language, his description remains vague enough to hint at a unique twist in the Pharisees' view of afterlife, for the soul of the good "passes over into another body" (singular). According to the parallel passage on Pharisees in *Antiquities* 18.14, the souls of the virtuous find "an easy path to living again" (ῥᾳστώνην τοῦ ἀναβιοῦν). On this point the Pharisees appear to depart from the Essene position, which envisions a spiritual home beyond Oceanus for the souls of the righteous—a view that Josephus explicitly compares with Greek notions (*War* 2.155). The difference may be only apparent, however, since elsewhere he speaks of good souls going *first* to a heavenly place and *from there* to "holy new bodies," in the revolution or succession of ages (ἐκ περιτροφῆς αἰώνων, *War* 3.375; *Ag. Ap.* 2.218). Those passages envisage an intervening period of the soul's existence before its reincarnation.

In any case, Josephus's emphases in all these passages on the holiness and singularity of the new body, its nature as *reward* for a good life (whereas reincarnation tends to be either generic necessity or punishment in Greek thought), and the notice that the transfer will occur (once?) in the succession of ages—so not as an ongoing process—create affinities with current pictures of *resurrection* (e.g., Paul in 1 Cor 15:35–51). If Josephus has bodily resurrection in view, he chooses not to make himself clear. His vague but evocative language would no doubt make such a view of afterlife sound more familiar to his audience. Whether this language reflects his own views or he obfuscates because straightforward talk of "bodily resurrection" might make audiences uncomfortable (cf. *Acts* 17:31–33; Celsus *ap.* Origen, *C. Cels.* 5.14; Augustine, *Civ.* 22.4–5) is impossible to say.

As in the other schools passages, in *War* 2.119–166 Josephus neither condemns nor praises the Pharisees' views. Affirmers of Fate, the soul, and judgment after death, they come off better than the Sadducean deniers of these things—since we know that Josephus is also an affirmer (*War* 2.158). But in this passage he has given much fuller attention to the Essenes' views, though these are quite similar to those of the Pharisees on key points, with unambiguous endorsement and admiration (2.158). Even his positive closing remark that, whereas the Pharisees are mutually affectionate (φιλάλληλοι) and cultivate harmony in the

---

[31] "That which lies in one's power" (*War* 3.389, 396; 5.59; *Ant.* 1.178; 5.110; 13.355; 18.215; 19.167). Souls are imperishable (*War* 3.372). Souls go into new bodies (*War* 3.375; *Ag. Ap.* 2.218). On language concerning the soul and afterlife throughout Josephus, see especially J. Sievers, "Josephus and the Afterlife," in *Understanding Josephus: Seven Perspectives* (ed by S. Mason; Sheffield: Sheffield Academic Press, 1998), 20–31.

assembly, the Sadducees are harsh even to one another (2.166), is relativized by 2.119: the Essenes outshine all others in their mutual affection (φιλάλληλοι . . . τῶν ἄλλων πλέον).

In *Antiquities*, the first school passage (13.171–173) gives us precious little content, though it again reveals interesting traits in our author. Restricting the comparison to the single issue of Fate, Josephus here constructs a simple three-point spectrum like Cicero's:

> [171] At about this time there were three philosophical schools among the Judeans, which regarded human affairs differently: one of these was the [school] of the Pharisees, another that of the Sadducees, and the third that of the Essenes. [172] The Pharisees, then, say that some things but not all are the work of Fate, whereas some—whether they happen or do not occur—fall to our account. The order of the Essenes, by contrast, posits Fate as the governess of all things, and [holds that] nothing whatsoever happens to humans that is not according to her determination. [173] Sadducees do away with Fate, reckoning that there is no such thing, and that human affairs do not reach fulfillment on her account, but everything rests with us, that indeed we were responsible for what is good and received evil from our own thoughtlessness. But concerning these things I have provided a more precise explanation in the second volume of the work *Judaica*.

As in *War* 2, Sadducees do away with Fate altogether, but now the Essenes take up the other pole position ("Fate is the Governess of everything, and nothing happens without her vote"). Where does that leave the Pharisees? To say that "some things are the work of Fate, but not everything, for some things happen—or not—because of us." Clearly, Josephus needs three schools for the spectrum, and the Sadducean position (denial of Fate) is a given. Whereas the Pharisees had been the Sadducees' polar opposites in *War* 2, that role must now be played by the Essenes, since they have been brought into the direct comparison, which leaves the Pharisees to find a middle way between the poles. Instead of taking *War*'s route, however, claiming that the Pharisees find Fate in every action *along with* human will, Chrysippus-like, Josephus now unhelpfully has them attribute *some* things (which?) to Fate and some to human choice. That these changes do not bother him, and indeed do not seem to matter (since he refers to *War* 2 for a more precise explanation), shows how little he wishes to be seen as the pedantic sort of philosopher. Broad strokes, changeable as needed for presentational reasons, suffice.[32]

Josephus's final schools passage aside from *Life* 10–11 (above) is the only one that ostensibly combines proportion (i.e., roughly equivalent space for each school) and a degree of comprehensiveness (i.e., several items are considered for each). Closer inspection shows, however, that very little is offered there concern-

---

[32] It is an intriguing question, why Josephus located the passage here. From a narrative point of view the opening chronological tag "at about this time" seems to date the appearance of the schools, though he does not spell this out. Certainly, the passage gives him a base from which to describe Pharisees and Sadducees at 13.297–298, and it is a device of his to plant a seed to which he will later return. For other proposals, see Sievers 2001.

ing the metaphysical positions of either Sadducees or Essenes; Josephus focuses rather on the practices and social position of those two schools. Only the postulates of the Pharisees receive any sustained treatment.

The most peculiar feature of *Ant.* 18.12–22 is the addition of a "Fourth Philosophy" (18.23–25)—the party of radical freedom represented by the followers of Judas the Galilean/Gaulanite—generated when Judea was annexed to the Roman empire in 6 C.E. As for the Fourth Philosophy, Josephus both abhors the innovation in the national heritage they represent, which will allegedly result in the destruction of Jerusalem, and admires the indomitable courage of its practitioners, in much the same way that he esteems the fearlessness of all Judean fighters and Essenes in *War*[33] and the nation as a whole in *Against Apion.*

Although scholars have often taken Josephus at face value and spoken of the Fourth Philosophy as if it were a real entity, it seems that we should consider it rather an *ad hoc* literary construction. Reasons: (a) To have a "fourth philosophy," one must have three, and Josephus is the only one we know to have positioned the three philosophies thus. Imagining the representatives of the Fourth Philosophy as a real group whose members understood themselves by such a description would be akin to expecting film characters to step off the screen into real life. (b) Before, during, and after this passage, Josephus will insist that there are (only) *three* Judean philosophies, even though he has always known about Judas the Galilean and his followers (*War* 2.119; *Ant.* 13.171; 18.11; *Life* 10–11). It does not occur to him elsewhere to mention a Fourth Philosophy. (c) Blaming the Fourth Philosophy for Judea's later ills is an *ex post facto* exercise, possible only with hindsight. It is unreasonable to imagine that later *sicarii,* Zealots, economic rebels, and other groups that emerged from particular conditions in the 40s through 60s (2.254, 651; 4.160–161) *understood themselves* to be members of such a philosophical school. (d) The Fourth Philosophy is not comparable to the others in having a distinctive set of views and way of life, admission procedures and membership requirements. Rather, Josephus claims that they agree with the Pharisees on all philosophical questions except the meaning of freedom (18.23). It seems, then, that he constructs a Fourth Philosophy for at least two reasons: as a novel means of exposing the aberrant character of the rebel mentality and as a way to drive home the ongoing theme of Judean courage (under the rubric of philosophy).

Like the other school passages, then, *Ant.* 18.12–25 is thoroughly conditioned by the demands of immediate narrative context. One decisive element of this context, rarely discussed by scholars, is the peculiar style of writing that Josephus adopts in *Ant.* 17–19, which Thackeray had credited to a literary assistant he dubbed the "Thucydidean hack."[34] Thackeray's notion that for *Antiquities* Josephus employed an array of literary assistants with different propensities has been rightly rejected, however, and we seem to be dealing with the author's

---

[33] *War* 2.50, 60, 152–153; 3.229–230, 472–488; 5.71–97, 277–278, 305–306, 315–316; 6.13–14, 33–53.

[34] Thackeray, *The Man and the Historian,* 107–15.

own experimentation with the literary possibilities of Greek.[35] In any case, *Ant.* 18.12–15 (on the Pharisees) uses the same stilted, quasi-poetic prose that one finds throughout these three volumes. Old Attic was characterized by "poetical coloring, forced and strange expressions, bold new coinages and substantivized neuters of participles and adjectives."[36] That *Ant.* 18.12–25 shares fully in the style of books 17–19 is another indicator that Josephus has written the passage himself or thoroughly reworked any sources used. The schools passage could not have been inserted bodily from another source.

What this language means for us is that, although Josephus devotes more words here than elsewhere to the Pharisees' views, we struggle in near futility to understand him. The strangely poetic character of his language may be seen in his new treatment of the Pharisees' unique tradition (*Ant.* 18.12b–c):

> They follow the authority of those things that their teaching deemed good and handed down;
> they regard as indispensable the observance of those things that it saw fit to dictate.
> Out of honor do they yield to those who precede them in age;
> Nor are they inclined boldly to contradict the things that were introduced.

All of this appears to mean no more than what we learned from *Ant.* 13.297–298, that the Pharisees observe a special "tradition from [their] fathers" (see the previous chapter in this volume). Obviously, embracing such a tradition assumes that they revere those predecessors. It may be that the third panel also indicates respect for *living* elders (though that would qualify the synonymous parallelism); if so, it only underscores the point made in *War* 2.166 that they live harmoniously, unlike the argumentative Sadducees; so also *Ant.* 18.16 has the Sadducees disputing even their own teachers. We do not have access to the historical reality of the Sadducees, but such a harsh evaluation might have been explained by insiders as nothing more than a tradition of vibrant exegetical debate.

The only straightforward statement in this paragraph is the one that opens it, and it is new: "The Pharisees restrain their regimen of life, yielding nothing to the softer side" (*Ant.* 18.12). Josephus does not contrast the Sadducees on this point, though their base among the elite might imply wealth (18.17; cf. 13.197–198; see also the previous chapter in this volume). Translating for the Loeb Classical Library, Louis Feldman notes a rabbinic parallel (*ARN* 5): "Pharisees deprive themselves in this world—foolishly, the Sadducees believe, because there is no other world." In the narrative of Josephus, it is striking that Josephus does not make more of this universally recognized virtue of simplicity in the case of the Pharisees, the way he does with the Essenes—both in this final school passage (18.20: they surpass all others) and in *War* 2. Shunning luxury certainly qualifies the Pharisees to be included among the philosophers (cf. *Ant.* 13.289), though Josephus does not celebrate this in their case.

---

[35] G. C. Richards, "The Composition of Josephus' *Antiquities*." *CQ* 33 (1939): 36–40; Shutt, *Studies*, 59–75; Rajak, *Historian*, 47–63, 233–36.

[36] Palmer, *Greek Language*, 159.

On the issue of Fate, Josephus's language is so garbled as to have caused copyists and translators much confusion:

> They reckon that everything is effected by Fate;
> Yet they do not thereby separate the intending of the human element from the initiative that rests with them [humans] (οὐδὲ τοῦ ἀνθρωπείου τὸ βουλόμενον τῆς ἐπ' αὐτοῖς ὁρμῆς ἀφαιροῦνται),
> It having seemed right to God that there be a fusion [or judgment or weighing against] (δοκῆσαν τῷ θεῷ κρίσιν]),
> And in the council-chamber of that one [Fate?] and [in] the one having willed of the humans, a siding with—with virtue and vice (καὶ τῷ ἐκείνης βουλητηρίῳ καὶ τῶν ἀνθρώπων τὸ ἐθελῆσαν [τῷ ἐθελήσαντι] προσχωρεῖν μετ' ἀρετῆς ἢ κακίας).

Although making sense of this confusion may be a worthwhile text-critical challenge, it is difficult to see the rewards for those who simply wish to understand Josephus's portrait of the Pharisees. The language appears deliberately crabbed and obscure, and we have no compelling reason to believe that there is much substance to be discovered. Apparently, Josephus abandons the simplified three-point scheme of *Ant.* 13.171–173, where the Pharisees hold a middle position of attributing "some things" to Fate and "some" to human volition, to return to the cooperation model of *War* 2.162–163. Fate is somehow involved in *every* action: her collaboration with human will is fancily framed but ultimately unfathomable. Since Josephus will not comment in this passage on the view of Fate held by either Sadducees or Essenes, he need not be concerned with maintaining a position for the Pharisees along a spectrum.

His description of the Pharisees' theory of souls is also awkwardly constructed, a sentence lacking a finite verb (finite verbs given below are either added for English translation or they represent infinitives in Josephus), though the general sense is clear (*Ant.* 18.14):

> That souls have a deathless power is a conviction of theirs (ἀθάνατόν τε ἰσχὺν ταῖς ψυχαῖς πίστις αὐτοῖς εἶναι),
> And that subterranean punishments, and also rewards (ὑπὸ χθονός δικαιώσεις τε καὶ τιμάς), are for those whose conduct in life has been either of virtue or of vice:
> For some, eternal imprisonment is prepared (ταῖς μὲν εἱργμὸν ἀίδιον προτίθεσθαι),
> But for others, an easy route to living again (ταῖς δὲ ῥᾳστώνην τοῦ ἀναβιοῦν).

Here too, the new quasi-poetic verbiage adds little to the spare prose of *War* 2.162–163. The eternal punishments (and possibly rewards), we now learn, are dispensed beneath the earth—so, the equivalent of Hades—and the envisaged eternal punishment is explained as an imprisonment or binding. This would come as no great surprise for Roman audiences, who would easily recall Odysseus's famous vision of Hades (*Od.* 11.576–600), where Sisyphus, Tantalus, and Tityus face unending torture in the netherworld. At *War* 2.156, indeed, Josephus mentions precisely those figures, including the similar character of Ixion, while elaborating the *Essene* view of post-mortem punishment.

War's "passing over to a new body" is now described by the similarly ambiguous "an easy passage to living again." It is on this point only that Sadducean philosophy will be briefly contrasted (18.16): "The doctrine of the Sadducees makes the souls disappear together with the bodies"—ironic phrasing, as if a doctrine could *make* souls disappear.[37] The closer parallel to the Sadducees, however, is the Essene doctrine, for with reciprocal irony those men "render souls deathless" (ἀθανατίζουσιν δὲ τὰς ψύχας, 18.18).

The relationship between Josephus's portraits and any actual Pharisee's articulation of his views must remain an open question, though we have good reason—in his accommodation of this passage to the style of *Ant.* 17–19 and in his generally free rearrangements—to think that literary artifice accounts for a great deal. In relation to *War* 2, there is nothing substantially new here.

A comparison of Josephus's Pharisees with his Sadducees and Essenes in this passage turns up three matters that deserve brief discussion. First, although his language for the other two groups has a similar poetic quality, it is more straightforward in structure and meaning. Second, and this is probably related, his descriptions of Sadducees and Essenes focus on ethical and practical questions: Sadducees recognize only what is in the laws and they are men of the highest standing (though Josephus dilates on the necessity of their public capitulation to Pharisaic law; 18.16–17); Essenes maintain special sacrifices and therefore are barred from the temple, but otherwise he praises their agricultural pursuits, unsurpassed virtue, common possessions, rejection of marriage and slavery, and provisions for leadership (18.18–22). Even the Fourth Philosophy, whose doctrine of radical political freedom Josephus repudiates, he mainly praises for their courage (18.23–25). Third, and the reverse of the same coin, Josephus says very little about the other schools' metaphysical views, mentioning only briefly the Sadducees' dissolution of the soul at death, the Essenes' attribution of all things to God and immortalization of souls, and the Fourth Philosophy's agreement with the Pharisees.

Is there any connection among these three features? If the impression of symmetry in this schools passage, which Josephus deliberately encourages—by proportionate sections, by the recurrence of "the doctrine" (ὁ λόγος) at the begin-

[37]Greek, Σαδδουκαίοις δὲ τὰς ψυχάς ὁ λόγος συναφανίζει τοῖς σώμασι—a statement worth investigating. The verb is sparsely attested before Josephus (Strabo, *Geogr.* 6.1.6; 8.6.23; 12.8.17; 17.3.12; Dionysius of Halicarnassus, *Ant. rom.* 1.1.2; Philo, *Leg.* 194; a fragment attributed to Pythagoras), and in these authors it is always in the middle or passive voice. Josephus uses it only here, and in the active voice. An intriguing possibility: the only writer in this group to speak of souls disappearing with bodies is the historian Dionysius, who in the prologue to his *magnum opus* speaks of historians not wanting their souls to disappear along with their bodies (hence they write memorials in the form of histories). Since Dionysius's twenty-volume *Roman Antiquities* was not only famous in Rome, but also a principal model for Josephus's twenty-volume *Judean Antiquities*, it is quite plausible (the means of proof elude us) that he intends a witty allusion to Dionysius's prologue here.

ning of the first three descriptions, by certain structural features (e.g., Σαδδουκαίοις δέ . . . Ἐσσηνοῖς δέ), and by a family resemblance of diction and word form—turns out to be undermined by such differences of content and emphasis, one might reason as follows. As Josephus shows on nearly every page of *Antiquities,* he is preoccupied with the Judean laws (or "constitution"), with those who observe or flout them, and thus with virtue and vice. He is no abstract philosopher. In the cases of Essenes and even Sadducees, he can easily identify praiseworthy aspects of their practical philosophy. With the Pharisees (18.15, 17; cf. the previous chapter in this volume), however, in spite of their enormous popularity and although he recognizes them *as* a philosophical school, he finds little to praise. After briefly noting their rejection of luxury he uses their space, as it were, for highly abstruse formulations of their positions on intractable questions of metaphysics. Although this surely does not constitute overt criticism, it fits with the lack of sympathy for the Pharisees that we found in the previous chapter.

Conclusions and Corollaries

In this chapter we have seen that Josephus's occasional presentations of the three Judean philosophical schools along a spectrum of metaphysical beliefs are the sort of thing one should expect from an elite representative of Judean culture. From a rhetorical point of view, they are much like his other digressions—on geography, military tactics, or botany. They display his erudition, resulting in part from his thorough training in all three schools, and yet at the same time his urbane superiority to any *parochialism, fanaticism, or pedantry*—even if he had forgivably indulged philosophical yearnings in adolescence. Like a Cicero (though with rather less philosophical intensity overall) or a Tacitus, this eastern nobleman can throw in such descriptions at opportune moments, as pleasant rest stops in the onward march of his historical narrative. The broadly philosophical character of the whole story, however, is much more prominent and important than such brief and murky outlines of the schools' beliefs.

In Josephus's case, because we have three such passages in his thirty-volume *oeuvre,* we can also see how freely he manipulates his material for momentary needs. In *War* 2, where he singles out the Essenes in order to extol the manly virtue that is the unifying theme of the book, Pharisees and Sadducees are left to occupy formulaically the pole positions of affirmers and deniers. In *Ant.* 13, where he opts to break the narrative with a short schematic of the three philosophies *On Fate,* he must rearrange the pieces. Essenes and Sadducees now occupy the extremes, with Pharisees attributing "some things" to Fate and "some things" to human volition. In *Ant.* 18, in the middle of his regrettable experiment with bold style, Josephus tries his hand at describing the schools in the new poetic prose—as in *Ant.* 13 referring to *War* 2 for greater precision. The many added words for the Pharisees are largely redundant, however, because of their opacity and the synonymous parallelism within this passage. They do confirm the notice in *Ant.* 13.297–298 concerning the Pharisees' special tradition, which had not appeared in *War* 2, and they include a new comment about the Pharisees' simple life. The rather technical-sounding descriptions penned for the Pharisees, however, stand in marked contrast to Josephus's open assessments of virtue among the other schools.

Josephus's handling of the three Judean philosophical schools should make us wary about using his descriptions of the Pharisees in these sketches for historical purposes.[38] Some aspects of Sadducean and Essene thought and life can be confirmed by, respectively, the New Testament and Philo (also Pliny). We may conclude from such independent witnesses that Sadducees rejected the afterlife and that Essenes lived in highly regimented "philosophical" communities that stressed simplicity of life (Philo, Pliny, *Nat.* 5.73). Of the Pharisees, the New Testament confirms that they observed a special legal tradition "from the fathers"[39] and that they believed in the afterlife; Josephus's language permits the notion of resurrection, even though he does not spell it out. Rabbinic literature on *Perushim* and *Tzadukim* presents considerable difficulties, both internally and in relation to the Pharisees and Sadducees of Josephus and the New Testament.[40] For the finer details of life and practice among these groups, however, we are frustrated partly by the general dearth of evidence, partly by an author who uses them as set pieces to be manipulated along with the rest of his material.

---

[38] Some important efforts to reach the historical reality of these three schools are: L. Wächter, "Die unterschiedliche Haltung der Pharisäer, Sadduzäer und Essener zur Heimarmene nach dem Bericht des Josephus." *ZRGG* 21 (1969): 97–114; G. Maier, *Mensch und freier Wille: Nach den jüdischen Religionsparteien zwischen Ben Sira und Paulus* (Tübingen: Mohr [Siebeck], 1981); Anthony J. Saldarini, *Pharisees, Scribes, and Sadducees in Palestinian Society: A Sociological Approach* (Wilmington: Michael Glazier, 1988); Sanders, *Practice and Belief;* Grabbe, *Judaism,* 2.463–554; G. Stemberger, *Jewish Contemporaries of Jesus: Pharisees, Sadducees, Essenes* (Minneapolis: Fortress, 1995); and A. I. Baumgarten, *The Flourishing of Jewish Sects in the Maccabean Era: An Interpretation* (Leiden: Brill, 1997).

[39] In particular, Baumgarten, "The Pharisaic Paradosis." *HTR* 80 (1987): 63–87.

[40] E. Rivkin, "Defining the Pharisees: The Tannaitic Sources." *HUCA* 40 (1969): 205–49; Neusner, *Rabbinic Traditions,* 3:304; also Saldarini, *Pharisees.*

Chapter 8

The Essenes of Josephus's *Judean War*: From Story to History

Recent vigorous disagreement[1] about the identity of the Qumran community[2] exposes in part the faulty method by which conclusions were initially drawn and permitted to ossify. Once the site of Qumran had been hypothetically identified as an Essene installation and the Dead Sea Scrolls as Essene productions, this nexus imposed constraints upon interpreters of the DSS, on the one hand, and of the Greek and Latin texts that purport to describe Essenes, on the other. Exegesis of both had now to fit the theory. And since the Scrolls had come to be regarded as *primary sources* for the Essenes, the texts that actually mention the *Essenoi / Esseni* by name[3] suffered the greater distortion. In a reversal of standard historical method, which begins with evidence clearly relevant to the phenomenon

---

[1]The heart of this chapter was originally presented at the 2004 International Josephus Colloquium in Dublin. I wish to thank Dr. Zuleika Rodgers for the opportunity to gain feedback from so many specialists, and the specialists themselves for helpful critique. The material will appear in full in my commentary to *War* 2, vol. 1b of *Flavius Josephus: Translation and Commentary* (ed. Steve Mason; Leiden: Brill, 2008).

[2]H. Stegemann, "The Qumran Essenes—Local Members of the Main Jewish Union in Late Second Temple Times." in *The Madrid Qumran Congress: Proceedings of the International Congress on the Dead Sea Scrolls, Madrid 18–21 March 1991* (ed. J. T. Barrerra and L. V. Montaner. Leiden: Brill, 1992), 83–166; N. Golb, *Who Wrote the Dead Sea Scrolls? The Search for the Secret of Qumran* (New York: Scribner, 1995); L. Cansdale, *Qumran and the Essenes: A Re-Evaluation of the Evidence* (Tübingen: Mohr [Siebeck], 1997); R. Donceel, "Qumran," in *The Oxford Encyclopaedia of Archaeology in the Near East* (ed. E. M. Meyers; Oxford: Oxford University Press, 1997), 392–96; Y. Hirschfeld, *Qumran in Context: Reassessing the Archaeological Evidence* (Peabody, Mass.: Hendrickson, 2004); essays in K. Galor, J.-B. Humbert, and J. Zangenberg. *Qumran: the Site of the Dead Sea Scrolls. Archaeological Interpretations and Debates.* Leiden: Brill, 2006; J.-B. Humbert, and J. Zangenberg. *Qumran: the Site of the Dead Sea Scrolls. Archaeological Interpretations and Debates.* Leiden: Brill, 2006.

[3]Various attempts have been made to find a Semitic root for the Essenes' name in the DSS. But all face the same limitation: unless there is a compelling reason, in the Scrolls themselves, to think that the term in question was the primary group label (rather than an ad hoc characterization) *and* unless specialists mainly agree that it is naturally rendered in Greek as *Essaioi* (conditions far from satisfied thus far), any proposal for a Semitic root must lean upon the Qumran-Essene hypothesis, so that its use as a basis for the hypothesis would entail a circular argument.

under investigation,[4] difficulties in aligning the Essene texts with these "primary sources" were now routinely explained away as the misunderstandings of outsiders.[5] Still today, the main published resources for the Dead Sea Scrolls or the Essenes, whether comprehensive studies[6] or specific treatments of Josephus's Essenes,[7] offer an item-by-item accommodation of the Essene passages to the Scrolls rather than a contextual reading of the Essene passages.

Such a circular method[8]—we interpret Josephus's statements about the Essenes in light of the DSS and then use the alleged parallels to prove the identity of the two groups[9]—could not generate stable results. A historical hypothesis identifying the DSS authors with Josephus's Essenes should have been required to show how adequately this posited Qumran-Essene phenomenon would explain both the Scrolls and the Essene narratives of Josephus, Philo, and Pliny. But in the 1950s, when the Authorized View was becoming established, there were no contextual interpretations of Josephus's Essene portrait, or of much else in his *oeuvre,* to be explained.[10] In the near absence of any appreciation of his works as compositions—of their structures, major and minor themes, language, or rhe-

---

[4]That is, evidence that clearly mentions "Essenes." Before 1947 there was considerable interest in the Essenes (cf. S. Wagner, *Die Essener in der wissenschaftlichen Diskussion: vom Ausgang des 18. bis zum Beginn des 20. Jahrhunderts; eine wissenschaftliche Studie* [Berlin: A. Töpelmann, 1960]), and attempts to understand who they were proceeded largely on this basis, though in the fashion of the day they were often assimilated to Hasidim, Pharisees, or other groups mentioned in rabbinic literature. K. Kohler's detailed 1905 article in the *Jewish Encyclopedia* is a model of the type.

[5]F. M. Cross (*The Ancient Library of Qumran and Modern Biblical Studies* [New York: Doubleday, 1961], 70): the Essene descriptions reveal an "exterior view or Hellenizing tendency"; cf. 76, 78; Sanders (*Practice and Belief,* 379): "Certainly his description does not convey adequately the flavour of the Scrolls."

[6]E.g., Black, "The Account"; A. Dupont-Sommer, *The Essene Writings from Qumran* (Cleveland: Word, 1961); A. Adam, *Antike Berichte über die Essener* (New York: de Gruyter, 1972); G. Vermes and M. D. Goodman, eds., *The Essenes According to the Classical Sources* (Sheffield: Sheffield Academic Press, 1989); J. C. VanderKam, *The Dead Sea Scrolls Today* (Grand Rapids: Eerdmans, 1994).

[7]T. S. Beall, *Josephus' Description of the Essenes Illustrated by the Dead Sea Scrolls* (Cambridge: Cambridge University Press, 1988), 3; R. Gray, *Prophetic Figures in Late Second Temple Jewish Palestine: The Evidence from Josephus* (New York: Oxford University Press, 1993), 5, but 81; Bergmeier, *Die Essener–Berichte,* 9, 51–2; T. Rajak, "Ciò Che Flavio Giuseppe Vide: Josephus and the Essenes," in *Josephus and the History of the Greco-Roman Period: Essays in Memory of Morton Smith* (ed. F. Parente and J. Sievers; Leiden: Brill, 1994), 143.

[8]Opponents of the Qumran-Essene hypothesis often find a similarly vicious circle in the assumed connection between Khirbet Qumran and the Scrolls from the nearby caves. See Hirschfeld, *Qumran,* 4–6.

[9]Put clearly by VanderKam (*The Dead Sea Scrolls,* 89): "It is reasonable to interpret the evidence in such a way that the sources [e.g., Josephus and the DSS] do not conflict." I cannot, however, see the historical method in such a principle.

[10]I mean by this that there was little or no attempt to figure out what the Essenes mean for Josephus's narratives—how they fit structurally or in terms of Josephus's characteristic themes, diction, and literary and rhetorical devices. See Bilde, *Josephus,* 71, 92, 102, 118 for the state of scholarship. Even at his time of writing, in the mid-1980s, he

torical devices—no one seems to have been demanding that the new hypothesis explain Josephus's portrait in its context, and so this crucial requirement was overlooked.

Now that the Qumran-Essene hypothesis is creaking under other pressures, while many students of Josephus's works have at last begun to attend to the compositional traits just mentioned, the time is right to re-evaluate Josephus's Essenes *in situ*—and without assuming a DSS referent. How would we understand his accounts if we examined them solely in light of his larger narratives and first audiences, the way we are beginning to analyze other material in his rich corpus? I do not imagine that trying to understand Josephus's Essenes could possibly settle the historical problems of either Essene or Qumran identity. Those are much larger investigations: this is a very limited and preliminary study of one part of one author's evidence, offered as an example of the much larger problems, though limited to one stage of the historical process. Nevertheless, it turns up some preliminary problems that must be dealt with by those who embark on those larger investigations.

Available space does not even permit a full discussion of Josephus's Essenes. It must suffice to consider the main passage, *War* 2.119–161—characterized by Josephus as his definitive statement (*Ant.* 13.173; 18.11; *Life* 10)—with some attention to the whole and a few examples of the parts. My thesis has two sides, namely, that *War*'s Essene passage is an integral part of this work's larger story, as of Josephus's entire literary output, and that understanding the way in which *War* uses the Essenes lays new obstacles before the Qumran-Essene hypothesis. The first claim may seem obvious or even trite to readers unfamiliar with the state of Josephus studies. Why would anyone imagine that any passage in Josephus's works was not intended to be there as integral part of the whole? Since, however, the Essene passage along with much else in Josephus has long been cheerfully credited to other hands entirely,[11] it is still necessary to ground one's interpretation of almost anything in this author with a defense of the proposition that he wrote it. Still, that task is incidental to our main goal of understanding the Essenes of Josephus's *War.*

Before turning to our main subject, I must address what might otherwise prove a distraction for readers. It is commonly proposed in literature advocating the Qumran-Essene hypothesis that (a) remarkable parallels between the DSS and Josephus's Essenes more or less confirm the hypothesis—some of these will be our main focus here—but (b) what settles the matter is the elder Pliny's notice (*Natural History* 5.73) concerning an Essene location. Now, if it were the case that Pliny's evidence independently established a connection between Essenes and Qumran, then the following study, which I offer as a preliminary contribution to

---

could still find little or no published research on the structures, aims, and audiences of Josephus's major compositions.

[11] For example, Black, "The Account"; Smith, "Description"; Bergmeier, *Die Essener-Berichte;* Gray, *Prophetic Figures,* 82. Different sorts of refutation are in Burchard, "Die Essener bei Hippolyt"; Baumgarten, "Josephus and Hippolytus"; Williams, "Authorship." But the dates of these clusters indicate the ongoing problem.

a new historical investigation of the Essenes, would be pointless. But does Pliny's description settle the question in advance?

After describing the region around Lake Kinneret (Gennesaret), naming the principal sites allegedly to the east, south, and west (*Nat.* 5.71), Pliny moves to the Dead Sea and follows the same pattern, describing Arabia to the east, Machaerus and Callirhoe to the south (as he mistakenly says), and finally the western region, which becomes his concluding comment on Judea:

> To the west [of Lake Asphaltitis, the Dead Sea], the Essenes completely shun the shores, which cause harm (*ab occidente litora Esseni fugiunt usque qua nocent*): a solitary tribe, wonderful beyond all others in the world, being without any women and renouncing all sexual desire, having no money, and with only palm trees as companions. Their assembly is born again daily from the crowds, tired of life and the vicissitudes of fortune, that crowd there for their manner of living. So for thousands of ages—remarkable to say—a tribe is eternal (*gens aeterna est*) into which no one is born! So fruitful for them is the reconsideration of life by others.
>
> Below these *was* the town of En Gedi (*infra hos Engada oppidum fuit*), second only to Jerusalem in fertility and groves of palm trees, but now a similar ruin (*nunc alterum bustum*). After that (*inde*) Masada, a fortress on a crag—for its part, not far at all from Asphaltitis (*et ipsum haut procul Asphaltite*). Thus is Judea.

Readers will be familiar with the ongoing debate, the main lines of which were established by the early 1960s, in light of the Dead Sea Scrolls,[12] over Pliny's meaning in locating *Esseni* to the west of the Dead Sea, with En Gedi "below them." For our purposes it is important to separate the two logically distinct questions: "What did Pliny mean?" and "What is the significance of his notice for historical hypothesizing about the Essenes?"

Pliny's works were widely read in antiquity, and were given extended life into the Middle Ages by a third-century plagiarist, C. Iulius Solinus, whose *Gallery of Remarkable Things* largely paraphrases parts of Pliny. When he comes to Pliny's Essenes, he rewords the crucial opening phrase to say that they occupy "the interior parts of Judea" on the west of the Dead Sea (*Interiora Iudaeae occidentem quae contuentur Esseni tenent. . . .*), below which was formerly the town of En Gedi (35.9, 12). Although Solinus does not appear to have independent knowledge of the region, his work is valuable as an early interpretation of Pliny's meaning. In modern scholarly literature too, before the Scrolls were found scholars assumed that Pliny had located the Essenes in the Judean wilderness west of the Dead Sea, around and above En Gedi. In marked contrast to the situation after 1950, scholarship of the time reveals no great debates about Pliny's meaning.

I cite three standard and detailed reference works prepared for different constituencies: the detailed article by Walter Bauer in the Pauly-Wissowa *Realency-*

---

[12]That is, although there were many differences in pre-DSS scholarship, this kind of focused debate did not occur there (see Audet, Jean-Paul. "Qumran et la notice de Pline sur les Esséniens." *RB* 68 (1961): 346–87; C. Burchard, "Pline et les Esséniens," *RB* 69 [1962]: 533–69).

clopädie (1924), for a classicist's perspective; from Jewish Studies, the fascinating article on Essenes by Kaufman Kohler in the *Jewish Encylopedia* (1905); and from the field of New Testament background, Emil Schürer's section on Essenes in his classic *Geschichte des jüdischen Volkes im Zeitalter Jesu Christi* (1901). Taken together, these should give us a fair sense of main-stream scholarly views in the early twentieth century. (Emphasis is mine throughout.) Without hinting at any controversy on the matter, Bauer understands Pliny as locating the Essenes "on the west side of the Dead Sea in and around the city of En Gedi."[13] Kohler speaks with similar ease about "the Essenes at En Gedi."[14] Most interesting is Schürer's assessment: after noting that Philo and Josephus both have Essenes widely dispersed throughout Judea, he remarks, "Hence we should be much mistaken if we were, *according to Pliny's description,* to seek them *only in the desert of Engedi* on the Dead Sea."[15]

With such a widely shared understanding of Pliny's meaning, and the realization that in any case the Essenes were more widely distributed than Pliny might be understood to suggest, it seems not to have occurred to those nineteenth-century explorers who described the surface remains at Khirbet Qumran at the north-west end of the Dead Sea to connect the site with Pliny's Essenes.[16] After surveying the various identifications of the remains proposed by these explorers—biblical Gomorrah, a Roman fort, or one of the cities mentioned in Josh 15:61—John Bartlett observes that "Kh. Qumran might never have been excavated had not shepherds of the Ta'amireh tribe accidentally stumbled on some leather scrolls in a cave north of Kh. Qumran in the winter of 1947–8."[17] That is, it was the discovery of the DSS, soon to be identified as Essene products—and not any prior assumption that Pliny intended to identify Qumran as Essene—that lent the site its subsequent importance.

Having not made a special study of the matter, I have no basis for declaring that no explorer ever proposed an area near Qumran in trying to locate Pliny's Essenes. Joan Taylor, who has recently surveyed that literature, has highlighted the account of travel-writer and co-founder of the Palestine Exploration Fund, W. H. Dixon, who came closest to at least including the Qumran area in his assessment. He understood the "chief seats" of the Essenes to have been in the area from Jerusalem to the Dead Sea, including the areas around Bethlehem, Mar Saba, En Gedi, and Ras el Feshka (near Qumran).[18] Much like other writers of

---

[13] That is, "auf der Westseite des Toten Meeres in der und um die Stadt Engada (Engeddi)" (*PWRE* 4:390).

[14] "Essenes," 231–32.

[15] Schürer, *Geschichte* 2:2.193–94. This is the translation of the German "3d–4th edition" of 1901, and the only one accessible to me while writing this essay.

[16] For early exploration of Qumran, see Cansdale, *Qumran,* 20, 26–7; J. R. Bartlett, *Archaeology and Biblical Interpretation* (London: Routledge, 1997), 67–70; J. Magness, *The Archaeology of Qumran and the Dead Sea Scrolls* (Grand Rapids: Eerdmans, 2002), 22–24; Hirschfeld, *Qumran,* 14–16.

[17] Bartlett, *Archaeology,* 70.

[18] W. H. Dixon, *The Holy Land* (2d ed.; London: Chapman and Hall, 1866), 279–80. See Taylor "Khirbet Qumran in the Nineteenth Century and the Name of the Site," *PEQ* 134 (2002): 156.

the period, he read Pliny as placing Essenes broadly to the west of the Dead Sea. After the Scrolls were found and identified as Essene products, however, there was a sharp turn in reading Pliny—and often, now insisting that he must have indicated Qumran as the Essene home.

At least some early DSS experts were still open-minded about Pliny's meaning. Sorbonne Semitics professor A. Dupont-Sommer (1950) fully recognized the standard reading (above), while proposing a new idea in suitably restrained language:

> *It is generally admitted* that the Essene colony described by Pliny was *situated near the spring of Engedi, towards the centre of the western shore of the Dead Sea; in fact the text of Pliny continues thus:* "Below them (*infra hos*) was the town of Engada . . . ." But I believe this means not that the Essenes lived in the mountains just above the famous spring, but that this was a little distance from their settlement, towards the south. Pliny then actually goes on to describe Masada, further to the south: "from thence (from Engada) one comes to Masada . . ." Thus from north to south we have the Essene "city," then Engada, then Masada. If Pliny's text is to be understood in this way, the Essene "city" would be found towards the north of the western shore; that is to say, precisely in the region of 'Ain-Feshka itself. *Should this explanation not be acceptable, it could be supposed that the Essenes possessed monasteries other than that mentioned by Pliny and Dio in the same Wilderness of Judea.*[19]

Dupont-Sommer thinks that he is suggesting—as a novelty—a north-south reading, on the basis of Masada's inclusion. Should this proposal not be accepted (a possibility he considers likely enough), he asks at least that Qumran be considered *another* possible Essene site, in addition to those identified by Pliny and Dio in the Judean wilderness.

Scholarly language on the subject would soon change, however, in both substance and tone. It is beyond the scope of this paper to explore the interpretation of Pliny in detail, but we may again focus on a few reference works.

I mentioned that Schürer was particularly interesting. That is because we have the luxury of comparing the revised version of his basic reference work, by an Oxford-based team in the 1970s and 80s, with his own work last revised in the first decade of the twentieth century. Although Schürer's revisers were generally conservative with respect to his main text, concentrating their updates in the extensive notes, in this case they revised the passage quoted above from the main text. Schürer had said that it would be a mistake to follow Pliny in seeking Essenes only in the desert of Engedi (above). The revisers offer: "It would accordingly be a mistake to be led by Pliny's description to look for them *only in the desert somewhere between Jericho and Engedi by the Dead Sea*"[20]—as though Pliny himself had located Essenes thus. A new footnote elaborates:

> The sites mentioned [by Pliny] are: *Jericho, the Essene settlement, En-gedi, Masada.* That is to say, the three known places are listed from north to south. Hence the Ess-

---

[19] A. Dupont-Sommer, *The Dead Sea Scrolls: A Preliminary Survey* (Oxford: Blackwell, 1952), 86 n. 1.

[20] Schürer-Vermes, *Jewish People,* 2:563.

> ene settlement lies south of Jericho and north of En-gedi and *the only location fitting this description is Qumran.*[21]

These are remarkable claims for at least two reasons. First, the new Schürer makes a conscious formal effort to distinguish cleanly between the classical evidence for the Essenes and the Dead Sea Scrolls, "as the identity of the Essenes and the Qumran sectaries is no more than a hypothesis—however probable."[22] But its significant reworking of Schürer's original, which (before the Qumran discoveries) had no such understanding of Pliny, shows plainly the influence of the hypothesis on the interpretation of what is proffered as independent evidence. This problem of contamination is endemic in scholarly reading of the Greek and Latin Essene sources, and particularly obvious in treatments of "Josephus's Essenes." Second, Pliny gives no such list of sites, from Jericho to the Essenes, En Gedi, and Masada (see his passage above). He does not mention a "place" or "settlement" of Essenes, let alone place it in a line between Jericho and En Gedi, such that only somewhere around Qumran could be intended. If he had done so, some earlier readers of Pliny, including the learned Schürer, would surely have noticed.

Yet similar claims abound in post-DSS reference works. Lester Grabbe's widely used textbook, *Judaism from Cyrus to Hadrian,* declares that "the sequence of listing is from north to south,"[23] and therefore "the statement of Pliny . . . *seems incompatible with any interpretation other than Qumran.*"[24] Geza Vermes's introduction to his English edition of the DSS comments on "the remarkable coincidence between the geographical setting of Qumran and Pliny the Elder's description of an Essene settlement near the Dead Sea *between Jericho and Engedi*" (emphasis added).[25] Likewise the noted Qumran expert Jodi Magness:

> Pliny's description of the Dead Sea appears to progress from north to south, *beginning with the Jordan River to* [sic] *the settlement of the Essenes to Ein Gedi and then to Masada.* This means that Ein Gedi lay downstream from or south of the settlement of the Essenes.[26]

Since Pliny says nothing of the sort, one must wonder how this notion entered scholarship. Pliny has mentioned Jericho only in the general description of Judea a few sentences earlier (*Nat.* 5.70), as the *first* of ten named toparchies. There is no linear movement from Jericho (or the Jordan) to En Gedi by way of Essenes.

Perhaps recent scholars have been unduly influenced by an odd passage in the reference work by Menachem Stern, *Greek and Latin Authors on Jews and Judaism* (1974), which Magness indeed quotes as a main support. I say "odd passage" because when Stern first discusses the location of the Essenes in his comments

---

[21] Ibid., 2:563 n. 6.
[22] Ibid., 2:561.
[23] Grabbe, *Judaism,* 492.
[24] Ibid., 494.
[25] G. Vermes, *The Dead Sea Scrolls in English* (London: Penguin, 1995), xxv.
[26] So Magness, *Archaeology,* 41.

on Pliny, he emphasizes Philo's and Josephus's superior knowledge of the group and their wide dispersal throughout Judea, rightly observing that Pliny does not mention a specific town or site where they lived:

> If he had, he would have contradicted Josephus, *BJ*, II, 124. In fact, the only information that may be derived from Pliny, and, for that matter, from Dio Chrysostom [*apud* Synesius, *Dio* 3.2], is that there was at one time a considerable concentration of Essenes *somewhere in the neighbourhood of the Dead Sea.*[27]

Stern goes on to criticize scholars who find in Pliny's *infra hos* a "decisive proof" of the Qumran-Essene hypothesis, for the matter cannot be settled by Pliny's language.[28] It is all the more surprising, then, when he proceeds without explanation to the passage cited by Magness (emphasis added):

> Moreover, the impression one gets from reading Pliny is that *he describes the Dead Sea by starting from the north,* and that 'En Gedi, which is mentioned after the Essenes, should therefore be located south of the Essene habitations. Similarly, Massada, which is *therefore* mentioned after 'En Gedi, indeed lies south of it.[29]

How one might get this impression from Pliny alone is far from clear, since the Roman author does not start from the north end of the Dead Sea. As we have seen, he deals with the Dead Sea region as he had covered the Kinneret region, ostensibly moving from *east to south to west.* If some sort of momentum in Pliny's description should suggest the meaning of *infra hos,* then we would need to locate them near the south of the Dead Sea, after Pliny's (erroneous) location of Callirhoe.

As for the final "thereafter [or "from there," *inde*] Masada," a site whose significance he does not elaborate in contrast to his comments on Essenes and En Gedi, Pliny's language indicates only that it also belongs in this western sector of the Dead Sea. Compare his mention on the east side of inland Machaerus before coastal Callirhoe (slightly north of Machaerus, though he says "south"), before he continues to the west. Pliny may mention Masada last, without elaboration, as a fitting end to his description of the region, because it was well known in Rome as the final act, associated with L. Flavius Silva Nonius Bassus, of the recently concluded war. Solinus's paraphrase similarly omits elaboration, giving *Massada castellum* its own sentence as the limit of Judea (35.12).

It would keep the discussion of evidence much clearer if scholars did not claim that Pliny more or less obviously located the Essenes in the Qumran area. He does not do so, as pre-Scrolls scholarship and, afterwards, some scholars important for the debate—Menachem Stern and Dupont-Sommer—realized.

If we seek to understand why so many post-DSS scholars have the impression that Pliny's description moves from Jericho or the Jordan to En Gedi by way

---

[27] M. Stern, *Greek and Latin Authors on Jews and Judaism: Edited with Introductions, Translations and Commentary* (3 vols.; Jerusalem: Israel Academy of Sciences, 1974–84), 2:479–80.

[28] Ibid., 2:480.

[29] Ibid., 2:481.

of the Essenes, when such a reading is impossible, we might conjecture a tacit awareness that Pliny's meaning cannot serve as the basis for the Qumran-Essene hypothesis if it is also determined by that hypothesis—or we would have a logical circle, thus: Pliny must intend Qumran because of the DSS discoveries there and the Qumraners must be Essenes because Pliny locates Essenes at Qumran. If one wishes to use Pliny in support of the hypothesis, he must himself, without any help from the Qumran-Essene hypothesis, locate Essenes in the Qumran area. Since, however, the "Jericho-Essenes-En Gedi-Masada" reading can only be achieved by violence to the text, and pre-Scrolls scholarship did not understand Pliny this way, the use of Pliny as a weight-bearing pillar of the Qumran-Essene hypothesis[30] *is* indeed circular.

Although it is clear that Pliny's *infra hos* most naturally indicates elevation (cf. his *supra* at 5.70)—in view of the general ancient usage of such terms (cf. Greek ἀνά, κατά) to indicate higher and lower elevations, up-or down-stream where the course of a river is being described (which amounts to the same thing),[31] and important cities (as in "up to" Rome or Jerusalem)—the central issue here is not what he "really meant," but one of method and argumentative logic. Pliny does not independently identify Qumran as the Essene base. If the Scrolls could be connected with Essenes on other grounds, one would then have the task of trying to understand Pliny accordingly: Could Qumran, if the Scrolls were known to be local Essene products, be construed as part of the Essene region west of the Dead Sea, above En Gedi, that Pliny had in view? But that issue arises only if the Scrolls are first shown to be Essene products; Pliny's statement cannot *ground* that hypothesis.

There are further problems.[32] Notice Pliny's clear implication that, wherever they live, the Essenes are thriving at his time of writing: "a tribe in which no one is born is eternal!" (*gens aeterna est;* cf. present-tense *fugiunt*), in pointed contrast to En Gedi, which *used to exist* (*fuit*) but is *now* a ruin (*nunc . . . bustum*). Pliny writes under Vespasian in the 70s, as he has just emphasized (5.69), soon after the destruction of Jerusalem, whose fate he connects with En Gedi's (5.73). But Qumran was destroyed as part of the same conflict, in 68 C.E. The paraphrase in Solinus makes the contrast even clearer: in contrast to the string of present-tense verbs describing the Essenes, he adds to Pliny's *fuit* of En Gedi, "but it has been destroyed" (*sed excisum est*). Magness recognizes the problem, resolving it with the surprising concession, given the weight that she places on this passage,

---

[30] So Burchard ("Pline," 534): *Given the disparity between the Greek portraits of the Essenes and the Scrolls,* the statement of Pliny is crucial for identifying the two groups ("Étant donné la disparité des récits de Philon et de Josèphe comparés entre eux et avec l'ensemble des manuscrits de Qumran, l'argument géographique est toujours le meilleur support de l'identification des anciens habitants de Kh. Qumran avec les Esséniens ou une branche du mouvement essénien."). On the crucial importance of Pliny's notice, see also VanderKam, *The Dead Sea Scrolls,* 71–5; Vermes, *The Dead Sea Scrolls,* xxv.

[31] E.g., Pliny, *Nat.* 4.83 (where both Pliny and those he purports to correct seem rather confused); 6.136 (the meaning of which is again uncertain); but both passages clearly follow the courses of rivers.

[32] For many astute observations on Pliny's passage, see R. A. Kraft, "Pliny on Essenes, Pliny on Jews," *DSD* 8 (2001): 255–61.

that Pliny "is somewhat confused."[33] But the remarkable vitality of these Essenes is the main point that he makes about them (taken over by Pliny), and his ostensible reason for mentioning them in his ethno-geographical tour, which typically highlights the interesting and unusual. If Pliny is confused about *this,* his main point, then we cannot get very far at all with his evidence.

On the subject of Pliny's complexities, it is also worth remembering (as pre-DSS scholars occasionally pointed out) that Pliny's *gens sola* and especially *gens aeterna* were not necessarily understood by him as native Judeans.[34]

So much for Pliny's meaning. As for the use of his description in historical reconstruction of the Essenes: any use of his evidence, no matter what it is taken to mean, must reckon with the fact that he displays little sound knowledge of Judea and the Dead Sea region, a body of water he describes as 100 Roman miles long and 75 across (*Nat.* 5.72), several times its actual area. Even if we could be certain of his meaning in locating Essenes—as we are certain that he makes Gamala (in the Golan) the highest town of Samaria (*Nat.* 5.69), that he places Bethsaida-Iulias along with Hippos *east* of the Kinneret (*Nat.* 5.71, though it is to the north) and Tarichaea *south* of the Kinneret (*Nat.* 5.71, misleading generations of scholars, since it is north of Tiberias on the west side), and that he situates Machaerus and Callirhoe *south* of the Dead Sea (*Nat.* 5.72, though they are further north on the eastern shore than En Gedi is on the west)—even then we would have no reason to assume that he knew what he was talking about. To prefer his claims to Josephus's evidence about Judean geography would be adventurous, to say the least.

I do not imagine that the foregoing is a complete or even partly adequate treatment of Pliny on the Essenes for general purposes, much less of the history of exploration in the Dead Sea region, which has been studied by others. The only reason I am dealing with Pliny here is to preclude a possible objection to the following study of Josephus, which treats the historical Essenes as an open question: But does not Pliny's location of the Essenes around Qumran already settle the Qumran-Essene identification? Since Pliny does not independently locate Essenes around Qumran, we may leave him[35] and proceed with our task of trying to

---

[33] Magness, *Archaeology,* 41.

[34] The point is stressed by Bauer ("Essener," 390, 421–22). That Essenes were known outside Judea but not necessarily understood to be Judeans may explain Josephus's emphatic opening remark (2.119) that Essenes "are Judeans by ancestry" (Ἰουδαῖοι μὲν γένος ὄντες); this may also help to explain Philo's use of them in *Every Good Man is Free* as exemplars of Judean and Stoic outlooks.

[35] Less prominent in scholarly discussion is the claim of the fifth-century Synesius (*Dio* 3.2) that Dio Chrysostom "somewhere praises the Essenes," an observation accompanied by notes on their lifestyle and location "by, near, beside, or beyond" the Dead Water (παρὰ τὸ Νέκρον Ὕδωρ). It is not clear, however, that anything other than the remembered praise comes from Dio (cf. Bauer, "Essener," 388). It is obviously not a quotation; the language (e.g., about εὐδαιμονία) is generally that of the later scholar; Synesius has the habit of briefly mentioning someone else's comment and then elaborating it himself; and the broken syntax suggests his elaboration of Dio's remembered remark "somewhere." Even Synesius's connection of Essenes with the Dead Sea might itself come (directly or indirectly) from the widely read Pliny or Solinus.

understand Josephus's portrait of the Essenes in his *Judean War*, as a preliminary contribution to a new historical investigation of the group.

Judean War and Its Essene Passage: Context, Aims, and Themes

In the opening sentences of the *War*, Josephus justifies his work by complaining that other writers either lack reliable information about the recent conflict or, if they have it, distort it in order to flatter the Romans and diminish the conquered Judeans (1.1–2). Those other accounts have not survived, but Josephus's assessment is perfectly plausible. Writing after the Parthian war of Lucius Verus a century later, the Syrian-Greek Lucian makes a similar complaint: "Most of them neglect to investigate what actually happened, but elevate their own leaders and generals to the sky while disparaging (καταρρίπτω) those of the enemy beyond all proportion" (*Hist. conscr.* 7). Josephus, for his part, accuses contemporary authors of bullying (καταβάλλω) and humiliating or diminishing (ταπεινόω) the Judeans (*War* 1.7). An abundance of material evidence from Flavian Rome, indications in literary texts,[36] and standard Roman attitudes toward enemies and troublemakers[37] render it antecedently probable that in Josephus's post-war Rome, the Flavians' much celebrated defeat of the Judeans meant the humiliation of the Judean ἔθνος.

Scholars have proposed many themes—or slogans—to account for the biases of Josephus's *War*. Throughout the twentieth century the work was most often considered Flavian propaganda directed primarily at the Parthians and any would-be allies.[38] Recently, critics have argued that the *War* attempts to protect Josephus and his aristocratic peers from guilt, by insisting that they had opposed the revolt,[39] or even to advance the claims of the surviving priesthood as a potential Judean government.[40] Yet the rich complexity of *War* seems to defy all efforts to distill such an uncomplicated thesis. A comprehensive interpretation would need to take account of the myriad twists and turns of the narrative, its many levels and productive tensions, and the values shared by Josephus and his Roman audience—extra-textual resources that help give coherence to the text. Even sketching the rudiments of an adequate interpretation would require a study of

---

[36]On the material and literary evidence, see the *Iudaea Capta* coins, the inscription from the lost arch of Titus (*CIL* 6.994), and the triumphal friezes of the current restored arch; for standard Roman attitudes to the enemy, A. Ziolkowski, "*Urbs Direpta,* or How the Romans Sacked Cities." in *War and Society in the Roman World* (ed. J. Rich and G. Shipley; London: Routledge, 1993), 69–91; for scholarly analysis of the Judean war as Flavian legitimization, B. Levick, *Vespasian* (London: Routledge, 1999), 53–4 and several essays in A. J. Boyle and W. J. Dominik, eds., *Flavian Rome: Culture, Image, Text* (Leiden: Brill, 2003); J. Edmondson, J. Rives, and S. Mason, eds., *Flavius Josephus and Flavian Rome* (Oxford: Oxford University Press, 2005).

[37]Mattern, *Rome,* (especially the first and last chapters).

[38]Laqueur, *Historiker* and Thackeray, *The Man and the Historian* set this durable theory in motion. The decisive challenges are Rajak, *Josephus* and Bilde, *Josephus.*

[39]Goodman, *Ruling Class,* 167; Price, *Siege,* xi; Mader, *Politics.*

[40]S. Schwartz, *Judaean Politics,* 81, 87.

its own. For the sake of economy I offer here only a few thoughts on some crucial features of *War* that help to situate the Essene passage.

1. With respect to both individuals and peoples, ancient analysts often assumed that inbred character or nature (ἦθος, φύσις, *natura, ingenium*) determined behavior. In the case of nations (ἔθνη) or at least their aristocracies, character was also reflected in the chosen constitution (πολιτεία). Plato famously links national characters with distinctive constitutions (*Resp.* 544d–591) and Xenophon opens his work on Athenian administration with the remark, "I have always thought along this line: that whatever the leaders of a state are like, so also is their constitution" (*Vect.* 1.1).[41] Ethnographers typically attributed distinct ethnic characters to disparate environmental conditions.[42] Polybius, Josephus's principal Greek model for *War,* regularly passes comment on the putative characters of whole peoples: morality, anger, treachery, jealousy, or love of freedom and piety (1.13.12; 3.3.3 7.1; 4.1.1–8, 53.5; 5.106). With the later neo-Platonists, this deeply entrenched theory of regional diversity would be subsumed under a sort of divine workflow chart, with tutelary deities governing each nation according to its distinctive character (cf. Celsus in Origen, *C. Cels.* 5.25). The emperor Julian will later speak eloquently of such diversity (*C. Gal.* 138a), holding that the codes of discipline developed by lawgivers merely reflect the innate dispositions of their various peoples (*C. Gal.* 131c).

If individuals and nations acted according to their characters, then to understand that character was already to know why they behaved as they did—for they *would* do that, wouldn't they? This principle was reflected at the personal level in the ubiquitous appeal to "probability" in court trials—the argument that it was not in a man's character (proven in part by ancestry and ancestors' achievements) to have done what he stands accused of doing.[43] The personal and the national are artfully combined by Polybius when he claims that Hasdrubal's character, marked by ambition and love of power and mirrored in his brother-in-law Hannibal, furnished the *real* cause of war with Rome (3.8). But Polybius distinguishes sharply between the personal character of these leaders and the national character of the Carthaginians. The more sophisticated authors, among whom we should include Josephus, were capable of such refinement.

There is no need to rehearse here the many attempts at characterizing the Judean *ethnos* through the four centuries (300 B.C.E.–100 C.E.) that separated Me-

[41] Within the context of Roman affairs, Tacitus observes (*Ann.* 4.33) that those who wish to understand the different states of the constitution during periods of plebeian or patrician ascendancy need to understand the nature of the masses (*vulgi natura*) and of the senate and aristocracy (*senatusque et optimatium ingenia*), respectively.

[42] The classic text for such geographical determinism is the Hippocratic *Airs, Waters, and Places.* Cf. Katherine Clarke, *Between Geography and History: Hellenistic Constructions of the Roman World* (Oxford: Clarendon, 1999), 27–28, 87–91, 150, 167–68; Isaac, *Invention,* 56–74.

[43] E.g., Aristotle, *Rhet.* 1.2.1–15.1356a; 2.1.2–3.1377b; Cicero, *De or.* 2.182; Quintilian, *Inst.* 5.12.10; Aulus Gellius, *Noct. att.* 4.18.3–5; May, *Trials,* 6–8; G. A. Kennedy, *A New History of Classical Rhetoric* (Princeton: Princeton University Press, 1994), 102–27.

gasthenes and Clearchus from Plutarch, Tacitus, and Juvenal—also Josephus.[44] It is enough to observe that when war with Rome erupted, many Greeks and Romans naturally linked its causes with their suppositions about the Judean character. This inference chain was anticipated by Cicero when he attributed the devastated condition of the Judeans in 59 B.C.E., after Pompey's subjection of Jerusalem, with their putative alien and abhorrent nature (*Flac.* 69)—after equally convenient disparagement of the Greek and Asiatic characters (*Flac.* 62–6). Strikingly similar is the extant section of Tacitus's build-up to his lost account of the war of 66–73 C.E.: the Judeans embrace customs and rites that are both reprehensible in themselves and at sharp variance with the Romans' *mos maiorum* (*Hist.* 5.4–5). That Judean character, in Tacitus's eyes, went some way toward explaining the Judean defeat at Roman hands (*Hist.* 5.2).[45]

This fundamental issue of the Judean character is Josephus's beginning point in *War.* Notice that his complaint about other writers, in keeping with the general principles of ancient historiography, is not as much about their factual inaccuracies as about their moral assessments: these so-called histories are filled with invective against the Judean people (*War* 1.2, 7–8). Redress will come not from factual accuracy in any modern sense, but from the correction of such partiality. Recognizing the centrality of the character question helps us to see the coherence of Josephus's entire corpus. It lays the groundwork for *Antiquities'* elaboration of the Judean constitution (1.5, 10) and Josephus's autobiographical treatment of his personal character (*Life* 430), and all of this reaches a summit in the *Against Apion*'s vigorous defense of the Judean character along with advocacy of the Mosaic constitution.

2. In Greco-Roman usage, good character or virtue (ἀρετή, *virtus*) was in the first instance about *manliness:* toughness, physical courage, endurance, and practical wisdom. Because it is so often observed that Socrates sublimated the category of ἀρετή, it perhaps needs to be stressed that the word nevertheless retained its deep associations with masculinity. Even ancient philosophy was largely about toughening oneself to become a real man—something that Josephus, among others, discusses (*Life* 10; Seneca, *Ep.* 108.14; Lucian, *Nigr.* 28). Well trained soldiers achieved by another route what philosophers pursued: they cultivated an equal contempt for pain and death, on the one hand, and for luxury and pleasure on the other. Plato indeed requires that the Guardians (φύλακες) of his ideal *polis* be both soldiers and philosophers (*Resp.* 7.525b).

This close connection between virtue and masculinity becomes clear in what we might call the Spartanization of political and moral philosophy (e.g., Aristotle, *Pol.* 1270a–b, 1333b).[46] We catch a glimpse of this process already in Xenophon's encomiastic descriptions of the Spartan warrior-king Agesilaus (*Ages.* 8.8; 9.5;

[44] The first volume of Stern, *Greek and Latin Authors* contains the essential material, which has been extensively analyzed.

[45] R. S. Bloch, *Antike Vorstellungen vom Judentum: der Judenexkurs des Tacitus im Rahmen der griechisch-römischen Ethnographie* (Stuttgart: F. Steiner, 2002).

[46] Tigerstedt, *Legend,* 1:228–309.

10.1–2) and of the philosopher Socrates (*Mem.* 1.2.1–4, 2.5–15; cf. 2.1.20; 3.1.6]), which are remarkably similar. The king was a model for those wishing to train in manly excellence (τοῖς ἀνδραγαθίαν ἀσκεῖν βουλομένοις) because he made a fortress *of his soul* and became a master of endurance (καρτερία). But the philosopher receives very similar praise for his tough regimen (δίαιτα [*Mem.* 1.3.5])—a word often associated with Spartan practice, and used by Josephus of Judeans and Essenes. Both men cultivated a steadfast imperviousness to external conditions: changes in weather, hardships, pleasures, and things feared by other men.

Cynics, Stoics, and other philosophers found in the Spartiates' rigorous training, simplicity of diet and lifestyle, displacement of marriage and family, communal masculine solidarity, rugged adaptability to all hardships, disdain for convention, keen sense of personal honor at all costs, and unflinching courage in the face of pain and death—albeit stripped of objectionably bellicose traits (Plato, *Leg.* 626c–d)—the realization of their own philosophical aspirations (Plutarch, *Lyc.* 31.1–2).[47] Indeed, the simple rough cloak that continued to mark out philosophers through Roman times was in origin the coarse τρίβων of the Spartans.[48]

Roman moralists found the Spartan model singularly appealing, exempting the city from their typical characterization of Greeks as effeminate, preening windbags. Irrespective of its recent woes, old Sparta seemed a model of Cato's virtues enacted through a whole society:[49] neither the attractions of money and sex nor the ultimate evil of death could turn the head of a man who had passed through the Spartan ἀγωγή or a true Roman. Polybius adduced crucial constitutional parallels between Rome and Sparta (6.10–11, 51), evidently regarding Sparta as the benchmark of wise government (6.50). The city remained largely decoupled from Greece's general fortunes, prospering as a Roman ally after the destruction of Corinth in 146 B.C.E. and, from Augustus to Nero, enjoying special favor and native rule under a *de facto* monarchy.[50] Although Nero's fondness for the other Greece temporarily reversed this trend, it seems that the Flavian period marked the beginning of a second recovery for the storied city.[51]

In Rome, masculine virtue had its own distinctive language. It seems that many Roman males lived in dread of being considered feminine in dress, deportment, gait, voice, gestures, or especially sexual behavior;[52] so it was perhaps inevitable that they should project these traits on rivals. A burgeoning library of modern studies on conceptions of barbarians, women, and sexuality has ex-

---

[47] Ibid., 1:228–2:30–48.

[48] Cf. P. Hadot, *The Inner Citadel: The Meditations of Marcus Aurelius* (Cambridge: Harvard University Press, 1998), 7–8.

[49] Wardman, *Rome's Debt,* 90–93.

[50] P. Cartledge and A. Spawforth, *Hellenistic and Roman Sparta: A Tale of Two Cities* (London: Routledge, 1989), 97–103.

[51] Ibid., 103. An inscription mentions Vespasian's donation to the city (*IG* v. 1. 691, SEG xi. 848).

[52] M. W. Gleason, *Making Men: Sophists and Self-Presentation in Ancient Rome* (Princeton: Princeton University Press, 1995); A. Corbeill, *Nature Embodied: Gesture in Ancient Rome* (Princeton: Princeton University Press, 2004), 122, 134.

posed a deep vein in the Roman male psyche, according to which men exercised *imperium*—both the right to control others, especially foreigners or women, and the obligation to control themselves—because of their superior *virtus* or maleness.[53] Writers from Cornelius Nepos to Pliny the elder connect the Romans' matchless *virtus* with their consequent *imperium*.[54] The logical consequence was that Rome's enemies, indeed all other nations and especially easterners—Greeks, Asians, Cypriots, Egyptians, and Parthians—were at best diminished specimens of masculinity, emasculated and rendered impotent by the Romans, and at worst outright effeminate. This is, to be sure, only one side of what has often been described as a contradiction or even schizophrenia in Greek and Roman views of barbarians—the combination of admiration for simplicity or innocent virtue with contempt for troublesome enemies.[55] But even where there was admiration for certain barbarian traits, in the aftermath of a lethal conflict it was clear where triumphant virtue lay.

Roman representation of defeated barbarians therefore consistently stressed their state of *aporia* and impotence in the face of Roman power. Often, artists made use of size discrepancies, so that for example in the IUDAEA CAPTA coins the seated and dejected figure of Judea, often female, rarely reaches half the height of the proud and vigorous Roman soldier. The miniaturization of the barbarian—which Josephus might conceivably have had in mind when he spoke of the diminution of his people—reached its extreme under Hadrian, who was given monstrous proportions in statue as he stepped on the back of a puny barbarian.[56] The frequent representation of conquered barbarians as helpless women, in juxtaposition to a towering Roman soldier, inescapably reinforces the Roman claim to superior masculinity. It has been plausibly argued (by comparing the remains of the Sebasteion of Aphrodisias) that the lost Forum of Augustus in Rome was constructed with a Portico of Nations depicting perhaps fifty conquered peoples in feminine caryatid form, precisely in order to generate "a coherent construction of Roman male power."[57] Ever since Crassus's disastrous campaign in Parthia in 53 B.C.E., the Parthians were often portrayed in effeminate terms: assumed to

---

[53]E.g., Amy Richlin, *The Garden of Priapus: Sexuality and Aggression in Roman Humor* (rev. ed.; Oxford: Oxford University Press, 1992); Ibid., *Pornography and Representation in Greece and Rome* (Oxford: Oxford University Press, 1992); Susan Deacy and Karen F. Pierce, *Rape in Antiquity* (London: Duckworth, 2002); C. A. Williams, *Roman Homosexuality: Ideologies of Masculinity in Classical Antiquity, Ideologies of Desire* (Oxford: Oxford University Press, 1999); I. M. Ferris, *Enemies of Rome: Barbarians through Roman Eyes* (Stroud: Sutton, 2000), 1–62.

[54]Williams, *Roman Homosexuality,* 135.

[55]See generally Edith Hall, *Inventing the Barbarian: Greek Self-Definition through Tragedy* (Oxford: Clarendon, 1989); R. M. Schneider, "Die Faszination des Feindes: Bilder der Parther und des Orients in Rom," in *Das Partherreich und seine Zeugnisse.* (ed. J. Wiesehöfer; Stuttgart: Franz Steiner, 1998), 95–146.

[56]See Ferris, *Enemies of Rome,* 85–86 and plate 19.

[57]Quoting Ferris, *Enemies of Rome,* 34, commenting on B. Kellum, "The Phallus as Signifier: The Forum of Augustus and Rituals of Masculinity," in *Sexuality in Ancient Art* (ed. N. B Kampen; Cambridge: Cambridge University Press, 1996), 170–83.

indulge in oriental luxury, they appeared on the leg carvings of Roman household tables as Ganymede-Peter Pan types.[58] I. M. Ferris has persuasively read the bizarre sculpture from the Sebasteion in Aphrodisias, of a naked Claudius towering over a female figure of Britannia, held by her hair and actively resisting but with one breast exposed, as a scene of imperial rape; with this he compares the sculpture from the same site of a naked Nero, looming over the supine female figure of Armenia.[59] After Trajan's later successes against the Parthians, with the more usual restraint his PARTHIA CAPTA coins personified the neighboring empire as cowering barbarians, often in the form of a kneeling woman.[60]

Even formerly virile Roman men could acquire the image of effeminacy if they spent too much time among the eastern barbarians, as we see in the propaganda against Marc Antony—portrayed as a slave at once to his passions, to Queen Cleopatra, and to eastern luxury. Freedom from the passions and from the fear of pain and death were not simply part of the enlightened life; they were *masculine* ideals. Valerius Maximus considers the craving for life, *cupiditas vitae*, a feminine trait (9.13.pr.) and contrasts those who faced death like men with those who were "spineless and effeminate" at the end.[61]

Making defeated enemies appear womanish is likely a universal tendency, as the jailing of a Malaysian opposition leader on sodomy charges and the sexually charged outrages at Abu Ghraib and Guantanamo Bay suggest. Perhaps the most vivid artistic representation from antiquity is on a famous Athenian wine pitcher from the 460s B.C.E., featuring the naked Athenian holding his erect penis as he prepares to penetrate a resigned, compliant, and bent-over Persian.[62] The Romans appear to have had an especially vigorous interest in this sort of vilification, or at least to have discussed it more openly. Because *virtus* and *imperium* implied control of others, one man's claim necessarily came at the expense of those whom he conquered or intimidated; the same held for Rome's dealings with foreign peoples.

The Flavian revival of Augustus's CAPTA coinage rendered Judea the latest manifestation of the eastern menace, the most recent counterpart to Egypt and Parthia whose subjection (likewise coincident with the termination of civil war) had been so important in Augustus's foundation of the principate.[63] Just as Octavian had transformed his defeat of an Egypt allied with his Roman rival Marc Antony into a victory over barbarians, the Flavian forces treated Vitellius's redoubt at Cremona as a foreign stronghold, sacking it, and Vespasian and Titus parleyed their quelling of a provincial rebellion in Judea into victory in a foreign war.[64] Their victory thus merited a neo-Augustan triumph, celebratory coins,

[58] Schneider, "Die Faszination," 106–110.

[59] Ferris, *Enemies of Rome*, 56–59 and plate 12.

[60] Schneider "Die Faszination," 100.

[61] Williams, *Roman Homosexuality*, 138–39.

[62] Summary discussion in Ferris, *Enemies of Rome*, 7.

[63] J. M. Cody, "Conquerors and Conquered on Flavian Coins," in *Flavian Rome: Culture, Image, Text* (ed. A. J. Boyle and W. J. Dominik; Leiden: Brill, 2003), 107–113.

[64] Mattern, *Rome*, 151, 168, 193; cf. Cody, "Conquerors," 109.

and a monumental building campaign that would reshape the city center (*forum pacis*, Flavian amphitheatre, arches honoring Titus).[65] Judeans were portrayed on Vespasian's IUDAEA CAPTA (provincial ΙΟΥΔΑΙΑΣ ΕΙΑΛΩΚΥΙΑΣ) coins as cowering in submission, often as a mourning woman alongside the God-like Roman conqueror.[66]

3. In Judean culture, for its part, the fullest paradigm of manly virtue, at both political and personal levels, was furnished by the "greatest generation": the leaders of the Hasmonean resistance against Antiochus IV, who had laid the foundation of the last independent state. The Hasmonean uprising was a primary source of inspiration for those who led the resistance to Roman rule and prosecuted the revolt of 66 C.E.[67] It had produced vivid and heart-rending stories of heroism, toughness, endurance, and contempt for torture and death—on the part of women as well as men (2 Macc 7; 4 Macc 5).[68] The Hasmonean literature also preserved claims to genetic links with Sparta (1 Macc 12:7). These associations help to explain Josephus's otherwise puzzling decision to begin his account of the war of 66–73 C.E. nearly a quarter of a millennium earlier, with the Hasmonean revolt (1.31). A proud priest who cherishes his own Hasmonean ancestry (*Life* 1–6), he will exploit that glorious heritage to depict the manly Judean character, while at the same time displaying the Hasmoneans' wise political leadership and the meaning of political "freedom" in relation to foreign powers.

4. Josephus wrote *Judean War*, then, as also his later works, to represent the Judean character after the failed revolt, when it was suffering intense ridicule as barbarian and womanish. There are many other things that one can and should say about *War* and its connected themes: *stasis* and tyranny; gubernatorial malfeasance; Judean governance and relations with Rome; debts to the Prophets, Thucydides, Polybius, and later Hellenistic historians; its place in relation to "Second Sophistic" literature; literary and rhetorical devices. But what lies beneath all of this and lends coherence to the whole corpus is Josephus's claim that the Judeans deserve respect as real men. The language of *War* is surprisingly often about *being a man*, and Josephus even contrasts the Roman and Judean claims on this score. He promises not to counter the chauvinist-Roman accounts with an equally jingoistic Judean statement, but only to give due credit to both sides (*War*

[65] A. J. Boyle, "Introduction: Reading Flavian Rome," in *Flavian Rome: Culture, Image, Text* (ed. A. J. Boyle and W. J. Dominik; Leiden: Brill, 2003), 1–67; Ronald Mellor, "The New Aristocracy of Power," in *Flavian Rome: Culture, Image, Text* (ed. A. J. Boyle and W. J. Dominik; Leiden: Brill, 2003), 69–101, e.g., chart some signal Augustan-Flavian parallels.

[66] Y. A. Meshorer, *Ancient Jewish Coinage* (2 vols.; New York: Amphora Books, 1982), 2:77–8, 288–89, plate 35; Cody, "Conquerors," 109, figs. 1, 3.

[67] Especially Farmer 1956; M. Hengel, *The Zealots: Investigations into the Jewish Freedom Movement in the Period from Herod I until 70 A.D.* (Edinburgh: T&T Clark, 1989).

[68] A. J. Droge and J. D. Tabor, *A Noble Death: Suicide and Martyrdom Among Christians and Jews in Antiquity* (San Francisco: Harper San Francisco, 1992); J. W. van Henten and Friedrich Avemarie, *Martyrdom and Noble Death: Selected Texts from Graeco-Roman, Jewish, and Christian Antiquity* (London: Routledge, 2002).

1.9). Nevertheless, his exploration of Judean virtues inevitably comes at some cost—within his writings—to the currently inflated Roman image. For a fuller discussion, see chapter 3 in this volume.

We have often been misled, I think, by Josephus's famous description of legionary training early in book 3, as if it were proof of Josephus's propagandistic activity on behalf of Rome.[69] This excursus claims in superlative language that because of their unbelievably strict and constant preparation, Roman soldiers *never* act impulsively and their commanders *never* leave anything to chance (3.98–101), with the result that they have *never* been beaten, whether by superior numbers or by stratagem, by difficult terrain or even by fortune (3.106–7). But this was the purest nonsense, as Josephus's audience, and any Roman familiar with the disasters of M. Licinius Crassus in Parthia (53 B.C.E.) and P. Quinctilius Varus in Germany (9 C.E.), knew. In Josephus's story itself, this excursus comes shortly after the shameful defeat of Cestius Gallus and his Twelfth Legion (τὸ Κεστίου πταῖσμα, *War* 1.21; *Life* 21; ἡ Κεστίου συμφορά, *War* 2.556) by Judean irregulars, which he has retold in detail (*War* 2.507–555). Like the principal speeches of *War* (even those attributed to Josephus), his digression on the legions is a farrago of half-truths and spin, configured to suit his artistic literary purposes. It builds the legions up for the dismantling of that reputation in the following narrative, which undermines any notion that they were masters of disciplined warfare.

The remarkable thing is that Josephus's habit of singling out Judean soldiers for honorable mention, as if in military dispatches, is not limited to his own campaign at Iotapata (3.229–230) or even to the period of the war's legitimacy under aristocratic direction, before the death of Ananus and Jesus (4.314–352). It continues through to the end of the narrative, even increasing in his account of the siege of Jerusalem, though he has no sympathy for the "tyrant" commanders. At *War* 6.147–148, for example, he will list the Judean heroes according to the faction to which they belonged: Simon's, John's, or the Idumeans.

When Titus arrives on Mt. Scopus and the Mount of Olives with his four imposing legions in glistening battle array, rather than being intimidated the Judeans unite their forces and rush out against the renowned *Legio X Fretensis* (*War* 3.65)—formerly commanded by M. Ulpianus Traianus (*War* 3.289), one of Vespasian's closest associates and among those honored by a consulship already in 70,[70] the father of a future emperor;[71] now led by A. Larcius Lepidus (*War* 6.237), another favorite of Vespasian's and future governor of Pontus-Bithynia. Josephus emphasizes, however, the confusion and disorder of this legion, the Judeans drive from its new camp—until Titus manages to restore order by his personal courage (5.71–84). Even when the Judeans are driven down the slope, they renew their attack, prompting most of the Tenth to flee *up the hill*—in spite of their ostensible advantage on higher ground; the men guarding Titus must advise him also to

[69] Programmatically, Thackeray, *The Man and the Historian*, 27–28.

[70] P. Gallivan, "The Fasti for A. D. 70–96." *CQ* 31.1 (1981): 187.

[71] B. Isaac and I. Roll ("A Milestone of A.D. 69 from Judaea: The Elder Trajan and Vespasian." *JRS* 66 [1976]: 15–19) describe a milestone on the Caesarea-Scythopolis road from 69 C.E., established by Traianus as *legatus* of *Legio* X and honoring Vespasian.

retreat (5.85–97). Josephus's ongoing comparisons frequently favor the Judeans.[72] Eventually, Titus will have to abandon the legions' risk-averse behavior and turn to castigate his troops for failing to dare like the Judeans, who do so without hope of victory but only to make a raw display of their manly courage (διὰ ψιλὴν ἐπίδειξιν ἀνδρείας, 6.42).

Recent interpretation of *War* has held that Josephus wrote to absolve the ruling class of complicity in the revolt.[73] In view of the foregoing survey, I find this an untenable position. The very first sentence (*War* 1.1–3) establishes Josephus's role as a general in the war, which was in any case well known in Rome (cf. Suetonius, *Vesp.* 4.5), and which he greatly elaborates in books 2 and 3. The many dignitaries who fled Jerusalem after the Cestian disaster he describes in the most unflattering terms: they deserted the city like those abandoning a sinking ship (2.556)—thus forsaking their most basic responsibilities as statesmen.[74] Of course, the deserters did not include either Josephus himself or the two men he admired most—the chief priests Ananus and Jesus (4.326–365; cf. 7.267). Rather than trying to avoid all responsibility for the war, Josephus demands respect for his people and their rightful aristocratic leaders, who made life exceedingly difficult for the Romans and would have done so even more—or they would have reached honorable terms—had the brilliant chief priests lived (4.320–321).

The narrative tendencies outlined here are considerably more prominent and structurally important than Josephus's occasional and *de rigueur*[75] flattery of Vespasian and Titus, which has received disproportionate attention. It was merely "the cost of doing business" in imperial Rome. Moreover, what might at first seem obsequious groveling may turn out to be something else entirely.[76]

5. Much of *War*'s characteristic language reinforces the ethos of Judean manly virtue, for example: contempt for death and terror (καταφρόνησις θανάτου, τῶν δεινῶν), endurance (καρτερία), and "in close order" (ἀθρόος). The collocation of καταφρόνησις or περιφρόνησις ("disdain, contempt") with θάνατος or τὰ δεινά ("death, terrors") is well attested in historians and moral philosophers of the Roman period.[77] But the author with the heaviest investment in this language is Josephus, for whom the disdain for terrors or death is a conspicuous Judean virtue. *War* introduces the theme in the person of Athrongeus, the rebel of 4 B.C.E. (2.60), though he was not otherwise an admirable figure.

---

[72] E.g., *War* 3.472–84, 87–88; 4.39–48, 91; 5.120–24, 315–16, 287–88; 6.11–14, 33–53, 285.

[73] E.g., Goodman, *Ruling Class,* 20, 154–60; Price, *Siege,* 31–33. For a fuller discussion, see chapter 4 in this volume.

[74] See Plutarch's contemporary essay on *Precepts of Statecraft.*

[75] Cf. his successful contemporary Pliny, *Nat.* praef.1–2.

[76] See ch. 3 in this volume.

[77] Cf. Warren, J. *Facing Death: Epicurus and His Critics.* Oxford: Clarendon, 2004. Of thousands of examples, Diodorus Siculus 5.29.2; 15.86.3; 17.43.6, 107.6; Dionysius of Halicarnassus, *Ant. rom.* 5.46.4; Philo, *Prob.* 30; *Abr.* 183; Musonius Rufus, *Diss.* 10; Epictetus, *Diatr.* 4.1.70, 71; Plutarch, *Brut.* 12.2; Lucian, *Peregr.* 13, 23, 33; Marcus Aurelius, *Med.* 4.50.1; 9.3.1; 12.34.1; Polyaenus, *Strat.* 5.14.1; Diogenes Laertius 1.6; Phalaris, *Ep.* 103.3; Appian, *Celt.* 1.9; *Bell. civ.* 5.4.36; Cassius Dio 43.38.1; 46.26.2, 28.5; 62.25.1.

Thereafter it becomes the chief characteristic of all Judean fighters (3.357, 475; 5.88, 458; 6.42; 7.406), which the Roman generals can only *try* to inculcate in their legions (6.33). Throughout *Antiquities* too Josephus features this Judean quality, beginning with an encomium on King Saul (*Ant.* 6.344–347). There we meet the only other example in Josephus, outside the Essene passage, of the rare agent-noun καταφρονητής· other would-be "despisers of terrors," he says, can learn from Saul's example. Most compelling are Josephus's remarks in *Against Apion:* the Judean constitution itself inculcates contempt for death (θανάτου περιφρόνησις), among other virtues (*Ag. Ap.* 2.146), and precisely in wartime Judeans despise death (θανάτου καταφρονεῖν, 2.294). Josephus's description of the Essenes thus embodies his vision of the entire Judean tradition.

Josephus's phrase καταφρονηταὶ τῶν δεινῶν, which he uses twice of the Essenes and once of Saul, is striking because this *nomen agentis* form ("despiser") hardly appears before his time,[78] though his contemporaries Epictetus (*Diatr.* 4.7.33) and Plutarch (*Brut.* 12.2; *Mor.* 84a, 1044a) begin to use it. Yet within the Essene passage he has it twice, predicated symmetrically of wealth (2.122) as well as terrors (2.151). Both Josephus and Plutarch characterize *good* men as despisers—of death and pleasures, the two conventional human motivators—shedding the usually negative associations of the word "disdain" (for the laws, gods, etc.). Plutarch also uses the cognate verb καταφρονέω, like Josephus, to portray those who despise the pleasures (*Mor.* 210a) and death (210f, 216c, 219e)—in Plutarch's case, the Spartans.

Endurance (καρτερία) was the most famous trait of the Spartans and the whole focus of their training,[79] emulated by philosophers (Xenophon, *Mem.* 1.2.1; 2.1.20; 3.1.6). This is also an important word group for Josephus, who uses it about 134 times, nearly half of these (63) in *War*—usually in relation to the endurance of the Judean fighters or the "steadfastness" of their defenses. In *Against Apion,* again, Josephus makes it a distinctive Judean trait (1.182; 2.146, 170, [225], 228, 273, 284), and three times (*Ag. Ap.* 2.225, 228, 273) he contrasts the Spartans' mere *reputation* for endurance with the undeniable Judean *display* of this virtue in the recent war. On Essene endurance during the war, see *War* 2.151–158, which we lack the space to discuss here.

As for the adjective ἀθρόος ("in concert") it occurs forty-five times in *War,* though only twelve times in Josephus's later works. Often he seems to employ the term to suggest that what the Roman legions must train themselves in—disciplined marching in columns—the Judeans achieve spontaneously when their laws are threatened (*War* 1.81, 84; 2.170, 174; 6.80, 82, 86). They stream together in unison.

6. The parallels we have already seen between *War*'s Essene passage and *Against Apion*'s portrait of the Judean nation could be developed at some length. Space limitations mandate brevity, but the crucial point is that these parallels confirm Josephus's use of the Essenes to exemplify larger currents in the *War* and in his larger

[78] LXX Hab 1:5; 2:5; Zeph 3:4; Philo, *Leg.* 322.

[79] Xenophon, *Ages.* 5.3; 10.1; 11.9; Plutarch, *Mor.* 208c, 210a, 237a; *Lyc.* 2.2; 16.5–6; 18.1; 29.5; *Ages.* 11.7; 30.3.

world-view. They are an integral part of his ongoing effort to explain the Judean character. Some parallels may be seen efficiently by a glance at the final sections of *Against Apion* (2.293–294), where Josephus idealizes Judean culture. Italicized phrases below match those that he applies to the Essenes in *War* 2.119–161:

> What greater beauty than inviolable *piety* (εὐσέβεια)? What greater *justice* (δικαιότερον) than obedience to the laws? What more beneficial than to *be in concord* with one another (πρὸς ἀλλήλους ὁμονεῖν), to be a prey *neither to disunion* (διίσασθαι) in adversity, *nor to arrogance* (ὑβρίζοντας) and *faction* (στασιάζειν) in prosperity; in war *to hold death in contempt* (θανάτου καταφρονεῖν); in peace *to devote oneself to crafts or agriculture* (τέχηναις ἢ γεωργίαις); and to be convinced that *everything in the whole universe* (πάντα δὲ καὶ πανταχοῦ) is under the eye and direction of God?

Just as concord becomes a national characteristic in the *Against Apion* (cf. *War* 2.122–123, 134, 145 on the Essenes), so also the solemnity, gravity, or dignity (Greek σεμνότης) that Josephus identifies as the outstanding Judean trait (*Ag. Ap.* 1.225; 2.223), most conspicuously exhibited by his good self (*Life* 258) but by precious few others,[80] happens to be the first general point he makes about the Essenes: they certainly are known for cultivating *gravitas* (*War* 2.119). In *Against Apion* 2.193–196, 199–202, 205, similarly, Josephus attributes other fundamental Essene characteristics to all Judeans, including simplicity of life and an insistence that marital sex be exclusively for procreation.

Again, Josephus introduces his "non-panegyric" on Judean culture in the *Against Apion* (2.145–146) thus:

> For I think it will become clear that we have laws optimally oriented towards piety (εὐσέβεια), towards community (κοινωνία) with one another, and towards humanity (φιλανθρωπία) among the world at large; yet further, towards justice (διακαιοσύνη), towards endurance in the course of struggles (ἡ ἐν τοῖς πόνοις καρτερία), and towards contempt for death (θανάτου περιφρόνησιν).

All of these qualities figure prominently in *War*'s Essene digression.

Lurking behind Josephus's implied connections between Essenes and all Judeans, then, is the ghost of Sparta. He displays great interest in the moral-philosophical aspects of the Spartan legend. In *War,* Sparta appears only incidentally as a fallen power from the past (1.425, 513, 532; 2.359, 381; 7.240–243). In the *Antiquities,* Josephus reproduces the letters from 1 Maccabees (12:5–23) that asserted an ancestral bond (ὡς ἐξ ἑνὸς εἶεν γένους, *Ant.* 12.26) between Judeans and Spartans (12.225–228; 13.164–171). Louis Feldman has recently itemized the remarkable parallels between Josephus's life of Moses and Plutarch's biography of the Spartan lawgiver Lycurgus.[81]

In *Against Apion* Josephus reconciles the positive and negative sides of his Spartan interest. Whereas Xenophon had enthused that everyone praised Spartan

---

[80] Cf. *War* 7.65 on Vespasian; *Ant.* 12.24 on the Tobiad Joseph.

[81] Louis H. Feldman, "Parallel Lives of Two Lawgivers: Josephus' Moses and Plutarch's *Lycurgus,*" 209–42.

customs, but no other city was willing to emulate them (*Lac.* 10.8), Josephus concedes that "everyone eulogizes Sparta" (*Ag. Ap.* 2.225) but insists that Judeans have the better of them on every score. Although the Spartans are admired as the most courageous and disciplined people ever (*Ag. Ap.* 2.130), he says, their reputation is not entirely deserved. They have long since abandoned their noble traditions and lost their sheen (*Ag. Ap.* 2.273), as Plutarch (*Mor.* 240a–b) also allows, such that the Judeans have a much longer and more impressive record of rigorous training (*Ag. Ap.* 2.172), discipline, endurance, and courage—as witnessed by the recent war (*Ag. Ap.* 2.225–231, 272–273). The Spartan constitution was defective in significant ways, among these in its military preoccupation and hostility toward others (hence Judean superiority in φιλανθρωπία), and it was therefore unsustainable (2.172, 226–230, 259; cf. Aristotle, *Pol.* 1333b). At the end of the day, the world-renowned Spartans are for Josephus only a benchmark (*Ag. Ap.* 2.259; compare Polybius's use above), in the same genetic line as, but inferior to, their Judean relations.

This three-way connection among all Judeans, Spartans, and Essenes in Josephus's thought receives confirmation from an unexpected quarter. Early in the fourth volume of Porphyry's third-century work *On Abstinence,* he examines the Spartans as a model of the regimented diet (*Abst.* 4.3.1–5.2). Shortly thereafter he turns to the Judeans and their famous food restrictions. For Porphyry, however, the best examples of the Judean way are the Essenes. Between brief introductory and concluding remarks on all Judeans (*Abst.* 4.11.1–2, 14.1–4), he focuses exclusively on the Essenes, borrowing nearly verbatim the passage that we are examining from *War* 2 (*Abst.* 4.11.3–13.10). Curiously, Porphyry gives his sources for the Essenes as not only *War 2* and the parallel in *Ant.* 18, but also the second book of Josephus's work "against the Greeks": i.e., *Against Apion.* Since *Against Apion* does not mention Essenes, Porphyry appears to have recognized the sorts of parallels that we have explored here, inferring that Josephus's description of *all* Judeans in *Ag. Ap.* 2.151–196 was really or especially about the Essenes. Perhaps he pragmatically assumed that an entire *ethnos* was incapable of living in such a disciplined way. Josephus himself, however, presents the Essenes as embodying the virtues of the entire nation.

7. *War* has a symmetrical structure, which enfolds the Essene passage, confirming in another way that it belongs fully to the narrative. At the beginning of *Antiquities* (1.7) Josephus reflects that he tried hard to "measure off" (συμμετρέω) the beginning and ending sections of *War,* symmetrically, and analysis of *War* shows that he did just that. The central panel or fulcrum is occupied by the fateful murder of Ananus and Jesus (4.326–365; cf. 7.267), which marked the beginning of the tyranny, irredeemable *stasis,* and catastrophe. At the beginning and end of the work are its only discussions of the temple at Leontopolis (1.33; 7.421), and there are many parallel stops along the way. Here I observe only that the Essene passage contributes to the overall symmetry. At *War* 2.154 Josephus describes the ascetics' view that at death the souls of the good return up to "the most refined ether" (ἐκ τοῦ λεπτοτάτου αἰθέρος). The only other occurrence of

"ether" in Josephus, except for a quotation at *Ag. Ap.* 2.11, comes in Titus's pep talk to the legions at 6.47—a roughly symmetrical location in the seven-volume work, with very similar nuances: Titus offers his troops the thought that souls released on the battlefield are welcome "into the purest element, ether" (τὸ καθαρώτατον στοιχεῖον αἰθήρ).

Essenes in the *Judean War*: General Considerations

The foregoing analysis already suggests important ways in which *War*'s Essene passage functions in that narrative and expresses Josephus's larger concerns. Before discussing a few specific points within the passage, we briefly consider its tenor and situation in *War* 2.

Context in War *2*

The Essene passage is bound securely to its immediate context both before and after. I once thought that the orderly and obedient philosophers were included chiefly as a foil for Judas the Galilean and his "school": whereas Judas rejected any recognition of mortal rulers and fomented revolt (2.118), the Essenes take an oath to maintain loyalty to those in charge (τοῖς κρατοῦσιν), because no one comes into leadership without God (2.140). But it seems from the context that the leaders intended there are Judean officials or the sect's own governors, rather than *world* rulers.[82] At any rate, many other connections with the narrative deserve mention.

The preceding material in book 2 (2.1–118) highlights the serious shortcomings of the later Herodians, whose long and bitter succession struggle ends with the egregious Archelaus as *ethnarch* of Judea, probationary to possible appointment as king should he prove worthy (2.93). Worthy he is not, and so he finds himself ignominiously exiled to Gaul (2.111). Josephus's interests are, typically, with moral questions. In his concluding remarks, he describes the lust that drove Archelaus to abandon his wife and take up with Glaphyra, widow of both Herod's son Alexander and the "Libyan" King Juba II. He also alleges this woman's wantonness, exposed in a dream by Alexander's ghost, which presages her death (2.114–116). It can hardly be a coincidence that the Essene passage provides immediate and sharp contrasts on all of these fronts. The first points Josephus stresses about the group are connected with their mastery of the passions, their awareness of women's "wantonness," and their utter lack of concern about natural succession (2.119–121). He goes on to emphasize their community of goods, opposition to personal distinction, and perspicuity when in positions of power (2.122–123, 140).

Josephus's association of vice and submission to the passions with women's influence, both in the Archelaus episode and in the opening lines of the Essene

[82] The counterpart to the same oath commits the Essene, should *he* come into a position of governance, not to distinguish himself by outward signs of power. The government in question must be local at most, possibly sectarian.

passage, is typical of his narrative tendencies. One small but clear example is the phrase "wanton ways of women" at *War* 2.121 (ἀσελγείαι γυναικῶν), which is hardly found before him,[83] though he uses it formulaically—of Herod's wife Mariamme (*War* 1.439), Jezebel (*Ant.* 8.3180), Cleopatra (*Ant.* 15.98), and transvestite Galilean Zealots in Jerusalem during the war (*War* 4.562). The portrayal of women as "faithless" and fickle in these two contiguous passages likewise matches his tendencies perfectly.[84]

Near the end of the Essene passage, the heroic endurance of these men, to the point of death if necessary (2.151–158), prepares linguistically for several examples of endurance in defense of the laws on the part of the Judean populace as a whole: under Pontius Pilate (2.169–177) and then in the face of Gaius Caligula's hubristic demands (2.184–205). Although the Essenes adopt a peculiar lifestyle, they embody Judean virtue in a concentrated form.

"Despisers of wealth and terrors": Ring Composition in the Essene Passage

We have noted the conspicuous double use of the agent-noun "despiser" (καταφρονητής) in this passage. As it happens, the two occurrences fall near the beginning (predicated of wealth) and near the end (of terrors) of the passage, prompting one to ask whether the excursus like *War* itself has a symmetrical or "concentric" arrangement. It does. The symmetry is established at the beginning and end by mention of the Pharisees and Sadducees (2.119, 162), and by discussion of women, marriage, and succession (2.119–121, 160–161). In this architecture, the central panel comprises the twelve oaths taken by initiates (2.139–142). The pivotal function of the central panel is emphasized by the matching verbs "reckon in" (ἐνκρίνω) and "reckon out" (ἐκκρίνω), which sit as gateways before and after the oaths (2.138, 143)—and appear only here in Josephus. Similarly, the reverence for the sun as a deity emerges in roughly parallel places (2.128, 148), as does the rare phrase "they make it a point of honor" (ἐν καλῷ τίθενται) at 2.123, 146.

Men at Work: The Tone of the Essene Excursus

In keeping with *War*'s ethos, the Essenes appear above all as tough, hard, and supremely courageous men. Modern readers may be predisposed to see such philosophers as meek pacifists, but that is not what Josephus says. They lead quiet lives, to be sure, free of what are characterized as feminine emotions and plea-

---

[83] Philo, *Vit. Mos.* 1.305; Dio Chrysostom, *1 Glor.* 2.56; and fragments of some astrological writers. Otherwise, wantonness was often attributed to *men* under the influence of drink and women (Polybius 10.38.2; 25.3.7).

[84] For the language, cf. *Ant.* 4.219; 13.430–31; 17.352; *Ag. Ap.* 2.201. On women in Josephus, see B. Mayer-Schärtel, *Das Frauenbild des Josephus: eine sozialgeschichtliche und kulturanthropologische Untersuchung.* Stuttgart: V. W. Kohlhammer, 1995; Tal Ilan, *Integrating Women into Second Temple History* (Tübingen: Mohr Siebeck, 1999), 85–125; S. Matthews, *First Converts: Rich Pagan Women and the Rhetoric of Mission in Early Judaism and Christianity* (Stanford: Stanford University Press, 2001).

sures, but that only contributes to their image of seriousness or *gravitas* (the first point made about them: 2.119).

1. The passage is filled with the language of martial order, reminiscent of the Spartans: τάγμα, προστάσσω, τάξις, εὐταξία, ἄσκησις, and δίαιτα. Only in the *War* context does Josephus call the Essenes a τάγμα· the word that he normally uses for Latin *legio* ("legion")—by far his most common use in *War*, where the word occurs roughly 128 times. Although he calls all of the schools by various names (ἅιρεσις, φιλοσοφία, μοῖρα, etc.), he uses τάγμα of the Essenes *five times* in this passage, and once of the Sadducees immediately afterward (2.122, 125, 143, 160, 161). Although he has the phrase ἐν τάξει only four times in all his writings, two of these are near each other in *War*'s Essene passage (2.130, 133): the Essenes do things in an orderly way. Josephus claims that they only take action when *ordered* to do so, using the cognates προστάσσω and ἐπίταγμα (2.134, 139). Other terms related to martial virtues that are conspicuously prominent in this passage are δίαιτα ("regimen")—five of *War*'s eleven occurrences are in this passage (this is a characteristic term elsewhere for *Spartan* life)—and ἄσκησις or ἀσκέω ("discipline," "training"—2.119, 150, 166 [cf. *Ant.* 1.6 and *Ag. Ap.* 2.192, where Josephus claims that Moses perfected training in virtue, ἄσκησις ἀρετῆς]). Since this usage is only in *War*, not in the Essene passages of *Antiquities*, it appears that Josephus has shaped his account to fit *War*'s overall martial outlook.

2. We have noted the importance of "endurance" (καρτερία) in Josephus's lexicon and the word's Spartan associations. At *War* 2.138 he says that endurance was the entire goal of the tough three-year Essene initiation. Then in 2.151–153 he gives (symmetrically) a vivid portrait of the results. Exhibiting a genuine contempt for death, during the war Essenes endured every kind of torture, and "smiled in their agonies." Although Josephus dwells on this physical and mental toughness, it tends to get ignored in scholarly assumptions about Essenes as pacifists. This section has particularly strong verbal associations with the Hasmonean accounts, and it reinforces the tone of manly courage.

3. Finally, analysis of Josephus's Essene passage reveals a concentration of words and phrases that most often appear in other literature, in such concentration, in descriptions of the Spartans. By making this connection I do *not* mean to suggest that Josephus presents Essenes as would-be Spartans or Spartan imitators. To the contrary, as we have seen, he considers the Judeans superior. The Spartan legend had profoundly shaped the discourse of masculine ideals, however, and Josephus, fully aware of this, draws from this same repertoire in describing the Essenes. See table 1 on page 278–79 below for examples.

Specific Items in Josephus's Description of the Essenes

It remains to survey a few particulars of the Essene passage in context, before drawing some conclusions that should be helpful for any historical use of this material.

Courage, Death, Afterlife

Because of the Qumran-Essene hypothesis, scholarly attention has focused most heavily on the first half of Josephus's Essene passage: the standard utopian features of shared goods, common meals, and simplicity. But what Josephus himself features—giving it by far the largest amount of space (one fifth of the forty Niese sections on celibate Essenes) and placing it in the climactic position—concerns the Essenes' courage and contempt for death, which he claims were illustrated in the recent war.[85] He connects all this with their Greek-like view of immortality and post-mortem rewards for the virtuous. Here is the clearest connection with *War* as a whole.

> [151] [They are] long-lived, most of them passing 100 years—as a result, it seems to me at least, of the simplicity of their regimen and their orderliness. Despisers of terrors, triumphing over agonies by their wills, considering death—if it arrives with glory—better than deathlessness. [152] The war against the Romans proved their souls in every way: during it, while being twisted and also bent, burned and also broken, and passing through all the torture-chamber instruments, with the aim that they might insult the lawgiver or eat something not customary, they did not put up with suffering either one: not once gratifying those who were tormenting [them] or crying. [153] But smiling in their agonies and making fun of those who were inflicting the tortures, they would cheerfully dismiss their souls, [knowing] that they would get them back again.
>
> [154] For the view has become tenaciously held among them that whereas our bodies are perishable and their matter impermanent, our souls endure forever, deathless: they get entangled, having emanated from the most refined ether, as if drawn down by a certain charm into the prisons that are bodies. [155] But when they are released from the restraints of the flesh, as if freed from a long period of slavery, then they rejoice and are carried upwards in suspension. For the good, on the one hand, sharing the view of the sons of Greece they portray the lifestyle reserved beyond Oceanus and a place burdened by neither rain nor snow nor heat, but which a continually blowing mild west wind from Oceanus refreshes. For the base, on the other hand, they separate off a murky, stormy recess filled with unending retributions.
>
> [156] It was according to the same notion that the Greeks appear to me to have laid on the Islands of the Blessed for their most courageous men, whom they call heroes and demigods, and for the souls of the worthless the region of the impious in Hades, in which connection they tell tales about the punishments of certain men—Sisyphuses and Tantaluses, Ixions and Tityuses—establishing in the first place the [notion of] eternal souls and, on that basis, persuasion toward virtue and dissuasion from vice. [157] For the good become even better in the hope of a reward also after

[85]Beall devotes just over seven pages of about one hundred (*Description*, 13–111) to this section. The German translation of Michel and Bauernfeind (Otto Michel and Otto Bauernfeind, *De Bello Judaico = Der jüdische Krieg: Griechisch und Deutsch* [3 vols. in 4; rev. ed.; Munich: Kösel, 1962]) includes little commentary in general, though it becomes extensive for *War*'s Essene passage as they suggest partial parallels with the DSS. Of the forty-eight notes there, four (nos. 79–82) are on this passage.

death, whereas the impulses of the bad are impeded by anxiety, as they expect that even if they escape detection while living, after their demise they will be subject to deathless retribution. [158] These matters, then, the Essenes theologize with respect to the soul, laying down irresistible bait for those who have once tasted of their wisdom.

Given space limitations, I offer only three observations about this fascinating passage. First, we have already observed the importance of the way in which philosophers face death as the acid test of their claims to enlightenment. In his epistle on holding death in contempt (*contemno mortem*), Seneca reflects that philosophy gets a bad name because people feel that its practitioners are all talk, and do not handle their own deaths well (*Ep.* 24.15). After describing the Essenes' way of life in some detail, accordingly, Josephus emphasizes the consequences of their philosophy for their confrontation of death. The recent war has proven this. Here I want to emphasize that Josephus approaches this matter, as he approaches his entire work, as a participant in the general elite discussion of these questions.

Seneca's brief letter is an excellent reference point, because the issues he covers are strikingly similar to those linked together here by Josephus. Trying to help Lucilius, who seems to have a number of fears, Seneca tries to help by reducing all of them to the worst that can happen: death (*Ep.* 24.3, 12, 15, 17). If one can handle death cheerfully, then all other fears must fade away. In canvassing his subject, Seneca discusses the nature of existence as a spirit dragged down by the body to which nature has bound one (24.17); the terrors evoked by instruments of torture designed to tear a man's flesh to pieces, with the groans and shrieks of those being torn on the rack (24.14); one's view of what happens after death—he raises the specters of Ixion and Sisyphus in Hades (24.18)—as giving one endurance (*patientia*) to face both life and death (24.24); examples of those who have faced death not only with courage, but even cheerfully (*fortiter, libenter,* 24.4), and of those who rose to meet death by confounding their torturers with aggressive bravery (24.5), who did not so much yield up their spirits as they dismissed them (*non emisit sed eiecit,* 24.7).

Josephus's description of the Essenes above puts him in the same world of discourse. Most impressive is the intellectual or worldly restraint that both authors display in connection with the afterlife. For Seneca, this means recalling the Socratic uncertainty principle about what awaits (*Apol.* 40a; later in Marcus Aurelius, *Med.* 7.32): whether death brings annihilation or transformation to spiritual freedom, it is nothing to be feared (*Ep.* 24.18). Although Seneca dares not reject the stories of Ixion and Sisyphus out of hand, he is notably hesitant about them (24.18). For Josephus, the same urbane restraint is suggested first by his remark that the Greeks "laid on" or "put up" (ἀνατίθημι) these images of the afterlife (*War* 2.156), "telling stories" (μυθολογέω) about the postmortem punishments of Ixion and Sisyphus in order to encourage virtuous behavior. His astonishingly explicit reflection here on the social utility of such beliefs, likely inspired by his model Polybius (6.56.7–12), appears downright Hobbesian. We seem far from the world of the Scrolls.

Second, I mentioned earlier the importance of the Hasmonean model for Judean manliness and courage. It is not coincidental that Josephus opens his narrative with an appreciative look back to the Hasmonean heroes. He portrays them, however, in a distinctive way: as men who (like *War*'s Herod and like Josephus himself) supplemented their remarkable personal courage with brilliant statecraft, bringing the nation to prosperity through a pattern of flexible alliances, in contrast to the one-sided image of them among many contemporaries as God's warriors. The Hasmonean substructure of his work becomes particularly clear in this passage, where the clustered key terms (twisted, torture, torture chamber, torment, test, endure, eating food contrary to custom, and dismissing souls to receive them back again) are found in such concentration elsewhere only in the courage-under-torture scenes of 2 and 4 Maccabees.[86] This again shows the deep level of integration of the Essene passage in his work.

Third, the language and themes of this passage bind it closely to Josephus's general outlook as narrator. Others who face death cheerfully (εὔθυμος) include Josephus himself (3.382), Titus's faithful soldiers (6.184), the Judean fighters (6.364), and Herod's brother Phasael (*Ant.* 14.369). According to *War* 3.320–321, Vespasian was deeply impressed with the courage of a Judean fighter captured at Iotapata: he held out under every kind of torture, and when he was finally crucified he "met death with a smile." The notion of souls coming from and returning to refined aether after their confinement in a physical body has many and varied parallels in Josephus: the views of the Pharisees, his character's ruminations on existence at Iotapata, Titus's battlefield speech, and Eleazar speaking to the rebels at Masada.[87]

In short, Josephus continues his self-representation—a worldly statesman fully conversant with the issues of the day and the deepest moral-philosophical questions—by featuring the Essenes among *War*'s profiles in manly courage. Although this fits perfectly well with his narrative, there is nothing in it to invite comparison with the Dead Sea Scrolls or Qumran, in substance, ethos, or geography.[88] But clearly we are not dealing here with a superficial "Hellenization" or translation into Greek. Josephus has absorbed at a profound level not only the language but also the categories, questions, and habits of thought of his Mediterranean peers. Whoever his Essenes were, they recommend themselves to this worldview.

A final small matter is again revealing for the question of Josephus's authorial control. The phrase ἔμοιγε δοκεῖν (literally, "to seem to me, at least"), which

---

[86] Thus, στρεβλ- words ("twist"), 4 Macc. 7:4, 14; 8:11, 13, 24; 9:17, 2; 12:3, 11; 14:12; 15:14, 24, 25; αἰκι- words ("torment"), 1:11; 6:9, 16; 7:4; 14:1; 15:19; ὑπομένω ("endure"), 1:11; 5:23; 7:9, 22; 9:8, 30; 15:30; 16:17, 22; 17:4, 12, 17, 23); βασανιστήριον ("torture-chamber") and "instruments" (ὄργανα) in that setting, 6:25; 9:20, 26; 10:5, 7, 18; getting souls "back again," 2 Macc 7:11, 14, 23, 29; esp. 14:46.

[87] *War* 2.163; 3.371–72; 6.47; 7.343–47. See in general Sievers, "Afterlife."

[88] See n. 85 above. The disproportionately brief commentary in Beall as in Michel-Bauernfeind is devoted to identifying Greek parallels and suggesting that the very different conceptions of the Scrolls might nevertheless be presented here in Greek "garb."

he uses above (2.151), is an almost unique stylistic trait of his *War*. The more expected finite-verb phrase, ἔμοιγε δοκεῖ ("it seems to me, at least"), is attested dozens of times in earlier authors. Josephus's phrase with the infinitive appears, outside *War*, only a couple of times before the second century C.E.[89] Yet he has it here and also at *War* 2.479; 3.302; 4.312; 6.4. Again, the Essene passage is deeply embedded in *Judean War*.

The following items I include also to suggest both how they fit neatly in Josephus's narratives and how difficult they are to understand if the group being described is that of the sectarian Scrolls.

Essenes Avoid Oil

> [123] They consider olive oil a stain, and should anyone be accidentally smeared with it he scrubs his body, for they make it a point of honor to remain hard and dry, and to wear white always.

Since olive oil was considered indispensable in ordinary life, and presses have been found even in small towns of Galilee,[90] Josephus's claim that the Essenes avoided it and bathed only in cold water (*War* 2.129) would make them seem remarkable ascetics to a Greek and Roman audience. The stative verb αὐχμέω ("be parched, hard and dry") normally has negative connotations ("be unwashed, squalid"), indicating a condition to be relieved through rain or washing,[91] but Josephus deliberately inverts this by making dryness "a point of honor." In light of our investigation thus far it is noteworthy that the Spartans were also remembered for considering their dry—and unwashed—skin a mark of their difference and toughness (Plutarch, *Lyc.* 16.6; *Mor.* 237b: αὐχμηροὶ τὰ σώματα). Both groups thus reject conventional standards of comfort, grooming, and the luxury of gymnasium-baths. The same general theme is continued in the Essenes' wearing of threadbare clothes (*War* 2.126; cf. the Spartans' [and philosophers'] τρίβων, above) and above all in their Spartan-like rejection of private ownership in favor of communal sharing and exchange as needed (2.122, 127; see table 1 below on pages 278–79).

There is more. Although Romans used oil for the necessities of life, some associated liberal use with Greek effeminacy. Tacitus characterizes Nero's distribution of oil to the equestrian and senatorial orders as "a Greek predilection (*Graeca facilitate*)" (*Ann.* 14.47), and Silius Italicus has a Roman commander encourage his troops to destroy the Greek soldiers of Sicily because they are effeminate: they practice the lazy pursuit of wrestling in the shade, where they love to gleam

89 Plato *Meno* (81a) and *Hippias Maior* (291a); it is also in the Orphic *Testimonia*, frag, 5.6, and Stobaeus, *Anth.* 4.1.114—both of the latter difficult to date.

90 P. Garnsey, *Food and Society in Classical Antiquity: Key Themes in Ancient History* (Cambridge: Cambridge University Press, 1999), 12–14; E. Leota Tyree and Evangelia Stefanoudaki. "The Olive Pit and Roman Oil Making," *Biblical Archaeologist* 59 (1996): 171–78.

91 *War* 4.457; *Ant.* 7.297; Plato, *Resp.* 606d; Plutarch, *Num.* 13.6–7; *Ages.* 30.3; *Mor.* 193a, 365d.

with oil (*Pun.* 14.134–138).[92] Similarly, in Josephus's *War*, men who have no shred of self-control indulge the use of oil. At 5.565–566, John of Gischala impiously distributes the sacred supplies of oil and wine from the temple to his men, who anoint themselves and drink heartily. This same rebel group, Josephus claims (4.561–562), went so far as to adopt women's ways: plaiting their hair, wearing women's clothes (but cf. *Ant.* 4.301), drenching themselves in perfume, applying make-up, giving in to "the passions of women," and indulging a "surfeit of wantonness." As surely as the tyrants' degeneracy produces a disgraceful demeanor, the Essenes' Spartan- and Roman-like discipline in physical appearance reflects their moral perspicuity.

Though Josephus features the Essene avoidance of oil, there is no known parallel in the DSS. The arguments of J. M. Baumgarten and Todd Beall for seeing in this passage an issue of oil's purity, to connect it with a particular manuscript reading of *CD* 12.15–17,[93] illustrate the methodological problem I seek to address. Josephus's account says nothing about purity concerns, but plainly links Essene avoidance of oil with a preference for dry, hard skin.

Election of Leaders

> [122] Hand-elected are the curators of the communal affairs, and indivisible are they, each and every one, [in pursuing] their functions to the advantage of all.

The adjective "hand-elected" (χειροτονητός) occurs only here in Josephus (cf. the participle χειροτονοῦντες at *Ant.* 18.22) and is rare elsewhere. The main alternative to being elected by show of hands was to be "lot-elected" (κληρωτός: Aeschines, *Tim.* 21; *Ctes.* 29; Aristotle, *Ath. pol.* 55.2), as some early Christian leaders reportedly were (Acts 1:26). Election by show of hands implies the conscious preference of one's peers rather than the choice of Fate (Aristotle, *Ath. pol.* 54.3; Lucian, *Nav.* 29).

It is unclear how this system of elected officials relates to the four-phase seniority system ("according to the duration of their training") indicated at the symmetrical counterpart to this notice, at 2.150. Did the senior members take direction from elected officials of lesser seniority? The tension is easily resolvable if Josephus describes here the election of leaders from among full-patch members only—a status achieved only after the three years of initiation (cf. 2.138)—whereas the four grades of 2.150 referred to those still proceeding through the phases of initiation. At *Ant.* 18.22 the text seems to imply that both the community's financial administrators and its priests—whose tasks are significantly confined to food preparation—are elected to their functions.

Contrast the DSS, which feature (a) an individual community leader known as the מבקר ("guardian": 1QS 6.12, 20; *CD* 9.18–22; 13.11, 16; 15.8–14) or פקיד

[92] Cf. Williams, *Roman Homosexuality*, 136.

[93] J. M. Baumgarten, "The Essene Avoidance of Oil and the Laws of Purity," *RevQ* 6 (1967): 183 and Beall, *Description*, 45, 142 n. 56; note the very different reading in Vermes, *The Dead Sea Scrolls*, 111.

("official": 1QS 6.14; *CD* 14.6)[94] and (b) group-rankings clearly dependent upon caste (priests, Levites, and others, possibly Israelites and proselytes, *CD* 14.3–6).[95] Among Josephus's Essenes, by contrast, neither the elected officials (plural, also at 2.129, 134) nor the four grades *according to time in the order* (at 2.150) have any connection with caste. He mentions priests exclusively in connection with a blessing over food in this passage (*War* 2.131), more generally in connection with food preparation at *Ant.* 18.22. Although Josephus himself was an immensely proud priest, the priests do not figure among either the ranks by seniority or the elected offices of his beloved Essenes.

Essenes Have No Center or Distinctive Settlement

[124] No one city is theirs, but they settle amply in each.

One of the clearest casualties of the Qumran-Essene hypothesis is Josephus's plain statement here. The context enhances this claim by continuing to speak about the Essenes' lack of possessions, their easy and frequent travel from one city to another, and their standing provisions for such constant movement, with *each community* appointing a special officer for the care of visitors (2.124–125). Josephus's portrait creates the impression that a visitor to Judea should expect to see these (celibate) Essenes frequently traveling the roads with worn-out clothes and shoes, sticks for protection, and little else. Significantly, every Essene he mentions by name—along with the Essene Gate and events involving the Essenes as a group—is connected with Jerusalem (*War* 1.78; 2.113, 567; 3.11; 5.145; *Ant.* 15.371–378; 17.346). This emphasis on the ubiquity of the Essenes in Judea fits with his use of the group as exemplary Judeans, widely dispersed throughout the land, their impressive regimen is easily seen and emulated by others. As we have seen, their way of life reflects general Judean values, only practiced at a higher level.

It hardly needs stressing (perhaps) that Josephus shows no awareness of Khirbet Qumran or any other center. To imagine such a small and remote base as "the place of the Essenes" would undermine everything Josephus writes about the group. Nevertheless, Qumran interference with reading Josephus has created the common picture of *celibate* Essenes based in Qumran (to match *1QS*) and married ones living in communities elsewhere (to account for the references to marriage in *CD*).[96] Such a proposal, however, in no way harmonizes Josephus with the Scrolls; it rather makes his narrative unintelligible. This passage is all about *celibate* Essenes (2.120–121: he will not mention the marrying kind until the end, 2.160–161), and it is *they* who are so fully mobile, lacking any particular place.

---

[94] Beall, *Description,* 46–47.

[95] Ibid., 99–100.

[96] Beall (ibid., 48–49) discusses scholarship on the problem of understanding this statement in relation to Qumran, and connects the non-Qumran locations with *CD*. Gray (*Prophetic Figures,* 81–89) puts Josephus's (celibate) Essenes at Qumran.

Essenes Revere the Sun as God

> [128] Toward the Deity, at least: uniquely pious [ways]. Before the sun rises, they utter nothing of the mundane things, but only certain ancestral prayers to him, as if begging him to come up. . . .
>
> [148] On the other days they dig a hole of a foot's depth with a trowel—this is what that small hatchet given by them to the neophytes is for—and wrapping their cloak around them completely, so as not to outrage the rays of God, they relieve themselves into it [the hole].

Essene reverence for the sun is emphasized by symmetrical reoccurrence and even celebrated by Josephus. The vivid phrase "the rays of God" (τὰς αὐγὰς τοῦ θεοῦ) recalls Euripides' *Heraclides* 749–50, where the Chorus calls upon the "luminous *rays of the God* who brings light to mortals," and Creon's admonition to Oedipus (Sophocles, *Oed. tyr.* 1423–1428) not to expose his uncovered, polluted head to "our Lord the Sun." It anticipates Julian's *Hymn to King Helios* (1.9), which gives a vivid sense of the piety that might be associated with sun-reverence.[97] Josephus's verb ἱκετεύω ("entreat, approach as supplicant") is common in his narratives, but its more than one hundred occurrences normally have God as the one petitioned. Taken together with "the rays of God" this is a strong statement of something approaching worship.

Josephus's comments on this matter have long puzzled interpreters who try to read this passage in light of the DSS. His words are either neutralized to match the Scrolls' "prayers at dawn"[98] or they encourage arbitrary source theories on the ground that no observant Jew could speak thus. Indeed, the *Temple Scroll* from Qumran only intensifies the biblical prohibition of sun-worship—on pain of death by stoning (11QTemple 55.15–21; cf. Deut 17:2–5; Ezek 8:16–19). We need, however, to read this passage in light of Josephus's narrative themes and audience values.

As in this passage, Josephus tends generally to personify the sun and to see it as a representation of God. Later in *War* he claims that the Zealots "polluted the Deity" when they left corpses unburied beneath the sun (*War* 4.382–383; cf. 3.377; 4.317). His Titus vows to bury the memory of Jerusalem's cannibalism in rubble, so that "the sun cannot look upon it" (*War* 6.217). In *Ant.* 1.282–283 God synonymously parallels *his* watching over the earth with the sun's: Abraham's children "shall fill *all that the sun beholds* of earth and sea. . . . *for it is I* who am watching over all. . . ." Moses positions the tabernacle, the special house of God (3.100), so as to catch the sun's first rays (3.115). He also directs the Israelites, once in Canaan, to create an altar oriented toward the sun (4.305). The high priest's upper garment is woven with gold to represent the ever-present rays of the sun

---

[97] Cf. *Hymn. homer. cer.* 35, 280; Nicander, frag. 74.39 (Gow and Scholfield); Athenaeus, *Deipn.* 15.31.42 (Kaibel). Philo of Alexandria speaks frequently, though metaphorically, of God as "the purest ray" or as rays of sun: *Fug.* 136; *Mut.* 6; *Somn.* 1.72, 116 ("the rays of God"), 239; *Praem.* 25; *Mos.* 1.66.

[98] Beall, *Description,* 52–54.

(3.184). God has made the Judeans the happiest people under the sun, says Balaam (4.114). Saul promises victory to allies, such that "the ascending sun should see them already victors" (6.76; cf. 216; 8.49; 9.225). It is telling that, while otherwise intensifying the biblical portrait of King Josiah's reforms (*Ant.* 10.268–270; cf. 2 Kgs 23:19–20), Josephus entirely omits the biblical reference to Josiah's destruction of horses and chariots *dedicated to the sun* by Menasseh and Amon (cf. 2 Kgs 23:11). In his paraphrase of 1 Maccabees, he changes the phrase "Far be it from me to do this deed!" in his source (1 Macc. 9:10) to "May the sun not look upon such a thing" (*Ant.* 12.424). And he has Marc Antony speak of the sun's looking away from the murder of Julius Caesar (14.309; cf. 16.99, 108; 18.46; *Ag. Ap.* 1.306). Josephus's portrayal of the Essenes thus matches his demonstrable narrative tendencies, and it should neither be attributed to his sources, as if it were "non-Jewish," nor explained as his misunderstanding.

For Josephus's Roman audience, Essene reverence for the sun would have been highly resonant. Sun-worship was widespread through the near and far east, at least since the emergence of Akhenaten ("glory of the [sun-disk] Aten") in the eighteenth Dynasty (fourteenth cent. B.C.E.). In early Greece, the informal worship of Helios was commonplace, reflected also in the popularity of Heliodorus ("gift of the sun") as a name. Anaxagoras's claim that the sun was merely a red-hot mass reportedly caused outrage (Diogenes Laertius 2.12). Hesiod (*Op.* 339) mentions offering sacrifices at both the rising and the setting of the sun (the "holy light"), and Plato speaks of Socrates' *prayers to the sun* (*Symp.* 220d; cf. *Leg.* 887d–e and Albinus, *Epit.* 14.6). The prestige of the sun for philosophers was helped along by the Stoic Cleanthes' (early third century B.C.E.) identification of it as the driving principle of the world (Diogenes Laertius 7.139; cf. Philo, *Opif.* 116; *Somn.* 187). In utopian literature after Alexander, sun-worship continued to have a prominent role, inspired partly by Plato's Atlantis (*Criti.* 113b–121c, esp. 115b), the travel narrative of Iambulus to an Island of the Sun (Diodorus Siculus 2.55–60), and the *Sacred Inscription* of Euhemerus, in which the Sacred Isle (Panchaia) was associated with the sun (Diodorus Siculus 5.41.4ff).[99] Worship of the sun was further catalyzed by its identification with Apollo (Euripides, *Phaethon* 225; Horace, *Saec.* 9)—incidentally, one of Sparta's chief deities[100]—a constant reminder of which in Josephus's Rome was the statue of Helios driving his chariot atop the Palatine temple of Apollo.[101] The native Roman god Sol Indiges would eventually be eclipsed by the Syrian import Sol Invictus (the Unconquered Sun), who remained dominant from the third century C.E. until the rise of Christianity (temporarily reversed by Julian's sun worship).

For Josephus, his audience, and his Essenes, reverence for the sun was an assumed component of respectable piety. We have no right or reason to interpret

---

[99] Cf. J. Ferguson, *Utopias of the Classical World* (London: Thames and Hudson, 1975), 104–6.

[100] Cartledge and Spawforth, *Sparta,* 193–94.

[101] Incidentally, Lycurgus is said to have established his constitution under the tutelage of Delphic Apollo, and reverence for Apollo remained customary among the Spartans (Herodotus 1.65; Plato, *Leg.* 674d; Xenophon, *Ages.* 1.34; 2.15, 17; *Lac.* 8.5).

Josephus in ways that render his Essenes more congenial to the DSS or some other writings. He speaks not about prayers "at dawn" but about reverence for the sun as in some sense the deity or the reflection of it.

Essenes are Devoted to the Compositions of the Ancients

> [136] They are extraordinarily keen about the compositions of the ancients, selecting especially those [oriented] toward the benefit of soul and body. On the basis of these and for the treatment of diseases, roots, apotropaic materials, and the special properties of stones are investigated.

As others have noted,[102] this passage has a close parallel in *Ant.* 8.44–49. There Josephus credits King Solomon with thousands of "compositions" (συντάσσω, 8.44–45). Those volumes recorded Solomon's comprehensive study of nature and the various properties (ἰδιώματα) of each form (8.44). In particular, they described the craft (τέχνη) of exorcism, "for the benefit and treatment" (εἰς ὠφέλειαν καὶ θεραπείαν) of humanity (8.55). Josephus even describes an instance of such *therapeia* (8.46) that he witnessed. The exorcist used a root (ῥίζα) prescribed by Solomon for the purpose (8.47). So again, Josephus's Essenes are admirable examples of the traits he claims for Judean culture as a whole.

Beall makes a good case for including among "the ancients" the pseudepigraphous *1 Enoch* and *Jubilees,* which mention cures through herbs and roots (*Jub.* 10.10–14; *1 Enoch* 7.1; 8.3; 10.4–8), and which were widely read by Judeans in the first century.[103] But there seems no reason to limit the ancients studied by the Essenes to Judeans. The study of roots for curative purposes had a long history in the Greco-Roman world. Aristotle's prolific student Theophrastus (fourth century B.C.E.) observes (*Hist. plant.* 9.8.1): "The powers of roots are many and for many [purposes], but the medicinal ones are especially sought out as being the most useful." The same Theophrastus devoted a work to stones and their "special properties" (*Lapid.* 3.5; 41.1; 48.1; cf. Galen, *Simpl. med. temp.* 12.207.2). The combination of roots and stones (the stones were typically broken and the fragments applied to certain roots) is found frequently in the medical and magical writers of antiquity, not least among Josephus's near contemporaries Dioscorides Pedanius,[104] Cyranides,[105] and Galen.[106] Another contemporary, Pliny the Elder, included in his *Natural History* detailed studies of plants and roots (*radices*) as remedies (*Nat.* 24–28). The "virtues of roots" were among the things of which King Solomon was alleged by some Judean authors to have had deep knowledge (Wis 7:20).

---

[102] See Thackeray's note in the Loeb to this passage.

[103] Beall, *Description,* 70–73.

[104] Pedanius, *Eup. simpl. med.* 1.133.1; 2.36.4, 118.2, 119.4; *Mat. med.* 1.78.2; 4.91.1; esp. 5.126.3.

[105] Cyranides 1.7.19, 8.26, 10.95, 17.16.

[106] *Simpl. med. temp.* 11.811.4; 12.41.13, 68.7.

Essenes Avoid Spitting—Middles and Right

> [147] And they guard against spitting into [their?] middles or to the right side and against applying themselves to labors on the Sabbath days, most distinctively of all Judeans: for not only do they prepare their own food one day before, so that they might not kindle a fire on that day, but they do not even dare to transport a container—or go to relieve themselves.

Although it is possible that the Essene prohibition of spitting into middles and the right has to do with simple politeness in a group setting, both the context and the verbal construction (τὸ πτύσαι εἰς μέσους ἢ τὸ δεξιὸν μέρος) make that unlikely. As for context, this "guarding [against]" shares a main verb (φυλάσσονται) with their guarding of the Sabbath from work, which Josephus illustrates by their avoidance of carrying pots or even of relieving themselves (2.147). None of this implies group activity, and defecation is emphatically private (2.148). As for the language about spitting, Josephus's two pointed restrictions—into middles (whatever that means)[107] and to the right side—obviously leave the other directions open: the left side, to begin with. It is inconceivable that Josephus has in mind a group context, in which it would be quite acceptable to spit at the people on one's left. And if there are people on one's right, there must be people on one's left. What, then, does he mean?

Spitting in general, but particularly into the middle area *of one's body* (Theophrastus, *Char.* 16.14; Pliny, *Nat.* 28.36)—the chest or torso (εἰς κόλπον πτύσαι; *in sinum spuendo*)—*or to the right side*—e.g., into the right shoe before dressing (Pliny, *Nat.* 24.172; 28.38; cf. Petronius, *Sat.* 74.13)—were behaviors popularly thought to prevent or cure illness. The custom of spitting for luck or health was grounded in a belief in the curative powers of human saliva (Pliny, *Nat.* 38.35–39). More likely, his μέσους ("middles") refers to the centers *of bodies*—torsos, equivalent to κόλπους[108]—rather than to a singular *group middle* as normally assumed. If this interpretation is valid, Josephus's Essenes reject spitting for good luck or to ward off disease, like other enlightened observers of the time, but not to clear one's throat.

It is commonly asserted that Josephus's remarks on Essene avoidance of spitting (albeit in two specified directions) is "strong evidence" for the Qumran-Essene hypothesis,[109] because the *Community Rule* (*1QS* 7.13–15) prescribes a month's penance for anyone who spits *into an assembly.* But the superficially similar expression in *1QS*, ואיש אשר ירוק אל תוך מושב הרבים ("and the man who

[107] Whatever it means, the unusual phrase "into middles" (εἰς μέσους) is a favorite of Josephus's. Outside of Dionysius of Halicarnassus, who employs it nine times, it appears only once or twice in each of four authors. Josephus has it a remarkable fifteen times (also *War* 4.216; 6.42; *Ant.* 3.13, 308; 5.54, 206; 9.56; 12.429; 17.130, 131; 19.261; *Life* 37, 251, 255).

[108] For this literal sense, cf. *Life* 326, where Josephus seizes an opponent wrestler-style, around the μέσος; cf. Herodotus 9.107; Aristophanes, *Eq.* 387; *Nub.* 1047.

[109] Beall, *Description,* 96; cf. Grabbe, *Judaism,* 2:495; VanderKam, *The Dead Sea Scrolls,* 87.

has spat into the assembled group" [will be punished for thirty days]), appears to be "a false friend." First, *1QS* 7 is listing a number of truly gauche behaviors, mostly in the context of group meetings, that make the culprit liable to fines or other penance: insulting one's companions, treating communal property recklessly, speaking foolishly, lying down and falling asleep in the meeting, going naked without good reason, *spitting into the group*, dressing so shabbily that one displays private parts, guffawing stupidly, and so forth. In such a context, being required to avoid spitting into the group seems only decent. If we had detailed rules for other communities (Jesus' followers, Pharisees, Baptists, trade guilds, philosophical schools), we should likely find them also prohibiting this kind of thing. Evidently the rule was necessary. (Several gyms to which I have belonged have needed signs reminding people not to spit in common areas, and indeed to control other bodily functions). The Talmud, with characteristic vividness, confronts the problem of spittle build-up during prayer—along with belching, yawning, and sneezing—and recommends ways to avoid spitting (*b. Ber.* 24a–b).

In Josephus, however, the context, content, and tone are entirely different. Both his directional indicators (middles and right) and his coupling of the spitting prohibition with scrupulous observance of the Sabbath (2.147) and extraordinary care in toilet practice (2.148) suggest high purpose, not penance for disgusting behavior in the group.

These few examples must suffice as a base for at least preliminary conclusions. Of the remainder—Josephus's treatments of women, marriage, and children in the Essene context, their community of goods, initiation, courage under torture, and sublime views of the afterlife (2.151–58)—much more could be said. But all such analysis would confirm that the Essenes of *War* 2 represent in concentrated form many characteristic features of Josephus's outlook. The passage is remarkable for its combination of parallels and evocations of material elsewhere in Josephus, in Hasmonean literature, and in Greek and Roman philosophy, history, and myth.

Conclusions and Historical Implications

This chapter has had two related goals: first to propose some rough, initial considerations for understanding Josephus's Essenes in context, as part of his narrative in the *Judean War;* second, to begin to think about the uses of that narrative for a historical reconstruction of the Essenes. The latter question has two dimensions: how Josephus's Essenes ought to function in *de novo* historical hypothesizing about the Essenes and, since there is already an established theory of Essene identity in the Qumran-Essene hypothesis, how Josephus's Essenes could be explained on that hypothesis. My conclusions follow.

1. *War*'s Essenes contribute both to this narrative and to Josephus's larger program in countless ways. His later works will describe few individuals—Moses,

Solomon, and of course himself—as the embodiment of Judean virtues. But no group other than the Essenes, not even the priesthood as a body, so perfectly illustrates the character of the Judean people as he wishes to present it. These are men's men, legionaries of the soul, engaged in the serious pursuit of the virtuous life: disciplined, courageous, perfectly just, and contemptuous of the pleasures as much as of the fears that drive ordinary men. They anticipate the values he will attribute to all Judeans in *Ag. Ap.* 2. It is no accident that Josephus's great portrait of the Essenes comes in the *War,* a work aimed largely at improving the post-war image of the Judean national character (1.1–8). The Essenes carry the torch lit by the Hasmoneans of the story's opening paragraphs.

Although many scholars have attributed Josephus's Essene passage to other hands, from whom he was thought to have borrowed either wholesale or in fragments that he then sewed together, the language and the description are demonstrably his (even if he was influenced by sources). Even the many *hapax legomena* in his Essene passage fit the patterns of his *hapax legomena* elsewhere, namely, they serve the purposes of linguistic variation, and they tend to be sparsely attested before his time but amply paralleled from his contemporary Plutarch onward. So they cannot plausibly come from a source, but rather illustrate Josephus's strenuous efforts throughout *War* to write in the fashionable new Atticism of the so-called "Second Sophistic."[110] The high-level Greek matches Josephus's implied posture throughout the work, which is that of the elite provincial statesman-aristocrat under Roman hegemony. He has clear debts to Thucydides, Polybius, and Strabo,[111] among others, and his work is often comparable to that of his near contemporaries Seneca (for moral philosophy), Plutarch, and Dio Chrysostom.

2. If we wish to reconstruct the historical Essenes in a new investigation, standard method would require us first to examine all Essene evidence in detail—this passage and the others in Josephus along with those in Philo and Pliny, along with the notice preserved from Dio in Synesius. Although each of these is as distinctive as Josephus's in their specific emphases and language, and although that careful work has not yet been done, I venture to suggest that it would not be extremely difficult to posit a historical picture of the Essenes to explain how each of these authors came up with his picture of the group, without much remainder. In all cases they appear as exemplary philosophers, dispersed through much of Judea, embodying in real life the familiar utopian-Spartan male regimen (stripped, as everyone agreed was necessary, of Sparta's warlike disposition): sharing goods, living with extreme simplicity in their fellowships, facing hardship and ultimately death with equanimity. Pliny and Dio both admired the Essenes, exclusively among Judean philosophical groups; Philo and Josephus independently chose to feature them as shining models of the Judean life. Whether other groups (certain groups of Jesus' followers, Baptists, Bannus's followers, Qumraners, etc.)

110 These observations will be fully documented in my commentary to *War* 2 (Leiden: Brill, 2008).

111 E.g., Eckstein, "Josephus and Polybius"; Shahar, *Josephus Geographicus.*

were also Essene must be be a secondary investigation, which can be tackled only when the Essenes themselves are reconstructed with some clarity on the basis of undisputed Essene evidence. The procedure is the same with other ancient phenomena: in studying the Pharisees, for example, we first come up with a picture on the basis of evidence for the Pharisees, only then speculating whether other texts that do not self-identify (e.g., Psalms of Solomon or Jubilees or Qumran's *CD*) are also Pharisaic.

3. The Qumran-Essene hypothesis presents a number of problems, beginning with the methodological difficulty that it "jumps the queue" by positioning a non-Essene source collection front and center, requiring evidence about the Essenes to accommodate itself to the Scrolls. It also seems to demand responses, with the status of default theory; scholars are defined as "for" or "against" this conclusion. But historical investigation knows no default theories. Our default position must always be one of not knowing, and unless we can build a compelling case from the ground up, by testing all hypotheses, we return to not knowing.

Substantively, the hypothesis requires us to believe that the historical phenomenon admired by Pliny and praised by Dio, described in glowing terms by Philo and then by Josephus, was the group(s) that produced and cherished the Dead Sea Scrolls. How plausible is that? Although a sound judgment on this matter could come only after a thorough historical investigation of the Essenes, and then a secondary exploration of all possible further affiliations, preliminary indications do not seem promising. Imagining that the sectarians of the Scrolls lie behind Josephus's descriptions faces roughly the same obstacles as imagining that he is describing certain early Christians or Baptists. To be sure, there are parallels in lifestyle (common meals, washing, community of goods), though these are not as close in language or in ethos as those between Josephus's Essenes and the men of the Alexandrian Mouseion, for example, or between them and the renowned Spartiates.

But there is a simpler and more obvious problem, namely, Why, given what we know of Josephus (*a fortiori,* what we know of Philo, Pliny, and Dio),[112] would he fasten upon the people of the Scrolls as his ideal Judeans, when the Scrolls-communities' mental, cultural, and social worlds are so completely at odds with his own? I am not a Scrolls specialist, but surveys by specialists of the central convictions reflected in these texts more or less agree on the general picture.[113] The Scrolls communities embrace rather sharp cosmic, anthropological, and temporal dualisms, and define themselves by these divisions: two ways and two spirits. They are a righteous remnant, led by Zadokite priests and also Levites, who understand themselves very much in opposition to a complacent and lax mainstream, the wicked, and the "seekers after smooth things" among others, especially the illegitimate Jerusalem aristocracy based in the temple—presumably, men such as the proud and worldly priest-aristocrat Josephus. Apocalyptically minded, if any

[112] See, e.g., the preceding seven chapters of this volume.

[113] E.g., VanderKam, *The Dead Sea Scrolls,* 110–19; Vermes, *The Dead Sea Scrolls,* 41–64.

group ever was, they see themselves living at the end of time and they eagerly anticipate the end of the present order in a decisive cosmic battle. Schooled in the ordinances of the Righteous Teacher, they await the anointed leaders ("messiahs") who will lead the vindication of their cause. Accordingly, they study scripture in a distinctive *pesher*-mode, applying its words to themselves as the righteous at the end of time.

It seems hard to imagine a less plausible group for even secondary identification with the Essenes beloved by the likes of Philo, Josephus, Pliny, and Dio—even if their Essenes also have initiations, eat meals together, and practice a simple regimen of life. Josephus, to speak only of him, is opposed to much of what the Scrolls appear to represent: he sees only pseudo-prophets and charlatans among those who promise the gullible an imminent end of the age. He himself could not be a more worldly, engaged, international figure, steeped in Greco-Roman rhetoric, historiography, and philosophy, now flourishing in Rome and trying to impress his audiences with the virtues of the Judean *ethnos*—and its ancient aristocratic-priestly constitution, of which he is the chief representative.

The Qumran-Essene hypothesis requires us to believe not only that Josephus (as Philo, Pliny, and Dio) for some reason became powerfully attracted to the people of the Scrolls; it also requires us to suppose that when he came to describe them in detail, he portrayed them not as the Scrolls do, with all of these distinctive traits, but in a much more generic, utopian-Spartan way. The mental gymnastics involved in this attraction followed by misrepresentation, multiplied for each classical author, are hard to credit.

I have no reason to insist *a priori* that the people of Qumran, or some group of Jesus-people or Baptists, could not conceivably constitute the historical reality behind Josephus's Essenes. Historians ought to care only about methods and evidence: conclusions come and go. But such an argument would need to be made, in place of the ongoing tendency to borrow individual items from the Essene sources without context. As it is, the hypothesis causes problems with understanding Josephus and his interests as an author. One needs to show, on any hypothesis about the historical Essene reality, how we ended up with all the ancient portraits that we have. When the Qumran-Essene hypothesis was first developed in the early 1950s, this problem was not recognized in this way because Josephus, in particular, was not viewed as an intelligent craftsman. Scholars felt free to select items from the buffet he seemed to provide, as if they were discrete nuggets, and reconfigure them as desired, dismissing those nuggets that seemed uncongenial as his misunderstanding of sources or as vaguely conceived "Hellenizations" requiring no further explanation. Those courses are no longer open to us, however, because they are demonstrably untenable. A historical hypothesis about the Essenes must now explain the Essene evidence, and this will mean, in the case of Josephus, showing how *ex hypothesi* (on any historical hypothesis) this craftsman came to his view of the group, why he described them as he did, and, especially, why he gave them such large play in his carefully constructed work on the *Judean War.*

Essenes	**Spartans**
The Essenes follow a prescribed *regimen* (δίαιτα), a word used in this philosophical sense conspicuously in the Essene passage (5 of 11 times in *War*); otherwise, it is used sparingly: of all Judeans in *Against Apion* (1.182; 2.173–74, 235, 240 and of the Pharisees (*Ant.* 18.12, 15).	Lycurgus laid down a comprehensive regimen (δίαιτα) for all Spartiates to follow (Xen., *Lac.* 5.1; 7.3; Plu., *Lyc.* 24.1; *Mor.* 209f, 210a, 225f, 226f, 227b), a discipline that Josephus elsewhere claims they were unable to maintain in spite of military prowess; contrast the Judeans (*Ag. Ap.* 2.235).
"Whereas these men shun the pleasures as vice, they consider self-control and not succumbing to the passions virtue" (2.120).	King Agesilaus, asked what benefit the laws of Lycurgus had brought Sparta, alleged replied, "contempt for the pleasures" (Plu., *Mor.* 210a).
As a sign of their immunity to the appeal of pleasures, Essenes avoid marriage and women altogether (2.120)—or (in the case of one group) minimize their implications by marrying only women of proven fertility, for the sole purpose of procreation (2.160–61).	The best indicator of the Spartan king Agesilaus's self-control is shown by his remarkable refusal to touch the one he loved (Xen., *Ages.* 5.4–6); Lycurgus's laws treat the indulgence of sexual feelings as very shameful (Xen., *Lac.* 2.12–14).
Marrying Essenes prove by their abstinence during pregnancy that they are coupled solely for the purpose of bearing children (τέκνων χρείαν, 2.161).	The Spartan constitution is radically oriented toward procreation: women's chief task is procreation (τεκνοποιία; Xen., *Lac.* 1.4). Although young men must marry, this is not for pleasure. They visit their wives only for brief conjugal visits, while still living with their male peers; wives and husbands can also be shared for maximum productivity (Xen., *Lac.* 1.5–10; Aristotle, *Pol.* 1270b).
Boys are adopted and raised with a rigorous training in the group's principles of character (2.120).	Boys are removed from their parents and raised by the community, to inculcate the values of simplicity and endurance (Xen., *Lac.* 2.2–6).
They are despisers of wealth (2.122). They practice community of goods (2.122).	Lycurgus forbade free Spartans from pursuing material gain; anyone found possessing gold or silver was fined (Xen., *Lac.* 7.1–6). He made wealth unenviable and dishonored (Plu., *Mor.* 239e).
Keeping their skin hard and dry (τὸ αὐχμεῖν), they make it a point of honor to avoid the use of oil (2.123).	Plutarch says that Spartiates kept their bodies hard and dry (αὐχμηροὶ τὰ σώματα), avoiding ointments and baths (Plu., *Mor.* 237a; *Lyc.* 16.6; *Ages.* 30.3).
They dress with extreme simplicity, wearing as few clothes as practicable and replacing them only when absolutely worn out (2.126).	Spartiates go without the customary Greek tunic and receive only one cloak each year (Plu., *Mor.* 237a). They punished a man who put a border on his sack coat (*Mor.* 239c).
They do not buy and sell, but take from each other and from the common store as needed (2.127).	Spartiates are forbidden to sell anything. If they need something, they freely take it from their neighbors (Plu., *Mor.* 238f).
They have a special reverence for the sun as divine, addressing prayers to it (him) in the morning and avoiding offense to the sun's rays (2.128, 148).	Spartans continue to revere Apollo—widely identified with the sun—who is the guarantor of their constitution (Herodotus 1.65; Plato, *Leg.* 674d; Xen., *Ages.* 1.34; 2.15, 17; *Lac.* 8.5).
Almost everything in their lives is ordered by their freely-chosen leaders (2.134).	Even the most important Spartans live under obedience to their leaders: for example, they run when called (Xen., *Lac.* 8.1–4)

Essenes	**Spartans**
The three-year Essene probation aims at producing endurance (καρτερία) and resistance to all hardship in its members (2.138; cf. 2.150–53). In *Against Apion* Josephus makes καρτερία a distinctive Judean trait, in explicit contrast to the *undeserved* Spartan reputation for this quality (*Ag. Ap.* 2. 225, 228, 273).	Καρτερία was a renowned Spartan trait, the goal of their whole system of training (Xen., *Ages.* 5.3; 10.1; 11.9 Plu., *Mor.* 208c, 210a, 237a; *Lyc.* 2.2; 16.5–6; 18.1; 29.5; *Ages.* 11.7; 30.3)
Essenes practice complete equality, never surpassing another in dress or other signs of advantage when in positions of authority (2.122, 140).	Lycurgus banished wealth and poverty, persuading the citizens to live together in equality (Plu., *Lyc.* 8.1–9.2). King Agesilaus insisted on using the worst bed and wearing simple dress (Xen., *Ages.* 4.2; 10.2; 11.11).
They share a special communal meal of simple food, admission to which is permitted only to full members, after probation and initiation (2.129–32, 137–42).	Lycurgus instituted communal meals, the most distinctive trait of Spartiate life (Plu., *Lyc.* 10–12); at these meals, candidates were assessed for initiation (*Lyc.* 12.5–6).
Their meals are free of unseemly noise (2.132).	Spartan communal meals are free of outrage, drunken uproar, shameful behavior or speech (Xen., *Lac.* 5.6).
They practice rare moderation in consuming food and drink, taking in only as much as necessary (2.133; cf. *Ag. Ap.* 2.195).	Lycurgus ordered that Spartiates receive just enough food and drink, not too much or too little (Xen., *Lac.* 5.3–4).
They swear to keep their internal affairs secret and they are closed to the outside world (2.129, 141).	Spartiates neither travel abroad nor accept foreign visitors (unless willing to adopt their constitution); what is said at their meetings remains secret (Plu., *Mor.* 236f, 238e).
They have an extremely high and severe standard of justice, including expulsion from the order (2.143–45).	Whereas other states punish only crimes against others, Lycurgus inflicted severe penalties on anyone failing to live the most virtuous life possible; those who fail to meet the standards of the νόμιμα are no longer included among the peers (Xen., *Lac.* 10.4–7).
They especially honor the lawgiver, as next in rank to God (2.145), in keeping with Josephus's claims elsewhere about Moses's super-human status (*Ant.* 3.180, 318–20; 4.329).	All Spartan kings have divine ancestry and are treated as demi-gods at death (Xen., *Lac.* 15.2, 9), but the lawgiver Lycurgus was honored above all, partly through a temple in his honor and annual sacrifices "as to a god" (Plu., *Lyc.* 5.3; 30.3).
They submit to the elders and to a majority (2.146).	Lycurgus, by making elders the ultimate judges over life and death, enhanced their prestige beyond that of all others (Xen., *Lac.* 10.1–3).
They are long-lived (2.151).	The only lawgiver listed in Lucian's essay on the long-lived (*Macr.* 28) is Lycurgus the Spartan.
They have trained themselves to be contemptuous of pain, suffering, and death itself (2.151–53). For Essenes, death with honor (τὸν θάνατον, εἰ μετ' εὐκλείας) is better even than deathlessness (2.151).	Lycurgus's most admirable achievement: causing the Spartans to regard noble death (τὸν καλὸν θάνατον) as better than a life in shame (Xen., *Lac.* 9.1)
They study "apophthegms of prophets" (2.159). "Apophthegm" is a rare term, used only here in Josephus, and most often associated in other literature with the compact Spartan way of speaking.	The Spartans detested lengthy speech and trained their young to speak, if at all, with extreme conciseness (Plu., *Lyc.* 19–20); collections of Laconian ("laconic") apophthegms circulated widely in antiquity.

Part III

CHRISTIAN ORIGINS

Chapter 9

Paul's Announcement (τὸ εὐαγγέλιον): "Good News" and Its Detractors in Earliest Christianity

I recently heard a television pundit remark that "What you read in the *New York Times* is not the gospel." Although the metaphor is commonplace, two things remain striking about it for students of the ancient world and Christian origins: first, that the word *gospel* has persisted through the ages to the world of popular discourse today; second, that the meaning of the word seems entirely unproblematic: it is a slightly exotic variant of "truth." Field-educated people, and churchgoers, know that "gospel" has at least two more technical senses. It is both the message proclaimed by the early church and the word normally used for the genre of the first four texts in the New Testament canon—the *gospels.* Still, "gospel" is generally assumed to have an obvious and well-established primary meaning: what the followers of Jesus taught and shared.

Scholars, of course, have a lot more to say about that gospel. The database of the American Theological Library Association (ATLA) lists some 25,754 books and articles[1] with the word in their titles alone. I have not read even a respectable fraction of this literature, but already from the basic and well-known scholarship on the origins of Christianity some surprising and possibly disconcerting facts emerge. For example, the New Testament gospels do not call themselves by this name;[2] they receive this label only from about the mid-second century, by the time of Marcion and Justin.[3] Further, usage of the Greek word translated "gospel" (εὐαγγέλιον) for some reason varies dramatically among New Testament authors—a phenomenon admitted by specialists to be "by no means easy to understand" and "enigmatic."[4] Moreover, before the New Testament, none of the *euangeli-* word group had

---

[1]On November 6, 2007. Here is an index of proliferating publication. When I prepared this essay as a guest lecture in late 2001, there were only 9,239 relevant entries.

[2]Cf. W. Marxsen, *Mark the Evangelist: Studies on the Redaction History of the Gospel* (Nashville: Abingdon, 1969), 149–50.

[3]E.g., Justin, *Apol.* 66.3, and Marcion, who may have been the innovator with his εὐαγγέλιον-and-ἀπόστολος proposal for a Christian canon, as reported in Origen, *Comm. Jo.* 5.7.1; Epiphanius, *Pan.* 2.123, 182. Marcion, incidentally, fully recognized the proprietary nature of Paul's εὐαγγέλιον language.

[4]H. Koester, *Ancient Christian Gospels: Their History and Development* (Philadelphia: Trinity Press International, 1990), 10.

significant currency. This is most glaringly obvious in the case of the Christian favorite: the neuter nominal form τὸ εὐαγγέλιον. In spite of all these learned complications, however, specialists go on to debate the "gospel genre," discussing whether gospels are unique faith-texts or like ancient biography or perhaps aretalogy; which texts should be recognized as "gospels"—what the limits of form may be;[5] and where the term originated. Was it borrowed from the Septuagint (adapting the verb in Isa 52:7), from Augustan propaganda, or where?[6]

Notwithstanding these refinements and debates, it seems that scholars generally, like the untutored population, regard the meaning and function of τὸ εὐαγγέλιον within early Christianity as more or less obvious. It means "good news," and it is translated that way in modern editions that seek an alternative to "gospel":[7] it was the *shared* early Christian proclamation about Jesus. Scholars say this even though we fully recognize the wide diversity of perspective, language, and viewpoint among the earliest followers of Jesus. The term εὐαγγέλιον, however, is not considered part of those early debates; it is what early Jesus- or Christ-followers of all varieties held in common. They may have disagreed about the *nature of* the good news, but surely no follower of Jesus objected in principle to the notion that Jesus brought, or his death and resurrection resulted in, "good news."

The point is obvious enough that I may cite just three prominent examples. Gerhard Friederich, in his famous *TDNT* article on εὐαγγέλιον, insists that the word was the common property of almost all early Christians, possibly even used by Jesus himself, and that the curious differences in usage "have been frequently noted but never explained."[8] Willi Marxsen, who devoted a programmatic chapter of his oft-cited monograph on Mark to *Euangelion,* proposed that although Paul may have introduced the term into Christian discourse, "by 'gospel' the primitive community understands the preaching of salvation as carried on in the community"—a view that Paul merely shared.[9] Harvard emeritus Helmut Koester, among the most authoritative scholars to have worked on εὐαγγέλιον in earliest Christianity, is also among the most emphatic on this point: Paul's εὐαγγέλιον was "the common gospel of the entire enterprise of the Christian mission."[10]

In this brief exploratory study I wish to reassess the evidence and propose a different hypothesis to explain the refractory evidence. Namely, in the first Christian generation (roughly 30–65 C.E.) it was indeed Paul who came up with the term εὐαγγέλιον. Wherever he got it from—and that seems impossible to determine—

[5]E.g., E. Pagels, *The Gnostic Gospels* (New York: Random House, 1979); R. Cameron, *The Other Gospels: Non-canonical Gospel Texts* (Philadelphia: Westminster, 1982); H. Koester, *Ancient;* B. L. Mack, *The Lost Gospel: The Book of Q and Christian Origins* (San Francisco: Harper San Francisco, 1993); R. J. Miller, *The Complete Gospels* (San Francisco: Polebridge, 1994).

[6]Cf. Koester, *Ancient,* 3–4; R. A. Burridge, *What are the Gospels? A Comparison with Graeco-Roman Biography* (Grand Rapids: Eerdmans, 2004).

[7]In texts as diverse as the NRSV, the *New Living Translation,* and the *Complete Gospels.*

[8]Friedrich, "εὐαγγέλιον." *TDNT* 2:727; cf. 734.

[9]Marxsen, *Mark,* 148–49.

[10]Koester, *Ancient,* 6.

he understood it as a proprietary and quasi-technical term of *his peculiar mission, outlook, and patronage circles.* Other followers of Jesus (or Christ) in the first generation also understood that this odd-sounding form was a *Stichwort* of Paul's. It was not at all shared vocabulary. In the second generation (ca. 65–100 C.E.), accordingly, it was only the first author to compose a narrative of Jesus' life, whom tradition calls "Mark" and who wrote in the spirit of Paul, who embraced τὸ εὐαγγέλιον in his work. Writers who borrowed heavily from Mark's material but were removed from its Pauline outlook did everything possible to remove this εὐαγγέλιον language or neutralize it by reconfiguration. Again, τὸ εὐαγγέλιον was not something shared by followers of Jesus in the first two generations. It would only come to be viewed this way from the third generation (from about 100 C.E.), in that movement toward homogeneity that we sometimes call "early catholicism."

It is simply not possible, in an essay attempting such a broad sketch, to interact much with the vast published scholarship on each of the texts surveyed here (indeed, on every particle of the New Testament). It would be counterproductive even to attempt it. I offer what follows as a different look at the primary evidence, fully aware that it risks dismissal from specialists for its bypassing of intense and long-standing debates, but nevertheless in the hope that it might add a slightly new perspective on a complex of issues.

The Problem of τὸ εὐαγγέλιον

First, let me try to sketch the contours of the problem. The current database of the *Thesaurus Linguae Graecae*[11] shows nearly 22,200 occurrences of *euangeli-* forms. But their distribution pattern is remarkable: the overwhelming majority (nearly 22,000) appear in Christian writings (including papyri) *after* the New Testament. For a daily user of the TLG, with its comprehensive coverage of classical and Hellenistic Greek texts, such a distribution is impressive. This is not to suggest that the word group was unknown before the Christians; it was simply not much used in normal Greek. The singular neuter εὐαγγέλιον, which is the main focus of our investigation, although it alone is attested 7,367 times in the TLG corpus, hardly appears before the Christians. Homer's *Odyssey* has two occurrences (14.152, 166), one in direct response to the other: in both cases the anarthrous form must mean in context, "*reward* [or gift] *for* a good piece of news"—that Odysseus is returning from Troy. The next non-Christian users come at the end of the New Testament's composition period: Josephus (*War* 2.420), who uses anarthrous εὐαγγέλιον ironically, of terrible news for Judea that is welcomed by a reprehensible governor as "a good report," and the plural in connection with Vespasian's acclamation (4.618, 656); and Plutarch, who has singular εὐαγγέλιον four times (*Ages.* 33.4; *Demetr.* 17.6; *Mor.* [*Glor. Ath.*] 347d twice). He supplies the article only once (in the second example), becoming the first attested non-Christian writer to do so. He uses the plural a dozen times. Though more common than

[11] The TLG project (http://www.tlg.uci.edu/) is based at the University of California, Irvine, and is directed by Prof. Maria Pantelia.

the singular, the plural εὐαγγέλια is also rare enough in pre-Christian literature that the examples may be listed. Aristophanes (*Eq.* 647, 656; *Plut.* 765), Isocrates (*Areop.* 10), Xenophon (*Hell.* 1.6.37; 4.3.14), Aeschines (*Ctes.* 60), Menander (*Perik.* 993), Diodorus Siculus (15.74.2), and the LXX (2 Sam 4:10)[12] have one, two, or three occurrences each—a pittance compared to the flood that is coming with the New Testament. Major and prolific authors such as Plato, Aristotle, Herodotus, Thucydides, and Polybius do not use any form of this word group. The LXX brings new popularity to the *verb* εὐαγγελίζομαι as well as the new feminine form εὐαγγελία (2 Sam 18:20, 22, 25, 27; 2 Kgs 7:9, for בשורה); together they account for twenty-seven of the LXX's twenty-eight cases of the word group; the anarthrous plural of εὐαγγέλιον appears once (2 Sam 4:10). But none of this helps much to explain the new Christian usage of τὸ εὐαγγέλιον.

In sum, before and around the rise of Christianity, the anarthrous plural εὐαγγέλια, though uncommon, was by far the more usual form of the noun. The singular εὐαγγέλιον was extremely rare, and outside of Christian circles was not found with the article in literature before Plutarch (who has it once). The cognate verb was favored by LXX translators, who also seem to have introduced the feminine noun.

This background, which ought to make us cautious about arguing for any external model, throws Christian usage into sharp relief. The small New Testament library includes seventy-six occurrences of the neuter singular. Of these, nearly all (i.e., seventy-two) include the definite article (τὸ εὐαγγέλιον). Something unusual is happening here, which calls for an explanation. Three of the four anarthrous instances are in Paul's letters, where the context requires its absence;[13] the fourth is in Rev 14:6. At about the time of the latest New Testament writings or shortly thereafter, Ignatius of Antioch uses the word group twenty-four times in his very limited group of letters, of which fully twenty-one also have the articular neuter τὸ εὐαγγέλιον. After Ignatius, Christian authors of the second century continue to use the word group eagerly. Among the Greek fathers, Origen, Eusebius, Cyril, Theodoret, John Chrysostom, and the Gregorys use the word group hundreds of times *each.* The pattern is clear: this language is markedly favored by early Christians from the second century, though hardly used by anyone else.

But the real peculiarities come *within* the New Testament collection, and this is the focus of the present chapter. The letters of Paul, both genuine and disputed, although they occupy significantly less than a quarter of the New Testament by word tally,[14] account for sixty of the seventy-six occurrences of the neuter singular. After Paul's letters, Mark is the heaviest user of it, with seven

[12] Koester (*Ancient,* 2 n. 3) counts 2 Sam (LXX 2 Kgs) 18:22, 25 as instances of εὐαγγέλιον (there plural), but he must be using a text other than Rahlfs, where they are printed as the feminine singular, just as 18:20, 27.

[13] At 2 Cor 11:4 and Gal 1:6 Paul sarcastically refers to "a different Announcement" as he attempts to combat defection. At Rom 1:1 he introduces this terminology to a new group.

[14] The New Testament has very roughly 138,000 words (depending upon variants and editions), the letters attributed to Paul (not including Hebrews) about 32,445.

occurrences: so together, Paul (with pseudo-Paul) and Mark account for sixty-seven of seventy-seven occurrences. Matthew, though it takes over more than 90 percent of Mark's text and adds about 50 percent, has only four occurrences of this noun; John has no trace of the word group in any form; and the sayings gospel Q (like *Gos. Thom.*) lacks the noun entirely. Curiously, although Luke omits the noun altogether and even Acts has it only twice, the *Doppelwerk* accounts for fully *half* of the fifty-two occurrences of the verb εὐαγγελίζω; Hebrews also omits the noun, though it has the verb twice.

In short, then, a triple movement needs explaining: first, why Paul and Mark seized upon the hitherto unused form τὸ εὐαγγέλιον so programmatically and consistently; second, why second-generation texts apart from Mark drew back and mainly dropped the term; and finally, why from the third generation onward it became extremely popular, indeed a fundamental component of Christian discourse across the board.

In order to get at the meaning and function of τὸ εὐαγγέλιον in the earliest strata of Christian history, it may help to re-alienate it by translating it as something other than the too-familiar "gospel," *a fortiori* by "good news." To begin with, the prefix εὐ did not necessarily mean that the news in question was good:[15] it might either have been semantically silent, as often with the cognate forms,[16] or it might have had to do with the faithfulness or truthfulness of the one reporting. Second, such translations overlook the unusual form of the construction. For analytical purposes we could simply call τὸ εὐαγγέλιον "X," but for aesthetic reasons let us call it something like *The Message, The [Good] Report,* or *The Announcement.* At the outset, that is, we need to recognize the oddity of the form, which tends to be obscured when we group all the forms (verb, singular and plural noun) together and say that they all have to do with "good news." Perhaps an analogy will help. We all know the English word "message" and we send *messages* constantly; there is nothing odd about the word. But if I were to ask a colleague what she was doing on the weekend, and she began to talk about *The Message,* how she aimed to study the *The Message* intently and help to disseminate it, I would quickly realize that she had in mind something very specific, unusual, and possibly a little weird. It is this oddity that Paul's first audiences heard when he began to use the unprecedented τὸ εὐαγγέλιον as something like a technical term. It was not "(good) news" (εὐαγγέλια) in general terms, but something very specific: The Announcement.

The Announcement in the First Generation (ca. 30–65 C.E.)

We begin with the earliest Christian text in existence today, 1 Thessalonians. When he writes this letter, Paul has recently begun his mission through mainland Greece. He has been traveling the Via Egnatia through Philippi with The Announcement, and has run into some sort of trouble; he then goes to Thessalonica,

[15] Paul's εὐαγγέλιον was evidently bad news for many or most: unbelievers (1 Thess 1:10) as well as his Christian opponents.

[16] See Koester, *Ancient,* 2 and n. 3.

where he faces further opposition, then south to Athens and Corinth, all the time propounding The Announcement (2:1–2). This very brief letter is in two parts. First, Paul has sent his associate Timothy back up to Macedonia to find out how these new believers, or trusters in The Announcement, are faring (3:1–6). Timothy has returned to him with a good report, and Paul writes to express his gratitude, to consolidate that good will (1 Thess 1:1–3:13 is dominated by thanksgiving and reminiscence). But Timothy has also apparently brought back a letter from the Thessalonians with at least three questions for Paul to address. The second part of 1 Thessalonians (from 4:1 or 4:9) comprises Paul's response to those questions in order, signified by the περὶ δέ ("Now concerning") formula at 4:9, 13; 5:1,[17] completed by final exhortations (5:12–28).

Because it comes so early in Paul's career and is unencumbered by the serious tensions among Jesus' followers that will come to the surface in later letters, 1 Thessalonians is crucial for understanding the nature of Paul's Announcement. Its mere four printed pages include six instances of τὸ εὐαγγέλιον. Notice both the content of The Announcement and Paul's proprietary language about it. At the very first occurrence of the term, Paul makes it proprietary (1 Thess 1:5): "*Our Announcement* came to you not in word only, but also in power and in the Holy Spirit and with full conviction." Conveniently for us, Paul goes on to reprise for his audience what it was that he announced to them when he had visited them (1:9–10): turn to serve the living God, trust in him, and wait for his son (Christ) from heaven, who will rescue or evacuate his followers from the impending divine wrath. While awaiting this salvation, Paul has emphasized that believers are to live pure, blameless lives (4:1–8) so that they will be ready "at the coming of our Lord Jesus Christ" (5:23–24). Paul had clearly left the impression that the saving climax would come very soon, and he now continues in this vein as he writes that "*we who are alive,* who remain, will be caught up in the clouds together with them [those who have meanwhile died "in Christ"] to meet the Lord in the air" (1 Thess 4:17). Paul expects the imminent end of the age, and this apocalyptically charged message is evidently the principal content of The Announcement.

The rest of the letter, including Paul's answers to the Thessalonians' questions, shows how simple and vivid this Announcement was. At least two of their three questions have to do with the length of time before the cataclysm arrives (at 5:1, they must have asked "*When* will at happen"; at 4:13, they have asked what happens to one who dies in the interim, before the cataclysm). Most impressive in this foundational letter is simply the frequency with which Paul reverts to The Announcement as his constant reference point; it is what he and Timothy are all about.

First Thessalonians appears to have been written from Achaia (3:1). The next time we meet Paul, a good deal of water has already passed under the bridge: he has established a group of followers in Corinth, left that city, written a letter to

[17] The point is not provable, but it is highly probable given the close parallel to the structure of 1 Corinthians, where Paul plainly states that he is replying to Corinthians' questions in series (1 Cor 7:1), and he uses just this formula (7:25; 8:1; 12:1; 15:1; 16:1, 12), and given the abrupt transitions to new topics in both texts.

them after his departure, now lost (cf. 1 Cor 5:9), and, having moved eastward to Ephesus in Asia, received two different pieces of information from the Corinthian believers (1 Cor 16:8, 17). One was an oral report from an ally of his in the group, a woman of some means named Chloe (1:11): she has sent slaves to him with the news that his followers have broken into factions, some of them now following other Christian teachers, notably one Apollos from Alexandria.[18] Paul seems to respond to that oral report concerning internal strife in the first six chapters. But he has also received a letter from the Corinthians with a list of questions (1 Cor 7:1, 25, etc.; 16:17). This time, however, the questions are not as simple as those from the Thessalonians. They are not naïve either, but clearly informed by another, alternative outlook on Christian issues, an outlook that seems to be associated with Apollos's group. So Paul responds to these rather aggressive questions. Remarkably, already at this relatively early point, he is in serious danger of losing much of his new following in Corinth to other Christ-teachers and potential patrons. The problem with these others, in Paul's characterization, is that they have too much of an investment in sophistry: rhetoric and wisdom, the values of the world (1:19–2:13). The main issue seems to be that they have come to think in terms of an internal spiritual transformation, and indeed resurrection, rather than being disposed to wait for a physical end of the age and resurrection of the dead (4:8–13; 15:12–51).

But there is a crucial social dimension to all this. In 1:17 Paul contrasts himself with the interloping teacher(s) by asserting that *he* alone was dispatched to declare The Announcement. In 4:15–17 we see this social dimension very plainly: in patronal language, Paul treats his converts as his children: "I became your father in Christ Jesus through The Announcement!" he will send his most faithful child Timothy to remind them of "my ways in Christ Jesus." These are not merely ideological issues; they are, perhaps above all, questions of authority and leadership: Paul is their *father* and must be properly respected. I pass over chapter 9 with little comment, though in a short space there he mentions The Announcement half a dozen times (9:21–23): he will play the part of a Judean or a Gentile, he says, whatever it takes to win people over to The Announcement.

First Corinthians 15:1–2 is crucial for our understanding of the place of Paul's Announcement in early Christianity. He invokes in typically proprietary terms "The Announcement that *I announced to you*" (τὸ εὐαγγέλιον ὃ εὐηγγελισάμην), using as often the cognate verb to reinforce the uniqueness of the message (other verbs are not entirely suitable).[19] As we have seen, many

[18] Apollos features much more prominently in 1 Corinthians than any other leader except Paul. Some are following him (1:12; 3:4) and Paul applies his elaborate contrasts between leaders and between worldly wisdom and "the cross" that he preaches to himself and Apollos. Paul established the group and yet Apollos has since come in (4:1–7; cf. 3:6–15). The Corinthians have even asked whether Apollos might return to them soon (16:12), whereas Paul must threaten them with a return visit (4:14–21—precisely in the context of rival leadership). Paul even makes a clever pun on Apollos's name by connecting it with the wisdom of the world that God "will destroy" (1:19).

[19] Also 1 Cor 9:14–16; 2 Cor 11:7; Gal 1:8, 11; Rom 1:15–16.

of his correspondents in Corinth have apparently begun to reinterpret Christ's resurrection—and therefore also salvation through Christ—in internal, spiritual, or perhaps philosophical, terms. In this way of thinking, one need not expect the heavenly apocalypse that Paul had portrayed. It is a fundamental issue, and in restating his case for imminent future salvation Paul will recall the foundation of his Announcement, which he received and passed on: Jesus died, was buried, and rose on the third day, from where he will soon return (15:3–11, 51–58). He lists several appearances of the risen Christ in support of a visible and programmatic resurrection, culminating with the appearance of Christ to Paul (15:5–8).

Now, Koester is in agreement with the preponderance of New Testament scholarship in insisting that this passage puts it beyond doubt that Paul understood τὸ εὐαγγέλιον as something he shared with other Christians, especially those in Jerusalem.[20] This is mainly because of the verbs used. At 1 Cor 15:2 Paul says that the Corinthians received (παραλαμβάνω) this from him previously, and at 15:3 he repeats that "I passed on to you (παρέδωκα) what I received (παρέλαβον)." What follows is considered by most scholars as a received tradition *from earlier followers of Christ.* Scholars point out that this language of reception and transmission, paralleled at 11:23, is standard in the Greek philosophical schools and in rabbinic literature (e.g., קיבל and מסר) for depicting "the chain of tradition."[21] Therefore, Paul plants himself in a line of tradition originating with the Jerusalem apostles, and his "gospel" also comes from them.

Although that inference seems reasonable, I would point out that it is not the only or perhaps the most likely option. At 1 Cor 11:23 Paul says explicitly that he received the Lord's Supper tradition "from the Lord." Similarly clear is Gal 1:6–12, where Paul's εὐαγγέλιον is again under fire from other teachers. Announcement-language is extremely dense in Gal 1:6–9: "I am amazed that your are so quickly turning from the one who called you in grace, to a different Announcement, which is not similar! But some are disturbing you and wanting to pervert The Announcement *of Christ.*" In that contested environment, Paul will use exactly the same παραλαμβάνω terminology to describe The Announcement that he received, which the Galatians then also shared from him: "I want you to know, brothers, about The Announcement that *was announced* by me, that it is *not human.* For I did not receive it from a human; nor was I taught it, but [it came] through a disclosure of Jesus Christ" (Gal 1:11–12). Precisely in response to the question, "*From whom* did he receive the content of The Announcement?" then, Paul insists that he did not get it from another human being. In the following sentences he will support this claim by noting that his own mission was well underway before he made his first brief visit to Jerusalem (1:15–24).

---

[20]Koester, *Ancient,* 6.

[21]I cite only three other scholars from very different perspectives to illustrate the strength of agreement on this point: G. Bornkamm, *Paul* (trans. D. M. Stalker; New York: Harper & Row, 1971), 113; L. Gaston, *Paul and the Torah* (Vancouver: University of British Columbia Press, 1987), 66–67; B. F. Meyer, *Christus Faber: the Master-Builder and the House of God* (Allison Park: Pickwick, 1992), 118, 140.

Back to 1 Cor 15:1–5, then: when Paul says that he handed on The Announcement as he received it, it seems most likely that he received it from Christ ("the Lord"), as he insists at 1 Cor 11:23 and in Galatians, and not from Jerusalem. It may be that scholars pass by this possibility because of the fairly detailed content of what Paul cites about the appearances of Jesus after his resurrection (15:3–5), and they are squeamish about supposing that Paul had such substantive discussions with the risen Christ. But there is a great deal that he claims to have learned from "the Lord" directly (e.g., 1 Thess 4:13–18; 1 Cor 15:51–58; 2 Cor 12:2–9). Whether such exchanges are historically plausible is not at issue here. Our goal is only to understand Paul's language and his perspective in using *euangelion*-terminology. Since he firmly insists that he received the εὐαγγέλιον from Christ and not from any human, that seems the best way to understand all of his verbally similar remarks on the subject.

Paul's brief letter to the assembly at Philippi also has a remarkably large number of εὐαγγέλιον-references (nine). The only point I wish to make here again concerns his proprietary tone in these passages. The Announcement evidently *began* with Paul and his mission; he thanks the Philippians for their "partnership in The Announcement from the first day until now" (Phil 1:5), and tellingly describes the outset of his own early travels as "the beginning of The Announcement, when I left Macedonia . . ." (Phil 4:15). Since he is now in prison, whether The Announcement will continue to flourish or not is an open question, all tied up with his personal fate (1:19–26): he is in prison for the defense of The Announcement (1:7), and is confident that his imprisonment will serve to advance it, because his guards have now heard of it and most of his associates have been strengthened through his predicament (1:12–14). Once again, Timothy is his most trusted associate, who his son in The Announcement (2.22), and Euodia and Syntyche have also striven together with him in The Announcement (4:2–3).

The same tone comes through in Paul's letter to Philemon: he is in custody because in the service of The Announcement (Phlm 13).

At about this time in Paul's career, he is beginning to face the issue that will continue to color his reputation, for good or ill, for centuries afterward: his conflict with Christ-teachers who understand allegiance to Jesus as something internal to Judean culture, such that if Gentiles wish to follow Jesus they need also to identify with Judean law and community, assuming the yoke of Torah to the extent of male circumcision (Phil 3:2–4; Gal 4:21; 5:2). This was a perfectly understandable consequence of both the Judean context of Jesus and his first students and general social conditions: Gentiles who embraced Paul's Announcement faced the social-political predicament, before the promised evacuation, of not having a place in the world,[22] and the obvious place to turn was Jesus' own long-established Judean culture, which was in any case receiving considerable interest from people of other nations.[23]

---

[22] See ch. 5 in the present volume.

[23] The primary evidence for such interest is extensive. I mention only passages as distinctive as Josephus, *War* 2.559; *Ant.* 20.17–96; *Ag. Ap.* 2.282–86, and Tacitus, *Hist.* 5.4. For

Paul's Announcement, however, was emphatically removed from Judean law, observance, or identity, and he quite pointedly renounced his own Judean past—counting it as "manure," he says—in order to follow Christ (Phil 3:4–9). So a conflict was inevitable, especially since his "super-apostle" opponents apparently had credentials that impressed Paul's wavering followers (Gal 1:6–9; 2 Cor 11:5–15): they seem to have included, if at some remove, Jesus' brother James and perhaps other brothers (Gal 2:12; 6:12–13; cf. Acts 21:17–22), as well as some of Jesus' original students, notably Peter (Gal 2:11–14). It is not clear from early evidence for his Announcement whether Paul had shown much interest in mentioning Judeans at all, though his earliest letter does include some brief, hostile remarks about them as killers of Christ (1 Thess 2:14–16). But certainly when the other leaders and their emissaries began to infiltrate his assemblies with their alternative vision of following Christ, the conflict exploded: it appears in Phil 3 and apparently 2 Cor 11, dominates Galatians, and provides the background for Romans. But for our present purposes, the main issue is how Paul speaks of τὸ εὐαγγέλιον also in these contexts.

Most scholars think that 2 Corinthians is a composite letter, compiled backwards in the New Testament, so that the later chapters were part of an earlier letter. I share this view, and so would consider first 2 Cor 10–11. Here Paul's proprietary attitude is again clear, as he castigates his followers for having been misled by other impressive teachers. But he was the first to travel all the way to them, he declares, "with The Announcement of Christ" (10:14). He feels a "divine jealousy" (11:2). He announced The Announcement of God to them without cost. *He* alone is the one who carries The Announcement. In 11:4–7 he makes the point sarcastically by accusing his erstwhile followers of having readily accepted another Jesus, another spirit, or another Announcement—*as if* there were others.

This same expression of an offended patron's deep hurt at the faithlessness of those in his care is equally vivid from the opening lines of Galatians, as we have seen. He thoroughly denounces his impressive opponents, even claiming with deliberate absurdity: "Even if we, or a messenger from heaven, should announce to you an announcement contrary to what we announced to you, let him be cursed!" (Gal 1:8). His personal investment as the only authentic bearer of The Announcement is perfectly clear, as we see again in 1:11: "The Announcement, which was brought by me." We have already observed Paul's claim of utter detachment from other mortals as he explains the source of his Announcement—from Christ alone. In 2:5 he also claims that, when he finally did visit the Jerusalem apostles after 14 or 17 years, he did not yield to pressure to change The Announcement. Again, it is proprietary and special to him.

Finally, in this section, we turn to Paul's letter to the Romans. This is where the thesis of this study becomes most clearly demonstrable, for Romans is the only one of Paul's undisputed letters written to a Christian community that he

different scholarly perspectives, see L. H. Feldman, *Jew and Gentile,* 177–446; M. Goodman, *Mission and Conversion: Proselytizing in the Religious History of the Roman Empire* (Oxford: Oxford University Press, 1994).

did not establish. (In chapter 10 I argue that the Christian community of Rome was Judean in character, values, and sympathies, though that argument is not necessary for this one.) Correspondingly, his use of τὸ εὐαγγέλιον is quite striking in this letter. We see throughout the assumption shared by him and readers in the world capital, although they too are followers of Christ, that The Announcement is something uniquely connected with Paul's mission. Thus in the opening sentence (1:1) he introduces himself, uniquely in his letters: "called as 'apostle set apart for an Announcement' of [or from] God." The quotation marks are justified by (a) the rare absence of the definite article, which will however appear in the occurrences soon to follow (i.e., it is hard to imagine him dropping the article for one of his own audiences, familiar with The Announcement), and (b) the novelty of the audience for Romans. Rather than referring to The Announcement as something known, he prefers to introduce it carefully. Evidently, this label is something that distinguishes him, and for which he is known; but he must now lay it out on his own terms. Again in 1:9 Paul identifies his service to Christ with The Announcement.

Most interestingly, in 1:13–16 he says to these followers of Christ in Rome that he would like to reap some harvest among them, which is to say that he would like bring The Announcement (εὐαγγελίσασθαι) to them *because*—note causal conjunction γάρ—he is not ashamed of τὸ εὐαγγέλιον.

Whoever said that Paul should be ashamed of The Announcement? This is not a prospect he raised at all in his confident letters to his own groups. To the extent that this whole long letter of Romans is indeed a defense of The Announcement, it shows over and over again that The Announcement was something peculiar to Paul and his assemblies. Paul is defending The Announcement against Judean-Christian accusations that it not only displaces but also implicitly maligns the Judeans, Moses, and Torah. He is at pains to show that he is fully cognizant of the claims of scripture (which he quotes an unparalleled sixty times in this letter) and that The Announcement does not disdain these things. It does not nullify God's promise to Israel or to Abraham; it does not make Torah observance a sin (Rom 2:25; 3:1; 4:1; 7:1, 7; 9:3; 11:1, 26). His opening sentence claims that The Announcement was promised long ago by the prophets (1:1–2).

But the crucial point for present purposes is that Paul considers τὸ εὐαγγέλιον to be his own responsibility. On the one hand, he declares it to be *his* in no uncertain terms. Note especially 2:16, referring to his apocalyptic scenario: "on the day when God judges the secrets of human beings, according to *my Announcement,* through Jesus Christ." At the closing of the letter (16:25)—which may belong after 14:23 according to some manuscripts—he similarly commends his readers to "the one who is able to strengthen you, *according to my Announcement* and the proclamation of Jesus Christ, according to the disclosure of the mystery kept secret for long times."

Consider also Rom 15:15–20. Just as in Galatians, The Announcement is something that Paul alone has been charged with disseminating, by Christ, among his Gentile "assemblies" (another distinctive term of his mission). He has spoken boldly because of his calling, in the service of The Announcement of (or from)

God. And so, by his efforts, The Announcement of Christ has been fulfilled from Jerusalem to Illyricum. In 15:20, note, he does not say that he brings The Announcement only where other people have not done so; rather, he brings The Announcement where *Christ has not been named.* There is a big difference, and it is the same distinction we saw in the letter opening, where he hoped to bring The Announcement to this group of Christ's followers (1:5). What the other people declare is not The Announcement, but only another way of speaking about Christ.

This is the other side of the coin of Paul's proprietary claim to The Announcement, and his language in Romans on the subject is truly remarkable. Although *euangeli-* words appear twelve times in Romans, a work addressed to followers of Christ, the word-group never once refers to *what the Romans already believe* or what they have been taught by other Christian leaders. It is not something shared between Paul and these readers. In all his other letters, as we have seen, Paul cites The Announcement without hesitation as the common bond between himself and his followers: they have worked together in it with him, they are established in it, and will be saved by it; he sends Timothy off to remind them of it; and he appeals to it as the basis of their relationship. In Romans, however, that bond through The Announcement simply does not exist; it is only something he hopes to create *when* he comes to them in the future and brings his Announcement.

It is almost humorous, therefore, to see how uncomfortable Paul is when he refers to what it is that the Roman Christians already believe. At Rom 6:17 he gives thanks that they, once slaves to sin, "have become obedient from the heart to the sort of teaching you were given" (εἰς ὃν παρεδόθητε τύπον διδαχῆς)—not to The Announcement. What a circumlocution! Paul is unable to say simply that they became obedient to The Announcement, as he would say of his own followers. Similarly at 16:17 he appeals to them to watch out for schismatics and scandals, in opposition to—not The Announcement, but—"the teaching that you learned." Romans makes it clear that τὸ εὐαγγέλιον is something peculiar to Paul, the thing for which he was designated or set apart.

If this seems obvious from the evidence, why is such a view not common in scholarship? There are at least two reasons. First, most scholars continue to see Romans as something like the flagship of Paul's corpus, or perhaps as his most mature statement, and not as something written for a very unusual audience in unique circumstances; they tend therefore to take the sharp edges off Paul's language by harmonizing Romans with his other letters. For Joseph Fitzmyer, "my gospel" means only "his personal way of announcing the good news"—not The Announcement itself.[24] Following time-honored practice in New Testament scholarship, others simply excise inconvenient phrases such as "my Announcement" as interpolations.[25] But there is no manuscript support for supposing an interpola-

[24]E.g., J. A. Fitzmyer *Romans: A New Translation with Introduction and Commentary* (AB 33; New York: Doubleday, 1993), 754; cf. 231–32, 714–15, 449, 746 on some of the other passages discussed. This will suffice for illustrative purposes because Fitzmyer also discusses previous scholarship on each verse.

[25]E.g., Koester, *Ancient,* 4–5 n. 4.

tion at 2:16, and for 16:25 it would be a long shot. At any rate, such measures do not solve the problem since the proprietary nature of The Announcement is clear throughout this letter, on the grounds sketched above.

At this point, we can summarize the main ingredients of Paul's Announcement. Positively, Paul understands Jesus in apocalyptic terms. Jesus died and rose to save humanity in some way, and this salvation will be completed in very concrete terms with Jesus' imminent return from heaven to evacuate his followers. Negatively, Paul is *against* any linkage between allegiance to Christ and Judaism, Torah observance, or Judean culture; he also rejects any special claim to authority by Jesus' family, brothers, or students. Finally, he repudiates any philosophical notion of Jesus' significance, any idea that Jesus was a wise teacher whose insights into life are what will save his followers. This brings us to the second generation.

The Announcement in the Second Generation (ca. 65–100 C.E.)

Although we do not know when the deutero-Pauline letters were composed, or even that they should be called deutero-Pauline (and not authentically Paul's), I side with the weight of critical opinion in finding Ephesians (perhaps with Colossians), on the one hand, and the Pastoral Epistles, on the other, as incompatible with the tone and content of Paul's genuine letters. On this view, Colossians and Ephesians represent a later effort to secure Paul's authority for an understanding of Christian life much like the one he vigorously opposed in 1 Cor 4:8–11 (a sort of internal, even proto-gnostic "realized eschatology"); the Pastorals, conversely, which show many parallels to Acts,[26] seek his support for later developments in church leadership and credal clarity. It is possible that Paul changed his views sufficiently over time that he himself could write Colossians (less likely Ephesians, which seems to borrow from it); but if he changed in that direction it is that much harder to imagine how he could have written the Pastorals. Our present interest in these texts must be severely restricted, however: only to observe that both sides apparently recognized the proprietary nature of Paul's Announcement and sought to exploit it in claiming Paul's authority. On the one hand, Colossians has an associate of Paul's (Epaphras) bringing The Announcement to this readership (1:5–7), and Paul claiming that "I, Paul, became [The Announcement's] minister" (1:23). Even more strikingly in the Pastorals, Paul speaks of "The Announcement of the glory of the blessed God, *with which I was entrusted*" (ὃ ἐπιστεύθην ἐγώ; 1 Tim 1:11). This clear and striking language continues at 2 Tim 1:10–11, where the author (albeit in language that does not sound Pauline) says that Christ "illuminated life and immortality through The Announcement, *for which I was placed as herald, apostle, and teacher.*" The same author admonishes "Timothy" to remember Christ "according to The Announcement of mine" (κατὰ τὸ εὐαγγέλιόν μου; 2 Tim 2:8). The language seems unmistakable: Paul and many others understood The Announcement to be his.

[26] S. G. Wilson, *Luke and the Pastoral Epistles* (London: SPCK, 1979).

The earliest narrative account of Jesus' life known to us is the one traditionally called Mark. But the title that the (anonymous) author himself gave the work appears in our text as Mark 1:1. We can recognize it as a title because it lacks a verb. And that title is fascinating: "The Origin of The Announcement of Jesus Christ." The foregoing discussion of serious contention over The Announcement in the first generation suggests that such a title is highly significant. As Martin Kähler famously observed in his late nineteenth-century attack on scholarly preoccupation with the historical Jesus,[27] Mark is by no means a proportionate account of Jesus' life. By about the half-way point (8:31–33) Jesus is vividly predicting his imminent and violent death, to be followed by resurrection, and the author increases anticipation by repeating the prediction in short order (9:31–32; 10:33–34). By chapter 11 of 16, Jesus has begun his final week in Jerusalem. And the first half of the book, rather than attempting a sequential account of Jesus' life, is arranged thematically: the author gives a few examples of Jesus' conflict stories (1:21–3:6, 20–34; chs. 11–12), his teaching in parables (4:1–34; ch. 13), and his miracles and cures (chs. 5–9). It seems that this thematic streamlining and lack of proportion are precisely what the author means to indicate by his title. Understanding the saving death, resurrection, and imminent return of Jesus *as* The Announcement, he writes to provide the immediate back-story to these pivotal events.

In a nutshell, Mark's explanation is that, shortly after his immersion by John, Jesus found himself in implacable and lethal conflict with the Judean leaders: hence the importance of the conflict stories in chapters 2 and 3, which end in 3:6 with those leaders already plotting to kill Jesus. Later in chapter 3 (3:20–22, 31–34), after that plot has been hatched, Jesus attributes to both the Judeans and his own family members—and the latter is extraordinary—the unforgivable sin of rejecting him. In return he pointedly rejects his family, saying that his true family are those who do his will; his real family, for their part, think that he is crazy (3:21). A little later the narrator takes the trouble to name the family members involved, including James and Jude (prominent in the first generation), and Jesus declares that prophets have no honor among their own (6:1–6). In this narrative Jesus also rejects Judean law, according to the narrator (adding his comment to a much less clear statement from Jesus), by instantly nullifying the dietary laws (7:19).

Moreover, Jesus' original students, later to be the Jerusalem apostles, are consistently disparaged in this story. They repeatedly fail to understand him or to recognize his saving mission, even though he patiently offers them repeated opportunities. Thus, Mark has Jesus first miraculously feed 5,000 men, but his students do not understand from this anything about his identity (ch. 6). Their hearts are hardened. Two chapters later he does almost the same thing again, feeding 4,000 men, and yet Mark's Jesus discovers that they are still hard-hearted and lacking all understanding (8:15–21; cf. 9:6, 18–29, 34; 10:32–45). Jesus will

[27] M. Kähler *The So-Called Historical Jesus and the Historic Biblical Christ* (trans. C. E. Braaten; Philadelphia: Fortress Press, 1964), 80 n. 11. Kähler applied the observation to each of the gospels, but began with Mark. Here his point is most easily confirmed.

even connect Peter very closely with Satan (8:33), and he explicitly approves a man who has nothing to do with the disciple group, but is effectively carrying out Jesus' work (9:38–41). What is astonishing is that this story never improves, but only gets worse. One of the students ends up betraying Jesus for money (14:10–11); they repeatedly fall asleep at his hour of greatest need (14:37–41); they all desert him at his arrest (14:27, 50); and Peter famously denies him at the crucial moment. The last we hear of Peter concerns his nervous breakdown after this betrayal (14:66–72). And the story ends on a desperate note: a group of women, plainly told by an angel to report Jesus' resurrection to his students, instead run away in fear and say *nothing to anyone* (16:8).

If we seek a place within early Christianity for such a text, it is easy enough to see that Mark has roughly the same positive and negative sensibilities as Paul. Positively, Mark is an apocalyptic narrative, giving story form to Paul's vision of imminent cosmic turmoil and evacuation of the faithful. This is how the kingdom of God, and thus salvation, will arrive. At 9:1 Mark's Jesus looks ahead to the end of the age: "There are some standing here who will not taste death before they see the kingdom of God come with power." The major block of Jesus' instruction in this narrative, which is famously sparing in elaborating such teaching, is the apocalyptic discourse of chapter 13. It promises the imminent end in dire terms, describing great cosmic upheaval as The Announcement is conveyed to the world, before the chosen are evacuated to heaven (13:13, 26–27). Negatively, Mark is relentlessly harsh on the very things that had posed the most serious challenges to Paul's Announcement: the Jerusalem apostles (Jesus' original students), status claims made by or for Jesus' family members, and the claims of Judean law on followers of Christ.

It is no surprise, then, that the author not only titles his work *The Origin of* The Announcement but even puts The Announcement—unqualified—in Jesus' mouth as the content of his own teaching. After his immersion (1:14–15), Jesus is said to have gone about "declaring The Announcement" and calling people to trust in it. At 8:34–35 and again 10:29 Mark's Jesus anticipates that his followers will persecution and loss "for the sake of The Announcement." At 13:10 Mark's Jesus even insists that The Announcement must be proclaimed *to all the Gentiles* before the end comes—just as Paul's letters show him setting out to do. And when the woman anoints Jesus in Bethany just before his death, Jesus remarks that her act will be remembered whenever The Announcement is proclaimed throughout the world. The author has a profound investment in The Announcement and, not coincidentally, shares Paul's outlook on following Jesus.

Just as Paul's use of τὸ εὐαγγέλιον was distinctive in his generation, so Mark's was unique in the second generation. The text we know as Matthew, although it borrows about 92 percent of Mark, taking both its basic framework and much of its content from the earlier work, manages to give an entirely different impression of what it means to follow Christ. The title of this work (1:1)—"The Book of the Genesis of Jesus, Messiah, son of David, son of Abraham"—already makes clear its different bent. It will plant Jesus firmly in the soil of biblical-Judean tradition. This is reinforced by the following genealogy (1:2–17), which traces Jesus to David and

Abraham, and then by the infancy narrative with its many evocations of Moses' birth story and explicit citations of scripture fulfilled (1:18–2:23).

The birth narrative also automatically raises the stature of Jesus' mother and family vis-à-vis Mark, and one of the few things Matthew omits outright from Mark is the paragraph about Jesus' family thinking he was crazy (Mark 3:20–21). Matthew stunningly overhauls Mark's grim portrayal of Jesus' students, unabashedly changing the endings of stories so that instead of being hard-hearted, blind, and dumb, they worship Jesus and fully recognize his identity (e.g., 14:28–33; 17:13); Matthew's Jesus even goes so far as to name Peter as the rock on which he will build his church (16:16–18). This is a major validation, over against Mark's dismal portrait of these men, and it completely recontextualizes those critical comments that Matthew retains. And of course the story ends with the comprehensive redemption of the disciples in the so-called "Great Commission" (28:16–20), where Jesus entrusts his ongoing mission to them.

As for Torah, not only does Matthew omit Mark's editorial remark about Jesus' canceling the dietary laws (Matt 15:17), but he also has Jesus insist at length (5:17–21) that he *did not come to abolish the law,* and that anyone who defaulted in even the least of the commandments or taught others to do so would be least in the kingdom. He even admires the Pharisees as teachers (not doers) and insists on the laws of tithing (23:2–3, 23). Matthew's Jesus was sent to "the lost sheep of the house of Israel" (10:6) and sees converts as coming to sit at table with the Patriarchs (18:11). *Abraham* appears six times, over against one appearance in Mark.

What becomes of The Announcement in this Judean-Christian narrative? This writer was much more apprehensive about the term than his Marcan source. Even though he followed Mark as conservatively as possible, he first removes any reference to The Announcement from his title, completely changing the framework. Next, whereas Mark had introduced Jesus right away as proclaiming The Announcement (unqualified), Matthew postpones this summary reference to 4:23, after the author has given full play to biblical citation and allusion. This author has Jesus talking instead about "The Announcement *of the kingdom*" (as also at 9:35; 24:14)—the "kingdom of heaven" being Matthew's preferred way of describing Jesus' teaching.[28] In the story of the woman's anointing Jesus for burial, Matthew borrows Mark's language, following it very closely. But whereas Mark had Jesus say that her deed would be told wherever The Announcement was proclaimed, Matthew slightly but significantly modifies it: it will be told wherever *this euangelion*—perhaps "this bit of good news"—is declared. So τὸ εὐαγγέλιον has been either dropped (only four remain of the eight in the much shorter text of Mark) or reworked so as to remove all traces of a εὐαγγέλιον that can be referred to absolutely as The Announcement.[29] This is a neat way for the author of Matthew

[28] The word "kingdom" (or "reign, sovereignty") appears some fifty-six times in Matthew, usually joined with "heaven." Mark has it only eighteen times, normally as the "kingdom of God" (of which Paul speaks a number of times), never kingdom of heaven.

[29] Whether through carelessness or charity, the author leaves just one reference to The Announcement, unqualified (Matt 26:13), but by that point the audience should understand "announcement of the kingdom."

to preserve his source while modifying it essentially for his own purposes—and distancing himself entirely from Paul's distinctive Announcement.

The Announcement in the Third Generation (ca. 100–135 C.E.)

I assign Luke-Acts to the third generation without great confidence, but because I have argued elsewhere that the author's knowledge of the later volumes of Josephus's *Antiquities,* at least perhaps as orally presented, best explains the peculiarities in their overlapping material. Since the *Antiquities* can be dated to 93/94 C.E., that would put Luke-Acts at least around 100 C.E.[30] And such a date, perhaps even a later one, would fit with the tendencies we are about to survey. Nevertheless, I do not wish to give the impression that I have an insupportable confidence about the date, which does not matter much for our purposes here.

In the two-volume Luke-Acts, we have a text that takes a different approach from both Mark and Matthew. On the one hand, in agreement with Matthew the author forcefully rejects the idea that Jesus himself had already broken with his Judean environment: Jesus is scrupulous in synagogue attendance and observance of the law, and he even likes to have dinner with the Pharisees—three times![31] But Luke-Acts also rejects Matthew's implication that Jesus issued *enduring* instructions that the Torah should be followed to the letter. The author achieves this balance by writing somewhat as a historian, and by writing two volumes. Having the luxury of one narrative for Jesus' career and another for the first Christian generation, he can show that different things were true and valid at different times, and they must be diachronically differentiated. The unique advantage of his narrative over other existing accounts, he claims, is that he will relate Jesus' deeds and sayings "in order" (1:1–4). During Jesus' lifetime, to be sure, he was a teacher who lived his life wholly within Judean culture and taught mainly about how to live, about reaching out to the poor and the marginalized. *After* his death and resurrection, however, everything changed, and the crucial requirement thereafter was to trust in his saving work. In a series of further revelations, although the apostles began their work in devoted attention to the temple and the law, Judean law was gradually sidelined as a requirement for all, and Gentiles were welcomed into salvation.

In the narrative of Luke, therefore, τὸ εὐαγγέλιον has no place, and it is utterly absent. As we have seen, the cognate verb is used remarkably often, but now in a clearly non-Pauline, non-technical, and familiar way. For example, Jesus declares that he has come *to bring good news*—not The Announcement—*to the poor* (Luke 4:18; 7:22). He does speak several times of bringing the good news (or announcement) of the kingdom of God, but for Luke this kingdom of God—during Jesus' lifetime—is also understood as largely immanent (rather than imminent), growing, and directed at the real poor above all (Luke 6:20; 10:9–11;

[30] S. Mason, *Josephus and the New Testament,* 251–95.

[31] See ch. 11 in the present volume.

11:20; 17:20–21; 18:16–17). Luke's omission of the noun τὸ εὐαγγέλιον cannot be accidental, given the range of material at the author's disposal, his use of Mark as a major source, and his knowledge of Paul's career and the first generation. It can only be the result of a deliberate program on the author's part to remain free of Mark's Pauline emphases and keep Jesus fully within the orb of Judean culture.

Like Matthew, or more so, Luke fully rehabilitates the disciples of Jesus, not only calling them *apostles* but also establishing the office of apostle as the foundation of the church, such that even when Judas shamefully defects, his "office" must be taken by another (Acts 1:20–21). Judas was aberrant, not an extreme example of the disciples' general untrustworthiness as in Mark. Peter is also fully redeemed: in the resurrection story he receives a personal appearance of the risen Jesus (Luke 24:34). In spite of his misguided denial, Peter will become the dominant leader in the first third of Acts, fearlessly leading the young church in its daring adventures.

Acts, rather than the narrative of Jesus' life in Luke, certainly has more of a Pauline flavor, in keeping with the author's plan of distinguishing the conditions of Jesus' life from what came later. Nevertheless, it does not concede to Paul the unique status that he claimed for himself; it does not even allow him the title of apostle—in the proper sense[32]—which Paul himself had consistently featured in his letters. Rather, Paul and his Announcement are entirely assimilated to the harmonious early Christian project, initiated by Peter and the Twelve. Here we have indeed the beginnings of "early catholicism," as many scholars have observed. Paul is domesticated and harmonized with the program.

In the *book of* Acts, τὸ εὐαγγέλιον appears only twice, and only once does it come from Paul (20:24). The first occurrence, and characteristic pride of place, is given to Peter. It is Peter (in Acts) who is the champion of the Gentile mission. Paul is present when the following scene occurs (15:7, emphasis added):

> After much debate had passed, Peter stood up and said to them: "Men, brothers! You know well that from the earliest days God made the choice among you that it would be *through my mouth* that the Gentiles would hear the message of The Announcement and believe!"

Here we see the utter displacement of Paul, and at the same time his domestication to a safe, apostolically grounded Christianity. He is allowed to mention τὸ εὐαγγέλιον once near the end of his story (20:24), but now as "The Announcement *of grace.*" Paul's distinctive language—as, presumably the large mission field that he had developed in Asia Minor and Greece—has been fully co-opted into a much more comprehensive, less urgently eschatological program, all under the authority of those claiming links to the Jerusalem apostles. Paul's hybrid status could not provide for an authentic succession.

---

[32]Of course, the word ἀπόστολος is used of Paul at Acts 14:4, 14. Since Barnabas is there named before Paul as an "apostle," however, and especially given this work's protection of the authoritative apostolic office for the Twelve (1:20–21), in these passages the word must have its non-technical sense of "missionary."

Luke-Acts is in this respect quite like its roughly contemporary third-generation texts: *1 Clement*, the *Epistle of Barnabas*, and the letters by Ignatius, bishop of Antioch. *1 Clement* almost sounds like Paul when it recalls his confrontation of Corinthian divisiveness by citing what he wrote "in the beginning of the εὐαγγέλιον" (*1 Clem.* 47.2), but this does not seem to indicate an awareness of Paul's unique Announcement, since the author has recently said that Christ sent all the apostles εὐαγγελιζόμενοι (42.3). *Barnabas* (5.9; 8.3) likewise understands τὸ εὐαγγέλιον to have been entrusted to the twelve apostles. Ignatius is the most liberal of this group in using τὸ εὐαγγέλιον in an absolute sense—an impressive twenty-one times, as we have observed. But everything has now changed from Paul's letters, for Ignatius too understands τὸ εὐαγγέλιον as something expected by the prophets,[33] taught by all the apostles, shared by all Christians, and supervised by bishops (*Phld.* 5:2: "the εὐαγγέλιον of our common hope"; cf. *Smyrn.* 6:5–8). Ignatius fills its meaning with an eclectic mix of ingredients from Paul, Matthew, and Hebrews—including everything from the virginal conception of Jesus (*Trall.* 9.1–2; *Smyrn.* 1.1) to the superiority of Christ's high-priesthood and the doctrine of incarnation (*Phld.* 9.1)—while downplaying or omitting completely Paul's characteristic emphasis on Jesus' imminent return.

Conclusion

From the methodological point of view, my principal aim has been to re-alienate the language of *gospel* in the study of early Christianity. We need to do this with early Christian language in general, which has long been so familiar that it has lost whatever shock value it may have had for the first generation of Jesus' followers; it is no longer easy to see the oddly formed peaks and crags through the fog of tradition. In the case of τὸ εὐαγγέλιον, the common view that it simply means "the good news" shared by all followers of Christ does not explain the evidence, the highly unusual form; Paul's proprietary tone and use of other language for other ways of following Christ; and resistance to Paul's mission-language except in the Pauline Mark. I do not care about the word "Announcement," but have used it as a place-holder to help analyze the pathways of this intriguing term.

I have argued, therefore, that Paul's letters show him proclaiming The Announcement as his personal mandate: he was given this Announcement—concerning the imminent evacuation of believers and punishment of the rest—directly by the risen Christ, and considered himself alone charged or "set aside" to deliver it. Both Paul and his contemporary Christian leaders understood this language to be distinctively his. His letters reveal plainly that he was jealous of

[33] Cf. Rom 1:1–2, where however the rhetorical context is entirely different, as Paul unusually tries to win recognition of The Announcement from a Judean-Christian group in Rome. By Ignatius's time (*Phld.* 8.2) it is important to show that the εὐαγγέλιον supervised by the bishop is fully grounded in scripture, but anyone who doubts this must yield to the bishop's authority.

it, and of those within his groups—once dedicated to The Announcement—who were defecting to follow other leaders with different teachings. From their side, Paul's Announcement was evidently offensive, or at least seriously deficient, for it undercut much of Jesus' own teaching and practice as his disciples understood it. Most importantly, The Announcement sidelined Jesus' closest associates from their positions of authority. In Romans, writing for a prominent Judean community in the world capital, Paul tried hard to defend it against its image of having departed, even recklessly, from Judean law and culture.

In the second generation, the anonymous follower of Paul who wrote Mark tried to establish the origin or back-story of τὸ εὐαγγέλιον in Jesus' allegedly immediate and lethal conflict with Judean leaders. Others, while borrowing his basic material, tried to improve upon his effort by creating radically new frameworks; this inevitably meant pruning away the more potent Pauline features, above all the conspicuously characteristic εὐαγγέλιον-language. The much longer Matthew preserves only a few instances of the term, and then only by neutralizing it with qualifications to remove its absolute status. John, Q, and *Thomas,* which all consider salvation largely a function of truly understanding Jesus' words or teachings, omit any trace of εὐαγγέλιον-language. How their authors would shudder to think that scholars have been so keen to label these works "gospels"!

Luke-Acts reflects the beginning tendency of third-generation texts to harmonize, homogenize, and domesticate the divergent streams of earliest Christianity. Luke removes τὸ εὐαγγέλιον utterly from Jesus' world, insightfully putting it off to the time of the apostles, where it is nonetheless robbed from Paul to pay Peter. At about the same time, *1 Clement, Barnabas,* and Ignatius reveal no hesitation in boldly using τὸ εὐαγγέλιον, but now it has been stripped of its most characteristic and divisive Pauline connotations, broadened to encompass aspects of all Christian outlooks, and thereby made safe as basic vocabulary of an incipient "orthodox," hierarchically administered, catholic church.

Chapter 10

"For I Am Not Ashamed of the Gospel" (Rom 1:16): The Gospel and the First Readers of Romans

In this chapter I argue that two old problems of scholarship on Romans—the question of audience and Paul's peculiar use of gospel language (εὐαγγέλιον / εὐαγγελίζομαι)—can be solved together. Paul uses the language of gospel with restraint because he is addressing a group of Christian Judeans (Ἰουδαῖοι),[1] whose manner of loyalty to Jesus does not yet correspond to Paul's *euangelion*.[2]

The Audience of Romans

The Problem

To call the audience of Romans a problem is admittedly special pleading on my part. In the celebrated "Romans debate" of recent years, the question of audience has not been a noteworthy bone of contention. Most critics recognize a conflict between the heart of the argument (1:16–11:36), which seems directed toward Judeans, and notices in the letter's opening and closing sections that seem to address Gentiles (1:1.5–6, 13–15; 11:13; 15:15–21). But this tension has usually been resolved by privileging the references to Gentiles: the audience is most commonly portrayed as essentially Gentile, with at best a vocal Judean minority.[3]

---

[1]To ancient ears, Ἰουδαῖος signified "Judean," no less than βαβυλώνιος and Αἰγύπτιος meant "Babylonian" and "Egyptian," respectively. Non-natives who had fully adopted Judean ways were also called "Judeans" by observers, who were certain that Judean culture was an alternative to one's own ancestral traditions (Epictetus, *Diatr.* 2.9.19–21; cf. Tacitus, *Hist.* 5.5; Juvenal, *Sat.* 5.14.96–106; Origen, *C. Cels.* 5.41.4–6). See ch. 5 in the present volume.

[2]To avoid *a priori* interpretation of the Greek term commonly rendered "gospel," I shall simply transliterate it as *euangelion*. For our purposes, one could as easily say, "let *euangelion* = X."

[3]Cf. K. P. Donfried, ed., *The Romans Debate* (Rev. and exp. ed; Peabody, Mass.: Hendrickson, 1991). The ten essays from the original volume (1977) all agree on a Gentile audience; of the thirteen new studies, only F. Watson, "The Two Roman Congregations: Romans 14:1–15:13" (pp. 203–15) proposes a Judean majority. Representative commentaries, which posit a Gentile majority, are: M. Black, *Romans* (NCB; London: Oliphants, 1973), 23; E.

This consensus is broad enough that recent monographs have tackled aspects of the purpose of Romans on the assumption of a Gentile readership.[4]

Still, it is not difficult to find admissions, from those who suppose a Gentile audience, that their supposition fits uncomfortably with the main argument of Romans. Thus P. Lampe:

> Methodologically, these unambiguous statements [*sc.* those referring to Gentiles] must take priority over the impression easily suggested by the rest of the letter's contents, that in Romans a chiefly Jewish-Christian readership is envisaged.[5]

Likewise J. A. T. Robinson finds a Gentile majority even while admitting that "the whole epistle presupposes a Jewish, Old Testament and rabbinic background and would be unintelligible to those who knew nothing of it."[6] Although W. G. Kümmel characterizes Romans as "essentially a debate between the Pauline gospel and Judaism, so that the conclusion seems obvious that the readers were Jewish Christians," he nevertheless deduces a Gentile readership because "the letter contains statements which indicate specifically that the community was Gentile-Christian."[7] Kümmel is adamant: "Any attempt to gain a picture of the readers of Rom[ans] must be made from this established point of view."[8]

It is odd, however, that contemporary scholars should attribute axiomatic importance to the introductory references to Gentiles, when F. C. Baur could make precisely the opposite assumption. Unlike most of his predecessors, the early Baur saw chapters 9–11 as the core ("germ and center") of the argument of Romans, and this only confirmed his reading of chapters 1–8, which made it "impossible to suppose that he [Paul] had any other readers than Jewish Christians before his mind."[9] This reasoning was so widely followed for a few decades that in 1876 H. J. Holtzmann could pronounce the demise of the "older opinion" that

---

Käsemann, *Commentary on Romans* (Grand Rapids: Eerdmans, 1980), 15; J. A. Fitzmyer, *Romans,* 33. It is curious that C. E. B. Cranfield's influential commentary (*A Critical and Exegetical Commentary on the Epistle to the Romans* [ICC; Edinburgh: T&T Clark, 1975], 1:20–21) has had so little influence on this score. Denying that 1:6, 13ff.; 15:15ff. implied a Gentile community, he argues that the community was mixed, with substantial groups of both Judeans and Gentiles.

[4] L. Gaston, *Paul and the Torah,* 22–23, 116; N. Elliott, *The Rhetoric of Romans: Argumentative Constraint and Strategy and Paul's Dialogue with Judaism* (JSNTS 45; Sheffield: Sheffield Academic Press, 1990), 20–21, 67, 95, 105, 167; L. A. Jervis, *The Purpose of Romans: A Comparative Letter Structure Investigation* (JSNTS 55; Sheffield: Sheffield Academic Press, 1991), 77, 103–104, 159–60.

[5] P. Lampe, *Die stadtrömischen Christen in den ersten beiden Jahrhunderten: Untersuchungen zur Sozialgeschichte* (WUNT 2/18; Tübingen: Mohr (Siebeck), 1989), 54. My translation.

[6] Wrestling with Romans (Philadelphia: Westminster, 1979), 7.

[7] W. G. Kümmel, *Introduction to the New Testament* (trans. H. C. Kee; Nashville: Abingdon, 1975), 309.

[8] Ibid., 310.

[9] F. C. Baur, *Paul, the Apostle of Jesus Christ: His Life and Work, His Epistles and His Doctrine; A Contribution to the Critical History of Primitive Christianity* (2 vols.; 2d rev. ed.; trans. E. Zeller; London: Williams and Northgate, 1876), 1:338.

Romans addressed a Gentile readership.[10] Today, however, Baur's thesis is almost universally dismissed as a curiosity. Scholars routinely cite against it the "clear" references to Gentiles in 1:1–15 and 11:13.[11]

What should we do, then, with a letter that, while apparently addressed to Gentiles in parts of the opening and closing, devotes itself to Judean concerns, namely, the distinction between Judeans and Greeks (1:18–2:16), circumcision and physical descent from Abraham (chs. 3–4), the status of Torah (chs. 6–8), and the election of Israel (chs. 9–11); and in which Paul calls his readers "people who know the law" (7:1), flatly states that they formerly lived under the law (7:4–6; 8:3), speaks to them as Judeans in the second and collective first person (2:17–29; 3:9, 27; 4:1), and expects them to appreciate an unparalleled abundance of scriptural allusions—even to such arcana as the mercy seat on the ark of the covenant (3:25)? Within the introduction itself, in spite of its putative address to Gentiles, Paul introduces a unique complex of references to the prophets of holy scripture (1:2) and King David (1:3). Why? Schmithals has formulated the problem with customary clarity: "The content of chs. 1–11 appears, in both its details and its whole thrust, to speak against the Gentile-Christian identity of the addressees."[12]

To make the common thesis of a Gentile majority more viable, scholars have tried in various ways to mitigate the force of chapters 1–11. Thus we have seen claims that the "law" known by the readers of Romans (7:1) could mean "law" in general[13]—even though it contains commandments such as "you must not covet," and is called the "holy" law under which Paul and his readers have lived, now supplanted by the coming of the spirit (7:5–12); that Gentiles could equally well be described as "those who know the law"; and that they too would have been concerned about scriptural interpretation and problems like the status of Israel.[14] Other scholars have understood the argument of Romans to be an epitome of Paul's previous teaching or a primer for his impending trip to Jerusalem—in either case, not specially relevant to concerns of the Gentile-Christian community in Rome, though addressed to them.[15]

Moreover, study of the diatribe and of rhetorical genres has been exploited to argue that because Paul's "interlocutor" is a rhetorical device, the typically Judean questions that Paul answers need not reflect the community's own problems at all. For example, when Paul disavows "sinning so that good may come" (6:1; 3:8), he is not responding to a Judean caricature of his own teaching, but is

---

[10] "Umschau auf dem Gebiet der neutestamentlichen Kritik," *Jahrbuch für protestantische Theologie* 2 (1876) 280; cited in W. Schmithals, *Der Römerbrief als historisches Problem* (SNT 9; Gütersloh: Gerd Mohn, 1975), 27.

[11] Schmithals, *Problem,* 27–28; W. Wiefel, "The Jewish Community in Ancient Rome and the Origins of Roman Christianity" in *The Romans Debate* (ed. Donfried), 85–86, 96.

[12] Schmithals, *Problem,* 11. My translation.

[13] Käsemann, *Romans,* 187.

[14] Cranfield, *Romans,* I, 18–19; Fitzmyer, *Romans,* 34. But see Schmithals, *Problem,* 87–88.

[15] T. W. Manson, "St. Paul's Letter to the Romans—and Others"; G. Bornkamm, "The Letter to the Romans as Paul's Last Will and Testament"; and J. Jervell, "The Letter to Jerusalem," in *The Romans Debate* (ed. Donfried), 3–15, 16–28, and 53–64.

himself ruling out an antinomian position among Gentile Christians.[16] Having defined Romans as epideictic rhetoric, D. Fraikin remarks on Rom 1:18–3:20:

> We are faced, then, with the interesting fact that Paul, in a discourse *whose goal is to strengthen the Gentiles in the gospel,* provides them with the arguments by which he would make his understanding of the gospel and its consequences credible *to Jews.*[17]

Fraikin explains Paul's tactics by suggesting that the Gentiles of Rome would have been deeply concerned about how Judeans viewed their faith, and so Paul provided them with a rationale. The most ambitious attempt to reinterpret the main argument of Romans along these lines is N. Elliott's revised dissertation, which contends that Paul's confrontation of Judean arguments is meant to serve as a paradigm for his Gentile readers, as a "protasis" to which they should supply the "apodosis": if the Judeans have no special claims against God's wrath, how much more shall *we Gentiles* lack them?[18]

Without dismissing *a priori* all future attempts to make Romans meaningful to Gentile readers, we may observe that these efforts have not so far proven compelling. The readers of Romans were not highly educated as a group,[19] and we should not credit them with the subtlety of doctorands. Elsewhere Paul is candid about his main points, and so we should assume that the language of Romans—including not only the "logic" that seems to enthrall interpreters, but also the sound of the words and phrases, the emotive tone with which Paul declares his esteem for Judean traditions (1:2–3; 3:1–2, 31; 7:12; 9:4–5; 11:25–36)[20]—was intended to find a ready reception. Paradoxically, it is the "rhetorical" approaches to Romans, with their debates about epideictic and deliberative kinds, or about where the *exordium* ends, that have become the worst offenders against the criteria of intelligibility and persuasiveness. It strains the imagination that Paul could have intended such indirect arguments to find any resonance with Gentile readers, no matter how well they understood the mechanics of the diatribe. Significantly, a specialist in rhetoric from outside the circles of NT scholarship supposes that in Romans Paul faces "two main rhetorical problems," *viz.,* his lack of personal acquaintance and "the probability that there will be among them [the readers] those clinging to the law and hostile to aspects of his message."[21]

---

[16] W. S. Campbell, "Romans III as a Key to the Structure and Thought of the Letter," in *The Romans Debate* (ed. Donfried), 261–62.

[17] D. Fraikin, "The Rhetorical Function of the Jews in Romans," in P. Richardson and D. Granskou, eds., *Anti-Judaism in Early Christianity* (ESCJ 2; Waterloo: Wilfrid Laurier University Press, 1986), 1:98. Emphasis added.

[18] N. Elliott, *Rhetoric,* 131–32, 141–42.

[19] Lampe, *Christen,* 135–63.

[20] N. Elliott, for example, seems to miss the crucial non-rational aspects of rhetoric when he suggests that Judeans would not have been persuaded by Paul's logic (*Rhetoric,* 171–73). W. Wuellner's oft-cited essay ("Paul's Rhetoric of Argumentation in Romans: An Alternative to the Donfried-Karris Debate over Romans," in *The Romans Debate* [ed. Donfried], 128–46) recognizes the importance of ethos, at least in principle (p. 133–34, 137).

[21] G. A. Kennedy, *New Testament Interpretation through Rhetorical Criticism* (Chapel Hill: University of North Carolina Press, 1984), 152. Kennedy is also sensitive to non-

Schmithals is right: a Gentile community receiving this letter should have sent it back as misdirected mail![22]

One clever strategy for increasing the Gentile readership of Romans requires that the word συγγενής, which is used of Andronicus, Junia, and Herodian in the greetings of chapter 16 (16:7, 11, 21), be read as a code for Judean Christians.[23] Lampe infers that therefore the other twenty or so names on the list (i.e., most of them) are Gentile.[24] But the word συγγενής ordinarily means "relative" or "kin," not "fellow national." In its six NT occurrences outside of Paul, it always refers to a *family member.*[25] In its only Pauline appearance outside of Romans 16, the word is likewise paired with ἀδελφός, "brother" (Rom 9:3). That both words refer to Israelites in that case (9:4) does not suggest that συγγενής should mean "Israelite" elsewhere, any more than ἀδελφός should. They are metaphors indicating filial affection. Paul includes everyone mentioned in Romans 16 under one or another term of endearment—my beloved (16:5, 8, 9, 12), brother/sister (vv. 14, 15, 17), fellow worker (vv. 3, 6, 9, 12), mother (v. 13), and relative (vv. 7, 11, 21)—effectively rotating these terms to suit the individual. Within this context, where he is trying to build bridges with affectionate language, we may not single out συγγενῆς and read it as a cipher for "Judean."[26]

Perceiving the difficulty in dissociating Paul's discussion of Judean issues (chs. 1–11) from the real needs of the readers, several critics have drawn the inevitable but problematic conclusion that the Gentile recipients themselves must have had a strong attachment to Judean ways.[27] Schmithals proposes that the readers had been Gentile adherents of the synagogue, like virtually all first-generation converts to Christianity,[28] but could not follow through as far as proselytism, and so found in Gentile Christianity an attractive alternative.[29] But what sort of Gentile Christians, who could be so matter-of-factly addressed *as* Gentiles (1:6, 13), would be inclined to think that God was the God of Judeans only (3:29), would be tempted to boast about their role as a light to the nations (2:17), could be grouped with Paul as *physical* descendants of Abraham (4:1), or would assume the indispensable importance of circumcision (2:25)? Gentiles who had

rational indices such as Paul's arrangement of words, including rhetorical questions, "to express emotion" (p. 155).

[22] Schmithals, *Problem,* 31–32.

[23] Cranfield, *Romans,* 1:18; Lampe, "The Roman Christians of Romans 16," in *The Romans Debate* (ed. Donfried), 224–25; F. Watson, "The Two Roman Congregations: Romans 14:1–15:13," in *The Romans Debate* (ed. Donfried), 208, 210–11.

[24] Lampe, "Romans 16," 224–25.

[25] Cf. Luke 1:58; 2:44; 14:12; 21:16; Acts 10:24; John 18:26, and LSJ *ad loc.*

[26] In 16:21 Paul identifies Timothy as ὁ συνεργός μου, and three other current companions—Lucius, Jason, and Sosipater—as συγγενῆς μου. Does he mean that the three (of uncertain identity) are Judeans, while Timothy, who was apparently born of a Judean mother and circumcised (Acts 16:1–3), is not?

[27] Schmithals, *Problem;* A. J. M. Wedderburn, "The Purpose and Occasion of Romans Again," in *The Romans Debate* (ed. Donfried), 196–97, 201 (with qualifications); and Fitzmyer, *Romans,* 33–36.

[28] Schmithals, *Problem,* 76–82.

[29] Ibid., 83–91.

embraced Christianity because it *lacked* the stringent requirements of Judean law would presumably not have adopted a traditional Judean standpoint over against Paul. We have several letters from Paul to Gentiles—also former God-fearers on Schmithals's view—and those letters are not like Romans.

The diplomatic solution of a mixed audience, with no clear Gentile or Judean majority, does not really help to explain the evidence.[30] For if there was an important enough Judean contingent to account for Romans 1–11, then Paul had no business addressing his readers without qualification as Gentiles, Greeks and barbarians. I suspect that many commentators recognize this problem, for they tend to speak of the Gentile audience only when discussing the introduction, but then casually allow references to a Judean minority when dealing with other parts of the letter.[31]

This is by no means an exhaustive account of the exegetical maneuvers that have been offered as plausible ways of explaining the Judean and Gentile references of Romans. Braver souls have attempted more comprehensive classifications.[32] My purpose is only to plead for a reappraisal. Given that, by most accounts, the heart of Romans 1–11 deals with Judean concerns, and in view of the inescapable rhetorical requirement that a letter resonate with its audience's sensibilities, are we really certain that the few references to Gentiles mean what they seem to mean at first glance? Would it not be more efficient to reexamine those three or four statements than to turn the whole letter inside out in defense of a Gentile readership?

External Evidence

Such external evidence as we possess for the earliest Christian community in Rome also poses formidable problems for the hypothesis of a Gentile community. Virtually everyone agrees that Christianity took root within the established Judean community of Rome. This consensus is grounded in the notice of Suetonius about the activities of one "Chrestus," which is plausibly, but by no means certainly, understood as a corruption of "Christus," in turn taken to mean "Christian teaching" (*Claud.* 25.4).[33]

---

[30] Ibid., 44–50.

[31] An example of this common slide is Kümmel (*Introduction*), who declares flatly that "community was Gentile-Christian" while discussing the greeting (p. 309) and then allows that it was "*not purely Gentile-Christian*" when discussing other features of the letter (p. 310).

[32] For the older and mainly German material, see Schmithals, *Problem,* 13–62. A synopsis of the newer studies is in Elliott, *Rhetoric,* 21–43. On the purposes of Romans in general, see Jervis, *Purpose,* 11–28; Donfried, *The Romans Debate,* xli–lxxii.

[33] It is easier to mention some dissenters: M. Sordi, *The Christians and the Roman Empire,* trans. A. Bedini (Norman: University of Oklahoma Press, 1986), 25–26; S. Benko, *Pagan Rome and the Early Christians* (Bloomington: Indiana University Press, 1984), 18. Suetonius's friends Pliny (*Ep.* 10.96) and Tacitus (*Ann.* 15.44) both know that *Christus* was the founder of Christianity, and Suetonius himself later mentions the *Christiani* (*Nero* 16.2). How, then, could he be so mistaken here?

However we interpret (or reconstruct!) Suetonius, other evidence confirms the Judean origins of Roman Christianity. First, the Christian community in Rome was not Pauline, and Paul understands himself as the pioneer in his "*euangelion* of the foreskin" (Gal 2:9). His self-understanding and the conflicts that he faced over this *euangelion* (cf. Gal 2:2; 1:10–11; Acts 21:21, 28) would be inexplicable if there had been a prior Gentile mission on the same terms. Peter and the others had gone to Judeans (Gal 2:7), he says, or had compelled Gentiles to Judaize (Gal 2:14; 6:12–13).[34] It is easiest, therefore, to envisage a non-Pauline community at Rome in the forties of the first century as Judean-Christian.

Second, Roman Christianity maintained a decidedly Judean ambience long after Paul's time.[35] This is indicated variously by *1 Clement* (90s C.E.?), with its "low Christology" and arsenal of Judean allusions;[36] Hebrews, which is often thought to have been addressed to Rome;[37] Christian borrowing of Judean burial customs;[38] the Marcionite prologue to Romans, which asserts that the Roman Christians had been taught the "law and prophets" by false apostles;[39] the assertion in Ambrosiaster's prologue that Roman Christianity began "according to a Judean rite";[40] widespread traditions that Peter preached in Rome under Claudius;[41] and Tacitus's evidence (below). Whatever the historical value of the patristic traditions, they at least agree on the surface with other indications that Roman Christianity took root in the synagogues, and this is the common scholarly view.

It is often argued, however, that the putative Gentile majority among Paul's readers in the 50s resulted from Claudius's expulsion of Judeans from Rome in 49 C.E. W. Wiefel asserts:

> Expulsion of the Jews from Rome also meant the end of the first Christian congregation in Rome, which up until then had consisted of Jewish Christians. In Paul's letter to the Romans, written a few years after these events, we meet a new congregation.[42]

---

[34] Antioch is no exception, for Paul is already at the scene when we first hear of Gentile Christians there (Gal 2:11). Cf. F. Watson, *Paul, Judaism and the Gentiles: A Sociological Approach* (Cambridge: Cambridge University Press, 1986), 50–56.

[35] In general, see Lampe, *Christen,* 58–63.

[36] H. B. Bumpus, *The Christological Awareness of Clement of Rome and Its Sources* (Cambridge: Cambridge University Press, 1972), 8–10.

[37] Kümmel, *Introduction,* 401.

[38] H. Leon, *The Jews of Ancient Rome* (Philadelphia: Jewish Publication Society, 1960; repr. Peabody, Mass.: Hendrickson, 1995), 55.

[39] That is, the traditional Vulgate prologue to Romans, from the third century or earlier, credited by some twentieth-century scholarship to followers of Marcion; see J. J. Clabeaux, "Marcionite Prologues to Paul," *ABD* 4:520–21. The Latin text is conveniently available in commentaries such as Cranfield, *Romans,* 1:20 n. 2.

[40] E.g., in Cranfield, *Romans,* 1:20 n. 1. The "Ambrosiaster" is the anonymous commentator whose work was attributed to Ambrose of Milan; for the original see *CSEL* LXXXI: Pars 1, cols. 5f. English translation is in Donfried, "A Short Note on Romans 16," in his *Romans Debate,* 47.

[41] Eusebius, *Hist. eccl.* 2.14.6–25.2 (citing Papias in support); Irenaeus (*Haer.* 3.1.1) has Peter and Paul laying the foundations of the church in Rome.

[42] Wiefel, "Community," in *The Romans Debate* (ed. Donfried), 93. Cf. W. Marxsen, *Introduction to the New Testament* (Philadelphia: Fortress, 1970), 95–104; Donfried, in his *Romans Debate,* xlv–xlvi, lxx–lxxi, 104–106; Elliott, *Rhetoric,* 51; Fitzmyer, *Romans,* 33.

When the Judeans returned following Nero's accession in 54, *ex hypothesi,* they found a Gentile community securely in place. The resulting tensions between the two groups are, according to some interpreters, reflected in Rom 14–15.[43] This reconstruction sometimes claims further support from Tacitus's notice that Nero punished Christians for the great fire of 64 (*Ann.* 15.44), which is taken to imply that (Gentile) Christians were clearly distinct from Judeans by that time.[44]

But there are serious problems with an expulsion of "all Judeans" under Claudius and the Neronian persecution of an obviously Gentile-Christian community.

Claudius's Expulsion of Judeans

However they reconstruct Claudius's policies with respect to Roman Judeans—as a single disciplinary action in 41 or 49,[45] or a ban on meeting in 41 followed by expulsion order in 49[46]—most recent writers agree that a wholesale expulsion of Roman Judeans under Claudius is improbable.[47] The evidence may be summarized as follows:

1. Expulsions of groups from the city tended to be haphazard and piecemeal affairs, more symbolic than comprehensive, with plenty of practical exceptions.[48]

2. Although an expulsion of some Judeans under Tiberius is well attested,[49] the literary evidence for Claudius's action is sparse and contradictory; but the movement of tens of thousands of Judeans could not have escaped attention.[50] The strongest statement comes from Suetonius's list of Claudius's policies pertaining to foreigners (*Claud.* 25), which asserts without elaboration that the emperor "expelled from Rome the Judeans who persistently rioted at the instigation of Chrestus" (*Iudaeos impulsore Chresto assidue tumultuantes Roma expulit;* 25.4). *If* "Chrestus" is a garbled reference to "Christian teaching," then Suetonius has a hazy picture of the event at best. Even if we arbitrarily took the rest of his statement at face value, the syntax would suggest only that militant Judeans were driven out.[51]

Describing the beginning of Claudius's reign, Cassius Dio stresses that the emperor did *not* expel the Judeans, because of their great numbers; he prohibited

---

[43] See the summary in Elliott, *Rhetoric,* 55–56.

[44] Fitzmyer, *Romans,* 35.

[45] V. M. Scramuzza, *The Emperor Claudius* (Harvard Historical Studies 44; Cambridge, Mass.: Harvard University Press, 1940), 151; Leon, *Jews,* 21–27; G. Lüdemann, *Paul, Apostle to the Gentiles: Studies in Chronology* (trans. F. S. Jones; Philadelphia: Fortress, 1984), 164–71; F. Millar in Schürer-Vermes, *Jewish People,* 3.1:77 n. 91.

[46] A. Momigliano, *Claudius: The Emperor and His Achievement* (trans. W. D. Hogarth; Oxford: Clarendon, 1934), 30–34; Fitzmyer, *Romans,* 32 and the works cited there.

[47] To the works mentioned in the two preceding notes add Baur, *Paul,* 1:328 (already!); Cranfield, *Romans,* 1:18; Lampe, *Christen,* 6–7; L. H. Feldman, *Jew and Gentile,* 96–97.

[48] See Tacitus, *Hist.* 1.22; R. Macmullen, *Enemies,* 125–26, 132–33.

[49] Josephus (*Ant.* 18.83–84), Tacitus (*Ann.* 2.85), Suetonius (*Tib.* 36), and Cassius Dio (*Roman History* 57.18.5).

[50] On the number of Judeans in Rome see Leon, *Jews,* 135.

[51] Since the participle qualifies *Iudaeos:* Leon, *Jews,* 24.

them from assembling, while permitting them to maintain their ancestral way of life (*Roman History* 60.6.6). It is possible that Dio later mentioned an expulsion of Judeans by Claudius, in the part of his narrative only partially preserved in Byzantine epitomes,[52] but that speculation would make the silence of Josephus and Tacitus (below) doubly problematic. And the hypothetical missing material would need to explain why an expulsion was feasible later, but not in 41. Further, in context (60.5.1–8.3), Dio seems to be describing hallmark policies that showed the character of Claudius's reign: they may have begun in 41 C.E., but they were not limited to that year.[53] Dio apparently understood Claudius's Judean policy to have involved something less than expulsion.

Josephus and Tacitus are utterly silent, even though Tacitus's account of this period is extant in full (*Ann.* 12), and he elsewhere relishes the punishments inflicted by Roman arms on the misanthropic Judeans (*Hist.* 5.1–13). Josephus's silence is most conspicuous. Rather than ignoring well-known events that might reflect badly on the Judeans, he usually explains them away as the fault of another group or a few untypical Judeans.[54] He could not have expected to make his points effectively by ignoring such an obvious counter-example to his main arguments. Moreover, he remembers Claudius as supportive of Judeans, even though he does not otherwise present Claudius in the best light, and other evidence for Claudius's dealings with Judeans generally confirms Josephus's impression.[55] Agrippa I, who had spent his early years in Rome with Gaius and Claudius (*Ant.* 18.143–146; 165–166), undertook dangerous negotiations to secure the reluctant Senate's endorsement of the new emperor (*Ant.* 19.236–247). Claudius rewarded Agrippa with a large kingdom (*Ant.* 19.274–275) and thereafter supported established Judean rights.[56]

If we discount the fifth-century Paulus Orosius's mistaken claim that Josephus mentioned an expulsion of the Judeans in the ninth year of Claudius's reign,[57] then the assertion of Acts 18:2, that Claudius had commanded all Judeans to leave Rome before Paul's visit to Corinth, is isolated. But the assertion fits the

[52] The epitomes begin with bk. 61.

[53] Cf. the games instituted on the birthdays of Claudius's parents (60.5.1), the prohibition of emperor worship (60.5.4), or the disbanding of the clubs (60.6.7).

[54] See Mason, *Josephus and the New Testament,* 52–84.

[55] Cf. Scramuzza, *Claudius,* 11–18.

[56] He issued a strong edict confirming Judean rights in the empire, in addition to the one that secured Judean civic status in Alexandria (*Ant.* 19.278–91; cf. 302–11). Josephus remarks, "By these edicts Claudius Caesar showed what he had decided about the Judeans" (*Ant.* 19.292). The rest of his narrative confirms this impression, for Claudius even overrules his governors in siding with the Judean positions (*Ant.* 15.407//20.7–14; *War* 2.245//*Ant.* 20.136; *War* 2.245//*Ant.* 20.136). Dio confirms Claudius's gratitude to the Judean Agrippa (60.8.2), and papyri show the emperor supporting Judean rights in Alexandria (P. London 1912) or condemning the anti-Judean activists Isidore and Lampon (*CPJ* 2.156; cf. Momigliano, *Claudius,* 35; Feldman, *Jew and Gentile,* 96–97).

[57] History Against the Pagans 7.6.15. A typical assessment of Orosius's work is that of G. F. Chesnut ("Eusebius, Augustine, Orosius, and the Later Patristic and Medieval Church Historians," in *Eusebius, Christianity, and Judaism* [ed. H. W. Attridge and G. Hata; Detroit: Wayne State University Press, 1992], 687–713): "a very bad history. It

known tendency of Luke-Acts to place Judeans at odds with Roman authorities and Christians alike,[58] and an exaggerated "all" is a feature of Lucan style.[59]

In sum, Claudius's measures, whatever they were, do not seem to have effected a decisive change in the life of the Judean community at Rome. Hence they offer no external support for the putative shift from Judean to Gentile Christianity. This conclusion is reinforced by Paul's own claim that he has longed to visit the Roman community, whose faith is known worldwide (1:8), for "many years" (15:23). Writing within three years of Nero's accession (54 C.E.),[60] which allegedly permitted Judeans to return to Rome, Paul addresses his readers as a well-settled community. And his main argument (chs. 1–11) continues to assume their Judean background. It is, as Baur recognized long ago, "opposed to all historic probability" that an edict of Claudius brought any essential changes to the constitution of the Roman Judean community.[61]

Nero's Persecution of Christians

Equally problematic is the supposition that Christians were clearly distinct from Judeans in Rome by Nero's time because Nero punished Christians and not Judeans for the great fire of 64. Although Tacitus is the only ancient author to connect the punishment of Christians with the fire, it seems that Nero did take action against some Christians at this time.[62] The problem is that, in doing so, he displayed a knowledge of Judean-Christian affairs that was ahead of its time, and that we should have expected only from an insider. Whereas Roman governors had difficulty distinguishing Christians from other Judean-based groups,[63] Judean authorities tended from the outset to see all forms of allegiance to the crucified Nazarene as alien.[64] It is this Judean perspective that Nero shares, and not that of his own elite Roman circles.

---

was neither well organized nor coherent, and constantly confused myth and legend with real historical events" (p. 697).

[58] See recently S. G. Wilson, "The Jews and the Death of Jesus in Luke-Acts" in *Anti-Judaism* (ed. Richardson), 1:155–64; J. T. Sanders, "The Jewish People in Luke-Acts" in *Luke-Acts and the Jewish People: Eight Critical Perspectives* (ed. J. B. Tyson; Minneapolis: Augsburg, 1988), 51–75.

[59] Lampe, *Christen,* 7.

[60] Suggested dates for Romans run from 51 (Lüdemann, *Paul,* 263) to 53 (Sordi, *Christians,* 23) to 55/56 (Cranfield, *Romans,* 1:14) to 57/58 (Fitzymer, *Romans,* 87). The date depends on how one assesses: the relation of Acts 18 to the Gallio inscription; the impact of (Felix's brother) Pallas's removal from Nero's court in 55; the date of Festus's arrival in Judea; and the interpretation of the "two years" in Acts 24:27.

[61] Baur, *Paul,* 1:329.

[62] Suetonius mentions the fire (*Nero* 38) and the punishment of Christians (16.2) but does not connect them. The claim that Nero persecuted Christians is widespread in Christian authors, e.g., Eusebius, *Church History* 2.25.

[63] This situation is presupposed by Acts 23:29; 24:5; 25:19; John 18:31; 19:6.

[64] Only so can we explain: the Judean Paul's persecutions of Christians (Gal 1:13); subsequent Judean opposition to the Christian Paul (Acts 21:21, 28); the deaths of Stephen and the two Jameses in Jerusalem (Acts 7; 12:2–3; Josephus, *Ant.* 20.200).

Writing some fifty years after the fire, the ex-consul Tacitus still knows the Christians as a sub-group of Judeans. He says that the superstition spread "not merely in Judea, the source of the disease (*originem eius mali*), but in the capital itself . . ." (*Ann.* 15.44). He goes on to charge the Christians with "hatred of the human race" (*odium humani generis*), which is the same accusation that he makes against Judeans in general (*Hist.* 5.5). Further, according to a famous passage from Sulpicius Severus, which is commonly thought to have originated with Tacitus, Titus reasoned that in destroying the temple in Jerusalem he would extinguish the Christians along with the other Judeans (*Sacred History* 2.30.6).[65] Whatever one makes of that very late passage, which may owe much to Sulpicius, even in the early second century Tacitus's aristocratic friends Pliny and Suetonius plainly know little about the Christians except their name. The spare material that they provide reflects only a dawning awareness of this "new superstition," even though they, like Tacitus, moved in the highest Roman circles.[66]

How, then, did Nero have such clear knowledge of the Christians as distinct from Judeans? This was precisely the period of his notorious marriage to Poppea Sabina (62–65 C.E.). Without deciding the precise significance of the term "God-fearer" (θεοσεβής) that Josephus applies to this woman (*Ant.* 20.195), we may recall that during her brief marriage to Nero both she and the Judeans enjoyed unusual influence in the imperial court.[67] Two separate embassies from Judea were able to secure important concessions from Nero at this time, both of which arguably ran counter to his immediate interests, and in both cases Josephus attributes Nero's favor to the mediation of Poppea (*Ant.* 20.195; *Life* 16).

The contrast between these successful Judean missions to Nero and his punishment of the Christians, at about the same time, suggests the ingredients for a solution. In looking for a scapegoat for the fire, Nero could plausibly have targeted any of the foreign groups based in the sectors of the city that remained intact, which probably included the transtiberine (Tacitus, *Ann.* 15.40). Christians, like other Judeans, would not likely have participated in his religious ceremonies to appease the gods, and so would have attracted further suspicion.[68] Since he apparently singled out the Christians with clarity of purpose, the circumstantial evidence suggests that he took advice from insiders, just when Poppea was at the height of her influence.[69] It is unnecessary to posit that Judean community leaders themselves initiated such actions,[70] but it seems plausible at least that a friend

[65]The admission in this same passage that the two *religiones* are opposed to each other may be the anti-Judean Sulpicius's own gloss; it does not seem to fit with the claim that they are a single *religio* or with Titus's logic on the temple, which should be credited to Suplicius's source.

[66]Pliny (an ex-consul), *Ep.* 10.96; Suetonius (secretary to the emperor Hadrian), *Nero* 16.2.

[67]On Poppea's influence in general, see M. T. Griffin, *Nero,* 101–3.

[68]Ibid., 133.

[69]Nero reportedly murdered her in 65, but he was so obsessed with her memory that he had Sporus castrated and renamed "Sabina" to play her role; Dio 62.27.4; 28.2–3; 63.13.1–2.

[70]Benko (*Pagan Rome,* 14–20): Judeans in Rome started the fire as a result of mounting tensions with Roman authority in Judea. They then blamed the Christians.

of the Judean community educated Nero on Judean-Christian differences. On this hypothesis, the name "Christian" was then aired for the first time in higher social circles. It would be remembered, however, only as the name of an egregious Judean faction until Pliny had occasion to investigate the group more fully.

Obviously, we lack the controls to make this or any other reconstruction of Nero's intentions compelling. But this much is clear: we cannot simply infer from Nero's reported action against the Christians that Roman Christianity was predominantly Gentile by 64. Tacitus's own description of this event confirms other external evidence that Roman Christianity maintained a strong Judean connection throughout the period in which Paul was active—in the 50s.

References to Gentiles in Romans

If the body of Romans seems to address Christian Judeans, and the external evidence tends to support that conclusion, then the few references to Gentiles in this letter carry a considerable burden. Schmithals puts the matter in sharp relief when he claims that the hypothesis of a Judean audience "runs aground on the simple fact—and *it is the decisive argument*—that the passages already noted, 1.5, 13ff.; 11.13; 15.15ff., admit no other meaning than this: Paul addresses his readers as Gentile Christians."[71] But are these passages so clear that we should go to any lengths to preserve the Gentile-Christian majority in Rome?

To be sure, the few advocates of a predominantly Judean readership have not often dealt with the references to Gentiles more convincingly than the majority have explained the "Judean" material. Baur held that the ἔθνη of the introduction, among whom the Romans seem to be included (1:5–6), should be understood not as "Gentiles" per se but only as the "nations." But granted that the same word has both nuances, in the immediate context Paul cites his apostleship to the ἔθνη in question (1:1); so one cannot avoid the "Gentile" connotation. Baur felt it necessary to concede that 11:13–36 was a digression directed at the Gentile *minority*.[72] J. C. O'Neill, for his part, simply excises some of the offending references to Gentiles (1:6, part of 1:15) as scribal glosses.[73] This is an extreme case of Matthean logic, on the removal of offending parts, though is perhaps still preferable to forfeiting the whole body. In support of his argument that Paul wrote Romans to persuade a Judean majority among the Roman Christians to adopt his gospel, Watson echoes a proposal of Baur's followers on 1:5–6,[74] and in another context I have suggested interpretations of all the Gentile passages that independently agree with this reading of 1:5–6, as follows.[75]

---

[71] Schmithals, *Problem,* 27. My translation; emphasis added.

[72] Baur, *Paul,* 1:332–34.

[73] J. C. O'Neill, *Paul's Letter to the Romans* (Harmondsworth: Penguin, 1975), 33, 37.

[74] Watson, *Paul,* 103.

[75] S. Mason, "Paul, Classical Anti-Judaism, and Romans," in *Approaches to Ancient Judaism,* New Series 4 (South Florida Studies in the History of Judaism 81; ed. J. Neusner; Atlanta: Scholars, 1993), 141–80, esp. 171–75.

1. In 1:5–6 Paul compares his own mission directly with that of the Roman Christians: he was called (κλητός) to be an apostle (1:1) "among all the Gentiles, *among whom you also are called* of Jesus Christ" (ἐν πᾶσιν τοῖς ἔθνησιν, . . . ἐν οἷς ἐστε καὶ ὑμεῖς κλητοὶ Ἰησοῦ Χριστοῦ). Paul does not say that the Romans *are* Gentiles any more than he says that he is a Gentile. Both he and his readers are called to be *among* the Gentiles. This is an appropriate way of describing dispersed Judeans who live in the capital of the pagan world.[76] That Paul means to evoke Israel's priestly mandate among the nations/Gentiles (Exod 19:4–6) seems likely also from his parallel remarks in 15:16: God called him "to be a servant (λειτουργόν) of Christ Jesus to the Gentiles (ἔθνη) in the priestly service (ἱερουργοῦντα) of the gospel of God." Thus, 1:5–6 does not imply that the Roman Christians are themselves Gentiles.

2. In 1:13 Paul indicates his desire to come to Rome "in order that I might harvest some fruit both among you, and even so among the remainder of the Gentiles" (καὶ ἐν ὑμῖν καθὼς καὶ ἐν τοῖς λοιποῖς ἔθνεσιν). This notice would indicate a Gentile readership at Rome, however, only if one assumed that "the remainder of the Gentiles" stood in relation to "you." Yet elsewhere in this letter, the "churches" (or assemblies, ἐκκλησίαι) of the Gentiles are distinct from the community at Rome—with the possible exception of 11:13, to which we shall return below. For example, Paul is carrying "the offering of *the* Gentiles [not 'of some Gentiles']" to Jerusalem (15:16)—and Paul does not so much as suggest a Roman contribution, even though he has bent every effort to get money from "the Gentiles" (1 Cor 16:1–2; 2 Cor 8–9). Again, his mission in the east has secured "the obedience of *the* Gentiles" (15:17). He even presumes to convey the gratitude of "*all* the churches of *the* Gentiles" to Prisca and Aquila (16:4), whom Acts portrays as Judeans (Acts 18:2). He also thinks that he has fully preached the gospel among the Gentiles of the east, and now wishes to head for Spain and the west (15:19).

Accordingly, I submit that "the remainder of the Gentiles" in 1:13 stands in contrast to the Gentiles of the east. This reading is supported also by the phrase ἐν τοῖς λοιποῖς ἔθνησιν, which must mean the remainder (cf. λοιπός) of the Gentiles—the ones who *are left*—and not merely "others."[77] He will harvest some fruit both among the Judean-Christians of Rome, in passing, and then continue the mission for which he was called among the western *Gentiles*. Paul's audience did not need to read the letter through to discover that he was planning to go to the remainder of the Gentiles in the west, for Phoebe and her entourage would have presented an oral report in bringing the letter, and associates like Prisca and Aquila doubtless knew his long-range intentions anyway.

3. Verses 1:14–15, which seem to premise Paul's intention to visit Rome on his obligation to "both Greeks *and* barbarians, both wise *and* foolish," are

[76]Cranfield (*Romans,* 1:20) accepts the plausibility of this reading.

[77]Pace Fitzmyer, *Romans,* 247, 250. Nor can the phrase easily apply to Gentiles already evangelized in the west; contra Cranfield, *Romans,* 1:20; Jervis, *Purpose,* 108.

an insufficiently recognized problem. The apparently easy conclusion, that the Christian community is therefore Gentile,[78] does not explain the τε καί construction of the two pairs (1:14): *both* Greek *and* barbarian, *both* wise *and* foolish. C. H. Dodd had to admit, perplexed, that the distinctions have "little real force in this setting."[79] The most natural grammatical readings, if they give full weight to both τε καί and οὕτως, seem excluded by their absurdity.[80] Paul cannot mean that he wants to meet foolish barbarians in Rome, after having dealt with wise Greeks for so long, or vice versa, or that he would like to visit a community with both elements. His work so far has been precisely in the classically Greek areas of the world, where wisdom was also a significant issue (1 Cor 1–4). If he means to apply these categories to his Roman readers, his words amount to a substantial insult. They also render improbable any explanation of the letter body, including the hypothesis of a mixed Gentile-Judean community.

Granting that the most obvious readings do not work well, we may proceed to several considerations that suggest another interpretation.

a. The derogatory categories "barbarians" and "foolish"[81] make better sense with reference to a third party than as a description of the readers themselves.

b. As is well known, the Roman empire was broadly divided along linguistic lines into the east, which was united by the Greek language after Alexander,[82] and the "barbarian" west, loosely linked by administrative Latin superimposed on the native languages. We have in the yet-unvisited western regions, then, a ready referent for Paul's statement.

c. This clause comes immediately after the one (1:13) in which Paul indicates his plan to go to the "remainder of the Gentiles," which I have taken to mean the Gentiles of the western Mediterranean. Though it would be extremely gauche for him to find barbarians and foolish persons among his current readers, it would make quite decent sense to contrast rhetorically the western Gentiles with those of the classically Greek regions in which he has worked thus far (Asia Minor, Macedonia, Achaia; Rom 15:19, 26). This referent would explain the τε καί: "I cannot rest content with the Greeks [in the east], but must proceed also to the *remainder* of the Gentiles, for I am obli-

---

[78] So Käsemann (*Romans*, 20—apparently); Jervis, *Purpose*, 104.

[79] C. H. Dodd, *The Epistle of Paul to the Romans* (London: Hodder and Stoughton, 1932), 8.

[80] Cranfield (*Romans*, 1:83–85) realizes that there is a problem but ends up with an implausible solution: Paul divides Gentile humanity in two different ways (v. 14) and then declares his intention to visit Rome because he is apostle to Gentiles (v. 15). But Cranfield has already rejected claims of a Gentile majority in Rome (p. 21). Fitzmyer (*Romans*, 251) searches for barbarians among Paul's converts in the east!

[81] See H. Windisch ("βάρβαρος," *TDNT* 1:548) on the unsavoury connotations of the word.

[82] On the pervasiveness of Greek in the east, see now F. Millar, *The Roman Near East, 31 BC-AD 337* (Cambridge, Mass.: Harvard University Press, 1993), 527–28.

gated to both Greeks *and* barbarians, both wise *and* foolish." With a touch of sarcasm that he hopes his (Judean) readers will appreciate, Paul employs the language—which had now lost much of its real force[83]—that Greek speakers had customarily used of others.

d. If this is what Paul has in mind, then οὕτως does not mean "I am coming to you because I am obligated both to Greeks and barbarians, and you people of course fit this description," but rather, "in fulfilling my obligation to both Greeks and barbarians, I must naturally pass through Rome; hence my desire and opportunity to visit you." This interpretation matches Paul's sense in 15:19–24 exactly: it is his mission to Spain that will bring him incidentally through Rome.

e. The adverb οὕτως can point forward to a following premise, as well as (or instead of) backward; it often does so in Paul.[84] Although the major English translations make verse 16 a new paragraph, that sentence begins with γάρ, which is a natural sequel to οὕτως.[85] And the substance of verse 16 serves rather well as justification for Paul's stopover in a Roman-Judean community, which will occur in spite of his normal obligation to Greeks and barbarians: "for I am not ashamed of the *euangelion,* for it is the power of God to everyone who trusts, to the Judean first and also to the Greek!" Although he has been entrusted with a *euangelion* for Gentiles, he is not ashamed for the Judean Christians to hear it as well (καὶ ὑμῖν). Indeed he believes that the *euangelion,* inasmuch as it levels all humanity before God, requires acceptance from Judean Christians too (below). That is why he does not hesitate to bring this gospel also to them (εὐαγγελίσασθαι; 1.15), whether in writing (the letter) or in person (the visit).

Thus we should arrange the four verses in question as part of the same paragraph, somewhat as follows:

> I do not want you to be ignorant, brothers, that I have often intended to come to you—and have been prevented from doing so until now—in order that I might have some fruit among you, just as also among the remainder of the *Gentiles.* [For] I am obligated to both Greeks *and* barbarians, to both wise *and* foolish. [That is why I plan to head west; cf. 15:19–24]. Hence the readiness *on my side* (τὸ κατ' ἐμὲ πρόθυμον) [but are *you* willing?] to bring the *euangelion* also (καί) to you who are in Rome: for I am not ashamed of the *euangelion;* it is the power of God for salvation to everyone who trusts, first the Judean and also the Greek.

Although still connected logically (by another γάρ), verse 17 introduces the revelation of God's righteousness and faith, and so fits more closely with the sequel (vv. 18ff.).

---

83 See A. Momigliano, *Alien Wisdom: the Limits of Hellenization* (Cambridge: Cambridge University Press, 1971), 7–11.

84 Rom 5:15, 18; 6:19–20; 10:6; 11:26; 1 Cor 4:1; 5:3–4.

85 Cranfield (*Romans,* 1:86) links v. 16a with what precedes.

4. For the next reference to Gentiles we must look all the way to 11:13, and this fact itself must be important for understanding the letter's audience. There Paul has just argued, with great delicacy and nuance, that by admitting Gentiles to salvation God has not forgotten his eternal covenant with Israel (9:1–11:12). That he speaks of Israel in the third person (9:3–5, etc.) does not imply that his audience is Gentile, since he also speaks of the Gentiles in the third person (9:24, 30; 11:11–12), and the particular Israelites in question are those who, unlike himself and the Judean-Christians (as I am arguing) of Rome, have not come to trust Christ (10:1; 11:1, 7). This whole part of his argument is in the abstract, dealing as it does with global questions of salvation history.

Paul has argued that the Gentiles were admitted to the promises by the sovereign act of God (9:14–24), because Israel was (by and large) blind and stubborn (11:3–10). Nevertheless, the admission of Gentiles is designed at least in part to provoke Israel to jealousy (9:23; 10:19; 11:11–12). Having just made this point using the third person for all parties concerned, Paul now adopts the second person: "Now I am speaking to you Gentiles" (11:13). After his excruciatingly careful argument addressing Judean concerns, he proceeds to warn the Gentiles bluntly not to become complacent, for just as they were "grafted in" to make Israel jealous, they too might be cut off if they prove faithless (11:17–25). He closes with a stunning revelation that accentuates the derivative and provisional place of the Gentiles. When the "full number" of Gentiles has come in, *all Israel* will be saved (11:25–26)! The entire argument of chapters 9–11 is thus a unity, defending Paul against charges that his gospel nullifies the promises *to Israel.*

Does this second-person aside to the Gentiles in 11:13–32 imply that his readership includes Gentiles? I think not. The context seems to require that the Gentiles in question are *not* those of any particular locale, but the ones he has been speaking about all along, namely,[86] the fruits of his Gentile mission who have come into salvation (9:30; 10:19; 11:11–12, 13b), the very ones among whom he has been performing the "priestly service," and from whom he has collected the offering for Jerusalem (15:16, 26–27). He addresses them directly here, in imaginary convocation, for obvious rhetorical effect. Having castigated Israel for failing to please God, he risks confirming his reputation for having dismissed Israel's heritage (3:8, 31; 6:15; 7:7; cf: Gal 4:30; Acts 21:21, 28). So he must balance the scale and reassure his Roman audience: the Gentiles have not taken over; they will be similarly punished if they should prove complacent. Although he could perhaps have made the same theoretical point by continuing to speak of the Gentiles in the third person, it is more effective to look his own converts in the eye *in absentia,* while his readers look on, and sternly caution them. In any case, the conclusion of the passage (11:25–36) reinforces the integrity of chapters 9–11, and

[86] M. Black is on the right track when he observes that Paul speaks through the Gentiles of Rome "to the whole Gentile world" (*Romans,* 144). Käsemann (*Romans,* 305) concurs: "These verses are directed to the Gentiles, without exclusively addressing the Roman readers." Evidently, these commentators only include Roman Gentiles among the readers because they have concluded from 1:5–6, 13 that the community included Gentiles.

so prevents us from treating 11:13 as a departure from his global reflection to speak of the internal situation in Rome; there is no break in the argument here.

5. The only other basis commonly cited for positing a Gentile majority among the Roman Christians is the content of chapters 14–15, in which some interpreters have found evidence of strained relations between the "weak" (hypothetically Judean-Christian) minority, who worry about dietary restrictions (14:2, 21) and calendar observance (14:5), and the "strong" (Gentile-Christian) majority, who have no such scruples. Paradoxically, however, even some of those who find a Gentile majority in Rome consider this passage rather a generalized *paraenesis* that does not deal with internal Roman problems,[87] while it is a proponent of the *Judean-majority* hypothesis who may be the most emphatic representative of the view that a Judean-Gentile conflict is in view.[88] We may assert at the outset with some confidence, then, that chapters 14–15 do not *require* a Gentile-Christian majority among the audience of Romans.

Abstinence from meat and wine, though a widely-admired (and seldom-practised) regimen in the ancient world, was by no means characteristic of Judeans; they were in fact known for their use of wine.[89] Watson is quite right that individual Judeans are said to have abstained in peculiar circumstances, when properly prepared food and drink were unavailable; but this observation cannot be applied to routine life in Rome, where there was such a large Judean population for nearly two centuries before Paul. Even if, as Watson speculates, Christian Judeans were no longer welcome in the transtiberine quarter (but how could they be excluded, since the quarter was not exclusively Judean?), the other parts of the city in which Judeans also lived—the Campus Martius and Subura—would have had the necessary services to support *kashrut*.[90] A vegetarian diet without wine could more easily be predicated of a heroic sub-group of either Judean or Gentile Christians than of Judean Christians as a bloc over against Gentiles.

In discussing these questions, we must bear in mind the overall shape of chapters 14–15. The main purpose of the general discussion of strong and weak is apparently to prepare for Paul's final appeal: "*Welcome one another, therefore,* as Christ has welcomed you" (15:7). It needs to be stressed, because it is often overlooked, that this exhortation is not evenhanded. The following two verses, beginning with γάρ, reiterate the point of the whole letter (1:2–4, 16; 3:29): Christ became a servant to the circumcised in order to confirm the ancient promises, *and so that the Gentiles might glorify God.* Paul is chiefly concerned that Judeans welcome the Gentiles of his mission, and thus recognize his particular "gospel." Accordingly, Paul supports his appeal with a string of biblical proof-texts for Gentile salvation, all of which feature the word *Gentiles* (15:9–12). Those who

---

[87] G. Klein, "Paul's Purpose in Writing the Epistle to the Romans," in *The Romans Debate* (ed. Donfried), 36; R. J. Karris, "Romans 14:1–15:3 and the Occasion of Romans," in *The Romans Debate* (ed. Donfried), 65–84.

[88] Watson, *Paul,* 94–98.

[89] Persius, *Sat.* 5.179–84; Plutarch, *Quaest. conv.* 4.6.2.

[90] See Leon, *Jews,* 137.

accept scripture as normative, evidently, should feel bound to accept the Gentiles. There is by contrast nothing here about *welcoming Judeans.* As throughout the earlier bulk of the letter, Paul continues a one-sided appeal to his Judean readers for consideration of Gentiles. Finally, and most important of all, this passage leads directly into Paul's summary of his "priestly work" among the Gentiles (15:14–29). The Gentiles of Paul's mission are the ones in need of welcome, and the whole letter is aimed at preparing that welcome.

To summarize thus far, whereas NT scholars have found the references to Gentiles in Romans so compelling that they have postulated a mixed community with a decisive Gentile majority, I have argued that the bulk of the letter, which should be given interpretative priority, indicates a Judean audience, that the few references to Gentiles can be more plausibly explained in other ways, and that the admittedly sparse external evidence also suggests a Judean form of Christianity in Rome at the time of this letter.

The criterion for assessing these proposals is not whether each one is immediately obvious. If they had been obvious, we should not have come to our current impasse. My argument is that, given the contradictory surface impressions created by Romans, and the dead ends that the Gentile hypothesis has created, we ought to ask whether that hypothesis is securely based. I would contend that the proposals above solve more difficulties than they create. Paul wrote the letter to persuade a Judean-Christian community to give his "gospel" for Gentiles a sympathetic hearing.

The Gospel in Romans

Peculiarities of Euangelion Language in Romans

With this argument in hand we may broach our second problem: Why does Paul uses *euangelion* language in such a peculiar way in Romans? Four peculiarities may be noted. (The following argument is contextualized by the broader survey in chapter 9 of this volume.)

1. Paul likes to use the noun *euangelion,* and does so thirty-eight times in the undisputed letters. But Romans, his longest letter, and the one that seems to be devoted to elaborating his *euangelion,* uses the word only nine times. Six of these instances occur in the opening and closing sections that we have discussed, with reference to his own mission and the faith of the Gentiles (1:1, 9, 16; 15:16, 19; 16:25). In the same proportion, two of the three occurrences of the verb *euangelizomai* in Romans fall within those same passages (1:15; 15:20), and the third is in a biblical quotation (10:15). Of the remaining three occurrences of *euangelion:* one falls within the short aside to Gentiles that we have discussed, speaking of the Gentiles' acceptance and Israel's rejection of the *euangelion* (11:28); in 10:16 Paul speaks in similar salvation-historical terms of the Judeans who have not believed the *euangelion;* and in the third case he appeals to "my *euangelion*" (2:16).

The upshot is that Paul nowhere speaks of the *euangelion* as something shared by him and his Roman Christian readers.

To appreciate the significance of this point one needs to recall the central role of the *euangelion* in Paul's other letters, where it is the explicit basis for his bond with his readers: "For you remember our labour and toil . . . while we preached to you the *euangelion* of God" (1 Thess 2:9); "For in Christ Jesus through the *euangelion* I gave birth to you" (1 Cor 4:15); " . . . thankful for your partnership in the *euangelion* from the first day" (Phil 1:5); "Let your manner of life be worthy of the *euangelion* of Christ . . . striving side by side for the faith of the *euangelion*" (Phil 1:27); "Even if *our* [shared] *euangelion* is veiled, it is veiled only to those who are perishing" (2 Cor 4:3); " . . . your obedience in acknowledging the *euangelion* of God" (2 Cor 9:13); "we did not yield . . . , that the truth of the *euangelion* might be preserved for you" (Gal 2:5). This sense of partnership between Paul and his readers in the *euangelion* is absent from Romans.

Its absence is the more striking because Paul has ample opportunity in this long letter to cite the *euangelion* when he speaks of what the Roman Christians have believed, obeyed, or been taught. Strangely, when these opportunities arise, Paul opts for awkwardly guarded locutions: "But thanks be to God that you who were slaves of sin have obeyed from your hearts *the sort of teaching to which you were given over* (ὃν παρεδόθητε τύπον διδαχῆς)" (6:17).[91] This exultant passage positively demands *euangelion,* but Paul conspicuously avoids it. Why? Similarly, he closes the letter with an admonition to beware of those who create disturbances, "contrary to the teaching which you have learned" (16:17). Although he recognizes their faith, and addresses them with terms of endearment, Paul does not cite the *euangelion* as the common basis of faith or ethics.

It is a rhetorical necessity that a writer or speaker establish common ground with his audience, and Paul does this at every opportunity in Romans. He cites a common scriptural heritage (1:2–3), physical descent from Abraham (4:1), commitment to Israel (3:1–2; 9:4–5), shared esteem for the law (3:31; 7:12), and common friends (ch. 16). But the *euangelion* is not common ground. Paul's assumption of a certain distance between this audience and his *euangelion* is highlighted by the phrase "my *euangelion,*" which he uses only in Romans (εὐαγγέλιον μοῦ; 2:16; 16:25).

2. That he associates this *euangelion* with himself and his Gentile converts, but not yet with his Roman readers, is indicated already by his opening self-identification: "Paul, slave of Jesus Christ, called as [or "to be"] apostle specially assigned to the *euangelion* of God" (κλητὸς ἀπόστολος ἀφωρισμένος εἰς εὐαγγέλιον θεοῦ 1:1). It is important here to clarify the sense of the perfect passive participle of ἀφορίζω—"set aside, reserve, appoint"—which I have with deliberate provocation rendered "specially assign."

Commentators have generally referred the phrase to an internal, psychological, or spiritual "consecration." Paul is thus portrayed as either reflecting upon

[91] Commentators, it is fair to say, do not make good sense of this line; R. Bultmann simply excised it as a "stupid insertion" (cited in Cranfield, *Romans,* 1:323).

his "conversion" to Christianity, in which he was separated by God from his Pharisaic past (cf. Phil 3:5–6), or piously recalling the language of Jeremiah about separation for God's work while still in the womb (cf. Jer 1:5; Gal 1:15).[92] But why make these points here and now, in this particular letter? What could they mean for these readers? No other letter opening presents Paul as "set apart."

Although purely theological senses are always possible, we ought to prefer one that relates Paul's language to the concrete situation of the letter. In this case, I would argue, Paul thinks of himself as specially assigned *vis-à-vis the other apostles* to the *euangelion* of God. This would entail a strong reading of the phrase, for if Paul were in his own mind the apostle responsible for the *euangelion* of God, then the *euangelion* would also in some sense also be reserved for him.[93]

We may note three data that support the stronger reading. First, the participle stands next to the noun "apostle." Although a comma is usually inserted between the two words, so that they are independently related back to "Paul," it seems at least equally plausible that the participle qualifies the immediately preceding "apostle"; he is "apostle assigned to the *euangelion* of God."[94] His *euangelion* distinguishes him from the other apostles.

Second, we know from Gal 2:7–9 that Paul really does consider himself the one apostle, in contrast to the others, who has been charged with the Gentile mission. And in that context he associates the word *euangelion* (explicitly) only with his mission (Gal 2:2, 5, 7). His letters elsewhere reflect his keen awareness of being different from the other apostles on account of his mission to the Gentiles (1 Cor 9:2; 15:9–10; 2 Cor 11:5). If *euangelion* has a special significance for the Gentile mission (below), then it would make sense for Paul to portray himself in Rom 1:1 as its special representative among the apostles.

Third, in Paul's only other self-referential use of the verb "set apart" (ἀφορίζω) he connects it with the *euangelion* and his Gentile mission: "when he who had set me apart since my mother's womb and had called me was pleased to reveal his son in me, so that (ἵνα) I might proclaim (εὐαγγελίζωμαι) him among the Gentiles . . ." (Gal 1:15–16). Whatever pious embellishments Paul might have bestowed on the term (e.g., his call "from the womb"), the point is clear enough that he considered himself specially reserved for the *euangelion* among the Gentiles.

---

[92]Black, *Romans,* 34; Cranfield, *Romans,* 1:53; Käsemann, *Romans,* 6; Fitzmyer, *Romans,* 229, 232.

[93]Cf. Josephus, *War* 2.488: successors of Alexander the Great "reserved" (ἀφώρισαν) for the Alexandrian Judeans their own quarter of the city.

[94]Cranfield (*Romans,* 1:53 n. 1) dismisses this possibility as "very clumsy" for reasons that escape me. In an unpunctuated text intended for oral presentation, it would be even clumsier to add a third qualifier to the original "Paul" (in addition to "slave . . ." and "called . . .") and expect the hearers/readers to ignore the immediately preceding words, which stand in the same case and number. While I might have preferred a definite article before "apostle" to make this reading absolutely clear, that would perhaps be too strong for the occasion; the customary reading would require, by contrast, an "and" between "apostle" and "set apart." Why not allow at least a dual apposition?

3. Another indicator of the distance between Paul and his Roman readers on the question of *euangelion* is the defensive posture of his opening statement, which colors the whole of the letter: "For I am not ashamed of the *euangelion*" (1:16). Why should he be ashamed, or even raise the rhetorical prospect of shame? In his letters to Gentiles, as we have seen, the *euangelion* is self-evidently true and decisive; shame is not a prospect. Possibly, he raises the issue in Romans only because he assumes the emphatic agreement of his readers—"Of course, Paul, one could never be ashamed of the *euangelion* that we all hold dear!"—as a way of establishing a common base. But overwhelming contextual indicators speak against such an interpretation. The whole letter is defensive, responding to real or alleged concerns from a Judean perspective (Rom 2:25; 3:1, 8, 27, 31; 4:1; 6:1, 15; 7:1, 7, 12; 8:2–3; 9:1–5; 11:25–36).

Further, we know—it is not a matter of speculation—that some Judean Christians *did* think that Paul should be ashamed of his *euangelion*.[95] They assumed that he had corrupted the apostles' teaching in order "to please men" (Gal 1:10–12), and that he had effectively written off Israel and its traditions (Acts 21:21, 28). In social terms, the appearance of having jettisoned one's ancestral laws and of having openly challenged the esteemed leaders of the group, who had in this case been associates and relatives of Jesus himself, would easily explain the charge of "disgrace."[96]

Scholars routinely note that the "sender" portion of Romans is much longer than usual in Paul's letters. They routinely suggest also that he has inserted an existing creed after the introduction of himself (1:2–3), and some allow that this must have been intended to cement the bond with his readers.[97] But these observations need to be focused more sharply, and as a problem: Why does Paul, immediately after mentioning his own name and his special *euangelion* (1:1) pile up clauses connecting that *euangelion* with Judean scripture and history? Why is it so untypically urgent for him to say this before he even gets to his "hello" (1:7)?

It seems to me that the attribution of 1:3–4 to a "pre-Pauline formula" has dulled our sensitivity to the defensive tone of this novel introduction. Paul says that the *euangelion* about Jesus was announced in the prophets of holy scripture, and that Jesus was a scion of David according to the *flesh*, yes (1:2–3); but his resurrection from the dead puts things on another plane entirely. Now designated son of God in *power* according to the *Holy Spirit*, he is the Lord who invites the obedience of Gentiles as well (1:4–5). That verses 2–3 are concessive is signaled by the vivid contrast between the boo-word "flesh" and the hurrah-word "spirit." The connotations of these categories would not be lost on any ancient reader, and elsewhere Paul applies them with rhetorical force precisely to the distinction between Judean Christianity and his *euangelion* (Phil 3:2–3, 18–20; 2 Cor 3:15, 18; Gal 3:1–5).

---

[95] See G. Lüdemann, *Opposition to Paul in Jewish Christianity* (trans. M. E. Boring; Minneapolis: Fortress, 1989), esp. 35–115.

[96] Cf. Josephus's assessment of Apion, *Ag. Ap.* 2.143–144.

[97] Dodd, *Romans*, 4–5; Cranfield, *Romans*, 1:57; Käsemann, *Romans*, 10–11; Fitzmyer, *Romans*, 228–30. Jervis (*Purpose*, 72–75, 85) draws attention to the unusual length of the "sender" field.

Paul is thus not arguing here for a balanced view of Jesus' human and divine pedigrees, or simply citing a creed.[98] He is making a programmatic statement that sets the pace for what will follow from verse 16, after the obligatory thanksgiving: he is out to explain and defend the "*euangelion* of God" among readers who have not yet accepted it.

4. Finally, just where we should most expect to find the *euangelion* invoked as common ground, in his otherwise generous thanksgiving, Paul confounds us by referring to "my intention to *bring the euangelion* also to (εὐαγγελίσασθαι) you who are in Rome" (1:15). What a thing to say in an otherwise diplomatic letter opening! In his typical letters to Gentiles, the verb consistently refers to the past, when Paul first established the community with his *euangelion*.[99] It is therefore unlikely that his Roman readers, who were already well established (1:8), valued the *euangelion* as a term of self-evident supreme good, in the way that Paul did. If they had done, his comment would have been a direct insult. We should rather conclude, in line with everything we have seen so far, that *euangelion*-language has special significance for Paul and his Gentile mission.

How do these peculiarities in Paul's *euangelion* language relate to the question of audience? A detached reading of K. Donfried's Romans *Debate* would show that they do not make good sense on the common hypothesis of a Gentile majority. G. Klein's proposal, that Paul intends to provide the Gentile Roman community with a proper apostolic foundation, is perhaps the most fully articulated.[100] It is also widely rejected.[101] It would be more plausible if Paul's apostleship had been evident to anyone but himself and his closest associates (cf. 1 Cor 9:2). In any case, it does not derive from a natural sense of *euangelizomai.*

The Gospel and Judean Christianity

If Paul's readers were Christian Judeans, we have a simple and probable solution to the difficulty—probable, because it hinges on a demonstrable trait in Paul's use of *euangelion.* He most closely approximates the possessive "my *euangelion*" of Romans when he deals with the Judaizing threat in his own churches.

In writing to Corinth and Galatia, as we have seen, Paul cites the *euangelion* as the basis of communion with his readers. He was the one who established them in the *euangelion,* and he encourages them to maintain their loyalty (*1 Cor* 4.15; 9.18; *2 Cor* 4.3; 9.13; *Gal* 2.14; 4.13). In both locations, however, Paul's teach-

[98] On this reading, I see no reason to suppose that Paul is using a creed at all. If he is, he has thoroughly adapted it to his current need.

[99] 1 Cor 1:17 (linked with baptizing); 9:16, 18; 15:1–2; 2 Cor 10:16; 11:7; Gal 1:8, 11, 16, 23; 4:13. He occasionally uses the verb, sarcastically, of others' activities in his churches (Gal 1:9).

[100] Klein, "Purpose," 29–43.

[101] Donfried, "Romans 16," 44–45; Watson, "Congregations," 213; P. Stuhlmacher, "The Purpose of Romans," in *The Romans Debate* (ed. Donfried), 241 n. 25; Elliott, *Rhetoric,* 22–23, 28–29; Jervis, *Purpose,* 26, 163 (although she does think that Paul wishes the Romans to accept him as "their apostle"); Fitzmyer, *Romans,* 76.

ing is challenged after his departure by advocates of a Judean Christianity that proves very appealing to his Gentile converts. Paul vehemently denounces these interlopers and their ideas.

His language is revealing. Where his opening thanksgiving would normally stand, an angry Paul marvels that his Galatian converts have so quickly turned to "a different *euangelion,* which is not merely another variety of the same" (εἰς ἕτερον εὐαγγέλιον, ὃ οὐκ ἔστιν ἄλλο; 1:6–7). The Judaizers, indeed, "wish to pervert *the euangelion of Christ.* But even if we ourselves or an angel from heaven should bring a *euangelion* different from the *euangelion* that we brought to you before, let him be accursed!" (1:8) In the face of this Judaizing challenge, he begins to use terms approaching the possessive "my *euangelion*" of Romans: he insists that "the *euangelion that was proclaimed by me*" comes directly from God (1:11). Similarly, he speaks of his dealings with the Judean-Christian leaders in Jerusalem: "I laid before them *the euangelion that I proclaim among the Gentiles*" (2:2). Does Paul really recognize any other *euangelion*? He seems plainly to identify "the *euangelion* of Christ" with what he preaches.

Most impressive, when Peter and the rest of the Judeans withdraw from common meals with Gentiles, to satisfy a delegation from James, Paul castigates them for not being "straightforward about 'the truth of *the euangelion*'" (2:14). Evidently, the scruples of these Judeans prevent them from embracing what Paul considers the *euangelion*—in spite of his exhortation that failure to do so involves rebuilding what has now been smashed to pieces (Gal 2:18) and nullifying the grace of God (2:21). Similarly, in the preceding sentences Paul has declared that he did not yield to certain "false brothers" who objected to the freedom that he took in Christ Jesus, "so that the 'truth of the *euangelion*' might remain among you" (Gal 2:5). Since the false brothers evidently promoted a Judean Christianity like Peter ("to enslave us," 2:5; "you compel Gentiles to judaize," 2:14), it is impossible to avoid associating the two events. For Paul, *the* truth of *the euangelion* is what he preaches among Gentiles.

We observe the same phenomenon in his correspondence with the Corinthians. Although he has given them birth through the *euangelion,* now in the face of a Judean challenge[102] he accuses them:

> If someone comes and proclaims another Jesus, whom we did not proclaim, or if you receive a different spirit, which you did not formerly receive, or a different (ἕτερον) *euangelion,* which you did not formerly accept, you happily adopt it! (2 Cor 11:4)

These passages seem to show that Paul is unwilling to connect full-blooded Judean Christianity—of the kind that would maintain a traditional Judean regimen in spite of the death and resurrection of Jesus—with his *euangelion.* And it is only in this context of conflict with "Judeanism" that Paul so qualifies his use of *euangelion.* Although he faces many other problems within his churches, he does not link those problems to a "different *euangelion*" (cf. 1 Corinthians).

---

[102] See Lüdemann, *Opposition,* 80–97.

I concede that Paul does not maintain an obvious and one-sided antipathy to Judean Christianity; nor does he withhold the term *euangelion* with perfect consistency. He is at least superficially ambivalent toward Christian Judeans. He formally acknowledges the apostleship of the Jerusalem leaders (1 Cor 9:5; 15:9; Gal. 2:2); he goes out of his way to reach a diplomatic agreement with them (Gal 2:1–10); he devotes a remarkable amount of energy, over several years, to the collection for the saints in Jerusalem (2 Cor 8–9; Rom 15:25–29); and he admits Judean believers as brothers and sisters. Within the context of the Jerusalem agreement, he implies that Peter's preaching to the "circumcision" parallels his own "*euangelion* of the foreskin" (Gal 2:7)—though he does not actually call Peter's preaching *euangelion*. Similarly, when he discusses apostles' finances, his quotation of Jesus' remark (1 Cor 9:14) seems to suggest that the other apostles too proclaim the *euangelion*. But he does not quite say it, and the sequel seems to isolate him and his *euangelion* from the others once again (9:15–18).

None of this, however, can obscure the fact that his most vehement repudiations of the law, circumcision, and those who advocate them arise out of disputes *within* the Christian camp (Philippians 3; *2 Corinthians* 3, 10–13; Galatians 3–4). He openly curses his Judean-Christian opponents, ridicules them, calls them names, and consigns them to perdition (Phil 3:2, 19; 2 Cor 11:3–4, 13–15, 26; Gal 1:8–9; 5:12; 6:12). He admits that the status of the Jerusalem apostles really means nothing to him after all (Gal 2:6). He counts his own Judean past as "dung" in the face of the new creation (Phil 3:7–8). Although we might prefer to think that he admits their teaching, at least grudgingly, as a "different kind of *euangelion*" (Gal 1:6; 2 Cor 11:4), we quickly realize that his language is sarcastic; for just as there is no Jesus or spirit other than the ones that he has preached, so there is no other *euangelion*.

It is not plausible, in my view, that Paul says all of this only because some Judaizers have interfered with his Gentile converts, and that he otherwise has no objection to Judean Christianity.[103] Such a conclusion does not adequately explain: his vigorous arguments for the end of the law in principle, even where he is not writing to his own converts (Rom 10:14); his consistent claim that the categories of Judean and Greek no longer apply in Christ (2 Cor: 5:17; Gal 3:28; Rom 10:14); his confrontation of Peter (implicitly also Barnabas, James, and others) for not abandoning what Peter understood as appropriate behavior for a Judean (Gal 2:11); his personal example of abandoning Torah observance in the light of Christ's coming (Phil 3:4–9); and the widespread impression that he encouraged other Judeans to follow suit (Acts 21:21, 28)—a charge that was hardly invented by the author of Acts (cf. Rom 3:8, 31; 7:7).[104] It is no coincidence that Paul's relations with Judea were always strained: originally driven out of Judea because of his preaching to the Gentiles (1 Thess 2:15–16), he returned only when absolutely necessary, for brief periods, and always with anxiety (Gal 1:18; 2:1; Rom 15:31–32).

---

[103] Pace K. Stendahl, *Paul Among Jews and Gentiles* (Philadelphia: Fortress, 1976), 2–3; Gaston, *Torah*, 137.

[104] See Lüdemann, *Opposition*, 55–59.

This ambivalence toward Judean Christianity, which seems to result from the tension between a clear ideology (Judaism per se has been supplanted by Christ) and political constraint (Paul must in practice get along with Judean Christians), is precisely what we find in Romans. On the rhetorical level, he is polite and even expresses the hope that he might learn something from his audience (1:12). He considers issues of importance to Judeans with great delicacy and nuance (1:16–11:36). But in the end, though he gives them as positive a face as he can, his positions are bad news for traditional Judean culture. In light of Christ's coming, circumcision, physical descent from Abraham, and Torah observance have lost their *crucial* significance (3:21; 4:14); in the current moment of salvation history "there is no distinction between Judean and Greek" (10:12; cf: 3:9).

Corresponding to this ambivalence, and wholly in keeping with the tendencies of his other letters, is Paul's use of *euangelion* in Romans. We have seen that he does not invoke it as a common basis with his readers. Nevertheless, in Rom 10:16 he seems to be referring to Israel when he quotes Isa 53:1 in support of his claim that "they have not all obeyed the *euangelion.*" If we applied rigorous logic, we should conclude that some Judeans therefore have obeyed the *euangelion,* and we should perhaps infer from this alone that Paul recognizes Judean Christianity as a form of *euangelion.* But even on such tight logic, he might only connect Judeans like himself—whom he will presently offer as a prime example of faithful Israel (11:2)—or Prisca and Aquila (16:3–5) with the *euangelion.* More to the point, we cannot employ rigorous logic in view of his demonstrable strategic flexibility when speaking to Judeans (cf. 1 Cor 9:21–22; 10:32–33). In spite of his posture of openness in this letter, Paul is disinclined to use the language of *euangelion* for what the readers have already believed.

Summary and Conclusion

I have set out to consider two problems: the audience of Romans and the peculiarities of Paul's *euangelion*-language in this letter. The former problem arises because the references to Gentiles in the opening and closing sections do not match the heart of the letter itself, which presupposes a Judean-Christian audience, or the external evidence, which attests to the Judean ambience of Roman Christianity through the first century. I have argued that these few references to Gentiles (a) *cannot* take methodological priority over the orientation of the letter as a whole and (b) *can* be plausibly understood in ways that do not involve a Gentile audience. It is much more economical to understand them this way than to interpret the rest of the letter as if it were addressed to Gentiles.

A case in point is Paul's peculiar use of "gospel" language in Romans, which was our second question. Paul's defensiveness about *his euangelion,* his desire to bring it to the Roman Christians as if it were something new, and his marked reluctance to call what they have already believed *euangelion,* are all difficult to explain by means of a Gentile-majority hypothesis. Yet these phenomena fit well with Paul's observable tendency in other letters to reserve *euangelion*-language for his unique mission to the Gentiles, and to withdraw it from shared discourse with his converts when they move toward Judean Christianity. The data make the best sense, in other words, if Romans is addressed to a group of Judean Christians. That Paul was the first Christian to use *euangelion*-language, and that he used it with a particular bearing on his Gentile mission, suggests that the word group was not as meaningful to non-Pauline Christians.[105]

Of course, there may have been some Gentiles among the Roman Christians, perhaps Judean sympathizers or even proselytes, but the letter does not deal with their particular concerns.

[105] This conclusion would have obvious implications for historical-Jesus research; but see already G. Friedrich ("εὐαγγέλιον," *TDNT* 2:727): "It is thus doubtful . . . whether Jesus ever spoke of εὐαγγέλιον."

Chapter 11

Chief Priests, Sadducees, Pharisees, and Sanhedrin in Luke-Acts and Josephus

It may seem odd at the end of the twentieth century that one should venture upon a new study of the Judean (traditionally "Jewish": see ch. 5 above) leaders in Acts. Acts and every other first-century source that mentions these groups have been known for nearly two millennia. If the object is to compare the portrayal in Acts with what is known historically about the chief priests, Sadducees, Pharisees, and Sanhedrin, has this not been done many times already? Remarkably, it is only within the last twenty years that scholars have begun seriously to study the function of the Judean leaders in the narrative of Acts. And it is no longer (or not yet) possible to speak of "what we know" historically about the Judean leaders.

These two phenomena are related, for the new focus on the roles of Judean leaders in particular texts results from the same intellectual forces that brought down the house of cards that formerly passed for historical knowledge. To be sure, intensive scholarly energy on our theme, following the rise of critical history and the emancipation of European Jews, produced great manuals of historical knowledge about the NT *Umwelt.* But since the turn of the century, broad intellectual movements exposing the problems of bias, perspective, context, construction, particularity, otherness, and diversity, have filtered through the academy.[1] These general intellectual tendencies have been catalyzed by particular advances. Jacob Neusner's reappraisal of the rabbinic corpus, which provided much of the fuel for old constructions of the Judean leaders, shows that this literature makes a coherent statement about its time of composition, not about the first century.[2] Archaeological discoveries, the recovery of lost writings, and the reappraisal of known texts have further helped to overturn the first critical syntheses, which tended to cobble together a monolithic system of thought from bits and pieces in a variety of sources.[3] The hallmark of our time is a profound historical agnosticism.[4]

---

[1] H. C. Kee, *Knowing the Truth: A Sociological Approach to New Testament Interpretation* (Minneapolis: Fortress, 1989) 1–64.

[2] J. Neusner, *The Rabbinic Traditions,* 3:234–38.

[3] Cf. M. Smith, "Palestinian Judaism"; Neusner, *Rabbinic Traditions,* 3:320–68; R. A. Kraft and G. W. E. Nickelsburg, eds., *Early Judaism,* 1–30; G. G. Porton, "Diversity in postbiblical Judaism," in *Early Judaism* (ed. Kraft and Nickelsburg), 57–80.

[4] S. Mason, "The Problem of the Pharisees in Modern Scholarship," in *Approaches to Ancient Judaism, New Series 3: Historical and Literary Studies* (SFSHJ 81; ed. J. Neusner; Atlanta: Scholars, 1993), 103–40.

This dissolution of reliable historical knowledge has rendered it all the more urgent to understand what is in each particular text. Since we do not possess the past itself, but only a few stories and physical remains from it, we should first try to understand what we have, rather than what we lack. So NT scholars have begun to return to the texts for their own sake, not merely as *sources* for patchwork historical reconstructions, and they have been greatly assisted by a new rapprochement with literary criticism.[5] They have begun to read the gospels and Acts more curiously, with attention to rhetoric,[6] plot and character, implied readers, narrators, and authors.[7] So we have seen a spate of studies on the Judean leaders not as historical figures but as *literary characters:* in Matthew,[8] Mark,[9] Luke-Acts,[10] Josephus,[11] and rabbinic literature.[12]

The new concern with texts as coherent stories does not preclude historical questioning. But it does mean that historical questions should not be asked too quickly, as they were before.[13] History can no longer be done positivistically, by looking at discrete statements in various authors and asking whether these statements are right or wrong as expressions of fact. Evidence only has meaning in context, as part of someone's story. If we do not know what it means in context, we cannot use it for historical purposes. In the wake of the collapse of old constructions of the Judean leadership groups, every new historical hypothesis must demonstrate a grasp of the stories from the period, show how an author chose to use the leaders in particular roles, and state how this particular historical reconstruction plausibly explains these many uses: if hypothesis X is right, then authors A, B, C, and D came to their views of the matter in this way.[14] The modern reconstruction will not be the same as any ancient story. But it must plausibly show how the ancient stories—the evidence to be explained—came into being.

---

[5]Cf. already N. Petersen, *Literary Criticism for New Testament Critics* (Philadelphia: Fortress, 1978).

[6]G. A. Kennedy, *Rhetorical Criticism.*

[7]E. P. Sanders and M. Davies, *Studying the Synoptic Gospels* (London: SCM, 1989), 224–51.

[8]D. R. A. Hare, *The Theme of Jewish Persecution of Christians in the Gospel According to St.* Matthew (SNTSMS 6; Cambridge: Cambridge University Press, 1967); S. van Tilborg, *The Jewish Leaders in Matthew* (Leiden: Brill, 1972).

[9]M. J. Cook, *Mark's Treatment of the Jewish Leaders* (Leiden: Brill, 1978).

[10]J. Ziesler, "Luke and the Pharisees," *NTS* 25 (1978–1979): 146–57; R. L. Brawley, *Luke-Acts and the Jews: Conflict, Apology, and Conciliation* (SBLMS 33; Atlanta: Scholars Press, 1987); J. T. Sanders, *The Jews in Luke-Acts* (Philadelphia: Fortress Press, 1987); R. P. Carroll, "Luke's Portrayal of the Pharisees," *CBQ* 50 (1988): 604–21; J. A. Darr, *On Character Building: The Reader and the Rhetoric of Characterization in Luke-Acts* (Louisville: John Knox, 1992).

[11]G. Baumbach, "The Sadducees in Josephus," in *Josephus, the Bible, and History* (ed. Feldman and Hata), 173–95; C. Thoma, "The High Priesthood in the Judgment of Josephus," in *Josephus, the Bible, and History* (ed. Feldman and Hata); Mason, *Josephus on the Pharisees,* 196–215.

[12]Neusner, *Rabbinic Traditions.*

[13]Neusner, *Rabbinic Traditions,* 3.320–68.

[14]Mason, *Josephus on the Pharisees,* 1–17.

These considerations make the following study of the Judean leaders in Luke-Acts quite different from what one might have come up with even fifty years ago, in spite of the fact that the "evidence" has remained constant. First, the author of Acts wrote the work as a sequel to the Gospel of Luke, so interpreters of Acts can only engage the story properly by first examining the Gospel. We cannot pull out Gamaliel's speech or some other episode as somehow reflective of Luke's community, but must start at the beginning and deal with the whole story. Second, we cannot assume any historical knowledge about the groups in question as an external referent. And since an original historical investigation would require prior analysis of all relevant texts, it is beyond our scope. Jacob Neusner,[15] Ellis Rivkin,[16] and Anthony Saldarini[17] have all tried their hands at historical reconstructions of the Pharisees (or several leadership groups)[18] in the new way—*after* first interpreting each relevant source in its own world—and they are to be applauded for realizing what is required. Still, none of their proposals yet commands sufficient support to serve as a secure body of knowledge. Strangely, the two most recent reconstructions of the Jewish groups,[19] while recognizing the negative implications of Neusner's work, do not seem to see the need to explain the ancient stories in any comprehensive way.[20]

Instead of comparing Acts with "history," which we do not have ready-made, it seems to me that we must begin to treat it as another kind of evidence, alongside the only contemporary Judean narratives that mention these Judean leaders—the writings of Flavius Josephus. Luke-Acts is arguably the most important early Christian statement on the Judean leaders, because of its unparalleled size and historical self-conception, and the Josephan corpus is without question the most important non-Christian witness. By developing interpretations of the Judean leaders in these two complex narrative sets, one might hope to establish a *prolegomenon* to historical reconstruction of the groups. Although in the original version of this essay[21] I tried to bring the two into comparison as wholes, space constraints here require me to abbreviate much of the Josephus section. Much of that material is represented in some way by other chapters in this volume (especially chapters 5 and 6 on a contextual reading of his Pharisees). I retain only enough of the second part and conclusion to suggest the lines of comparison.

The secondary literature on Luke, Acts, Josephus, and each of the Judean groups is so vast that responsible interaction would have produced a

[15] J. Neusner, *From Politics to Piety: The Emergence of the Pharisaic Judaism* (Englewood Cliffs: Prentice-Hall, 1973).

[16] Rivkin, *Revolution.*

[17] Saldarini, *Pharisees.*

[18] Ibid.

[19] Sanders, *Practice and Belief,* 317–490; Grabbe, *Judaism,* 2:463–554.

[20] See S. Mason, "Revisiting Josephus's Pharisees," in *Judaism in Late Antiquity,* pt. 3: *Where We Stand: Issues and Debates in Ancient Judaism* (4 vols.; ed. J. Neusner and A. J. Avery-Peck; Leiden: Brill, 1999), 23–56.

[21] S. Mason, "Chief Priests, Sadducees, Pharisees and Sanhedrin in Acts," in *The Book of Acts in its Palestinian Setting* (ed. R. Bauckham; vol. 4 of *The Book of Acts in its First-Century Setting,* ed. B. W. Winter. Grand Rapids: Eerdmans, 1995), 115–77.

multi-volume book rather than a chapter. In the available space I can only summarize three recent and comprehensive interpretations of the Judean leaders in Luke-Acts, before proceeding with my own analysis of the primary texts. Parenthetical notes indicate studies that I have found unusually helpful, whether I agree with them or not.

The State of the Question

In 1987 Robert L. Brawley and Jack T. Sanders[22] published the first two comprehensive studies of the Jewish leaders in Acts. Each knew the other's work in progress, but they came to quite different assessments of Luke's overall purpose and of his use of the Jewish leaders. Five years later, John A. Darr[23] tried to refine their efforts with closer attention to narratological method. The common concern of all three to identify the literary function of Jewish leadership groups in Luke-Acts marks an advance over previous work and provides a useful starting point.

Jack T. Sanders

Sanders's interpretation of Luke's social context follows that of Robert Maddox.[24] This Gentile-Christian community faces an identity crisis caused by the competing claims of Judaism to the same texts and tradition. Luke and his readers share a Pauline outlook.[25] The legitimacy of the young church's interpretation of scripture with reference to Christ is challenged by the established Jewish community and by Jewish Christians who call for Torah observance.[26] Luke's response is to show that the Jewish people are misguided, that they have both rejected God and been rejected by God. Gentile inclusion is now divinely authorized; non-Christian Jews and Jewish Christians who seek to remain observant have been written off by God.[27]

Sanders arrives at these conclusions after considering first how the main leadership groups and Jerusalem function in Luke-Acts (chs. 1–2). With the exception of two incidental references to high priests (Luke 3:1; Acts 19:14), the chief priests and elders along with their associated scribes are consistently hostile to Jesus and the young church.[28] The attitude of these leaders provides one important reference point for Luke's view of the Jews. Luke even implies that it was Jews who executed Jesus; here and elsewhere he imagines Jewish soldiers directed

---

22 See n. 10 above.
23 See n. 10 above.
24 R. Maddox, *The Purpose of Luke-Acts* (Edinburgh: T&T Clark, 1982).
25 Sanders, *Luke–Acts,* 316–17.
26 Ibid., 130, 314.
27 Ibid., 54, 110–11, 317.
28 Ibid., 20.

by the chief priests.[29] The four Herods in Luke-Acts also persecute Jesus' group (John the Baptist, Jesus, James) when behaving as Jews; when acting as secular leaders, however, they tend to acquit (Jesus and Paul).[30] Jerusalem functions as the "*locus classicus* of hostility to God, to his purposes, to his messengers."[31] Luke normally uses the term Sanhedrin (*synedrion*) for a place, the "courtroom" of the Jewish council, though he can also use it of the assembled body.[32]

Acknowledging the apparent ambivalence of Luke-Acts toward the Jewish people, who sometimes support Jesus and the church but sometimes oppose them, Sanders proposes that one look first at the speeches to determine Luke's fundamental view. There he finds a consistent portrait: "the Jews are and always have been willfully ignorant of the purposes and plans of God expressed in their familiar scriptures. . . ." This view is "repeated over and over in every possible way *ad nauseam*."[33] Jesus' keynote sermon in Nazareth (Luke 4:16–27) and Paul's final assessment (Acts 28:25–28) serve to frame the other speeches as declarations of Jewish rejection. Although there was a time in which the prospect of repentance and salvation was duly offered, by Stephen's speech in Acts 7 repentance is no longer an option.[34] If one then interprets the Jews' narrative actions in light of the speeches one finds that, in spite of early support for Jesus and the church, ultimately "the Jews have *become* what they from the first *were*":[35] intransigent opponents of the divine will who are rejected by God.[36]

With this portrait of the Jewish leaders and people in hand, Sanders turns to the Pharisees. The problem is that they appear quite friendly to Jesus throughout the Gospel, with their dinner invitations, warning to flee Herod Antipas, and absence from the passion narrative.[37] Most of their disputes concern the proper interpretation of the Law.[38] In Acts, the Pharisees remain basically friendly, as the speech of Gamaliel and their siding with Paul in the Sanhedrin indicate; strangely, the only obstructionist Pharisees are the Christian Pharisees of Acts 15:5, who insist that Gentile Christians be circumcised and observe Torah, and whose views Luke rejects.[39]

Sanders finds in this episode the key to Luke's use of the Pharisees. In the Gospel and here in Acts, "Pharisees" stand for those Jewish Christians who dismiss Gentile Christianity (and Luke's community) as illegitimate; Luke's stories about Jesus' eating with sinners and Sabbath freedom are meant to confront those Jewish Christians.[40] The Pharisees/Jewish-Christians appear to desire Jesus'

---

[29] Ibid., 9–12.
[30] Ibid., 20–2.
[31] Ibid., 26.
[32] Ibid., 4–5.
[33] Ibid., 63.
[34] Ibid., 54–5.
[35] Ibid., 81.
[36] Ibid., 81–3.
[37] Ibid., 85–8.
[38] Ibid., 90–1.
[39] Ibid., 94–5.
[40] Ibid., 95.

company, but they do not understand him or his program. They are therefore the hypocrites whose leaven must be avoided, and Luke dismisses them along with non-Christian Jews.[41] But Luke also uses the friendly non-Christian Pharisees of Acts, Gamaliel and the others on the council, to "underscore the linkage between Christianity and the ancestral Israelite religion."[42] Thus, Pharisees fulfill two roles in Luke's effort to exclude Judaism from Christianity: they represent Christians who do not see the implications of Jesus' coming for Judaism (in Pauline terms) and they serve as sort of official Jewish greeters and guarantors of the Christian movement.[43]

Sanders devotes nearly half of his book[44] to a linear reading of Luke-Acts in order to justify his thematic analysis *in situ*.

Robert L. Brawley

Brawley agrees with Sanders that Luke-Acts comes from a Pauline church, but the rest of his analysis is diametrically opposite. Far from providing a rationale for the severance of Christianity from Judaism, Brawley's Luke seeks to reunite Pauline Christianity with Judaism, to draw "authentic Jews toward Christianity and authentic Christians toward Judaism."[45] This rapprochement requires the rehabilitation of Paul, which is the main burden of Acts. In the face of Jewish and Jewish Christian criticism, Paul must be shown a faithful Jew, in direct continuity with the unimpeachably Jewish Peter.[46] In Brawley's view, Jewish repentance and salvation remain options through to the very end of Acts; even Acts 28 claims that some of the Roman Jews were "persuaded" by Paul (Acts 28:24).[47]

In support of his thesis, Brawley takes a minimalist approach to the text. That is, whereas most scholars have seen particular figures and situations as paradigmatic of the Jewish/Christian problem at Luke's time of writing, Brawley insists that they be confined to their plain sense. Thus, the rejection at Nazareth does not foreshadow *universal* Jewish rejection, but reflects only the rejection of some people at one place and one time.[48] Acts does not show a steady movement away from Jerusalem to the ends of the earth, because there is a constant return to Jerusalem throughout.[49] Acts 1:8 ("to the ends of the earth") remains unfulfilled in the text itself. Unlike Paul's own letters, Luke-Acts knows of no Pauline Gentile mission; Paul has a *diaspora* mission, which includes Jews and Gentiles, and he puts more effort into the Jewish mission.[50] Most important, the "architectonic"

---

[41] Ibid., 110–1.
[42] Ibid., 97.
[43] Ibid., 112.
[44] Ibid., 156–299.
[45] Brawley, *Luke-Acts,* 159.
[46] Ibid., 42–3; 66–7.
[47] Ibid., 141.
[48] Ibid., 26.
[49] Ibid., 36.
[50] Ibid., 49.

structure of Acts highlights not the spread of *Christianity*, but the parallel between Peter (ch. 1–12) and Paul (chs. 13–28).[51] The many standard legitimation techniques of Hellenistic literature used by Luke confirm that Luke is out to defend Paul.[52]

How do the Jewish-Judean leaders fit in Luke's agenda? Like many others,[53] Brawley is impressed by the friendliness of the Pharisees in Luke-Acts—a disposition that confounds the form-critical staple that hostility to the Pharisees increases as the Synoptic Tradition develops.[54] Although Luke is critical of their character, tosses in a stock slander (Luke 16:14), and takes over some negative comments from his sources, he has a marked concern to present the Pharisees as "respected and authoritative representatives of Judaism who can hover close to the edge of Christianity. Moreover, Luke likely expects some of his readers to identify favorably with the Pharisees, and he uses them as a point of contact."[55] Brawley notes Luke's assumption that the Pharisees are the most eminent Jewish group, to which he finds parallels in Josephus and rabbinic literature.[56]

By contrast, the Sadducees are inauthentic representatives of Israel, who are unmasked by the Pharisee Gamaliel, "the genuine Jew on the verge of affirming Christianity."[57] Brawley parallels Gamaliel's speech, which implicitly makes the Sadducees "God-fighters" for their determination to expunge Christianity, with Josephus's portrait of the Sadducees as rejecting divine intervention in human affairs.[58] He suggests that Josephus and the rabbis exaggerate when they claim that the Pharisees dominate the Sadducees in public life (cf. Josephus, *Ant.* 18.17), proposing rather that the Sadducees controlled the Sanhedrin through most of the first century, though they must have accommodated the Pharisees somewhat.[59]

Most closely allied with the Sadducees in Luke-Acts are the chief priests, the leading antagonists of Jesus and the church.[60] Luke distinguishes ordinary priests, such as the Baptist's father Zechariah (cf. also Acts 6:7), from these wealthy aristocrats.[61] Jerusalem and the temple, which Luke sees as interchangeable, are important for him not primarily as the locus of opposition to God (*contra* Sanders) but as the navel of the earth, the meeting point between heaven and earth.[62]

As for the Jewish people, Brawley disagrees with Sanders's claim that their response can be categorized as univocal rejection. He finds two responses, depending upon whether they act on their own or are led by the chief priests. In the

---

[51] Ibid., 42–3.
[52] Ibid., 51–67.
[53] Cf. Ziesler, "Luke and the Pharisees," 146–57.
[54] Brawley, *Luke–Acts*, 85–6.
[55] Ibid., 84.
[56] Ibid., 95–6.
[57] Ibid., 97–8.
[58] Ibid., 117.
[59] Ibid., 113.
[60] Ibid., 111.
[61] Ibid., 110–1.
[62] Ibid., 127–30.

former case they repent, and repentance remains a live option through the end of Acts (28:24). There is no final repudiation of the Jews in Acts.

John A. Darr

Darr's work brings the question of Luke's characters to a new plane of sophistication. He seeks to develop "a reader-response (or pragmatic) model attuned to the Greco-Roman literary culture of the first century."[63] Of the Jewish groups, Darr discusses only the Pharisees; yet his crucial methodological observations warrant attention here.

Against both formalist and reader-oriented literary theory, Darr holds that the meaning of texts is produced by the dialogue between text and reader. When a text is read, it becomes a literary "work." Texts necessarily assume some knowledge on the part of readers because they leave all sorts of gaps to be filled in. The reader's extra-textual resources—here, knowledge of Greek language, ancient Mediterranean cultural scripts, classical literature, literary conventions and reading rules, and common historical and geographical data—are indispensable to the operation the work, a symbiosis of author and reader. The first-time reader is tractable, open to change in light of new information as the narrative progresses. She or he "builds characters" with each new engagement. The reader does not compare Luke-Acts with Mark or Q, but tries to create a coherent view from the text itself. Critical interpretation of Luke-Acts, therefore, requires the scholarly reconstruction not of the text's historical community but of the most plausible dialogue between text and reader.

How, then, does Darr read the Pharisees of Luke-Acts? First, he criticizes the studies of Sanders and Brawley for atomizing the narrative in redaction-critical fashion. They try to isolate what is characteristically Lukan by comparing Luke with his sources and by valuing the end of the story more highly than the beginning.[64] Over against his sources, and especially in Acts, Luke seems to present the Pharisees positively. Darr contends, however, that a linear reading of the text creates a much more complex picture of these characters. They provide a "paradigm of imperceptiveness," ironically *observing* Jesus and his followers but failing to *perceive* their significance.[65] In Luke's rhetorical world, characters are graded according to their level of perception; of all the *dramatis personae,* the reader is persuaded to reject the faulty attitudes of the Pharisees. They "become *caricatures of a morality to be avoided,* for it blinds and deafens one to God."[66]

To fill out this reading, Darr walks through each major episode involving the Pharisees. Luke encourages the reader to think of them from the beginning (Luke 5:17) as a homogenous group, each of whose members knows what the

---

[63] Darr, *Character,* 14.
[64] Ibid., 86–9.
[65] Ibid., 86–7.
[66] Ibid., 92; emphasis original.

others know.[67] Collectively, they criticize Jesus because of their failure to perceive (Luke 5:22).[68] The opening conflict stories of Luke 5–6 establish a contrast between two models of response to Jesus—that of the unrepentant Pharisees and that of the repentant sinner—which will operate throughout the Gospel.[69] The Pharisees grumble against Jesus[70] and reject God's purpose.[71] Whereas many scholars have found redeeming value in the Pharisees' three dinner invitations to Jesus, Darr contends that Luke deliberately confounds the reader's expectations of a *symposium* in these stories by silencing Jesus' Pharisaic companions, emphasizing their unworthiness to share narrative space with him.[72] Their warning to flee Herod Antipas (Luke 13:31) Darr interprets as an expression of nefarious motives, because they have themselves plotted against Jesus (11:53–54) and the narrative has not prepared the reader for any friendliness on their part.[73] In the famous "kingdom of heaven" saying (Luke 17:20–21) Darr finds Jesus denouncing not heavenly signs but the Pharisees' practice of "observing" without perceiving (cf. παρατηρέω in 6:7; 14:2). The final episodes of the Pharisee and toll-collector (Luke 18:9–14) and the triumphal entry (19:39) confirm the Pharisees in their collective role as imperceptive, arrogant, "unmarked graves" full of internal filth.[74]

Although Acts omits any strong criticism of the Pharisees, Darr proposes that the reader who knows the Gospel must interpret Acts's Pharisees in a "highly ironical" way.[75] Thus, Luke's claim that Gamaliel was "well respected by the people" is no compliment, given the fickleness of the people.[76] He and the council free Peter only out of fear, not because of justice.[77] And the implicit contrast between Gamaliel and council-member Joseph of Arimathea (Luke 23:50) does not help Gamaliel's image: "the Pharisaic leader suffers in comparison with the Arimathean."[78] The council's actions are tragically ironic, "sadly misguided, presumptuous, even ludicrous."[79] Gamaliel reinforces the readers' perception of Pharisees as seeing but not perceiving.[80] The Pharisaic believers who precipitate the apostolic conference (Acts 15:5) are clearly on the wrong side of God's plan.[81] And Paul's "Pharisaic defense" (Acts 23:1–10; 26:4–5) is a clever ad hoc strategy suited to his situation before the Sanhedrin, which no

67 Ibid., 93.
68 Ibid., 94.
69 Ibid., 95, 102.
70 Ibid., 96.
71 Ibid., 100.
72 Ibid., 103, 106.
73 Ibid., 106.
74 Ibid., 114–15.
75 Ibid., 116.
76 Ibid., 116.
77 Ibid., 117.
78 Ibid., 118.
79 Ibid., 119.
80 Ibid., 120.
81 Ibid., 121.

more reveals his true thinking than does his appeal to Greek philosophy when on trial in Athens (Acts 17:22).[82]

Thus, Darr finds in Luke-Acts a consistent portrayal of the Pharisees as dramatic representatives of attitudes not to be followed.

Luke-Acts: An Interpretation of the Story

It is a commonplace to observe that the interpretation of parts requires constant attention to the whole, and vice versa. My interpretation of the chief priests, Sadducees, Pharisees, and Sanhedrin differs from those mentioned in part because I have a different conception of "parts" and "whole." Before considering the particular passages of interest to us, therefore, I should sketch my interpretation of the larger story.

Whenever a Greek or Latin text contains a prologue, we should pay careful attention to it because that was the place, at the very opening of the roll, where the author was expected to reveal something germane about the aim and scope of the work.[83] In spite of its brevity, the prologue to Luke-Acts contains the standard features found in historical prefaces:[84] importance of the subject, weakness of previous treatments, unique credentials of the author, author's efforts to secure the truth, and the author's thesis. Thus:

> Since many people have taken it upon themselves (ἐπεχείρησαν) to draw up an account of the events that have been fulfilled among us, even as those who from the outset were eyewitnesses and attendants of the word passed them down to us, it seemed only fitting that I, who have investigated everything precisely (ἀκριβῶς) from the start, should write in an orderly manner (καθεξῆς) for you, most excellent Theophilus, so that you might know the reliable foundation (τὴν ἀσφάλειαν) of the things that you have been taught. (Luke 1:1–4)

Since Luke bases his eagerness to write on the fact that others have already written, he must find their work defective.[85] Elsewhere in Luke-Acts the verb ἐπιχειρέω, which he uses of the earlier works, has the sense of futile, misguided, or presumptuous effort (Acts 9:29; 19:13). Luke promises that he will demonstrate "the reliable foundation" (ἀσφάλεια) of what Theophilus has learned. The three occurrences of the cognate adjective ἀσφαλής in Luke-Acts (Acts 21:34; 22:30; 25:26) refer to sorting out the truth in the midst of *competing claims;* this parallels the common use of the term in both historical work and philosophical quests for truth (Plutarch, *Superst.* 171 E; Justin, *Dial.* 8.1). Luke says, in effect: "you have heard various accounts; now I shall tell you what really happened." His story is meant to outshine those of his predecessors.

---

[82] Ibid., 124.

[83] Earl, "Prologue-Form," 856.

[84] A. J. Toynbee, *Greek Historical Thought: From Homer to the Age of Heraclitus* (New York: New American Library, 1952), 29–97.

[85] Sterling, *Historiography.*

How so? Because only Luke has researched everything "with precision (or accuracy)," only he is in a position to write "in an orderly manner." The adverb καθεξῆς appears five times in Luke-Acts (also Luke 8:1; Acts 3:24; 11:4; 18:23), but nowhere else in the NT. We conclude that he intends *orderly progression* to be the distinguishing feature of his narrative.[86]

Luke's concern with proper sequence operates at many levels. Most obviously, his unique inclusion of a second volume dealing with the young church allows him to make distinctions unavailable to other gospel writers. Whereas they tend to present Jesus himself in cosmic conflict with Judean culture, making him overturn the dietary laws (Mark 7:19), speak of the "church" (Matthew 16:18; 18:17), or openly discuss his identity (John 3:11–21 etc.), only Luke's Gospel can afford to leave Jesus wholly within the Judean world because it awaits a second volume. Luke postpones until then the cancellation of dietary laws (Acts 10:14; 11:9), use of church language (Acts 5:11; 7:38, etc.), and open discussion of Jesus' identity until after the resurrection (2:36; 4:11, etc.). Luke's treatment of the Baptist and his students in their relationship to Jesus' group is likewise distinguished by development (Luke 3:2–22; 7:18–23; Acts 19:1–7).

His concern with sequence also functions at a basic stylistic level.[87] It becomes clear first in the abrupt shift at Luke 1:5 from the business-like historical prologue to the scene with Zechariah in the Jerusalem temple. Luke sets the stage with authentic "period language" that creates an old-fashioned atmosphere, filled with angelic appearances, where actors spontaneously break into poetic verse. Throughout the entire two-volume work he will quietly adjust his language to suit the scene, from synagogues to governor's courts to a shipwreck.

Corresponding to Luke's dynamic style is his constantly evolving narrative. The golden prehistory of the birth narratives, in which characters compose poetry on the spot, establishes the conditions of irony by having incontrovertible authorities declare who Jesus is—the descendant of David and son of God, who will restore Israel's glory and defeat its enemies (Luke 1:32–33, 69–70)—in advance of the story. In 3:1, however, Luke retreats to a "real" world in which Jesus' identity is not yet an issue of open debate. This is a fairly stable environment in which he spends his time helping the poor, the sick, and the sinners. When Jesus arrives in cold and barren Jerusalem, however, the situation quickly deteriorates. He is arrested, beaten, paraded before Herod Antipas, bitterly denounced by the Jerusalem leaders, and executed. This intense suffering and conflict, though vividly described, occupies a relatively short section of the story (chs. 19–23).

Jesus' resurrection recaptures the air of peace (Luke 24:36) and hope. But the story has taken a decisive turn, for his identity is now clear from scripture (24:26–27, 44–47). References to Jesus in Acts maintain this two-stage scenario: he *was* a righteous teacher, healer, and prophet, whom God declared or *made* Messiah by raising him from the dead (Acts 2:36; 10:38; 13:27–31). The days of

---

[86] L. T. Johnson, "Luke-Acts, Book of," *ABD* 4:404–20 (here 405).

[87] J. M. Dawsey, *The Lukan Voice: Confusion and Irony in the Gospel of Luke* (Macon: Mercer, 1986), 1–41.

ambiguity are now over: it is imperative to repent and trust in the risen Jesus for forgiveness of sins, for outside of him there is no salvation (Acts 4:12). A succession of divine revelations to Jesus' followers is matched by their increasing separation from Judaism: the conflict leading to Stephen's death, on (false) charges of attacking fundamental Judean institutions; Peter's reluctant mission to the Gentile Cornelius, in which God declares the Judean dietary laws null and void (Acts 10:14; 11:9); and the divine decision, finally ratified by the apostles, to admit Gentiles without requiring that they adopt Judean cultural markers (15:12–29).

The remainder of the book (chs. 13–28) portrays the exploits of the recent convert Paul. We cannot infer from this focus, I think (against Brawley), that the rehabilitation of Paul was Luke's major concern. The narrowing of group history to the characterization of individual lives was a well-established strategy, which allowed writers to develop psychological motives and build rounded characters.[88] Paul was an obvious choice for one who wished to describe the separation of Christianity from Judaism—if we may use these problematic terms for this purpose.

Luke's constantly evolving narrative makes any articulation of his "theology" hazardous.[89] In view of these constant shifts, it is important to notice where the story ends. We find in Acts 28 that the Judeans have proven unresponsive, so "this salvation" has gone out to the Gentiles (28:25–28). For some time now, Luke has begun to speak of "the Jews" without qualification as opponents of the Christians (12:3, 11; 14:4–5), even while allowing that many Judeans believed (13:43; 14:4). By the end of Acts the reader has come to associate the term "Judean" with unbelief and opposition. This is where Mark and John *begin* Jesus' story, but Luke delays hardened opposition until the end. Only *his* readers will know that it was not always so, that the story was much more complex.

It is surprising that the dynamic qualities of Luke-Acts, which have been well known for so long,[90] have had relatively little impact on studies of Luke's overall aim or his presentation of the Judean leaders, which usually posit a static view of some kind. I conclude from the preface and the story itself, however, that these obvious shifts are the point. Over against other Christian authors, Luke sees himself charting a *gradual development* of Christianity from Judean roots. He writes as a historian, seeking to correct accounts that confused Jesus before and after the resurrection. This is the "reliable foundation" that he offers Theophilus. We need not suppose, then, that his Pharisees or other Judean leaders have any direct correspondence to figures known to his readers; he uses these figures because he thinks that they were important in Jesus' career.

Critics have identified many other themes in Luke-Acts. For our examination of the Judean leadership, one is particularly germane: Jesus appears as a

---

88 Thus Feldman has been able to study Josephus's biblical paraphrase as the history of key figures (see his *Rewritten Bible*).

89 Johnson, "Luke-Acts," 405.

90 Cf. M. Dibelius, *Studies in the Acts of the Apostles* (London: SCM, 1956), 123–37.

philosopher,[91] and his students as a school of Judean philosophy.[92] Even though Luke does not call Jesus a philosopher, or Christianity a philosophy, it is not a daring thesis that he assumes the category. Our identification turns on the author's and readers' shared extra-textual resources. If these characters behave as philosophers were known to behave, then the reader will have perceived them as philosophers. [See chapter 7 in this volume.]

Recall that first-century "philosophy" was not primarily a matter of abstract reasoning. Philosophers of all stripes called for a simple lifestyle, free of conventional worries. Over against the entrenched class system, they railed against the prestige of birth and especially against wealth and luxury (Seneca, *Ep.* 17, 108.9–12). They promised true happiness (εὐδαιμονία) only to those who lived the philosophical life—advocated by their school.[93] Against the pervasive rhetorical tradition, they demanded that words and actions accord, that one really *be* what one *seemed* to be; thus, hypocrisy or false living was a primary target of their preaching (Seneca, *Ep.* 20.2). They disavowed philosophers who taught ineffective clichés or pointless abstractions, and above all those who asked for money. Epictetus complained bitterly about philosophers unworthy of the name, who delighted in abstract reasoning. He insisted that true philosophy was a cure for the soul. It required that the "sick" person first realize his illness and then seek help (*Diatr.* 2.9; 19; 3.21.30–38; Seneca, *Ep.* 15.1). The acid tests of effective philosophy were παρρησία, the ability to speak the truth no matter what the consequences, and contempt for death.[94]

Many aristocrats acquired a broad knowledge of philosophical issues during their tertiary education,[95] but it was generally understood that they should hold themselves apart from serious commitment to a particular school. Real commitment to the philosophical life, such as Epictetus demanded of his audiences and Lucian delighted in satirizing, required virtual "conversion" (μετάνοια, ἐπιστροφή) to a counter-cultural lifestyle (βίος).[96] This might involve a change in dress, diet, and demeanour (Seneca, *Ep.* 5.2; 14.4). Serious pursuit of philosophy, therefore, required a degree of detachment from public affairs, (Quintilian, *Orator* 11.1.35; 12.2.7; Seneca, *Ep.* 7–8; Lucian, *Nigr.* 3–37), though such retirement was unbecoming to Roman nobility (Seneca, *Ep.* 108.22; Tacitus, *Agr.* 4.3). In Rome itself, philosophy had long provided a home to vestigial republican sentiments, and these affiliations only complicated the philosophers'

---

[91] C. H. Talbert, *Literary Patterns, Theological Themes and the Genre of Luke-Acts* (SBLMS 20; Missoula: Scholars Press, 1974), 89–98; Brawley, *Luke-Acts,* 56–62.

[92] S. Mason, "Greco-Roman, Jewish, and Christian Philosophies," *Approaches to Ancient Judaism, New Series 4: Religious and Theological Studies* (SFSHJ 81; ed. J. Neusner; Atlanta: Scholars, 1993), 1–28.

[93] H.-F. Weiss, "Pharisäismus und Hellenismus: zur Darstellung des Judentums im Geschichtswerk des jüdischen Historikers Falvius Josephus," *OLZ* 74 (1979): 427–29.

[94] R. MacMullen, *Enemies,* 63–69.

[95] H. I. Marrou, *Education,* 206–16.

[96] Nock, *Conversion,* 173.

ambiguous social position.[97] Opposition between zealous philosophers and rulers was proverbial (Epictetus, *Diatr.* 1.29.10; Cassius Dio 65.12.1–2; 13.1).

So, while the philosophers of bygone ages were esteemed in public imagination and a certain philosophical literacy was *de rigueur* in polite society, the figure of the philosopher as gadfly, endlessly attacking social convention, was unattractive to those who had a stake in the status quo.

Luke does not need to call his characters philosophers for the first-century reader to understand their philosophical overtones. John the Baptist leads an extremely simple life, repudiates the privileges of birth from Abraham, demands a change of thinking (μετάνοια), and calls for ethical behavior (Luke 3:2–14). Before long, his fearless speech lands him in trouble with an ostensibly powerful ruler—in reality, a "reed shaken by the wind" who prefers soft clothing and comfort (3:19–20; 7:24–25). And the established philosophers of the day are impervious to his teaching. These images were familiar to Luke's readers: whatever else he was, John was a Judean philosopher. Josephus presents him in somewhat the same way (*Ant.* 18.116–119).

Similarly, notwithstanding Jesus' classically Judean, messianic, and prophetic identifications in Luke-Acts, he appears in first-century Galilee as a philosopher, a teacher who gathers students. In spite of humble origins among the poor, this teacher is quickly recognized for his effectiveness. Other teachers respect and consult him, though he is critical of them and prefers to teach among the socially undesirable fringe groups. For them, his message has a powerful ethical thrust. He demands that the wealthy erase time-honored social distinctions and include the outcasts in their own lives. He requires that his own followers leave their homes and sell their goods. This ascetic behavior is necessary if they are to be effective "salt"—a metaphor, like that of the gadfly, which emphasises their countercultural role. He is frank in his criticism of the established philosophers for being ineffective: hypocrites, lovers of money, irrelevant logic-choppers, concerned with outward appearance and not reality.

Luke's Jesus and his students, by contrast, bring effective teaching, always accompanied by deeds, a combination that preserves them from the philosopher's biggest pitfall—hypocrisy.[98] For Luke, Jesus is a physician in Epictetus's sense: his words and those of his followers pierce the heart of the hearer and bring about a conversion (μετάνοια). Like Socrates, Jesus is brought to trial for causing an upheaval in the society of his day. He faces death with perfect equanimity.

In Acts the philosophical overtones are even more striking. Like the Pythagoreans and the Judean Essenes, the early Christians practice communal ownership. They speak out before crowds and authorities with perfect freedom (παρρησία). Following Jesus' example, Stephen faces death without fear, even asking forgiveness for his judges. In Athens, Luke's Paul has no qualms about ranging Christian

[97] MacMullen, *Enemies,* 46–94.

[98] Healing and exorcism were certainly not incompatible with a philosopher's vocation (Josephus, *War* 2.136 [on Essenes]; *Ant.* 8.41–44 [on Solomon]; Philostratus, *Life of Apollonius of Tyana* 4.20. 45).

alongside Stoicism and Epicureanism. Paul is a model of Christian effectiveness when, by his composure in the face of death, he saves his ship-mates from drowning and casually shakes off a deadly snake. These are the marks of a true philosopher. The Pharisees, Sadducees, and Christians (Nazarenes) are described as αἱρέσεις, a term often used of philosophical schools.[99]

Admittedly, many of Luke's categories—prophet, Holy Spirit, Messiah, scripture—do not fit the typical language of the *Greek* philosophical schools. Yet Philo and Josephus are instructive here, for they present Judaism as a philosophical culture while also preserving its biblical connections (*Ant.* 1.25). Josephus portrays Abraham, Moses, Solomon, Daniel, and other Judean figures as great philosophers, and claims that the Greek philosophers borrowed from Moses. This does not prevent him from talking simultaneously about the laws, the priesthood and temple, or prophecy. In the same way, Luke's evocation of philosophical themes does not compromise his much-discussed biblical motifs.[100]

Chief Priests, Sadducees, Pharisees, and Sanhedrin in Luke-Acts

With this background in view, we turn to the particular passages in Luke-Acts that mention chief priests, Sadducees, Sanhedrin, and Pharisees.

In Luke

Pharisees

Unlike Mark (12:13) and Matthew (3:7; 16:6; 21:45, etc.), the Gospel of Luke keeps the Pharisees quite separate from the Sadducees and chief priests, who appear only in Jerusalem. The Pharisees operate in the broad expanse of Jesus' work among the common people before that final conflict. No doubt, this distinction reflects Luke's concern for correct order.

We first meet the Pharisees when Jesus has summoned a circle of his own students. The reader sees, first, that the Pharisees are coupled with teachers of the law (νομοδιδάσκαλοι), or perhaps that they *are* teachers of the law if this construction is epexegetical.[101] Luke uses νομοδιδάσκαλοι only here in the Gospel, substituting "scribes" or "their scribes" hereafter (5:30); this suggests that he uses the descriptive term to help explain who the Pharisees were at their first appearance. The reader learns further that they have a broad base in the Judean world: they have come from "every village of Galilee and Judea and Jerusalem" to observe the new teacher (Luke 5:17). They appear, therefore, as established teachers,

[99] Mason, *Josephus on the Pharisees,* 128.

[100] Cf. now C. A. Evans and J. A. Sanders, *Luke and Scripture: The Function of Sacred Tradition in Luke-Acts* (Minneapolis: Fortress, 1993).

[101] The only other occurrence of the word is in Acts 5:34, where Gamaliel is called both a Pharisee and a νομοδιδάσκαλος.

who assume the responsibility to scrutinize other teachers. No other teachers will surface outside of Jerusalem.

Tension builds quickly when Jesus declares a paralytic forgiven. The scribes and Pharisees first accuse him of "blasphemy" (5:21)—not a technical charge in Luke, but generally improper speech (cf. Luke 22:65; 23:39; Acts 13:45; 18:6). The tension is resolved for the moment when Jesus demonstrates his virtue by curing the man, at which point "ecstasy seized them all and they glorified God" (Luke 5:26).

Another problem follows, however, when Jesus associates with toll collectors and sinners, whom, it now appears, the Pharisees consider unworthy associates for a teacher (5:30). Jesus' response to this challenge seems important for understanding Luke's view of the Pharisees: "Those who are well have no need of a physician, but rather those who are ill; not for the righteous have I come, but to call the sinners to a change of thinking" (5:31–32). In context, this saying implies that the Pharisees and their associates—the healthy and the righteous—do not need what Jesus has to offer. Jesus does not yet condemn the Pharisees, but clearly distinguishes his aims from theirs.

Three further controversies show significant differences between Jesus and the Pharisees, and indicate that he is an enigma to them. But the issues remain unresolved as far as the reader knows. The Pharisees ask why his students do not fast, as do their own and the Baptist's (5:33); they ask why his students are allowed to pluck grain on the Sabbath, when this is "not permitted" (6:2), though his counter-argument from scripture suggests that this action *is* permitted (6:3); and they watch to see if they can accuse him for curing a man on the Sabbath (6:7), but his combination of cure and argument confounds them. Luke finishes this block of five conflicts with the remark that the Pharisees were thoroughly discomfited; they were "filled with incomprehension, and discussed with one another what they should do in the case of Jesus" (6:11). Their mission of inspection has failed to give them a basis for judging the new teacher, so the reader awaits the sequel.

We next encounter Pharisees after Jesus has given his powerful speech on the plain, in which he outlines the consolation that awaits the suffering and the suffering that awaits the comfortable (6:20–26), after he has cured a foreign soldier's servant, revived a widow's dead son (7:1–17), and lauded John the Baptist's work. Here Luke interjects that, whereas the people and the toll collectors gladly accepted John's immersion, the Pharisees and "lawyers" (or "legists" [J. T. Sanders], for νομικοί) set aside the will of God by refusing immersion (7:30). This aside, important because it reliably conveys the author's view, is the strongest note of condemnation so far. It is not only that the recognized Judean teachers have different aims from Jesus, but at least in their response to John's teaching they are out of step with God's will.

Luke's criticism is soon followed, however, by a leading Pharisee's invitation to Jesus to join him for dinner (7:36). This odd juxtaposition sets in motion a pattern that will continue throughout the Gospel. Jesus will criticize the Pharisees at every opportunity, but they nonetheless continue to treat him as a respected colleague. Their cooperation with this gadfly who never stops challenging them reinforces Luke's picture of the Pharisees as obtuse: they simply do not understand the criticism.

The Pharisee who invites Jesus appears as a man of substance, since the guests "recline" for dinner; the house in view was not the typically cramped apartment of a town dweller but a residence large enough to accommodate couches for eating. That the woman should hear of Jesus' meal at the Pharisee's house while she was in town, and that she should know where to find it (Luke 7:37) confirms that this was an affair of high society on the local scene. Simon the Pharisee is among the relatively few comfortable residents of Galilee.

Although hosts might invite a wide range of guests, from prospective patrons to their own clients, Jesus appears in this story at least as an fellow teacher, perhaps a guest of honor, who might be invited to discourse after dinner for entertainment (Martial, *Epigrams* 11.52).[102] Simon's unspoken shock at Jesus' behavior in acknowledging the sinful woman[103] indicates that he expected something else, that he had viewed Jesus as a worthy colleague. This surprise would be perfectly intelligible to the reader in view of the erotic connotations of the woman's action, and the traditional associations of women who attended banquets.[104] Jesus' vehement response to Simon, in which he points out the host's failings in contrast to the woman's self-effacing love, is left unanswered by the Pharisee (7:44–47). In the light of Jesus' previous encounters with Pharisees, we should probably put this down to Simon's utter perplexity, which the reader might well share. The last we hear of him, Simon addresses Jesus respectfully and seems willing to take correction from him (7:40). If he was a poor host, the reader also sees that Jesus is not a typical honored guest, consorting with a woman and publicly accusing the host. Luke's story is much more sophisticated than simple castigation of the Pharisees or exaltation of Jesus.

Pharisees do not appear again explicitly until Jesus worked a good deal more among the people, when another Pharisee invites him to dine (Luke 11:37). Since Luke has closely associated Pharisees and legists, however, we should note that it was a legist who tested Jesus' knowledge by asking him what he must do "to inherit eternal life," and then, "who is my neighbour?"—the question that elicited the parable of the good Samaritan (10:25). The former question shows that the legist accepts the notion of an afterlife, as do Jesus, the Pharisees, and the people. He also "seeks to justify himself" (10:29), which is typical behavior of the Pharisees in Luke.

In the second meal scene, a Pharisee invites Jesus to a luncheon—or perhaps simply to "dine" (ἀριστάω). Luke's variation of the language at least indicates that we are dealing with a common occurrence in Jesus' life. Again, the guests

---

[102] P. Veyne, *A History of Private Life*, vol. 1: *From Pagan Rome to Byzantium* (Cambridge, Mass.: Harvard University Press, 1987), 188–89.

[103] K. E. Corley, *Private Women, Public Meals: Social Conflict in the Synoptic Tradition* (Peabody, Mass.: Hendrickson, 1993), 63, 124.

[104] Corley, *Private Women*, 24–79.

recline (ἀναπίπτω) in comfortable circumstances (11:37). Here too the Pharisee is surprised at this teacher's behavior, and Jesus responds with a customarily stinging attack. Luke says that "when the Pharisee saw it, he was amazed that he [Jesus] was not first immersed [οὐκ . . . ἐβαπτίσθη] before the meal" (11:38). Within the narrative world, of course, Luke's choice of word is significant. The reader has already learned that the Pharisees were not immersed by John, a serious violation of divine will (7:30); yet here they criticize Jesus for not being immersed before dinner, a routine issue that exposes their pettiness.

But what should Luke's readers have understood by this immersion that Jesus failed to perform? Commentators often imagine that, because the Pharisees were involved, and Mark mentions Pharisaic hand-washing (Mark 7:3), Luke also refers here to "ceremonial hand-washing."[105] This conclusion seems strained, however, in view of what the passage actually says. The word βαπτίζω connotes drenching or immersion, and there is no reference to hands. Jesus goes on to talk about washing the inside and the outside, where the inside clearly has to do with human motives (11:39–41). Therefore, the issue seems to be the inside and outside of the *person,* not hands. And the implicit comparison with John's immersion only strengthens this sense of washing the whole body.

Now, it was common enough for a host to invite a dinner guest to visit the baths with him before the meal, thus providing a whole afternoon and evening of activity (Martial, *Epigrams* 11.52). I submit that all of the narrative clues so far about the Pharisees' comfortable circumstances would incline the reader to understand the charge thus: an upscale Pharisee host is offended at Jesus' declining a friendly invitation to bathe before dinner. That much would be intelligible to any Mediterranean reader. In addition, some readers perhaps knew that in Judean culture full immersion was required to remove common kinds of impurity (Lev 15:13–27). If so, Luke may be suggesting that the Pharisee was scandalized at Jesus' failure to take advantage of his private immersion pool before eating. Though immersion before dinner was not mandated in scripture, and we do not know to what extent it was a Pharisaic norm, the assumption may simply be that most teachers would be happy for the chance to purify themselves as often as possible.[106] In any case, the issue seems to be a full immersion, and the Pharisee's shock that Jesus should demonstratively decline the proffered opportunity. Jesus' behavior might be shocking also to the reader, whether as simple refusal of a host's offer or as an implicit challenge to common piety. Jesus continues to behave as a gadfly.

The ensuing discussion contains three woes against the Pharisees and three against their colleagues the legists, who are also present at this impressive meal. Under the general charge of being concerned with external convention rather than thoughts and attitudes—the eternal complaint of the philosopher—Jesus

---

[105] P. F. Esler, *Community and Gospel in Luke-Acts: The Social and Political Motivations of Lucan Theology* (Cambridge: Cambridge University Press, 1987), 122; Darr, *Character,* 103.

[106] Sanders, *Practice and Belief,* 217–30.

accuses the Pharisees specifically of worrying about tithing insignificant herbs while neglecting important issues of justice, and of loving honors (11:41–43). Most interestingly, he describes the Pharisees as "indistinct memorials [or tombstones], which pedestrians walk all over without knowing" (11:44). This image is quite different from Matthew's *whitewashed* tombs (Matthew 23:27). It seems from Matthew's note that Judeans marked tombs so that pedestrians could avoid corpse uncleanness;[107] as reputedly exact teachers, the Pharisees would presumably be among the more careful in this respect. Jesus' charge would then mean that while the Pharisees worry about marking other graves, they fail to mark *themselves* out as places to be avoided! (Cf. the similar association of them with leaven to be avoided at 12:1.) Without such knowledge of Pharisaic custom, the reader might simply infer that they, in contrast to Jesus and his students, fail to distinguish themselves from society as a whole; they are ineffective set pieces like the sophists of Greek culture.

This biting dinner speech offends (ὑβρίζω) the legists as well, but their respectful complaint ("Teacher . . . ") only invites Jesus to turn on them with even sharper invective (11:45). Rather than helping people, he alleges, they burden them with unreasonable tasks; they block the path to knowledge (γνῶσις) and do not find it themselves. Their obstructionist behavior leads them to oppose true prophets and apostles—the name that Jesus has given a few of his leading students (6:13)—just as their counterparts in biblical history did (11:47–51). There is a considerable overlap between the "false prophets" or court prophets of biblical history and the sophists of Greek culture. While Luke's explicit language puts the Pharisees in continuity with these biblical predecessors, the first-century Greek reader could not avoid associating them with Sophists.

The close relationship between Pharisees and legists is confirmed by Luke's closing remark, that when Jesus had left the house following this confrontation, they together (now called "scribes and Pharisees") began "to bear a serious grudge, and to draw him out with questions concerning many other matters, laying an ambush to trap him with something that might come from his mouth" (11:53–54). Rather than taking the criticism to heart and examining whether they might actually change their ways, the offended philosophical elite simply look for ways to show up this new teacher. Their opposition is nothing like the chief priests' later effort to kill Jesus; it is at the level of academic debate between "safe" philosophers who have long secured an established place in the status quo and a small group of upstarts who challenge that order.

This conflict is developed in the following paragraph. Jesus' teaching and healing draw "tens of thousands of people," for they find real help from him. But he warns them *not* to seek help from the Pharisees. "Watch out for the leaven of the Pharisees, which is pretense!" (12:1). Seeking out leaven was a basic Judean custom for the Passover season, quite possibly familiar to Luke's readers from scripture (Exod 13:6–8). As recognized teachers, the Pharisees themselves would presumably have given guidelines for ensuring that all leaven was scrupulously

[107] Ibid., 72.

removed. Jesus' warning is again sarcastic: the Pharisees are the leaven that one needs to worry about! That he bothers to warn the people about the Pharisees agrees with many other indications in the story that at the people generally considered the Pharisees *their* teachers. Jesus presents his own more effective teaching as an alternative to their established way.

The Pharisees' offense at Jesus' criticism does not, surprisingly, lead to hatred. Luke presents their motivation as the normal human psychology of affront and envy. For soon after, when push comes to shove, some Pharisees come to warn Jesus that Herod Antipas "wants to kill" him (13:31). This notice out of the blue seems important for maintaining the reader's perspective on the relationships among the characters. Jesus has been in almost daily contact with the Pharisees, yet in spite of his regular and sharp criticism, the only revenge that they are either interested in or capable of is the satisfaction that might be found in embarrassing him on the basis of some teaching or other. Herod Antipas operates on the quite different plane of raw power. He has hardly appeared in the story at all, yet we learn first that he imprisoned and executed the Baptist (3:19–20; 9:9) and now that he wishes to kill Jesus. The reader understands that such major political figures have a different scale of values and means at their disposal. Jesus' students and the Pharisees are, comparatively speaking, in the same boat here. They both live and function among the common people. Herod is most closely matched by the Jerusalem authorities, who actually control some machinery of government. There is no good reason (*pace* Darr) to see the Pharisees' warning as duplicitous; all of the contextual indicators point the other way.

In particular, the following paragraph has Jesus invited yet a third time to dine with "one of the leading Pharisees," this time at a Sabbath meal (14:1). Again, it is a lavish affair with a large number of guests and many couches, typically arranged in order of honor. Again, the philosopher Jesus proceeds to challenge the whole banquet etiquette of his fellow guests (cf. Lucian, *Symp.* 8–9), by proposing that those eager to sit at the most honored places—closest to the host—go first to the least desirable couches, from which they may be summoned (14:7–11). Then again, they may not be summoned—a large risk for those concerned about their image, but not a concern to those who truly know themselves! These are precisely the sorts of social conventions exposed by true philosophy (Lucian, *Nigr.* 3–37).

An even more devastating critique of dinner culture comes when Jesus next discusses whom to invite (14:12–14). His insistence that hosts not invite their friends, brothers, relatives, or rich neighbours, who might repay them with a reciprocating invitation, was as radical as his coming demand that potential students abandon their homes. Hosts might invite some humble folk to dinner out of patronal obligation, perhaps feeding them less expensive fare than the others. But it was widely accepted that one should seek out equals and more distinguished guests, and that one might justifiably be offended if they accepted another invitation instead (Pliny, *Ep.* 1.15). Jesus' criticism would only make sense if he too had been invited as a respectable teacher. In the first-century Mediterranean context, his insistence that hosts seek out as dinner guests "the poor, the disabled, the lame, and the blind" was no less peculiar than it would be today. Although the Christian reader will side with Jesus, Luke is evidently not trying to present the Pharisees as evil, only as insensitive to the magnitude of human need and unwilling to take the extreme steps needed to become effective "salt" (below).

How did the Pharisees respond? We learn first that they were still watching Jesus carefully when he came to the house (14:1). Either en route or soon after his arrival, a man with dropsy confronted him. Jesus, after challenging the Pharisees on the question of Sabbath cures (14:3), cured the man with a touch and dismissed him (14:4)—apparently indicating that the man was not part of the banquet. The Pharisees' response is ambiguously stated: "They were incapable of answering back to these things" (14:6). Did he, then, win them over? At least, he dominated the rest of the dinner-time discussion. And when he made his observations about inviting the disabled to dinner, one of his fellow diners enthusiastically agreed that future reward was vastly more desirable than present repayment (14:15).

By this point, the reader is getting a fairly well rounded picture of Luke's Pharisees. They are much more complex than simply "friends" or "enemies" of Jesus. A complex of further encounters in chapters 14–18 solidifies the reader's understanding of the Pharisees. The first comes immediately after the banquet with Pharisees, and provides a striking contrast between Jesus' way and the Pharisees'. He makes frightfully clear the conditions of becoming *his* student (14:25–35): utter disdain for the most basic social categories (father, mother, wife, children, brothers, sisters, one's own self), "carrying one's own cross"—a vivid image of suffering in the first-century Mediterranean, and abandoning *all* of one's possessions (14:33). Only so can one become effective salt, not the kind of salt that has become useless (μωρανθῇ)—like the Pharisees (14:34–35)!

On hearing Jesus' itemization of student requirements, the Pharisees grumbled, while characteristically missing the point of this ascetic regimen, that he included among his pupils toll collectors and sinners, the most unworthy sorts of people. This complaint confirms their assumption that he is a fellow teacher, for if they were rabid opponents like the later chief priests and Herod Antipas, they would not care what sort of students he chose.

The whole complex of parables in 15:3–16:13 comes in response to the Pharisees' grumblings; at the end (16:14) they have been "listening to all these things." Without detailed analysis here, we observe that the first three parables have a common and simple point, namely, there will be more celebration over the lost who are found than over the ones who have always been safe. These parables are transparent allegories, in which the ninety-nine sheep who stay on the path are equated with the "righteous who have no need of rethinking" (15:7), whereas both the lost sheep and the lost coin are interpreted as the sinner who has a change of mind (15:7, 10). The gripping story of the lost son is equally clear: the Pharisees are the older son (ὁ πρεσβύτερος), who have served the father for countless years and never once transgressed his commandment (οὐδέποτε ἐντολήν παρῆλθον), while this son who has associated with *harlots* is celebrated (15:29–31). The father generously allows that the older son has always been cherished, and has always had access to everything of the father's (15:32). All of this confirms that the Pharisees are the safe, righteous, and healthy, who do not need Jesus' teaching, though in other contexts he finds them culpable for having squandered their privileged position.

When, at the conclusion of the final parable of the group, Jesus declares that one cannot serve God and mammon (16:13), "the Pharisees, being lovers of money (φιλάργυροι), turned up their noses at him" (16:14). The charge of loving money was a stock accusation of some philosophers against others from at least the time of Socrates (Diogenes Laertius 6.56).[108] It fits so precisely with the image of the Pharisees that Luke and the reader have been building so far, as complacent sophists who hold lavish banquets among their friends, that the reader might wonder at Luke's failure to launch this attack before now.

Similarly, Jesus' following words reprise all of the previous Pharisee stories: "You are those who justify yourselves before people, but God knows your hearts; for what is exalted by people is an abomination before God" (16:15). This observation sums up the Pharisees' place in the whole scheme of "high and low, honor and shame, internal and external, truth and convention, reality and appearance," which runs as a subtext throughout the Gospel of Luke, and which was of paramount concern to ethical philosophers of Luke's time. The Pharisees have entirely lost their bite by allying themselves uncritically with the wrong sides of these pairs.

Jesus' most compassionate statement to the Pharisees comes when they next inquire of him, still the respected teacher, "when the kingdom of God comes" (17:20). In this famous passage, Jesus responds that the kingdom does not come "after observation, nor will they say, 'Look, here it is!' or 'There it is!' But look, the kingdom of God is *within you*" (17:22). Evidently, the Pharisees do not understand, and Jesus quickly turns to his students. Although the kingdom saying has caused endless discussion, it presents no real difficulties in the portrait of the Pharisees that we have been building. Jesus is declaring that the Pharisees have the kingdom in themselves, as the "older brother" with heaven's resources at their disposal, as the righteous and healthy of society; but as we have seen time and again, they squander their potential. They are not the ones to do it.

Their preoccupation with appearance and self-justification is exposed one more time in the famous parable of the Pharisee and the toll collector (18:9–14). Here, Pharisees are understood to typify those who "are persuaded that they themselves are righteous and vilify everyone else" (18:9).

The utter incomprehension of the Pharisees is illustrated again by their final scene in the Gospel. Standing with Jesus at the eastern approach to the temple, they heard the large crowd of joyful students praising God and citing Ps 118:26:[109] "Blessed is the king who comes in the name of the Lord" (19:38). Some of the Pharisees among the crowd said, "Teacher, admonish your students." They still call him teacher, but they do not understand his program or the momentous events unfolding before them.

---

[108] Brawley, *Luke-Acts*, 61, 86.

[109] Cf. J. A. Sanders, "A Hermeneutic Fabric: Psalm 118 in Luke's Entrance Narrative," in *Luke and Scripture* (ed. Evans and Sanders), 140–53.

Chief Priests, Sadducees, and Sanhedrin

Chief priests, Sadducees, and Sanhedrin may be treated together because they are closely related in the Gospel, appearing only in the climactic Jerusalem narrative (Luke 19:45–24:53). Luke's reference to the serving high priest(s) (ἀρχιερεύς) at Luke 3:1 is simply a chronological marker. In Luke 9:22, shortly before the travel narrative, he has Jesus predict that the Son of Man will be tried and killed by the "elders and chief priests and scribes." This points ahead to the Jerusalem narrative. The other thirteen occurrences of ἀρχιερεύς, along with every occurrence of Sadducee (Σαδδουκαίος; once) and Sanhedrin (συνέδριον; once), come in the Jerusalem story.

These basic narrative facts already begin to shape the reader's evaluation of the chief priests, Sanhedrin, and Sadducees. They stand in stark contrast to the only other significant Judean leaders of this narrative, the Pharisees. In Jerusalem, there is no more debating over modes of Sabbath observance or association with sinners, but only lethal conflict. Unlike the Pharisees, the temple-based leadership controls a police force, and it can execute its will immediately.

Jesus' "passion predictions" do not dominate the story here as they do in Mark. The two predictions after 9:22 (9:43–45; 18:31–34) mention only "men" and " Gentiles" rather than the temple leadership as Jesus' killers. Since the Pharisees themselves do not plot Jesus' death (contrast Mark 3:6), and since Luke includes much special material of a general ethical nature in the body of the work, the effect of the passion predictions on the reader is to create *dissonance*. Why must Jesus die, when he is doing so much good, and getting along so well with other teachers who respect him? The opening statement of the travel narrative (9:51) and the lament over Jerusalem (13:33–35) confirms that things will be *different* there.

This difference is closely related to the theme of reversal that runs through the entire Gospel. Jesus set out to bring good news to the poor, sick, and sinners, but this message is bad news for the rich, the powerful, and the self-satisfied righteous. Since the bulk of his career has been among the common people, he has mainly spoken good news and hope. Jerusalem is different because it represents the seat of power in Judean life, the home of the central Judean government (even the Roman governor and Galilean tetrarch are there), and the economic heart of Judean society. Whereas Jesus has been bringing good news to the deprived, he will now confront the powerful with bad news (cf. Luke 6:20–26).

Once Jesus arrives at the gates of Jerusalem, there is no more leisure for general ethical observations. From the eastern gate he predicts the city's destruction because it remains oblivious to the time of its "inspection" (19:44). As soon as he enters the temple, he drives out the merchants and begins to teach (19:45). Within two sentences of describing his entry, the narrator brings us face to face with the authorities we have vaguely expected all through the story: "The chief priests and the scribes, even the highest ranking of the people, sought to kill him" (19:47). Jesus' life has taken a decisive turn; this is no longer the world of the common people and Pharisees. For Luke's readers, who understand the Romans' ruthless intolerance of upheaval in the provinces, and who possibly also know that the Jerusalem temple was a regular scene of trouble (cf. Josephus, *War* 2.43, 224), the temple incident would suffice to make the chief priests' actions plausible. It is not clear that Luke means to *condemn* the Jerusalem leadership. His portrayal seems more resigned: they were completely blind to Jesus' significance, and acted as one might have expected of them.

Chapter 20, immediately following this announcement of the chief priests' aims, comprises six conflict stories. It is worth comparing these with the earlier controversies involving the Pharisees and the ordinary people in Luke 5–6. There, the issues were academic (definition of Sabbath observance, appropriate times for fasting, Jesus' right to announce forgiveness of sins, his choice of associates), and nothing came of them. Now, however, the chief priests, who have already decided to kill Jesus, are in his audience (20:1). Their first question goes to the heart of the matter: Who are you, that you should teach here (20:2)? It is not *what* Jesus teaches in the temple that causes problems, for we are told only that he was teaching (19:47; 20:1); that activity is the point of the controversy. Jesus' authority had never been a serious issue in his dealings with the Pharisees. They did wonder about his forgiveness of sins at their first encounter (Luke 5:26), but he temporarily convinced them by his actions; their later surprise at his actions came precisely because they accepted him as a fellow teacher. Here, the chief priests assume an exclusive right to teach in the temple, and so they want to know what he is doing here. Since they have determined to kill him, and are not likely to be persuaded by any answer, their question is sarcastic.

Jesus answers enigmatically, but then boldly relates an allegory that challenges *their* legitimacy. In failing to recognize his mission, he says, they are like wicked tenant farmers, who have abandoned their accountability to the vineyard owner and so dismiss or kill his messengers, even his son. With this provocation, the "scribes and chief priests sought to lay hands on him at that moment" (20:19). But in contrast to Jesus, who speaks fearlessly though he lacks any protection from visible authority, these well-armed and seemingly powerful figures are actually powerless to execute their wishes because "they feared the people" (20:19). Their paralysis only confirms Jesus' judgment of them.

To protect their image from further damage, these weak authorities must engage in subterfuge: withdrawing from the scene, they send in spies who pretend (ὑποκρίνομαι) to be decent (δίκαιος) people (20:20), just as the chief priests themselves pretend to be divinely ordained rulers. These spies blatantly lie, claiming that they accept Jesus' teaching as from God (20:21). Once again, Jesus represents the philosophical ideal of absolute integrity and fearlessness over against the sham of the social structure. With perfect composure, he sees through the chief priests' machinations (20:23). The chief priests and their spies, since they are paralyzed by fear of their own people, hope to frame Jesus by finding something that will persuade the Roman governor to take action (20:21).[110] Contrary

[110] In supposing that the governor would be present in Jerusalem, Luke seems here to anticipate his later note (22:1) that the feast of Passover was near.

to plan, however, the spies themselves are both intimidated by the people and amazed at Jesus' answer to their question (20:26).

Enter the Sadducees, for their only scene in the Gospel. They are "one-trick ponies," whose sole noteworthy characteristic is that they go around saying "there is no resurrection" (20:27). In doing so, they seem to represent the empty theology of the Jerusalem establishment who, like the rich man of Luke 16:25, already have their consolation. The Sadducees present a clever scenario to Jesus, in which a woman who has married several times dies. Whose wife will she be in heaven? Jesus, who has always assumed the resurrection in his earlier teaching, in agreement with the people and the Pharisees, has no difficulty exposing the silliness of the question (for Luke). The witless Sadducees are reduced to silence, after conceding, "Teacher, you spoke well" (20:39). This failure of the Jerusalem establishment to convict Jesus by his words only focuses attention more closely on the chief priests' motives. Why, then, *do* they wish to kill him?

Jesus now takes the offensive, driving home the theme of reversal by exposing the (alleged) greed of the temple authorities. He asserts that the scribes like to "devour widows' houses" and then cover up their rapacity with a façade of piety (προφάσει; 20:47). He illustrates this story with the example of a poor widow who is just then depositing two small coins in the temple treasury, while the rich deposit their large gifts (21:1–3). Although Jesus simply remarks on the relative abundance of the widow's gift, without explicitly condemning the temple authorities (21:4), the context seems to convey Jesus' general criticism of the temple's financial affairs. He proceeds immediately to predict the destruction of the whole temple edifice, in response to those who are naïvely impressed by its superficial beauty and votive offerings (21:5–6).

Following this prediction, we are reminded that, whereas the people are eager to hear Jesus' teaching (21:38), the chief priests and scribes are looking for a way to kill him, though they fear the people (22:2). They find their means in Judas, whom Satan enters just at this time (22:4–5). After Jesus' final meal, a crowd of "chief priests and captains of the temple and elders" (22:52) comes secretly to arrest him on the Mount of Olives. Once again, Jesus fearlessly exposes their cowardice. This apparent small triumph of the authorities represents the reign of darkness (22:52–53).

From the Mount of Olives Jesus is ushered to the very heart of the Jerusalem establishment, the residence of the high priest (22:54). After he had been held overnight, "the Senate (πρεσβυτέριον)[111] of the people convened, chief priests and also scribes, and they led him into their council chamber (συνέδριον)" (22:66). Inasmuch as this *synedrion* is distinguished from the persons involved as a place to which one can go, we conclude with Sanders that Luke uses the term here of a building or room. Unlike the other Gospels, Luke does not place this trial by Judean authorities in the high priest's house. Perhaps he knows that trials were conducted in a special chamber.

[111] This is the only occurrence of the word in Luke, though it appears also in Acts 22:5 as a term for the council.

Interestingly enough, although Luke seems to assume that the high priest led the πρεσβυτέριον, since Jesus goes from the high priest's house to the court (and cf. Acts 5:17, 21; 7:1; 23:2), nothing is said of the high priest himself during Jesus' trial. All of the council's statements are collective (Luke 22:67; 23:2, 10, 13), though the other Gospels put the same words in the high priest's mouth (e.g., Mark 14:61, 63). It is possible, given his confusing statements about the high priest's identity elsewhere (Luke 3:1; Acts 4:6), that Luke did not know who the high priest was, and did not want to put his whole narrative under suspicion by naming the wrong man. Or we might suppose that he intends to broaden the blame for Jesus' death to the whole chief-priestly college. Perhaps he thinks that chief-priestly cliques were more central to the operation of the Senate than any particular high priest.

Although Luke is not explicit here, he seems to suggest that Pilate handed Jesus over to soldiers under the chief priests' control: "Jesus he handed over (παρέδωκεν) to their will" (23:25).[112] We hear no more of the chief priests by name, but the context suggests that they are the principal members of "the rulers" (οἱ ἄρχοντες) who ridicule Jesus on the cross (23:35). Nothing in the narrative so far has prepared us for the notice in Luke 23:50–52 that a "good and righteous" member of the council (βουλευτής), who was awaiting the kingdom of God (a Pharisee?), should ask to give Jesus a proper burial. Luke's claim that Joseph of Arimathea had not consented to the council's decision highlights Luke's earlier rhetorical exaggeration in making the *whole* council responsible (23:1).

We conclude that the chief priests function in the Gospel of Luke as the embodiment of the powerful who have bad news awaiting them (Luke 6:24–26). Whereas Jesus has been very successful among the people, in spite of his constantly criticizing the Pharisees, his encounter with the supremely hypocritical chief priests brings him immediately into fatal conflict. They want him executed on *any* charge because he challenges their authority by assuming a teaching role in the temple. They hold the city and the temple in their hands, and they have police at their disposal. But they are paradigms of pretense, worried about appearances, weak and fearful in spite of their instruments of power, while the apparently powerless Jesus confronts them with perfect composure. The chief priests are the driving force in the Judean council led by the high priest, and they meet in a συνέδριον. The Sadducees are flat characters in Luke, vaguely associated with the Jerusalem leadership.

In Acts

We have considered the Gospel of Luke at some length because it provides the indispensable literary context for the Book of Acts. We have seen that a great deal changes in Acts, following the death and resurrection of Jesus. It is in many ways a new world, for Jesus' identity as Messiah is now openly declared by his apostles. Still, the story remains based in Jerusalem and the chief priests, Saddu-

[112] Sanders, *Luke and Scripture,* 9–12.

cees, Sanhedrin, and Pharisees continue to play important secondary roles that build upon their earlier roles in Jesus' career. Because the Pharisees often appear together with the others in Acts, it will be unnecessary to treat the leadership groups under separate heads.

Since this story begins in Jerusalem, the reader of the Gospel knows enough to anticipate some trouble for Jesus' followers from the very group that executed Jesus himself. That opposition is not long in coming. Jesus' followers explode upon the scene when they receive power from heaven, which enables them to proclaim Jesus' resurrection boldly, and to confirm their teaching with spectacular cures. They quickly attract 3,000 followers to their group, who sell off their possessions and join in this counter-cultural school initiated by Jesus (Acts 2:1–47). One of their cures involved a lame man who used to sit begging by one of the temple gates, where the only help he had ever received from Judean leaders and passersby was in the form of charitable donations. His healing at the hands of Peter and John caused a commotion in Solomon's Portico, at which they began to proclaim Jesus' resurrection, the need for a change of mind, and trust in this new revelation from God (3:11–26).

It comes as no surprise to the reader that, "the priests, the commander (στρατηγός) of the temple (guard) and the Sadducees came upon them, greatly exercised on account of their teaching the people, and their proclaiming in Jesus the resurrection of the dead" (4:1–2). There are two issues here: (a) that Jesus' students are teaching the people without authorization in the temple area, and (b) that they are talking about resurrection in the case of Jesus. Both issues recall Jesus' experience in the temple, where his authority to teach was questioned, and the Sadducees confronted him on the issue of resurrection. The added twist here is their teaching in Jesus' name. Since his crucifixion was engineered by the chief priests, they are indignant that his students are still active. Also in keeping with the reader's expectations, these nameless, rather flat figures exercise their power quickly. They arrest Peter and John and hold them over for interrogation the next day (4:3). In spite of the arrest, however, 5,000 more men believe as a result of the apostles' teaching (4:4), which underscores the leaders' helplessness in the face of divine action.

On the next day, "the leaders and the elders and the scribes in Jerusalem" gather to try Jesus' students. Strangely, it is only now that Luke troubles to mention some names. In the opening of the main Gospel narrative he had confusingly dated the Baptist's career to the time when "Annas was high priest and Caiaphas" (Luke 3:2)—confusingly, because the reader expects one high priest's name. In the narrative of Jesus' days in Jerusalem, the serving high priest plays no role. Yet now, in discussing the trial of Peter and John, Luke allows that among those gathered were "Annas the high priest, and Caiaphas and John and Alexander and as many as were of the high priest's family" (4:6). This passage seems to confirm that Luke thinks of Annas as serving high priest, but that only makes it more problematic in relation to Josephus's account (below).

What the temple-based authorities—leaders, chief priests, scribes, elders, and Sadducees—wish to know is the where these men get their authority to teach

(4:7). As in Jesus' case, they demand confirmation of what they already know, that they do not want these men teaching in the temple. The apostles' reply cites the same irritating passage from Ps 118:22 that Jesus had used in his conflict with these leaders (4:11; cf. Luke 20:17), concerning the stone that the builders rejected. The temple leaders quickly make the connection, realizing that the apostles' remarkable boldness of speech (παρρησία), the philosopher's prized virtue, comes from their study with Jesus (4:13). Their deliberations take place in a room called a *synedrion,* which people can enter and exit (4:15).

As in the Jerusalem narrative of the Gospel, the leaders are in a political predicament. They realize their inability to deny the cure of the lame man because it is now well known to the people (4:16). Nor are they able to punish Peter and John "because of the people" (4:21). But instead of giving even the slightest attention to what the miracle might mean about the new teaching, they stubbornly proceed with their plans to silence Jesus' group by forbidding them to teach "on the basis of Jesus' name" (4:18). The issue here seems to be practical and political: they do not want the name of a recently crucified troublemaker perpetuated as a rallying call in the temple area. Peter and John, for their part, are *unable* to cease speaking of what they have seen and heard (4:20). This divinely revealed teaching is inevitable, in spite of the powerful chief priests' designs.

The point is reinforced by what happened next. When the apostles continued their teaching in spite of the warning, "the high priest and all those with him, the school of the Sadducees then current (ἡ οὖσα αἵρεσις τῶν Σαδδουκαίων), were filled with zeal and laid hands on the apostles, and placed them in the public prison" (5:17). Once again the authorities used their visible powers to effect their goals, "but an angel of the Lord" opened the prison doors and told the apostles to return to teaching the people in the temple, which they did. The reader must smile as he or she sees the exalted high priest convening "the *synedrion* [here, the body more than the place] and the whole Senate of the sons of Israel" to try the apostles again, but finds the cell guarded, locked, and empty (5:23)! Instead of asking what this might mean and pondering the divine will, the high priest stubbornly uses the force at his disposal, the commander (στρατηγός) of the temple guard with his officers, to arrest the apostles. Again, the commander must seize them carefully, without visible force, so as not to arouse the ire of the people (5:26). When the apostles appear before the *synedrion* (both the room and the place are suggested), they make the same point as before: they are simply obeying God (5:29). The temple leadership is ignorant of God's will; it was responsible for killing the one whom God himself has exalted as prince and savior (5:31). "Those who heard [those meeting in the *synedrion*] became infuriated and wanted to kill them" (5:33).

What comes next is a complete surprise to the reader—even more than Joseph of Arimathea's appearance after the *collective* council action against Jesus (Luke 23:1, 51). Whereas he has consistently separated the popular Pharisees from the aristocratic Sadducean-priestly leadership of Jerusalem, Luke now introduces a Pharisee in the Sanhedrin! "Now a certain Pharisee in the *synedrion* by the name of Gamaliel, *a teacher of the Law honored by all the people,* stood up and ordered the men to be taken outside for a moment." (5:34). On the one hand, this first reference to a Pharisees in Acts fits everything we remember about them from the Gospel: they are the esteemed popular teachers of Jesus' world. On the other hand, what is this Pharisee doing in the Jerusalem council led by the high priest, which both the Gospel and Acts have thus far portrayed as a chief-priestly and Sadducean preserve? The Pharisees' presence in the council will become increasingly important as the narrative of Acts proceeds. It seems doubtful that Luke means to highlight the tension; rather, he is quietly introducing Pharisees in the council for a new rhetorical situation. This can only mean that he has always known about their presence, but suppressed that information when discussing the events related to Jesus' death. And this implies that he has a specific role for the Pharisees in his narrative, which he does not wish to confuse with the Sadducean chief priests' role.

Gamaliel's speech provides further clues about the Pharisees' perspective. It also shows Luke's concern for verisimilitude. Although the Christians would not see themselves as a faction comparable to the followers of Judas or Theudas, Gamaliel compares these groups as a councillor might plausibly do. He is the only councillor we have met who has the slightest interest in discussing the Christians' claims, and this alone sets him apart from the chief-priestly councillors, just as the Pharisees of the Gospel, who loved to debate issues, were different from the chief priests there.

This is the first occasion in which chief priests and Pharisees come into direct contact, and the result is illuminating. Against the chief priests' wish to kill the apostles, this popular teacher insists, "Consider carefully what you are about to do to these men!" After recounting the examples of Theudas and Judas, whose movements came to nought, he concludes, "So also now I am saying to you, leave these men alone and let them be. For if this scheme or this effort is of human origin, it will be smashed to pieces. But if it is from God, you will not be able to smash them—lest you be found God-fighters" (5:38–39). This lone Pharisaic voice in what we had thought was a chief-priestly Senate then *persuades* the others (5:39). How can this be? Luke does not explain. Perhaps Gamaliel was a uniquely skilled orator, or admired by the other councillors. But the narrative indicators point in another direction, namely, the leaders are afraid of the people, and the Pharisee Gamaliel is highly respected by the people. The reader's most likely assumption, I submit, would be that Gamaliel carries disproportionate weight because he represents the popular will. His position is opposed to that of the council majority, but they defer to him because of his popular standing. As always, they must temper their own aims by considering the people; only now we learn that the people's school is represented in Senate.

To conclude from Gamaliel's articulation of the narrator's own view here—Christianity cannot be stopped—that Gamaliel stands on the verge of Christian faith would be to miss Luke's narrative indicators.[113] He is no more a partisan of the Christians than he is of the other popular groups mentioned. But it is equally

[113] Contra Brawley, *Luke-Acts,* 97–98.

misguided to see him as a wicked man motivated by fear, or to contrast him with Joseph of Arimathea in Luke 23:51—a bit of a stretch.[114] Why must each character be a paradigm of good or evil? Luke has a historian's concern for verisimilitude. Gamaliel appears as a shrewd popular politician, weighing popular piety against administrative needs. Like the Pharisees of the Gospel, he adopts a cautious wait-and-see approach, which does not preclude a sound flogging at the *synedrion* (5:40).

At this point, the narrative could go one of two ways: the presence of an influential Pharisee in the Senate might portend increasing openness to Christianity on the part of the chief priests, or the Pharisees and people might increasingly assimilate to the obstructionist tradition of the Senate.

The death of Stephen marks a significant shift. Up to that point, many thousands of the people have believed. Even a *large* number of priests have accepted the new faith (6:8). These are not chief priests, but they are linked with the temple establishment. When Stephen begins to preach in Greek-speaking synagogues, however, his opponents instigate false witnesses who allege that he speaks against Moses, the laws, and the temple (6:11–13). Although the reader knows the charge to be mischievous, in view of Luke's pronounced emphasis thus far on Law-observance among Jesus' students, we see an ominous change now, for the false witnesses are able to stir up the *people* against Stephen (6:12). When Stephen is brought before the *synedrion,* the high priest has broad support for his execution; there is no question of fearing the people or dealing with the Pharisees. Stephen accuses the whole people (7:51–53), and one of those who consents to Stephen's death is Saul (8:1), who turns out to be a Pharisee (26:5).

Christianity has been tarred with the accusation that it aims to overturn Judean tradition, and this charge brings the Pharisees, who otherwise have quite different interests from the chief priests, into cooperation with them on the Christian problem. A major persecution of Christians breaks out in Judea (8:1–3). Whereas until now the high priest's authority has seemed limited to Jerusalem, on this issue he public cooperation for a nation-wide disciplinary action (8:3; 9:1–2). The temple-based opposition to Christianity is now solidifying with the apparent inclusion of Pharisees and many of the people.

Paradoxically, we soon see that there is something to the charge that Christianity overturns Judean custom, though this was not yet true when Stephen died. In a pivotal revelation to Peter, God declares all food and all humanity *clean* (10:15, 28; 11:9). The abrogation, or drastic relativization, of the dietary laws constitutes a massive break with even the most popular forms of Judean observance. It is no coincidence that, of the eighty-three occurrences of Ἰουδαῖος in Luke-Acts, seventy-three come after the revelation to Peter. Only now are "the Judeans" mentioned without qualification as a body distinct from, and basically hostile to, Christians (e.g., 12:3, 11; 13:5, 45; 14:1; 17:5; 18:12; 22:30; 23:12, 20; 24:9). Unbelieving Judeans are more and more allied with the Jerusalem leadership as a stubborn bloc. The apostolic council, by recognizing the divine directive to

[114]Contra Darr, *Character,* 116–17.

admit Gentiles without circumcision (15:8–10, 28), seals the non-Judean (or not necessarily Judean) character of Christianity. As the Judeans collectively fail to follow the successive revelations of God's will, they and the Christians appear headed toward complete mutual isolation.

An incident retold in chapter 19 illustrates the distance between Judeans and Christians by that point. Among the traveling Judean exorcists in Ephesus are allegedly seven sons of a high priest (or chief priest) named Sceva, who resort to using Jesus' name in their exorcisms. But even the demon can see through them and ridicules their ineffectiveness: "Jesus I'm acquainted with and Paul I know, but who are you?" (19:15). The story continues the old theme of the chief priests' uselessness, but now they now appear as a spent force, an object of derision more than even a minor irritant.

Yet this growing momentum toward separation also highlights Luke's effort to *prevent* any final schism. While tending to speak of Judeans without qualification as non-Christians, he nonetheless insists that "many Judeans" continued to trust in Jesus (13:43; 14:1; 17:4, 11–12; 18:8; 19:9; 20:20; 28:24). Everywhere Paul goes on his Mediterranean mission, even when taken to Rome in chains, he seeks out the local Judean-expatriate community to convince its membership that Jesus is their Messiah (13:5, 14:1; 16:13; 17:2–3; 28:23). He typically grounds his teaching in Judean (biblical) history, and both he and the apostles continue to observe Judean Law in general—notwithstanding the relativization of the dietary laws (15:10; 18:18; 24:16–17). Luke has the proconsul Gallio in Corinth recognize that the question of Paul's faith is an internal Judean matter (18:14–15). Even as many priests have already adopted the new faith, so also many "from the school of the Pharisees" believe (15:5).

An essential element of Luke's strategy to unite Christianity and Judean culture is his portrayal of the church as a Judean *philosophical school* alongside the Pharisees and Sadducees. In the earlier chapters of Acts, both Pharisees (15:5) and Sadducees (4:17) have been called by the name associated with philosophical schools: αἵρεσις. When Paul is arrested on his final trip to Jerusalem, his encounter with the *synedrion* (here signifying the council more than the place) affords Luke an opportunity to forge this link between Christianity and Judean culture.

In this case, the *synedrion* is called together by the Roman tribune holding Paul. The high priest Ananias heads the Senate now (23:2). Paul claims not to know that he is the high priest when he lets loose an insulting remark after being struck in the mouth (23:3), but his ignorance may well be feigned. Although Luke has never divulged this before, it suddenly serves his rhetorical purpose to have Paul realize that the *synedrion* is divided between Sadducees and Pharisees: "the one section comprises Sadducees and the other Pharisees" (23:6). Paul seizes on this fact to create a diversion. He claims to be a Pharisee on trial simply because of his belief in resurrection—which, Luke reminds us, the Sadducees reject, along with angels and spirits (23:8). Paul's claim causes "great commotion" as the two schools square off against each other, with the Pharisees conceding that Paul might indeed have heard from an angel or a spirit (23:9)!

The story is filled with irony and sarcasm. Since its main point seems to be that Paul cleverly devises a ruse to save himself, we should not put too much weight on particular items. The whole narrative of Luke-Acts has told us that Christianity is essentially different from Pharisaism, and that Jesus' resurrection is a unique case abundantly supported by evidence and divine demonstration. In light of all that has happened, the Pharisees and Sadducees would be truly stupid to fall for Paul's claim. The author is making sport of these Judean schools. Nevertheless, the joke has a serious side. First, the Pharisees' belief in resurrection confirms that Christianity belongs in the orbit of Judean philosophical culture—even though resurrection might seem strange to Gentile philosophers (17:32). Second, the Pharisees' openness to Paul, comical though it is, recalls Gamaliel's more serious openness and the Pharisees' lost opportunities of bygone days; now, their academic debates with the Sadducees about resurrection are ludicrous, given their incomprehension of Jesus' significance. Luke's *division* of the Senate into only two parties fits his narrative here, but we know that can present it otherwise in different situations; it is unclear exactly how he really perceives the council's make-up.

More clues for understanding the church's relationship to Judean leaders are furnished by Paul's defense before Felix at Caesarea. The high priest, *still* relying on outward human measures while blithely ignoring God's will, enlists the aid of an orator (ῥήτωρ) named Tertullus. The appearance of an *orator* on the high priest's team gives the story of the Judean leaders a sense of closure, with no little humor. Luke's readers know that truth is not be found in rhetoric. There had always been a stand-off between those interested in the truth, whether philosophers or historians, and orators, whose talent lay in making the worse case appear the better. And now, finally, the high priest has employed an orator in his service—a fitting move for the "whitewashed wall" (23:3)! Tertullus's speech, typical of a servile golden mouth, reeks with obsequiousness toward this notoriously impious governor (as the readers perhaps understand).[115] Still, Luke has Tertullus call Christianity a *school* (αἵρεσις) alongside the other Judean schools: Paul is "a ringleader of the school of the Nazarenes" (24:5). The Christians appear as a philosophical school within Judean culture, bearing the standard of truth against the rhetoric and sophistry of the others. They are persecuted in the same way that all truth-telling philosophers have always been persecuted by sophists.

Admittedly, Luke's Paul implicitly rejects the label of a "school" ("the Way, which they call a school"; 24:14), but that is because for him Christianity is now the only way, and not simply one "choice" (cf. αἱρέομαι). His reluctance does not stem from disagreement that Christianity belongs within Judean culture, for he protests his fidelity to the Judean people (24:16–18). By putting the term on

[115]Luke's Paul, by contrast, directly confronts Felix on issues of righteousness, self-control, and coming judgement (24:25). His brief flattery of Agrippa II at 26:3 seems intended as sharp sarcasm, in view of the presence of Agrippa's lover-sister Berenice (25:23), who serves no narrative function if not to make the reader recall their widely rumoured liaison.

Tertullus's lips, Luke can claim that Christianity is at least accepted by Judeans as a one of their own schools, which identification helps to locate it socially within the Mediterranean world.

That the word carries no negative connotation is shown by Paul's use of it again in his defense before Agrippa. This scene draws together many aspects of Luke's treatment of the Judean leadership groups and so provides a fitting conclusion to our survey of Luke-Acts on this question. Paul says in part:

> All the Judeans know my way of life right from my youth, which was spent from the beginning among my people and in Jerusalem; they have known me all along, if they are willing to declare it, that according to *the most precise school* of our [Judean] piety I lived as a Pharisee (κατὰ τὴν ἀκριβεστάτην αἵρεσιν τῆς ἡμετέρας θρησκείας ἔζησα φαρισαῖος). (Acts 26:5)

So the Pharisees are, as the reader has come to suspect, the most famous and precise of the Judean schools. At least for someone in Paul's position, not being a priest, there seem to be no stronger Judean credentials than alliance with the Pharisees.

Paul continues:

> And now it is on the basis of our forefathers' hope in the promise given by God that I stand on trial, for which hope our twelve tribes earnestly worship night and day, aspiring to grasp it. Concerning this hope I am accused by the Judeans, O King. But why is it thought incredible by all of you that God raises the dead? (Acts 26:6–8)

Thus far Paul stresses the closeness between the Christians' root claim, that Jesus was raised, and Pharisaic belief. In doing so, perhaps he recalls for the reader the whole Gospel of Luke and the early part of Acts, in which the Pharisees maintained a cautiously critical interest in the new teaching. They shared the belief of Jesus and his students in a future resurrection in which rewards and punishments would be meted out. In one of its two basic claims (the dying Messiah is a more contentious issue not raised here), Christianity stands in continuity with the views of the most exacting school. But this theoretical point of agreement has long passed by the time of Luke's Paul, as God's successive revelations were missed by most Pharisees and other Judeans.

Paul goes on:

> Indeed I myself thought it necessary to put up strong opposition against the name of Jesus of Nazareth. That is what I did among the Jerusalemites: I locked up many of the holy ones in prisons, having received the authority to do so from the chief priests, and as they were being killed I cast a vote against them. And often punishing them in synagogues everywhere I tried to coerce them into repudiating [this name]—I was boiling over with rage to the extent that I pursued them even into other regions. (Acts 26:9–12)

He recalls here his own entry into the Christian story, right at the moment when Judeans as a whole began to turn against Stephen and the other Christians because of rumors that they were overturning Judean tradition in the name of this

Jesus. Saul the Pharisee was a vital part of this coherent Judean effort led by the chief priests. The usual gulf between chief priests and Pharisees (with the people) assumed in the Gospel and as late as Gamaliel's speech, had now been overcome for the sake of the Christian problem. Nevertheless, Paul goes on, God compelled this member of the Pharisaic school to accept Jesus as Messiah, and he could not disobey the heavenly revelation (26:12–19). The reader knows that some other Pharisees also believed.

Thus, on the one hand, Luke's view is that Christianity is the only way, the only proper response to God's revelations, which stand in complete continuity with the biblical heritage and promises. Nevertheless, from a social perspective, the main stream of Judeans see it as a new "school" alongside those of the Pharisees and Sadducees. Luke's own use of "Judeans" without qualification to mean non-Christians belies this claim. The two communities are indeed separate by his day, and Christian groups are mainly Gentile. But this basic narrative assumption throws into relief Luke's efforts to plead the church's genuinely Judean heritage. The church may be understood as the school that fearlessly proclaims the truth, though it is opposed by complacent sophists in positions of power, who are stereotypically unwilling to examine themselves or change their thinking (μετάνοια).

Conclusion

The Book of Acts, then, opens with the same impression of Judean leaders that the Gospel had developed. After Jesus' resurrection, the Judean *people* continue to respond faithfully to the message of Jesus' followers, accepting Jesus' messiahship in the tens of thousands. This broad popular response is predictably opposite to that of the Sadducean, temple-based leadership, whose antagonism operates at several levels. Politically, they are upset at the continued propagation of Jesus' name. Socially, they reject the untutored apostles' ambition to teach the people in the temple precincts. Theologically, they find the doctrine of resurrection absurd. Their comically futile attempts to stamp out the budding Christian movement in the face of divine intervention, reinforce their image as powerless pretenders, always fearful of popular resentment.

Between the people and the Jerusalem leaders stand the Pharisees. They are popular teachers, widely respected for their precision (ἀκρίβεια). Only now do we learn, however, that the Pharisees are represented in the Jerusalem council. At the outset, things still look hopeful as the influential Pharisee Gamaliel is able to persuade the council that the Christians should be left alone for the time being—a view that accords with his roles as both pragmatic councillor and mediator of popular sentiment. The reader will ultimately discover that Pharisees constitute one of the two major blocs in the council, a fact suppressed by Luke to serve his earlier points, but Luke never abandons his basic assumption that the two parties represent different constituencies and views.

This essential difference of outlook between the schools intensifies the drama when, after some false reports about Stephen's teaching, the whole Judean people begin to unite behind a bipartisan coalition on the Christian problem. The sort of basic conflict between Christians and "the Judeans" that is assumed as basic in other gospels develops *only now,* late in the day; the gulf is widened by Christian relativization of the dietary laws and full inclusion of uncircumcised Gentiles. Significant numbers of priests and Pharisees trust Jesus as Messiah, and pockets of the Judean diaspora supplement their numbers, but this leaves a large residue of hardening Judean opposition. While conceding this growing separation, Luke nonetheless tries to maintain the church's position within the orbit of Judean culture by casting it as another *school* in addition to the Pharisees and Sadducees. In reality it is more than a school, since it alone has been faithful to successive divine revelations, but it is at least perceived as a school by other Judeans.

Luke has nothing to say about the vexed question of the Judean Senate's competence to inflict the death penalty. But he assumes throughout his narratives that the council can both condemn and execute offenders against Judean law. The Senate led by the chief priests plans to kill Jesus, the apostles, and Paul; they do kill Stephen without impediment. Their decision to have Jesus tried by Pilate, we have seen, stems not from an inability to try capital cases (cf. John 18:31) but from their customary fear of the people (19:48; 20:6, 19). When this fear prevents them from seizing Jesus themselves, they send spies to ask him about tribute to Caesar, hoping that his answer will provide grounds for a trial by the governor (20:20). That would remove Jesus but still leave them free of popular resentment for the move. The reader concludes that they would have seized and executed Jesus had it not been for this pervasive fear.

Although we cannot offer detailed assessments of other scholarship on our theme, the foregoing interpretation of the Judean leaders in Luke-Acts may serve as tacit confirmation of some points and disconfirmation of others in the work of Sanders, Brawley, and Darr. In my view, their common oversight is their desire to make the Pharisees a static symbol of some kind, though Luke's whole narrative seems to resist static identifications. To make sense of all the narrative indicators, one must respect Luke's avowed *historical* interest—in describing how things got to be the way they now are—and shed the old form-critical bugbear that requires each item in the story to correspond to some aspect of the reading community's life.

In Josephus

We are fortunate indeed to possess the narratives of the first-century Judean historian Josephus. They also discuss the Judean leadership groups in question, but from an entirely different perspective. Whereas Luke disdains the Jerusalem establishment, Josephus is a proud member of it. Luke could never have written these words:

> What could be more beautiful or just than to have placed God as governor of the whole universe, to assign to the common priesthood the administration of the

> greatest affairs, and to have entrusted to the high priest the governance of all the other priests? (*Ag. Ap.* 2.185)

With the aristocrat Josephus we enter a new world of values, which may be contrasted with Luke's according to the following scheme of their differing value systems (though it should not be pressed for other purposes):

LUKE-ACTS	JOSEPHUS
God	God
Jesus and his followers	The Chief Priests, Priesthood, Sadducees
The Judean People—and the Pharisees	Essenes
Chief Priests and Sadducees	The Judean "mob"—admirers of the Pharisees

Whereas Luke-Acts contains 38 references to chief priests, 6 to Sadducees, and 35 to Pharisees (so Pharisees and chief priests appear about equally), Josephus has 372 references to chief priests, 13 to Sadducees, and 44 to Pharisees. His work thus has *much* more to do with priestly circles; he has much less interest than Luke, proportionately, in the Pharisees. This divergence of perspective comes through in all of Josephus's narratives, which we shall now briefly summarize. This basic difference between Luke and Josephus should, however, make us all the more aware of any *shared assumptions* about the realities of Judean society, which are all the more useful for historical reflection because they come from such diverse perspectives.

Judean War

In post-war Rome, the captured Judean general Josephus first wrote an account of the war, to combat the anti-Judean histories that had already appeared. Although those histories have not survived, we may infer from later Roman accounts (Tacitus, *Hist.* 5.1–13) and from Josephus's own story (e.g., *War* 1.2, 7–9) that they at least (a) presented the revolt as a typical expression of the rebellious Judean national character and (b) portrayed the Roman victory as another triumph of Roman Fortune, which defeated the Judean God. Josephus argues, by contrast, that (a) the revolt was an untypical action, engineered by a handful of power-seeking "tyrants" who duped the masses—against the whole train of Judean tradition, which advocated peaceful observance of the laws (*War* 1.9–12)—and (b) it was the all-powerful God worshiped by the Judeans who used the Romans, to whom he had entrusted world power at this moment of history, to punish his people for their sins, particularly for the rebels' pollution of the temple in Jerusalem. As a priest of the conquered nation (1.3), Josephus will offer an authoritative Judean account to help alleviate post-war hostilities.

In this temple-centered history, the chief priests play a critical role. From the beginning of the Hasmonean story through the Herodian and subsequent periods, the reader is regularly informed about the identity of the serving high priest (1.31, 56, 68, 109, 194, etc.). Josephus assumes everywhere that the high priest and his associates are the authorized rulers of the nation. These chief priests regularly appear in epexegetical union with "the powerful" (οἱ δυνατοί) and "the eminent" (οἱ γνώριμοι) (2.243, 301, 316, 318, 336, 410, 422, etc.). These groups are often called simply "the leaders" (οἱ ἄρχοντες) (2.237, 333, 405, 407, etc.). A first-century reader would quickly understand that these are the wealthiest and most educated Judeans, the aristocratic leaders of society.

Occasionally they are mentioned alongside "the council" (ἡ βουλή), which seems to be largely their preserve (2.331, 336). When this Senate first appears in the narrative, Josephus mentions it casually, as if it needs no explanation that Jerusalem should have its own βουλή, as Rome and other cities had theirs (1.284, 285; 7.65, 107). The Jerusalem council, Josephus claims, had a meeting chamber—also called a βουλή here—beside the Xystus, or public meeting place (5.145; cf. 2.344; 4.243; 6.354). One scribe (ὁ γραμματεύς) of the council, a priest, is mentioned by name (5.532). Josephus also mentions incidentally a commander (στρατηγός) of the temple precincts, to whom the sentries report (6.294). Interestingly, the word συνέδριον in *War* .consistently refers to an ad hoc official meeting; Josephus almost always speaks of its being convened (ἀθροίζω) or dissolved (διαλύω) on a single occasion (1.559, 571, 620, 640; 2.25, 81, 93; 6.342).

The significance of the chief priests for this narrative lies in the fact that they anchor the "moderate" position over against the rebels. As the proper guardians of the temple and its program, they understand the importance of sustaining the temple service at all costs, even though they too are deeply offended by the behavior of Roman officials in Judea. Their insistence on peace brings them into direct conflict with Josephus's rogues' gallery: Eleazar son of Yair and the Sicarii, Menahem, John of Gischala, Simon son of Giora, the Idumeans, and Zealots. Already during Felix's tenure as governor, in the fifties, the *sicarii* murder the high priest Jonathan (2.256). When Gessius Florus plunders the temple and some of the Judeans mock him, the chief priests intercede to alleviate Florus's anger and maintain peace (2.301–304). When he then callously slaughters Judeans in the upper market area, the chief priests implore the incensed people not to retaliate (2.316). They themselves represent the people's complaints to Agrippa, to try to have Florus removed (2.336), but continue to plead with the people not to lead them into open rebellion (2.411–416). The reader knows that the chief priests will be ineffective, however, when one of their own younger members joins the revolutionaries (2.409), and Josephus notes that "not one of the revolutionary party would listen" to the aristocrats' pleas (2.417).

From this point onward, the chief priests and their associates become the object of deliberate and violent opposition from the rebels. Some rebels set fire to the high priest's house along with the royal palace and public archives where debts were recorded (2.427). They murder the chief priests Ananias and Ezechias (2.441), and the Idumeans later kill Jesus and Ananus (4.314–318). Josephus's editorial eulogy on the last two leaders makes clear his sympathy for their position: their love of the temple and its service, their commitment to peace and national honor (4.319–325). The rebels crown their impiety by electing to the high priesthood a simpleton from the countryside who was "not even descended from high priests" (4.155–157). Josephus complains throughout the narrative that his own views and those of the chief priests were unappealing to the common people, who saw hopes of political, social, economic, and religious salvation in the rebels' vain promises (e.g. 6.286–287; cf. 2.4, 427, 253–260).

Pharisees and Sadducees do not play a significant role in the main drama of *War,* appearing only in the first two volumes as part of the backdrop. This literary fact is itself important: the Pharisees, Sadducees, and Essenes represent old and, if we may use the term in this context, "normal" Judaism—the kind that obtained before the revolt. The rebels represent a radical departure from all such customary Judean thinking. This does not mean that Josephus himself is fond of either Pharisees or Sadducees. (Please see chapters 5 and 6 in this volume for an overview.)

The Sadducees will not appear again in *War.* Nor will the "Essenes" under that precise name, though Josephus will mention that John the "*Essaios*" (perhaps from the same group, or someone from Essa?) entered the conflict on much the same terms as he himself did (2.567; 3.11). The Pharisees make one further brief but telling appearance, when their "most eminent" members join forces with the chief priests and powerful ones to dissuade the people from revolt (2.411). This casual notice reflects Josephus's continued assumption that the Pharisees are the most prominent of the "schools," since Sadducees and Essenes are not mentioned here, but the reader is left to speculate on their exact social status. The prominent Pharisees are no more able than the chief priests and their associates to stem the revolutionary tide. In this struggle for the hearts and minds of the people, the Pharisees appear on the leaders' side over against the rebels, but this whole coalition is sadly unable to divert the nation from ruin.

Judean Antiquities, Life, *and* Against Apion

We may treat together Josephus's magnum opus, *Judean Antiquities,* and his autobiography, *Life,* which he wrote as an appendix to the longer work. In concluding this survey, I shall also include a note on Josephus's last known composition, the *Against Apion,* which mentions only the priesthood.

The preface to *Antiquities* identifies it as a sequel to the *Judean War* (*Ant.* 1.1–4), but in a somewhat different rhetorical context. Rather than writing primarily to refute false accounts, Josephus now addresses those who, like Ptolemy Philadelphus and his patron Epaphroditus, are "eager" to learn of Judean antiquity and culture (1.9–10). Outside of his writings there is abundant evidence that some Romans at the end of the first century were attracted in varying degrees to Judean culture.[116] For such an audience Josephus describes Judaism as the noblest and "most philosophical" way of life ever devised, far superior to the readers'

[116]H. J. Leon, *Jews,* 10–35.

own unreasonable native mythologies (1.18–26). Only the laws of Moses bring what is most sought after by the philosophical schools: happiness (εὐδαιμονία) (1.14, 20). On the basis of these laws, God rewards virtue and punishes crime with perfect consistency. Josephus's presentation of Judaism as an effective system in contrast to all others provides an interesting parallel to Luke's portrayal of *Christian* teaching as uniquely effective.

As in *War*, the chief priests are visible everywhere in the narrative of *Antiquities-Life*. In the preface Josephus takes as his model the high priest Eleazar, who consented to the translation of Judean scripture into Greek (1.11–12); Eleazar appears as the authorized leader of the nation. In summarizing the measures revealed to Moses at Sinai, Josephus details the high priest's clothing and its cosmic significance (3.159–187) and describes the appointment of Aaron as the first supreme priest (3.188–192). Stones on the high priest's clothing used to shine, he says, to indicate God's presence with his people (3.214).[117] When Moses had finished receiving the laws, he consigned them to the priests for safeguarding; the high priest and his subordinates administer the Judean laws (4.304). As he wends his way through the biblical era and down to his own day, Josephus again identifies the reigning high priest at each period (4.152; 5.318; 6.122, 242, etc.; 10.150–152; 11.73, 90, 121, 158, 297, 300, 306, etc.). At the end of the book, moreover, he recapitulates the entire high-priestly succession (διαδοχή; 20.261) from Aaron through the period following Archelaus's removal (20.224–251). In casting Judaism as a philosophical culture founded by Moses and the high priests as "successors," Josephus recalls the language of the philosophical schools, which typically traced a list of true successors who preserved the teachings of the founding philosopher intact (Diogenes Laertius 6.13, 19; Seneca *Ep.* 40.3).[118]

Josephus differs from Luke on the identity of the serving high priest at the time of Jesus and his first followers. He has Annas I as high priest in the period 6–15 C.E., and Caiaphas as his fourth successor (*Ant.* 18.34–35, 95), whose tenure from 18–37 C.E. would cover the period of Jesus' death and the church's origin (cf. Matt 26:57). Although Luke implies that Annas was the serving high priest then, Josephus can be almost equally confusing when he calls an individual "high priest" long after his term of office (*War* 2.441; *Ant.* 20.205; *Life* 193); but unlike Luke, he usually provides enough context to clarify the matter. According to Josephus, Annas was a particularly distinguished high priest, whose five sons all subsequently served in the office (*Ant.* 20.197–198); his family was thus a major force in chief-priestly circles through the whole period from 6 to 70 C.E. So it is conceivable that a later writer could also see him as the power behind the office even in Caiaphas's time, though one would have expected Luke to be clearer in Luke 3:2. Luke concurs with Josephus that Ananias was high priest during Paul's Jerusalem trial (*Ant.* 20.103, 131; Acts 23:2).

The new rhetorical situation in *Antiquities* dictates a somewhat different use of the high priests as characters over against *War*. Now, in keeping with his theme,

---

[117] Thoma, "High Priesthood," 196–99.

[118] Mason, *Josephus on the Pharisees*, 235–39.

Josephus must distinguish good and bad actions of high priests. The errant high priests include the greedy and mean-spirited Onias, who brought the nation to the brink of disaster in the Ptolemaic period (12.58), and the later Hasmonean high priests who fell dramatically from their ancestors' glory through their selfish intrigues (13.300–319, 431–432). But the most striking examples of transgressors are those whom Josephus had praised effusively in *War,* when he was using them as foils to the rebel leaders. In *Antiquities* the moderate Ananus is accused of injustice for convening the Judean council without the Roman governor's permission (20.199), and King Agrippa II deposes him for this reason (20.200–203). This same chief priest accepts bribes to have Josephus ousted from command of the Galilee (*Life* 193, 196). And on the eve of the revolt the former high priest Ananias (also praised in *War*) has his servants rob the poorer priests of their tithes, leaving them to starve to death (20.206–207). These actions, together with Ananias's use of bribery to maintain his power (20.213), are a major cause of subsequent divine punishment (20.214, cf. 218).

As in *War,* Josephus assumes that the high priest heads a council or Senate. Moses tells the people that such an aristocracy (ἀριστοκρατία), rather than a monarchy, is the best possible constitution (4.223).[119] When the people implore later Samuel to appoint a king, he is deeply upset because, being a righteous man, he hates kingship and is "strongly committed to aristocracy" (6.36). Josephus alters the biblical narrative of Joshua's time to make the great commander consult the high priest and his Senate (γερουσία) (5.15, 43, 55). Interpreting the cycles of sin depicted in Judges, Josephus asserts that "the aristocracy was falling into corruption: no longer did they appoint the Senates or the leadership formerly legislated," which failure resulted in discord and, ultimately, civil war (5.135). When the Judeans return from captivity, they live under a government that is "aristocratic, with the rule of the few" (ἀριστοκρατικῇ μετὰ ὀλιγαρχίας) (11.111). A letter from Antiochus III mentions the Judean Senate as the governing body (12.138, 142), and Jonathan the Hasmonean writes as high priest, on behalf of "the Senate and body of priests" (13.166, 169). Although the later Hasmonean princes create a monarchy (11.111), and so begin the decline of the dynasty (13.301), the Roman Gabinius restores the *aristokratia* when he sets up regional councils in Judean territory (14.91). The emperor Claudius again writes to the "rulers, council, and people of Jerusalem" (20.11). This body judges at least some capital cases (*Ant.* 14.167; 20.200–202).

Josephus makes much of the fact that Herod and Archelaus altered tradition by appointing "insignificant persons" (ἄσημοι) to the high priesthood, not those from the Hasmonean line. With the death of Herod and Archelaus's departure, however, "the high priests were entrusted with the leadership of the nation" (τὴν δὲ προστασίαν τοῦ ἔθνους; 20.251). These notices confirm that for him the nation is properly an aristocracy, and that Herod's rule was an aberration. This view may explain the virtual disappearance of the council led by the high priest during Herod's reign.

[119] Thoma, "High Priesthood," 201.

Outside of Herod's reign, the term συνέδριον in *Antiquities* often means the regular Judean Senate led by the high priest. This usage begins when Gabinius establishes five *synedria* of which Jerusalem is the first (14.91). That the Jerusalem *synedrion* was continuous with the older Senate led by the high priest (in Josephus's story) is indicated by the complaint of the Judean leaders to the high priest Hyrcanus II that Herod has killed bandits in Galilee without a trial before the *synedrion,* as *the Law* requires (14.167). Bowing to their pleas, Hyrcanus convenes the *synedrion* (14.168, 170, 171, 177–180). In this story, one of the councillors—who turns out to be a Pharisee (15.3–4), though Josephus chooses not to say so here—fruitlessly insists that Herod be punished, against the will of the majority. Paradoxically, when Herod becomes king he kills all the members of the *synedrion* except this one (or two? 14.175; 15.4). That is not the end of this council, however, for (according to one version known to Josephus) Herod later pressured it to approve the execution of the high priest Hyrcanus (15.173). Once Herod becomes king, *Antiquities* uses *synedrion* of the ad hoc meetings convened by him (16.357–367; 17.46). It is not clear whether the *synedrion* that later permitted the Levites to wear linen was the standing council or another ad hoc group (20.216–217). But clearly, Josephus assumes that the Judeans were normally governed by a council led by the high priest (cf. also *Ag. Ap.* 1.30; 2.185).

Early in the sixties, the high priest Ananus's convening of a (the?) *synedrion* in the absence of a Roman governor leads to his removal (20.200, 202). Even though the council was still led by the high priest, he did not have the power to convene it without Roman approval. Note that in Acts the Roman tribune can summon the council (Acts 22:30).

The clearest picture we get of the inner workings of *any* Jerusalem council in Josephus comes in his account of John of Gischala's attempt to have him withdrawn from the Galilee (*Life* 189–198). Whether this body, τὸ κοινὸν τῶν Ἱεροσολυμιτῶν, was the regular Senate is not immediately clear.[120] The serving high priest, who seems to have been Matthias son of Theophilus (*Ant.* 20.223), does not surface in the proceedings; the leading figures are the former high priests Ananus and Jesus. One gathers from the parallel in *War* that the rebels (mysteriously) won over those members of the ruling class that remained in Jerusalem and then appointed them leaders (*War* 2.556–568). Since the individuals involved were also the customary leaders of the people, however, this group appears as a makeshift war cabinet, a subset of the regular leadership (cf. 2.411).

In any case, our question concerns the function of τὸ κοινὸν τῶν Ἱεροσολυμιτῶν in the story of the *Life.* Josephus can call this *koinon* "the *synedrion* of Jerusalem" (*Life* 62), or simply "the leaders" (οἱ πρῶτοι) of the people (*Life* 28). His terms appear interchangeable. He seems to favor the expression τὸ κοινὸν τῶν Ἱεροσολυμιτῶν in the *Life* as a way of insisting upon the legitimacy of his military appointment (65, 72, 190, 254, 267, 309, 341, 393). He was selected by "the body politic of the Jerusalemites." The *Life* gives us no reason to suppose that the war council was essentially different from the ordinary Senate

[120] Price, *Siege,* 63–67.

that governed the state under the high priest's leadership. Elsewhere in Josephus, τὸ κοινόν can refer to a standing council headed by the high priest (*Ant.* 6.17; 13.366), though the meaning of the phrase is flexible.

No matter how typical this particular council was, it is significant that John reportedly tried to use his influence with Simon son of Gamaliel, a leading and respected Pharisee on the council from a "very illustrious family," to effect his aims. In response to John's request Simon "tried to persuade (ἔπειθεν) the chief priests Ananus and Jesus, son of Gamalas, and some others of their bloc (στάσεως) . . ." (193). The situation assumed here has some parallels to what we found in Luke-Acts: chief priests and Pharisees have different constituencies and aims; the Pharisees are not the official powers but are able to sway the chief priests often enough that the Galilean considers it worthwhile trying to use Gamaliel's influence here. Josephus claims, however, that Ananus pointed out the difficulties involved in persuading the council to take such action, since "many of the chief priests and leaders (οἱ προεστῶτας) of the people" would testify to his ability as commander. Unfazed, the eminent Pharisee allegedly resorted to bribery in order to accomplish his goal. Finally persuaded by these underhanded means, "Ananus and those with him" sent a delegation of three Pharisees and one other to replace Josephus (196–198). The Pharisee succeeded, one way or another.

In comparison with the chief priests, the Pharisees and Sadducees receive little attention in *Antiquities-Life*. Please see chapters 5 and 6 in this volume.

Josephus's *Against Apion* offers a brief, systematic rebuttal of Judaism's literary defamers along with a positive statement of the culture's principles. The priesthood and its leadership play an important role as guardians of this peerless heritage. The Jews' ancestors put in charge of their records "the most excellent men (οἱ ἄριστοι)," namely, priests (1.30; cf. *Life* 1). In Judean culture, the greatest precautions are taken to ensure that the priestly *aristoi* remain ancestrally pure (1.31). Judean records, accordingly, contain the names of their high priests in succession through 2,000 years (1.36). In his famous discussion of the Judean "theocracy" (2.165), Josephus further celebrates the priests' care for the laws: "This responsibility included the precise administration of the Law and of the other pursuits of everyday life; the priests were charged with supervision of all affairs, the settlement of legal disputes, and the punishment of those condemned" (2.187). His emphasis on the condemnation of criminals reflects his view that only the Judean laws deal effectively with crime (2.276–278; cf. *Ant.* 1.20–22). The priests, supervised by the high priest (2.185), are the agents of this uniquely effective system.

Conclusions

In Acts we have the second volume of a work that seeks to chart the development of Jesus' followers from a movement within Judaism to a largely Gentile group rejected by most Judeans. To sketch and justify this development, Luke makes extensive use of certain Judean groups—the chief priests, Sadducees, Pharisees, and *synedrion*—as background characters. Our chief aim has been to understand how these groups function in the story of Luke-Acts. Although we have an ultimately historical interest, that history does not exist anywhere in advance. We can only try to recreate the history once we understand the evidence that needs explaining, of which Luke-Acts is a significant part. Luke's contemporary Josephus wrote the only non-Christian narratives of the time that mention the groups in question. So, instead of trying to compare Luke-Acts to "history," I have propose a comparative analysis with Josephus's narratives as a way of throwing Luke's portrayal into relief.

Luke and Josephus present radically different viewpoints. For the Christian author, Jesus brought his divinely authorized teaching to the common people, and especially to the outcasts among them. In doing so, he had to contend with the Pharisees, who completely dominated popular piety outside of Jerusalem. Jesus was severely critical of these established teachers for forfeiting their responsibilities by failing to help the people. They were the salt that had lost its flavor, righteous guardians of conventional piety who were blind to the people's needs and Jesus' effectiveness. He, by contrast, summoned a group of students who lived heroically countercultural lives while bringing real help to the masses. The Pharisees, though often alarmed at Jesus' actions, remained cautiously open to this popular teacher.

When he came to Jerusalem, however, he encountered an altogether different group of leaders: the aristocratic, Sadducean, God-denying, chief priests, with their executive council and police force. Their immediate opposition to Jesus was intended to be lethal, though Luke makes fun of their impotence. They finally managed to arrest and execute Jesus, with unacknowledged supernatural intervention. The Jerusalem establishment was very far indeed from God's will. These lofty authorities lived in constant fear of popular sentiment, to which they regularly acceded.

In Acts, the story has fundamentally changed as a result of Jesus' resurrection, which makes acceptance of his messiahship a divine requirement. At the outset, the common people support the new teaching in large numbers and the Pharisees continue their role as cautious observers. With the circumstances that lead to Stephen's death, however, the Pharisees (who now appear in the Jerusalem council itself!) and the people close ranks with the chief priests, to present a more or less galvanized Judean opposition, in spite of cross-overs through the remaining narrative. While acknowledging this growing separation, Luke insists that the Christians only did what was required by God, and that they have by no means abandoned the Judean heritage. The Judeans view the "Nazarenes" as a philosophical school alongside the Pharisees and Sadducees. As a self-conscious historian, Luke has tried to correct the pictures of the Judean leaders in the other Christian texts known to him.

Josephus, in marked contrast to Luke, is an enthusiastic spokesman for the Judean aristocracy. He believes that the laws delivered to Moses by God are the finest in the world; the priestly *aristoi* led by the chief priests are the authorized guardians of this cosmic treasure. He looks on the common people with a combination of pity and contempt because they are vulnerable to whatever self-appointed leaders come along, who often create serious problems for the duly established leadership. In *War,* this tension plays itself out in the struggle between the chief priests and the rebel leaders for the people's hearts and minds; Josephus admits that the chief priests failed. In *Antiquities,* which deals with Judaism in more stable times, the Pharisees are the people's troublesome advocates, though they are not as bad as the rebel leaders. Josephus's later works elaborate his portrait of the chief priests as guardians of the nation's glorious tradition, even while conceding that some chief priests have brought God's punishment on the people (*Antiquities*).

The basic divergence of religious perspective between Luke and Josephus makes their agreement in basic assumptions remarkable. This coincidence may be summarized as follows:

1. The chief priests were the traditional Judean aristocracy, who had supreme control of national affairs from their base in Jerusalem. They were the highest Judean authorities in the land when there was no king, exercising control over the temple service, promulgating the laws, and trying cases. They typically ruled by means of a council or Senate headed by the serving high priest, which had a designated meeting place in or near the temple precinct. Neither author claims that this council had always ruled on the same terms, but both assume conciliar aristocratic rule as the norm. The council envisioned need not fit the old picture of an independent, representative parliament,[121] but Luke and Josephus both assume that it was a regular body with an executive function. The chief priests had security or police forces at their disposal, tried capital cases, and executed offenders. In spite of their visible authority, however, the chief priests always had to be concerned about popular sentiment, often mediated by the Pharisees, which frequently hampered their own program. We note, incidentally, that most ancient ruling bodies were profoundly concerned to conciliate the people, even in Rome, the center of world power.[122]

2. Luke and Josephus describe more of what the Sadducees did not think than what they did think. For both, they were a philosophical school holding sceptical views. They had a tiny base in the aristocracy, including at least some members of the family of Ananus (Annas), though Luke estimates Sadducean influence in chief-priestly circles more highly than Josephus. According to both writers, Sadducees denied life after death and consequently the notion of post-mortem rewards and punishments. Their rejection of the Pharisees' special traditions along with their different social status led to the ongoing conflicts that Luke and Josephus describe. Luke's claim that the Sadducees recognized "neither angel nor spirit" (Acts 23:8) would fit broadly with their rejection of immortality and non-biblical tradition if the reference is to a more elaborate, extrabiblical angelology and demonology accepted by the Pharisees. If Luke indicates a categorical

[121] Thus far Goodman, *Ruling Class,* 113–18; Sanders, *Practice and Belief,* 472–81.
[122] MacMullen, *Enemies,* 172–73.

rejection of ἄγγελοι, even those of the Pentateuch itself, his claim stands alone. Both authors lack any sympathy for Sadducean positions.

3. Luke and Josephus understand the Pharisees as a philosophical school occupying a middle ground between the chief-priestly aristocracy and the masses. Their roots were with the people, among whom they enjoyed a long-standing reputation for precision in the laws and great piety. Their influence does not appear as authoritative control, but arises from shared aspirations, an important part of which was the hope for resurrection and judgement. The common people (Luke: largely outside of Jerusalem) had little to do with chief priests, but treated the Pharisees as authorized teachers. Yet the most eminent Pharisees, those from distinguished families such as Gamaliel's family, held positions in the Senate. Because they were perceived to represent popular opinion, they were often (Josephus: routinely) able to sway the council's decisions, though both authors suggest that they constituted a minority in the council. In the face of certain popular leaders, such as militants and charismatics who precipitated the revolt (in Josephus) or Jesus of Nazareth (in Luke), even the Pharisees failed to maintain the people's complete confidence.

These agreements are striking even if, as I think likely, Luke was familiar with the later volumes of Josephus's *Antiquities*.[123] Whether he knew Josephus's work or not, Luke's account of Jesus' relationship with the Pharisees and chief priests is independent, reflecting assumptions that he at least partly acquired from elsewhere. It is important for historical consideration that these agreements are in matters *assumed* by Luke and Josephus: neither author is interested in the Pharisees, Sadducees, or Sanhedrin in and of themselves; they use these figures as part of the understood scenery of first-century Palestine. Far from inflating the Pharisees' influence out of a desire to support them, for example, both authors assume it in order to *complain* about it. This must be explained by scholars who wish to argue that historically the Pharisees enjoyed no such influence. Similarly, their shared assumption that the high priest ordinarily headed a council of some sort requires explanation, even if the notion of a standing "Sanhedrin," such as the Mishnah tractate of that name presents, does not match the evidence of these Greek texts.

This summary of agreements between Luke and Josephus is of course not yet historical reconstruction. My goal has been to help *prepare* for historical reasoning about the Judean leadership groups by clarifying their functions in two of the most important narrative collections on the issue. Historical hypotheses must account for these and all other relevant stories. Even some recent reconstructions of the Judean leadership groups do not show how the hypotheses advocated would explain the narratives as we have them—on *any* comprehensive interpretation of those narratives. Paradoxically, nearly two thousand years after the chief priests, Sadducees, Pharisees, and Jerusalem court flourished, we await satisfactory explanations of their lives and times.

---

[123] Mason, *Josephus and the New Testament,* 251–95.

Bibliography

Ackroyd, P. R., and C. F. Evans, eds. *From the Beginnings to Jerome*. Vol. 1 of the *Cambridge History of the Bible*. 3 vols. Cambridge: Cambridge University Press, 1963–70.

Adam, A. *Antike Berichte über die Essener*. New York: de Gruyter, 1972.

Ahl, F. "The Art of Safe Criticism in Greece and Rome." *American Journal of Philology* 105 (1984): 174–208.

Albright, W. F., and C. S. Mann. "Qumran and the Essenes: Geography, Chronology, and Identification of the Sect." Pages 11–25 in *The Scrolls and Christianity: Historical and Theological Significance*. Edited by M. Black and W. F. Albright. London: S.P.C.K, 1969.

Alon, G. *Jews, Judaism, and the Classical World*. Jerusalem: Magnes, 1977.

Amir, Y. "The Term *Ioudaismos* (ʾΙΟΥΔΑΙΣΜΟΣ): A Study in Jewish-Hellenistic Self-Identification." *Immanuel* 14 (1982): 34–41.

Amit, D., J. Patrich, and Y. Hirschfeld, eds. *The Aqueducts of Israel*. Portsmouth: Journal of Roman Archaeology, 2002.

Ando, C. *Imperial Ideology and Provincial Loyalty in the Roman Empire*. Berkeley: University of California Press, 2000.

Ashton, J. "The Identity and Function of the ʾΙΟΥΔΑΙΟΙ in the Fourth Gospel." *Novum Testamentum* 27 (1985): 40–75.

Attridge, H. W. "Josephus and his Works." Pages 185–232 in *Jewish Writings of the Second Temple Period: Apocrypha, Pseudepigrapha, Qumran Sectarian Writings, Philo, Josephus*. Edited by M. E. Stone. Philadelphia: Fortress, 1984.

———. *The Interpretation of Biblical History in the Antiquitates Judaicae of Flavius Josephus*. Missoula: Scholars Press, 1976.

Audet, Jean-Paul. "Qumran et la notice de Pline sur les Esséniens." *Revue Biblique* 68 (1961): 346–87.

Aune, D. E. *Prophecy in Early Christianity and the Ancient Mediterranean World*. Grand Rapids: Eerdmans, 1983.

Aune, D. E. "Romans as a *Logos Protreptikos*." Pages 278–96 in *The Romans Debate*. Rev. and exp. ed. Edited by K. P. Donfried. Peabody, Mass.: Hendrickson, 1991.

Aviam, M. "Yodefat/Jotapata: The Archaeology of the First Battle." Pages 121–33 in *The First Jewish Revolt: Archaeology, History, Ideology*. Edited by A. Berlin and A. Overman. London: Routledge, 2002.

Bacher, W. *Die exegetische Terminologie de jüdischen Traditions-literatur*. Hildesheim: Georg Olms, 1965.

Baeck, L. *Paulus, die Pharisäer und das Neue Testament.* Frankfurt: Ner-Tamid, 1961.

Balme, M., ed. *Menander: The Plays and Fragments.* Oxford: Oxford University Press, 2001.

Balsdon, J. P. V. D. *Romans and Aliens.* Chapel Hill: The University of North Carolina Press, 1979.

Bamberger, B. J. *Proselytism in the Talmudic Period.* Cincinnati: Hebrew Union College, 1939.

Barclay, J. M. G. "Josephus v. Apion: Analysis of an Argument." Pages 195–221 in *Understanding Josephus: Seven Perspectives.* Edited by S. Mason. Sheffield: Sheffield Academic Press, 1998.

Barnes, T. D. *Tertullian: A Historical and Literary Study.* Oxford: Clarendon, 1971.

Barnes, T. D. "The Sack of the Temple in Josephus and Tacitus." Pages 129–44 in *Flavius Josephus in Flavian Rome.* Edited by J. Edmondson, J. Rives, and S. Mason. Oxford: Oxford University Press, 2005.

Barrett, C. K. *A Commentary on the Epistle to the Romans.* London: Adam & Charles Black, 1962.

Bartlett, J. R. *Archaeology and Biblical Interpretation.* London: Routledge, 1997.

Barton, J. *Oracles of God: Perception of Ancient Prophecy in Israel after the Exile.* Oxford: Oxford University Press, 1986.

Bartsch, S. *Actors in the Audience: Theatricality and Doublespeak from Nero to Hadrian.* Cambridge, Mass.: Harvard University Press, 1994.

Bauer, W. "Essener." Pages 386–430 in vol. 4 of *Paulys Realenzyklopädie der Classischen Altertumswissenschaft.* 49 vols. Edited by A. F. Pauly, G. Wissowa, et al. Munich: A. Druckenmüller, 1924.

Baumbach, G. "The Sadducees in Josephus." Pages 173–95 in *Josephus, the Bible, and History.* Edited by L. H. Feldman and G. Hata. Detroit: Wayne State University Press, 1989.

Baumgarten, A. I. *The Flourishing of Jewish Sects in the Maccabean Era: An Interpretation.* Leiden: Brill, 1997.

———. "Josephus and Hippolytus on the Pharisees." *Hebrew Union College Annual* 55 (1984): 1–25.

———. "Josephus on Essene Sacrifice." *Journal of Jewish Studies* 45.2 (1994): 169–83.

———. "The Name of the Pharisees." *Journal of Biblical Literature* 102 (1983): 418–28.

———. "The Pharisaic Paradosis." *Harvard Theological Review* 80 (1987): 63–87.

Baumgarten, J. M. "The Essene Avoidance of Oil and the Laws of Purity." *Revue de Qumran* 6 (1967): 183–92.

———. "The 'Halakha' in Miqsat Ma'ase ha-Torah (MMT)." *Journal of the American Oriental Society* 16.3 (1996): 512–16.

———. "The Unwritten Law in the Pre-Rabbinic Period." *Journal for the Study of Judaism in the Persian, Hellenistic, and Roman Periods* 3 (1972), 7–29.

Baur, F. C. *Paul, the Apostle of Jesus Christ: His Life and Work, His Epistles and His Doctrine; A Contribution to the Critical History of Primitive Christianity.*

2 vols. Translated by E. Zeller. 2d rev. ed. London: Williams and Northgate, 1876.

———. [1866]. *Paulus, der Apostel Jesu Christi.* Osnabrück: O. Zeller, 1968.

Beall, T. S. *Josephus' Description of the Essenes Illustrated by the Dead Sea Scrolls.* Cambridge: Cambridge University Press, 1988.

Beard, M., J. North, and S. Price. *Religions of Rome.* 2 vols. Cambridge: Cambridge University Press, 1998.

Beck, N. *Mature Christianity: The Recognition and Repudiation of the Anti-Jewish Polemic in the New Testament.* London: Associated University Press, 1985.

Beebe, H. K. "Caesarea Maritima: Its Strategic and Political Importance to Rome." *Journal of Near Eastern Studies* 42 (1983): 195–207.

Begg, C. *Josephus' Account of the Early Divided Monarchy (AJ 8, 212–420): Rewriting the Bible.* Bibliotheca ephemeridum theologicarum Iovaniensium 108. Leuven: Leuven University Press, 1993.

———. *Josephus' Story of the Later Monarchy.* Bibliotheca ephemeridum theologicarum Iovaniensium 155. Leuven: Leuven University Press, 2000.

———. *Judean Antiquities 5–7.* Vol. 4 of *Flavius Josephus: Translation and Commentary.* Edited by Steve Mason. Leiden: Brill, 2004.

Beilner, W. "Der Ursprung des Pharisäismus." *Biblische Zeitschrift* 3 (1959): 235–51.

Bell, A. "Josephus and Pseudo-Hegesippus." Pages 349–61 in *Josephus, Judaism, and Christianity.* Edited by L. H. Feldman and G. Hata. Detroit: Wayne State University Press, 1987.

Benko, S. *Pagan Rome and the Early Christians.* Bloomington: Indiana University Press, 1984.

Bergmeier, R. *Die Essener-Berichte des Flavius Josephus: Quellenstudien zu den Essenertexten im Werk des jüdischen Historiographen.* Kampen: Kok Pharos, 1993.

Berlin, A., and A. Overman, eds. *The First Jewish Revolt: Archaeology, History, Ideology.* London: Routledge, 2002.

Betz, H. D. *Galatians: A Commentary on Paul's Letter to the Churches in Galatia.* Hermeneia. Philadelphia: Fortress, 1979.

Bickerman, E. J. *God of the Maccabees: Studies in the Meaning and Origin of the Maccabean Revolt.* Leiden: Brill, 1979.

———. "La chaine de tradition pharisienne." Pages 256–69 in vol. 2 of *Studies in Jewish and Christian History.* 2 vols. Leiden: Brill, 1980.

Bilde, P. "The Causes of the Jewish War According to Josephus." *Journal for the Study of Judaism in the Persian, Hellenistic, and Roman Periods* 10.2 (1979): 179–202.

———. *Flavius Josephus between Jerusalem and Rome: His Life, his Works, and Their Importance.* Sheffield: JSOT Press, 1988.

Birnbaum, E. *The Place of Judaism in Philo's Thought: Israel, Jews, and Proselytes.* Atlanta: Scholars Press, 1996.

Black, M. "The Account of the Essenes in Hippolytus and Josephus." Pages 172–82 in *The Background of the New Testament and its Eschatology.* Edited by W. D. Davies and D. Daube. Cambridge: Cambridge University Press, 1956.

———. "Judas of Galilee and Josephus's Fourth Philosophy." Pages 45–54 in *Josephus-Studien: Untersuchungen zu Josephus, der antiken Judentum und dem Neuen Testament, Otto Michel zum 70. Gerburtstag gemidwet.* Edited by O. Betz, K. Haacker, and M. Hengel. Göttingen: Vandenhoeck & Ruprecht, 1974.

———. "Pharisees." Pages 774–81 in vol. 3 of *The Interpreter's Dictionary of the Bible.* 4 vols. Edited by G. A. Buttrick. Nashville: Abingdon, 1962.

———. *Romans.* New Century Bible. London: Olliphants, 1974.

———. *The Scrolls and Christian Origins: Studies in the Jewish Background of the New Testament.* New York: Charles Scribner's Sons, 1961.

Blenkinsopp, J. "Prophecy and Priesthood in Josephus." *Journal of Jewish Studies* 25 (1974): 239–62.

Bloch, H. *Die Quellen des Flavius Josephus in seiner Archäologie.* Leipzig: Wiesbaden: M. Sändig, 1968.

Bloch, M. *The Historian's Craft.* Translated by P. Putnam. New York: Knopf, 1953.

Bloch, R. S. *Antike Vorstellungen vom Judentum: der Judenexkurs des Tacitus im Rahmen der griechisch-römischen Ethnographie.* Stuttgart: F. Steiner, 2002.

Blumell, L. "A Jew in Celsus' True Doctrine? An Examination of Jewish Anti-Christian Polemic in the Second Century." *Studies in Religion* 36.2 (2007): 297–316.

Boatwright, M. T., D. J. Gargola, and R. J. A. Talbert. *The Romans: From Village to Empire.* Oxford: Oxford University Press, 2004.

Bodde, D., ed. *A Short History of Chinese Philosophy.* New York: Macmillan, 1948.

Boers, H. "The Form-Critical Study of Paul's Letters: 1 Thessalonians as a Test Case." *New Testament Studies* 22 (1975–76): 140–58.

Bond, H. *Pontius Pilate in History and Interpretation.* Cambridge: Cambridge University Press, 1998.

Bonz, M. P. "The Jewish Donor Inscriptions from Aphrodisias: Are They Both Third-Century, and Who Are the *Theosebeis*?" *Harvard Studies in Classical Philology* 96 (1994): 281–99.

Bornkamm, G. "The Letter to the Romans as Paul's Last Will and Testament." Pages 17–31 in *The Romans Debate.* Rev. and exp. ed. Edited by K. P. Donfried. Peabody, Mass.: Hendrickson, 1991.

———. *Paul.* Translated by D. M. Stalker. New York: Harper & Row, 1971.

Bousset, W. *Die Religion des Judentums im späthellenistischen Zeitalter.* Tübingen: Mohr (Siebeck), 1964.

Bowersock, G. W. *Greek Sophists in the Roman Empire.* Oxford: Clarendon, 1969.

———. *Hellenism in Late Antiquity.* Ann Arbor: University of Michigan Press, 1990.

Bowersock, G. W., and T. Cornell, eds. *A. D. Momigliano: Studies on Modern Scholarship.* Berkeley: University of California Press, 1994.

Bowie, E. L. "The Greeks and Their Past in the Second Sophistic." *Past and Present* 46 (1974): 3–41.

Bowker, J. *Jesus and the Pharisees*. Cambridge: Cambridge University Press, 1973.

Bowman, S. "Josephus in Byzantium." Pages 362–85 in *Josephus, Judaism, and Christianity*. Edited by L. H. Feldman and G. Hata. Detroit: Wayne State University Press, 1987.

Boyle, A. J. "Introduction: Reading Flavian Rome." Pages 1–67 in *Flavian Rome: Culture, Image, Text*. Edited by A. J. Boyle and W. J. Dominik. Leiden: Brill, 2003.

Boyle, A. J., and W. J. Dominik, eds. *Flavian Rome: Culture, Image, Text*. Leiden: Brill, 2003.

Brandt, H. D., ed. *Immanuel Kant: Was ist Aufklärung? Ausgewählte kleine Schriften*. Hamburg: F. Meiner Verlag, 1999.

Braun, M. *Griechischer Roman und hellenistische Geschichtschreibung*. Frankfurt: V. Klostermann, 1934.

———. *History and Romance in Graeco-Oriental Literature*. Oxford: Blackwell, 1938.

Braund, D. C. "Cohors: The Governor and his Entourage in the Self-Image of the Roman Republic." Pages 10–24 in *Cultural Identity in the Roman Empire*. Edited by R. Laurence and J. Berry. London: Routledge, 1998.

Brawley, R. L. *Luke-Acts and the Jews: Conflict, Apology, and Conciliation*. Atlanta: Scholars Press, 1987.

Bringmann, K. *Hellenistische Reform und Religionsverfolgung in Judäa*. Göttingen: Vandenhoeck & Ruprecht, 1983.

Broshi, M. "The Credibility of Josephus." *Journal of Jewish Studies* 33 (1982): 379–84.

Brown, F., S. R. Driver, et al. *A Hebrew and English Lexicon of the Old Testament*. Oxford: Clarendon, 1906.

Bruce, F. F. *The Epistle to the Galatians: A Commentary on the Greek Text*. NIGTC. Grand Rapids: Eerdmans, 1981.

———. *The Epistle of Paul to the Romans*. TNTC. Grand Rapids: Eerdmans, 1963.

Brunt, P. A. *Roman Imperial Themes*. Oxford: Oxford University Press, 1990.

Buck, C., and G. Taylor. *Saint Paul: A Study of the Development of His Thought*. New York: Charles Scribner's Sons, 1969.

Buehler, W. W. *The Pre-Herodian Civil War and Social Debate*. Basel: Friedrich Reinhardt, 1974.

Bultmann, R. *The History of the Synoptic Tradition*. New York: Harper & Row, 1963.

Bumpus, H. B. *The Christological Awareness of Clement of Rome and Its Sources*. Cambridge: Cambridge University Press, 1972.

Burchard, C. "Die Essener bei Hippolyt: Hippolyt, REF. IX 18, 2–28, 2 und Josephus, Bell. 2, 119–61." *Journal for the Study of Judaism in the Persian, Hellenistic, and Roman Periods* 8.1 (1977): 1–41.

———. "Pline et les Esséniens." *Revue biblique* 69 (1962): 533–69.

Burgmann, H. "Der Grunder der Pharisaergenossenschaft: der Makkabaer Simon." *Journal of Jewish Studies* 29 (1978): 153–91.

———. "The Wicked Woman: Der Makkabaer Simon?" *Revue de Qumran* 8 (1972): 323–59.

Burkert, W. *Ancient Mystery Cults.* Cambridge, Mass.: Harvard University Press, 1987.

———. *Greek Religion.* Translated by J. Raffan. Cambridge, Mass.: Harvard University Press, 1984.

Burridge, R. A. *What are the Gospels? A Comparison with Graeco-Roman Biography.* Grand Rapids: Eerdmans, 2004.

Cameron, R. *The Other Gospels: Non-canonical Gospel Texts.* Philadelphia: Westminster, 1982.

Campbell, W. S. "Romans III as a Key to the Structure and Thought of the Letter." Pages 251–64 in *The Romans Debate.* Rev. and exp. ed. Edited by K. P. Donfried. Peabody, Mass.: Hendrickson, 1991.

Cansdale, L. *Qumran and the Essenes: A Re-Evaluation of the Evidence.* Tübingen: Mohr (Siebeck), 1997.

Cape, R. W., Jr. "Persuasive History: Roman Rhetoric and Historiography." Pages 212–28 in *Roman Eloquence: Rhetoric in Society and Literature.* Edited by W. J. Dominik. London: Routledge, 1997.

Carroll, R. P. "Luke's Portrayal of the Pharisees." *Catholic Biblical Quarterly* 50 (1988): 604–21.

Cartledge, P., and A. Spawforth. *Hellenistic and Roman Sparta: A Tale of Two Cities.* London: Routledge, 1989.

Chapman, H. "Spectacle and Theater in Josephus's Bellum Judaicum." PhD diss., Department of Classics, Stanford University, 1998.

Charles, R. H. *Eschatology: the Doctrine of a Future Life in Israel, Judaism, and Christianity.* New York: Schocken Books, 1963.

———. *Religious Development between the Old and New Testaments.* London: Oxford University Press, 1914.

Charlesworth, J. H., ed. *Apocalyptic Literature and Testaments.* 2 vols. New York: Doubleday, 1983.

Chesnut, G. H. "Eusebius, Augustine, Orosius, and the Later Patristic and Medieval Church Historians." Pages 687–713 in *Eusebius, Christianity, and Judaism.* Edited by H. W. Attridge and G. Hata. Detroit: Wayne State University Press, 1992.

Cioffari, V. "Fortune, Fate, and Chance." Pages 225–36 in vol. 2 of *The Dictionary of the History of Ideas.* 5 vols. Edited by P. P. Wiener. New York: Scribner, 1973.

Clabeaux, J. J. "Marcionite Prologues to Paul." Pages 520–1 in vol. 4 of *The Anchor Bible Dictionary.* 6 vols. Edited by D. N. Freedman. New York: Doubleday, 1992.

Clarke, Catherine. *Between Geography and History: Hellenistic Constructions of the Roman World.* Oxford: Clarendon, 1999.

Clarke, M. L. *Higher Education in the Ancient World.* London: Routledge, 1971.

Cody, J. M. "Conquerors and Conquered on Flavian Coins." Pages 103–23 in *Flavian Rome: Culture, Image, Text.* Edited by A. J. Boyle and W. J. Dominik. Leiden: Brill, 2003.

Cohen, N. G. "Josephus and Scripture: Is Josephus' Treatment of the Scriptural Narrative Similar Throughout Antiquities I–XI?" *Jewish Quarterly Review* 54 (1963–64): 311–32.

Cohen, S. J. D. *Beginnings of Jewishness: Boundaries, Varieties, Uncertainties*. Berkeley: University of California Press, 1999.

———. "History and Historiography in the Against Apion of Josephus." Pages 1–11 in *Essays in Jewish Historiography*. Edited by A. Rapoport-Albert. Middletown: Wesleyan University Press, 1988.

———. "᾿ΙΟΥΔΑΙΟΣ ΤΟ ΓΕΝΟΣ and Related Expressions in Josephus." Pages 23–28 in *Josephus and the History of the Greco-Roman Period*. Edited by J. Sievers and F. Parente. Leiden: Brill, 1994.

———. *Josephus in Galilee and Rome: His Vita and Development as a Historian*. Leiden: Brill, 1979.

———. "Masada, Literary Traditions, Archaeological Remains, and the Credibility of Josephus." *Journal of Jewish Studies* 33 (1982): 385–405.

———. Respect for Judaism by Gentiles According to Josephus. *Harvard Theological Review* 80 (1987): 409–30.

Colautti, F. M. *Passover in the Works of Flavius Josephus*. Leiden: Brill, 2002.

Collingwood, R. G. *The Idea of History*. London: Oxford University Press, 1976.

Collins, J. J. "A Symbol of Otherness: Circumcision and Salvation in the First Century." Pages 163–86 in *To See Ourselves as Others See Us*. Edited by J. Neusner and E. S. Frerichs. Chico, Calif.: Scholars Press, 1985.

Collins, R. F. *Studies on the First Letter to the Thessalonians*. Leuven: Leuven University Press, 1984.

Connor, W. R. *Thucydides*. Princeton: Princeton University Press, 1984.

Conte, G. B. *Latin Literature: A History*. Baltimore: Johns Hopkins University Press, 1994.

Conzelmann, H. *The Theology of St. Luke*. London: Faber, 1961.

Cook, M. J. *Mark's Treatment of Jewish Leaders*. Leiden: Brill, 1978.

Corbeill, A. *Controlling Laughter: Political Humor in the Late Roman Republic*. Princeton: Princeton University Press, 1996.

———. *Nature Embodied: Gesture in Ancient Rome*. Princeton: Princeton University Press, 2004.

Corley, K. E. *Private Women Public Meals: Social Conflict in the Synoptic Tradition*. Peabody, Mass.: Hendrickson, 1993.

Cotter, W. "The Collegia and Roman Law: State Restrictions on Voluntary Associations." Pages 74–89 in *Voluntary Associations in the Graeco-Roman World*. Edited by J. S. Kloppenborg and S. G. Wilson. London: Routledge, 1996.

Cranfield, C. E. B. *A Critical and Exegetical Commentary on the Epistle to the Romans*. International Critical Commentary. 2 vols. Edinburgh: T&T Clark, 1974.

Cribiore, R. *Gymnastics of the Mind: Greek Education in Hellenistic and Roman Egypt*. Princeton: Princeton University Press, 2001.

Cross, F. M. *The Ancient Library of Qumran and Modern Biblical Studies*. New York: Doubleday, 1961.

Culpepper, R. A. "The Gospel of John and the Jews." *Review and Expositor* 84 (1987): 273–88.

Dalman, G. H. *Aramaisch-Neuhebraisches Handworterbuch zu Targum, Talmud, und Midrash.* Frankfurt am Main: J. Kaufmann, 1922.

———. *Grammatik des jüdisch-palastinischen Aramaisch.* Darmstadt: Wissenschaftliche Buchgesellschaft, 1960.

Danielou, J. *A Theology of Jewish Christianity.* Philadelphia: Westminster, 1964.

Darr, J. A. *On Character Building: The Reader and the Rhetoric of Characterization in Luke-Acts.* Louisville: John Knox Press, 1992.

Daube, D. "Typology in Josephus." *Journal of Jewish Studies* 31 (1980): 18–36.

Davidson, I., and D. J. Penslar, eds. *Orientalism and the Jews.* Hanover: Brandeis University Press, 2005.

Davies, W. D. "Apocalyptic and Pharisaism." Pages 19–30 in *Christian Origins and Judaism.* Edited by W.D. Davies. London: Longman & Todd, 1962.

Davis, M., ed. *Israel: Its Role in Civilization.* New York: Seminary Israel Institute of the Jewish Theological Seminary of America, 1956.

Davis, N., C. M. Kraay, et al. *The Hellenistic Kingdoms: Portrait Coins and History.* London: Thames & Hudson, 1973.

Dawsey, J. M. *The Lukan Voice: Confusion and Irony in the Gospel of Luke.* Macon: Mercer, 1986.

Deacy, S., and K. F. Pierce. *Rape in Antiquity.* London: Duckworth, 2002.

Deissmann, A. *Paul: A Study in Social and Religious History.* New York: Harper & Row, 1957.

Derenbourg, J. *Essai sur l'histoire et la geographie de la Palestine.* Hildesheim: H.S. Gerstenberg, 1975.

Destinon, J. von. *Die Quellen des Flavius Josephus in der Jüd. Arch. Buch XII–XVII—Jüd. Kreig. Buch I.* Kiel: Lipsius, 1882.

Dibelius, M. *An die Thessalonicher I–II. An die Philipper.* Tübingen: Mohr (Siebeck), 1937.

———. *Studies in the Acts of the Apostles.* London: SCM, 1956.

Dixon, W. H. *The Holy Land.* 2d ed. London: Chapman and Hall, 1866.

Dodd, C. H. *The Epistle of Paul to the Romans.* London: Hodder & Stoughton, 1932.

Dominik, W. J., ed. *Roman Eloquence: Rhetoric in Society and Literature.* London: Routledge, 1997.

Donaldson, T. L., ed. *Religious Rivalries and the Struggle for Success in Caesarea Maritima.* Waterloo: Wilfrid Laurier Press, 2000.

Donceel, R. "Qumran." Pages 392–96 in *The Oxford Encyclopaedia of Archaeology in the Near East.* Edited by E. M. Meyers. Oxford: Oxford University Press, 1997.

Donfried, K. P. "1 Thessalonians 2:13–16 as a Test Case." *Interpretation* 38 (1986): 242–53.

Donfried, K. P., ed. *The Romans Debate.* Rev. and exp. ed. Peabody, Mass.: Hendrickson, 1991.

Dörrie, H. "Was ist 'spätantiker Platonismus'? Überlegungen zur Grenzziehung zwischen Platonismus und Christentum." *Theologische Rundschau* 36 (1971): 285–302.

Dover, K. J. *Greek Homosexuality.* London: Duckworth, 1978.

Drexler, H. "Untersuchungen zu Josephus und zur Geschichte des jüdischen Aufstandes." *Klio* 19 (1925): 277–312.

Droge, Arthur J., and James D. Tabor. *A Noble Death: Suicide and Martyrdom Among Christians and Jews in Antiquity.* San Francisco: Harper San Francisco, 1992.

Droysen, J. G. *Geschichte des Hellenismus.* Hamburg: F. Perthes, 1836.

Dubnow, S. *Weltgeschichte des jüdischen Volkes.* Berlin: Jüdischen Verlag, 1925–29.

Dupont-Sommer, A. *The Dead Sea Scrolls: A Preliminary Survey.* Oxford: Blackwell, 1952.

———. *The Essene Writings from Qumran.* Cleveland: Word, 1961.

Eagleton, T. *Literary Theory: An Introduction.* Minneapolis: University of Minnesota Press, 1996.

Earl, D. C. "Prologue-Form in Ancient Historiography." *ANRW* 1.2:842–56. Edited by H. Temporini and W. Haase. New York: de Gruyter, 1972.

Eck, W. *The Age of Augustus.* Oxford: Blackwell, 2003.

Eck, W., and H. Cotton. "Josephus' Roman Audience: Josephus and the Roman Elites." Pages 37–52 in *Flavius Josephus and Flavian Rome.* Edited by J. Edmondson, J. Rives, and S. Mason. Oxford: Oxford University Press, 2005.

Eckstein, A. M. "Josephus and Polybius: A Reconsideration." *Classical Antiquity* 9 (1990): 175–208.

———. *Moral Vision in the Histories of Polybius.* Berkeley: University of California Press, 1995.

Edmondson, J., J. Rives, and S. Mason, eds. *Flavius Josephus and Flavian Rome.* Oxford: Oxford University Press, 2005.

Ehrlich, E. L. "Zur Geschichte der Pharisäer." *Freiburger Rundbrief* 29 (1977): 46–52.

Elbogen, I. *Die Religionsanschauungen der Pharisäer.* Berlin: H. Itzkowski, 1904.

———. "Einige neuere Theorien uber den Ursprung der Pharisäer und Sadduzäer." Pages 135–48 in *Jewish Studies in Memory of Israel Abrahams.* New York: Jewish Institute of Religion, 1927.

Elliott, N. *The Rhetoric of Romans: Argumentative Constraint and Strategy and Paul's Dialogue with Judaism.* Sheffield: Sheffield Academic Press, 1990.

Ellis, E. E. *The Old Testament in Early Christianity.* Tübingen: Mohr (Siebeck), 1991.

Eriksen, A. "Redefining Virtus: The Setting of Virtue in the Works of Velleius Paterculus and Lucan." Pages 111–22 in *Greek Romans and Roman Greeks.* Edited by E. N. Ostenfeld. Aarhus: Aarhus University Press, 2002.

Esler, P. F. *Community and Gospel in Luke-Acts: The Social and Political Motivations of Lucan Theology.* Cambridge: Cambridge University Press, 1987.

———. *Galatians.* London: Routledge, 1999.

Evans, C. A., and J. A. Sanders. *Luke and Scripture: The Function of Sacred Tradition in Luke-Acts.* Minneapolis: Fortress, 1993.

Eyben, E. *Restless Youth in Ancient Rome.* Translated by Patrick Daly. London: Routledge, 1993.

Fantham, E. *Roman Literary Culture: From Cicero to Apuleius.* Baltimore: Johns Hopkins University Press, 1996.

Farmer, W. R. *Maccabees, Zealots, and Josephus; an Inquiry into Jewish Nationalism in the Greco-Roman Period.* Westport: Greenwood, 1956.

Feeney, D. *Literature and Religion at Rome: Cultures, Contexts, and Beliefs.* Cambridge: Cambridge University Press, 1998.

Feldman, L. H. *Jew and Gentile in the Ancient World: Attitudes and Interactions from Alexander to Justinian.* Princeton: Princeton University Press, 1993.

———. *Josephus and Modern Scholarship (1937–1980).* New York: de Gruyter, 1984.

———. *Josephus's Interpretation of the Bible.* Berkeley: University of California Press, 1998.

———. *Judean Antiquities 1–4.* Vol. 3 of *Flavius Josephus: Translation and Commentary.* 10 vols. Edited by S. Mason. Leiden: Brill, 2000.

———. "Parallel Lives of Two Lawgivers: Josephus' Moses and Plutarch's Lycurgus." Pages 209–42 in *Flavius Josephus and Flavian Rome.* Edited by J. Edmondson, S. Mason, and J. Rives. Oxford: Oxford University Press, 2005.

———. "Prophets and Prophecy in Josephus." *Journal of Theological Studies* 41 (1990): 386–422.

———. "Proselytes and 'Sympathizers' in Light of the New Inscription from Aphrodisias." *Review de études juives* 48 (1989): 265–305.

———. "Proselytism by Jews in the Third, Fourth and Fifth Centuries." *Journal for the Study of Judaism in the Persian, Hellenistic, and Roman Periods* 24 (1993): 1–58.

———. "Use, Authority, and Exegesis of Mikra in the Writings of Josephus." Pages 455–517 in *Mikra: Text, Translation, Reading and Interpretation of the Hebrew Bible in Ancient Judaism and Early Christianity.* Edited by M. J. Mulder and H. Sysling. Minneapolis: Fortress, 1988. Repr., Peabody, Mass.: Hendrickson, 2004.

———. "Some Observations on the Name of Palestine." *Hebrew Union College Annual* 61 (1996): 1–23.

———. *Studies in Josephus' Rewritten Bible.* Leiden: Brill, 1998.

Feldman, L. H., and G. Hata, eds. *Josephus, the Bible, and History.* Detroit: Wayne State University Press, 1989.

Feldman, L. H., and J. R. Levison, eds. *Josephus' Contra Apionem: Studies in its Character and Context with a Latin Concordance to the Portion Missing in Greek.* Leiden: Brill, 1996.

Feldman, L. H., and H. Schreckenberg. *Josephus: A Supplementary Bibliography.* New York: Garland, 1986.

Ferguson, J. "Classical Religions." Pages 749–65 in *The Roman World.* Edited by J. Wacher. 2 vols. London: Routledge, 2002.

———. *Utopias of the Classical World.* London: Thames & Hudson, 1975.

Ferris, I. M. *Enemies of Rome: Barbarians through Roman Eyes.* Stroud: Sutton, 2000.

Finkelstein, L. "The Origin of the Pharisees." *Conservative Judaism* 23 (1969): 25–36.

———. *The Pharisees: The Sociological Background of Their Faith.* 2 vols. Philadelphia: Jewish Publication Society, 1938.

Fischel, H. A. Story and History: Observations on Greco-Roman Rhetoric and Pharisaism. Pages 59–78 in D. Sinor, ed., *American Oriental Society-Middle West Branch: Semi-Annual Volume.* Bloomington: University of Indiana Press, 1969.

Fitzmyer, J. A. *Romans: A New Translation with Introduction and Commentary.* Anchor Bible 33. New York: Doubleday, 1993.

Foerster, W. "Der Ursprung des Pharisäismus." *Zeitschrift für die neutestamentliche Wissenschaft* 34 (1935): 35–51.

———. "εὐσεβέια." Pages 176–77 in vol 7 of *The Theological Dictionary of the New Testament.* 10 vols. Edited by G. Kittel and G. W. Bromiley. Grand Rapids: Eerdmans, 1985.

Fornara, C. W. *The Nature of History in Ancient Greece and Rome.* Berkeley: University of California Press, 1983.

Fowler, D. "God the Father (Himself) in Vergil." *Proceedings of the Vergil Society* 22 (1996): 35–52.

———. *Readings in Postmodern Latin.* Oxford: Oxford University Press, 2000.

Fraikin, D. "The Rhetorical Function of the Jews in Romans." Pages 91–105 in vol. 1 of *Anti-Judaism in Early Christianity.* 2 vols. Edited by P. Richardson and D. Granskou. Waterloo: Wilfrid Laurier University Press, 1986.

Franxman, T. W. *Genesis and the Jewish Antiquities of Flavius Josephus.* Rome: Biblical Institute Press, 1979.

Friedlander, I. The Rupture Between Alexander Jannai and the Pharisees. *Jewish Quarterly Review* 4 (1913–14): 443–8.

Friedrich, G. "εὐαγγέλιον." Pages 707–37 in vol. 2 of *The Theological Dictionary of the New Testament.* 10 vols. Edited by G. Kittel and G. W. Bromiley. Grand Rapids: Eerdmans, 1985.

Frier, B. W. "Roman Demography." Pages 85–109 in *Life, Death, and Entertainment in the Roman Empire.* Edited by D. S. Potter and D. J. Mattingly. Ann Arbor: University of Michigan Press, 1999.

Frova, A. "L'Iscrizione di Pontio Pilato a Cesarea." *Rendiconti Istituto Lombardo* 95 (1961): 419–34.

Furnish, V. P. *II Corinthians.* Anchor Bible 32a. New York: Doubleday, 1984.

Gager, J. G. *The Origins of Anti-Semitism: Attitudes Toward Judaism in Pagan and Christian Antiquity.* Oxford: Oxford University Press, 1983.

Galinsky, K. *Augustan Culture: An Interpretive Introduction.* Princeton: Princeton University Press, 1996.

Gallivan, P. "The Fasti for A.D. 70–96." *Classical Quarterly* 31.1 (1981): 186–220.

Galor, K., J.-B. Humbert, and J. Zangenberg. *Qumran: the Site of the Dead Sea Scrolls. Archaeological Interpretations and Debates.* Leiden: Brill, 2006.

Garnsey, P. *Food and Society in Classical Antiquity: Key Themes in Ancient History.* Cambridge: Cambridge University Press, 1999.

Gaston, L. "Paul and Jerusalem." Pages 61–72 in *From Jesus to Paul: Studies in Honour of Francis Wright Beare.* Edited by P. Richardson and J. C. Hurd. Waterloo: Wilfrid Laurier University Press, 1984.

———. *Paul and the Torah.* Vancouver: University of British Columbia Press, 1987.

Gay, P. *The Enlightenment: An Interpretation.* New York: Knopf, 1969.

Gehrke, Hans-Joachim. *Stasis : Untersuchungen zu den inneren Kriegen in den griechischen Staaten des 5. und 4. Jahrhunderts v. Chr.* München: C. H. Beck, 1985.

Geiger, A. *Das Judentum und seine Geschichte. Vol 1: Bis zur Zerstörung des zweiten Tempels.* Breslau: W. Jacobson, 1865.

———. *Urschrift und Übersetzungen der Bibel: in ihrer Abhängigkeit von der Entwicklung des Judentums.* Frankfurt: Madda, 1928.

Geller, M. "Alexander Jannaeus and the Pharisees Rift." *Journal of Jewish Studies* 30 (1979): 203–10.

Gelzer, M. "Die Vita des Josephos." *Hermes* 80 (1952): 67–90.

Genesius, W. *Hebräische Grammatik.* Hidelsheim: Georg Olms, 1962.

Gerber, C. *Ein Bild des Judentums für Nichtjuden von Flavius Josephus: Untersuchungen zu seiner Schrift Contra Apionem.* Leiden: Brill, 1997.

Gleason, M. W. "Elite Male Identity in the Roman Empire." Pages 67–84 in *Life, Death, and Entertainment in the Roman Empire.* Edited by D. S. Potter and D. J. Mattingly. Ann Arbor: University of Michigan Press, 1999.

———. *Making Men: Sophists and Self-Presentation in Ancient Rome.* Princeton: Princeton University Press, 1995.

Golb, N. *Who Wrote the Dead Sea Scrolls? The Search for the Secret of Qumran.* New York: Scribner, 1995.

Goldhill, S. *Being Greek under Rome: Cultural Identity, the Second Sophistic, and the Development of Empire.* Cambridge: Cambridge University Press, 2001.

Goldstein, J. A. *I Maccabees.* Anchor Bible 41. New York: Doubleday, 1976.

———. *II Maccabees.* Anchor Bible 41a. New York: Doubleday, 1983.

Goodman, M. "Josephus as Roman Citizen." Pages 329–38 in *Josephus and the History of the Greco-Roman Period: Essays in Memory of Morton Smith.* Edited by F. Parente and J. Sievers. Leiden: Brill, 1994.

———. *Mission and Conversion: Proselytizing in the Religious History of the Roman Empire.* Oxford: Oxford University Press, 1994.

———. "A Note on the Qumran Sectarians, the Essenes, and Josephus." *Journal of Jewish Studies* 46 (1995): 161–66.

———. *The Ruling Class of Judaea: The Origins of the Jewish Revolt against Rome AD 66–70.* Cambridge: Cambridge University Press, 1987.

Grabbe, Lester L. *Judaism from Cyrus to Hadrian: The Persian and Greek Periods.* 2 vols. Minneapolis: Fortress, 1992.

Graetz, H. *Geschichte der Jüden von den altesten Zeiten bis auf die Gegenwart.* Leipzig: Oskar Leiner, 1905.

Graf, F. *Magic in the Ancient World.* Cambridge, Mass.: Harvard University Press, 1997.

Gray, R. *Prophetic Figures in Late Second Temple Jewish Palestine: The Evidence from Josephus.* New York: Oxford University Press, 1993.

Griffin, M. T. *Nero: The End of a Dynasty.* London: B. T. Batsford, 1984.

Groningen, B. van. "EKDOSIS." *Mnemosyne* 16 (1963): 1–17.

Gruen, E. S. *Culture and National Identity in Republican Rome.* Ithaca: Cornell University Press, 1992.

———. *Diaspora: Jews amidst Greeks and Romans.* Cambridge: Cambridge University Press, 2002.

———. *The Last Generation of the Roman Republic.* Berkeley: University of California Press, 1995.

Guignebert, C. *The Jewish World in the Time of Jesus.* London: Routledge, 1939.

Guterman, S. L. *Religious Toleration and Persecution in Ancient Rome.* London: Aiglon, 1951.

Guttmann, A. *Rabbinic Judaism in the Making.* Detroit: Wayne State University Press, 1970.

Hadas, M. *Hellenistic Culture: Fusion and Diffusion.* New York: Columbia University Press, 1959.

Hadot, P. *The Inner Citadel: The Meditations of Marcus Aurelius.* Cambridge, Mass.: Harvard University Press, 1998.

Hall, E. *Inventing the Barbarian: Greek Self-Definition through Tragedy.* Oxford: Clarendon Press, 1989.

Hall, J. M. *Ethnic Identity in Greek Antiquity.* Cambridge: Cambridge University Press, 1997.

———. *Hellenicity: Between Ethnicity and Culture.* Chicago: University of Chicago Press, 2002.

Hands, A. R. "Sallust and Dissimulatio." *Journal of Roman Studies* 49 (1959): 56–60.

Hanson, P. D. "Apocalypticism." Pages 28–31 in *The Interpreter's Dictionary of the Bible Supplement.* Edited by G. A. Buttrick. Nashville: Abingdon, 1976.

Hardwick, M. E. *Josephus as an Historical Source in Patristic Literature through Eusebius.* Atlanta: Scholars Press, 1989.

Hare, D. R. A. *The Theme of Jewish Persecution of Christians in the Gospel According to St. Matthew.* Society for New Testament Studies Monograph Series 6. Cambridge University Press, 1967.

Harland, P. A. *Associations, Synagogues, and Congregations: Claiming a Place in Ancient Mediterranean Society.* Minneapolis: Fortress, 2002.

Harnack, A. *Das Wesen des Christentums.* Stuttgart: Ehrenfried Klotz, 1950.

Harrington, D. J. *The Maccabean Revolt: Anatomy of a Biblical Revolution.* Wilmington: Michael Glazier, 1988.

Harris, M. History and Significance of the Emic/Etic Distinction. *Annual Review of Anthropology* 5 (1976): 329–50.

Harris, W. V. *Ancient Literacy.* Cambridge, Mass.: Harvard University Press, 1989.

Harrison, P. *"Religion" and Religions in the English Enlightenment.* Cambridge: Cambridge University Press, 1990.

Hata, G. "Is the Greek Version of Josephus' 'Jewish War' a Translation or a Rewriting of the First Version?" *Jewish Quarterly Review* 66 (1957): 89–108.

Hecht, R. D. "Philo and Messiah." Pages 139–68 in *Judaisms and Their Messiahs.* Edited by J. Neusner. Cambridge: Cambridge University Press, 1987.

Hedrick, C. W. *Ancient History: Monuments and Documents.* Oxford: Blackwell, 2006.

Heller, B. "Grundzüge der Aggada des Flavius Josephus." *Monatsschrift für Geschichte und Wissenschaft des Judentums* 80 (1936): 237–46.

Henderson, J. *Fighting for Rome: Poets and Caesars, History and Civil War.* Cambridge: Cambridge University Press, 1998.

Hengel, M. "Die Synagogeninschrift von Stobi." *Zeitschrift für die neutestamentliche Wissenschaft und die Kunde der älteren Kirche* 57 (1966): 145–83.

———. *Jews, Greeks, and Barbarians: Aspects of the Hellenization of Judaism in the Pre-Christian Period.* Philadelphia: Fortress, 1980.

———. *Judaism and Hellenism: Studies in Their Encounter During the Early Hellenistic Period.* London: SCM, 1974.

———. *The Zealots: Investigations into the Jewish Freedom Movement in the Period from Herod I until 70 A.D.* Edinburgh: T&T Clark, 1989.

Henten, J. W. van, and R. Abusch. "The Depictions of the Jews as Typhonians and Josephus's Strategy of Refutation in Contra Apionem." Pages 2671–309 in *Josephus' Contra Apionem: Studies in its Character and Context with a Latin Concordance to the Portion Missing in Greek.* Edited by L. H. Feldman. Leiden: Brill, 1996.

Henten, J. W. van, and F. Avemarie. *Martyrdom and Noble Death: Selected Texts from Graeco-Roman, Jewish, and Christian Antiquity.* London: Routledge, 2002.

Herford, R. T. *The Pharisees.* New York: Macmillan, 1924.

Hershkowitz, D. *Valerius Flaccus' Argonautica: Abbreviated Voyages in Silver Latin Epic.* Oxford: Oxford University Press, 1998.

Hicks, R. D., ed. *Diogenes Laertius, Lives of the Eminent Philosophers.* Cambridge, Mass.: Harvard University Press, 1925.

Hirschfeld, Y. *Qumran in Context: Reassessing the Archaeological Evidence.* Peabody, Mass.: Hendrickson, 2004.

Hoffmann, R. J. *Julian's Against the Galileans.* Amherst: Prometheus, 2004.

Hölscher, G. "Josephus." Pages 1934–2000 in vol. 18 of *Paulys Realenzyklopädie der Classischen Altertumswissenschaft.* 49 vols. Edited by A. F. Pauly, G. Wissowa, et al. Munich: A. Druckenmüller, 1916.

Holtzmann, "O. Der Prophet Malachi und der Ursprung des Pharisaerbundes." *Archiv für Religionswissenschaft* 29: 1–21, 1931.

Hornblower, S. *Thucydides.* London: Duckworth, 1984.

Horsley, R. A. "Josephus and the Bandits." *Journal for the Study of Judaism in the Persian, Hellenistic, and Roman Periods* 10.1 (1979): 37–63.

Horsley, R. A., and J. S. Hanson. *Bandits, Prophets, and Messiahs: Popular Movements at the Time of Jesus.* New York: Harper & Row, 1988.

Horst, P. vander, ed. *Ancient Jewish Epitaphs*. Kampen: Kok Pharos, 1991.

Hurd, J. C. "Paul Ahead of his Time: 1 Thess. 2:13–16." Pages 117–33 in vol. 1. of *Anti-Judaism in Early Christianity*. 2 vols. Edited by P. Richardson and D. Granskou. Waterloo: Wilfrid Laurier University Press, 1986.

———. "The Sequence of Paul's Letters." *Canadian Journal of Theology* 14 (1968): 189–200.

Hussey, M. D. "The Origin of the Name Pharisee." *Journal of Biblical Literature* 39 (1920): 66–69.

Iggers, G. G. *The German Conception of History: the National Tradition of Historical Thought from Herder to the Present*. Middleton, Conn.: Wesleyan University Press, 1968.

Ilan, T. *Integrating Women into Second Temple History*. Tübingen: Mohr Siebeck, 1999.

Inowlocki, S. "The Citations of Jewish Greek Authors in Eusebius of Caesarea's *Praeparatio Evangelica* and *Demonstratio Evangelica*." M. Litt. Thesis, University of Oxford: Faculty of Oriental Studies, 2001.

Ireland, S., ed. *Menander: The Bad-Tempered Man (Dyskolos)*. Warminster: Aris and Phillips, 1995.

Isaac, B. H. *The Invention of Racism in Classical Antiquity*. Princeton: Princeton University Press, 2004.

———. *The Near East under Roman Rule: Selected Papers*. Leiden: Brill, 1998.

Isaac, B. H., and I. Roll. "A Milestone of A.D. 69 from Judaea: The Elder Trajan and Vespasian." *Journal of Roman Studies* 66 (1976): 15–19.

Jacob, B. *In Namen Gottes: Eine sprachliche und religionsgeschichtliche Untersuchung zum Alten und Neuen Testament*. Berlin: S. Cavalry, 1903.

Jaeger, W. *Paideia: The Ideals of Greek Culture*. 3 Vols. Oxford: Oxford University Press, 1973.

James, W. *The Varieties of Religious Experience: A Study in Human Nature*. London: Longmans, Green, and Co, 1928.

Jastrow, M. *A Dictionary of the Targumim, the Talmud Babli and Yerushalmi, and the Midrashic Literature*. New York: Pardes, 1950.

Jeremias, J. *Jerusalem zur Zeit Jesu*. Göttingen: Vandenhoeck & Ruprecht, 1958.

Jervell, J. "The Letter to Jerusalem." Pages 53–64 in *The Romans Debate*. Rev. and exp. ed. Edited by K. P. Donfried. Peabody, Mass.: Hendrickson, 1991.

Jervis, L. A. *The Purpose of Romans: A Comparative Letter Structure Investigation*. Sheffield: Sheffield Academic Press, 1991.

Jervis, L. A., and P. Richardson, Eds. *Gospel in Paul: Studies on Corinthians, Galatians, and Romans for Richard N. Longenecker*. Sheffield, Sheffield Academic Press, 1994.

Jewett, R. K. *A Chronology of Paul's Life*. Philadelphia: Fortress, 1979.

———. *The Thessalonian Correspondence*. Philadelphia: Fortress, 1986.

Johnson, L. T. "Luke-Acts, Book of." Pages 404–20 in vol. 4 of *The Anchor Bible Dictionary*. Edited by D. N. Freedman. 4 vols. New York: Doubleday, 1992.

Jones, B. W. *The Emperor Domitian*. London: Routledge, 1992.

Jones, B. W., and R. Milns, eds. *Suetonius: The Flavian Emperors, A Historical Commentary.* London: Bristol Classical Press, 2002.

Jones, C. P. "*Ethnos* and *Genos* in Herodotus." *Classical Quarterly* 46 (1996): 315–20.

Josephus. Translated by H. St. J. Thackeray et al. 10 vols. LCL. Cambridge, Mass: Harvard University Press, 1926–1965.

Juster, J. *Les Juifs dans l'empire romain.* New York: Burt Franklin, 1914.

Kähler, M. *The So-Called Historical Jesus and the Historic Biblical Christ.* Translated by C. E. Braaten. Philadelphia: Fortress, 1964.

Kajanto, I. *God and Fate in Livy.* Turku: Turun Yliopiston Kustantama, 1957.

Karris, R. J. "Romans 14:1–15:13 and the Occasion of Romans." Pages 65–84 in *The Romans Debate.* Rev. and exp. ed. Edited by K. P. Donfried. Peabody, Mass.: Hendrickson, 1991.

Käsemann, E. *Commentary on Romans.* Grand Rapids: Eerdmans, 1980.

Kasher, A. "The *Isopoliteia* Question in Caesarea Maritima." *Jewish Quarterly Review* 68 (1977): 16–27.

———. *Jews and Hellenistic Cities in Eretz Israel: Relations of the Jews in Eretz-Israel with the Hellenistic Cities During the Second Temple Period (332–70 CE).* Tübingen: Mohr (Siebeck), 1990.

Kautzsch, E., ed. *Die Apokryphen und Pseudepigraphen des Alten Testaments.* Tübingen: Mohr (Siebeck), 1900.

Kee, H. C. *Knowing the Truth: A Sociological Approach to New Testament Interpretation.* Minneapolis: Fortress, 1989.

Keitel, Elizabeth. "Principate and Civil War in the Annals of Tacitus." *American Journal of Philology* 105 (1984): 306–25.

Kellum, B. "The Phallus as Signifier: The Forum of Augustus and Rituals of Masculinity." Pages 170–83 in *Sexuality in Ancient Art.* Edited by N. B Kampen. Cambridge: Cambridge University Press, 1996.

Kennedy, G. A. *A New History of Classical Rhetoric.* Princeton: Princeton University Press, 1994.

———. *New Testament Interpretation through Rhetorical Criticism.* Chapel Hill: University of North Carolina Press, 1984.

Kenney, E. J., and W. V. Clausen, eds. *The Cambridge History of Classical Literature.* 5 vols. Cambridge: Cambridge University Press, 1982–89.

Kienle, P. *Die Berichte über die Sukzessionen der Philosophie. Dissertation.* Berlin: Freie Universität Berlin, 1961.

Kierkergaard, S. *The Concept of Irony: With Constant Reference to Socrates.* New York: Harper & Row, 1965.

Kieval, P. "The Talmudic View of the Hasmonean and Early Herodian Periods in Jewish History." PhD diss., Waltham: Brandeis University, 1970.

Klausner, J. *The Messianic Idea in Israel.* London: George Allen and Unwin, 1956.

Klein, G. "Paul's Purpose in Writing the Epistle to the Romans." Pages 32–49 in *The Romans Debate.* Rev. and exp. ed. Edited by K. P. Donfried. Peabody, Mass.: Hendrickson, 1991.

Kloppenborg, J. S. "Collegia and Thiasoi: Issues in Function, Taxonomy, and Membership." Pages 16–30 in *Voluntary Associations in the Graeco-Roman World.* Edited by J. S. Kloppenborg and S. G. Wilson. London: Routledge, 1996.

Kloppenborg, J. S., and S. G. Wilson, eds. *Voluntary Associations in the Graeco-Roman World.* London: Routledge, 1996.

Knox, J. *Chapters in a Life of Paul.* Nashville: Abingdon, 1950.

Knox, N. "On the Classification of Ironies." *Modern Philology* 70 (1972): 53–62.

Koester, H. *Ancient Christian Gospels: Their History and Development.* Philadelphia: Trinity Press International, 1990.

Kohler, K. "Essenes." Pages 224–32 in vol. 5 of *Jewish Encyclopedia.* 12 vols. Edited by I. Singer. New York: Funk & Wagnalls, 1901–1906.

———. "Pharisees." Pages 661–66 in vol. 9 of *Jewish Encyclopedia.* 12 vols. Edited by I. Singer. New York: Funk & Wagnalls, 1901–1906.

Kokkinos, N. *The Herodian Dynasty: Origins, Role in Society and Eclipse.* Sheffield: Sheffield Academic Press, 1998.

Konstan, D. "Defining Ancient Greek Ethnicity." *Diaspora* 6 (1997): 97–110.

Kraeling, C. H. "The Episode of the Roman Standards at Jerusalem." *Harvard Theological Review* 35 (1942): 263–89.

Kraemer, H. "προφήτης." Pages 783–96 in vol. 6 of *The Theological Dictionary of the New Testament.* 10 vols. Edited by G. Kittel and G. W. Bromiley. Grand Rapids: Eerdmans, 1985.

Kraemer, R. S. "On the Meaning of the Term 'Jew' in Greco-Roman Inscriptions." *Harvard Theological Review* 82 (1989): 35–53.

Kraft, R. A. "Pliny on Essenes, Pliny on Jews," *Dead Sea Discoveries* 8 (2001): 255–61.

Kraft, R. A., and G. Nickelsburg, eds. *Early Judaism and its Modern Interpreters.* Atlanta: Scholars Press, 1986.

Kramer, W. R. *Christ, Lord, Son of God.* London: SCM, 1966.

Kraus, C. S. "From Exempla to Exemplar? Writing History around the Emperor in Imperial Rome." Pages 181–200 in *Flavius Josephus and Flavian Rome.* Edited by J. Edmondson, J. Rives, and S. Mason. Oxford: Oxford University Press, 2005.

Kraus, C. S., and A. J. Woodman. *Latin Historians.* Oxford: Oxford University Press, 1997.

Krenkel, M. *Josephus und Lukas.* Leipzig: H. Haessel, 1894.

Krieger, Klaus-Stefan. *Geschichtsschreibung als Apologetik bei Flavius Josephus.* Texte und Arbeiten zum neutestamentlichen Zeitalter 9. Tübingen: Francke, 1994.

Kümmel, W. G. *Introduction to the New Testament.* Translated by H. C. Kee. Nashville: Abingdon, 1975.

———. *The New Testament: A History of the Investigation of its Problems.* Nashville: Abingdon, 1972.

Kurke, L. "Charting the Poles of History: Herodotos and Thoukydides." Pages 118–22 in *Literature in a Greek World.* Edited by O. Taplin. Oxford: Oxford University Press, 2000.

Ladouceur, D. J. "Josephus and Masada." Pages 95–133 in *Josephus, Judaism, and Christianity.* Edited by L. H. Feldman and G. Hata. Detroit: Wayne State University Press, 1987.

———. "The Language of Josephus." *Journal for the Study of Judaism in the Persian, Hellenistic, and Roman Periods* 14.1 (1983): 18–38.

Lamberton, R. *Plutarch.* New Haven: Yale University Press, 2001.

Lampe, P. "The Roman Christians of Romans 16," Pages 216–30 in *The Romans Debate.* Rev. and exp. ed. Edited by K. P. Donfried. Peabody, Mass.: Hendrickson, 1991.

Lampe, P. *Die stadtrömischen Christen in den ersten beiden Jahrhunderten: Untersuchungen zur Sozialgeschichte.* 2d ed. Wissenschaftliche Untersuchungen zum Neuen Testament 2/18. Tübingen: Mohr (Siebeck), 1989.

Laqueur, R. *Der jüdische Historiker Flavius Josephus: Ein biographischer Versuch auf neuer quellenkritischer Grundlage.* Darmstadt: Wissenschaftliche Buchgesellschaft, 1970.

Lateiner, D. *Sardonic Smile: Nonverbal Behavior in Homeric Epic.* Ann Arbor: University of Michigan Press, 1995.

Lauterbach, J. Z. The Pharisees and Their Teachings. *Hebrew Union College Annual* 6 (1929): 69–140.

———. "The Sadducees and the Pharisees." *Central Conference of American Rabbis Yearbook* 23: 176–98, 1913.

Lebram, J. "Der Idealstaat der Juden." Pages 233–53 in *Josephus-Studien: Festschrift für Otto Michel.* Edited by O. Betz. Göttingen: Vandenhoeck & Ruprecht, 1974.

Leeman, A. D. "Structure and Meaning in the Prologues of Tacitus." *YCS* 23 (1973): 169–208.

Leiman, S. Z. *The Canonization of Hebrew Scripture: The Talmudic and Midrashic Evidence.* Hamden: Archon, 1976.

———. "Josephus and the Canon of the Bible." Pages 50–58 in *Josephus, the Bible, and History.* Edited by L. H. Feldman and G. Hata. Detroit: Wayne State University Press, 1989.

Leipoldt, J., and W. Grundmann *Umwelt des Urchristentums.* Berlin: Evangelische Verlagsantalt, 1965–1966.

Leon, H. J. *The Jews of Ancient Rome.* Philadelphia: Jewish Publication Society, 1960, Repr. Peabody, Mass.: Hendrickson, 1995.

Leppin, H. *Histrionen: Untersuchungen zur sozialen Stellung von bühnenkünstlern im Westen des römischen Reiches zur Zeit der Republik und des Principats.* Bonn: Habelt, 1992.

Leszynsky, R. *Pharisäer und Sadduzäer.* Frankfurt am Main: J. Kaufmann, 1912.

Leveau, P. "Aqueduct Building: Financing and Costs." Pages 85–101 in *Frontinus' Legacy: Essays on Frontinus' de aquis urbis Romae.* Edited by D. R. Blackman and A. T. Hodge. Ann Arbor: University of Michigan Press, 2001.

Levick, B. *Vespasian.* London: Routledge, 1999.

Levine, L. I. *The Ancient Synagogue: The First Thousand Years.* New Haven: Yale University Press, 2000.

———. *Caesarea under Roman Rule.* Leiden: Brill, 1975.

———. "The Jewish-Greek Conflict in First Century Caesarea." *Journal of Jewish Studies* 25 (1974): 381–97.

———. "On the Political Involvement of the Pharisees under Herod and the Procurators." *Cathedra* 8 (1978): 12–28.

Lieberich, H. *Studien zu den Geschichtsschreiber in der griechischen und byzantinischen Geschichtsschreibung I: Die griechischen Geschichtsschreiber.* Munich: J.G. Weiss, 1899.

Lieu, J. *Image and Reality: The Jews in the World of the Christians in the Second Century.* Edinburgh: T&T Clark, 1996.

Lindner, H. *Die Geschichtsauffassung des Flavius Josephus im Bellum Judaicum. Gleichzeitig ein Beitrag zur Quellenfrage.* Leiden: Brill, 1972.

Lintott, A. W. "Civil Strife and Human Nature in Thucydides." Pages 25–32 in *Literary Responses to Civil Discord.* Edited by J. H. Molyneux. Nottingham: University of Nottingham, 1993.

———. *Imperium Romanum: Politics and Administration.* London: Routledge, 1993.

———. *Violence, Civil Strife and Revolution in the Classical City, 750–330 BC.* London: Croom Helm, 1982.

Livy. *History of Rome, Books 1–2.* Translated by B. O. Foster. LCL. Cambridge, Mass.: Harvard University Press, 1967–1984.

Lohse, E. *Umwelt des Neuen Testaments.* Göttingen: Vandenhoeck & Ruprecht, 1971.

Long, A. A. *Hellenistic Philosophy: Stoics, Epicureans, Sceptics.* London: Duckworth, 1974.

Lönnqvist, K. "Pontius Pilate—An Aqueduct Builder?—Recent Findings and New Suggestions." *Klio* 82 (2000): 458–74.

Lowe, M. F. "Who Were the ΙΟΥΔΑΙΟΙ?" *Novum Testamentum* 18 (1976): 103–30.

Luce, T. J. *Livy: The Composition of His History.* Princeton: Princeton University Press, 1977.

Lüdemann, G. *Opposition to Paul in Jewish Christianity.* Minneapolis: Fortress, 1989.

———. *Paul, Apostle to the Gentiles: Studies in Chronology.* Philadelphia: Fortress, 1980.

Luther, Heinrich. *Josephus und Justus von Tiberias: Ein Beitrag zur Geschichte des jüdischen Aufstandes.* Halle: Wischan & Burkhardt, 1910.

Luz, M. "Eleazar's Second Speech on Masada and its Literary Precedents." *Rheinisches Museum* 126 (1983): 25–43.

Macfie, A. L. *Orientalism.* London: Pearson, 2002.

Mack, B. L. *The Lost Gospel: The Book of Q and Christian Origins.* San Francisco: Harper San Francisco, 1993.

MacMullen, R. *Enemies of the Roman Order: Treason, Unrest, and Alienation in the Empire.* London: Routledge, 1966.

———. *Paganism in the Roman Empire.* New Haven: Yale University Press, 1981.

Maddox, R. *The Purpose of Luke-Acts.* Edinburgh: T&T Clark, 1982.

Mader, Gottfried. *Josephus and the Politics of Historiography: Apologetic and Impression Management in the Bellum Judaicum.* Leiden: Brill, 2000.

Magness, J. *The Archaeology of Qumran and the Dead Sea Scrolls.* Grand Rapids: Eerdmans, 2002.

Maier, G. *Mensch und freier Wille: Nach den jüdischen Reliogionsparteien zwischen Ben Sira und Paulus.* Tübingen: Mohr (Siebeck), 1981.

Malherbe, A. J. "Gentle as a Nurse: The Cynic Background to I Thess II." *Novum Testamentum* 12 (1970): 203–17.

———. *Paul and the Thessalonians: The Philosophic Tradition of Pastoral Care.* Philadelphia: Fortress, 1987.

———. *Paul and the Popular Philosophers.* Minneapolis: Fortress, 1989.

Malingrey, A. M. *Philosophia: Étude d'un groupe de mots dans la littérature greque, des presocratiques au IV siècle après J.C.* Paris: C. Klincksieck, 1961.

Mandelkern, S. *Veteris Testamenti Concordantiae: Hebraicae atque Chaldiaicae.* Graz: Akademische Druck und Verlagsanstalt, 1955.

Manson, T. W. "Sadducee and Pharisee: the Origin and Significance of Their Names." *Bulletin of the John Rylands University Library of Manchester* 21 (1938): 144–59.

———. "St. Paul's Letter to the Romans—and Others." Pages 1–16 in *The Romans Debate.* Rev. and exp. ed. Edited by K. P. Donfried. Peabody, Mass.: Hendrickson, 1991.

Mantel, H. "The Sadducees and the Pharisees." Pages 99–123 in vol. 7 of *The World History of the Jewish People.* Edited by M. Avi-Yonah and Z. Baras. Jerusalem: Massada, 1977.

Marincola, J. *Authority and Tradition in Ancient Historiography.* Cambridge: Cambridge University Press, 1997.

Marrou, H. I. *A History of Education in Antiquity.* Translated by G. Lamb. Madison: University of Wisconsin Press, 1956.

Martinez, F. G., ed. *The Dead Sea Scrolls Translated: the Qumran Texts in English.* Leiden: Brill, 1996.

Marxsen, W. *Mark the Evangelist: Studies on the Redaction History of the Gospel.* Nashville: Abingdon, 1969.

Marxsen, W. *Introduction to the New Testament.* Philadelphia: Fortress, 1970.

Mason, S. "Chief Priests, Sadducees, Pharisees and Sanhedrin in Acts," in *The Book of Acts in its Palestinian Setting.* Edited by R. Bauckham. Vol. 4 of *The Book of Acts in its First-Century Setting.* Edited by B. W. Winter. Grand Rapids: Eerdmans, 1995, 115–77.

———. "The Contra-Apionem in Social and Literary Context: An Invitation to Judean Philosophy." Pages 143–86 in *Josephus' Contra Apionem: Studies in its Character and Context with a Latin Concordance to the Portion Missing in Greek.* Edited by M. Goodman and J. Levison. Leiden: Brill, 1996.

———. "Contradiction or Counterpoint? Josephus and Historical Method." *Review of Rabbinic Judaism* 6 (2003): 145–88.

———. "An Essay in Character: The Aim and Audience of Josephus's Vita." Pages 31–77 in *Internationales Josephus-Kolloquium Münster 1997.* Edited by F. Siegert and J. Kalms. Münster: LIT, 1998.

———. "Figured Speech and Irony in the Works of T. Flavius Josephus." Pages 243–88 in *Flavius Josephus and Flavian Rome.* Edited by J. Edmondson, J. Rives, and S. Mason. Oxford: Oxford University Press, 2005.

———. "Flavius Josephus in Flavian Rome: Reading on and between the Lines." Pages 559–89 in *Flavian Rome: Culture, Text, Image.* Edited by A. J. Boyle and W. J. Dominik. Leiden: Brill, 2003.

———. *Flavius Josephus on the Pharisees. A Composition-Critical Study.* Leiden: Brill, 1991.

———, ed. *Flavius Josephus: Translation and Commentary.* 10 vols. Leiden: Brill, 2000–.

———. "'For I am Not Ashamed of the Gospel': The Gospel and the First Readers of Romans," Pages 254–87 in *Gospel in Paul: Studies on Corinthians, Galatians and Romans for Richard N. Longenecker.* Edited by L. Ann Jervis and P. Richardson. Sheffield: Sheffield Academic Press, 1994.

———. "Greco-Roman, Jewish, and Christian Philosophies." Pages 1–28 *Approaches to Ancient Judaism, New Series 4: Religious and Theological Studies.* South Florida Studies in the History of Judaism 81. Edited by J. Neusner. Atlanta: Scholars Press, 1993.

———. "Introduction to the Judean Antiquities." Pages ix–xxxvi in *Judean Antiquities 1–4, Translation and Commentary* by L. H. Feldman. Vol. 3 in *Flavius Josephus: Translation and Commentary.* 10 vols. Edited by S. Mason, ed., Leiden: Brill, 2000.

———. *Josephus and the New Testament.* 2d rev. ed. Peabody, Mass.: Hendrickson, 2003.

———. "Josephus, Daniel, and the Flavian House." Pages 161–91 in *Josephus and the History of the Greco-Roman Period: Essays in Memory of Morton Smith.* Edited by F. Parente and J. Sievers. Leiden: Brill, 1994.

———. "Josephus, the Greeks, and the Distant Past." in *Antiquity in Antiquity.* Edited by K. Osterloh and G. Gardner. Tübingen: Mohr (Siebeck), forthcoming.

———. "Josephus on Canon and Scripture." Pages 217–35 in *Hebrew Bible/Old Testament: The History of Interpretation.* Edited by M. Saebo. Göttingen: Vandenhoeck & Ruprecht, 1996.

———. "Josephus on the Pharisees Reconsidered: A Critique of Smith/Neusner." *Studies in Religion* 17 (1988): 455–69.

———. *Life of Josephus: Translation and Commentary.* Vol. 9 in *Flavius Josephus: Translation and Commentary.* 10 vols. Edited by Steve Mason. Leiden: Brill, 2001.

———. "Of Despots, Diadems, and *Diadochoi:* Josephus and Flavian Politics." in *Writing Politics in Imperial Rome.* Edited by W. J. Dominik and J. Garthwaite. Leiden: Brill, forthcoming.

———. "Paul, Classical Anti-Judaism, and Romans." Pages 141–80 in *Approaches to Ancient Judaism, New Series 4: Religious and Theological Studies.* South Florida Studies in the History of Judaism 81; Edited by J. Neusner. Atlanta: Scholars Press, 1993.

———. "Priesthood in Josephus and the Pharisaic Revolution." *Journal of Biblical Literature* 107 (1988): 657–61.

———. "The Problem of the Pharisees in Modern Scholarship." Pages 103–40 in *Approaches to Ancient Judaism, New Series 3: Historical and Literary Studies.* South Florida Studies in the History of Judaism 81. Edited by J. Neusner. Atlanta: Scholars Press, 1993.

———. "'Should Any Wish to Enquire Further' (Ant. 1.25): The Aim and Audience of Josephus's Judean Antiquities/Life." Pages 64–103 in *Understanding Josephus: Seven Perspectives.* Edited by S. Mason. Sheffield: Sheffield Academic Press, 1998.

———. *Understanding Josephus: Seven Perspectives.* Sheffield: Sheffield Academic Press, 1998a.

———. "Was Josephus a Pharisee? A Re-examination of Life 10–12." *Journal of Jewish Studies* 40.1 (1989): 31–45.

———. "What Josephus Says about the Essenes in His Judean War." Pages 434–67 in *Text and Artifact in the Religions of Mediterranean Antiquity: Essays in Honour of Peter Richardson.* Edited by S. G. Wilson and M. Desjardins. Waterloo: Wilfrid Laurier Press, 2000.

Mattern, S. P. *Rome and the Enemy: Imperial Strategy in the Principate.* Berkeley: University of California Press, 1999.

Matthews, S. *First Converts: Rich Pagan Women and the Rhetoric of Mission in Early Judaism and Christianity.* Stanford: Stanford University Press, 2001.

May, J. M. *Trials of Character: The Eloquence of Ciceronian Ethos.* Chapel Hill: University of North Carolina, 1988.

Mayer, R., and C. Moeller "Josephus—Politiker und Prophet." Pages 239–62 in *Josephus-Studien: Untersuchungen zu Josephus, dem antiken Judentum, und den Neuen Testament.* Edited by O. Michel. Göttingen: Vandenhoeck & Ruprecht, 1974.

Mayer-Schärtel, B. *Das Frauenbild des Josephus: eine sozialgeschichtliche und kulturanthropologische Untersuchung.* Stuttgart: Verlag W. Kohlhammer, 1995.

Mazar, A. "A Survey of the Aqueducts to Jerusalem." Pages 210–42 in *The Aqueducts of Israel.* Edited by D. Amit, J. Patrich, and Y. Hirschfeld. Portsmouth: Journal of Roman Archaeology, 2002.

McLaren, J. S. *Turbulent Times? Josephus and Scholarship on Judaea in the First Century.* Sheffield: Sheffield Academic Press, 1998.

Meeks, W. *The First Urban Christians.* New Haven: Yale University Press, 1983.

Meier, C. *Caesar.* London: Fontana, 1982.

Mellor, R. "The New Aristocracy of Power." Pages 69–101 in *Flavian Rome: Culture, Image, Text.* Edited by A. J. Boyle and W. J. Dominik. Leiden: Brill, 2003.

———. *Tacitus.* London: Routledge, 1993.

Meredith, A. "Later Philosophy." Pages 288–307 in *The Roman World*. Edited by J. Boardman, J. Green and O. Murray. Oxford: Oxford University Press, 1988.

Meshorer, Y. A. *Ancient Jewish Coinage*. 2 vols. New York: Amphora Books, 1982.

Meyer, B. F. *Christus Faber: The Master-Builder and the House of God*. Allison Park: Pickwick, 1992.

Meyer, E. *Ursprung und Anfänge des Christentums*. Stuttgart: J. G. Cotta, 1921–1923.

Meyer, R. "Bermerkungen zum literargeschichtlichen Hintergrund der Kanontheorie des Josephus." Pages 285–99 in *Josephus-Studien: Untersuchungen zu Josephus, dem antiken Judentum, und den Neuen Testament*. Edited by O. Michel. Göttingen: Vanderhoeck & Ruprecht, 1974.

Meyer, R., and H.-F. Weiss "φαρισαῖος." Pages 11–48 in vol. 9 of *The Theological Dictionary of the New Testament*. 10 vols. Edited by G. Kittel and G. W. Bromiley. Grand Rapids: Eerdmans, 1985.

Meyer-Zwiffelhoffer, E. *πολιτικῶς ἄρχειν*: Zum Regierungstil der senatorischen Statthalter in den kaiserzeitlichen griechischen Provinzen. Stuttgart: F. Steiner, 2002.

Michel, O., and and O. Bauernfeind. *De Bello Judaico = Der jüdische Krieg: Griechisch und Deutsch*. 2d ed. 3 vols. in 4. Munich: Kösel, 1962.

Migliario, E. "Per l'interpretazione dell' Autobiografia di Flavio Giuseppe." *Athenaeum* 69.1–2 (1981): 92–137.

Millar, F. "Last Year in Jerusalem: Monuments of the Jewish War in Rome." Pages 101–28 in *Flavius Josephus and Flavian Rome*. Edited by J. Edmondson, J. Rives, and S. Mason. Oxford: Oxford University Press, 2005.

———. *The Roman Near East, 31 BC-AD 337*. Cambridge, Mass.: Harvard University Press, 1993.

Miller, R. J. *The Complete Gospels*. San Francisco: Polebridge, 1994.

Misch, G. *A History of Autobiography in Antiquity*. 2 vols. London: Routledge, 1950.

Moehring, H. R. "Joseph ben Matthia and Flavius Josephus." *ANRW* 2.21.2:864–917. Edited by H. Temporini and W. Haase. New York: de Gruyter, 1984.

———. "Novelistic Elements in the Writings of Flavius Josephus." PhD diss., University of Chicago, 1957.

———. "Review of Shaye J.D. Cohen, Josephus in Galilee and Rome: His Vita and Development as a Historian." *Journal of Jewish Studies* 32 (1980): 240–42.

Momigliano, A. *Alien Wisdom: The Limits of Hellenization*. Cambridge: Cambridge University Press, 1971.

———. "J. G. Droysen Between Greeks and Jews. Pages 1447–61 in *A. D. Momigliano: Studies in Modern Scholarship*. Edited by G. Bowersock and T. J. Cornell. Berkeley: University of California Press, 1994.

———. *Claudius: The Emperor and his Achievement*. Oxford: Clarendon, 1934.

———. *Quarto Contributo alla Storia degli Studi Classici e del Mondo Antico*. Rome: Edizioni di Storia e Letteratura, 1969.

Moore, G. F. "Fate and Free Will in the Jewish Philosophies According to Josephus." *Harvard Theological Review* 22 (1929): 371–89.

———. *Judaism: In the First Centuries of the Christian Era*. New York: Schocken Books, 1958.

Muecke, D. C. *The Compass of Irony*. London: Methuen, 1969.

Mueller, J. G. *Des Flavius Josephus Schrift gegen den Apion*. Hildesheim: Georg Olms, 1967.

Mulder, M. J., and H. Sysling, eds. *Mikra: Text, Translation, Reading and Interpretation of the Hebrew Bible in Ancient Judaism and Early Christianity*. Minneapolis: Fortress, 1988. Repr., Peabody, Mass.: Hendrickson, 2004.

Munck, J. *Paul and the Salvation of Mankind*. Richmond: John Knox, 1959.

Munn, M. *The School of History: Athens in the Age of Socrates*. Berkeley: University of California Press, 2000.

Munson, R. V. *Telling Wonders: Ethnographic and Political Discourse in the Work of Herodotus*. Ann Arbor: University of Michigan Press, 2001.

Myers, J. L. "Μηδίζειν : Μηδισμός." Pages 97–105 in *Greek Poetry and Life: Essays Presented to Gilbert Murray on His Seventieth Birthday*. Edited by C. Bailey. Oxford: Clarendon, 1936.

Nadon, C. *Xenophon's Prince: Republic and Empire in the Cyro*paedia. Berkeley: University of California Press, 2001.

Neusner, J., ed. *Approaches to Ancient Judaism*. University of South Florida Studies in Religion. Atlanta: Scholars Press, 1991–99.

———. *Eliezer ben Hyrcanus: The Tradition and the Man*. Leiden: Brill, 1973.

———. *From Politics to Piety: The Emergence of Pharisaic Judaism*. Englewood Cliffs: Prentice Hall, 1973.

———. "Judaism after Moore: A Programmatic Statement." *Journal of Jewish Studies* 31 (1980): 141–56.

———. *Judaism as Philosophy: The Method and Message of the Mishnah*. Columbia: University of South Carolina Press, 1991.

———. "Pharisaic-Rabbinic Judaism: A Clarification." *History of Religions* 12.3 (1973): 250–70.

———. *The Philosophical Mishnah*. Atlanta: Scholars Press, 1988–1989.

———. *The Rabbinic Traditions About the Pharisees Before 70*. 3 vols. Leiden: Brill, 1971.

———. *Studying Classical Judaism: A Primer*. Louisville: Westminster John Knox, 1991.

Neusner, J., and A. J. Avery-Peck, eds. *Where We Stand: Issues and Debates*. Pt. 3 in vol. 1 of *Judaism in Late Antiquity*. 4 vols. Edited by Jacob Neusner and Alan J. Avery-Peck. Leiden: Brill, 1999–2000.

Neyrey, Jerome H. "Josephus' Vita and the Encomium: A Native Model of Personality." *Journal for the Study of Judaism in the Persian, Hellenistic, and Roman Periods* 25 (1994): 177–206.

Nicolson, F. W. "The Saliva Superstition in Classical Literature." *Harvard Studies in Classical Philology* 8 (1897): 23–40.

Niese, B. "Der Jüdische Historiker Flavius Josephus." *Historische Zeitschrift* 40 (1896): 193–237.

Nock, A. D. *Conversion: The Old and the New in Religion from Alexander the Great to Augustine.* Baltimore: Johns Hopkins University Press, 1998.

Nodet, É. *Flavius Josephe: Les Antiquités Juives.* Paris: Les Éditions du Cerf, 1990.

———. *La Bible de Josèphe.* Paris: Les Éditions du Cerf, 1996.

Noy, D., ed., *Jewish Inscriptions of Western Europe.* Cambridge: Cambridge University Press, 1993–1995.

O'Gorman, E. *Irony and Misreading in the Annals of Tacitus.* Cambridge: Cambridge University Press, 2000.

O'Neill, J. C. *Paul's Letter to the Romans.* Harmondsworth: Penguin, 1975.

Oesterley, W. O. E. *The Jews and Judaism during the Greek Period.* London: S.P.C.K, 1941.

Ogilvie, R. M. *The Romans and Their Gods.* London: Chatto & Windus, 1969.

Ory, G. *A la recherche des Esséniens.* Paris: Le Cercle Ernest-Renan, 1975.

Osborn, E. F. *Tertullian, First Theologian of the West.* Cambridge: Cambridge University Press, 1997.

Otis, B. "The Uniqueness of Latin Literature." *Arion* 6 (1967): 185–206.

Pagels, E. *The Gnostic Gospels.* New York: Random House, 1979.

Palmer, L. R. *The Greek Language.* London: Faber, 1980.

Paret, H. "Über den Pharisaismus des Josephus." *Theologische Studien und Kritiken* 29: 809–44, 1856.

Parkes, J. F. *The Foundations of Judaism.* London: Valentine-Mitchell, 1960.

Parkin, T. G. *Demography and Roman Society.* Baltimore: Johns Hopkins University Press, 1992.

Paul, A. "Flavius Josèphe et les Esséniens." Pages 127–38 in *The Dead Sea Scrolls: Forty Years of Research.* Edited by U. Rappaport. Leiden: Brill, 1992.

Pearce, S. "Review of Flavius Josephus: Translation and Commentary vol. 3." *Journal of Jewish Studies* 55: 169–70, 2004.

Pearson, B. "1 Thessalonians 2:13–16: A Deutero-Pauline Interpolation." *Harvard Theological Review* 64 (1971): 79–94.

Pelletier, A. *Flavius Josèphe, adapteur de la lettre d'Aristée.* Paris: Klincksieck, 1962.

———. Josephus, the Letter of Aristeas, and the Septuagint. Pages 97–115 in Louis H. Feldman & Gohei Hata, eds., *Josephus, the Bible, and History.* Leiden: Brill, 1989.

Pelling, C. *Literary Texts and the Greek Historian.* London: Routledge, 2000.

Petersen, N. *Literary Criticism for New Testament Critics.* Philadelphia: Fortress, 1978.

Pfeiffer, R. H. *History of New Testament Times.* London: Adam and Charles Black, 1949.

Pike, K. L. *Language in Relation to Unified Theory of the Structure of Human Behavior.* Glendale: Summer Institute of Linguistics, 1954.

Plass, P. *Wit and the Writing of History: The Rhetoric of Historiography in Imperial Rome.* Madison: University of Wisconsin Press, 1988.

Polish, D. "Pharisaism and Political Sovereignty." *Judaism* 19 (1970): 415–18.

Porton, G. "Diversity in Post-Biblical Judaism." Pages 57–80 in *Early Judaism and Its Modern Interpreters.* Edited by R. A. Kraft and G. Nickelsburg. Atlanta: Scholars Press, 1986.

Potter, D. S. *Literary Texts and the Roman Historian.* London: Routledge, 1999.

Preisker, H. *Neutestamentliche Theologie.* Berlin: A. Topelmann, 1937.

Price, J. J. *Jerusalem under Siege: The Collapse of the Jewish State, 66–70 C.E.* Leiden: Brill, 1992.

———. *Thucydides and Internal War.* Cambridge: Cambridge University Press, 2001.

Rabin, C. Alexander Jannaeus and the Pharisees. *Journal of Jewish Studies* 7 (1956): 5–10.

Räisänen, H. *Paul and the Law.* Philadelphia: Fortress, 1983.

———. "Paul's Conversion and the Development of His View of the Law." *New Testament Studies* 33 (1987): 404–19.

Rajak, T. "The Against Apion and the Continuities in Josephus's Political Thought." Pages 222–46 in *Understanding Josephus: Seven Perspectives.* Edited by S. Mason. Sheffield: Sheffield Academic Press, 1998.

———. "Ciò Che Flavio Giuseppe Vide: Josephus and the Essenes." Pages 141–60 in *Josephus and the History of the Greco-Roman Period: Essays in Memory of Morton Smith.* Edited by F. Parente and J. Sievers. Leiden: Brill, 1994.

———. *Josephus: The Historian and His Society.* London: Duckworth, 1983.

———. "Justus of Tiberias." *Classical Quarterly* 23 (1973): 345–68.

Rajak, T., and D. Noy "*Archisynagogoi:* Office, Title, and Social Status in the Greco-Jewish Synagogue." *Journal of Roman Studies* 83 (1993): 75–93.

Rappaport, S. *Agada und Exegese bei Flavius Josephus.* Vienna: A. Kohut Memorial Foundation, 1930.

Rasp, H. Flavius Josephus und die jüdischen Religionsparteien. *Zeitschrift für die neutestamentliche Wissenschaft* 23 (1924): 27–47.

Reicke, B. *Neutestamentliche Zeitgeschichte.* Berlin: A. Topelmann, 1965.

Reinach, T. *Textes d'auteurs grecs et romains relatifs aux Judaisme.* Hildesheim: G. Olms, 1963.

Rengstorf, K. H. *A Complete Concordance to Flavius Josephus.* 4 vols. Leiden: Brill, 1973–1975.

Reynolds, J., and R. Tannenbaum. *Jews and Godfearers at Aphrodisias.* Cambridge: Cambridge Philological Society, 1987.

Richards, G. C. "The Composition of Josephus' *Antiquities.*" *Classical Quarterly* 33 (1939): 36–40.

Richardson, P. *Herod: King of the Jews, Friend of the Romans.* Columbia: University of South Carolina Press, 1996.

———. *Israel in the Apostolic Church.* Cambridge: Cambridge University Press, 1969.

Richardson, P., and D. Granskou et al., eds. *Anti-Judaism in Early Christianity.* 2 vols. Waterloo: Wilfrid Laurier University Press, 1986.

Richlin, A. *The Garden of Priapus: Sexuality and Aggression in Roman Humor.* Revised edition. Oxford: Oxford University Press, 1992.

———. *Pornography and Representation in Greece and Rome.* Oxford: Oxford University Press, 1992.

Rist, M. "Apocalypticism." Pages 157–61 in vol. 1 of *The Interpreter's Dictionary of the Bible.* 4 vols. Edited by G. A. Buttrick. Nashville: Abingdon, 1962.

Rives, J. "Christian Expansion and Christian Ideology." Pages 15–41 in *The Spread of Christianity in the First Four Centuries: Essays in Explanation.* Edited by W. V. Harris. Leiden: Brill, 2005.

———. "Flavian Religious Policy and the Jerusalem Temple." Pages 145–66 in *Flavius Josephus and Flavian Rome.* Edited by J. Edmondson, J. Rives, and S. Mason. Oxford: Oxford University Press, 2005.

———. *Religion in the Roman Empire.* Oxford: Blackwell, 2006.

Rivkin, E. "Defining the Pharisees: The Tannaitic Sources." *Hebrew Union College Annual* 40 (1969): 205–49.

———. *A Hidden Revolution.* Nashville: Abingdon, 1978.

———. "Pharisees." Page 658 in *The Interpreter's Dictionary of the Bible Supplement.* Edited by K. R. Crim and G. A. Buttrick. Nashville: Abindgon, 1962.

Robinson, J. A. T. *Wrestling with Romans.* Philadelphia: Westminster, 1979.

Robinson, J. M. *The Nag Hammadi Library.* New York: Harper & Row, 1977.

Roetzel, C. J. *The Letters of Paul: Conversations in Context.* Louisville: John Knox, 1991.

Rogan, E. L., and A. Shlaim, eds. *The War for Palestine: Rewriting the History of 1948.* Cambridge: Cambridge University Press, 2001.

Rogers, C. L. *The Topical Josephus: Historical Accounts that Shed Light on the Bible.* Grand Rapids: Zondervan, 1992.

Roller, M. B. *Constructing Autocracy: Aristocrats and Emperors in Julio-Claudian Rome.* Princeton: Princeton University Press, 2001.

Romano, A. C. *Irony in Juvenal.* Hidelsheim: Georg Olms, 1979.

Rorty, R. *Contingency, Irony, and Solidarity.* Cambridge: Cambridge University Press, 1989.

Roth, C. "The Pharisees in the Jewish Revolution of 66–73." *Journal of Semitic Studies* 7 (1962): 63–81.

Rudich, V. *Dissidence and Literature under Nero: The Price of Rhetoricization.* London: Routledge, 1997.

———. *Political Dissidence under Nero: The Price of Dissimulation.* London: Routledge, 1993.

Russell, D. S. *The Jews from Alexander the Great to Herod.* Oxford: Clarendon, 1967.

———. *The Method and Message of Jewish Apocalyptic.* Philadelphia: Westminster, 1964.

Rutgers, L. V. *The Jews in Late Ancient Rome: Evidence of Cultural Interaction in the Roman Diaspora.* Leiden: Brill, 1995.

Said, E. W. *Orientalism.* New York: Random House, 1978.

Saïd, S. "The Discourse of Identity in Greek Rhetoric from Isocrates to Aristides." Pages 275–99 in *Ancient Perceptions of Greek Identity.* Edited by I. Malkin. Cambridge, Mass.: Harvard University Press, 2001.

Saldarini, A. J. *Pharisees, Scribes, and Sadducees in Palestinian Society: A Sociological Approach.* Wilmington: Michael Glazier, 1988.

Salles, C. *Lire à Rome.* Paris: Les Belles Lettres, 1992.

Sandbach, F. H. *The Stoics.* London: Chatto & Windus, 1975.

Sanders, E. P. *Jesus and Judaism.* Philadelphia: Fortress, 1985.

———. *Jewish Law from Jesus to the Mishnah: Five Studies.* London: SCM, 1990.

———. *Judaism, Practice and Belief, 63 BCE–66 CE.* Philadelphia: Trinity Press International, 1992.

———. *Paul and Palestinian Judaism.* Philadelphia: Fortress, 1977.

———. *Paul, the Law, and the Jewish People.* Philadelphia: Fortress, 1983.

Sanders, E. P., and M. Davies, *Studying the Synoptic Gospels.* London: SCM, 1989.

Sanders, J. A. "A Hermeneutic Fabric: Psalm 118 in Luke's Entrance Narrative." Pages 140–53 in *Luke and Scripture: The Function of Sacred Tradition in Luke-Acts.* Edited by C. A. Evans and J. A. Sanders. Minneapolis: Fortress, 1993.

Sanders, J. T. *The Jews in Luke-Acts.* Philadelphia: Fortress, 1987.

———. "The Jewish People in Luke-Acts" in *Luke-Acts and the Jewish People: Eight Critical Perspectives.* Edited by J. B. Tyson. Minneapolis: Augsburg, 1988, 51–75.

Sardar, Z. *Orientalism.* Buckingham: Open University Press, 1999.

Satran, David. "Daniel: Seer, Prophet, Holy Man." Pages 33–48 in *Ideal Figures in Ancient Judaism: Profiles and Paradigms.* Ed. J. J. Collins and G. W. E. Nickelsburg. Chico, Calif.: Scholars Press, 1980.

Schäfer, P. *Geschichte der Juden in der Antike.* Stuttgart-Neukirchen: Katholisches Bibelwerk, 1983.

———. *Judeophobia: Attitudes Toward the Jews in the Ancient World.* Cambridge, Mass.: Harvard University Press, 1997.

Schäfer, P., and M. R. Cohen. *Toward the Millenium: Messianic Expectations from the Bible to Waco.* Leiden: Brill, 1998.

Schalit, Abraham. "Josephus und Justus." *Klio* 26 (1933): 67–95.

———, ed., *Namenwörterbuch zu Flavius Josephus.* Leiden: Brill, 1968.

Schechter, S. *Aspects of Rabbinic Theology: Major Concepts of the Talmud.* New York: Schocken Books, 1961.

Schiffman, L. H. *The Halakhah at Qumran.* Leiden: Brill, 1975.

———. *Who Was A Jew? Rabbinic and Halakhic Perspectives on the Jewish Christian Schism.* Hoboken: Ktav, 1985.

Schlatter, A. *Die Theologie des Judentums nach dem Bericht des Josephus.* Gütersloh: C. Bertelsmann, 1932.

Schlegel, A. W. *A Course of Lectures on Dramatic Art and Literature.* London: H. G. Bohn, 1846.

Schmidt, D. "1 Thess 2:13–16: Linguistic Evidence for an Interpretation." *Journal of Biblical Literature* 102 (1983): 269–79.

Schmithals, W. *Der Römerbrief als historisches Problem.* Studien zum Neuen Testament 9. Gütersloh: Gerd Mohn, 1975.

———. *Paul and the Gnostics.* Nashville: Abingdon, 1972.

Schneider, R. M. "Die Faszination des Feindes: Bilder der Parther und des Orients in Rom." Pages 95–146 in *Das Partherreich und seine Zeugnisse.* Edited by J. Wiesehöfer. Stuttgart: Franz Steiner, 1998.

Schoeps, H. J. *Paul: The Theology of the Apostle in the Light of Jewish Religious History.* Philadelphia: Westminster, 1961.

Schreckenberg, H. *Die Flavius-Josephus-Tradition in Antike und Mittelalter.* Leiden: Brill, 1972.

Schreckenberg, H. *Rezeptionsgeschichtliche und textkritische Untersuchungen zu Flavius Josephus.* Leiden: Brill, 1977.

Schubert, K. *Die Religion des nachbiblischen Judentums.* Vienna: Herder, 1955.

———. "Jewish Religious Parties and Sects." Pages 79–98 in *The Crucible of Christianity.* Edited by A. Toynbee. London: Thames & Hudson, 1969.

Schürer, E. *Geschichte des jüdischen Volkes im Zeitalter Jesu Christi,* 3.–4. Auflage. Leipzig: J. C. Hinrichs, 1901–1909.

Schürer, E. *A History of the Jewish People in the Time of Jesus Christ.* 5 vols. Edinburgh: T&T Clark, 1896–1901.

Schürer, E. *The History of the Jewish People in the Age of Jesus Christ (175 B.C.–A.D. 135).* 3 vols. in 4 pts. Revised and edited by G. Vermes, F. Millar, and M. Goodman. Edinburgh: T&T Clark, 1973–1987.

Schwartz, D. R. *Agrippa I: The Last King of Judaea.* Tübingen: Mohr (Siebeck), 1990.

———. "Herodians and *Ioudaioi* in Flavian Rome." Pages 63–78 in *Flavius Josephus and Flavian Rome.* Edited by J. Edmondson, J. Rives, and S. Mason. Oxford: Oxford University Press, 2005.

———. "Josephus and Nicolaus on the Pharisees." *Journal for the Study of Judaism in the Persian, Hellenistic, and Roman Periods* 14 (1983): 157–71.

———. "Josephus on the Jewish Constitutions and Community." *Scripta Classica Israelica* 7: 30–52, 1983–1984.

———. *Studies in the Jewish Background of Early Christianity.* Tübingen: Mohr (Siebeck), 1992.

Schwartz, S. "The Composition and Publication of Josephus' *Bellum Judaicum* Book 7." *Harvard Theological Review* 79 (1986): 373–86.

———. *Imperialism and Jewish Society 200 B.C.E. to 640 C.E.* Princeton, Princeton University Press, 2001.

———. *Josephus and Judaean Politics.* Leiden: Brill, 1990.

Schweizer, A. *Paul and His Interpreters.* New York: Schocken Books, 1964.

Scramuzza, V. M. *The Emperor Claudius.* Cambridge, Mass.: Harvard University Press, 1940.

Segal, M. H. *A Grammar of Mishnaic Hebrew.* Oxford: Clarendon, 1958.

Sevenstern, J. N. *The Roots of Pagan Anti-Semitism in the Ancient World.* Leiden: Brill, 1975.

Shahar, Y. *Josephus Geographicus: The Classical Context of Geography in Josephus.* Tübingen: Mohr (Siebeck), 2004.

Shanks, H., ed. *Christianity and Rabbinic Judaism: A Parallel History of Their Origins and Early Development.* Washington, D.C.: Biblical Archaeological Society, 1996.

Shelton, J.-A. *As the Romans Did.* Oxford: Oxford University Press, 1988.

Shutt, R. J. H. *Studies in Josephus.* London: S.P.C.K, 1961.

Sider, R. D. *Ancient Rhetoric and the Art of Tertullian.* Oxford: Oxford University Press, 1971.

Sievers, J. "Josephus and the Afterlife." Pages 20–31 in *Understanding Josephus: Seven Perspectives.* Edited by S. Mason. Sheffield: Sheffield Academic Press, 1998.

Sievers, J. "Josephus, First Maccabees, Sparta, the Three Haireseis—and Cicero." *Journal for the Study of Judaism in the Persian, Hellenistic, and Roman Periods* 32 (2001): 241–51.

Smallwood, E. M. *The Jews Under Roman Rule, from Pompey to Diocletian: A Study in Political Relations.* Leiden: Brill, 1981.

———. "The Legislation of Hadrian and Antoninus Pius Against Circumcision." *Latomus* 18: 568–92, 1959.

———. "Philo and Josephus as Historians of the Same Events." Pages 114–32 in *Josephus, Judaism, and Christianity.* Edited by L. H. Feldman and G. Hata. Leiden: Brill, 1987.

Smith, J. Z. "Religion, Religions, Religious." Pages 269–84 in *Critical Terms for Religious Studies.* Edited by M. C. Taylor. Chicago: University of Chicago Press, 1998.

Smith, M. "The Description of the Essenes in Josephus and the Philosophoumena." *Hebrew Union College Annual* 35 (1958): 273–93.

———. "Palestinian Judaism in the First Century." Pages 67–81 in *Israel: Its Role in Civilization.* Edited by M. Davis. New York: Harper & Brothers, 1956.

Smith, M., F. Parente, et al. *Josephus and the History of the Greco-Roman Period: Essays in Memory of Morton Smith.* Leiden: Brill, 1994.

Smith, W. C. *The Meaning and End of Religion.* New York: Macmillan, 1963.

Sordi, M. *The Christians and the Roman Empire.* Norman: University of Oklahoma Press, 1986.

Southern, P. *Domitian: Tragic Tyrant.* London: Routledge, 1997.

Stambaugh, J. E. *The Roman City.* Baltimore: Johns Hopkins University Press, 1988.

Stanley, C. "Neither Jew nor Greek." *Journal for the Study of the New Testament* 64 (1996): 101–24.

Starr, R. J. "The Circulation of Texts in the Ancient World." *Mnemosyne* 40 (1987): 213–23.

Stegemann, H. "The Qumran Essenes—Local Members of the Main Jewish Union in Late Second Temple Times." Pages 83–166 in *The Madrid Qumran Congress: Proceedings of the International Congress on the Dead Sea Scrolls, Madrid 18–21 March 1991.* Edited by J. T. Barrerra and L. V. Montaner. Leiden: Brill, 1992.

Stemberger, G. *Jewish Contemporaries of Jesus: Pharisees, Sadducees, Essenes.* Minneapolis: Fortress, 1995.

Stendahl, K. *Paul Among Jews and Gentiles.* Philadelphia: Fortress, 1976.

Sterling, G. E. *Historiography and Self-definition: Josephus, Luke-Acts, and Apologetic Historiography.* Leiden: Brill, 1992.

———. "The Invisible Presence: Josephus's Retelling of Ruth." Pages 104–71 in *Understanding Josephus: Seven Perspectives*. Edited by S. Mason. Sheffield: Sheffield Academic Press, 1998.

Stern, M. *Greek and Latin Authors on Jews and Judaism: Edited with Introductions, Translations and Commentary*. 3 vols. Jerusalem: Israel Academy of Sciences, 1974–1984.

———. "The Jews in Greek and Latin Literature." Pages 1101–59 in *The Jewish People in the First Century*. Edited by M. Stern and S. Safrai. Philadelphia: Fortress, 1976.

Steuernagel, C. "Pharisäer." Columns 1825–1935 in *Paulys Realenzyklopädie der Classischen Altertumswissenschaft* 38. Stuttgart: Alfred Druckenmüller, 1938.

Stone, M., ed., *Jewish Writings of the Second Temple Period: Apocrypha, Pseudepigrapha, Qumran Sectarian Writings, Philo, Josephus*. Philadelphia: Fortress, 1984.

Strecker, G. *Der Weg der Gerechtigkeit: Untersuchung zur theologie des Matthaus*. Göttingen: Vandenhoeck & Ruprecht, 1962.

Suggs, M. J. "The Word is Near You: Romans 10:16 within the Purpose of the Letter." Pages 289–312 in *Christian History and Interpretation*. Edited by W. R. Farmer. Cambridge: Cambridge University Press, 1967.

Sundberg, A. C. "The Old Testament: A Christian Canon," *Canadian Biblical Quarterly* 30 (1968): 43–55.

Swain, S. *Hellenism and Empire: Language, Classicism and Power in the Greek World, AD 50–250*. Oxford: Oxford University Press, 1996.

Sweet, W. E. *Sport and Recreation in Ancient Greece*. Oxford: Oxford University Press, 1987.

Syme, R. "Domitian: The Last Years." *Chiron* 13 (1983): 121–46.

———. *The Roman Revolution*. Oxford: Oxford University Press, 1939.

———. *Tacitus*. 2 vols. Oxford: Clarendon, 1958.

———. *Ten Studies in Tacitus*. Oxford: Clarendon, 1970.

Syon, D. "Gamla: City of Refuge." Pages 134–54 in *The First Jewish Revolt: Archaeology, History, Ideology*. Edited by A. Berlin and A. Overman. London: Routledge, 2002.

Tabor, J. D., and E. V. Gallagher *Why Waco? Cults and the Battle for Religious Freedom in America*. Berkeley: University of California Press, 1995.

Talbert, C. H. *Literary Patterns, Theological Themes, and the Genre of Luke-Acts*. Missoula: Scholars Press, 1975.

Taylor, J. E. "Khirbet Qumran in the Nineteenth Century and the Name of the Site," *Palestine Exploration Quarterly* 134 (2002): 144–64.

Tcherikover, V. *Hellenistic Civilization and the Jews*. Philadelphia: The Jewish Publication Society of America, 1966.

———. "Jewish Apologetic Reconsidered." *Eos* 48 (1956): 169–93.

Thackeray, H. St. J. *Josephus: The Man and the Historian*. New York: Ktav, 1967.

Thoma, C. "The High Priesthood in the Judgment of Josephus." Pages 196–215 in *Josephus, the Bible, and History*. Edited by L. H. Feldman and G. Hata. Leiden: Brill, 1989.

Thomas, R. *Herodotus in Context: Ethnography, Science, and the Art of Persuasion.* Cambridge: Cambridge University Press, 2000.

Thomson, J. A. K. *Irony: An Historical Introduction.* London: Allen & Unwin, 1926.

Tigerstedt, E. N. *The Legend of Sparta in Classical Antiquity.* 2 vols. Stockholm: Almquist & Wiksell, 1974.

Tilborg, S. van. *The Jewish Leaders in Matthew.* Leiden: Brill, 1972.

Timothy, H. B. *The Early Christian Apologists and Greek Philosophy: Exemplified by Irenaeus, Tertullian, and Clement of Alexandria.* Assen: van Gorcum, 1973.

Torrey, C. C. "Apocalyptic." Pages 669–71 in vol. 1 of the *Jewish Encyclopedia.* 12 vols. Edited by I. Singer. New York: Funk & Wagnalls, 1901.

Toynbee, A. *Greek Historical Thought: From Homer to the Age of Heraclitus.* New York: New American Library, 1952.

Trebilco, P. *Jewish Communities in Asia Minor.* Cambridge: Cambridge University Press, 1991.

Trilling, W. "Die Taufertradition bei Matthaus." *Biblische Zeitschrift* 3: 282–84, 1959.

Turner, C. H. "Apostolic Succession." Pages 93–214 in *Essays on the Early History of the Church and the Ministry.* Edited by H. B. Swete. London: Macmillan, 1918.

Tyree, E. L., and E. Stefanoudaki. "The Olive Pit and Roman Oil Making." *Biblical Archaeologist* 59 (1996): 171–78.

Tyson, J. B., ed. *Luke-Acts and the Jewish People: Eight Critical Perspectives.* Minneapolis: Augsburg, 1988.

Unnik, W. C. van. *Flavius Josephus als historischer Schriftsteller.* Heidelberg: Schneider, 1978.

Urbach, E. E. *The Sages and Their Concepts and Beliefs.* Jerusalem: Magnes, 1975.

VanderKam, J. C. *The Dead Sea Scrolls Today.* Grand Rapids: Eerdmans, 1994.

Vermes, G. *The Dead Sea Scrolls in English.* London: Penguin, 1995.

Vermes, G., and M. D. Goodman, eds. *The Essenes According to the Classical Sources.* Sheffield: Sheffield Academic Press, 1989.

Veyne, P., ed. *A History of Private Life.* Vol. 1: *From Pagan Rome to Byzantium.* Cambridge: Harvard University Press, 1987.

Vogel, M. "Vita 64–69, das Bilderverbot, und die Gailäapolitik des Josephus." *Journal for the Study of Judaism in the Persian, Hellenistic, and Roman Periods* 30 (1999): 65–79.

Wacher, J., ed. *The Roman World.* London: Routledge, 2002.

Wacholder, B.-Z. *Nicolaus of Damascus.* Berkeley: University of California Press, 1962.

Wächter, L. "Die unterschiedliche Haltung der Pharisäer, Sadduzäer und Essener zur Heimarmene nach dem Bericht des Josephus." *Zeitschrift für Religions- und Geistesgeschichte* 21 (1969): 97–114.

Wagner, S. *Die Essener in der wissenschaftlichen Diskussion: vom Ausgang des 18. bis zum Beginn des 20. Jahrhunderts; eine wissenschaftliche Studie.* Berlin: A. Töpelmann, 1960.

Walzer, R. *Galen on Jews and Christians.* Oxford: Oxford University Press, 1949.

Wardman, A. *Rome's Debt to Greece.* Bristol: Bristol Classical Press, 1976.
Warfield, B. B. "Tertullian and the Beginnings of the Doctrine of the Trinity." Pages 3–109 in *Studies in Tertullian and Augustine.* Edited by B. B. Warfield. New York: Oxford University Press, 1930.
Warren, J. *Facing Death: Epicurus and His Critics.* Oxford: Clarendon, 2004.
Watson, F. *Paul, Judaism, and the Gentiles: A Sociological Approach.* Cambridge: Cambridge University Press, 1986.
Watson, J. "The Two Romans Congregations: Romans 14:1–15:13." Pages 203–15 in *The Romans Debate.* Rev. and exp. ed. Edited by K. P. Donfried. Peabody, Mass.: Hendrickson, 1991.
Weber, F. *Jüdische Theologie auf Grund des Talmud und verwandter Schriften.* Leipzig: Dorffling & Franke, 1897.
Weber, W. *Josephus und Vespasian: Untersuchungen zu dem Jüdischen Krieg des Flavius Josephus.* Hildesheim: Georg Olms, 1973.
Weçowski, M. "Ironie et histoire: le discours de Socles (Herodote V 92)." *Anc. Soc.* 27 (1996): 205–58.
Wedderburn, A. J. M. "The Purpose and Occasion of Romans Again." Pages 195–202 in *The Romans Debate.* Rev. and exp. ed. Edited by K. P. Donfried. Peabody, Mass.: Hendrickson, 1991.
Weeber, K.-W. *Luxus im alten Rom: Die Schwelgerei, das süsse Gift.* Darmstadt: Primus Verlag, 2003.
Weiss, H.-F. "Pharisaismus und Hellenismus: Zur Darstellung des Judentums im Geschichtswerk des jüdischen Historikers Flavius Josephus." *Orientalistische Literaturzeitung* 74 (1979): 421–34.
Wellhausen, J. "The Attitude of the Pharisees to Roman Rule and the House of Herod." Pages 18–47 in *Jews, Judaism, and the Classical World.* Edited by G. Alon. Jerusalem: Magnes, 1977.
———. "Did the Jewish People and Its Sages Cause the Hasmoneans to Be Forgotten?" Pages 1–17 in *Jews, Judaism and the Classical World.* Edited by G. Alon. Jerusalem: Magnes, 1977.
———. *Die Pharisäer und die Sadducäer: eine Untersuchung zur inneren jüdischen Geschichte.* Greifswald: Bamburg, 1874.
Wheeler, K. *German Aesthetic and Literary Criticism: The Romantic Ironists and Goethe.* Cambridge: Cambridge University Press, 1984.
Whiston, W., ed. *The Works of Josephus: Complete and Unabridged.* Peabody, Mass.: Hendrickson, 1987.
White, P. "The Friends of Martial, Statius, and Pliny, and the Dispersal of Patronage." *Harvard Studies in Classical Philology* 79 (1975): 265–300.
Whittaker, C.R. *Rome and Its Frontiers: The Dynamics of Empire.* London: Routledge, 2004.
Whittaker, M. *Jews and Christians: Graeco-Roman Views.* Cambridge: Cambridge University Press, 1984.
Wiefel, W. "The Jewish Community in Ancient Rome and the Origins of Roman Christianity." Pages 65–88 in *The Romans Debate.* Rev. and exp. ed. Edited by K. P. Donfried. Peabody, Mass.: Hendrickson, 1991.

Wilken, R. L. "Collegia, Philosophical Schools, and Theology." Pages 268–91 in *The Catacombs and the Colosseum: The Roman Empire as the Setting of Primitive Christianity*. Edited by S. Benko and J. J. O'Rourke. London: Oliphants, 1972.

Williams, C. A. *Roman Homosexuality: Ideologies of Masculinity in Classical Antiquity, Ideologies of Desire*. Oxford: Oxford University Press, 1999.

Williams, D. S. "Josephus and the Authorship of *War* 2.119–161 (on the Essenes)." *Journal for the Study of Judaism in the Persian, Hellenistic, and Roman Periods* 25.2 (1994): 207–21.

Williamson, G.A. *The World of Josephus*. Boston: Little Brown, 1964.

Willis, W. L. *Idol Meat in Corinth*. Chico, Calif.: Scholars Press, 1985.

Wilson, S. G. "The Jews and the Death of Jesus in Luke-Acts." Pages 155–64 in vol. 1 of in *Anti-Judaism in Early Christianity*. 2 vols. Edited by Richardson, P. and D. Granskou et al. Waterloo: Wilfrid Laurier University Press, 1986.

———. *Luke and the Pastoral Epistles*. London: SPCK, 1979.

———. *Related Strangers: Jews and Christians 70–170 C.E.* Minneapolis: Fortress, 1995.

Windisch, H. "βάρβαρος." Pages 546–53 in vol 1 of *The Theological Dictionary of the New Testament*. 10 vols. Edited by G. Kittel and G. W. Bromiley. Grand Rapids: Eerdmans, 1985.

Wiseman, T. P. *Clio's Cosmetics: Three Studies in Greco-Roman Literature*. Leicester: Leicester University Press, 1979.

———. *Death of an Emperor: Flavius Josephus*. Exeter: University of Exeter Press, 1991.

———. *Roman Political Life: 90 B.C.–A.D. 69*. Exeter: University of Exeter Press, 1985.

———. *Roman Studies: Literary and Historical*. Liverpool: F. Cairns, 1987.

Woodman, A. J. *Rhetoric in Classical Historiography: Four Studies*. London: Croom Helm, 1988.

Wuellner, W. "Paul's Rhetoric of Argumentation in Romans: An Alternative to the Donfried-Karris Debate over Romans." Pages 128–46 in *The Romans Debate*. Rev. and exp. ed. Edited by K. P. Donfried. Peabody, Mass.: Hendrickson, 1991.

Yavetz, Z. *Plebs and Princeps*. Oxford: Oxford University Press, 1969.

———. "Reflections on Titus and Josephus." *Greek, Roman, and Byzantine Studies* 16 (1975): 411–32.

Zagagi, N. *The Comedy of Menander: Convention, Variation, and Originality*. London: Duckworth, 1994.

Zanker, P. *The Power of Images in the Age of Augustus*. Translated by Alan Shapiro. Ann Arbor: The University of Michigan Press, 1988.

Zeitlin, S. *The Rise and Fall of the Judean State*. Philadelphia: Jewish Publication Society of America, 1962–1978.

Ziesler, J. "Luke and the Pharisees." *New Testament Studies* 25 (1978–1979): 146–57.

Ziolkowski, A. "*Urbs Direpta*, or How the Romans Sacked Cities." Pages 69–91 in *War and Society in the Roman World*. Edited by J. Rich and G. Shipley. London: Routledge, 1993.

Index of Modern Authors

Index of Ancient Persons and Places

NB: Judea/Judeans and Rome/Romans are omitted because of their ubiquity. Josephus is indexed only for the third part of the book, on Christian origins, for the same reason.

Index of Ancient Sources